ZAGATSURVEY®
25TH ANNIVERSARY

2004

NEW YORK CITY RESTAURANTS

D0066809

Editors: Curt Gathje and Carol Diuguid

Coordinator: Larry Cohn

Published and distributed by
ZAGAT SURVEY, LLC
4 Columbus Circle
New York, New York 10019
Tel: 212 977 6000
E-mail: newyork@zagat.com
Web site: www.zagat.com

Acknowledgments

Thanks to the following, each of whom edited sections of this guide: Kelly Alexander, Stephanie Clifford, Erica Curtis, Daphne Dennis, Dara Furlow, Lynn Hazlewood, Gwen Hyman, Nancy Jones, Bernard Onken, Tanya Steel and Miranda Van Gelder.

This guide would not have been possible without the hard work of our staff, especially Betsy Andrews, Augustine Chan, Reni Chin, Liz Daleske, Griff Foxley, Schuyler Frazier, Jeff Freier, Shelley Gallagher, Michael Gitter, Randi Gollin, Katherine Harris, Natalie Lebert, Mike Liao, Dave Makulec, Donna Marino, Lorraine Mead, Laura Mitchell, Jennifer Napuli, Emily Parsons, Rob Poole, Benjamin Schmerler, Troy Segal, Robert Seixas, Daniel Simmons, Yoji Yamaguchi and Sharon Yates.

Contents

About This Survey 4
What's New 5
Ratings & Symbols 7
Most Popular 9
TOP RATINGS:
    Food, Decor, Service, Best Buys 10
RESTAURANT DIRECTORY:
    Names, Addresses, Phone Numbers, Web
    Sites, Ratings and Reviews 23
INDEXES:
  Cuisines 226
  Locations 245
  Special Features
    Breakfast 263
    Brunch 263
    Buffet Served 264
    BYO 264
    Celebrity Chefs 264
    Cheese Trays 264
    Chef's Table 265
    Child-Friendly 265
    Cool Loos 265
    Critic-Proof 266
    Dancing/Entertainment 266
    Fireplaces 266
    Game in Season 267
    Gracious Hosts 267
    Historic Places 267
    Holiday Meals 268
    Hotel Dining 269
    "In" Places 270
    Jacket Required 270
    Jury Duty 271
    Late Dining 271
    Meet for a Drink 272
    Natural/Organic 272
    Noteworthy Newcomers/Closings 273
    Outdoor Dining 275
    People-Watching/Power Scenes 276
    Pre-Theater/Prix Fixe Menus 277
    Private Rooms 277
    Pubs/Microbreweries 278
    Quick Bites 278
    Quiet Conversation 279
    Raw Bars 279
    Romantic Places 279
    Senior Appeal 280
    Singles Scenes 280
    Sleepers 280
    Sunday – Best Bets 281
    Tasting Menus 281
    Tea Service 281
    Theme Restaurants 282
    Transporting Experiences 282
    Visitors on Expense Account 282
    Winning Wine Lists 282
Wine Chart 284

About This Survey

Here are the results of our *2004 New York City Restaurant Survey*, covering some 1,918 restaurants as tested, and tasted, by 29,361 avid local restaurant-goers (up from 25,922 last year). This marks the 25th year that Zagat Survey has reported on the shared experiences of diners like you.

What started in 1979 in New York as a hobby involving roughly 200 friends rating local restaurants has come a long way: Today we have over 250,000 surveyors with hundreds of thousands more registered to vote worldwide. And over the past 25 years we have branched out to publish guides to nightlife, entertaining, hotels, resorts, spas, shopping, golf, movies, theater and music. Most of these guides are also available at **zagat.com**, where you can vote and shop as well.

By regularly surveying large numbers of regular customers, we hope to have achieved a uniquely current and reliable guide. A quarter-century of experience has verified this. This year's NYC participants dined out an average of 3.4 times per week, meaning this *Survey* is based on roughly 5.2 million meals. Of these surveyors, 54% are women, 46% men; the breakdown by age is 21% in their 20s; 28%, 30s; 18%, 40s; 19%, 50s; and 14%, 60s or above. We sincerely thank each of these surveyors; this book is really "theirs."

To help guide our readers to NYC's best meals and best buys, we have prepared a number of lists. See Most Popular (page 9), Top Ratings (pages 10–19), Best Buys (page 20) and Bargain Prix Fixe Menus (pages 21–22). In addition, we have provided 48 handy indexes and have tried to be concise. Also, for the first time, we have included Web addresses. Finally, it should be noted that our editors have synopsized our surveyors' opinions, with their comments shown in quotation marks.

To join any of our upcoming *Surveys*, just register at zagat.com. Each participant will receive a free copy of the resulting guide when it is published. Your comments and even criticisms of this guide are also solicited. There is always room for improvement with your help. You can contact us at newyork@zagat.com or by mail at Zagat Survey, 4 Columbus Circle, New York, NY 10019. We look forward to hearing from you.

New York, NY
October 20, 2003

Nina and Tim

Nina and Tim Zagat

What's New

In the past year Gotham restaurants struggled to deal with a sluggish economy, the lingering aftermath of 9/11 and a new ban on smoking. Here's what's happening:

More Smoke Than Fire: A statewide smoking ban in all indoor public spaces has stirred much debate since its inception early this year. However, from what we can tell, the controversy has produced more smoke than fire. Indeed, most diners seem pleased by the clearing of the air: 23% of our surveyors report that it has prompted them to go out more often than before – particularly to "authentic" (i.e. "smoky") French bistros, which they once shunned. Only 4% say that the smoking law has deterred their restaurant-going.

Comfort Dining Closer to Home: The uncertain economic climate has showed a warming trend as more low-key residential restaurants sprouted all over town. Boasting neither big-name chefs nor well-known designers, neighborhood places like Celeste, Efendi, Five Front, Mermaid Inn and Westville succeeded by providing comfort both on the plate and in the pocketbook. Of the new openings this year, fully 74% fit our BATH ("Better Alternative to Home") definition, to wit: 1) modest prices; 2) casual ambiance; and 3) homey, hearty food.

Top Spots: Le Bernardin recaptured the *Survey*'s No. 1 Food rating from its perennial competitor Daniel (now No. 2), while 1991–1996 frontrunner Bouley continued its recovery, jumping from No. 11 in 2003 to No. 5 this year. After a 19-year run as the town's top Italian, Il Mulino was overtaken by Babbo. Proving that good things can come in small packages, the 30-seat West Village storefront Mexicana Mama was voted Top Mexican, while Brooklyn's The Grocery made the biggest upward move from No. 36 to No. 7.

Loyalty Oaths: NYC's Most Popular list had few major changes: Union Square Cafe was back on top, followed by Gramercy Tavern, Daniel, Gotham Bar & Grill and Nobu. The Upper West Side's two-year-old Ouest enjoyed the biggest climb, from 45 to 27. While Rocco DiSpirito was busy televising the opening of Rocco's 22nd Street, his Union Pacific took the biggest loss, down 11 slots from 21 to 32.

Hello and Goodbye: Despite the troubled economy, there were 174 noteworthy openings and 91 closings this year. Last year's figures were 186 and 104, respectively. The most notable new arrivals included 'Cesca, the latest gift to the Upper West Side from Tom Valenti; the stylish Lever House; Mix in New York, showcasing the joint talents of Alain Ducasse and Jeffrey Chodorow; Schiller's, the latest hipster destination from Keith McNally; 66, Jean-Georges Vongerichten's decidedly upscale Chinese TriBeCan; and WD-50, Wylie Dufresne's follow-up to 71 Clinton Fresh Food. As for closings, Lespinasse was the most prominent casualty in a field that included Butterfield 81, Campagna, Chicama, Pazo, Pico, Sushisay, The Tonic and Two Two Two.

Coming Attractions: The coming year looks highly promising, spearheaded by the opening of Time Warner's Columbus Circle complex that will showcase the return of Lespinasse's Gray Kunz, a new steakhouse from Jean-Georges Vongerichten, as well as offshoots of LA's Ginza Sushi-Ko and Thomas Keller's renowned French Laundry. The Meatpacking District will continue to heat up with the arrival of Spice Market, a collaboration between Vongerichten and Kunz; Vento Trattoria, a new Steve Hanson project; Ono, a Japanese via restaurateur Jeffrey Chodorow; and Terre, a Country French boîte from chef Christian Delouvrier. Also in the works is Lucy, a Mexican specializing in Oaxacan cuisine from restaurateur Phil Suarez, and Riingo, a Japanese-American from Aquavit chef Marcus Samuelsson.

The Prix Fixe Is In: In response to the jittery economy, a number of newcomers, including Chubo, Dish, Kitchen 22 and 360, have opened offering a concept of prix fixe–only meals, value priced in the $20–$25 range. In addition, NYC & Company's successful Restaurant Week promotion seems to have evolved into Restaurant Year, with many prominent participants extending their deals year-round (see also our Bargain Prix Fixe listings, pp. 21–22).

Low Inflation: A positive side of the slow economy is that the average cost of a NYC meal held steady, with a marginal 0.3% increase to $37.06 from $36.95. Though higher than the U.S. average of $30.32, New York is a real bargain compared to other world capitals such as London ($51.15), Paris ($53.29) or Tokyo ($66.60).

What Gaul: France's decision not to support the U.S. war with Iraq brought diplomatic affairs to the dining table when a boycott of French restaurants was proposed in the heat of wartime patriotism. This embargo proved short-lived, as most diners realized that NYC's so-called French restaurants are in fact run and staffed by Americans, serve American products and pay American taxes.

Asian Shuffle: The growing popularity of Japanese food continues unabated, with 15% of our surveyors naming it their favorite cuisine this year (up from 4% in 2001). Thai food showed a similar surge of popularity, especially with younger diners, and boasted two of the year's showiest newcomers, SoHo's Peep and Williamsburg's SEA. On the other hand, Chinese cooking inexplicably continues to decline in popularity, with only 7% calling it their favorite ethnic food. Indeed, an astonishing 18 Japanese places received food ratings that exceeded the highest rated Chinese restaurant. Here's rooting for a Chinese renaissance.

New York, NY
October 20, 2003

Nina and Tim Zagat

Ratings & Symbols

Name, Address, Phone Number & Web Site

Zagat Ratings

Hours & Credit Cards

F	D	S	C
▽ 23	9	13	$15

Tim & Nina's ◗ 🖾 ⌀
4 Columbus Circle (8th Ave.), 212-977-6000;
www.zagat.com

🗹 Open 24/7, this 25-year-old "literal dive" located in
the Columbus Circle IND station offers a "one-of-a-kind"
Chinese-German dining experience where an "hour after
you eat you're hungry for more sweet-and-sour schnitzel";
fans ignore its "Bauhaus meets Mao's house" look and
the staff's "yin-yang" uniforms (lederhosen for men,
cheongsam for women) and say it's "some cheap trip",
even if you must "shout when the A train comes in."

Review, with surveyors' comments in quotes

Restaurants with the highest overall ratings and greatest
popularity and importance are printed in CAPITAL LETTERS.

Before reviews a symbol indicates whether responses
were uniform ■ or mixed 🗹.

Hours: ◗ serves after 11 PM
　　　　🖾 closed on Sunday

Credit Cards: ⌀ no credit cards accepted

Ratings: Food, Decor and Service are rated on a scale of
0 to **30**. The Cost (C) column reflects our surveyors' estimate
of the price of dinner including one drink and tip.

F	Food	D	Decor	S	Service	C	Cost
23		9		13		$15	

0–9　poor to fair　　　　**20–25**　very good to excellent
10–15　fair to good　　　**26–30**　extraordinary to perfection
16–19　good to very good　▽　low response/less reliable

For places listed without ratings or a numerical cost estimate,
such as an important newcomer or a popular write-in, the
price range is indicated by the following symbols.

I	$15 and below	**E**	$31 to $50
M	$16 to $30	**VE**	$51 or more

Most Popular

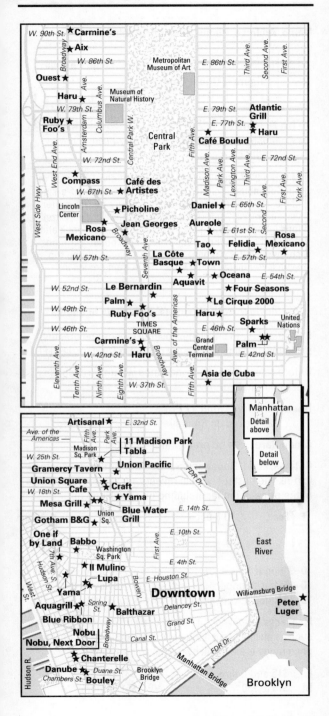

W. 90th St. ★Carmine's

★ Aix
W. 86th St.

Ouest ★

Metropolitan
Museum of
Art

E. 86th St.

Haru ★
W. 79th St.

Museum of
Natural History

Ruby
Foo's ★

Central
Park

E. 79th St.

Atlantic
Grill

E. 77th St. ★ Haru

★ Café Boulud

W. 72nd St.

E. 72nd St.

Compass ★

Café des
★ Artistes
W. 67th St.

Daniel ★

E. 65th St.

Lincoln
Center

★ Picholine

Aureole

E. 61st St.

Rosa
Mexicano ★

Jean Georges ★

Rosa
Mexicano ★

★ Tao Felidia

W. 57th St.

La Côte
★ Basque ★ Town

E. 57th St.

Le Bernardin ★

Aquavit ★

★ Oceana

E. 54th St.

★ Four Seasons

W. 52nd St.

Palm ★

W. 49th St.

Ruby Foo's ★

★ Le Cirque 2000

Haru ★

TIMES
SQUARE

W. 46th St.

E. 46th St.

Sparks
★★

United
Nations

Carmine's
★

W. 42nd St. Haru ★

Grand
Central
Terminal

Palm ★★
E. 42nd St.

Asia de Cuba
★

W. 37th St.

Manhattan
Detail
above

Detail
below

Artisanal ★
E. 32nd St.

Ave. of the
Americas

Fifth
Ave.

Park
Ave.

11 Madison Park
Tabla

W. 25th St.

Madison
Sq. Park

Union Pacific

Gramercy Tavern ★

Union Square ★
Cafe
W. 18th St.

★ Craft

Mesa Grill ★★

★ Yama

Gotham B&G
★

Union
Sq.

Blue Water
Grill

E. 14th St.

One if
by Land
★

Babbo
★

Washington
Sq. Park

E. 10th St.

E. 4th St.

★ Il Mulino

★ Lupa

Yama
★

Aquagrill ★★

Spring
St.

Blue Ribbon

★ Balthazar

E. Houston St.

Downtown

Delancey St.

Williamsburg Bridge
★

Peter
Luger ★

Nobu
Nobu, Next Door

Grand St.

Canal St.

★ Chanterelle

Danube ★★ Duane St.
Chambers St. Bouley

Brooklyn
Bridge

Manhattan Bridge

East
River

FDR Dr.

Brooklyn

Most Popular

Each of our surveyors has been asked to name his or her five favorite restaurants. The following list reflects their choices, followed in parentheses by last year's ranking:

1. Union Square Cafe (2)
2. Gramercy Tavern (1)
3. Daniel (4)
4. Gotham Bar & Grill (3)
5. Nobu (5)
6. Blue Water Grill (9)
7. Jean Georges (7)
8. Babbo (10)
9. Peter Luger (6)
10. Le Bernardin (8)
11. Balthazar (12)
12. Bouley (18)
13. Aureole (11)
14. Eleven Madison Pk. (14)
15. Chanterelle (15)
16. Four Seasons (16)
17. Tabla (20)
18. Picholine (17)
19. Artisanal (22)
20. Atlantic Grill (30)
21. Aquavit (13)
22. Il Mulino (23)
23. Craft (26)
24. Café des Artistes (25)
25. Rosa Mexicano (29)
26. Carmine's (24)
27. Ouest (45)
28. Le Cirque 2000 (31)
29. Asia de Cuba (19)
30. Mesa Grill (32)
31. Aquagrill (28)
32. Union Pacific (21)
33. Felidia (44)
34. Lupa (40)
35. Palm (34)
36. La Côte Basque (36)
37. Danube (27)
38. Yama (33)
39. One if by Land (42)
40. Café Boulud (41)
41. Oceana (35)
42. Compass (–)
43. Ruby Foo's (38)
44. Blue Ribbon (–)
45. Sparks (39)*
46. Town (–)
47. Aix (–)
48. Haru (–)
49. Tao (–)
50. Nobu, Next Door (–)

It's obvious that many of the restaurants on the above list are among the city's most expensive, but New Yorkers also love a bargain. Fortunately, our city has an abundance of wonderful ethnic restaurants and other inexpensive spots that fill the bill. Thus, we have listed 100 Best Buys on page 20 and over 200 Prix Fixe and Pre-Theater Menus on pages 21–22. Also bear in mind that New York's outer borough restaurants include many venues at prices that are often a third or less than what you'd expect to pay in Manhattan.

---

* Indicates a tie with restaurant above.

Top Ratings

Visit zagat.com for complete listings in each category.

Top 50 Food

28 Le Bernardin
Daniel
Peter Luger
Nobu
Bouley
Jean Georges
Grocery
27 Gramercy Tavern
Gotham Bar & Grill
Nobu, Next Door
Chanterelle
Tomoe Sushi
Pearl Oyster Bar
Alain Ducasse
Jewel Bako
Babbo
Veritas
Café Boulud
Danube
Oceana
Il Mulino
Union Square Cafe
Sushi Yasuda
Aureole
Grimaldi's

Picholine
26 Sushi of Gari
March
Atelier
Trattoria L'incontro
Il Giglio
La Caravelle
L'Impero
Aquagrill
La Grenouille
Four Seasons
Union Pacific
Milos
Montrachet
La Côte Basque
Tocqueville
Honmura An
Craft
Annisa
Lupa
Scalini Fedeli
Aquavit
25 Erminia
Felidia
Scalinatella

By Cuisine

American
28 Grocery
27 Gramercy Tavern
Gotham Bar & Grill
Veritas
Union Square Cafe
Aureole

American (Regional)
27 Pearl Oyster Bar/NE
25 Cooking with Jazz/Cajun
24 Mesa Grill/SW
23 Mary's Fish Camp/NE
Tropica/FL
21 Michael's/CA

Barbecue
22 Pearson's Texas BBQ
Kang Suh
21 Kum Gang San
Virgil's
19 Blue Smoke
17 Hog Pit

Brasseries
23 Artisanal
Balthazar
22 L'Absinthe
21 Brasserie 8½
City Hall
One C.P.S.

Cafes
27 Café Boulud
Union Square Cafe
25 River Cafe
Park Avenue Cafe
24 Duane Park Cafe
22 Café des Artistes

Caviar & Champagne
26 La Grenouille
24 Caviar Russe▽
Petrossian
Caviarteria▽
20 FireBird
18 King Cole Bar

Excluding places with low voting except as indicated by ▽.

Chinese
24 Canton
Shun Lee Palace
23 Phoenix Garden
Mr. K's
Shun Lee West
Chin Chin

Coffeehouses
22 Ferrara
21 Grey Dog's Coffee
Once Upon a Tart
Le Pain Quotidien
20 Cafe Lalo
19 Omonia Cafe

Delis
23 Barney Greengrass
Second Ave. Deli
Katz's
21 Carnegie
19 Sarge's
18 Ben's Kosher

Dessert
25 La Bergamote
24 Payard Bistro
23 Veniero's
Sweet Melissa
Amy's Bread
22 City Bakery

French
28 Le Bernardin
Daniel
Bouley
Jean Georges
27 Chanterelle
Alain Ducasse
Café Boulud
26 Atelier
La Caravelle
La Grenouille
Montrachet
La Côte Basque
Tocqueville

French (Bistro)
25 Le Gigot
24 db Bistro Moderne
JoJo
Bistro St. Mark's
Le Tableau
Jarnac

Greek
26 Milos
25 Periyali
24 Taverna Kyclades
23 Elias Corner
Avra Estiatorio
Snack

Hamburgers
24 db Bistro Moderne
Corner Bistro
23 burger joint
22 Wollensky's Grill
Island Burgers
21 '21' Club

Indian
25 Tabla
24 Chola
Bread Bar at Tabla
Jackson Diner
Tamarind
23 Dawat

Italian
27 Babbo/*multi*
Il Mulino/*Aquila*
Roberto's/*Naples*
26 Trattoria L'incontro/*Abruzzi*
Il Giglio/*Rome*
L'Impero/*multi*
Lupa/*multi*
Scalini Fedeli/*multi*
25 Erminia/*Rome*
Felidia/*Trieste*
Scalinatella/*Capri*
Don Peppe/*multi*
Piccolo Angolo/*Genoa*

Japanese
28 Nobu
27 Nobu, Next Door
Kuruma Zushi
Tomoe Sushi
Jewel Bako
Sushi Yasuda
Sushi Sen-nin
26 Sushi of Gari
Sugiyama
Sushi Seki
Honmura An
25 Sushi Zen
Blue Ribbon Sushi

Korean
25 Hangawi
22 Woo Lae Oak
Kang Suh
21 Kum Gang San
Do Hwa
Gam Mee Ok

Kosher
24 Prime Grill
23 Second Ave. Deli
Pongal
20 Le Marais
Box Tree
Darna

Top Food

Mediterranean
27 Picholine
23 Aesop's Tables
   Red Cat
   Il Buco
   Harrison
   Verbena

Mexican
25 Mexicana Mama
24 Maya
23 Hell's Kitchen
   Alma
22 Rocking Horse
   Mi Cocina

Middle Eastern
23 Zaytoons
22 Turkish Kitchen
21 Oznot's Dish
   Pasha
   Beyoglu
   Moustache

Noodle Shops
26 Honmura An
23 Sobaya
22 Big Wong
   Great NY Noodle
21 Sweet-n-Tart Rest.
20 Sweet-n-Tart Cafe

Pizza
27 Grimaldi's
25 Lombardi's
24 Joe's Pizza
   Nick's
   Lil' Frankie's Pizza
23 Totonno Pizzeria

Seafood
28 Le Bernardin
27 Pearl Oyster Bar
   Oceana
26 Aquagrill
   Milos
25 Manhattan Ocean Club

South American
24 Patria
22 Calle Ocho
   SushiSamba
   Chur. Plataforma
   Pampa
21 Coco Roco

Southern/Soul
22 Maroons
20 Amy Ruth's
   Kitchenette
   Shark Bar
   Pink Tea Cup
19 Great Jones Cafe

Spanish
23 Sevilla
22 El Cid
   Bolo
   Marichu (Basque)
   El Faro
   Solera

Steakhouses
28 Peter Luger
25 Strip House
   Sparks
   Uncle Jack's
24 MarkJoseph
   Post House
   Prime Grill
   Palm
   Nick & Stef's
   Del Frisco's
23 Pietro's
   Morton's
   Keens

Tapas
22 El Cid
   Bolo
   Marichu
   Solera
21 Xunta
20 Pipa

Thai
24 Vong
23 Joya
22 SEA
   Planet Thailand
   Elephant
   Wondee Siam

Vegetarian
25 Hangawi
   Gobo
23 Pongal
22 Vatan
21 Candle Cafe
20 Angelica Kitchen

Vietnamese
23 Saigon Grill
22 Nam
21 O Mai
   Nha Trang
20 Le Colonial
   New Pasteur

Wild Cards
27 Danube/*Austrian*
26 Aquavit/*Scandinavian*
25 Wallsé/*Austrian*
   Convivium/*Iberian-Italian*
24 Roy's/*Asian-Seafood*
   Aki/*Japan.-Jamaican*

By Special Feature

Breakfast
28 Jean Georges
26 Atelier
25 Norma's
24 Mark's
   Payard Bistro
23 Balthazar

Brunch
26 Aquagrill
   Aquavit
25 River Cafe
   Eleven Madison
   Town
   Park Ave. Cafe

Buffets
26 Aquavit (Sun.)
24 Chola
22 Bukhara Grill
   Dumonet (Sun.)
   Turkish Kitchen (Sun.)
21 Water Club

Business Dining
28 Le Bernardin
27 Gotham Bar & Grill
   Union Square Cafe
26 Four Seasons
   Milos
25 Bayard's

Child-Friendly
22 Zum Stammtisch
21 Virgil's Real BBQ
20 Carmine's
19 Serendipity 3
16 Benihana
15 Tavern on the Green

Hotel Dining
28 Jean Georges/Trump
27 Alain Ducasse/Essex Hse.
   Café Boulud/Surrey
26 Atelier/Ritz-Central Park
25 Norma's/Parker Meridien
   Town/Chambers

"In" Places
27 Pearl Oyster Bar
   Sushi Yasuda
26 Atelier
25 Tasting Room
   Gobo
23 Joya
22 66
   fresh.
21 Peep
20 Dos Caminos
   Otto

Late Dining
27 Nobu, Next Door
25 Blue Ribbon Sushi
   Blue Ribbon
24 Corner Bistro
23 Blue Water Grill
   'ino

Lunch ($20)
28 Nobu
   Jean Georges
27 Aureole
26 Union Pacific
   Montrachet (Friday)
   Tocqueville

Meet for a Drink
27 Gramercy Tavern
   Gotham Bar & Grill
26 L'Impero
25 Town
   Bond Street
24 Mark's

Most Improved
28 Grocery
26 Tocqueville
25 Fleur de Sel
   Fiamma Osteria
   Bayard's
24 Nick & Stef's

Newcomers: Rated
25 Gobo
23 Aix
   Jefferson
   Sage
22 66
   Amuse

Newcomers: Others
   Capitale▽
   'Cesca
   Lever House
   Mermaid Inn▽
   Mix in New York
   Nice Matin▽
   OLA▽
   Rocco's 22nd St.
   Schiller's
   Sueños
   WD-50▽

Party Sites
28 Nobu
   Jean Georges
26 Four Seasons
25 Le Cirque 2000
24 One if by Land
   Del Frisco's

Top Food

People-Watching
24 Elio's
23 Balthazar
22 Mercer Kitchen
Il Cantinori
Nam*
21 Da Silvano

Power Scenes
28 Daniel
Peter Luger
Nobu
Jean Georges
26 Four Seasons (lunch)
25 Le Cirque 2000

Private Rooms
28 Le Bernardin
Daniel
27 Gramercy Tavern
Alain Ducasse
Picholine
25 Bayard's

Pub Dining
23 Keens Steakhse.
22 Wollensky's Grill
20 J.G. Melon
Knickerbocker B&G
17 Joe Allen
St. Andrews

Quick Bites
23 Amy's Bread
22 City Bakery
Dishes
21 BB Sandwich Bar
Once Upon a Tart
20 F & B

Quiet Conversation
28 Le Bernardin
27 Chanterelle
Alain Ducasse
Picholine
26 Atelier
La Caravelle

Raw Bars
26 Aquagrill
23 Blue Water Grill
Shaffer City
Ocean Grill
22 Atlantic Grill
Mercer Kitchen

Singles Scenes
25 Town
Blue Ribbon
24 Bread Bar at Tabla
Mesa Grill
23 Artisanal
Balthazar

Sleepers▽
28 Di Fara
25 Eliá
Arabelle
23 Giovanni
22 Sesumi
Kam Chueh

Sunday's Best
28 Bouley
26 Lupa
25 River Cafe
Ouest
24 Shun Lee Palace
23 Balthazar

Tasting Menus
28 Le Bernardin ($98)
Daniel ($120)
Bouley ($75)
Jean Georges ($118)
Grocery ($65)
27 Gramercy Tavern ($85)

Trips to the Country
29 Xaviar's/NY
28 Ryland Inn/NJ
Arch/NY
La Panetière/NY
Mill River Inn/LI
27 Rest. du Village/CT

24-Hour
22 Kang Suh
21 Kum Gang San
Gam Mee Ok
20 Wo Hop
Bereket
Gray's Papaya

Winning Wine Lists
27 Gotham Bar & Grill
Babbo
Veritas
Union Square Cafe
26 Montrachet
25 Bayard's

By Location

Chelsea
25 La Bergamote
24 Da Umberto
23 Red Cat
22 El Cid
　　 Rocking Horse
　　 Le Zie 2000

Chinatown
24 Canton
23 New Green Bo
　　 Oriental Garden
22 Grand Sichuan
　　 Ping's Seafood
　　 Big Wong

East Village
27 Jewel Bako
25 Tasting Room
24 Hasaki
　　 Le Tableau
　　 Lil' Frankie's Pizza
　　 Il Bagatto

East 40s
27 Kuruma Zushi
　　 Sushi Yasuda
26 L'Impero
25 Sparks
24 Grifone
　　 Prime Grill

East 50s
27 Oceana
26 March
　　 La Grenouille
　　 Four Seasons
25 Felidia
　　 Le Cirque 2000

East 60s
28 Daniel
27 Aureole
26 Sushi Seki
25 Scalinatella
　　 Park Avenue Cafe
24 rm

East 70s
27 Café Boulud
26 Sushi of Gari
25 Lusardi's
24 Mark's
　　 Campagnola
　　 Payard Bistro

East 80s
25 Erminia
　　 Etats-Unis
24 Elio's
　　 Primavera
23 Sirabella's
　　 Totonno Pizzeria

East 90s & Up (below Harlem)
21 Table d'Hôte
　　 Sarabeth's
20 Vico
　　 Pascalou
19 Bistro du Nord
　　 Yura & Co.

Financial District/Seaport
25 Bayard's
24 MarkJoseph Steak
　　 Roy's NY
22 Au Mandarin
21 Bridge Cafe
　　 55 Wall

Flatiron/Union Square
27 Gramercy Tavern
　　 Veritas
　　 Union Square Cafe
26 Tocqueville
　　 Craft
25 Fleur de Sel

Garment District
24 Nick & Stef's Steak
23 Keens Steakhouse
22 Kang Suh
21 Kum Gang San
　　 Gam Mee Ok
　　 Frankie & Johnnie's

Gramercy/Madison Park
26 Union Pacific
25 Tabla
　　 Eleven Madison Park
　　 Yama
24 Bread Bar at Tabla
　　 Novitá

Greenwich Village
27 Gotham Bar & Grill
　　 Tomoe Sushi
　　 Pearl Oyster Bar
　　 Babbo
　　 Il Mulino
26 Annisa

Top Food

Harlem
- *24* Charles' Southern▽
- *21* Rao's
- Patsy's Pizzeria
- *20* Amy Ruth's
- *19* Bayou
- *18* Jimmy's Uptown

Little Italy
- *25* Il Palazzo
- *24* Pellegrino's
- *23* Il Cortile
- Nyonya
- *22* Angelo's of Mulberry
- Ferrara

Lower East Side
- *25* 71 Clinton Fresh Food
- *23* Katz's Deli
- *22* Alias
- *21* Salt
- *20* Grilled Cheese NYC
- Paladar

Meatpacking District
- *22* Old Homestead
- Macelleria
- *21* Paradou
- Frank's
- *20* Pastis
- Son Cubano

Murray Hill
- *27* Sushi Sen-nin
- *25* Hangawi
- *23* Artisanal
- Asia de Cuba
- *22* Pizza 33
- Mishima

NoHo
- *25* Bond Street
- *23* Il Buco
- *22* Five Points
- *21* Sala
- *19* Great Jones Cafe
- *18* NoHo Star

NoLita
- *25* Lombardi's
- *22* Bread
- Café Habana
- Peasant
- *20* Le Jardin Bistro
- *18* Mexican Radio

SoHo
- *26* Aquagrill
- Honmura An
- *25* Blue Ribbon Sushi
- Blue Ribbon
- Fiamma Osteria
- *24* L'Ecole

TriBeCa
- *28* Nobu
- Bouley
- *27* Nobu, Next Door
- Chanterelle
- Danube
- *26* Il Giglio

West Village
- *25* Mexicana Mama
- Piccolo Angolo
- Wallsé
- Taka
- *24* Corner Bistro
- Jarnac

West 40s
- *25* Sushi Zen
- Ilo
- *24* db Bistro Moderne
- Sea Grill
- Del Frisco's
- *23* Esca

West 50s
- *28* Le Bernardin
- *27* Alain Ducasse
- *26* Atelier
- La Caravelle
- Sugiyama
- Milos

West 60s
- *28* Jean Georges
- *27* Picholine
- *23* Shun Lee West
- *22* Gabriel's
- Café des Artistes
- Rosa Mexicano

West 70s
- *23* Ocean Grill
- *22* Scaletta
- Compass
- Pomodoro Rosso
- *21* Pasha
- La Grolla

West 80s
- *25* Ouest
- *23* Aix
- Barney Greengrass
- Nëo Sushi
- *22* Calle Ocho
- Celeste

West 90s & Up
- *24* Gennaro
- *23* Saigon Grill
- Max
- *22* Métisse
- Terrace in the Sky
- Yuki Sushi

Outer Boroughs

Bronx
27 Roberto's
25 Enzo's∇
23 Dominick's
21 El Malecon
   Mario's
   F & J Pine Rest.

Brooklyn: Bay Ridge
24 Areo
23 Tuscany Grill
22 Chianti
21 Chadwick's
   Embers
20 101

Brooklyn: Heights/Dumbo
27 Grimaldi's
25 River Cafe
   Henry's End
24 Queen
23 Noodle Pudding
21 La Bouillabaisse

**Brooklyn: Carroll Gardens/
Boerum Hill/Cobble Hill**
28 Grocery
26 Saul
24 Osaka
23 Joya
   Sweet Melissa
   Zaytoons

Brooklyn: Park Slope
25 Blue Ribbon Sushi
   Blue Ribbon
   Al Di La
   Convivium Osteria
24 Rose Water
   Bistro St. Mark's

Brooklyn: Williamsburg
28 Peter Luger
23 Bamonte's
22 SEA
   Planet Thailand
   Diner
21 Oznot's Dish

Brooklyn: Other
23 Totonno Pizzeria
   Nyonya
22 L&B Spumoni Gardens
   Gargiulo's
   Gage & Tollner
21 À Table

Queens: Astoria
26 Trattoria L'incontro
25 Piccola Venezia
24 Taverna Kyclades
23 Elias Corner
   Christos Hasapo
   Stamatis

Queens: Other
25 Don Peppe
   Cooking with Jazz
   Uncle Jack's Steak
24 Nick's
   Jackson Diner
   Park Side

Staten Island
25 Carol's Cafe
24 Trattoria Romana
23 Aesop's Tables
   Denino's Pizzeria
22 Angelina's
21 American Grill

Top 50 Decor

28 Danube
Daniel
River Cafe
27 One if by Land
Four Seasons
La Grenouille
Rainbow Room
Alain Ducasse
Suba
FireBird
26 Hangawi
Le Bernardin
Chanterelle
Le Cirque 2000
Tao
Café des Artistes
Chez Es Saada
Café Botanica
Water's Edge
Jean Georges
Bouley
Gramercy Tavern
Eleven Madison Park
Aureole
Union Pacific

Kings' Carriage Hse.
25 Town
March
Aquavit
Tabla
Atelier
Scalini Fedeli
Guastavino's
Asia de Cuba
Gotham Bar & Grill
AZ
Bayard's
Erminia
La Caravelle
Terrace in the Sky
Boat House
66
La Côte Basque
Tavern on the Green
Fiamma Osteria
Oceana
L'Impero
Fifty Seven Fifty Seven
Honmura An
Box Tree

Gardens

Aesop's Tables
Barbetta
Barolo
Bistro St. Mark's
Blue Hill
Bottino
Bryant Park Grill
Convivium Osteria
Dolphins
Gascogne
Grocery
Hudson Cafeteria
I Coppi

I Trulli
Le Jardin Bistro
March
Miracle Grill (E. Village)
Paradou
Park
Patois
Surya
Tavern on the Green
Va Tutto!
Verbena
ViceVersa
Vittorio Cucina

Great Rooms

Alain Ducasse
Aureole
Balthazar
Barbetta
Bayard's
Café des Artistes
Capitale
Chanterelle
Craft
Daniel
Danube
Dumonet
Eleven Madison
FireBird

Four Seasons
Gramercy Tavern
Jean Georges
La Grenouille
Le Bernardin
Le Cirque 2000
Lever House
March
Milos
Mix in New York
Rainbow Room
66
Tao
Torre di Pisa

subscribe to zagat.com

Romance

Aureole
AZ
Balthazar
Barbetta
Café des Artistes
Chanterelle
Chez Es Saada
Chez Josephine
Chez Michallet
Danube
Erminia
FireBird
Il Buco
Jezebel
JoJo
King Cole Bar
Kings' Carriage Hse.
La Grenouille
L'Impero
Mark's
March
One if by Land
Petrossian
Primavera
Provence
Rainbow Room
River Cafe
Scalini Fedeli
Tavern on the Green
Terrace in the Sky
Top of the Tower
Water's Edge

Views

American Park
Boat Basin
Boat House
Bryant Park Grill/Cafe
Deck
55 Wall
F.illi Ponte
Foley's Fish House
14 Wall Street
Harbour Lights
Lobster Box
Marina Cafe
Métrazur
Michael Jordan's
Pete's Downtown
Rainbow Room
River Cafe
Sea Grill
Tavern on the Green
Terrace in the Sky
Top of the Tower
View
Water Club
Water's Edge

Top 50 Service

27 Daniel
Alain Ducasse
Le Bernardin
Chanterelle
Gramercy Tavern
Danube
26 Jean Georges
Union Square Cafe
Four Seasons
March
Bouley
La Grenouille
Picholine
Aureole
Veritas
Gotham Bar & Grill
La Caravelle
Tasting Room
25 Jewel Bako
Café Boulud
La Côte Basque
Eleven Madison Park
Oceana
Mark's
Grocery

Union Pacific
Atelier
Hangawi
Scalini Fedeli
Mr. K's
Aquavit
24 Erminia
Tabla
River Cafe
Le Cirque 2000
Montrachet
Fifty Seven Fifty Seven
Tocqueville
L'Impero
One if by Land
Le Perigord
Blue Hill
Nino's
Babbo
Acappella
Nobu
Honmura An
Bayard's
Sushi Yasuda
Petrossian

Best Buys

Full-Menu Restaurants

1. Mama's Food Shop/*American*
2. Bereket/*Turkish*
3. Olive Vine Cafe,/*Middle Eastern*
4. Zaytoons/*Middle Eastern*
5. Pump/*Health Food*
6. Big Wong/*Chinese*
7. Bo-Ky/*Vietnamese*
8. Joya/*Thai*
9. El Malecon/*Dominican*
10. Sweet-n-Tart Café/*Chinese*
11. X.O./*Chinese*
12. Pho Bang/*Vietnamese*
13. La Taza de Oro/*Puerto Rican*
14. Wild Ginger/*Thai*
15. Goody's/*Chinese*
16. New Pasteur/*Vietnamese*
17. Alice's Tea Cup/*Eclectic*
18. Old Devil Moon/*Southern*
19. Dojo/*Health Food*
20. Rice/*Asian-Eclectic*
21. Nha Trang/*Vietnamese*
22. Friendhouse/*Chinese*
23. SEA/*Thai*
24. Flor de Mayo/*Peruvian*
25. New Green Bo/*Chinese*
26. Pepe . . . To Go/*Italian*
27. Veselka/*Ukrainian*
28. A/*French-Caribbean*
29. L & B Spumoni/*Italian*
30. Saigon Grill/*Vietnamese*
31. Sobaya/*Japanese noodles*
32. Nyonya/*Malaysian*
33. Vegetarian Paradise/*Chinese*
34. Kitchenette/*American*
35. Spice/*Thai*
36. Cafe Mogador/*Moroccan*
37. Symposium/*Greek*
38. Great NY Noodle/*Chinese*
39. Cafe Luluc/*French*
40. Gam Mee Ok/*Korean*
41. Republic/*Asian*
42. Planet Thailand/*Thai*
43. Sweet-n-Tart Rest./*Chinese*
44. Shanghai Cuisine/*Chinese*
45. Route 66 Cafe/*Eclectic*
46. Angelica Kitchen/*Vegetarian*
47. Gobo/*Vegetarian*
48. Wo Hop/*Chinese*
49. Jackson Diner/*Indian*
50. Viand/*Coffee Shop*

Specialty Shops

1. Krispy Kreme/*doughnuts*
2. Emack & Bolio's/*ice cream*
3. Gray's Papaya/*hot dogs*
4. Joe's Pizza/*pizza*
5. Papaya King/*hot dogs*
6. BB Sandwich Bar/*cheese steak*
7. Little Italy Pizza/*pizza*
8. Pizza 33/*pizza*
9. La Bergamote/*bakery*
10. F & B/*European hot dogs*
11. Grilled Cheese NYC/*sandwich*
12. Ess-a-Bagel/*deli*
13. Pie/*pizza*
14. Amy's Bread/*baked goods*
15. burger joint/*burger*
16. Eisenberg/*sandwiches*
17. Grey Dog's Coffee/*coffeehse.*
18. Blue 9 Burger/*burger*
19. Sweet Melissa/*pastry*
20. Peanut Butter & Co./*sandwich*
21. DT.UT/*coffeehouse*
22. Hale & Hearty/*soup*
23. Veniero's/*Italian pastry*
24. Panino'teca 275/*sandwich*
25. Cosmic Cantina/*Mexican*
26. Chop't Creative/*salad*
27. Corner Bistro/*burger*
28. Dishes/*salad & sandwich*
29. Johnny Rockets/*burgers*
30. Hampton Chutney/*dosas*
31. Once Upon a Tart/*pastry*
32. Caffe Reggio/*coffeehouse*
33. 71 Irving Place/*sandwich*
34. Burritoville/*Mexican*
35. Ferrara/*Italian pastry*
36. Cosi/*sandwiches*
37. Cozy Soup & Burger/*burger*
38. Two Boots/*pizza*
39. Better Burger/*burger*
40. Island Burgers/*burger*
41. Denino's Pizzeria/*pizza*
42. A Salt & Battery/*fish 'n' chips*
43. Grimaldi's/*pizza*
44. City Bakery/*Amer. bakery*
45. Hill Diner/*Diner*
46. ChipShop/*fish 'n' chips/curry*
47. Edgar's Cafe/*coffeehouse*
48. Cafe Lalo/*coffeehouse*
49. Nick's/*pizza*
50. Omonia Cafe/*desserts*

Bargain Prix Fixe Menus
Lunch

Ambassador Grill	25.00	Le Perigord	28.00
Aquavit	30.00	Le Zinc	20.04
Arqua	20.00	L'Orto	29.95
Artisanal	20.04	Lumi	22.00
Aureole	20.00	Lutèce	24.00
Avra Estiatorio	24.95	Luxia	16.00
Bay Leaf	12.95	Madison Bistro	21.25
Beacon	19.95	March	39.00
Becco	16.95	Maria Pia	19.95
Bistro du Nord	14.95	Marichu	25.00
Bombay Palace	12.95	Mark's	28.00
Bouley	35.00	Métrazur	20.04
Brasserie 8½	25.00	Molyvos	22.50
Café Botanica	24.00	Montrachet (Fri.)	20.04
Café Boulud	36.00	Mr. K's	25.00
Café des Artistes	25.00	Nick & Stef's	20.04
Cafe Nosidam	21.95	Nobu	20.04
Capsouto Frères	20.04	Novitá	19.99
Chanterelle	38.00	Osteria del Circo	25.00
Chiam	20.50	Park Bistro	23.50
Chin Chin	20.00	Patria	20.04
Chola	13.95	Patroon	20.04
Chur. Plataforma	27.95	Payard Bistro	28.00
Cibo	25.95	Petrossian	20.04
Citarella	35.00	Pierre au Tunnel	19.00
Compass	20.04	Pó	25.00
D'Artagnan	20.00	Primola	15.50
db Bistro Moderne	29.00	Quatorze Bis	16.00
Delegates' Dining	22.50	Queen	23.99
Diwan	12.95	Rain	20.04
Downtown	35.00	René Pujol	23.00
Duane Park Cafe	20.04	Salaam Bombay	12.95
Eleven Madison Park	25.00	San Domenico	20.04
Felidia	29.50	Sapphire Indian	11.95
Fleur de Sel	25.00	Shaan	13.95
Frère Jacques	22.00	Shaffer City	19.99
Gage & Tollner	20.00	Shun Lee Palace	20.04
Gascogne	19.50	Sushiden	25.00
Giorgio's/Gramercy	15.00	Sushi Yasuda	20.50
Gotham Bar & Grill	25.00	Tabla	25.00
Halcyon	29.00	Tamarind	20.04
Hangawi	19.95	Tavern on the Green	20.04
Heartbeat	25.00	Terrace in the Sky	25.00
Honmura An	24.00	Thalia	16.95
Icon	20.04	Tocqueville	20.04
I Trulli (Enoteca)	20.00	Tse Yang	25.75
Jackson Diner	6.95	'21' Club	32.00
Jean Georges	20.00	Ulrika's	22.00
Jewel of India	13.95	Union Pacific	20.04
JoJo	20.00	Vago	19.95
La Metairie	25.00	ViceVersa	20.04
La Palapa	9.95	Vong	20.00
La Petite Auberge	15.75	Water Club	20.04
L'Ecole	20.04	Water's Edge	29.00
Lenox	20.04	Zoë	20.04

Bargain Prix Fixe Menus
Dinner

Where applicable, the first price is for pre-theater, the second for normal dinner hours.

Algonquin Hotel†	35.00	Le Gigot†	29.00
Alouette†	22.00	Lenox†	25.00
Arqua	30.00	Le Père Pinard†	13.99
Artisanal	30.04	Le Pescadou†	25.00
Bay Leaf†	20.95	Le Tableau†	25.00
Beacon†	35.00	Levana	29.95
Becco	21.95	Le Zinc	30.03
Bistro du Nord†	18.95	Le Zoo†	21.00
Bistro Les Amis†	19.95	Lima's Taste†	16.95
Brasserie 8½†	32.00	Luxia†	27.00
Bryant Park Grill†	25.00	Madison Bistro	31.00
Café Botanica†	35.00	Mamlouk	30.00
Cafe Luxembourg	38.50	Manhattan Grille	24.95
Cafe Nosidam†	21.95	Marchi's	38.90
Candela†	19.99	Maria Pia	19.95
Capsouto Frères	30.04	Mark's†	35.00
Chelsea Bistro†	25.00	Métisse†	25.00
Chez Michallet	23/30	Métrazur	30.04
Chin Chin	30.00	Metro Fish	25.00
Chubo	24.00	Metronome†	30.00
Cibo	29.95	Michael's†	38.00
Compass	30.00	Molyvos†	34.50
Cooking w/Jazz†	17.50	Montrachet	30.04
Culinaria†	35.00	Osteria del Circo†	39.00
db Bistro Moderne†	39.00	Ouest†	26.00
Del Frisco's†	34.95	Park Bistro†	23.50
Dolphins†	20.00	Pasha†	22.95
Downtown	35.00	Payard Bistro†	34.00
Etrusca†	32/39	Petrossian	28/39
FireBird	38.00	Pierre au Tunnel	34.00
Florent	20/22	Remi	30.04
Frère Jacques†	25.00	Russian Samovar†	28.00
Gage & Tollner†	23.95	San Domenico†	32.50
Garden Cafe	25.00	Sea Grill	39.00
Gascogne†	27.00	Shaan†	21.95
Halcyon†	39.00	Sharz Cafe†	18.50
Hangawi	29.95	Sushiden	35.00
Henry's End†	21.99	Sushi Yasuda	18.50
Icon	30.04	Table d'Hôte†	22.50
Ilo†	30.00	Taka†	11.95
Indochine†	25.00	Tavern on the Green†	30.04
Jewel of India†	21.95	Tocqueville†	38.00
Joanna's†	29.75	Torre di Pisa†	26.95
Kitchen 22/82	25.00	'21' Club†	37.00
La Baraka	24/32	Uncle Jack's†	29.95
La Mediterranée	22/30	Vago†	26.00
La Metairie†	25.00	Vatan	21.95
La Petite Auberge	23.95	Verbena	30.00
Lavagna†	25.00	ViceVersa†	30.04
Le Boeuf à la Mode	35.00	Vivolo†	21.95
L'Ecole	29.95	Vong†	38.00
Le Colonial†	24.00	Water Club	39.00

† Pre-theater only

Restaurant Directory

A 🌱✏

22	10	22	$22

947 Columbus Ave. (bet. 106th & 107th Sts.), 212-531-1643

◾ Everything's "tiny" except the flavor and hospitality at this "friendly", "inexpensive" Morningside Heights BYO French-Caribbean "shoebox"; the digs are "funky" enough to "bring out the East Village in anyone."

Abigael's

19	16	18	$44

1407 Broadway (bet. 38th & 39th Sts.), 212-575-1407; www.abigaels.com

◾ "Who knew kosher could be creative?" marvel mavens of this Garment District New American whose "very decent" menu "takes the boring out" of the genre; still, kvetchers grumble that the "not-bad" noshes come at some price considering the "bland" decor.

Above

19	19	19	$49

Hilton Times Sq., 234 W. 42nd St., 21st fl. (bet. 7th & 8th Aves.), 212-642-2626

◾ "Above the fray" of 42nd Street dwells this "classy" (if "somewhat sterile"-looking) New American boasting "spectacular" views of the "new Times Square"; something of a "sleeper" for pre-theater dining, suits say it's also tops "for business lunches" and breakfasts.

Acappella 🌱

24	20	24	$63

1 Hudson St. (Chambers St.), 212-240-0163; www.acappella-restaurant.com

◼ Though not as widely known as it deserves to be, this "dark, romantic" TriBeCa Northern Italian "strikes high notes" with its "amazing" classic dishes and "attentive" black-tie staff; not surprisingly for such a "special-occasion" haven, it has high tabs, but at least the "spine-tingling" gratis grappa will leave one "warbling."

Acme Bar & Grill ◑

15	12	14	$23

9 Great Jones St. (bet. B'way & Lafayette St.), 212-420-1934

◼ NoHo's own little Acadiana may "look like a truck stop", but it can't be beat for "big piles of cheap" Cajun "comfort" "basics"; no wonder it attracts "large gatherings" who troop downstairs after dinner to hear live bands at Acme Underground.

Acqua

18	17	18	$32

718 Amsterdam Ave. (bet. 94th & 95th Sts.), 212-222-2752

◾ The "neighborhood's hurting for reasonably priced Italian" eateries like this West 90s newcomer according to denizens delighted with its "reasonable", "straightforward" fare and "pretty space"; others see "such potential", but feel it still "has kinks to work out."

Acqua Pazza

▽	24	21	23	$49

36 W. 52nd St. (bet. 5th & 6th Aves.), 212-582-6900; www.acquapazzanyc.com

◼ "Sure to be a hit", this "civilized" new Midtown Italian seafooder is luring area lunchers with its "scrumptious" "fresh fish" and "deft service"; the early word is it's also "great for dinner with colleagues" – particularly if they're paying.

Adä

▽	21	23	22	$55

208 E. 58th St. (bet. 2nd & 3rd Aves.), 212-371-6060; www.adarestaurant.com

◼ "Looks like France, tastes like India" is the lowdown on this "beautiful, modern" Eastsider where "your mouth will think you're in paradise" given the creative "haute" subcontinental cuisine; wallet-watchers protest prices that seem "expensive" for the genre.

Aesop's Tables 🌱

23	19	20	$44

1233 Bay St. (Maryland Ave.), Staten Island, 718-720-2005; www.aesopstables.net

◼ For a "springtime" "fairytale eating experience", Slers hit the "delightful" back garden blooming with "flowering plants" at this "tiny, quaint" Med–New American bistro; enjoyed inside or out, the kitchen's handiwork is deemed "excellent and original."

Afghan Kebab House
18 | 10 | 16 | $21

2680 Broadway (102nd St.), 212-280-3500
764 Ninth Ave. (bet. 51st & 52nd Sts.), 212-307-1612
1345 Second Ave. (bet. 70th & 71st Sts.), 212-517-2776
155 W. 46th St. (bet. 6th & 7th Aves.), 212-768-3875
74-16 37th Ave. (bet. 74th & 75th Sts.), Queens, 718-565-0471
■ "Tender, succulent kebabs" and other "down-home Afghan eats" are available all over town thanks to this "friendly" chain whose "no-frills" setup deters few, especially given a "spice-to-price" ratio, paired with a BYO policy that adds up to "penny-pincher paradise."

Agave
18 | 19 | 17 | $35

140 Seventh Ave. S. (bet. Charles & W. 10th Sts.), 212-989-2100
☑ "New and trying hard", this West Villager's "off to a good start" with its "attractive" faux-"pueblo" digs and "solid" Southwestern fare reflecting a "creative twist" or two; as for the "warm" staff, a few feel they're "still working out the kinks."

Agozar
▽ 18 | 17 | 16 | $36

324 Bowery (bet. Bleecker & Bond Sts.), 212-677-6773; www.agozarnyc.com
☑ "Small, spicy dishes served in a small, spicy space" is the word on this *muy* "fun" new NoHo Cubano, where "creative tapas", Havana-style mix with "pitchers of mojitos" for all-around "good vibes"; still, a few note all those "tiny portions" can get "expensive."

Aigo
– | – | – | E

1608 First Ave. (bet. 83rd & 84th Sts.), 212-327-4700
Named after a Provençal garlic soup and simmering with a sunny color scheme, this ambitious Upper Eastsider features a pricey Mediterranean menu topped off by a how-did-they-do-that soufflé filled with ice cream.

AIX
23 | 24 | 22 | $59

2398 Broadway (88th St.), 212-874-7400; www.aixnyc.com
■ "Aix marks the spot" for chef Didier Virot's "exceptionally creative" French newcomer, one of the rare reasons "to dine out on the Upper West Side"; its "adult" bi-level space and "pro service" add other reasons that have kept it full since day one despite Midtown prices.

aka Cafe ❶
20 | 15 | 18 | $28

49 Clinton St. (bet. Rivington & Stanton Sts.), 212-979-6096; www.akacafe.com
■ Aka "71 Junior", this "funkier", "cheaper" chip off the Lower East Side block "just oozes cool", and its "innovative", "freaking awesome" Eclectic "sandwiches and snacks" "hold up to the hip factor"; "tiny" portions make for perfect "grazing" with a "tasty" cocktail or two.

Aki
24 | 14 | 21 | $37

181 W. Fourth St. (bet. Barrow & Jones Sts.), 212-989-5440
■ Only in NY (ok, only in the Village) could you find Japanese-Jamaican cuisine – notably "simply fabulous" sushi that's "not to be missed for inventiveness alone"; selfish regulars hope the "obscure" address will prevent its sliver of a room from becoming overrun.

Aki Sushi
19 | 11 | 17 | $28

366 W. 52nd St. (bet. 8th & 9th Aves.), 212-262-2888
1425 York Ave. (bet. 75th & 76th Sts.), 212-628-8885
☑ These West Side–East Side Japanese "neighborhood locals" slice "big, fresh, reasonably priced" sushi in "no-ambiance" quarters; no wonder many go for the "fast delivery" or "convenient takeout."

ALAIN DUCASSE ⌧ | 27 | 27 | 27 | $185

Essex House, 155 W. 58th St. (bet. 6th & 7th Aves.), 212-265-7300; www.alain-ducasse.com
■ If you can get over the price at what is the city's most expensive restaurant, you'll find that Michelin 9-star chef Alain Ducasse delivers the "ultimate" in "sybaritic" French multicourse dining; his "rapture"-inducing cuisine is "impeccably" served amid surroundings "calibrated for sophistication, luxury and elegance", and at least this "dream-come-true" experience is cheaper than flying to his restaurants in Paris and Monte Carlo; N.B. dinner only; if you can't handle the tab, try his less expensive eatery Mix a block east.

Al Bustan | 21 | 15 | 19 | $40

827 Third Ave. (bet. 50th & 51st Sts.), 212-759-5933
■ "Freshness is the key" to the appeal of this "rare" (in NY, anyway) upscale Lebanese on the East Side that's especially beloved for its "scrumptious" meze; "tasteful" (if "bland") decor and "gracious" service make it fine for "taking a client", while the $21.95 lunch menu is the answer for anyone who finds it "too expensive."

Al Di La | 25 | 17 | 20 | $39

248 Fifth Ave. (Carroll St.), Brooklyn, 718-783-4565; www.aldilatrattoria.com
■ "Substitute the Gowanus Canal for the Grand Canal" and you've got this Park Slope Venetian, where "rich, delicious", "sophisticated"-yet-"simple" cuisine comes in a "casual" "storefront"; among the "best in the neighborhood" – heck, "the whole city" – its "popularity" and "no-reservations policy" spell "lines around the block."

Aleo | ▽ 24 | 21 | 23 | $35

7 W. 20th St. (5th Ave.), 212-691-8136; www.aleorestaurant.com
■ Fans of the former Flatironer Bondi appreciate that nothing's changed much decorwise since this Med-Italian "great newcomer" took its place (including the "beautiful little garden"); early visitors are "pleasantly surprised" by the ambitious offerings and sincere service.

Alfama | 20 | 19 | 21 | $44

551 Hudson St. (Perry St.), 212-645-2500; www.alfamarestaurant.com
■ "Lisbon would be proud" of the "classy" cuisine at this "pretty" West Village Portuguese, where "surprisingly lovely dining experiences" are bolstered by a "deep" wine/port list, not to mention "gorgeous waiters" clad in sailor suits; N.B. there's live fado on Wednesdays.

Alfredo of Rome | 18 | 18 | 20 | $45

4 W. 49th St. (bet. 5th & 6th Aves.), 212-397-0100; www.alfredos.com
☑ "Order the fettuccine Alfredo and you won't be disappointed" say fans of this big, "friendly" Rockefeller Center Italian that's both a "tourist destination" and a "business" lunch standby; the less-impressed shrug "ok", but "nothing to write Roma about."

Algonquin Hotel | 16 | 22 | 18 | $51

Algonquin Hotel, 59 W. 44th St. (bet. 5th & 6th Aves.), 212-840-6800; www.algonquinhotel.com
☑ Come "soak up the memories" along with a "perfect martini" at this "historic" Midtown "warhorse" whose "'30s-throwback" interior "feels as if Dorothy Parker et al. might show up at any moment"; the lobby "can't be beat for a drink", and the Oak Room's "ace" for cabaret, but the American fare is only "passable" and pricey to boot.

Alias ⌧ | 22 | 16 | 20 | $40

76 Clinton St. (Rivington St.), 212-505-5011
■ "By any other name" it would still be darn "good eating" at this "small", "way cool" Lower East Side American sibling to 71 Clinton,

whose "great-value" menu bursts with "creative" flavors; equally "hip" is the "sleek interior", which you'd never guess was behind its "authentic bodega front."

Alice's Tea Cup
18 | 22 | 15 | $21 |

102 W. 73rd St. (bet. Amsterdam & Columbus Aves.), 212-799-3006; www.alicesteacup.com

◪ Enter a "testosterone-free zone" at this "adorable" West Side tearoom pouring 100-plus varieties to go with its "yummy sandwiches and pastries"; "flaky" service (did she "fall down the rabbit hole"?) and "long waits" aside, all agree it's "just so much fun."

Allioli ◕
▽ 24 | 19 | 19 | $36 |

291 Grand St. (bet. Havemeyer & Roebling Sts.), Brooklyn, 718-218-7338; www.allioli.net

■ "Not your everyday tapas" joint, this "hipster"-friendly Williamsburg Spaniard mixes "Iberian traditions with modern flavors" to "delicious" effect, while the "*muy bueno*" sangria has "trustafarian and sandalista" patrons "dreaming of Spain"; P.S. "sit in the garden" if weather permits.

Alma
23 | 21 | 19 | $32 |

187 Columbia St. (DeGraw St.), Brooklyn, 718-643-5400; www.almarestaurant.com

■ "A taste of real Mexico" awaits at the border – the Carroll Gardens–Red Hook border, that is – where this "exciting" eatery produces "high-end" dishes that taste all the better thanks to the "view of Manhattan" from its "rooftop patio"; in short, it "has fun written all over it."

Alma Blue
– | – | – | M |

179 Prince St. (bet. Sullivan & Thompson Sts.), 212-471-2345

Quietly opening in a restaurant-filled zone of SoHo, this moderately priced Mediterranean provides streetside people-watching and a simple but tasteful interior; there's nothing understated about the menu, however, which features the likes of gnocchi made with broccoli rabe.

Alouette
19 | 17 | 17 | $41 |

2588 Broadway (bet. 97th & 98th Sts.), 212-222-6808

■ In an area awash in bodegas and fast-food eateries, this West 90s French bistro stands in "charming" "relief" with its "pleasant" fare and "quiet" vibe; for such "fine dining" at "fair prices", denizens don't mind if service can be "stuffy" and the "tiny" quarters "*coude à coude.*"

Alphabet Kitchen ◕
20 | 19 | 16 | $33 |

171 Ave. A (bet. 10th & 11th Sts.), 212-982-3838; www.alphabetkitchen.net

■ "Tapas with an interesting twist" plus "serious sangria" and modest prices have East Villagers in "love" with this "sultry" Spaniard, which also boasts "model-y hostesses" and an "outdoor garden you can smoke in"; as to the noise level, one diner's "lively" is another's "loud."

Amaranth ◕
▽ 18 | 16 | 16 | $50 |

21 E. 62nd St. (bet. 5th & Madison Aves.), 212-980-6700

◪ Break out your "gold card and heels" for visits to this "chichi" East Side "Euro"-magnet, where the "air-kiss crowd" collects for "good times" and "nothing-special" Mediterranean bites; non-"socialites" detect "a little too much attitude" and "noise", but there aren't many better places to show off your tan.

Amarone ◕
18 | 13 | 18 | $35 |

686 Ninth Ave. (bet. 47th & 48th Sts.), 212-245-6060

◪ Ideal for "catching a meal before the show", this "dependable", "reasonably priced" Hell's Kitchen Italian is appreciated more for its "fresh, handmade pasta" and "friendly", "get-you-there-in-time" service than for its "tired-looking" interior.

Ambassador Grill

18	17	17	$52

Millennium UN Plaza Hotel, 1 UN Plaza (44th St., bet. 1st & 2nd Aves.), 212-702-5014

◪ "Diplomats and expense-account" types favor this "classy" American across from the UN for "quiet, private" "business" dining, as well as its "incredible Sunday champagne brunch"; if some "love the atmosphere", more say its "mirrored-disco look" "needs updating."

America

14	14	14	$28

9 E. 18th St. (bet. B'way & 5th Ave.), 212-505-2110; www.arkrestaurants.com

◪ All America, including "teens, tots and tourists", converges at this stadium-size Flatironer whose "huge" menu includes "PB&J, tenderloin and just about everything in between"; though definitely "not gourmet", it's sure to "please everyone's wallet", if not their ears – these "decibel levels" "put the 'din' in dinner."

American Grill

21	17	21	$44

420 Forest Ave. (bet. Bard Ave. & Hart Blvd.), Staten Island, 718-442-4742; www.americangrill.org

■ "Staten Island's place to see and be seen" is this "classy", "pricey" source for "real American food at its best" ("chops, fish") and service that "makes everyone feel at home"; no wonder local "politicos" and luminaries grace its "cozy" interior as well as its wall of "caricatures."

American Park

18	22	18	$46

Battery Park (opp. 17 State St.), 212-809-5508; www.americanpark.com

◪ You're sure to "impress out-of-towners" at this Battery Park "version of Tavern on the Green", where the American food's "acceptable" and "every table has a good view" of "Lady Liberty"; it's a "fabulous experience on a lovely day", but expect to "pay for the location, baby."

Amici Amore I

20	17	20	$35

29-35 Newtown Ave. (30th St.), Queens, 718-267-2771; www.amiciamore1.com

■ "Flavorful, painstakingly prepared" Italian classics and "upbeat, courteous service" have regulars of "gracious" chef-owner Dino Redzic's Astoria trattoria wanting to "keep this treasure to themselves"; too bad, because it'll likely be busier "now that MoMA Queens" is only a short drive away.

Amma

▽ 23	20	21	$33

246 E. 51st St. (bet. 2nd & 3rd Aves.), 212-644-8330

■ The "chic" decor and matching prices "let you know you're in Midtown" at this superior East 50s Indian newcomer; the "high-quality" cuisine's "explosion of flavor", "warm" service and "best-value" lunch are further reasons it's "welcome" to the scene.

Amuse ●◪
(fka The Tonic)

22	22	21	$44

108 W. 18th St. (bet. 6th & 7th Aves.), 212-929-9755; www.amusenyc.com

■ Tickling the fancy of Chelseaites, this "sexy" "revamp of The Tonic" offers a "scintillating" New American menu with "different portion sizes" to encourage "sampling and sharing"; overall it's a "clever" (if "pricey") concept that's obviously appreciated by the "active crowd" at its handsome 100-year-old mahogany bar.

Amy Ruth's

20	11	16	$22

113 W. 116th St. (bet. Lenox & 7th Aves.), 212-280-8779

■ Southern "home cooking" so "heavenly" it'll "make you slap yo' mama" is the specialty at Carl Redding's "artery-clogging" Harlem soul fooder that's best known for some of "the best" and cheapest ribs and fried chicken around; service is "sweet" and "slow as molasses", but "large portions and lots of seasoning" make it "well worth" any wait.

Amy's Bread   23 11 16 $12

Chelsea Mkt., 75 Ninth Ave. (bet. 15th & 16th Sts.), 212-462-4338
972 Lexington Ave. (bet. 70th & 71st Sts.), 212-537-0270
672 Ninth Ave. (bet. 46th & 47th Sts.), 212-977-2670 ⊟
www.amysbread.com
■ It's "carb heaven" at this "fantastic" bakery/cafe trio where "killer" "artisan" breads and baked goods are the star attractions, but "interesting" sandwiches and soups are also "standouts"; "tiny", "cramped" quarters mean many "grab a loaf and run."

Anche Vivolo ●⊠   18 15 20 $42

222 E. 58th St. (bet. 2nd & 3rd Aves.), 212-308-0112;
www.vivolonyc.com
☑ An "old-style Italian that has withstood the test of the time", this East Side "neighborhood haunt" "near Bloomie's" may have "staid" surroundings, but its "doting service" and "fabulous early-bird special" ($21.95) make it a natural for its "older clientele."

Angelica Kitchen ⊟   20 14 16 $22

300 E. 12th St. (bet. 1st & 2nd Aves.), 212-228-2909
☑ "It'll get you addicted to veggies" warn regulars of this East Village vegan whose "vibrant" all-natural offerings ("no plain old Boca burgers" here) are served up in digs like a "'50s diner gone holistic"; the less-Zen disdain "ashram-chic" decor and "spacey" servers.

Angelina's   22 19 19 $53

26 Jefferson Blvd. (Annadale Rd.), Staten Island, 718-227-7100;
www.angelinasristorante.com
☑ Hostess-with-the-mostest Angelina is "always roaming to make sure things are going well" at this "upscale" SI Italian; its "strip-mall" setting is often "crowded" and "loud", but "exceptional" (if "expensive") traditional fare and "old-school" service make it all "tolerable."

Angelo & Maxie's   21 18 18 $48

1285 Sixth Ave. (bet. 51st & 52nd Sts.), 212-459-1222
233 Park Ave. S. (19th St.), 212-220-9200 ●
www.mootwo.com
☑ "Solid performers in the testosterone-and-cholesterol genre", these "straightforward", "best-value" steakhouses appeal to "young" "carnivores" with "humongous" steaks and "meet-market" bar scenes; "brash service" and "crowded", "damn noisy" conditions mean they're not for the faint-of-heart.

Angelo's of Mulberry Street   22 15 19 $39

146 Mulberry St. (bet. Grand & Hester Sts.), 212-966-1277;
www.angelomulberry.com
☑ "Remains a classic" laud lovers of this "famous" Little Italy Italian, where the red-gravy fare is "heavenly" and the "pro" waiters "steal the show"; the crowd may be "touristy" and the "old-style" decor in need of "freshening up", but regulars respect it "for what it is."

Angelo's Pizzeria   20 12 16 $22

1043 Second Ave. (55th St.), 212-521-3600
117 W. 57th St. (bet. 6th & 7th Aves.), 212-333-4333
☑ "Massive brick ovens" turn out "damn good" "thin-crust pizza" at this "cheap-and-reliable" Midtown twosome known for "fresh, flavorful toppings"; it's "great for a quick fix", but beware "chaotic", "noisy" digs and "slow" service at peak times.

Angus McIndoe ●
▽ 18 | 17 | 21 | $37

258 W. 44th St. (bet. B'way & 8th Ave.), 212-221-9222;
www.angusmcindoe.com

■ "After a show you never know who you'll see" at this tri-level Theater District American that's "always swimming with B'way celebs"; the food's "solid", prices "decent" and staff "very friendly", but that's not the reason "stargazers" call it a "sure bet."

Anju ⊠
▽ 16 | 22 | 15 | $40

36 E. 20th St. (bet. B'way & Park Ave. S.), 212-674-1111; www.anjuny.com

☑ Offering "more lounge than dining", this "hip", "bi-level" Flatiron Asian tenders a "sexy" "loft" space, "potent" potables and a "pricey", "small menu" of mostly "finger food"; though the "scene dominates", some still seek out the Korean-style "cook-at-your-table" BBQ.

Annie's
16 | 14 | 15 | $27

1381 Third Ave. (bet. 78th & 79th Sts.), 212-327-4853

☑ Upper Eastsiders agree that the "chintz-filled farmhouse setting" of this "glorified diner" makes "a wonderful place to have brunch", which explains why it's "crazed" on weekend mornings; parents protest the "no-stroller policy" as "not baby-friendly."

ANNISA
26 | 23 | 23 | $62

13 Barrow St. (bet. 7th Ave. S. & W. 4th St.), 212-741-6699;
www.annisarestaurant.com

■ "Culinary powerhouse" Anita Lo's "provocative combinations" at her "refined" Greenwich Village New American are complemented by a list of "women-made wines", a "serene", "Zen-like" setting and "amicable" "pro service"; for such "wonderful experiences", it's no surprise the "price tag's high."

A.o.c.
– | – | – | M

(fka Grove)

314 Bleecker St. (Grove St.), 212-675-9463

Its name is short for *l'aile ou la cuisse* ('the wing or the thigh'), but there's more than chicken offered at this midpriced Village French bistro, e.g. classics like steak frites and salade niçoise; set in the no-frills space fka Grove, it's inherited its predecessor's spacious back patio that's long been a weekend brunch magnet.

A.O.C. Bedford
– | – | – | E

14 Bedford St. (bet. Downing & Houston Sts.), 212-414-4764;
www.aocbedford.com

Not to be confused with the similarly named nearby Villager, this new arrival takes its moniker from the French *appellation d'origine contrôlée* system of designating regional foods and wines; the menu borrows from the cuisines of France, Italy and Spain, and, as the name suggests, emphasizes high-quality, suitably priced ingredients.

ápizz ⊠
20 | 20 | 18 | $37

217 Eldridge St. (bet. Rivington & Stanton Sts.), 212-253-9199; www.apizz.com

■ Located in a "rustic, candlelit" Lower East Side converted garage, this unpronounceable, "unpretentious" Italian's cooked dishes (notably "fabulous" pizzas) acquire their "deep, robust flavor" in the "tremendous" wood-fired oven that doubles as the room's "focal point."

AQ Cafe ⊠
▽ 20 | 18 | 14 | $20

Scandinavia House, 58 Park Ave. (bet. 37th & 38th Sts.), 212-847-9745;
www.aquavit.org

■ It's "Aquavit at McDonald's prices", or almost, at this "cheerful" Midtown lunch-only Scandinavian, where the light-of-wallet and short-of-time can "sample chef Marcus Samuelsson's handiwork", albeit in a self-serve, "cafeteria-style" milieu "reminiscent of Ikea."

AQUAGRILL
26 | 19 | 22 | $51

210 Spring St. (6th Ave.), 212-274-0505

■ You often have to squeeze in to this "stylish", steeply priced SoHo "seafood mecca" in order to sample its "deliciously prepared", "couldn't-be-fresher" fish, plus its "above-and-beyond raw bar"; "friendly service" assures that everything goes swimmingly.

AQUAVIT
26 | 25 | 25 | $65

13 W. 54th St. (bet. 5th & 6th Aves.), 212-307-7311; www.aquavit.org

■ "Dream meals" are the province of this "civilized" Midtown Scandinavian where the "astonishingly beautiful" main dining room (complete with birch trees and a "two-story waterfall") and "impeccable service" befit the "inspired" cuisine that's a "veritable symphony of taste sensations"; yes, you'll need "deep pockets", but all agree it's worth it because chef Marcus Samuelsson is "a genius"; P.S. the casual upstairs cafe is more affordable.

Arabelle
▽ 25 | 25 | 25 | $71

Plaza Athénée Hotel, 37 E. 64th St. (Madison Ave.), 212-606-4647; www.arabellerestaurant.com

☑ A "beautiful" "way to escape the hustle-and-bustle" is this "elegant" East Side "quiet oasis" in the Hotel Plaza Athénée, where the "delicate", "delicious" French cuisine is served in gilt-and-Venetian-glass splendor; slightly "stuffy" service and "expensive" tabs are par for the course; N.B. closed at press time.

Areo
24 | 18 | 19 | $47

8424 Third Ave. (bet. 84th & 85th Sts.), Brooklyn, 718-238-0079

■ If you "don't mind the high hair and pinky rings", it's well "worth making a trip" to this Bay Ridge Italian, because the pastas and other classics are "to die for"; just know it's a "boisterous" place, and "if you're not Tony Soprano, you'd better be prepared to wait for a table."

Arezzo ⓢ
23 | 17 | 21 | $50

46 W. 22nd St. (bet. 5th & 6th Aves.), 212-206-0555; www.arezzonyc.com

☑ Fans report that "talented" chef Margherita Aloi's "fresh pastas are second to none" at this "casual but upscale-feeling" Flatiron Northern Italian; the service is "terrific" too, but some grumble it's "overpriced", especially considering the "noisy, stark" setup.

Arqua
21 | 19 | 22 | $50

281 Church St. (White St.), 212-334-1888

■ Long a "neighborhood family" "fixture" for "delicious", "simple" Northern Italian, this TriBeCa favorite's "well-spaced tables", sunny decor and "very attentive service" also make it a suitable candidate for "business" meals; you can't get closer to Tuscany in the U.S.

Arté
18 | 18 | 19 | $41

21 E. Ninth St. (bet. 5th Ave. & University Pl.), 212-473-0077

■ "Every neighborhood should have" a "reliable", "welcoming" "haunt" like this Village Italian, where the fireplace feels "homey" in winter and the back garden's "charming" in summer; so what if the "solid" fare is a bit on the "unimaginative" side.

Artie's Deli
17 | 10 | 14 | $20

2290 Broadway (bet. 82nd & 83rd Sts.), 212-579-5959; www.arties.com

■ "Deli-icious" declare devotees of this low-budget, "kid-friendly" knishery that may not score points for its "basic diner atmosphere", but does for its "friendly, chatty staff" and pastrami sandwiches "you can hardly wrap your mouth around"; in short, it's pretty much "what an Upper West Side deli should be."

ARTISANAL
23 | 21 | 19 | $50

2 Park Ave. (enter on 32nd St., bet. Madison & Park Aves.), 212-725-8585

■ At Terrance Brennan's Murray Hill French brasserie–cum–"cheese-lover's paradise", "even a mouse could OD" given the "remarkable" selection, matched by a "strong" wine list packed with by-the-glass choices; if service can be "snooty" and acoustics "noisy", hearts still melt at the "bargain" prix fixes and "fantastic" fromagerie selling wedges to go.

Arturo's Pizzeria ◑
20 | 12 | 14 | $22

106 W. Houston St. (Thompson St.), 212-677-3820

■ "Deservedly famous coal-oven pizza" is just part of the "fun" at this affordable "vintage" Village Italian where "kitschy", "old-world" decor and "live jazz and piano" add up to "great experiences"; no wonder it's often "cramped" and "cacophonous", with "long waits" on weekends.

A Salt & Battery
19 | 10 | 14 | $15

112 Greenwich Ave. (bet. 12th & 13th Sts.), 212-691-2713
80 Second Ave. (bet. 4th & 5th Sts.), 212-254-6610
www.asaltandbattery.com

☑ The "next best thing to London", this "chippie" duo's "cheeky" Brit staff batters up the "best damn fish 'n' chips around", both at the West Village take-out original (with a few stools) and its eat-in East Village offshoot; critics carp it's "pricey for fast food."

ASIA DE CUBA ◑
23 | 25 | 20 | $54

Morgans Hotel, 237 Madison Ave. (bet. 37th & 38th Sts.), 212-726-7755;
www.ianschragerhotels.com

☑ The "brilliant Starck-white decor" is a perfect foil for the "Euros" and "skinny 20-year-olds" who nibble "sensational", "pricey" bites at this "sexy" Murray Hill Asian-Cuban amid a "loud, brash", "South-Beach-comes-to-NY" ambiance; "snooty" tendencies aside, most find it a "very hot" scene, even if some sophisticates shrug "once cool", now "post-peak."

Assaggio
18 | 17 | 19 | $36

473 Columbus Ave. (bet. 82nd & 83rd Sts.), 212-877-0170

■ "Pleasant", "reasonable" pastas, a "welcoming atmosphere" and "even some elbow room" make this West Side Italian "neighborhood favorite" a "happy discovery" "near the Museum of Natural History"; insiders say it's "nicer in the summer when you can eat outside."

À Table
21 | 17 | 17 | $33

171 Lafayette Ave. (bet. Adelphi St. & Clermont Ave.), Brooklyn,
718-935-9121; www.atable.org

■ "Vive la Fort Greene" cheer Francophiles after sampling this "simple" Gallic country inn's "*délicieux et bon marché*" "hearty bistro fare" served at "big, wooden" communal tables; its "sharp, young" crowd tends to ignore any "attitude" lapses from the "no-nonsense" "Euro" staff.

ATELIER
26 | 25 | 25 | $89

Ritz-Carlton Central Park, 50 Central Park S. (6th Ave.), 212-521-6125;
www.ritzcarlton.com

■ Last year's "best new restaurant of the year", this "first-class-all-the-way" "phenom" in the Central Park South Ritz-Carlton is a "spacious", suitably "ritzy" showcase for chef Gabriel Kreuther's "exquisite", "creative" New French cuisine and impressive 900-label wine list; an "impeccable" pro staff that "treats you like royalty" is the crowning touch that makes it "well worth every penny" of the "$$$" tab.

ATLANTIC GRILL ◐

| 22 | 19 | 19 | $46 |

1341 Third Ave. (bet. 76th & 77th Sts.), 212-988-9200;
www.brguestrestaurants.com

■ "Another Steve Hanson treasure", this "big", "always crowded" Upper East Side "seafood haven" is prized nearly as much for its "bustling", neighborly ambiance as for its "wonderfully fresh fish"; just keep in mind that all that "energy" generates plenty of "noise", and "plan on a long wait" in the "crazy" (in a good way) bar.

Au Mandarin

| 22 | 17 | 20 | $31 |

World Financial Ctr., 200-250 Vesey St. (B'way), 212-385-0313

■ "Yay, they're back!" cheer Wall Street workers of this reopened "upscale" Chinese that excels at producing "classics for the American palate" and "attentive" service; "quick delivery" makes it a godsend "when working late."

AUREOLE ⊠

| 27 | 26 | 26 | $76 |

34 E. 61st St. (bet. Madison & Park Aves.), 212-319-1660;
www.aureolerestaurant.com

■ Charlie Palmer may be spending most of his time in Napa these days, but his team "continues to dazzle" at his East Side "flagship", where chef Dante Boccuzzi's "meticulously prepared" New American cuisine and desserts "almost too beautiful to eat" find their match in "polished-but-not-stuffy" surroundings and "superb" service; "just call it heaven" declare its "posh" patrons, who gladly "skip a mortgage payment" to savor "the essence of fine dining."

Avenue

| 19 | 15 | 15 | $37 |

520 Columbus Ave. (85th St.), 212-579-3194; www.avenuebistro.com

◩ The closest the Upper West Side comes to a Parisian neighborhood bistro, this Gallic perennial "favorite" sends out "solid" standards (including "unforgettable hot chocolate") amid "casually" "chic" environs; "slow service" and "close quarters" let you catch all of "your neighbor's conversation."

Avenue A Sushi ◐

| 18 | 17 | 14 | $27 |

103 Ave. A (bet. 6th & 7th Sts.), 212-982-8109

■ Aka "Disco Sushi" thanks to its "strobe lights" and "loud music" from nightly DJs, this East Village Japanese's "young", "hip" crowd comes as much for the "dy-no-mite" vibe as the "super" ("for the price") fish; think of it as "a party and dinner rolled into one."

Avra Estiatorio ◐

| 23 | 22 | 20 | $50 |

141 E. 48th St. (bet. Lexington & 3rd Aves.), 212-759-8550;
www.avrany.com

■ Eastsiders consider this Greek seafooder a "breath of briny sea air", thanks to its "exceptional" fish in preparations both "traditional" and "modern"; "upscale" quarters and a "caring" crew have many calling it "one of the best" in Manhattan, though the "by-the-pound pricing" "can add up."

Az

| 23 | 25 | 21 | $61 |

21 W. 17th St. (bet. 5th & 6th Aves.), 212-691-8888; www.aznyc.com

■ Though its Food rating is uncertain due to the post-*Survey* departure of chef Patricia Yeo, fans say that this "pricey" Flatiron restaurant's "creative" Asian-accented New American cuisine offers a "wonderful dining experience" "from A to Z"; its "beautiful, Zen-like" dining room, complete with glass "retractable roof" (reached via a "futuristic elevator" ride), ups the "value" quotient.

Azafran
▽ 24 | 23 | 21 | $42

77 Warren St. (bet. Greenwich St. & W. B'way), 212-284-0578;
www.myazafran.com

■ "Creative", "diverse", "delicious" tapas and "ultramodern" design have early visitors declaring this "bright" new Spaniard a "beautiful addition to TriBeCa"; "fast, cheerful" service and an "eye candy" crowd are other appeals, but "expensive" tabs can be a turnoff.

Azalea ◐
– | – | – | E

224 W. 51st St. (bet. B'way & 8th Ave.), 212-262-0105

Offering interesting Italian dishes from Parma and the Amalfi Coast, this airy Theater District newcomer (in the former Trionfo space) presents a fresh option for ticket-holders and business diners, with an attractive $35 pre-theater prix fixe to boot.

Azul Bistro
▽ 20 | 18 | 19 | $35

152 Stanton St. (Suffolk St.), 646-602-2004

■ "Go late, stay long" is the M.O. of mavens who favor this Lower East Side Argentinean, where, naturally, "excellent" "meat is the main" attraction; "enthusiastic service" and "interesting" decor also contribute to its overall "great value."

Azuri Cafe ⇗
▽ 24 | 4 | 8 | $13

465 W. 51st St. (bet. 9th & 10th Aves.), 212-262-2920

☑ "Some of the best Israeli food around" – notably "incredible" falafel – for just a few shekels is why lunchtime lines form at this "shacklike" Midtowner; just "watch out" for the "moody" owner (he can "make the soup Nazi seem welcoming").

BABBO ◐
27 | 23 | 24 | $68

110 Waverly Pl. (bet. MacDougal St. & 6th Ave.), 212-777-0303;
www.babbonyc.com

■ "Mario Batali has the Midas touch" (as does his partner Joe Bastianich) and it shows at his Village "crown jewel" that, after 19 years, has edged out Il Mulino as the "best Italian in NYC"; "crowds, noise" and prices notwithstanding, "heavenly experiences" here consist of "rich", "exotic", "truly original" cuisine backed by a "dream" wine list, a "sophisticated, yet casual", two-floor carriage house setting and "knowledgeable" (some say "snobbish") service; those wishing to go must "pray" and keep "hitting redial" because "it's easier to win the lottery than get a reservation."

Baci
▽ 23 | 18 | 22 | $41

7107 Third Ave. (71st St.), Brooklyn, 718-836-5536

■ "If he's in the mood", the "opera-singing owner" of this "tiny", "homestyle" Bay Ridge Italian will "serenade" you "while you eat" (and "he's isn't bad"); given the "*delizioso*" classic dishes and "quaint", "romantic" ambiance, locals croon it's "a find."

Baldoria
20 | 17 | 19 | $54

249 W. 49th St. (bet. B'way & 8th Ave.), 212-582-0460; www.baldoriamo.com

☑ "If you can't get into Rao's – and who can?" – "chip-off-the-old-block" Frank Pellegrino Jr.'s "Sinatra"-worthy Theater District duplex Italian "is the next best thing"; "big", "terrific" red-sauce portions, a "fun", jukebox-aided vibe and "helpful" service lead most to take in stride the "noisy" acoustics and "expensive" tabs.

Baldo Vino ◐
▽ 18 | 23 | 21 | $34

126 E. Seventh St. (bet. Ave. A & 1st Ave.), 212-979-0319

■ The old country comes to the East Village via this "charming" new "farmhouse"-style Italian wine bar/eatery full of "personality" as well as lots of "rustic" Tuscan chandeliers and knickknacks; "surprisingly

tasty and original pastas" are among the "light", "homespun" offerings
served up by the cordial staff.

Bali Nusa Indah
19 | 9 | 17 | $24

651 Ninth Ave. (bet. 45th & 46th Sts.), 212-265-2200

◪ For a "good introduction" to Indonesian food, this "authentic"
Theater District "bargain" is "one of the few" options in the city; if the
decor cries out for a "freshening-up", "eager" staffers who help
navigate the many "exotic" options compensate.

BALTHAZAR ◐
23 | 23 | 19 | $50

80 Spring St. (bet. B'way & Crosby St.), 212-965-1414;
www.balthazarny.com

◼ "Still hip, still gorgeous" and "still a scene", this "crowded", "noisy"
SoHo "quintessential" French brasserie ("without the smoke or
attitude") is "the quickest way to Paris now that the Concorde is no
longer flying"; sure, a few "tourists" have joined the "celebs" and
"beautiful people" at its "close, small" tables, but given the "superb"
classic fare and "fabulous" ambiance, few dispute that this "hot spot"
is "aging well."

Baluchi's
18 | 14 | 15 | $25

283 Columbus Ave. (bet. 73rd & 74th Sts.), 212-579-3900
224 E. 53rd St. (bet. 2nd & 3rd Aves.), 212-750-5515
1431 First Ave. (74th St.), 212-396-1400
1149 First Ave. (63rd St.), 212-371-3535
1724 Second Ave. (bet. 89th & 90th Sts.), 212-996-2600
1565 Second Ave. (bet. 81st & 82nd Sts.), 212-288-4810
104 Second Ave. (6th St.), 212-780-6000
361 Sixth Ave. (Washington Pl.), 212-929-2441
193 Spring St. (bet. Sullivan & Thompson Sts.), 212-226-2828
240 W. 56th St. (bet. B'way & 8th Ave.), 212-397-0707
Additional locations throughout the NY area
www.baluchis.com

◼ "Currying favor" all over town with its "well-spiced", well-priced
"reliable" dishes, this "above-par" Indian chain is also appreciated
for its "prompt" service and "half-price lunch deal" that lets you "eat
like a maharaja without spending like one."

Bambou
21 | 23 | 19 | $44

243 E. 14th St. (bet. 2nd & 3rd Aves.), 212-358-0012;
www.bambounyc.com

◪ For an instant "island escape", travel to this "upscale" East Village
French-Caribbean, whose "dark", "languorous" interior seems all
the more "romantic" after an "exotic" cocktail or two; focus on the
"interesting" cuisine and you'll hardly notice if the staff's "a bit flaky."

Bamonte's
23 | 16 | 21 | $38

32 Withers St. (bet. Lorimer St. & Union Ave.), Brooklyn,
718-384-8831

◼ "Some things never change – and that's a good thing" at this more
than 100-year-old Williamsburg Italian frequented by an "old-time"
"cast of characters" who all "seem to know each other"; sample the
"real-deal" "red-sauce" classics delivered by waiters "older than
your grandfather" and you'll agree "you can't beat the nostalgia."

Banania Cafe ⇝
22 | 17 | 18 | $30

241 Smith St. (Douglass St.), Brooklyn, 718-237-9100

◼ A "Smith Street pioneer still holding its own", this "easygoing",
"affordable" Cobble Hill French bistro "never fails" to please with its
"intriguing" roster of "comforting, delicious" dishes; often "crowded",
it's really "popular" for its "delightful" weekend brunch.

Bandol Bistro

19	17	19	$43

181 E. 78th St. (bet. Lexington & 3rd Aves.), 212-744-1800;
www.bandolbistro.com

◪ This "quaint, little" Upper East Side French bistro "caters to locals" who detect a "hint of Paree" in its "pleasant" cooking and "interesting" regional wine list; a less-enchanted minority shrugs "pleasant enough" but "nothing spectacular", adding it's "expensive for what it is."

Banjara ◐

22	16	19	$29

97 First Ave. (6th St.), 212-477-5956

■ "Don't be put off by the location", because this East Village Indian is a "true standout" from the Curry Row competition thanks to its "unexpected" dishes both "delicious" and "authentic"; other pluses are "attentive" service and a room that, while a bit "dark", is "better than most" on the strip.

Bann Thai

22	21	20	$30

69-12 Austin St. (Yellowstone Blvd.), Queens, 718-544-9999;
www.bannthairestaurant.com

■ Somewhat "obscurely located" "toward the quieter end of Austin Street" in Forest Hills, this "tiny" Thai "packs 'em in" nonetheless with its fairly priced, "flawlessly" prepared dishes, "charming" "jewel box" space and "friendly" staff; locals feel "lucky to have it."

Bao 111 ◐

∇ 22	20	19	$38

111 Ave. C (7th St.), 212-254-7773

■ "Cool food in cool digs" is the early word on this new East Village Vietnamese whose slim, "simple-yet-chic" interior has been packed from day one with "hipsters"; "incredibly fresh" "nouveau" cuisine and a "hospitable" vibe should keep them coming.

Baraonda ◐

18	17	15	$40

1439 Second Ave. (75th St.), 212-288-8555; www.baraondany.com

◪ "Dancing on the tables keeps the calories down" for the "skinny" "Euros" who go "Macarena crazy" "after hours" at this "festive", "noisy", "tightly" packed East Side Italian; though the pastas and such are "decent enough", you're there "for the scene, not the food."

Barbalùc

∇ 17	21	17	$58

135 E. 65th St. (Lexington Ave.), 212-774-1999

◪ "Chichi" Eastsiders are clicking their Manolos with delight over this "sophisticated" new Northern Italian and its "strikingly" "sleek" decor, "interesting" dishes from the Friuli region and "elegant" upstairs bar; admirers see "lots of potential", but the less-convinced simply call it "too pricey."

Barbetta ⊠

20	23	20	$56

321 W. 46th St. (bet. 8th & 9th Aves.), 212-246-9171;
www.barbettarestaurant.com

■ "Approaching 100", this "lovely townhouse" Theater District Italian "has only improved with age" according to partisans of its "palazzo"-like interior, "glorious" statuary-filled garden, "satisfying" authentic fare and "doting" service; some say it's "superannuated" and "overpriced", but legions of loyalists laud it as "a holiday from modern times."

Bar 89 ◐

16	23	16	$29

89 Mercer St. (bet. Broome & Spring Sts.), 212-274-0989

◪ "Freak out" visiting friends with a trip to this "noisy", "energetic" SoHo American's claim-to-fame "cool bathrooms", whose "clear-glass doors" fog when you lock them ("they can't see you . . . or can they?"); as for the moderately priced "dressed-up bar fare", it's strictly secondary to the "mean" cocktails.

Barking Dog ⊐

Dumont Plaza Hotel, 150 E. 34th St. (bet. Le...
1678 Third Ave. (94th St.), 212-831-1800
1453 York Ave. (77th St.), 212-861-3600

■ "Sit! stay!" and "chow down" at these "d...
friendly" East Side Americans where the "two-foo...
legged" brave "stroller pileups" for "basic" "com...
"cheap"; if the staff needs a little "obedience training",...
who line up for weekend brunch don't growl about it.

Barney Greengrass ⊐

| 23 | 7 | 13 |

541 Amsterdam Ave. (bet. 86th & 87th Sts.), 212-724-4707

■ "Ridiculous lines" at brunch, "cranky-but-lovable" service and "agita"-inducing prices are all part of the "experience" at this circa-1908 Upper West Side "landmark"; look for bagels and "delicious smoked fish" plus an ambiance that's "old NY at its bustling best" – and if the seriously "dated" digs "ain't elegant", that's deliberate.

Barolo ◐

| 19 | 22 | 18 | $47 |

398 W. Broadway (bet. Broome & Spring Sts.), 212-226-1102;
www.nybarolo.com

☑ On a fine "summer evening", there are few more "lovely" places than this "stylish" SoHo Italian's "splendorous" garden, where a "fun" "twenty"-something "scene" flourishes; while the "food and service don't quite measure up", the "expensive" prices are every bit as "grand", ditto the "superb wine list."

Bar Pitti ◐⊐

| 21 | 14 | 17 | $33 |

268 Sixth Ave. (bet. Bleecker & Houston Sts.), 212-982-3300

■ "Pitti there's not one of these places on every corner" because this Village Italian's "fresh" pastas, "good value", summer sidewalk seating and "model/celeb" scoping spell "long lines" nightly; insiders suggest "come early or late" to avoid the wait.

BarTabac ◐

| 17 | 19 | 15 | $28 |

128 Smith St. (Dean St.), Brooklyn, 718-923-0918

■ Could be "the set of *Amélie*" say "Francophiles" of this "cute", "more-French-than-France" Boerum Hill bistro beloved by locals for its "solid-deal" "standards" and "free foosball"; just consider it "Bar*Non*Tabac" now that "Bloomberg's new law" is in place.

Basil, The

| 19 | 18 | 18 | $35 |

206 W. 23rd St. (bet. 7th & 8th Aves.), 212-242-1014

■ Holy Basil's "more upscale" new Chelsea Thai "offshoot" makes "a welcome addition" to the area according to admirers of its "exquisitely presented", "inventive", "tasty" fare and "stylish, clean" aesthetic; still, some fear it may be a bit "undervalued and overlooked."

Basso Est ◐

| ▽ 24 | 18 | 26 | $35 |

198 Orchard St. (Stanton St.), 212-358-9469

■ The name means 'Lower East' (a nod to its way-Downtown address), and this "cheerful" Italian newcomer is certainly neighborhood appropriate: small, "cozy" and *basso*-priced, yet ambitious in the cooking department; the few surveyors who've visited so far pronounce it "fantastic", especially the *simpatico* service.

Basta Pasta

| 21 | 16 | 20 | $36 |

37 W. 17th St. (bet. 5th & 6th Aves.), 212-366-0888

■ "Japan-ized Italian" (think "*Iron Chef*" "al dente") is the "quirky" concept at this "sleek" Flatiron "fusion pasta" joint where the Boot-rific dishes with a "subtle" "Asian influence" come out of an "immaculate open kitchen"; "service as memorable as the food" seals the deal.

| | | 25 | 24 | $64 |

`...com`

...Bayou "wonderful", if ... the "magical" ...ered" due to its ...e Bernardin and ...al cuisine that's ...old-world", and ...ble" pro service; ...omenal party site.

| | 18 | 19 | $34 |

...ington & 3rd Aves.), 212-871-3300

...oggy-themed", "kid- ...ted" and the "...ort food" on the ...the "crowds"

17 | 14 | 15 | $21 | $24

...average" cuisine and caring ... ...popular" with the "Midtown business crowd"; if the dinner menu... ...ghtly "pricey", the $12.95 lunch buffet is one of the city's "best bargains."

Bayou
19 | 15 | 17 | $32

308 Lenox Ave. (bet. 125th & 126th Sts.), 212-426-3800;
www.bayouinharlem.com

☑ Locals feel "gungho about the gumbo" and other "reliable", "spicy" Crescent City favorites at this Harlem Creole specialist; though an authentically "welcoming", "funky joint", it does spin something of a "NYC twist" (a few feel it's "a bit overpriced" for the genre).

BB Sandwich Bar ◐
21 | 4 | 13 | $7

120 W. Third St. (bet. MacDougal St. & 6th Ave.), 212-473-7500

☑ "Get extra napkins – you'll need 'em" at this Village "hole-in-the-wall" that serves just one "perfect creation": a "messy", slightly "spicy", "heavenly" riff on the Philly cheese steak; purists may sniff it's "not the original", but even they agree for a "quick, cheap" bite it's hard to beat.

Beacon
23 | 22 | 21 | $55

25 W. 56th St. (bet. 5th & 6th Aves.), 212-332-0500

■ Waldy Malouf's Midtown New American "temple to wood-fired" cookery is a "triumph" according to addicts of its "hearty" fare and "handsome", "multilevel", "Frank Lloyd Wright"–inspired room centered around an "open kitchen"; wallet-watchers who protest its "pricey" dinner tabs endorse the "terrific $19.95 lunch" prix fixe.

Becco ◐
21 | 17 | 19 | $39

355 W. 46th St. (bet. 8th & 9th Aves.), 212-397-7597; www.becconyc.com

■ At this Italian "Theater District star", "you can't go wrong" with the $21.95 "all-you-can-eat pasta" dinner and "$20-a-bottle wine list", though there are also lots of other "delicious" options; a recent expansion should help with the pre-curtain "overcrowding."

Bella Blu ◐
19 | 16 | 16 | $42

967 Lexington Ave. (bet. 70th & 71st Sts.), 212-988-4624;
www.bellablu.com

☑ No one "leaves feeling blue" from this "fun" East Side Northern Italian, given its "energetic", "young" scene and "better-than-expected" pastas and wood-oven pizzas; service may be "uneven" and acoustics "really loud", but that doesn't keep the "crowds" away.

Bella Donna
18 | 9 | 15 | $24

307 E. 77th St. (bet. 1st & 2nd Aves.), 212-535-2866
1663 First Ave. (bet. 86th & 87th Sts.), 212-534-3261

■ What these "too-small" East Side Italian "carbo-loaders" "lack in decor", they "make up for in tasty food", "friendly" service and "unbeatable" prices; locals count them as "major neighborhood assets"; N.B. 77th Street is BYO.

Bella Luna
17 | 15 | 17 | $32

584 Columbus Ave. (bet. 88th & 89th Sts.), 212-877-2267

☑ "Loyal customers" tout this "newly renovated" Upper West Side "neighborhood favorite" for "solid" Italian cooking, "friendly", "hardworking" service and pricing that's "light on the wallet"; however, critics call it "unremarkable."

Bella Via
▽ 18 | 16 | 18 | $29

47-46 Vernon Blvd. (48th Ave.), Queens, 718-361-7510

■ "Who would expect" "wonderful thin-crust pizza" just a stone's throw from "the entrance to the Midtown Tunnel"?; this "friendly", affordable Italian is a "welcome addition to Long Island City" indeed, offering pastas and other classics along with the coal-fired pies that are its star attraction.

Bellavista Cafe
▽ 19 | 17 | 19 | $31

554 W. 235th St. (bet. Johnson & Oxford Aves.), Bronx, 718-548-2354

■ "Cozy, homey and friendly", this moderately priced Riverdale Italian's "inviting" vibe is enhanced by blooms from an adjacent flower shop; its traditional dishes are "a notch up" from the ordinary, but some locals consider it "a little pricey for the neighborhood."

Bellini 🅳
22 | 20 | 22 | $52

208 E. 52nd St. (bet. 2nd & 3rd Aves.), 212-308-0830

■ "Expense-accounters" and other deep pockets find "la dolce vita" at this "refined", "old-school" Midtown Neapolitan known for its "expensive", "first-rate" fare and "accommodating" staff; a further allure is the "warm hospitality" of "charming" owner Donatella Arpaia.

Bello 🅳
20 | 15 | 19 | $40

863 Ninth Ave. (56th St.), 212-246-6773; www.bellorestaurant.com

■ Ok, maybe it is "your father's Italian", but that's not a bad thing at this "solid, steady" Hell's Kitchen "standby" serving *bello* classics in "generous portions"; its "quiet", "white-linen" milieu makes for a "pleasant" "pre-theater bite", and the "free parking is a real plus."

Belluno 🅳
20 | 19 | 21 | $42

340 Lexington Ave. (bet. 39th & 40th Sts.), 212-953-3282; www.bellunoristorante.com

■ "Much-needed" in its "underserved" corner of Murray Hill, this "airy", "multilevel" Italian is still something of a "sleeper"; "solid" standard fare, "gracious", "unobtrusive" service and "romantic digs" perfect "for quiet conversation" result in romeos relying on it as a "great date" place.

Ben Benson's
22 | 16 | 20 | $59

123 W. 52nd St. (bet. 6th & 7th Aves.), 212-581-8888

■ "When only gin and cholesterol will do", try this "venerable", "expense account"–friendly Midtown meat manor's mega-martinis and "giant" "slabs of beef"; if the "attentive" waiters can be "cranky" and the blond wood–paneled quarters "cramped" and "noisy", "old-boy" regulars would expect nothing less.

Benihana of Tokyo
16 | 14 | 18 | $37

120 E. 56th St. (bet. Lexington & Park Aves.), 212-593-1627
47 W. 56th St. (bet. 5th & 6th Aves.), 212-581-0930
www.benihana.com

☑ Good "cheesy fun" is in the air at this moderately priced, "dinner-and-a-show-rolled-into-one" Japanese steakhouse chain, where "families and groups" go to be "entertained by the chefs" with "knives and food flying at you"; it's especially "wonderful for kids and tourists", who don't mind if the theatrics are "better than the food."

Benny's Burritos

17 | 9 | 13 | $16

93 Ave. A (6th St.), 212-254-2054 ●
113 Greenwich Ave. (Jane St.), 212-727-0584

■ "So big they need their own zip code" attest admirers of the "cheap", "wholesome" "tasty" burritos that are the trademark of these separately owned Downtown Mexican "holes-in-the-wall"; given the "no-frills", nearly "no-service" setup, many make it "takeout."

Ben's Kosher Deli

18 | 11 | 14 | $21

209 W. 38th St. (bet. 7th & 8th Aves.), 212-398-2367
Bay Terrace, 211-37 26th Ave. (211th St.), Queens, 718-229-2367
www.bensdeli.net

◪ "Mouthwatering", "overstuffed sandwiches" have kosher-keepers kvelling over these Garment District–Queens outlets of a national deli chain; others kvetch "there are better places", but they're cheap enough and will "do in a pinch."

Beppe ⊠

22 | 21 | 20 | $52

45 E. 22nd St. (bet. B'way & Park Ave. S.), 212-982-8422; www.trulytuscan.com

■ Italophiles "longing for the tastes of Tuscany" travel to Cesare Casella's Flatiron Italian for "inspired" "rustic" cooking that "brings back memories of Siena"; given the "romantic", "serene" setting and "knowledgeable" service, most "leave feeling peppe", if poorer.

Bereket ●⊅

20 | 4 | 12 | $11

187 E. Houston St. (Orchard St.), 212-475-7700

■ Despite "zero ambiance", the "diverse" crowd at this 24/7 Lower East Side "cafeteria-style" Turkish "kebab joint" happily "ignores its appearance"; "moist" grilled goods, "animated" slam-bang service and "dirt-cheap prices" add up to "late-night-munchie" "perfection."

Beso

∇ 19 | 13 | 16 | $26

210 Fifth Ave. (Union St.), Brooklyn, 718-783-4902

■ "Funky" Slopers line up for "loud, crowded" "fabulous brunches" at this Nuevo Latino known for its "rich, delicious" cooking; it's "rarely crowded" at dinner because the "simple decor" is a bit "lacking" ("change the lighting and these guys would do sensationally").

Better Burger ●

16 | 10 | 15 | $14

178 Eighth Ave. (19th St.), 212-989-6688
565 Third Ave. (37th St.), 212-949-7528
www.betterburgernyc.com

◪ "Organic" burgers and hot dogs with "air-baked fries" and a "fat-free shake" let you "satisfy fast-food cravings" "without the guilt" at these "virtuous" Murray Hill–Chelsea "joints"; the unconverted sense "something's missing" ("better than what?").

Beyoglu ●

21 | 17 | 18 | $31

1431 Third Ave. (81st St.), 212-650-0850

■ "Deservedly popular" for its "out-of-this-world" meze (think "Turkish tapas") and kebabs, this Upper East Side newcomer gets as "crowded" and "noisy" as "a bazaar"; still, "moderate" prices and a staff that "treats you like a pasha" provide "much to love."

Bice ●

20 | 19 | 18 | $55

7 E. 54th St. (bet. 5th & Madison Aves.), 212-688-1999

◪ At this stylish Midtown Northern Italian "institution", the "flashy, Eurotrashy", "air-kissing" "floor show" comes "with no cover charge", though the "dependable" but "expensive" dishes may set you back a ways; service that's "welcoming for regulars" has the hoi polloi calling it "pretentious with a capital 'P.'"

Bienvenue 🄩   ▽ 20 14 22 $40
21 E. 36th St. (Madison Ave.), 212-684-0215

■ "Adorable", "motherly" "French waitresses" "take care of you" at this "small" Murray Hill Gallic bistro, and the kitchen's "solid" standards complete the "pleasantly" "homey" experience; every neighborhood should "have such a standby."

Big Nick's Burger Joint ●   18 5 12 $14
2175 Broadway (77th St.), 212-362-9238

☑ At this "dumpy-but-lovable" 24/7 Upper West Side "dive", the "encyclopedic menu" (especially the "sumo-size" burgers) and "taste-for-value" ratio are "beyond compare"; however, given the decor and service – or lack thereof – many opt to "order out."

Big Wong ⊅   22 3 11 $12
67 Mott St. (bet. Bayard & Canal Sts.), 212-964-0540

☑ "Better for the adventurous diner", this "bustling" Chinatown Cantonese is famed for its "inner warmth"–inspiring congee and noodles; regulars happily "ignore" the "rough" service and "dingy", "no-decor" quarters, focusing on the "super-cheap", "authentic" eats.

Bill Hong's   20 12 18 $44
227 E. 56th St. (bet. 2nd & 3rd Aves.), 212-751-4048;
www.billhongs.com

☑ "A loyal following" patronizes this circa-'55 Midtown Chinese that "captures the spirit" of Cantonese eateries "of yesteryear" with its "classic" cuisine and "time-warp" decor; the prices are as "rich" as its history, but nonetheless it's "always busy."

Billy's ●   16 12 18 $42
948 First Ave. (bet. 52nd & 53rd Sts.), 212-753-1870

☑ For "real" "old-fashioned chophouse atmosphere", the "50-plus crowd" favors this circa-1870 Sutton Place "saloon" where "plain, wholesome" pub fare is served by a staff nearly "as old as the restaurant"; if upstarts claim it's "pricey" and "beyond its prime", devotees declare it "deserves discovery by the next generation."

Biricchino 🄩   20 10 18 $33
260 W. 29th St. (8th Ave.), 212-695-6690

☑ It *is* possible to find "great eats near the Garden" thanks to this plain but "friendly" Chelsea "stalwart" known for its "homey", "reasonable" Italian menu featuring super "sausage choices"; wags wink it's "much easier to stomach than the Rangers."

Bistro du Nord   19 17 18 $44
1312 Madison Ave. (93rd St.), 212-289-0997

■ "You're in Paris" claim Carnegie Hill clients of this "adorable" French bistro where "delicious" cooking and a "cramped", "jewel-box" interior make for a transporting time; if the regular menu's "a little pricey", there's always the "bargain prix fixe."

Bistro Les Amis ●   21 17 20 $37
180 Spring St. (Thompson St.), 212-226-8645;
www.bistrolesamis.com

■ To "bring back memories" of pre-"Prada" SoHo, try this "low-key" French bistro whose "hearty", "midpriced" dishes and "cozy, dimly lit" quarters (plus sidewalk seats "in kind weather") add up to "comforting" meals minus the "trendiness."

Bistro Le Steak ◑
18 | 14 | 17 | $40

1309 Third Ave. (75th St.), 212-517-3800

Ok, "it's not the Palm", but this "noisy", "informal" East Side "steak-frites joint" is a "solid" "neighborhood" choice; the interior may need "sprucing up" and the staff an "attitude" adjustment, but the fact that it's always "crowded" speaks for itself.

Bistro St. Mark's
24 | 19 | 19 | $39

76 St. Mark's Ave. (Flatbush Ave.), Brooklyn, 718-857-8600

Located on an "out-of-the-way" Park Slope block, this "jewel" of a French bistro is resoundingly voted "worth the trip", thanks to Johannes Sanzin's "subtle"-yet-"inventive" cuisine; its "hip" loftlike interior is supplemented by a "fabulous", "funky" garden, and the service is "pleasant" (if "slow").

Bistro Ten 18
19 | 18 | 19 | $34

1018 Amsterdam Ave. (110th St.), 212-662-7600

"Tasty", "homestyle" French classics, moderate prices and "pretty, romantic" decor account for this "comfortable" Morningside Heights bistro's popularity with Columbia U. types; the view of St. John the Divine is a big bonus.

Black Duck
∇ 20 | 17 | 17 | $44

Park South Hotel, 122 E. 28th St. (bet. Lexington Ave. & Park Ave. S.), 212-448-0888; www.parksouthhotel.com

Named for a Prohibition era rum-running ship, this "maritime-themed" Gramercy New American sails on the power of its "solid", seafood-oriented fare and "dimly seductive" digs; with live jazz on weekends, romeos recommend it as a "first-date place."

Bleu Evolution ◑
∇ 17 | 22 | 16 | $27

808 W. 187th St. (Fort Washington Ave.), 212-928-6006; www.metrobase.com/bleu

One part "Moulin Rouge", one part "tag sale", this Washington Heights French-Moroccan's "funky" interior casts a "seductive" spell, even if its "eclectic" cuisine can be "hit-or-miss" and its staff "slow"; locals, "grateful" for this "oasis", urge "don't miss the back garden."

Blue 9 Burger ◑₽
17 | 5 | 10 | $8

92 Third Ave. (12th St.), 212-979-0053

"Succulent", "fresh", "California-style burgers" "cooked to order" have Left Coast "expats" calling this "cheap", no-frills East Villager "as close to In-N-Out Burger as you'll find east of Vegas"; on the downside, service is "slow for fast food" and there's "not much atmosphere" unless "grease" counts for decor.

bluechili
∇ 23 | 25 | 20 | $38

251 W. 51st St. (bet. B'way & 8th Ave.), 212-246-3330; www.bluechilinyc.com

The owner of Red Garlic has gone "trendy" with this new Theater District Pan-Asian, whose "very cool, all-white" interior sports a waterfall and lighting that changes hue as the night wears on; its "killer drinks" and "inventive" dishes have met with early approval.

Blue Fin ◑
22 | 23 | 19 | $52

W Hotel Times Sq., 1567 Broadway (47th St.), 212-918-1400; www.brguestrestaurants.com

"When you want to feel glamorous", impress "out-of-towners" or just "watch the Times Square crowd go by", Steve Hanson's "buzzing" seafooder is just the ticket; given the "ultra-mod" bi-level space and "fintastic" fare, its "beautiful" habitués (plus the odd "fanny-packed tourist") are undeterred by "pricey" tabs, sometimes-"amateurish" service and "can't-hear-yourself-chew" acoustics.

Blue Hill
25 | 22 | 24 | $61

75 Washington Pl. (bet. 6th Ave. & Washington Sq. W.), 212-539-1776;
www.bluehillnyc.com

■ "Intelligence and taste" prevail at this "elegant, yet low-key" Village New American, where chefs Daniel Barber and Michael Anthony create "complex", "exquisite" seasonal cuisine reflecting "integrity and a commitment to local producers"; figure in a "personable" staff and "very cool", "minimalist" setting (complete with garden seating in summer), and few wince at the "expensive" bill.

BLUE RIBBON ●
25 | 19 | 22 | $47

97 Sullivan St. (bet. Prince & Spring Sts.), 212-274-0404
280 Fifth Ave. (bet. 1st St. & Garfield Pl.), Brooklyn, 718-840-0404

■ "Thank you, Brombergs" enthuse "loyal followers" of brothers/owners Bruce and Eric and their "SoHo institution" (with a new, larger Park Slope outpost), whose "glorious" New American menu ensures that it's perpetually "jammed"; "amazing" at any hour, it's possibly "the best place in NY to get a serious meal after midnight" (till 4 AM), though it "doesn't take reservations", so "expect to wait."

Blue Ribbon Bakery ●
24 | 18 | 20 | $38

33 Downing St. (Bedford St.), 212-337-0404

■ "Grazers with wide-ranging tastes" gravitate toward this Greenwich Village New American that offers myriad "mouthwatering choices" (plus "breadbaskets to die for") to go with its "fantastic sidewalk-watching" from the street level room's "huge windows"; closely spaced "small tables" create a "European" feel, though "long waits" for the "fabulous" weekend brunch are very NYC.

Blue Ribbon Sushi
25 | 19 | 21 | $48

119 Sullivan St. (bet. Prince & Spring Sts.), 212-343-0404 ●
278 Fifth Ave. (bet. 1st St. & Garfield Pl.), Brooklyn, 718-840-0408 ⊠

■ "Fresh, fresh, fresh" fish and a "wicked sake assortment" ensure that this "hip" SoHo sushi specialist is still "jamming" "after all these years", and now there's a "roomier" Park Slope offshoot that's become "quite the Fifth Avenue scene"; despite an expansion, the original remains "tight" and its "no-reservations" policy spells "long waits" – thankfully in good company.

Blue Smoke
19 | 17 | 19 | $39

116 E. 27th St. (bet. Lexington & Park Aves.), 212-447-7733;
www.bluesmoke.com

◪ Proving that nobody's perfect, not even Danny Meyer, many surveyors were "disappointed" at the outset that his Gramercy "haute BBQ" didn't cut it, but most agree that it "has improved" a lot since then; now 'cue-nnoisseurs tout the ribs and sides here, and suggest that you bring your dancing shoes to this "deliberately unfancy" joint since after eating, you can "work it off jiving downstairs" at the Jazz Standard; P.S. vegetarians need not apply.

BLUE WATER GRILL ●
23 | 22 | 20 | $48

31 Union Sq. W. (16th St.), 212-675-9500; www.brguestrestaurants.com

■ At Steve Hanson's Union Square "perennial favorite", "superior seafood" comes in a "gorgeous", "soaring" (and "a tad noisy") "converted bank" setting; figure in a "hot" crowd, "sultry downstairs jazz room", and "impeccable" raw bar, and it's deemed a "bankable" bet for a "marvelous" experience, with plenty of "bang for the buck."

Boat Basin Cafe ●
11 | 20 | 11 | $22

W. 79th St. (Hudson River), 212-496-5542; www.boatbasincafe.com

◪ With "unbeatable decor" "provided by the Hudson River" and "boats bobbing" in the marina, this "atmospheric" "hangout" in Riverside Park "impresses even hardened New Yorkers"; the Traditional American fare may be "just ok", but the burgers are "good", the cocktails "strong" and the "view priceless"; N.B. open mid-April–October.

Boat House
16 | 25 | 16 | $46

Central Park, enter on E. 72nd St. (Central Park Dr. N.), 212-517-2233; www.thecentralparkboathouse.com

☑ "Even jaded locals" go misty over the "tranquil", "romantic" setting of this New American "oasis" "tucked away" beside Central Park's boat pond, and a recently added glass wall ensures that its "magical" view can now be enjoyed "in any season"; oh, yes, and the "food's pretty good" too.

Bobby Van's Steakhouse ☒
23 | 17 | 21 | $59

230 Park Ave. (46th St.), 212-867-5490; www.bobbyvans.com

☑ "Huge, juicy steaks" "as thick as your arm" are the forte of this Midtown "manly man" red meatery, and if the "prices cost you that, plus your leg", carnivores don't complain much given the "generous cocktails" and "personable", real "noo yawk" staff; all in all it's a "solid entry", if "not quite in the first tier of Manhattan steak palaces."

Boca Chica
20 | 14 | 16 | $27

13 First Ave. (1st St.), 212-473-0108

■ "Small, loud and lotsa fun", this East Village South American is a magnet for "festive", "young" sorts who gamely "squeeze in" for "humongous portions" of "affordable", *muy* "tasty" fare; just watch those "plenty-strong tropical drinks" – they "pack a punch."

Bo-Ky ⊅
19 | 5 | 11 | $12

80 Bayard St. (bet. Mott & Mulberry Sts.), 212-406-2292

☑ "Big bowls of steaming soup" have slurpaholics standing in line at this "bustling" Vietnamese noodle shop; devotees deem it a true "Chinatown experience", complete with "fast", no-frills service and "unbeatable prices", "so why worry" about "shabby" decor?

Bolo
22 | 19 | 21 | $51

23 E. 22nd St. (bet. B'way & Park Ave. S.), 212-228-2200; www.bolorestaurant.com

☑ "Flay, *olé*" cheer fans of "celeb chef" Bobby Flay and his "colorful", "classy-yet-casual" Flatiron Spaniard that spins "delectable" "twists" on the classics (including a "terrific new tapas" menu), served by "attentive" staffers; despite grumbles over "pricey" tabs, the majority maintains it's "worthy of the buzz."

Bombay Palace
18 | 17 | 18 | $34

30 W. 52nd St. (bet. 5th & 6th Aves.), 212-541-7777

☑ Could be the "best deal in Midtown" swear "bargain"-hunters of this "old-style" Indian's $12.95 "savory" lunch buffet; at dinner, the "refined" air and "unrushed staff" notwithstanding, there are complaints about the "unchanging menu" and slightly "expensive" prices.

Bond Street ◑
25 | 23 | 18 | $59

6 Bond St. (bet. B'way & Lafayette St.), 212-777-2500

☑ "Decide to be fabulous" and join the "hip and chic" at this pricey NoHo Japanese where the "chichi sushi" is as "exquisite" as the "sleek", "minimalist" space; both are in danger of being upstaged by the "gorgeous clientele" (especially in the "downstairs lounge").

Bonita
▽ 22 | 21 | 17 | $19

338 Bedford Ave. (bet. S. 2nd & 3rd Sts.), Brooklyn, 718-384-9500

☑ Providing "fresh", "slightly nouveau", moderately priced Mexican fare, this budget-friendly yearling from the owners of nearby Diner boasts a "cool space" complete with outdoor seating; the "too-hip vibe can be a turnoff", but what do you expect? – it's Williamsburg.

Borgo Antico ●
18	18	20	$38

22 E. 13th St. (bet. 5th Ave. & University Pl.), 212-807-1313;
www.borgoanticonyc.com

■ "Almost like Florence", this "sweet" Village Italian is "dependable" for "hearty", "rustic" pastas; "charming owners", an "obliging" staff and a "comfortable" "upstairs dining room" make it "return-worthy."

Bottino
19	19	17	$43

246 10th Ave. (bet. 24th & 25th Sts.), 212-206-6766; www.bottinonyc.com

■ "Art-world" types, "fashionistas" and "Euros" lend a "Calvin-Klein-campaign-come-to-life" feel to this "cool" Northern Italian in West Chelsea's gallery district; the fare's "sleek and simple, like the decor", and served by "gorgeous" (if "snooty") staffers to regulars who vie for "coveted tables" in the "glorious" back garden.

Bouchon
22	17	21	$37

41 Greenwich Ave. (bet. Charles & Perry Sts.), 212-255-5972

■ Locals in-the-know uncork the kudos when describing this "adorable", midpriced Village bistro whose "delicious", "really French" classics taste all the better for the "refreshingly friendly" service; habitués hope the rest of the world "won't catch on."

BOULEY ●
28	26	26	$82

120 W. Broadway (Duane St.), 212-964-2525; www.bouley.net

■ Devotees may debate whether he's "a god", "a genius" or simply "the most inventive chef in NYC", but most agree that David Bouley's TriBeCa New French provides "transcendent experiences" featuring "exquisitely creative" and "complex" cuisine, a "romantic" "vaulted" interior and "attentive" pro service; dinner prices are "not for the faint of heart", but the "sumptuous" $35 prix fixe lunch is a "bargain."

Bouterin
21	23	20	$57

420 E. 59th St. (bet. 1st Ave. & Sutton Pl.), 212-758-0323

■ "Ah, to be in Provence" sigh sojourners to this "beautiful" Sutton Place Gallic whose sunny, "fresh flower"–filled "country French" digs threaten to outshine the "tasty" cuisine; "peaceful and serene", it's a "great place to take the parents" or throw a "bridal shower."

Box Tree
20	25	22	$73

250 E. 49th St. (bet. 2nd & 3rd Aves.), 212-758-8320;
www.boxtreerestaurant.com

◪ Back on the scene after years of labor disputes, "you'd never know" that this "exquisite" Midtown townhouse – a "romantic trysting spot" that's "the perfect place for proposing" – is now "kosher at its finest" (kosher French, that is); "very high prices" mean most reserve it for very "special nights."

Branzini
∇ 20	15	18	$41

Library Hotel, 299 Madison Ave. (41st St.), 212-557-3340

■ "Go for the namesake" sea bass recommend regulars of this casual, midpriced Med that also serves as a "respite from the hustle-and-bustle" near Grand Central; it also offers "decent" salads and the like, but foes note the "tight" quarters make for "too much togetherness."

Brasserie ●
20	23	19	$46

100 E. 53rd St. (bet. Lexington & Park Aves.), 212-751-4840;
www.restaurantassociates.com

■ "Strike a pose" while strutting the "neon-lighted runway" entrance to this Midtown "modern twist on the classic brasserie"; the "cool elegance and futuristic vibe", not to mention "terrific" cuisine, ensure it's "still one of the hippest" ways to "impress a guest or client."

Brasserie 8½
21 | 24 | 21 | $50

9 W. 57th St. (bet. 5th & 6th Aves.), 212-829-0812; www.restaurantassociates.com

■ "Burberry-Bulgari-Bergdorf" shoppers share real estate with "*Sex and the City*" sorts at this "stunning" Midtown brasserie whose "spacious" "mid-century modern" dining room always elicits "wows", as do the bills; chef Julian Alonzo's food is "delicious", but the "after-work" set mostly comes for the "gorgeous" bar/lounge.

Brasserie Julien
18 | 18 | 17 | $41

1422 Third Ave. (bet. 80th & 81st Sts.), 212-744-6327

■ Few can say *non* to an "easy, casual" "neighborhood" French bistro like this Yorkville "gem" run by a "charming" couple; "terrific" burgers and other "enjoyable" fare, "soothing" live jazz on Saturday nights and recently added sidewalk seating cinch the deal.

Brasserie 360
18 | 17 | 16 | $46

200 E. 60th St. (3rd Ave.), 212-688-8688

☑ To discover "what sushi has to do with French brasserie" cooking, try this "promising" bi-level newcomer "across from Bloomie's", where so far the "schizo" "Paris-Asia" concept "seems to work"; it's just the thing for an "after-shopping" breather, even if the service "could use improvement."

Bravo Gianni ●
21 | 15 | 20 | $59

230 E. 63rd St. (bet. 2nd & 3rd Aves.), 212-752-7272

☑ Bring "a big appetite" and a fat wallet to fully enjoy this "clubby" East Side "old-school Italian", and say *ciao* to chef/owner Gianni, who's "always at the door to welcome you"; the "reliably tasty" "traditional" fare outshines the "tired decor", as does the "friendly" staff.

Brawta Caribbean Café
▽ 19 | 11 | 14 | $22

347 Atlantic Ave. (Hoyt St.), Brooklyn, 718-855-5515

☑ "Slow down, mon", because while the "authentic", "cheap" Caribbean eats at this "extra-small" Boerum Hill BYO have "flavor and spice to spare", "the wait can be long"; "the food's the thing" at this "no-decor" delight, but the prices add allure.

Bread
22 | 14 | 16 | $20

301 Church St. (Walker St.), 212-334-8282
20 Spring St. (bet. Elizabeth & Mott Sts.), 212-334-1015

■ "Wanna-be models" and "hipsters" find "wonderfully crusty" panini for not too much bread at this bite-size NoLita cafe serving "heavenly" goods from Balthazar Bakery; those who gripe about the "cramped" space can now head to a roomier, full-menu TriBeCa sibling that opened post-*Survey.*

Bread Bar at Tabla
24 | 23 | 22 | $39

11 Madison Ave. (25th St.), 212-889-0667

■ It's a naan-stop "sharing festival" report those who gather at Tabla's "more-affordable" downstairs "little sister" on Madison Square to munch "creative", "luscious" Indian-inspired mini-dishes and flatbreads while sipping "exotic cocktails"; it sets the standard for "distinctive" "upscale-casual" dining, especially "out on the patio."

Brennan & Carr ●⊟
– | – | – | I

3432 Nostrand Ave. (Ave. U), Brooklyn, 718-646-9559

The aroma of fried food permeates this low-budget, 66-year-old Sheepshead Bay fast-fooder where nearly everyone orders the signature roast beef sandwich; it's a toss-up whether the wood-paneled walls or the well-seasoned staff are more craggy.

Bricco
19 | 17 | 18 | $37

304 W. 56th St. (bet. 8th & 9th Aves.), 212-245-7160; www.bricconyc.com
■ Ladies, "don't forget to leave a lipstick kiss on the ceiling", as required by tradition at this "low-key" West Midtown Southern Italian where the "thin-crusted" pizzas and other "better-than-reliable" eats inspire smooches; no wonder it's a "pre-theater" "favorite."

Brick Cafe
▽ 19 | 22 | 22 | $30

30-95 33rd St. (31st Ave.), Queens, 718-267-2735
■ Further evidence that "Astoria is getting hip", this Northern Italian newcomer's "charmingly rustic" interior and "tasty", "Queens-priced" classics have locals labeling it "the best place to come around in a long time"; other pluses include sidewalk seating in summer and a "cozy" next-door lounge.

Brick Lane Curry House
21 | 15 | 17 | $28

342 E. Sixth St. (bet. 1st & 2nd Aves.), 212-979-2900
■ "Named for London's Indian [dining] district", this "upscale" yearling on the East Village's Curry Row was a "front-runner" from day one due to its "fresh", "well-spiced" dishes; just watch out for the "woo-hoo hot" phaal curry ("there's a reason they offer a free beer if you can finish it").

Bridge Cafe
21 | 16 | 20 | $40

279 Water St. (Dover St.), 212-227-3344
■ "Taste NYC history" along with "delicious" New American cuisine at this "quiet" brick-walled "hideaway" housed in a circa-1794 building under the Brooklyn Bridge; yes, it's "a bit out of the way", but most consider it "worth the search."

Bright Food Shop
19 | 10 | 15 | $25

216-218 Eighth Ave. (21st St.), 212-243-4433; www.kitchenmarket.com
☑ It sounds like "a weird combo", but devotees of this Chelsea Asian-Mexican report that it provides "inventive" fare that'll "wake up your taste buds"; too bad the "loosey-goosey" staff and "drab" decor don't have the same "zing", though a post-*Survey* expansion may have "added some ambiance."

Brio
18 | 14 | 19 | $38

786 Lexington Ave. (61st St.), 212-980-2300; www.brionyc.com
■ This "comfy" East Side Italian makes the "perfect place" to "unwind after shopping" Bloomingdale's, thanks to its "wholesome" classic dishes and "unrushed" vibe; for more of "a quick bite", patrons pop "around the corner" for "killer pizza" at its sibling, Brio Forno Cafe.

Brooklyn Diner USA ❍
16 | 13 | 15 | $29

212 W. 57th St. (bet. B'way & 7th Ave.), 212-977-2280; www.brooklyndiner.com
☑ Ok, so "it's not in Brooklyn" and "it's not really a diner", but Shelly Fireman's "retro" Midtowner is "very popular" anyway for "surprisingly good comfort food" in "gigantic portions"; if some "seasoned NYers" sniff it's an "overpriced parody", even more opine "it's a fun place."

Brother Jimmy's BBQ ❍
16 | 10 | 13 | $23

428 Amsterdam Ave. (bet. 80th & 81st Sts.), 212-501-7515
1485 Second Ave. (bet. 77th & 78th Sts.), 212-288-0999
1644 Third Ave. (93rd St.), 212-426-2020
www.brotherjimmys.com
☑ "Dress down" because it "gets messy" at these "loud, crowded" Southern BBQ pits where "ribs rule" and "twentysomethings" kick up

a "rowdy" "frat-party" scene (especially "watching ACC games"); parents willing to venture in appreciate that kids under 12 "eat free."

Bruculino
20 | 15 | 20 | $34

225 Columbus Ave. (70th St.), 212-579-3966

■ Spared the "crazy waits" at its "down-the-street" "sister" Pomodoro, this more "mellow" West Side Italian is a local "favorite" for its "hearty" "classic" dishes in "generous servings" at reasonable prices; add "pleasing" service and boosters croon "*bellissima!*"

Brunelli
19 | 16 | 20 | $40

1409 York Ave. (75th St.), 212-744-8899

■ "First-timers feel like regulars" at this "thumbs-up" Yorkville Italian where "the service is genuine", the "old-country" dishes are "always good" and the "portions are huge"; it's a "festive", "family"-oriented kind of place (i.e. "take your mother, not your date").

Bruno ⧄
20 | 18 | 21 | $53

240 E. 58th St. (bet. 2nd & 3rd Aves.), 212-688-4190; www.brunosnyc.com

■ "Stay until Danny begins his show" in the piano bar recommend regulars of this "upscale", "no-surprises" Midtown Italian near the Queensboro Bridge, whose "interesting, tough-guy crowd" is looked after by "attentive" black-tie "pro waiters"; come more than once and owner Bruno "will know your name."

Bryant Park Grill/Cafe
16 | 21 | 15 | $41

behind NY Public Library, 25 W. 40th St. (bet. 5th & 6th Aves.), 212-840-6500; www.arkrestaurants.com

☑ Food's "not really the point" at these "delightful" "Midtown escapes", where the "solid" American fare is "outclassed" by the "splendid" "park view", whether in the more formal "glass-walled" Grill or more casual alfresco Cafe; they're "pickup city" after work, when singles suffer "sticker shock" and "slightly daft" service.

B. Smith's Restaurant Row
18 | 19 | 18 | $44

320 W. 46th St. (bet. 8th & 9th Aves.), 212-315-1100; www.bsmith.com

☑ "Good energy" abounds at this "hoppin'" Restaurant Row Eclectic, especially when "beautiful" owner Barbara Smith is there to add "spark" to the "souped-up Southern" fare; just know it's "popular with tourists" and can get "a little noisy" around curtain time.

Bubby's
19 | 14 | 15 | $27

120 Hudson St. (N. Moore St.), 212-219-0666; www.bubbys.com

☑ The "ultimate in comfort food", this "kid-friendly", "no-frills" TriBeCa American "institution" offers "celeb-spotting" (is that "J.Lo and Ben"?) along with its "upscale", but moderately priced diner eats; "terrible acoustics" and staffers who're "a bit dizzy" don't deter the "hordes" who queue up for the brunch "hullabaloo."

Bukhara Grill
22 | 17 | 20 | $35

230 E. 58th St. (bet. 2nd & 3rd Aves.), 212-339-0050
217 E. 49th St. (bet. 2nd & 3rd Aves.), 212-888-2839

■ It's "worth the extra rupee" to sample specialties "so different from typical Indian fare" at these "well-spiced" Midtown subcontinentals; the "elegant, carefully" presented lunch buffet is "an incredible deal" at $13.95, but just don't be "overwhelmed" by the "doting" staff.

Bull & Bear ◐
20 | 22 | 20 | $54

Waldorf-Astoria, 570 Lexington Ave. (49th St.), 212-872-4900;
www.waldorfastoria.com

■ "Tradition abounds" at the Waldorf-Astoria's "classic" "old-school" beef house, where "waiters at least 100 years old" serve seriously priced, "solid steaks" to "suits" in "handsome" quarters; a "younger business" crowd convenes at the bar for "after-the-close drinks."

Bull Run ☒   17 | 16 | 17 | $43

Club Quarters Hotel, 52 William St. (Pine St.), 212-859-2200

☑ "Looks and feels like a Wall Street hangout" say surveyors of this "pricey" Financial District New American; foes shrug "satisfactory" but "nothing special", while the more bullish say it's a "reliable", "attractive choice for business meals"; N.B. closed weekends.

Burger Heaven   16 | 8 | 13 | $16

9 E. 53rd St. (bet. 5th & Madison Aves.), 212-752-0340
20 E. 49th St. (bet. 5th & Madison Aves.), 212-755-2166 ☒
804 Lexington Ave. (62nd St.), 212-838-3580
536 Madison Ave. (bet. 54th & 55th Sts.), 212-753-4214
291 Madison Ave. (bet. 40th & 41st Sts.), 212-685-6250 ☒
www.burgerheavenny.com

☑ Possibly "the fastest decent hamburgers" around come off the grill of these "great-value" Midtown "lunchtime staples", and the "get-'em-in, get-'em-out" service suits supporters just fine given the "tightly packed, noisy" digs; others simply opine "heaven, it ain't."

burger joint at   23 | 11 | 13 | $12
Le Parker Meridien ●≠

Le Parker Meridien, 119 W. 56th St. (bet. 6th & 7th Aves.), 212-708-7414

■ "Follow your nose" through the Parker Meridien's lobby and "past the curtain" to this "most incongruous" "hidden greasy spoon" imaginable, where "perfect", "juicy", "grilled-to-order" burgers and "ethereal" fries await; you may not believe this place could exist, but it's already "crowded" enough that "you'll stand in line at lunch."

Burritoville   17 | 6 | 12 | $12

298 Bleecker St. (7th Ave. S.), 212-633-9249 ●
144 Chambers St. (bet. Greenwich St. & W. B'way), 212-571-1144
625 Ninth Ave. (44th St.), 212-333-5352 ●
1487 Second Ave. (bet. 77th & 78th Sts.), 212-472-8800 ●
141 Second Ave. (bet. 8th & 9th Sts.), 212-260-3300 ●
866 Third Ave. (52nd St.), 212-980-4111
36 Water St. (Broad St.), 212-747-1100
166 W. 72nd St. (bet. Amsterdam & Columbus Aves.), 212-580-7700 ●
352 W. 39th St. (9th Ave.), 212-563-9088
264 W. 23rd St. (bet. 7th & 8th Aves.), 212-367-9844 ●
Additional locations throughout the NY area
www.burritoville.com

☑ "Vegans and carnivores" alike find "tasty", "big, fat burritos" and other "mongo-sized" Tex-Mex meals at this "convenient", "super-fast" chain; "economical" pricing means most forgive the "dive" decor, though others opt for delivery or takeout.

Bussola Ristorante ☒   ▽ 21 | 15 | 18 | $45

65 Fourth Ave. (bet. 9th & 10th Sts.), 212-254-1940

■ It's a "mystery" why this "lovable" "classic" Village "neighborhood" Italian is such a "secret" say supporters who swear by its "surprisingly well-prepared" cuisine and recent renovation; P.S. its "can't-be-beat" gelato is available at the next-door cafe.

Butter ●☒   18 | 24 | 16 | $57

415 Lafayette St. (bet. Astor Pl. & 4th St.), 212-253-2828;
www.butterrestaurant.com

☑ It's "models, models everywhere" at this "sexy" Village New American sporting a "simply stunning" "all-wood" dining room, where "hot", "young" things stop in for "lilliputian" bites before hitting nearby

"Pangaea or Rehab"; critics complain of "attitudinous" service and "banker"-worthy prices, and note it's "more scene than cuisine."

Cabana ●
20 18 18 $32

South Street Seaport, 89 South St., Pier 17, 3rd fl. (bet. Fulton & John Sts.), 212-406-1155
1022 Third Ave. (bet. 60th & 61st Sts.), 212-980-5678
107-10 70th Rd. (bet. Austin St. & Queens Blvd.), Queens, 718-263-3600
■ "*Caliente!*" describes both the "exciting" flavors and the "sexy" scene at this "festive" Nuevo Latino mini-chain that's perpetually "packed" with "tourists" and "twentysomethings"; "reasonable" prices and free-flowing "fruity drinks" fuel the "lighthearted" mood.

Cafe Asean ⊅
21 16 18 $25

117 W. 10th St. (bet. Greenwich & 6th Aves.), 212-633-0348
■ A longtime "solid performer", this "bargain" Village Southeast Asian woks up "terrific", "fresh" dishes amid "cozy" (some say "cramped"), "shabby-chic" environs; when warm weather rolls around, locals know to ask for a table in the "cute" "back garden."

Cafe Atlas
▽ 22 22 23 $56

40 Central Park S. (bet. 5th & 6th Aves.), 212-759-9191
■ Atlas shrugged, then "cleverly reinvented itself" as this "smart" Midtown New American, a "less-formal", "less-expensive" (though not much) "fine-dining" establishment; "original" cuisine, "excellent service" and a "lovely" setting leave visitors glad it's back on the map.

Café Bar ●⊅
▽ 21 23 13 $21

32-90 36th St. (34th Ave.), Queens, 718-204-5273;
www.cafebar-lic.com
☑ Astoria's "young" and "arty" gravitate to this "hipster hangout"–cum–Greek eatery where the "fun", "retro"-"'70s" look is as "delicious" as the inexpensive, standard dishes; just keep in mind the "mellow, cool vibe" extends to the terminally "laid-back" service.

CAFÉ BOTANICA
20 26 22 $55

Essex House, 160 Central Park S. (bet. 6th & 7th Aves.), 212-484-5120
☑ "Try for a window table" to best enjoy the "fabulous Central Park South vista" from this "lush" ground-floor Med–New American, which, together with the "reliably lovely" cuisine and "pampering" service, makes for "an all-around elegant experience"; yes, it's "expensive", but there's always the "bargain" $35 dinner prix fixe.

CAFÉ BOULUD
27 22 25 $73

Surrey Hotel, 20 E. 76th St. (bet. 5th & Madison Aves.), 212-772-2600;
www.danielnyc.com
■ Though some consider it the "poor man's Daniel", this "cozy, casual version" of Daniel Boulud's flagship still ranks "among the finest" restaurants in the city (and is still "expensive" enough to require an "unlimited expense account"); "brilliant", "low-key haute" French-Eclectic cuisine, "elegant" modern quarters and "stellar service" consistently add up to "exquisite dining experiences."

Cafe Centro ⊠
21 19 20 $42

MetLife Bldg., 200 Park Ave. (45th St. & Vanderbilt Ave.), 212-818-1222;
www.restaurantassociates.com
■ Located "steps up from Grand Central" and proffering a "varied" menu of "well-crafted" fare, this "bustling" midpriced Midtown Med brasserie has long been a magnet for "commuters" and "corporate" types; although the "suits" kick up "high decibel" levels at lunch, by evening it's more "quiet" and "relaxed."

Cafe Con Leche
17 | 10 | 14 | $21

424 Amsterdam Ave. (bet. 80th & 81st Sts.), 212-595-7000
726 Amsterdam Ave. (bet. 95th & 96th Sts.), 212-678-7000

☑ Westsiders "satisfy rice-and-bean cravings" at this "basic" Cuban-Dominican duo whose "tasty" fixes of "homestyle cooking" and cafe con leche – "the best this side of Havana" – come at "Santo Domingo prices"; "fussy" types who find the digs "less-than-desirable" get it "to go."

Café de Bruxelles ◑
20 | 15 | 17 | $38

118 Greenwich Ave. (13th St.), 212-206-1830

■ "Faithful" renditions of "your Flemish favorites" are the forte of this "feels-like-old-Europe" West Village Belgian long known for its "fantastic" moules frites and "huge selection" of imported brews; no wonder it's "always bustling with diners enjoying themselves."

CAFÉ DES ARTISTES ◑
22 | 26 | 22 | $62

1 W. 67th St. (bet. Columbus Ave. & CPW), 212-877-3500;
www.cafenyc.com

■ It's "as enchanting as ever" at George and Jenifer Lang's West Side slice of "old NY", where Howard Christy Chandler's "heavenly" murals of "luscious nudes" and "lots of fresh flowers" contribute to the "magical" atmosphere; though "few artists could afford it" (save the $25 prix fixe lunch), the "delicious" French food and "pampering" service make it the perfect place "to propose – or apologize."

Cafe du Pont
18 | 13 | 17 | $38

1038 First Ave. (bet. 56th & 57th Sts.), 212-223-1133

■ "Escape the hustle and bustle" of the city in this "low-key", "postage stamp–size" Sutton Place bistro offering "consistently good" fare; it's "quiet and satisfying", especially for senior types who appreciate its early-bird prix fixe dinner.

Cafe Español ◑
19 | 13 | 17 | $31

172 Bleecker St. (bet. MacDougal & Sullivan Sts.), 212-505-0657
78 Carmine St. (bet. Bedford St. & 7th Ave. S.), 212-675-3312

☑ "Tasty" but "sneaky sangria" will have you "giggling through the meal" at these separately owned Village Spaniards that dish out "tons" of "delish" paella at "phenomenal prices"; the "loud, fun" mood makes up for iffy faux-"fiesta" digs.

Café Frida
21 | 18 | 17 | $33

368 Columbus Ave. (bet. 77th & 78th Sts.), 212-712-2929

■ A "notch above the typical", this "lively" Upper West Side "gourmet Mexican" is locally favored for its "killer guac" "made tableside" and "scrumptious margaritas"; plus, "you can't beat the price", especially considering the "low-key", "pleasing atmosphere."

Café Habana ◑
22 | 11 | 13 | $22

17 Prince St. (Elizabeth St.), 212-625-2001

☑ "Hipsters" "litter the sidewalk, waiting to get into" this "diner-esque" NoLita Cuban-Mexican "shoebox" for "cheap", "delicious" eats (including "legendary" grilled corn-on-the-cob); just "be patient" – or check out the take-out cafe around the corner.

Cafe Joul
19 | 15 | 17 | $40

1070 First Ave. (bet. 58th & 59th Sts.), 212-759-3131

■ For "French without the attitude", Sutton Place denizens duck into this "tiny" bistro run by a "lovely" husband-and-wife team and dine on "enjoyable" classics; most find the "little-bit-of-Paris" milieu "congenial" enough, but a few feel "the price is just a bit too high" for "a neighborhood place."

F   D   S   C

Cafe Lalo ◐⇄
20 | 18 | 12 | $19

201 W. 83rd St. (bet. Amsterdam Ave. & B'way), 212-496-6031; www.cafelalo.com

☑ "Sweet tooths" "shoehorn" themselves into this "mobbed", "noisy-as-all-get-out" Upper West Side "temple to pastry" (of *You've Got Mail* fame) to savor "decadent desserts"; the only sour notes are "glaring" lighting, "frazzled" service and those "absurdly long lines."

Cafe Lebowitz ◐
17 | 16 | 14 | $29

14 Spring St. (Elizabeth St.), 212-219-2399

☑ NoLita "intelligentsia" "meet and greet" over "tasty" standards at this "hip" French bistro that's been a "local favorite" from day one; still, some "disappointed" with the "unoriginal" menu and overly "laid-back" service expected more, given the Brian McNally pedigree.

Cafe Loup ◐
18 | 17 | 18 | $39

105 W. 13th St. (bet. 6th & 7th Aves.), 212-255-4746

■ "Nothing surprising, nothing disappointing" in the way of French bistro classics is what the neighbors want from this "trusted Village standby"; "comfy", "vintage photo"–filled digs, "feel-good" service and a "grown-up bar" are other reasons it's "still a winner."

Cafe Luluc ◐⇄
21 | 18 | 18 | $24

214 Smith St. (Baltic St.), Brooklyn, 718-625-3815

■ "Grooving" from "early-morning breakfast till late-evening for snacks" this "cute", "unfussy" Cobble Hill Banania Cafe offshoot "succeeds at being all things to all people" with its "lively" vibe and "affordable", "flavorful" French bistro fare "made with style."

Cafe Luxembourg ◐
21 | 18 | 19 | $46

200 W. 70th St. (bet. Amsterdam & West End Aves.), 212-873-7411

■ "Still buzzing after all these years", this Lincoln Center–area French bistro "mastered the classics" long ago, and its "glam" art deco setting still "makes everyone look good"; "potential star sightings" go a long way in making up for the "sardine" seating, "loud" acoustics and high pricing.

Cafe Mogador ◐
22 | 15 | 17 | $22

101 St. Marks Pl. (bet. Ave. A & 1st Ave.), 212-677-2226

☑ "Holding up amid the East Village's yuppie invasion", "this "busy" yet "relaxed" Moroccan still pulls in "arty, alterna" types with its "earthy, aromatic" and "cheap" tagines and such; if the staff can be "ditzy", at least they "never rush you."

Cafe Nosidam
16 | 16 | 17 | $46

768 Madison Ave. (66th St.), 212-717-5633

■ Gold-card holders "exhausted from shopping" vie with the "Viagra and Botox" set for "sidewalk" tables at this "fab" East Side Italian-American; the "expensive" bites may be "pretty good", but they're secondary to the Madison Avenue "people-watching."

Cafe Picasso
▽ 18 | 14 | 15 | $24

359 Bleecker St. (bet. Charles & W. 10th Sts.), 212-929-4774

☑ "Excellent thin-crust pizza" from a wood-burning oven is the masterwork of this often crowded, "rustic" West Village Italian, a favorite of backpacking "Euros" and other "low-budget" sorts; in warm weather, the "cute" back garden feels like "a work of art."

Café Pierre
▽ 22 | 26 | 26 | $64

Pierre Hotel, 2 E. 61st St. (5th Ave.), 212-940-8195; www.fourseasons.com

■ Exuding "grand, old-world" "elegance" on the "Versailles" model, this East Side French dining room's "soothing" virtues include "very

52   subscribe to zagat.com

fancy" (and "very expensive") cuisine and "disc[...]
"couldn't be more lovely" purr pleased patrons [...]
4 PM" in the Rotunda and imagine they're "r[...]
duchesses" as they nibble "scones and cucumbe[...]
hearty breakfasts to late-night dining to Kathl[...]dis cabaret
stylings, this is one of "the ultimate NY experiences."

Cafe Ronda
▽ | 21 | 14 | 19 | $33

249-251 Columbus Ave. (bet. 71st & 72nd Sts.), 212-579-9929
☒ "A great addition to the neighborhood" declare Upper Westsiders
of this "friendly" Med–South American that's a welcome source for
"affordable", "casual" eats (burgers, grilled items, etc.); windows that
open onto the sidewalk add to the atmosphere.

Café Sabarsky
20 | 24 | 19 | $37

Neue Galerie, 1048 Fifth Ave. (86th St.), 212-288-0665;
www.wallserestaurant.com
■ It "could be a cafe on the Ringstrasse" declare devotees of this
"*wünderbar*" Viennese in the Neue Galerie, who endure long "lines"
to be "transported" by the "gorgeous" decor and Kurt Gutenbrunner's
"divine" Austrian fare; insiders "save their calories" (and wallets) by
coming in the "off hours" for "fabulous pastries and coffee."

Cafe S.F.A. ☒
17 | 16 | 15 | $27

Saks Fifth Ave., 611 Fifth Ave., 8th fl. (bet. 49th & 50th Sts.),
212-940-4080
■ "Ladies who shop" meet "ladies who lunch" at Saks' "surprisingly
good" American "in-store cafe", snaring "seats by the window" to
take in the "view out over St. Pat's"; it's a "most civilized" way "to
recharge", despite the "long" line to get in.

Cafe Spice
18 | 15 | 15 | $26

Grand Central, lower level (42nd St. & Vanderbilt Ave.),
646-227-1300
72 University Pl. (bet. 10th & 11th Sts.), 212-253-6999
www.cafespice.com
■ "Undergrads" study up on "tasty", "non-threatening" Indian at
the "innovatively decorated", inexpensively priced Village branch of
this "cut-above-Sixth-Street" twosome; the Grand Central "take-out"
outpost's ideal for "curry fans" on the go.

Café St. Barts
17 | 21 | 16 | $32

109 E. 50th St. (Park Ave.), 212-888-2664; www.cafestbarts.com
☒ Perhaps the "basic" eats at this Midtown American "won't inspire
religious devotion", but in fine weather its "heavenly" "garden setting"
alongside St. Bartholomew's draws a faithful following; P.S. "be sure
to reserve on nice days."

Cafe Steinhof
17 | 17 | 16 | $25

422 Seventh Ave. (14th St.), Brooklyn, 718-369-7776
■ This "*gemütlich*" Austrian keeps waltzing along with "stick-to-your-
ribs" classics (including "the best Wiener schnitzel") and "great beers",
all at "good prices"; given its location in an "otherwise" culinarily
"barren" stretch of Park Slope, locals aren't complaining.

Cafeteria ◗
17 | 17 | 13 | $30

119 Seventh Ave. (17th St.), 212-414-1717
☒ "Don't be fooled by the name" – you won't find any "plastic trays" or
"hair nets" at this "slick" 24/7 Chelsea American where the "amazing
mac 'n' cheese" and other "easy-on-the-wallet" "comfort" fare is
"perfect after clubbing"; just beware the "major 'tude" of its "wanna-
be model waiters."

Cafe Topsy
(fka Papillon)

▽ 17 | 18 | 19 | $26

575 Hudson St. (bet. Bank & 11th Sts.), 646-638-2900; www.cafetopsy.com

This once-radical Villager has put its days of haute cuisine behind it and now focuses on "basic" British pub classics like fish 'n' chips, which suits fine the British expat crowd that haunts its Guinness-soaked bar; sidewalk seating in warm weather is another appeal.

Cafe Trevi ●

▽ 21 | 16 | 23 | $50

1570 First Ave. (bet. 81st & 82nd Sts.), 212-249-0040; www.cafetrevi.com

When a "reliable old standby" changes hands, "it needs to prove itself"; so far, early visitors report that the "new ownership" of this longtime Upper East Side Northern Italian is "maintaining its service and food standards"; a "friendly" feeling all around bodes well – if only they hadn't maintained the prices.

Cafe Un Deux Trois ●

15 | 14 | 16 | $39

123 W. 44th St. (bet. B'way & 6th Ave.), 212-354-4148;
www.cafeundeuxtrois.biz

"Chaotic" and "noisy" it may be, but this perennial "Theater District favorite" French bistro "has its act together" and will "get you to the show on time"; for a "winning" experience, insiders say "stick to basics" and face up to the "crowded", "touristy" scene.

Caffe Buon Gusto ●

18 | 14 | 17 | $28

236 E. 77th St. (bet. 2nd & 3rd Aves.), 212-535-6884
1009 Second Ave. (bet. 53rd & 54th Sts.), 212-755-1476
151 Montague St. (bet. Clinton & Henry Sts.), Brooklyn, 718-624-3838
www.caffebuongusto.com

At this "casual", "unpretentious" trattoria trio, "reliable" mix-and-match pastas, "decent prices" and a "pleasant attitude" go a long way in offsetting "cramped" conditions and overly "relaxed" service.

Caffe Cielo

18 | 15 | 17 | $40

881 Eighth Ave. (bet. 52nd & 53rd Sts.), 212-246-9555

"Let's hear it for consistency" cheer fans of the "basic", "fair"-price pastas and such served up at this "solid" Theater District Italian; the "open-air feeling" suits "leisurely" diners, while ticket-holders appreciate that the staff "gets you out in time."

Caffe Grazie

18 | 15 | 19 | $42

26 E. 84th St. (bet. 5th & Madison Aves.), 212-717-4407

Aesthetes weary "after a day of museum-hopping" hit this "lovely" East Side townhouse Italian for "straightforward", "well-prepared" fare dispensed by a "considerate" staff; insiders suggest "sit upstairs" and try not to notice that it "could be a little roomier."

Caffe Linda ⊠

19 | 14 | 18 | $28

145 E. 49th St. (bet. Lexington & 3rd Aves.), 646-497-1818

Patrons are "packed in" to this "friendly", "shoebox"-size Midtown Italian, "but who cares?" when you can get "fresh", "homestyle" basics at reasonable prices; the fact that it's nearly "devoid of tourists" doesn't hurt either.

Caffé on the Green

21 | 22 | 19 | $50

201-10 Cross Island Pkwy. (bet. Clearview Expwy. & Utopia Pkwy.),
Queens, 718-423-7272; www.caffeonthegreen.com

"Permanent Christmas lights" add "twinkle" to this Bayside Italian set in "Rudolph Valentino's old home"; add "delish" dishes and a "wonderful" view and it's "ideal for all sorts of big get-togethers"; if only the "Manhattan ambiance" didn't come at "Manhattan prices."

Caffe Rafaella ◐
17 | 17 | 11 | $21

134 Seventh Ave. S. (bet. Charles & W. 10th Sts.), 212-929-7247

◪ "Sinfully gorgeous desserts" have "salivating" patrons "skipping dinner" and going straight for the pastry case at this "comfy couch"–filled Village Italian; most don't mind "watching the world go by" while wondering "where's my waiter?"

Caffe Reggio ◐⇗
16 | 19 | 14 | $15

119 MacDougal St. (bet. Bleecker & W. 3rd Sts.), 212-475-9557; www.caffereggio.com

■ "Late at night" you "can feel the ghosts" at this circa-1927 Village Italian coffeehouse, where the "classic pastries" and java come "cheap", and the "old-NY" ambiance is free; regulars threaten "open mutiny" if "they ever try to spruce it up."

California Pizza Kitchen
16 | 11 | 15 | $21

201 E. 60th St. (bet. 2nd & 3rd Aves.), 212-755-7773; www.cpk.com

◪ Those Californians sure put "some strange things on their pizza", but still "kids love" the "wide selection" of pies and "free refills" on soda at this East Side link of the West Coast chain; parents go for the "low prices", if not the "factory" feel and "distracted" service.

Calle Ocho
22 | 23 | 20 | $45

446 Columbus Ave. (bet. 81st & 82nd Sts.), 212-873-5025

■ A "glittering" West Side crowd of twentysomethings toys with "knockout" tropical drinks and kicks up a "high-energy" scene at this Nuevo Latino, whose "soaring" setting "balances hip with come-hither"; as to the "innovative" cuisine, those who can focus on it declare it "delicious."

CamaJe ◐
∇ 19 | 16 | 14 | $35

85 MacDougal St. (bet. Bleecker & Houston Sts.), 212-673-8184; www.camaje.com

◪ "Rendezvous with your true love" at this "sweet", "intimate" Village French bistro, where the "ambitious" meals follow a "relaxed" pace; romantics relish the "laid-back" atmosphere, but eat-and-run types wish the service weren't so "slow"; P.S. "try the cooking classes" offered three days a week.

Campagnola ◐
24 | 18 | 22 | $58

1382 First Ave. (bet. 73rd & 74th Sts.), 212-861-1102

■ At this "clubby" East Side stalwart, the "amazing" Italian cuisine is as "full of flavor and character" as its "crowded" dining room and "hopping" piano bar; word is the professional service gets even better when you're a "regular", but no matter how often you show up, the prices remain "off the charts."

Canaletto
20 | 17 | 20 | $45

208 E. 60th St. (bet. 2nd & 3rd Aves.), 212-317-9192

■ "Convenient to Bloomie's", this "spry little" East Side Italian "hideaway" makes a perfect "shoppers' rest stop" thanks to its "reliably" "tasty" fare and "pleasant" vibe; regulars plead "shhh – keep it to yourself."

Candela
18 | 22 | 18 | $40

116 E. 16th St. (bet. Irving Pl. & Park Ave. S.), 212-254-1600; www.candelarestaurant.com

◪ The "cavernous", "candles-everywhere" "goth" interior of this Union Square New American has casanovas calling it an "ideal date place" (just "bring a flashlight if you want to see your date" or "read the menu"); if the fare's "just ok" and service "lackadaisical", most are in too "glowing" a mood to mind.

Candle Cafe/Candle 79 21 13 18 $27
1307 Third Ave. (bet. 74th & 75th Sts.), 212-472-0970
154 E. 79th St. (bet. Lexington & 3rd Aves.), 212-537-7179
www.candlecafe.com
✓ "Fantastic vegan dining experiences" draw "alternative" eaters
to this "inventive" Eastsider whose "healthy" fare has supporters
swearing they'd "eat grass" if it were on the menu; critics of the
"earthy" decor and "cramped" seating welcome the bigger, more
upscale branch soon to open nearby.

Canteen ◐ 18 20 17 $41
142 Mercer St., downstairs (Prince St.), 212-431-7676; www.canteennyc.com
✓ It's "the granddaddy of" the "hip", "upscale comfort food" eateries
now all over town, and this "subterranean" "retro"-"'60s" American
is still "grooving" along; perhaps "it's not the hot spot it was", but it's
still "fun" "after a day of shopping in SoHo."

Canton ⊘ 24 13 21 $41
45 Division St. (bet. Bowery & Market St.), 212-226-4441
■ "Close your eyes" and don't "bother with the menu" – "just let owner
Eileen Leong pick for you" at her "sedate" Chinatowner whose "fresh"
food "sets the gold standard for Cantonese"; its prices are a bit "steep",
but rapturous reviewers report it's "well worth it."

Canyon Road 20 17 16 $33
1470 First Ave. (bet. 76th & 77th Sts.), 212-734-1600; www.arkrestaurants.com
■ "Attractive" "young" things fill this "upbeat", "adobe"-style East Side
Southwesterner, sipping margaritas to "knock your sombrero off" and
chowing down on "flavorful" fare; it's "crowded and noisy", but that's
what the regulars expect from this never-ending "party."

Capitale ∇ 21 28 21 $65
130 Bowery (bet. Broome & Grand Sts.), 212-334-5500; www.capitaleny.com
■ It's "worth the trip just to see" this "spectacular" Little Italy
newcomer set in an 1893 bank designed by Stanford White; early
visitors are putting their money on its "vast", "breathtaking space",
Corinthian columns and all, because the "fresh" New American fare,
no matter how good, would have a pretty hard time "matching" such
an "amazing" setting.

Capsouto Frères 23 23 22 $53
451 Washington St. (Watts St.), 212-966-4900; www.capsoutofreres.com
■ "Hard to find" but "worth seeking out", this airy, brick-walled TriBeCa
French bistro is a "perfect place to pop the question" thanks to its
"genuinely hospitable" pro service and "lovely" setting that's "quiet"
enough for a tête-à-tête; the final "romantic" touch is "subtle",
"delectable" cuisine from "a kitchen dedicated to capturing your heart."

Cara Mia 19 14 17 $32
654 Ninth Ave. (bet. 45th & 46th Sts.), 212-262-6767;
www.caramianyc.com
✓ If only "they could stretch the walls" of this "sweet" Hell's Kitchen
Italian, because its "tiny" digs are often "way too crowded", especially
"pre-theater"; surveyors of its "flavorful" meals at "won't-break-the-
bank" prices aren't surprised that "it's so popular."

Carino 19 13 20 $31
1710 Second Ave. (bet. 88th & 89th Sts.), 212-860-0566
■ A "warm, familylike setting" (down to the "checkered tablecloths"),
"simple", "affordable" Southern Italian "homecooking" and the
presence of iconic Mama Carino herself ensures this "small" Upper
Eastsider remains a beloved "neighborhood joint."

CARMINE'S
20 | 15 | 17 | $34

2450 Broadway (bet. 90th & 91st Sts.), 212-362-2200
200 W. 44th St. (bet. B'way & 8th Ave.), 212-221-3800
www.carminesnyc.com

☑ "Gargantuan platters" of "garlicious" Italian dishes served "family-style" keep these "noisy" pasta "factories" "packed" with "big groups" of carbophiles, "bargain"-hunters and "tourists"; at the Times Square branch, gripes about "interminable waits" should abate now that a second floor has doubled its capacity; P.S. it's a good idea to "split" orders unless you want to see the world's largest doggy bag.

Carne ◐
18 | 17 | 16 | $34

2737 Broadway (105th St.), 212-663-7010

☑ Always "crowded" with "young" "carnivores", this "attractive" Columbia-area "budget steakhouse" has a "cool" "SoHo" vibe to go with its "good, solid" beef; service can be "disorganized" and acoustics "noisy as hell", but it's still "a rare treat above 96th Street."

Carnegie Deli ◐≠
21 | 8 | 12 | $24

854 Seventh Ave. (55th St.), 212-757-2245; www.carnegiedeli.com

☑ To experience "NY between two slices of bread" try this Midtown deli "legend" where you sit "shoulder-to-shoulder" with "tourists", "showbiz hangers-on" and other partakers of the "platinum standard" of pastrami, pickles and cheesecake; the "enormous sandwiches" may come via "surly" waiters, but that's "part of the charm", especially when you see Soon-Yi and Woody treated the same way as you.

Carol's Cafe ☒
25 | 18 | 19 | $51

1571 Richmond Rd. (bet. Four Corners Rd. & Seaview Ave.), Staten Island, 718-979-5600

■ "Fresh, dynamic dishes" prepared by a "real perfectionist" – chef-owner Carol Frazzetta – draw "sophisticated" Staten Islanders to this "comfortable, quaint" Eclectic that's voted the borough's "best"; no surprise it's on the "pricey" side, but the same meal would cost a lot more in Manhattan.

Carriage House ◐
▽ 17 | 20 | 17 | $49

136 W. 18th St. (bet. 6th & 7th Aves.), 212-647-8889

☑ The old-fangled name and 19th-century exterior might imply the contrary, but this Chelsea newcomer (from the folks behind Cafeteria) sports a slick, "desert"-themed interior and an equally modern (pricewise and otherwise) New American menu; early voters found it "better than expected" given the "trendy" milieu.

Casa ◐☒
▽ 22 | 18 | 21 | $38

72 Bedford St. (Commerce St.), 212-366-9410

■ "Authentic" "Brazilian delicacies" draw a Portuguese-speaking "young crowd" to this "tiny" West Villager where "killer caipirinhas" go down easy with the "fresh" regional dishes; "enthusiastic" service and modest prices complete the "thoroughly enjoyable" experience.

Casa Di Meglio ◐
18 | 17 | 19 | $35

235-237 W. 48th St. (bet. B'way & 8th Ave.), 212-582-6577

■ "Low-key places" aren't easy to find in the center of the Theater District, but this "unpretentious" Italian fills the bill with its "pleasantly" "quiet" ambiance; if live wires find it "a little dull", most are grateful for the "simple" fare offered at quite "reasonable prices."

Casa La Femme ◐
15 | 26 | 16 | $58

150 Wooster St. (bet. Houston & Prince Sts.), 212-505-0005

☑ "Cleopatra is the only thing missing" at this "exotic" SoHo "night at the Casbah", where diners "recline on pillows" "in their own tents", and "belly dancers and hookahs" complete the "sexy", "atom-bomb-of-date-weapons" vibe; some say the Egyptian cuisine and "disorganized" staff "could use some help, but most guests are too busy to notice.

Casa Mia   20 | 16 | 19 | $33

225 E. 24th St. (bet. 2nd & 3rd Aves.), 212-679-5606
■ For Gramercy "locals", this "lovely, little" family-run Italian's a "secret" they're "too glad to keep"; "friendly" welcomes, "inexpensive" cooking "like mama's" and "living room"–esque decor make everyone feel "right at home" (but here "you don't have to do the dishes").

Caserta Vecchia   ∇ 20 | 17 | 24 | $28

221 Smith St. (bet. Baltic & Butler Sts.), Brooklyn, 718-624-7549; www.casertavecchiarestaurant.com
■ After being damaged by fire only days after it opened in 2002, this affordable Carroll Gardens Italian is back in business, offering a wide array of brick-oven pizzas and "uncomplicated" Neapolitan dishes amid pleasant, brightly lit digs.

Casimir ●   21 | 20 | 15 | $32

103-105 Ave. B (bet. 6th & 7th Sts.), 212-358-9683
■ The "East Village stylo-tron" set collects at this "dim", "sultry" Alphabet City bistro whose "mouthwatering" fare is "as French as it gets" – as is the "curt" service; "budget-minded foodies" sigh "you'll think you died and went to Marseilles."

Caviar Russe ⌧   ∇ 24 | 21 | 23 | $93

538 Madison Ave., 2nd fl. (bet. 54th & 55th Sts.), 212-980-5908; www.caviarrusse.com
■ You may "have to hock your jewelry" for a trip to this "posh" Midtowner that "feels more like a private club than a restaurant", but devotees declare it worth the "splurge"; those who "love that caviar" can't get enough of the "beluga"-heavy New American fare.

Caviarteria   ∇ 24 | 12 | 17 | $57

Trump Park Ave., 502 Park Ave. (59th St.), 212-759-7410
☑ For "quick caviar and champagne fixes", hit this "tiny" Midtown "den" where the "excellent" eggs and other delicacies come at prices more "reasonable" than the competition; those opposed to "no atmosphere" get it to "take home" at the well-stocked retail counter.

Celeste ⌿   22 | 14 | 17 | $31

502 Amsterdam Ave. (bet. 84th & 85th Sts.), 212-874-4559
■ "It's been discovered", meaning this "tiny" Upper West Side Italian is "always packed", but sanguine locals "wait forever for a table" and "play sardine" once inside for its "delicious pizzas and pastas"; if the "cash-only policy's painful", "bargain prices" are celestial.

Cellini ⌧   20 | 18 | 21 | $49

65 E. 54th St. (bet. Madison & Park Aves.), 212-751-1555
■ During lunch it's "more business than pleasure" at this "classy" Midtown Northern Italian, where "superior" servers guide suits as they select from a "list of specials as long as the menu"; come evening, the "civilized", "country inn"–like interior inspires "romance."

Cendrillon   ∇ 23 | 19 | 20 | $37

45 Mercer St. (bet. Broome & Grand Sts.), 212-343-9012; www.cendrillon.com
■ "Amazing flavors" abound at this "truly distinctive" SoHo "sleeper", perhaps the city's only source for "exotic" Filipino-Asian "fusion" fare; "tastefully" "clean, open" design and "a laid-back atmosphere" make it "perfect for an intimate meal."

Centolire
20 | 23 | 19 | $56

1167 Madison Ave. (bet. 85th & 86th Sts.), 212-734-7711

☑ It's "another Pino Luongo winner" declare the "very Upper East Side" regulars of this "elegant" Italian beloved for its "beautiful" duplex setting (especially the "more serene upstairs" dining room); still, many find the kitchen's flavorful mix of "classics old and new" somewhat "inconsistent" and "expensive."

'Cesca
– | – | – | M

164 W. 75th St. (Amsterdam Ave.), 212-787-6300

Chef Tom Valenti of Ouest returns to his hearty Southern Italian roots at this comfortable new West Side eatery; although it's just opening at press time, its culinary pedigree, moderate prices and stylish decor all give reason for optimism.

Chadwick's
21 | 18 | 21 | $39

8822 Third Ave. (89th St.), Brooklyn, 718-833-9855

■ Known in Bay Ridge as "a great place to meet for meat", this "cozy neighborhood" steakhouse has long been a source for "hearty portions" of "good American eats" in "comfortable" "pub"-like environs; the only tough part is the parking.

Chango
16 | 16 | 15 | $36

239 Park Ave. S. (bet. 19th & 20th Sts.), 212-477-1500

☑ "Food's not the focus" of this "happening", "midpriced" Flatiron Mexican; still, its "young", "good looking" crowd says between "killer" cocktails you can sample some "surprisingly good" bites.

Chanpen Thai
19 | 14 | 18 | $25

761 Ninth Ave. (51st St.), 212-586-6808

☑ "Don't be scared by the garish decor" – this Hell's Kitchen Thai is a "tasty" "treat, especially for the beginner"; if naysayers find it "underspiced", few find fault with the "reasonable prices" given its Theater District–adjacent address.

CHANTERELLE ☒
27 | 26 | 27 | $89

2 Harrison St. (Hudson St.), 212-966-6960; www.chanterellenyc.com

■ "A golden glow" suffuses the "deeply satisfying" dining experiences at this "well-oiled" TriBeCa French where David and Karen Waltuck's "passion is evident in everything" "from the floral arrangements and the synchronized service" to the "sublime", "swoon"-inducing cuisine and even the original artist-designed menus; "beautiful" by day, "exquisite by night", "if it were any more romantic, it would be illegal"; P.S. the $38 prix fixe lunch is one of the "best bargains in the city."

Charles' Southern-Style Kitchen
▽ 24 | 5 | 13 | $16

2839 Eighth Ave. (151st. St.), 212-926-4313
83 W. 165th St. (Woodycrest Ave.), Bronx, 718-681-8800

■ "Mm-mm!" exclaim visitors to this "friendly", low budget Harlem soul fooder (with a Bronx take-out arm) – its "spectacular" "greaseless fried chicken" alone is "worth the trek", not to mention the "bargain" "all-you-can-eat" buffet; it "has zero ambiance" (think "employee cafeteria"), but devotees shrug "so what?"

Charlotte
18 | 19 | 19 | $47

Millennium Broadway Hotel, 145 W. 44th St. (bet. B'way & 6th Ave.), 212-789-7508; www.millenniumhotels.com

☑ "Theatergoers" look to this attractive New American for "quiet", "less-harried" dining right near Times Square; "dependable, if not stellar", cuisine and a "reasonable" pre-theater prix fixe is what they find, though the regular menu strikes some as "overpriced."

Chat n' Chew ●

| 17 | 13 | 14 | $21 |

10 E. 16th St. (bet. 5th Ave. & Union Sq. W.), 212-243-1616

☑ "A hoot and a half", this "schlocky" little "dive" off Union Square "doesn't disappoint" for "comfort food at comfort prices"; "transplanted Southerners" and others go mad for "best-ever mac 'n' cheese" delivered by a "ditzy" but "kid-friendly" staff that prefers chewing and chatting to serving and smiling.

Chef Ho's Peking Duck Grill

| 20 | 14 | 17 | $28 |

1720 Second Ave. (bet. 89th & 90th Sts.), 212-348-9444

☑ Eastsiders don't have to "schlep to Chinatown" for "delicious" Peking duck and "cut-above" Hunan specialties, thanks to this affordable "white-linen-tablecloth" spot that's just "upmarket" enough to feel like "a night out", if not a fancy one.

Chelsea Bistro

| 22 | 19 | 20 | $46 |

358 W. 23rd St. (bet. 8th & 9th Aves.), 212-727-2026

■ Loyal locals laud this "romantic" Chelsea French bistro for its "charming" interior complete with a fireplace in winter and garden in summer; the "sophisticated" cuisine and "gracious" service take the edge off "not-cheap" prices.

Chelsea Grill

| 17 | 13 | 16 | $26 |

135 Eighth Ave. (bet. 16th & 17th Sts.), 212-242-5336

☑ "Huge", "juicy burgers" are the starring attraction of this "down-to-earth" Chelsea "pub" that's a "neighborhood staple" for "good, plain American food" "well prepared and reasonably priced"; P.S. the "year-round garden is a real plus" since the interior is its weak spot.

Chelsea Ristorante

| 20 | 17 | 20 | $35 |

108 Eighth Ave. (bet. 15th & 16th Sts.), 212-924-7786; www.chelsear.com

■ A "welcoming" staff bearing "lots of free nibbles" pre-meal sets the tone at this "relaxed" Chelsea Northern Italian, "a quiet gem" that proffers "well-prepared" fare "without an ounce of pretension"; a recent redo (which may outdate the above Decor score) has "vastly improved" its looks.

Chez Brigitte ⊄

| ▽ 17 | 6 | 17 | $18 |

77 Greenwich Ave. (bet. Bank St. & 7th Ave. S.), 212-929-6736

☑ "Quick, cheap" bistro meals can be had for "cheap" if you're lucky enough to score one of the "11 stools" at this "teeny-tiny" West Village "glorified French diner"; locals depend on its "honest, freshly cooked" basics and shrug you "gotta love" its "zero-atmosphere" digs.

CHEZ ES SAADA ●▣

| 18 | 26 | 17 | $44 |

42 E. First St. (bet. 1st & 2nd Aves.), 212-777-5617; www.chezessaada.com

☑ "Follow the rose-petal" path to the "dreamy" downstairs "caverns and fountains" of this "dark and sexy" East Village Moroccan; clearly "it's all about the mood" here, but the "exotic" food is "tasty" too, if dispensed in "pricey", "miniscule" portions.

Chez Jacqueline

| 20 | 18 | 19 | $45 |

72 MacDougal St. (bet. Bleecker & Houston Sts.), 212-505-0727

■ An "old-time" "taste of Provence" in the Village, this "*très Français*" bistro remains "engaging" thanks to its "rich", "enjoyable" (some say "overpriced") standards and "on-target" service; if it offers "no surprises", that suits its "traditionalist" fan base just fine.

Chez Josephine ●▣

| 20 | 21 | 21 | $47 |

414 W. 42nd St. (bet. 9th & 10th Aves.), 212-594-1925; www.chezjosephine.com

■ "Who can resist" "colorful", "campy" owner Jean-Claude Baker and his Theater District French bistro dedicated to his adoptive mother, the renowned Josephine; praise for the "surprisingly good food", live piano–fueled ambiance straight "out of the Folies Bergeres" and "pampering, flirty service" drowns out gripes about "cramped" seating.

Chez Michallet
23 | 19 | 22 | $49

90 Bedford St. (Grove St.), 212-242-8309; www.chezmichallet.com

■ "Cute as a button, and not much bigger", this "extraordinarily romantic" West Village French bistro warms hearts with its "excellent" traditional bistro fare and "friendly service"; if a few find it "a bit overpriced", most say it's perfect for a "secluded rendezvous."

Chez Napoléon ⌧
18 | 13 | 19 | $39

365 W. 50th St. (bet. 8th & 9th Aves.), 212-265-6980; www.cheznapoleon.com

◪ "The kind of bistro Paris used to abound with", this tiny Theater District "time warp" has been persisting in its "unpretentious", "old-style French" ways since 1959; considering the "bargain pre-theater" prix fixe, most people simply ignore the "tired", "nondescript" digs.

Chez Oskar ●
▽ 19 | 18 | 18 | $32

211 DeKalb Ave. (Adelphi St.), Brooklyn, 718-852-6250; www.chezoskar.com

◪ "Dependable French bistro fare" at "reasonable prices" keeps "diverse", "good-looking" locals coming to this "enjoyable" Fort Greene "dimly lit hideaway"; generally considered "solid" all around, it's particularly "popular" for "weekend brunch."

Chiam Chinese Cuisine ●
21 | 18 | 21 | $40

160 E. 48th St. (bet. Lexington & 3rd Aves.), 212-371-2323

■ "High-quality ingredients and clever preparations", a "fancy" modern setting and "exceptional" service add up to a "cut-above" experience at this Midtown Chinese; if "upscale pricing" raises a few eyebrows, diners mostly focus on the "outstanding" "dim sum brunch."

Chianti
22 | 17 | 19 | $38

8530 Third Ave. (86th St.), Brooklyn, 718-921-6300

■ "You can't beat the generous portions" (ordered individually or "family-style") dished out at this Bay Ridge bastion of Italian "homestyle cooking" and a natural "meeting place for family and friends"; if the finicky fume it's "noisy" and "crowded", that's the price of popularity.

Chickenbone Cafe ●
– | – | – | I

177 S. Fourth St. (Driggs Ave.), Brooklyn, 718-302-2663

Chef Zak Pelaccio's "inventive" New American–Eclectic cuisine comprising organic, locally sourced ingredients at way-low prices (most menu items are under $10) means this hip Williamsburg newcomer is already a culinary standout; the savvy wine list and classic cocktails are other strong suits.

Chick-Inn ●
– | – | – | I

(fka Anglers & Writers)

420 Hudson St. (St. Luke's Pl.), 212-675-0810

Americana still reigns at this West Villager (fka Anglers & Writers) that has been reinvented as an old-time country road stop, right down to the Rheingold Beer wall art; the budget-priced, homespun menu includes hot dogs, burgers and, naturally, roast chickens.

ChikaLicious ●
– | – | – | I

203 E. 10th St. (bet. 1st & 2nd Aves.), 212-995-9511; www.chikalicious.com

East Villagers are crowding in to this tiny new dessert bar that just serves sushi-size portions of sweets, in three-course prix fixes with optional wine pairings; targeted to ladies, it features ingenious touches such as hooks for handbags under the counter.

Chimichurri Grill
21 | 14 | 20 | $42

*606 Ninth Ave. (bet. 43rd & 44th Sts.), 212-586-8655;
www.chimichurrigrill.com*

■ "Plan to eat too much" and "bring on the Malbec" at this "tiny",
"welcoming" Hell's Kitchen Argentinean whose "flavorful" steaks are
"exquisitely prepared" and "as big as your head", but in truth "anything"
would taste "terrific" slathered with the namesake "sauce."

China Grill
22 | 21 | 19 | $51

CBS Bldg., 60 W. 53rd St. (bet. 5th & 6th Aves.), 212-333-7788

■ "Don't dress down" for trips to this perennially "noisy, vibrant" (and,
yes, "pricey") Midtown Asian, where the "swanky, chic" set collects
over "creative" fusion fare in "huge, sharable" portions, followed by
desserts that are as "architecturally splendid" as the "soaring" space;
"go with a group" and "listen to the roar of the crowd."

Chin Chin ●
23 | 18 | 21 | $44

216 E. 49th St. (bet. 2nd & 3rd Aves.), 212-888-4555

■ Waiters bearing platters of "tremendously toothsome" dishes
(including "fab Grand Marnier shrimp") "treat you like an emperor" at
this "upscale", "unpretentious" Midtown Chinese; for such "gourmet"
experiences, expect to "take it on the chin" when the bill comes.

Chipper, The ⌿
∇ 19 | 9 | 15 | $13

*41-28 Queens Blvd. (42nd St.), Queens, 718-729-8730;
www.thechipper.net*

☑ This basic Brit-style "little chip shop" arrived in Sunnyside not long
ago, and in addition to "the best cod" serves just about "anything in the
world battered and fried"; pub-crawlers love that it's cheap and open
"late-night" (till 5 AM on weekends), but its stand-and-eat counter setup
makes the weary "wish they had tables."

ChipShop/CurryShop ⌿
19 | 14 | 18 | $19

*381-383 Fifth Ave. (bet. 6th & 7th Sts.), Brooklyn, 718-832-7701;
www.chipshopnyc.com*

☑ "Ex-pats" and "Anglophiles" "satisfy cravings" "on a shoestring"
at this "funky" Park Sloper that unites the twin pillars of "British
comfort food" under one roof: half of the place is devoted to "real-
deal" fish 'n' chips, the other to "delicious" Indian curries; both go
down well with the "Boddingtons on tap."

Cho Dang Gol
∇ 23 | 15 | 17 | $26

55 W. 35th St. (bet. 5th & 6th Aves.), 212-695-8222

☑ "Delicious BBQ" and all the "traditional", "spicy" sides are on
hand, but what really makes this cheap, "cozy" Garment District
Korean "unforgettable" are its many dishes made with "heavenly
homemade tofu" "so good it's like eating clouds."

Chola
24 | 16 | 22 | $37

*232 E. 58th St. (bet. 2nd & 3rd Aves.), 212-688-4619;
www.fineindiandining.com*

■ A "dazzling array" of "delicious and unusual regional specialties"
makes this "upscale" East Side Indian appealing to those who've
"outgrown Sixth Street", as does the "gracious" staff and "softly lit
surroundings"; P.S. "try the lunch buffet" that's a "great deal" at $13.95.

Chop't Creative Salad ⊠
21 | 9 | 15 | $14

24 E. 17th St. (bet. B'way & 5th Ave.), 646-336-5523

☑ You feel "healthier just standing in line" at this salubrious saladeer off
Union Square where an "endless variety" of the "freshest ingredients"
are tossed and chopped to order in "humongous" portions; if some

budget-minded lunchers find it "a bit pricey" for the genre, to most it's "definitely worth it."

Choshi
18 | 11 | 17 | $30

77 Irving Pl. (E. 19th St.), 212-420-1419; www.cho-shi.com

☑ "Great everyday sushi" "with no pretense" is sliced and rolled at this "best-buy" Gramercy Japanese that's often "jammed" with "spillover" crowds from nearby Yama; weather permitting, "try for an outdoor table" and enjoy the "people-watching."

Chow Bar
20 | 19 | 16 | $38

230 W. Fourth St. (W. 10th St.), 212-633-2212

☑ "Dark and sexy" in a "Shanghai-in-the-'40s" kind of way, this West Village Pan-Asian pulls a "twentysomething" crowd for "surprisingly tasty" bites and "plum sakatini"–fueled "good times"; still, a few feel the "fun" vibe would be even more so if the staff got an "attitude" fix.

Christos Hasapo-Taverna ●
23 | 16 | 20 | $41

41-08 23rd Ave. (41st St.), Queens, 718-777-8400;
www.christossteakhouse.com

■ "Butcher shop by day", "friendly" steakhouse by night, this Astoria Greek is locally renowned for its "top-notch" beef "at fair prices"; "you're-in-Athens" surroundings and "better-than-you'd-expect" wines are other reasons it's "worth a detour."

Chubo
– | – | – | M

6 Clinton St. (bet. Houston & Stanton Sts.), 212-674-6300;
www.chubonyc.com

This "pretty" Lower East Side newcomer is the latest to offer the "good idea" of a budget-minded, prix fixe–only menu, where $24 buys you three courses; the Eclectic offerings span the globe, while the service is universally "accommodating."

Church & Dey
– | – | – | E

Millenium Hilton, 55 Church St., 3rd fl. (Dey St.), 212-312-2000

Regional American favorites like Yankee pot roast fill out the menu at this new Financial District arrival in the recently reopened Millenium Hilton; it's fast becoming a tourist favorite given its unobstructed view of the World Trade Center site.

Churrascaria Plataforma ●
22 | 17 | 20 | $50

316 W. 49th St. (bet. 8th & 9th Aves.), 212-245-0505;
www.churrascariaplataforma.com

■ It's easy to "eat yourself silly" at this "festive" (i.e. "loud") Theater District Brazilian that's filled with "big groups" savoring the "ample salad bar" and "delicious" skewered "meat, meat and more meat" borne by "an endless procession of waiters"; P.S. a new TriBeCa branch is soon to open.

Cibo
20 | 20 | 20 | $42

767 Second Ave. (bet. 41st & 42nd Sts.), 212-681-1616

■ An "oasis" in an area that's something of a restaurant "desert", this Tudor City Tuscan–New American ensconced in the old Daily News Building may not make headlines, but its "sophisticated" fare, "spacious" setup and fair pricing make it a "no-risk" local favorite.

Cicciolino ●⌖
∇ 22 | 18 | 19 | $27

108 E. Fourth St. (bet. 1st & 2nd Aves.), 212-260-3105

■ Punchy colors and a sense of humor set the tone at this "tiny", kitschy new East Village Italian, whose name aptly translates as 'cute little thing'; its "gently priced" menu is divided into three categories: Tiny Things; Little, Good Things; and Bigger, Even Better Things.

Cilantro ●

17 | 15 | 16 | $28

244 E. 79th St. (2nd Ave.), 212-537-7745
1321 First Ave. (71st St.), 212-537-4040
1712 Second Ave. (bet. 88th & 89th Sts.), 212-722-4242
www.cilantronyc.com

▣ If the "simple" Southwest fare "isn't the star" of this "friendly" Upper East Side trio, no one minds much considering the "sizzling" margaritas, "festive" mood and "affordable" prices; in warmer months the sensitive-of-ear escape the "noise" by seeking "outdoor" seats.

Cinque Terre

∇ 19 | 16 | 19 | $44

Jolly Madison Towers, 22 E. 38th St. (bet. Madison & Park Aves.), 212-867-2260; www.jollymadison.com

▣ Locally lauded as an "undiscovered gem", this Northern Italian "tucked inside" a recently renovated Murray Hill hotel specializes in "well-prepared" Ligurian dishes; "warm" service and "good value" compensate for a setting that some find "blah."

Cipriani Dolci

20 | 21 | 18 | $43

Grand Central, West Balcony (42nd St. & Vanderbilt Ave.), 212-973-0999; www.cipriani.com

▣ "Architecture" buffs and "people-watchers" alike report "the view is beautiful" from this "classy" Italian's balcony overlooking Grand Central's main concourse; but while all agree it's "great for drinks", the "pricey" nibbles inspire mixed reviews.

Circus

19 | 19 | 19 | $43

808 Lexington Ave. (bet. 62nd & 63rd Sts.), 212-223-2965

■ "For a convivial night out", Eastsiders hit this "relaxed", "enjoyable" Brazilian near Bloomie's, where "slightly eccentric" decor featuring "terrific circus art" contributes to the "upbeat" mood, and "flavorful", midpriced dishes come via a "laid-back" staff.

Citarella ▣

23 | 21 | 21 | $59

1240 Sixth Ave. (49th St.), 212-332-1515; www.citarella.com

■ Fluctuating from "terrific to spectacular" is the word on this "posh" tri-level Radio City seafooder's "fresh, imaginatively prepared" fish and "lovely desserts"; it lures a "sophisticated crowd", which takes in stride the "Rockefeller prices", if not the sometimes "snooty" service.

Cité ●

21 | 20 | 21 | $57

120 W. 51st St. (bet. 6th & 7th Aves.), 212-956-7100; www.citerestaurant.com

■ The "can't-be-beat" "after 8 PM" prix fixe with "unlimited wine" is one reason this "clubby" Theater District steakhouse is usually "bustling" and "festive"; "bottomless-glass" dinners aside, this is one place that can be counted on for culinary contentment.

Cité Grill ●

20 | 17 | 19 | $47

120 W. 51st St. (bet. 6th & 7th Aves.), 212-956-7262; www.citerestaurant.com

■ Known as the "dress-down version of Cité", this "casual" Midtown chophouse is "faster" and a bit more "economical" than its next-door neighbor, making it a natural "business-lunch staple"; in the evenings, its "huge", "fabulous" burgers come with "a free floor show" via the "noisy, active" bar scene.

Citrus Bar & Grill

19 | 18 | 16 | $34

320 Amsterdam Ave. (75th St.), 212-595-0500; www.citrusnyc.com

■ "Schizophrenic, but it works" say fans of this Upper Westsider's "offbeat" Nuevo Latino–Asian fusion concept (e.g. "the sushi-quesadilla combo"); its "cool, modern" digs are "always packed" with a "young", juicy couture crowd downing "fruity drinks" and kicking up a "loud", "hopping" scene.

City Bakery
22 13 13 $18
3 W. 18th St. (bet. 5th & 6th Aves.), 212-366-1414
☑ You can "satisfy all kinds of cravings" amid the "mild-mannered chaos" of Maury Rubin's "hip" Flatiron bakery/cafe; famed as a "pastry-lover's heaven", it also proffers "delicious" sandwiches, soups and a "salad bar like you've never seen"; less-sweet are "flaky" service and "long lines."

City Crab/Lobster
17 14 15 $39
121 W. 49th St. (bet. 6th & 7th Aves.), 212-354-1717
235 Park Ave. S. (19th St.), 212-529-3800
☑ Even if a few crab about the "franchise" feel and all-at-sea service, this Flatiron seafooder and its new Midtown twin thrive as "great after-work" "singles scenes"; almost incidentally, they're also "reliable" for "crustacean favorites" at "reasonable prices."

City Grill ●
16 15 16 $27
269 Columbus Ave. (bet. 72nd & 73rd Sts.), 212-873-9400
☑ "Delivers what it promises" declare West Side denizens of this "no-nonsense" American whose comfort offerings are "never great, but never bad either"; an "easygoing", "pubby feel" and a "lively bar" are other reasons it remains a "popular neighborhood" "asset."

City Hall ⌧
21 22 21 $52
131 Duane St. (bet. Church St. & W. B'way), 212-227-7777
■ "If only the real City Hall took care of its constituents as well" as this "truly hospitable" TriBeCa American whose "big, brassy", "old-NY" milieu and "excellent" surf 'n' turf menu draws an "elite" mix of "politicos" and "Wall Streeters" for "power-scene lunches" (with matching "power tabs"); those in-the-know request an "outdoor" table in clement weather or a private room when partying.

Coco Pazzo
20 19 19 $56
23 E. 74th St. (bet. 5th & Madison Aves.), 212-794-0205
Time Hotel, 224 W. 49th St. (bet. B'way & 8th Ave.), 212-320-2929
☑ "Excellent" Tuscan fare and "velvet-gloved" service draw a "see-and-be-seen" clientele to Pino Luongo's perennially "popular" East Side Northern Italian (and its now separately owned Times Square offshoot); "unknowns" shouldn't be surprised if they have to "pay for the privilege" to get "seats by the kitchen"; N.B. following the closure of his restaurant Campagna, Mark Strausman has returned here as chef.

Coco Roco
21 14 15 $24
392 Fifth Ave. (bet. 6th & 7th Sts.), Brooklyn, 718-965-3376
■ "Lima comes to Park Slope" via this "busy, noisy", no-frills Peruvian that has amigos "chowing down" on "perfect rotisserie chicken" and "tasty seviches"; "distracted" service deters few considering the "cheap", "heaping portions" that amount to "amazing value."

Cocotte
21 19 19 $39
337 Fifth Ave. (4th St.), Brooklyn, 718-832-6848
■ From the owners of Fort Greene's Loulou comes this "cozy", "charming" Park Slope French–New American yearling whose "memorable" cooking, "fair prices" and "friendly service" have locals lauding it as a "wonderful addition" to the area.

Coffee Shop ●
16 14 11 $27
29 Union Sq. W. (16th St.), 212-243-7969
☑ Still a "scene and a half", this Union Square "late-night" vet is a coffee shop "in name" only, featuring "funky" Brazilian-accented American fare and "fun drinks"; just know that the famously "model-esque" staff is "purely decorative" and "long waits" are the norm.

Col Legno

▽ | 20 | 12 | 19 | $33 |

231 E. Ninth St. (bet. 2nd & 3rd Aves.), 212-777-4650

☑ "What homecooking must be like in Tuscany" comes from the "open kitchen" of this East Village "neighborhood" Italian known for its "wood-fired pizzas" and other such "simple pleasures"; its "rustic" room may be bare-bones, but there's no bones about the fact that the "zany" owner exudes "warmth."

Columbus Bakery

19 | 12 | 11 | $16 |

474 Columbus Ave. (bet. 82nd & 83rd Sts.), 212-724-6880
957 First Ave. (bet. 52nd & 53rd Sts.), 212-421-0334
www.arkrestaurants.com

☑ "Stroller"-pushers and "work-at-home types" populate this crosstown cafe-bakery pair, "reading the paper" over "big cups o' joe" and ignoring the "cutthroat competition" for tables; the cafeteria-style setup and minimal service don't distract from the "tempting" treats.

Comfort Diner

14 | 10 | 13 | $19 |

214 E. 45th St. (bet. 2nd & 3rd Aves.), 212-867-4555
25 W. 23rd St. (bet. 5th & 6th Aves.), 212-741-1010

☑ "The name says it all" sigh contented customers of this "retro" diner duo paying "kitschy" homage to "'50s"-style comfort classics; "enormous portions" and a "family-friendly" vibe ensure it's always "busy", despite gripes about "new millennium" prices.

COMPASS

22 | 23 | 20 | $54 |

208 W. 70th St. (bet. Amsterdam & West End Aves.), 212-875-8600;
www.compassrestaurant.com

■ Though the post-*Survey* departure of chef Neil Annis hurts, the interior of this West Side New American remains as "fabulous" as ever, and the arrival of new toque Mark Andelbradt (formerly of Chicago's Tru) indicates that the needle is pointed "in the right direction."

Cono & Sons O'Pescatore

▽ | 21 | 13 | 19 | $36 |

301 Graham Ave. (Ainslie St.), Brooklyn, 718-388-0168

■ "Crowded and boisterous", this Williamsburg Italian dispenses lotsa "fresh" pesce and other "home"-style cooking at "amazing" prices; those in-the-know wonder why more "spaghetti-and-meatball" mavens haven't "stumbled upon" it.

Convivium Osteria

25 | 23 | 22 | $43 |

68 Fifth Ave. (bet. Bergen St. & St. Mark's Ave.), Brooklyn, 718-857-1833

☑ "In a class by itself" declare devotees of this "farmhouse"-like Park Slope "gem" whose "talented kitchen" delivers a "magnificent" and "unique combination of cuisines" – Portuguese, Italian and Spanish – matched with the "best little wine list"; regulars report it also has "one of Brooklyn's nicest gardens."

Cooking with Jazz ⌧⊅

25 | 13 | 20 | $36 |

1201 154th St. (12th Ave.), Queens, 718-767-6979; www.cookingwithjazz.com

■ "It ain't New Orleans, but it sure is close" say surveyors of this "total dive" "tucked away" in Whitestone; its specialty is "incredible" Cajun fare "with zing" (the chef "trained with Paul Prudhomme, and it shows"); a "friendly" vibe and "live jazz" are other reasons it attracts a "herd on weekends."

Coppola's ◑

20 | 15 | 17 | $32 |

378 Third Ave. (bet. 27th & 28th Sts.), 212-679-0070
206 W. 79th St. (bet. Amsterdam Ave. & B'way), 212-877-3840
www.coppolas-nyc.com

☑ Dispensing "delicious" "red-sauce" Italian in "portions your grandma would approve of", this "crowded, noisy", "no-attitude" duo is the kind of "comfortable" choice where you can "tuck your napkin into your shirt" and *mangia*; "very fair prices" seal the deal.

Cornelia Street Cafe ●
17 | 15 | 18 | $31

29 Cornelia St. (bet. Bleecker & W. 4th Sts.), 212-989-9319;
www.corneliastreetcafe.com

■ At this "classic Village cafe", "music, poetry and readings" are as much a part of the "bohemian" scene as the "decent" "value"-priced American eats and "popular Sunday brunch"; "it's been around forever" as a place to "meet, eat and be merry."

Corner Bistro ●⊉
24 | 9 | 12 | $14

331 W. Fourth St. (Jane St.), 212-242-9502

☑ Despite "dark", "dingy" digs, this "old-time" West Village drinking hole is "packed noon and night" with "carnivores" craving "heavenly" burgers served on "paper plates" at "'50s throwback prices"; far-flung fans "wish my corner had this bistro."

Cosette
21 | 16 | 20 | $36

163 E. 33rd St. (bet. Lexington & 3rd Aves.), 212-889-5489

☑ "Simple", "hearty French cooking" "triumphs" at this modestly priced Murray Hill bistro whose menu of "classics" would make a Gallic mother "proud"; as for the "minute" space, most consider it "intimate."

Cosi
17 | 11 | 12 | $13

2160 Broadway (76th St.), 212-595-5616 ●
841 Broadway (13th St.), 212-614-8544 ●
60 E. 56th St. (bet. Madison & Park Aves.), 212-588-1225
Paramount Plaza, 1633 Broadway (51st St.), 212-397-9838 ●
257 Park Ave. S. (21st St.), 212-598-4070
498 Seventh Ave. (bet. 36th & 37th Sts.), 212-947-1005
700 Sixth Ave. (23rd St.), 212-645-0223 ●
504 Sixth Ave. (13th St.), 212-462-4188 ●
11 W. 42nd St. (bet. 5th & 6th Aves.), 212-398-6662
World Financial Ctr., 200 Vesey St. (West Side Hwy.), 212-571-2001
Additional locations throughout the NY area
www.getcosi.com

☑ "Addictive" flatbread sandwiches with choose-your-own fillings "aren't for those on Atkins", but "long lunch lines" bespeak this "quick" chain's "popular" appeal; less endearing are "burned-out" counter folk and tabs that have some dubbing it "Costli."

Cosmic Cantina ●⊉
19 | 7 | 12 | $11

101 Third Ave. (13th St.), 212-420-0975

■ The "healthier" way to "get your Mexican fix", this "fresh, fast" eat-in/take-out East Village burrito joint (a "delicious import" from North Carolina) uses organic ingredients and offers a host of "low-fat" options; as to the "laid-back" setting – "don't even call that decor."

Cotto ⊉
– | – | – | M

131 Ave. C (bet. 8th & 9th Sts.), 212-777-8600

Since the East Village's appetite for low-key, midpriced Italians shows no sign of waning, this no-frills newcomer is likely to find a following for its pleasant, no-surprises selection of standards; a good beer selection, amiable staff and snug back patio are added virtues.

Counter
▽ 23 | 22 | 21 | $27

105 First Ave. (bet. 6th & 7th Sts.), 212-982-5870

■ "Not your usual crunchy-granola" Vegetarian, this "stylishly" spare East Village newcomer features "sophisticated" dishes that make even inveterate "carnivores forget" where they are; the front wine bar confirms the impression with a "wonderful", all-"organic" wine list.

Country Café

▽ 19 | 16 | 17 | $33

69 Thompson St. (bet. Broome & Spring Sts.), 212-966-5417;
www.countrycafesoho.com

■ A little taste of the "French countryside" in SoHo, this "romantic" standby's "solid" Gallic fare comes at "fair prices" that "make it even more enjoyable"; area workers note it's mostly "undiscovered at lunch."

Cowgirl

16 | 18 | 15 | $25

519 Hudson St. (W. 10th St.), 212-633-1133

■ "Campy comfort food" à la Frito pie and "kitschy" "rodeo" decor make for "festive" "fun" at this West Village Southwestern; though you may have to "lasso" your server to get your order in, the mac 'n' cheese is a surefire "hit with the kids", while the "strong margaritas" "do the trick for the grown-ups."

Cozy Soup & Burger ●

19 | 9 | 14 | $14

739 Broadway (Astor Pl.), 212-477-5566

☑ "A little less greasy" but still "down and dirty" after a recent "face-lift" and expansion, this 24/7 Village diner remains a "classic" for "large burgers, large fries" and large numbers of "NYU kids" taking advantage of the "always-there-for-you" hours.

CRAFT

26 | 24 | 23 | $67

43 E. 19th St. (bet. B'way & Park Ave. S.), 212-780-0880

■ "Exquisitely simple, perfectly prepared" cuisine comprising "pristine" seasonal ingredients is the hallmark of Tom Colicchio's "sublime" Flatiron New American, which takes the "choose-one-from-each-column" format to "mind-blowing" heights; "refined", "hip-to-be-spare" surroundings and "knowledgeable" service add up to supremely "sumptuous" dining that "foodies" find more than "worth the wait for a reservation", lamenting that they can only "afford to go once a year."

Craftbar

21 | 20 | 21 | $39

47 E. 19th St. (bet. B'way & Park Ave. S.), 212-780-0880

☑ Aka "Craft Jr.", this "cheaper" next-door New American may offer a limited menu, "but what's there is cherce"; despite "crammed" conditions and long "waits", "outstanding" sandwiches and such enjoyed in "sleek", "minimalist" digs have most rating it the "best spin-off since *The Jeffersons*."

Cripplebush Road ●

– | – | – | M

168 Wythe Ave. (N. 7th St.), Brooklyn, 718-387-5855

A 6,000-sq.-footer festooned with historic memorabilia, this new, midpriced Williamsburg Mediterranean also has two pleasantly aromatic wood-burning ovens, one for pizza and the other for specials like wild boar; in addition, there's an all-Greek wine list.

Crispo ●

22 | 18 | 18 | $42

240 W. 14th St. (bet. 7th & 8th Aves.), 212-229-1818

☑ West Villagers wish to keep this year-old Italian "winner" "a secret", but most realize it's already "too late"; "wonderful" "housemade" pastas and other "well-priced" choices mean its "cozy" room is often "crowded and noisy", but that's all part of the "friendly" vibe.

Crudo ☒

– | – | – | M

54 Clinton St. (bet. Rivington & Stanton Sts.), 646-654-0116;
www.crudobar.com

The Lower East Side's restaurant rep continues to grow with the arrival of this new seafooder from the owners of 1492 Food; it's already garnering good buzz thanks to its offbeat raw-fish menu (available in either large or small plates) and its sprawling backyard garden.

Cuba Libre ❶
18 | 15 | 16 | $36

165 Eighth Ave. (bet. 18th & 19th Sts.), 212-206-0038;
www.cubalibreonline.com

☑ Its "great new space" across the street did not slow the "festive" feel of this "very Chelsea" "Nuevo Cubano" where the "*muy caliente* mojitos" and "little-piece-of-Havana" eats come courtesy of an "occasionally snarky" guyabera-clad staff; "ay-yi-yi" noise levels have some packing "Advil."

Cub Room
20 | 20 | 18 | $44

131 Sullivan St. (Prince St.), 212-677-4100; www.cubroom.com

■ Elbow past the "lively" "bar scene up front" and discover the "comfy" charms of this consistently fine SoHo New American that's also prime for "people-watching"; P.S. the "next-door cafe" offers "simpler" fare for "half the price."

Cucina
20 | 19 | 19 | $44

256 Fifth Ave. (bet. Carroll St. & Garfield Pl.), Brooklyn, 718-230-0711;
www.cucinarestaurant.com

☑ Voters divide over this "venerable" Park Slope Italian that has seen several chef changes in recent years and a sharp ratings drop since the last *Survey*; fans feel it "still delivers" "solid" fare in "quiet", upscale environs, but detractors declare it's "now only middle-of-the-pack."

Cucina di Pesce ❶≠
18 | 15 | 18 | $24

87 E. Fourth St. (bet. Bowery & 2nd Ave.), 212-260-6800;
www.cucinadipesce.com

■ Seekers of "quality" Italian "on a budget" turn to this "busy" East Village "old reliable" whose $10.95 "early-bird dinner" may qualify as an "urban miracle"; the "charming" "back garden" also earns points, though a few feel the overall look seems "lost in 1967."

Culinaria ⓩ
▽ 23 | 16 | 19 | $50

202 W. 40th St. (bet. 7th & 8th Aves.), 212-869-0725

■ A "friendly" new addition to the culinarily challenged Garment District, this "spare but comfortable" bi-level Italian turns out "well-executed" dishes inspired by ancient Roman recipes and dispensed in "decidedly non-fashion portions"; early visitors say it's "a find" that "deserves to be discovered" by those who can afford it.

Cupping Room Café ❶
17 | 15 | 15 | $28

359 W. Broadway (bet. Broome & Grand Sts.), 212-925-2898;
www.cuppingroomcafe.com

☑ When you're in SoHo and "don't want a trendy place", this "homey", affordable American and its "hearty" basics fill the bill; on weekends, it's "packed" and "noisy" with brunchers "fueling up" before "shopping it up"; N.B. it offers Mediterranean food and music on Wednesday and Friday nights.

Curry Leaf
20 | 11 | 18 | $25

99 Lexington Ave. (27th St.), 212-725-5558; www.curryleafnyc.com

■ It's "a cut above the standard" on "Curry Hill" declare devotees of this pleasingly priced Indian from the owners of the nearby specialty foods shop Kalustyan's; observant curry fans appreciate that its "delicious", "delicately spiced" dishes are both kosher and halal.

Cyclo
20 | 15 | 17 | $30

203 First Ave. (bet. 12th & 13th Sts.), 212-673-3975

■ "Fresh, beautifully prepared" Vietnamese fare, "serene", "candlelit" digs and "reasonable" tabs have romantics rating this East Villager a "great" "first-date" place; if it can be "cramped" and "too dark to read the menu", that's all part of the "charm."

Da Andrea
22 | 16 | 21 | $33

557 Hudson St. (bet. Perry & W. 11th Sts.), 212-367-1979; www.biassanot.com

■ "*Buonissimo*" declare West Village denizens of this "family-run" Northern Italian that's as well-loved for its "sweet" service as for its "wonderful" "housemade" pastas at "affordable" prices; given the "teensy" digs and large following, consider it "reservations-essential."

Da Antonio ◪
20 | 16 | 21 | $53

157 E. 55th St. (bet. Lexington & 3rd Aves.), 212-588-1545

■ "Hearing the list of specials" as recited by "welcoming" owner Antonio Cerra "is a treat in itself" at this "civilized" Midtown Italian where "mature" types find "delicious" pastas and "exceptionally" "warm" service; "lively" tunes from a piano player help take the sting out of "pricey" tabs.

Da Ciro
21 | 16 | 18 | $37

229 Lexington Ave. (bet. 33rd & 34th Sts.), 212-532-1636; www.daciro.com

◪ Locally known for its "delicious" focaccia robiola and pizzas from a "wood-burning oven", this "crowded" bi-level Murray Hill Italian is "more than just a red-sauce emporium"; still, there are a few grumbles about "high-level" noise and prices.

Dae Dong ◐◪
▽ 20 | 15 | 17 | $30

17 W. 32nd St. (bet. B'way & 5th Ave.), 212-967-1900

■ "In the heart of" the Garment District's "K-Town", this tad-"classier" Korean saves you a trip "to Flushing – or Seoul" – with its multiplicity of "authentic" "home"-style dishes plus tabletop BBQ; just "be prepared to smell like the food when you leave."

Da Filippo
21 | 17 | 21 | $49

1315 Second Ave. (bet. 69th & 70th Sts.), 212-472-6688

■ Functioning as a "neighborhood dining room", this "surprisingly good", "expensive" East Side Northern Italian "always seems to pack 'em in"; perhaps the secret is that "excellent" owner-host Carlo is usually there "running the show."

Daily Chow
18 | 16 | 16 | $22

2 E. Second St. (Bowery), 212-254-7887; www.dailychow.com

■ The latest from the Kin Khao clan, this "playful" East Village Pan-Asian provides its "young crowd" with "fast doses" of "tasty", "great-value" eats, notably the "make-your-own" Mongolian BBQ; all in all it's a "fun" find, especially "for a group."

Dakshin Indian Bistro
▽ 20 | 13 | 19 | $23

1713 First Ave. (bet. 88th & 89th Sts.), 212-987-9839
741 Ninth Ave. (50th St.), 212-757-4545

■ This East Side–West Side Indian duo wins hearts – er, stomachs – with its "moderately priced" "fresh" fare and "pleasant" staff; midday diners call the lunch buffet's "array of dishes" a "best-buy."

Dallas BBQ ◐
14 | 8 | 13 | $19

3956 Broadway (166th St.), 212-568-3700
261 Eighth Ave. (23rd St.), 212-462-0001
132 Second Ave. (St. Marks Pl.), 212-777-5574
1265 Third Ave. (bet. 72nd & 73rd Sts.), 212-772-9393
27 W. 72nd St. (bet. Columbus Ave. & CPW), 212-873-2004
132 W. 43rd St. (bet. B'way & 6th Ave.), 212-221-9000
21 University Pl. (8th St.), 212-674-4450
www.bbqnyc.com

◪ "Masses" "looking to gorge" inexpensively stampede to this BBQ chain for "Texas-size" chicken-'n'-rib "pig-outs" at "Deep-South prices"; "franchise" atmosphere and "assembly-line" service are part of the "bargain" – but this many people can't be totally wrong.

Danal
21 | 21 | 18 | $34

90 E. 10th St. (bet. 3rd & 4th Aves.), 212-982-6930

⬛ Think French "country kitchen", East Village–style and you've got this "funky", "lived-in" Provençal with a "romantic" back garden; though its brunch is "one of the city's most charming", expect "long waits"; P.S. heed the owner's "no–cell phone policy", or else.

Da Nico
22 | 17 | 19 | $35

164 Mulberry St. (bet. Broome & Grand Sts.), 212-343-1212

⬛ "Better than most in Little Italy", this affordable "old-school" Italian serves brick-oven pizzas and other classics that pack in everyone from "tourists" to "former mayors" ("hey, Rudy!"); if surveyors are split over service, there's no debating the fact that it's best "in the summer when the garden is open."

DANIEL ⬛
28 | 28 | 27 | $100

60 E. 65th St. (bet. Madison & Park Aves.), 212-288-0033; www.danielnyc.com

⬛ "Star" chef Daniel Boulud "continues to shine" at his "luxe" East Side "formal" French where "masters of the universe" enjoy meals of near-"perfection" "all the way around", from the "spectacularly" "creative", "flawlessly" executed cuisine to the "regal" surroundings and "unparalleled service"; voted at or near the top in every category covered by this *Survey*, it can only be described as "breathtaking" – not least "when you get the check."

Daniella
21 | 13 | 19 | $39

320 Eighth Ave. (26th St.), 212-807-0977

⬛ "Blink" and "you'll miss" this "hole-in-the-wall" Italian not too far from Madison Square Garden; its "decent", "reasonably" priced standards come as a "pleasant surprise" in an area short on options; N.B. a recent chef change may outdate its Food score.

DANUBE ◑⬛
27 | 28 | 27 | $85

30 Hudson St. (bet. Duane & Reade Sts.), 212-791-3771; www.thedanube.net

⬛ Run, don't "waltz" to David Bouley's supremely "soigné" TriBeCa "masterpiece", voted No. 1 for Decor in this *Survey* thanks to its "evocative", "Klimt-inspired" "jewel-box" dining room that, together with the "refined", "sensuous" Viennese cuisine, "transports" diners "to another era" (though surely "the Hapsburgs never had it this good"); given such "romantic" repasts, it's "particularly *willkommen*" to couples, if not to wallets (expect to spend some "serious" Do-Re-Mi).

Darna
20 | 20 | 15 | $36

600 Columbus Ave. (89th St.), 212-721-9123

⬛ "Breaking preconceived notions of what kosher is", this Upper West Side glatt kosher Moroccan offers "tasty", "original" fare complemented by a "good wine list"; the only bone is "slooow" service that optimists suggest is still a "work in progress."

D'Artagnan ⬛
20 | 16 | 19 | $51

152 E. 46th St. (bet. Lexington & 3rd Aves.), 212-687-0300; www.dartagnan.com

⬛ "There's nothing better" "when it's cold out" than a meal at Ariane Daguin's Midtown "cardiologist's nightmare" of a French bistro known for its "delicious" foie gras, cassoulet and other "hearty" (and pricey) Gascogne fare; still, snobs snipe its "unintentionally campy" "Musketeer" motif "has got to go."

Da Silvano ❶

21 | 16 | 17 | $53

260 Sixth Ave. (bet. Bleecker & Houston Sts.), 212-982-2343;
www.dasilvano.com

■ Nonstop "celebrity sightings" and reliably good Tuscan fare are the reasons you'll need to "trade your firstborn for a sidewalk table" at Silvano Marchetto's "high-energy" Villager; it's a perpetual "scene" where prices are as "rich" as the proprietor's "leather pants", but then there's always the "cheaper" Cantinetta next door.

Da Tommaso ❶

19 | 12 | 18 | $42

903 Eighth Ave. (bet. 53rd & 54th Sts.), 212-265-1890

☑ "Good pasta", "dated decor" is the lowdown on this "old-fashioned", midpriced Theater District Northern Italian whose "solid" fare earns it "standby" status with many; regulars report the trick is to "stick with the specials."

Da Umberto ☒

24 | 18 | 21 | $56

107 W. 17th St. (bet. 6th & 7th Aves.), 212-989-0303

☑ You "feel like you're eating in Firenze" at this "atmospheric" Chelsea Northern Italian that loyalists "love" for its genuine Italian ambiance, "*bellissimo*" cuisine and "attentive" service; the less-enamored claim it's "overpriced" with "standoffish" service (unless you are a friend of owner Umberto).

Dawat

23 | 18 | 21 | $44

210 E. 58th St. (bet. 2nd & 3rd Aves.), 212-355-7555

☑ Its "sublime" "upscale" Indian cuisine, "subtle" surroundings and "attentive" staff ensure this East Midtown "perennial standout" is "still one of the best" subcontinentals in town ("with prices to match"); still, a cutting minority contends it's "lost its edge" in recent years.

db Bistro Moderne

24 | 21 | 22 | $59

City Club Hotel, 55 W. 44th St. (bet. 5th & 6th Aves.), 212-391-2400;
www.danielnyc.com

■ Daniel Boulud "has done it again" with this Theater District French bistro that's a "happening", more "affordable" (if still "pricey") "alternative to its more formal sibling", Daniel; yes, the "famous" $29 foie gras–laced burger has an "obscene" price tag, but it's "worth every cent"; P.S. the $39 pre-theater prix fixe is a "wonderful" value.

Deborah

21 | 16 | 20 | $34

43 Carmine St. (bet. Bedford & Bleecker Sts.), 212-242-2606;
www.deborahlifelovefood.com

■ "Homecooking much better than home" is the concept at this "tiny but jovial" Village New American where chef-owner Deborah Stanton often "emerges from her kitchen to greet" you; for such "loving" treatment, not to mention "fair prices", most ignore the "narrow", "dark" setting.

Deck, The

– | – | – | E

Chelsea Piers, Pier 59 Studios, 2nd level, W. 18th St. (Hudson River), 212-741-3183

Outdoor types are likely to enjoy this new Chelsea Piers arrival, a Southern Italian on a palm tree–lined deck overlooking the Hudson (with an equally inviting interior); given that it adjoins Pier 59 photography studio, you can expect a crowd of supermodels and their posses.

Dee's Brick Oven Pizza

22 | 14 | 19 | $24

104-02 Metropolitan Ave. (71st Dr.), Queens, 718-793-7553;
www.deesbrickovenpizza.com

■ "Addictive thin-crust" pizzas with "tremendous toppings", "cheery" service and "reasonable" prices mean this "always-crowded" Forest

Hills brick-oven specialist is particularly popular with "families"; those who eschew the "noisy", no-frills digs get their fixes "takeout."

DeGrezia ☒   22 | 21 | 22 | $54

231 E. 50th St. (bet. 2nd & 3rd Aves.), 212-750-5353

◪ "They know how to take care of you" at this "quiet", "flower-filled", "downstairs" East Midtown "hideaway", where the "high-quality, high-priced" Northern Italian fare is backed by an 800-label wine list; in short, it's just the place for a business meal or even to "take mother."

Delegates' Dining Room ☒   ▽ 20 | 19 | 18 | $39

United Nations, 4th fl. (1st Ave. & 45th St.), 212-963-7626

▉ "Wear a tie", "survive security" and you too can "mingle with delegates" while surveying the "stunning" 180-degree "view of the East River" at this weekday-lunch-only buffet in the UN; the "elaborate" Eclectic spread changes regularly to trot out dishes from "different parts" of the globe.

Del Frisco's ◐   24 | 23 | 22 | $63

McGraw Hill Bldg., 1221 Sixth Ave. (49th St.), 212-575-5129;
www.lonestarsteakhouse.com

▉ "The '80s" "power scene" lives at this "spacious" Midtown-does-Dallas chophouse where "beef lovers" and "Atkins fans" feast on "top-of-the-line" steaks in "gargantuan portions" – with "Texas"-size tabs to match; in "after-work" hours there's a "noisy" "scene" at the "massive" downstairs bar; on top of all this, a choice of handsome private rooms invites party-givers and -goers.

Delhi Palace   ▽ 23 | 15 | 18 | $22

37-33 74th St. (bet. Roosevelt & 37th Aves.), Queens, 718-507-0666

▉ "Stiff competition for the Jackson Diner", this "worthwhile" Jackson Heights Indian just "down the block" turns out "first-rate" dosas and other fairly priced classic dishes from all over the subcontinent.

Delmonico's ☒   20 | 21 | 21 | $55

56 Beaver St. (William St.), 212-509-1144; www.delmonicosny.com

◪ "The ghost of Diamond Jim Brady" haunts this steeply priced reincarnation of the "NYC landmark" steakhouse, a "clubby Wall Street den" whose "solid" steaks fuel "multimillion-dollar deal"-making; still, while "old boys" may feel at home here, others say it's time to bring this period piece into the "21st century"; N.B. closed Saturday.

Delta Grill   20 | 16 | 18 | $29

700 Ninth Ave. (48th St.), 212-956-0934

◪ "Holy alligator" – it's like "a brief trip to Cajun country" at this "raucous" Hell's Kitchen "Big Easy facsimile" specializing in affordable "N'Awlins favorites prepared well", with live weekend music to boot; skeptics sniff "Southerners know better."

Denino's Pizzeria ⊘   23 | 9 | 15 | $17

524 Port Richmond Ave. (bet. Hooker Pl. & Walker St.), Staten Island, 718-442-9401

▉ Interboro travelers claim "it's worth the schlep" to this "rustic" Staten Island pizza "legend" famed for its "amazing" thin-crust beauties dished out on "paper plates"; just "get there early" or "join dozens of other families" vying for a booth; P.S. for a summer "1-2 punch", "walk across the street" afterward for ices at Ralph's Famous.

Dervish Turkish ◐   20 | 17 | 19 | $33

146 W. 47th St. (bet. 6th & 7th Aves.), 212-997-0070

▉ 1,001 bites can be had for a "reasonable price" at this "Turkish delight" whose "mild, but intriguingly spiced" cuisine and "warm" service make it a "rewarding" Theater District "find"; as for the slightly "dark" setting, it's "nothing to write home to Istanbul about."

Di Fara ⇗
△ | 28 | 5 | 14 | $10 |

1424 Ave. J (bet. 14th & 15th Sts.), Brooklyn, 718-258-1367

■ "What pizza should be" comes from the oven of this 40-year-old Midwood "institution" where you won't find any "tubs of pre-shredded cheese"; "dumpy" digs notwithstanding, come watch owner Dominic De Marco make your "phenomenal" pie "while you wait" (and wait).

Dim Sum Go Go
| 20 | 14 | 14 | $22 |

5 E. Broadway (Chatham Sq.), 212-732-0797

☑ Don't look for carts at this "funky" "neo-Chinese" take on Chinatown dim sum, because it's strictly "order-off-the-menu", "steamed-fresh" here; never mind if the service and decor are "no-nonsense" – most customers are ready to "go-go again" and soon due to the high quality and low prices.

Diner ◐
| 22 | 16 | 18 | $27 |

85 Broadway (Berry St.), Brooklyn, 718-486-3077

■ "Surprisingly refined" fare comes in a "funky" 1920s Pullman car at this "well-priced" Williamsburg American where the specials are "written on the tablecloths" nightly; its "arty", "black-glasses" crowd seems not to mind the "flighty", "hipster-dreamboat" staff.

Dish ◐
△ | 18 | 14 | 19 | $26 |

165 Allen St. (bet. Rivington & Stanton Sts.), 212-253-8840;
www.dish165.com

■ "Dressed-up" New American "comfort food" is the concept at this "hip, diner-style" Lower East Side newcomer, where there's a "mix-and-match" selection of sides to go with your entree (think the "poor man's Craft"); "zero attitude" and "affordable" prices are other pluses.

Dishes
| 22 | 10 | 12 | $14 |

47 E. 44th St. (bet. Madison & Vanderbilt Aves.), 212-687-5511 ⊠
Grand Central, lower level (42nd St. & Vanderbilt Ave.),
212-808-5511 ⇗

☑ "Not your typical salad bar", this weekday-only East Midtown eat-in/ take-out duo is a corporate "crowd-pleaser" thanks to its "abundant", "supreme-quality" breakfast and lunch offerings; less popular are its "maddening lines", "slow service" and "pricey" tabs.

District
| 21 | 22 | 21 | $52 |

Muse Hotel, 130 W. 46th St. (bet. 6th & 7th Aves.), 212-485-2999;
www.themusehotel.com

☑ "Lovely" decor shares the spotlight with Sam DeMarco's "creative" cuisine at this "sophisticated", albeit expensive, Times Square New American that proves "you don't have to compromise your taste to make it to the show on time"; critics "don't know what all the raves are about."

Divino ◐
| 18 | 13 | 19 | $38 |

1556 Second Ave. (bet. 80th & 81st Sts.), 212-861-1096

■ Deemed "pleasant", if "not *divino*", this Upper East Side Italian "staple" is known for its "reliable classic dishes" with "live music" on the side (weekends only); for many it makes a good "midweek dinner filler" or "Sunday supper", but, as its ratings show, the decor could use some help.

Diwan
| 21 | 18 | 18 | $36 |

148 E. 48th St. (bet. Lexington & 3rd Aves.), 212-593-5425

■ It "keeps changing names" but the cuisine remains as "amazing" as ever at this "upscale" (with "corresponding prices") Midtown

Indian; "bargain"-hunters ballyhoo its $12.95 lunch buffet "taken to new heights" and recent "swank" redo.

Django ⓈⒾ · 20 | 24 | 19 | $51

480 Lexington Ave. (46th St.), 212-871-6600

■ "It's a winner" declare East Midtowners of this "hip", "spacious" French-Med yearling on an "otherwise" "sparse" stretch of Lex; ok, maybe the "pricey" brasserie fare's "standard" and the service a bit "slow", but "that's made up for" by the "sleek" bi-level space.

Docks Oyster Bar · 19 | 16 | 17 | $44

2427 Broadway (bet. 89th & 90th Sts.), 212-724-5588
633 Third Ave. (40th St.), 212-986-8080
www.docksoysterbar.com

◪ "Like shooting fish in a barrel", these "time-tested", "nothing-fancy" seafood houses are "always a shore thing" for midpriced "fresh" fin fare in "classic" preparations; "crazy-loud", "chaotic" conditions and "crabby" service don't deter devotees from swimming here in schools.

Do Hwa · 21 | 21 | 17 | $37

55 Carmine St. (bet. Bedford St. & 7th Ave. S.), 212-414-1224

■ "Delicious" seasonal Korean eats, including tabletop BBQ, a "handsome, slick" setting and a DJ (Thursday–Saturday) lure the "beautiful people" to this Greenwich Villager; the tabs may be slightly "pricey" for the genre, but fans don't seem to mind.

Dojo ⌽ · 15 | 8 | 12 | $14

24-26 St. Marks Pl. (bet. 2nd & 3rd Aves.), 212-674-9821
14 W. Fourth St. (Mercer St.), 212-505-8934 ◓

■ "When you need a tofu-hijiki burger", this straight-outta-"Berkeley" Village Veggie duo fills the bill; for such "cheap, cheap" Asian-influenced "hippie concoctions", "student types" happily overlook the "rundown" digs and "spacey" service.

Dok Suni's ⌽ · 21 | 16 | 15 | $28

119 First Ave. (bet. 7th St. & St. Marks Pl.), 212-477-9506

◪ "Hipsters abound" at this "dark, sexy", "always-packed" East Village Korean, where the "mouthwatering" fare is served with a dash of "attitude"; though there's "always a wait", it's deemed "a godsend when you don't want to trek to K-town."

Dolphins ◓ · 18 | 19 | 19 | $35

35 Cooper Sq. (bet. 5th & 6th Sts.), 212-375-9195

■ A "lovely garden" "made for summer nights" may be its "greatest asset", but this "quiet", "civilized" Cooper Square seafooder's "incredible-bargain" $20 early-bird dinner is also a serious "draw"; well-wishers wonder why this "sleeper" doesn't net more attention.

Dominic ⓈⒾ · – | – | – | M

(fka Pico)

349 Greenwich St. (bet. Harrison & Jay Sts.), 212-343-0700

After closing his ambitious TriBeCa Portuguese, Pico, chef-owner John Villa has reopened it as this less-expensive neighborhood Italian offering food in three sizes (appetizer, entree, family-style); a priced-to-move wine list and curved booths are further enhancements.

Dominick's ⌽ · 23 | 8 | 18 | $32

2335 Arthur Ave. (bet. Crescent Ave. & E. 187th St.), Bronx, 718-733-2807

■ "Don't make the mistake of asking for a menu" at this cash-only Bronx Italian "classic", just "order what the strangers" at your "communal table" are having, and wait for the "heaping platters of delicious" food to arrive; it feels sort of like a paesano "family reunion", though "long weekend lines" are also part of the "experience."

Don Giovanni ◑
18 | 11 | 15 | $24

214 10th Ave. (bet. 22nd & 23rd Sts.), 212-242-9054
358 W. 44th St. (bet. 8th & 9th Aves.), 212-581-4939
www.dongiovanni-ny.com

☑ "Reliable brick-oven pizza" and other "cheap" Italian standards turn these "casual" Westsiders into "neighborhood necessities"; aesthetes avoid the "dingy" digs with sidewalk seating or "delivery."

Don Pedro's
▽ 21 | 20 | 22 | $30

1865 Second Ave. (96th St.), 212-996-3274

■ In a culinarily underserved corner of the Upper East Side, this "impressive" new Latino-Carribean is striving to fill the area's "refined" dining gap; a "friendly" vibe and "reasonable" bilingual menu spiced with "interesting specials" have locals celebrating its arrival.

Don Peppe ⊟
25 | 10 | 19 | $37

135-58 Lefferts Blvd. (135th Ave.), Queens, 718-845-7587

■ Definitely "worth the taxi ride" to Ozone Park, this veteran Italian's "excellent" eats served "family-style" and clientele worthy of a "*Sopranos* casting call" "more than make up" for the "lack of decor"; "bring friends" – you'll "go home with leftovers anyway" – and remember that this "garlic heaven" is "cash-only."

Dos Caminos
20 | 23 | 19 | $44

373 Park Ave. S. (bet. 26th & 27th Sts.), 212-294-1000 ◑
475 W. Broadway (Houston St.), 212-277-4300
www.brguestrestaurants.com

☑ Steve Hanson has "another winner" with these Gramercy-SoHo "*muy* cool" Mexicans, "cavernous" magnets for "eye-candy" "young professionals" who may dig its "fabulous" look and "100+ tequila" list even more than the "tasty" "upscale" fare; if it gets "chaotic" and "downright deafening", never mind – it's all part of the "scene."

Downtown ◑
20 | 19 | 18 | $62

376 W. Broadway (bet. Broome & Spring Sts.), 212-343-0999;
www.cipriani.com

☑ It "helps to be rich, beautiful or speak with an accent" at this "chicer-than-chic" SoHo Northern Italian where the food "sings Venice", but "it's surprising anyone actually eats" given all the "air-kissing" going on; yes, it's "expensive", but at least you "get clipped in style."

Downtown Atlantic
– | – | – | M

364 Atlantic Ave. (bet. Bond & Hoyt Sts.), Brooklyn, 718-852-9945

Boerum Hill's Atlantic Avenue antiques district continues to sprout bars and eateries, and among the latest is this old photograph–filled New American that draws shoppers and neighborhood noshers on a budget; other pluses are an on-site bakery and live weekend jazz.

Dr-K
▽ 23 | 23 | 19 | $32

114 Dyckman St. (Nagle Ave.), 212-304-1717

■ The few who've discovered this affordable new Washington Heights Nuevo Latino say "wow!" – "there should be more like this Uptown"; the "surprisingly good" cuisine and "elegantly over-the-top" surroundings are providing a "much-needed" culinary "spark in the neighborhood."

Druids ◑
▽ 19 | 16 | 19 | $29

736 10th Ave. (bet. 50th & 51st Sts.), 212-307-6410

■ Now that the smoke has cleared, "what looks like" just a "typical" Irish pub in Hell's Kitchen turns out to offer a wee bit more, including a wallet-friendly American menu with a few "grander ambitions", a "friendly" vibe and a "sweet back garden" ("the way to go" in summer).

DT.UT ◐   17 | 18 | 14 | $13

1626 Second Ave. (bet. 84th & 85th Sts.), 212-327-1327; www.dtut.com

■ Gen-Yers who "miss the student union" flock to this East Side coffee-and-dessert house packed with "comfy chairs" and the "budding novelists" and "first dates" who hog them; it's a "hangout" to rival "Central Perk", raising the question "what's going to happen when *Friends* ends?"; N.B. a new East Village branch is in the works.

Duane Park Cafe   24 | 20 | 23 | $51

157 Duane St. (bet. Hudson St. & W. B'way), 212-732-5555

■ "When you can't figure out where to go" in TriBeCa, there's always this New American "perennial" "sleeper", an "oasis for grown-ups" seeking "delicious", "well-executed" cuisine, "gracious" service and a "serene" ambiance allowing "quiet conversation"; admirers always wonder "why isn't it busier?"

Due ◐⇪   21 | 17 | 20 | $39

1396 Third Ave. (bet. 79th & 80th Sts.), 212-772-3331

■ "Everybody's dream" of a "neighborhood" Northern Italian, this "quiet", "affordable" Upper Eastsider pleases its "loyal" "over-50" following with "cut-above" cooking, "quaint" Mediterranean decor and "welcoming" service; too bad it doesn't "take plastic."

Duke's   16 | 12 | 14 | $23

99 E. 19th St. (Park Ave. S.), 212-260-2922

■ "Frat life continues" at this Gramercy "roadhouse", where "comfy Southern food" at "ridiculously low prices" plus "Pabst Blue Ribbon in a bucket" equals a "young, loud" scene; those who abhor the "bad decor" and "TVs always on sports" cease "to notice" once they've "thrown back a few."

Dumonet   22 | 25 | 25 | $75

(fka Carlyle Restaurant)

Carlyle Hotel, 35 E. 76th St. (Madison Ave.), 212-744-1600; www.thecarlyle.com

■ It has a new moniker to go with its subtly "renovated" dining room and updated menu, but this East Side bastion of "graciousness and civility" remains as "exquisite" as ever, thanks to its "cosseting" service and chef Jean-Louis Dumonet's modern French fare; whether for a "sumptuous" breakfast or brunch or an "elegant" "formal" dinner, "if you can afford it," "it doesn't get much better than this."

DuMont   ▽ 21 | 18 | 18 | $26

432 Union Ave. (bet. Devoe St. & Metropolitan Ave.), Brooklyn, 718-486-7717

■ Possibly "the best burgers in Williamsburg" (well, after Peter Luger) draw "the über-hip" to this "friendly", "bargain"-oriented American, whose menu may be "small", but at least "everything [on it] is good"; its appealing "dim, modest" space is "always crowded", but a patio and back bar ease the crush.

Dylan Prime   22 | 22 | 20 | $57

62 Laight St. (Greenwich St.), 212-334-4783; www.dylanprime.com

■ "Heavy on the portions, easy on the eyes", this TriBeCa "Atkins paradise" sure isn't "your father's steakhouse" given the "inventive" menu putting a "fresh spin on the classics" and "slick atmosphere"; no surprise it pulls in a "young", "corporate" clientele, who say "the only drawback is" the out-of-the-way Holland Tunnel–area location.

East
16 11 15 $26

210 E. 44th St. (bet. 2nd & 3rd Aves.), 212-687-5075
354 E. 66th St. (bet. 1st & 2nd Aves.), 212-734-5270
365 First Ave. (bet. 21st & 22nd Sts.), 212-689-8898
366 Third Ave. (bet. 26th & 27th Sts.), 212-889-2326
71 University Pl. (bet. 10th & 11th Sts.), 212-673-0634
253 W. 55th St. (bet. B'way & 8th Ave.), 212-581-2240 ◐

■ "Straightforward" Japanese "cheap eats" "from sushi to sukiyaki" draw the budget-minded to this "no-frills" chain for "acceptable" if "undistinguished" dining (though Gramercy boasts a "cool" self-serve conveyor belt); aesthetes avoid the "drab" digs via "fast takeout and delivery."

East Lake ◐⊟
21 12 13 $26

42-33 Main St. (Franklin Ave.), Queens, 718-539-8532

☑ A "classic" in Flushing's C-town, this "no-atmosphere" Cantonese seafooder offers some "unusual dishes" plus "Sunday dim sum to die for"; it's "very busy", but "the lines go fast" and the staff, if "rude", is so "quick" "it takes longer to park than eat."

East of Eighth ◐
15 15 16 $28

254 W. 23rd St. (bet. 7th & 8th Aves.), 212-352-0075;
www.eastofeighth.com

■ This "Chelsea standby" "still packs in the beautiful boys" for "good, casual, cheap" Eclectic eats best enjoyed out in the "darling garden"; if service is "slow", most don't mind since it's remarkably "without attitude" given the neighborhood.

East Post ◐
19 18 17 $30

92 Second Ave. (bet. 5th & 6th Sts.), 212-387-0065

■ "Bring a date" because it's "affordable" enough to pick up the tab at this "busy but not noisy" East Village Italian offering "tasty", "homestyle" dishes in a "friendly" atmosphere; better still, it's "easier to get into than Frank" two doors down.

E.A.T.
19 11 13 $35

1064 Madison Ave. (bet. 80th & 81st Sts.), 212-772-0022; www.elizabar.com

☑ Eli Zabar's sandwich shop may be the "most expensive in the known universe", however, breakfasting and lunching "kings and queens" of the Upper East Side hardly notice because "ya can't beat" it when it comes to "taste"; for the same reason, most people take the "lousy" service and "no-ambiance" setup in stride.

Eatery ◐
18 16 15 $30

798 Ninth Ave. (53rd St.), 212-765-7080; www.eaterynyc.com

■ "Where the hipsters go" in Hell's Kitchen, this "relaxed", "spare" American grooves to "'70s disco tunes" as its "friendly" (if "harried") staff dispenses "value"-packed, "trendy comfort food"; insiders tout "eating outside" in summer.

Ecco ⊠
21 19 20 $48

124 Chambers St. (bet. Church St. & W. B'way), 212-227-7074

■ "It never fails us" declare devotees of this longtime "little bit of Italy" in TriBeCa, where the 19th-century "saloon" setting is a "friendly" backdrop for "old-school" meals with "gracious service"; if a finicky few suggest it's getting a bit "dingy", regulars retort just "*mangia!*"

Ecco-la ◐
16 14 15 $25

1660 Third Ave. (93rd St.), 212-860-5609

☑ Upper Eastsiders favor this "quaint" Italian "standby", whose "cheap, reliable" eats dished out in "cozy, Village-esque" digs make it a local "favorite" even "after all these years"; "tight quarters" are par for the course.

Edgar's Cafe ●⊅

| 18 | 17 | 15 | $18 |

255 W. 84th St. (bet. B'way & West End Ave.), 212-496-6126
■ "Poe-etic desserts" make "great date" fodder at this affordable Upper West Side cafe whose "House of Usher"–meets–"old-fashioned ice cream parlor" interior is "worthy" of its gothic author namesake; lunchers also tout its "cheap, interesting" sandwiches.

Edison Cafe ⊅

| 15 | 8 | 13 | $18 |

Edison Hotel, 228 W. 47th St. (bet. B'way & 8th Ave.), 212-840-5000
■ Aka the "Polish Tea Room", this "last-of-its-kind" Theater District "greasy spoon" sustains everyone from "celebrities" to the "down-and-out" with its ultra-"cheap", "Jewish comfort food" dispensed by a "fast", "crusty" crew; though the eats are "so-so" at best, "where else can you get matzo brei in Midtown?"

Edward's ●

| 17 | 16 | 17 | $30 |

136 W. Broadway (bet. Duane & Thomas Sts.), 212-233-6436
■ A "great place to enjoy a drink and watch the people go by", this "cheery little TriBeCa bistro can be "counted on" for "plentiful portions" of "comfy food" American-style; a "child-friendly" vibe and "easygoing" service add appeal.

Efendi ●⊅

| 20 | 11 | 15 | $21 |

1030 Second Ave. (bet. 54th & 55th Sts.), 212-421-3004
■ This new BYO Turk's arrival has Eastsiders singing "oh happy day" over its flavorsome, "homestyle fare" and "bargain" prices; however, "confusing" "no-menu" ordering and "deli"-like digs have others opting out – as in "takeout."

Eight Mile Creek ●

| ▽ 21 | 16 | 22 | $39 |

240 Mulberry St. (bet. Prince & Spring Sts.), 212-431-4635;
www.eightmilecreek.com
■ "Try the 'roo, mate" advise the "handsome, ridiculously friendly" expat staffers who stand in for decor at this Little Italy Aussie; it boasts "exotic" dishes (think "emu carpaccio") and "amazing" wines, plus a "great bar downstairs" for "pub food and beers."

Eisenberg Sandwich Shop ⌧⊅

| 19 | 9 | 16 | $11 |

174 Fifth Ave. (bet. 22nd & 23rd Sts.), 212-675-5096
☑ "Perfect tuna sandwiches" and "great egg creams" explain why this circa-1929 Flatiron "institution" is "the real McCoy" of "old New York luncheonettes"; if a few find it "hole-in-the-wall ugly", most see only "character."

EJ's Luncheonette

| 17 | 11 | 14 | $20 |

447 Amsterdam Ave. (bet. 81st & 82nd Sts.), 212-873-3444 ⊅
432 Sixth Ave. (bet. 9th & 10th Sts.), 212-473-5555
1271 Third Ave. (73rd St.), 212-472-0600 ⊅
☑ A "notch above the usual neighborhood diner" declare "stroller"-pushing supporters of this "bustling", "faux '50s" trio, where the American staples give "comfort", even if the "slow" service and "crazy" brunch lines don't; "cheap" tabs secure its "winner" status.

Elaine's ●

| 12 | 13 | 14 | $47 |

1703 Second Ave. (bet. 88th & 89th Sts.), 212-534-8103
☑ Owner Elaine Kaufman is an "institution" and her Upper East Side Italian-American eatery–cum–writers' magnet is often still a "scene"; however, critics call it "overhyped" and "overpriced", citing "snobbish" service, "lousy" food and a "wanna-be, used-ta-be" clientele.

El Charro Español
▽ 19 | 12 | 18 | $38

4 Charles St. (bet. Greenwich Ave. & 7th Ave. S.), 212-242-9547

■ After nearly 80 years building "a loyal following", this Spanish Villager is still "a favorite" for its "consistently good" "traditional" dishes, "helpful" service and "joyful" vibe; just "make a reservation" because it's "small" and usually full of folks "having a good time."

El Cid
22 | 13 | 18 | $33

322 W. 15th St. (bet. 8th & 9th Aves.), 212-929-9332

◪ Paella partisans "pack in like sardines" at this "teeny" Chelsea Spaniard favored for its "killer sangria" and "garlicky", "cid-licious" tapas; its interior's a little "cheesy" ("dim the lights, please"), but it's "loads of fun" and "well worth the wait."

Elephant, The ●
22 | 17 | 15 | $34

58 E. First St. (bet. 1st & 2nd Aves.), 212-505-7739

■ "Make sure your friends are skinny" when trying to squeeze into this "funky", "sexy" East Village "matchbox", where "sultry" Thai-French flavors and "the best litchi martinis" lure the "young and hip"; "not-so-fabulous" service and serious "noise" come with the territory.

Elephant & Castle ●
17 | 14 | 15 | $24

68 Greenwich Ave. (bet. 6th & 7th Aves.), 212-243-1400

■ A longtime local "standby" for "cheap" and "charming" meals, this "comfy", "pub-grub-and-Guinness" Village American is also "fun with kids"; given the "informal" vibe, no one minds much if the premises "could use some sprucing up."

ELEVEN MADISON PARK
25 | 26 | 25 | $61

11 Madison Ave. (24th St.), 212-889-0905

■ "Artful without pretension, swanky but not stuffy", Danny Meyer's Madison Park New American is "all class", from Kerry Heffernan's "superb", "clean" cuisine (and equally "interesting" wine list) to the "really ace" service to the "gorgeous", "soaring" landmark space; for those who can't swing the "expensive" tabs, there's always the "bargain" $25 lunch prix fixe, not to mention the restaurant's hot dog cart parked across the street.

El Faro
22 | 9 | 17 | $35

823 Greenwich St. (Horatio St.), 212-929-8210

◪ "Tiny and ancient", this circa-1927 West Village Spaniard "looks like nothing from the outside (and inside too)", but its paella and other classics so "garlicky" they'd "kill a vampire at 10 paces" are "pure ecstasy" with a glass of sangria; it's often "crowded and noisy", but regulars say "who cares?"

Eliá
▽ 25 | 20 | 23 | $48

8611 Third Ave. (bet. 86th & 87th Sts.), Brooklyn, 718-748-9891

■ You've landed in "Santorini" upon entering this "intimate", "elegant" Bay Ridge Greek that has yet to be discovered by most surveyors; "friendliest-ever" service and "unbelievably good" fish and lamb dishes have those who know it claiming they'd come every night if it weren't for the "high prices."

Elias Corner ●卍
23 | 9 | 14 | $32

24-02 31st St. (24th Ave.), Queens, 718-932-1510

◪ "The fish is first class" at this bit of the "Aegean in Astoria" that's legendary for "well-priced", "simply prepared", "terrifically fresh" Greek seafood, and its "fantastic terrace in summer"; there are "no frills, reservations or credit cards" (not to mention elbow room or menus), and service comes "with an opinion", but still most shrug "what's not to like?"

Elio's ◐
24 | 17 | 19 | $54

1621 Second Ave. (bet. 84th & 85th Sts.), 212-772-2242

☑ "Cosmetically enhanced Eastsiders" and "tycoons" "from the covers of *Forbes*" "air kiss" over "melt-in-your-mouth" classics at this "energetic", "pricey", "old-school" Italian; outsiders complain service is "terrific" only for "regulars", while insiders confirm once you're a "steady" "everything works."

El Malecon
21 | 6 | 15 | $15

764 Amsterdam Ave. (bet. 97th & 98th Sts.), 212-864-5648
4141 Broadway (175th St.), 212-927-3812 ◐
5592 Broadway (231st St.), Bronx, 718-432-5155 ◐

☑ "Hearty" portions of "basic Dominican fare" and "the best cafe con leche" earn these "friendly", strictly no-frills Uptowners "heaven-in-the-'hood" status; they're "a big bargain", and the Washington Heights branch is even "open 24/7."

elmo ◐
14 | 20 | 14 | $33

156 Seventh Ave. (bet. 19th & 20th Sts.), 212-337-8000

☑ "The best-looking dishes" are downing "strong cocktails" at the bar at this "retro-chic" Chelsea New American crowded with "fashionistas and boys in love"; the look is "sleek", and the "late-night" and weekend brunch scenes hopping, so few care that the "cavernous" space is "cacophonous" and the food "forgettable."

El Parador Cafe ⌧
20 | 15 | 21 | $38

325 E. 34th St. (bet. 1st & 2nd Aves.), 212-679-6812

■ This "dark" Murray Hill Mexican's been a "neighborhood staple" since the '50s; though it may "need a face-lift", its "mega-margaritas", "oh-so-good" classic dishes and "friendly" service have regulars hoping "it'll stay open another 40 years."

El Pote ⌧
21 | 12 | 19 | $35

718 Second Ave. (bet. 38th & 39th Sts.), 212-889-6680

☑ "Consistently good food" and "very fair prices" keep the regulars regular at this veteran Murray Hill Spaniard; the "small quarters "look like nothing" but staffers who treat customers "like family" still maintain a "jovial atmosphere."

El Quijote ◐
19 | 13 | 17 | $36

226 W. 23rd St. (bet. 7th & 8th Aves.), 212-929-1855

☑ "Garlicky", "bib"-worthy "el grande lobsters" at "two-for-one" prices and "knockout sangria" fuel the "circus" scene at this Chelsea Spaniard known for its "anachronistic" "mock"-Andalusian digs; for such "characterful" "fun", amigos amiably endure "unbearable" waits, "indifferent" service and "noisy" acoustics.

El Teddy's
14 | 17 | 14 | $36

219 W. Broadway (bet. Franklin & White Sts.), 212-941-7071

☑ Look for "Lady Liberty" "overhead" and you can't miss this "wacky" TriBeCa Mexican, whose Dali-inspired "acid-trip" interior brims with bevies of "broker types" and "bachelorette parties" downing "killer margaritas" and "passable" edibles.

Emack & Bolio's ◐≠
24 | 8 | 15 | $6

389 Amsterdam Ave. (bet. 78th & 79th Sts.), 212-362-2747
56 Seventh Ave. (bet. 13th & 14th Sts.), 212-727-1198
www.emackandbolios.com

■ "Calories be damned – full feed ahead" cry fans of these "celestial" ice cream shops "imported" from Boston; "they charge a lot", but as the "lines out the door" attest, they scoop "the most unique flavors you'll find anywhere."

Embers
21 | 13 | 17 | $40

9519 Third Ave. (bet. 95th & 96th Sts.), Brooklyn, 718-745-3700

◪ The "quality" beef in "big Brooklyn portions" is "an unbelievable bargain" at this Bay Ridge "family" steakhouse for the "leisure-suit-and-cell-phone" set; maybe the decor's deficient and service "nothing great", but at least you – and your wallet – will "leave full."

Empire Diner ●
14 | 13 | 13 | $23

210 10th Ave. (22nd St.), 212-243-2736

◪ Thanks to its "standard" fare served 24/7, West Chelsea's "retro" "black-and-chrome" diner has become an "institution" for "after clubbing" and for lunch while "gallery-hopping"; in clement weather the outdoor seating's "perfect for people-watching", but "be careful" lest the "casual-at-best" staffers "forget you exist."

Empire Szechuan ●
15 | 8 | 14 | $21

4041 Broadway (bet. 170th & 171st Sts.), 212-568-1600
2642 Broadway (100th St.), 212-662-9404
2574 Broadway (97th St.), 212-663-6004
193 Columbus Ave. (bet. 68th & 69th Sts.), 212-496-8778
15 Greenwich Ave. (bet. Christopher & W. 10th Sts.), 212-691-1535
173 Seventh Ave. S. (bet. Perry & W. 11th Sts.), 212-243-6046
381 Third Ave. (bet. 27th & 28th Sts.), 212-685-6215
251 W. 72nd St. (bet. B'way & West End Ave.), 212-873-2151

◪ "Dependable but unspectacular", this ubiquitous Chinese chain "will never surprise" but does present a "huge menu" at "cheap" prices; those who find the "no-frills" venues "depressing" note "they deliver anywhere."

Ennio & Michael
∇ 22 | 17 | 23 | $42

539 La Guardia Pl. (bet. Bleecker & W. 3rd Sts.), 212-677-8577

▣ They "make everyone feel special" at this "solid" NoHo Italian, whose "rich", "old-school" specialties come in a "relaxed, refreshingly un-trendy" space; the money-minded may rate it "expensive", but regulars who are treated "like *familigia*" don't mind.

Enzo's
∇ 25 | 13 | 20 | $32

1998 Williamsbridge Rd. (Neill Ave.), Bronx, 718-409-3828

▣ "Huge portions" of "excellent red-sauce" Italian make it tough to "get a table" at this Bronx traditionalist, where service is "attentive" and the premises, though "plain", possess a certain "authenticity"; "discerning locals" ask "what more could you want?"

Epicerie ●
∇ 18 | 18 | 14 | $30

170 Orchard St. (bet. Rivington & Stanton Sts.), 212-420-7520

▣ "Like a street corner in France", this Lower East Side Gallic bistro's facade resembles a "cute" collection of shops; apart from erratic service, once inside it proves to be "great for a cozy brunch" or "solid" dinner, while its "lively bar" hosts a "hipster scene" with nightly DJs and live bands.

Epices du Traiteur
20 | 16 | 20 | $36

103 W. 70th St. (Columbus Ave.), 212-579-5904

▣ "Unusual" "North African specialties" make this Lincoln Center–area Med-Tunisian a "change of pace"; "sweet" if "small" digs, "friendly" service and tabs "that don't spoil your appetite" also win kudos.

ERMINIA ▨
25 | 25 | 24 | $60

250 E. 83rd St. (bet. 2nd & 3rd Aves.), 212-879-4284

▣ "Dark" and "intimate", this Italian has Eastsiders "falling in love" with its "romantic", "candlelit" space, "exceptional" Roman fare and "first-class" treatment from servers "who know how to remain available, yet out of the way"; just "bring lots of cash."

Esca
23 19 20 $61

402 W. 43rd St. (9th Ave.), 212-564-7272

☑ The only "problem is getting a reservation" at Mario Batali and Joe Bastianich's "glorious", albeit "expensive", Theater District Italian where chef David Pasternack turns out "killer branzino", "excellent" crudo and other seafood specialties; if voters are split on service and looks, all agree it's a "restaurant to return to again and again."

Esperanto ◗
20 16 15 $30

145 Ave. C (9th St.), 212-505-6559

■ An "instant vacation" awaits at this "popular", "friendly" East Village Nuevo Latino "party" where "loud", "young" locals down "potent" tropical drinks and "feast" on "spicy", *delicioso* fare; if service is "lackadaisical", at least everything's "reasonably priced."

Esperides ◗
22 16 21 $34

37-01 30th Ave. (37th St.), Queens, 718-545-1494

■ "Beautifully grilled fish" and "amazing meze" delivered by "attentive, kind" staffers keep the "older", "local" crowd happy at this "gracious", "moderately priced" Astoria Greek; "informal" yet "classy", overall it's deemed "satisfying and authentic."

ESPN Zone
12 19 13 $27

1472 Broadway (42nd St.), 212-921-3776; www.espnzone.com

☑ "A must for the tourist/sports fan" who longs "to watch every game on the planet simultaneously", this Times Square "theme" behemoth boasts "TVs everywhere" (even the "bathroom stalls"), plus copious "suds", "noise" and "long lines"; the affordable American eats are strictly "mediocre" and ditto the service, but "what do you expect from a sports bar?"

Ess-a-Bagel
23 6 13 $9

359 First Ave. (21st St.), 212-260-2252
831 Third Ave. (bet. 50th & 51st Sts.), 212-980-1010
www.ess-a-bagel.com

☑ "The hell with Atkins" – this deli duo's "basketball"-size bagels are "a perfection of starch", and, when topped with lox and a "schmear", quite possibly "proof of the existence of God"; though served with "a side of attitude", purists say "the shtick is worth" it.

Essex
∇ 20 18 17 $30

120 Essex St. (Rivington St.), 212-533-9616; www.essexnyc.com

☑ The New American food at this Lower Eastsider is "cheap and good", the $12 brunch with "unlimited" (well, up to three) drinks "the best" and the soaring Essex Street Market space "great"; still, some say the bustling "bar is the main focus" here.

Etats-Unis
25 16 22 $54

242 E. 81st St. (bet. 2nd & 3rd Aves.), 212-517-8826

■ A "small, well-edited menu" of "dynamic" cuisine plus "interesting wines" and "super-pleasant service" make this "quiet" East Side New American a beacon in "a sea of cookie-cutter" eateries; it's "teeny", but the "brilliant" fare is "worth" the squeeze, as well as "the bucks"; N.B. it has a cheaper, more casual wine bar just across the street.

Ethiopian Restaurant
∇ 19 11 21 $26

1582 York Ave. (bet. 83rd & 84th Sts.), 212-717-7311

■ You "eat with your fingers" (well, with injera bread) at this new "family-run", "authentic-as-you-can-get" East Side Ethiopian; a "small, simple" place offering "great lunch specials" and some of "the friendliest service anywhere", it's welcomed as a "needed" local change-of-pace.

Ethos
_ | _ | _ | M |

495 Third Ave. (bet. 33rd & 34th Sts.), 212-252-1972
Murray Hill's lack of Greek eateries is answered by this new, moderately priced Hellenic that already has the feeling of a neighborhood vet; look for fast-moving waiters carrying large plates of salads, clay-pot specialties and whole fish priced by the pound in a bustling setting.

Etoile
▽ 18 | 18 | 20 | $47 |

Lombardy Hotel, 109 E. 56th St. (bet. Lexington & Park Aves.), 212-750-5656; www.etoilerestaurant.com
■ This "classy" American is plushly appointed "like a private club" and offers "pleasing" classics dispensed with "personal service"; insiders tout the $25 dinner prix fixe.

Etrusca
_ | _ | _ | E |

Hilton NY, 125 W. 53rd St. (bet. 6th & 7th Aves.), 212-261-5750; www.hilton.com
Following a complete revamp a couple of years ago, this Midtown Northern Italian resplendent with terra cotta, limestone and marble evokes the charms of Tuscany; the rustic (yet decidedly upscale) cuisine is matched with a Boot-centric wine list.

Euzkadi
▽ 21 | 17 | 17 | $33 |

108 E. Fourth St. (1st Ave.), 212-982-9788
■ Its name may be "unpronounceable", but the kitchen "certainly knows how to cook fish" and other "traditional" Basque fare at this "cute" East Village boîte exuding a "friendly", "very European" feel; it's a "good value" too.

Evergreen Shanghai
17 | 11 | 15 | $24 |

785 Broadway (10th St.), 212-473-2777
10 E. 38th St. (bet. 5th & Madison Aves.), 212-448-1199
63 Mott St. (bet. Bayard & Canal Sts.), 212-571-3339 ⊅
1378 Third Ave. (bet. 78th & 79th Sts.), 212-585-3388
☑ "Juicy dumplings" are the stars at this Chinese quartet offering "cheap", "reliable dim sum" plus a "good-for-all-tastes" "hodgepodge" of other Asian specialties, including sushi at a couple of branches (there's even karaoke by reservation at Murray Hill).

Excellent Dumpling House ⊅
18 | 4 | 10 | $15 |

111 Lafayette St. (bet. Canal & Walker Sts.), 212-219-0212
☑ "Stick to the dumplings" and you won't go wrong at this "aptly named", "super-cheap", "always dependable" Chinatown stop; "communal tables", "surgical fluorescent" lighting and "dour" service have even intrepid admirers admitting "takeout is better."

Faan ◗
18 | 19 | 18 | $23 |

209 Smith St. (Baltic St.), Brooklyn, 718-694-2277; www.faanonline.com
■ At this "arty", "exotic" Cobble Hill Pan-Asian, the DJ-enhanced "young vibe" is "hip" enough to "make anyone feel chic", while the "solid" fusion fare (including sushi) is "cheap" enough for any budget; "outdoor seating" that's glassed-in winter and "a great bar" are also faan.

Fairway Cafe/Steakhouse
20 | 8 | 13 | $28 |

Fairway, 2127 Broadway, 2nd fl. (74th St.), 212-595-1888
☑ "A little miracle above the market", Mitchel London's "bare-bones" West Side mezzanine cafe serves "fab" brunches and lunches by day,

but come sundown it becomes a BYO steakhouse offering a "deal" of a dinner for $35; yes, it's "loud and chaotic" with "rushed" service, "just like everything at Fairway."

F & B   20 | 13 | 15 | $10
269 W. 23rd St. (bet. 7th & 8th Aves.), 646-486-4441; www.gudtfood.com
■ Besides "fancy franks", this cheap Chelsea "wiener wonderland" dispenses "Euro" street snacks (frites, fish 'n' chips), "excellent beers" and even champagne; "snappy" counter service in "simple, narrow" digs makes it possibly the "most elegant fast food in town."

F & J Pine Restaurant ⌽   21 | 14 | 18 | $29
1913 Bronxdale Ave. (bet. Morris Park Ave. & White Plains Rd.), Bronx, 718-792-5956
■ Adorned with "game-worn jerseys" and other "memorabilia", this Bronx Italian "Yankee hangout" hits to all fields with "pounds of pasta" and other "old-fashioned", "value"-oriented classics served "family-style"; for best results "go with a crowd", "bring cash" and remember that "you can wait forever" on a game day.

Fanelli's Cafe ◐   15 | 14 | 13 | $24
94 Prince St. (Mercer St.), 212-226-9412
■ A "laid-back" "refuge" from the "tourists" and "SoHo froufrou", this "dark, gritty" circa-1872 pub "institution" has long been a "local hangout" for "drinks and burgers"; now that the "smoke" has cleared, regulars say the "honest bar food" turns out to be "surprisingly good."

FELIDIA ⊠   25 | 22 | 23 | $65
243 E. 58th St. (bet. 2nd & 3rd Aves.), 212-758-1479; www.lidiasitaly.com
■ "Lidia Bastianich is the queen" and reigns supreme at her "gracious" East Side "townhouse" Italian, where "inventive" pastas and other dishes supply "gastronomic bliss", the wine list is "unmatched" and the service "knowledgeable and entertaining"; loyal subjects "love to see the owner" "work the room", "but the prices – mama mia!"

Félix ◐   16 | 18 | 14 | $38
340 W. Broadway (Grand St.), 212-431-0021; www.felixnyc.com
◪ To "throw back some champagne with the Euros", make "the scene" at this SoHo brunch favorite, which is at its best "in warm weather" when the "large windows" are open; the bistro fare's "good, and the prices fair", so most overlook the less-than-felix-itous service.

Ferdinando's Focacceria ⊠⌽   ▽ 21 | 15 | 16 | $20
151 Union St. (bet. Columbia & Hicks Sts.), Brooklyn, 718-855-1545
■ "You want authentic, you gotta come" to this Carroll Gardens "turn-of-the-last-century" Sicilian whose "signature" chickpea fritters come with small price tags and "heaps of atmosphere"; P.S. "hours are sporadic" (dinner Fridays and Saturdays only).

Ferrara   22 | 15 | 16 | $17
195 Grand St. (bet. Mott & Mulberry Sts.), 212-226-6150 ◐
Roosevelt Hotel, 363 Madison Ave. (bet. 45th & 46th Sts.), 212-599-7800
www.ferraracafe.com
◪ Serving "some of little Italy's best sweets" – notably "cannoli beyond compare" – this 1892 "landmark" Little Italy pasticceria (with a Midtown outpost) is still "the place to go for dessert" and coffee; just keep in mind it's "always noisy, crowded" and "touristy."

Ferrier Bistro ◐   18 | 14 | 15 | $44
29 E. 65th St. (bet. Madison & Park Aves.), 212-772-9000
■ "Squeeze past the beautiful people" at the bar in order to dine at this tiny East Side French, where the bistro fare's "good", but strictly

F D S C

secondary to the "loud", "late"-raging "Euro scene"; bargain-seekers ballyhoo the $21 pre-theater prix fixe.

Fiamma Osteria
25 | 25 | 23 | $59

206 Spring St. (bet. 6th Ave. & Sullivan St.), 212-653-0100; www.brguestrestaurants.com

■ "The jewel in Steve Hanson's crown", this "sexy" SoHo Italian more than "lives up to its press clippings" with "breathtaking, deceptively simple" cuisine, a "superb" wine cellar, "sophisticated" "multilevel" quarters and "gracious" pro service; if the bill can be "discomforting", most willingly open their wallets because "this place is on fire."

55 Wall
21 | 22 | 21 | $51

Regent Wall St., 55 Wall St. (bet. Hanover & William Sts.), 212-699-5555; www.regenthotels.com

■ "Enjoy a civilized meal and drink away those trading losses" at this "tasteful" Financial District New American boasting a "great alfresco" terrace, "well-prepared" fare and "deluxe" service; if a few feel it's just "a bit boring" for the "hip" hotel setting, all agree it's a welcome "respite from the frenzy of the Street."

Fifty Seven Fifty Seven
23 | 25 | 24 | $63

Four Seasons Hotel, 57 E. 57th St. (bet. Madison & Park Aves.), 212-758-5757; www.fourseasons.com

■ A "Zen-meets-NY" "visual feast" courtesy of "I.M. Pei", this "swank" New American in Midtown's foremost hotel is the ultimate in "corporate cool"; "both refined and relaxed", it's "a good place to show off" (especially over "power breakfasts") while savoring "premium", "*très expensif*" fare and "impeccable" service; P.S. watch the "power players" and "entertainment types" "strut" in the adjacent bar.

F.illi Ponte
20 | 21 | 20 | $61

39 Desbrosses St. (West Side Hwy.), 212-226-4621; www.filliponte.com

☑ "Ask for a table with a view of the river" because this "out-of-the-way" ("use MapQuest") TriBeCa Italian's "one of the best" for "sunset-watching"; the classic cuisine and wines also are "delightful", as is the "old-time" feel that's almost "like dining with Sinatra and Martin" (right down to the "pricey" tab); P.S. "valet parking is a definite plus."

Fino
▽ 19 | 18 | 21 | $46

4 E. 36th St. (bet. 5th & Madison Aves.), 212-689-8040 Ⓢ
1 Wall Street Ct. (Pearl St.), 212-825-1924

☑ Long a "class act" for "wonderful" service and "surprisingly good" (if "pricey") traditional fare, this Murray Hill Italian has been joined by a new Financial District outpost; some say the "stuck-in-the-'70s" original could use an "HGTV" makeover, but its capacious offspring's "open and attractive."

Fiorello's Cafe ◗
19 | 16 | 19 | $44

1900 Broadway (bet. 63rd & 64th Sts.), 212-595-5330; www.cafefiorello.com

■ On opera nights you'd better "book early" to get in this Lincoln Center–area Italian, which elicits bravos for its "great antipasti bar" and "paper-thin pizza", as well its "efficient" "curtain"-conscious staff; "cramped" and "noisy" inside, the sidewalk seats provide plentiful space and prime people-watching in good weather.

Fiorentino's
▽ 20 | 14 | 17 | $30

311 Ave. U (bet. McDonald Ave. & West St.), Brooklyn, 718-372-1445

☑ "Now this is real Brooklyn": a "relaxed", "no-frills" Gravesend "family favorite" dishing up "killer" platefuls of Neapolitan "classics" at "pizza-parlor prices"; plan on "waiting" with the "loud crowd" unless you "go early."

FIREBIRD 20 | 27 | 21 | $59
365 W. 46th St. (bet. 8th & 9th Aves.), 212-586-0244
■ "A true Russian gem", this "opulent" bit of "old St. Petersburg" on Restaurant Row will have you "convinced you're Anna and Vronsky" given the "sumptuous" duplex townhouse setup, caviar-studded cuisine and "exquisite" service; à la carte prices may set "your wallet on fire", but the $20 lunch and $38 dinner prix fixes are a "wonderful" "value."

Firenze ⬤ 19 | 17 | 19 | $41
1594 Second Ave. (bet. 82nd & 83rd Sts.), 212-861-9368
☒ Reminiscent of those "small restaurants around Florence", this East Side Tuscan serves up its "homey" "traditional fare" in "cozy" (if "tight") "candlelit" surroundings; "welcoming" service takes the bite out of what some consider "elevated" prices.

First ◐ 20 | 19 | 17 | $41
87 First Ave. (bet. 5th & 6th Sts.), 212-674-3823
■ "Grab one of the big booths" and "get a really good nosh on" at Sam DeMarco's "dark", "loud" and "funky" East Village New American where a "mixed crowd" of "late-night gourmands" tipple "tiny 'tinis" and feast on "tasty" fare; "who knew dining could be so much fun?"

Fish ◐ 19 | 13 | 16 | $38
280 Bleecker St. (Jones St.), 212-727-2879
☒ "Full of life", this Village "neighborhood" seafooder offers the rare combination of "reasonable prices" and "fresh", "well-prepared" fish (plus loads of raw-bar choices) from the owner's "daily catch"; it recently got a "fun new menu", but the digs are as "cramped" as ever.

Five Front ▽ 21 | 21 | 20 | $35
5 Front St. (Old Fulton St.), Brooklyn, 718-625-5559
■ "Good dining has finally arrived in Dumbo" say early visitors to this "hip", "accommodating" newcomer; blessed with "sexy lighting", a "beautiful garden" and "consistently tasty", affordable New American dishes, it also offers a "bargain" $20 dinner prix fixe three days a week.

Five Points ◑ 22 | 22 | 21 | $44
31 Great Jones St. (bet. Bowery & Lafayette St.), 212-253-5700
■ NoHo locals give the "high five" to this "friendly" New American, which, despite an "unassuming location", produces "sophisticated" cuisine in "Zenful" quarters centered around a "trickling stream of water"; "a joy" for dinner, mavens maintain it's "even better for brunch."

Fives ▽ 26 | 28 | 26 | $65
Peninsula Hotel, 700 Fifth Ave. (55th St.), 212-903-3918; www.peninsula.com
■ "Wonderful" but "totally overlooked" say supporters of this "gorgeous", "quiet" French–New American bastion of "old-world", "elegant dining" and "top-rate" cuisine; the less-expensive adjacent wine bar makes an "excellent" choice for "a simple Midtown meal."

Flea Market Cafe ◐ 19 | 18 | 16 | $30
131 Ave. A (bet. 9th St. & St. Marks Pl.), 212-358-9282
■ "Good bistro food and true East Village prices" are the draw at this "casual" Tompkins Square Park French; its "shabby-chic" quarters get "loud" and "crowded", and service can be "laissez-faire", but most don't mind lingering awhile given the amiable, "laid-back" atmosphere.

Fleur de Sel 25 | 21 | 23 | $58
5 E. 20th St. (bet. B'way & 5th Ave.), 212-460-9100; www.fleurdeselnyc.com
■ Cyril Renauld's Flatiron French "model bistro" is "like being in Normandy, only with better food"; "lovingly prepared" cuisine,

"sincere" service and "civilized" environs enlivened with "artwork by the chef" add up to "*magnifique*" (if "expensive") experiences.

Flor de Mayo ◐
21 | 9 | 16 | $18

484 Amsterdam Ave. (bet. 83rd & 84th Sts.), 212-787-3388
2651 Broadway (101st St.), 212-663-5520
◪ The pollo a la brasa is "*muy delicioso*" at these "packed" West Side Chinese-Peruvians dishing out "good food and plenty of it" for "almost no money"; "dive" decor ("renovations" at the Uptown branch notwithstanding) and "gruff" service have some seeking "takeout."

Flor de Sol ◐⊠
20 | 22 | 18 | $40

361 Greenwich St. (bet. Franklin & Harrison Sts.), 212-366-1640
◪ Even though it's often "crowded" and "loud", this TriBeCa Spanish "perfect date" place's "million candle"–filled interior is just the "hot" setting for a "sangria-fueled seduction"; those focusing on the tapas and other "light bites" rate them "above average", especially when savored in the "sidewalk seats."

Florent ◐⇄
19 | 13 | 14 | $28

69 Gansevoort St. (bet. Greenwich & Washington Sts.), 212-989-5779;
www.restaurantflorent.com
■ "Sober up with fill-'er-up" bistro fare at "the original" Meatpacking District "French diner"; "hectic" and "waaay too crowded" around the clock, it's "not as fringe as it used to be", but still serves as a "refuge" from "gentrification" for "suits", "leather daddies" and everyone in between.

Flor's Kitchen
21 | 9 | 15 | $20

149 First Ave. (bet. 9th & 10th Sts.), 212-387-8949;
www.florskitchen.com
◪ "Big", "delicious", "homestyle" flavors emerge from this East Village Venezuelan's "mighty-mite" kitchen, while its "miniscule" (18 seats) digs burst with "friendly Latin vibes"; devotees overlook "long waits", "rickety chairs" and "zero decor" because it's "worth the hassle."

Foley's Fish House
21 | 23 | 20 | $52

Renaissance NY Hotel, 714 Seventh Ave. (bet. 47th & 48th Sts.),
212-261-5200; www.foleysfishhouse.com
■ "Get a table by the window" at this Times Square seafooder and you've got "the lights" of Broadway "at your feet"; it's "all about the view" here, but the "piscatory platters" are "tasty" and the environs "civilized and quiet", so even if it's "a little expensive", most declare it a pre-theater "winner."

Fontana di Trevi ⊠
▽ 20 | 16 | 20 | $45

151 W. 57th St. (bet. 6th & 7th Aves.), 212-247-5683; www.fontanaditrevi.com
■ A "golden oldie" across from Carnegie Hall, this "traditional" Italian serves up "big portions" of "satisfying" fare at more or less "reasonable prices"; while the atmosphere's "a bit grandparenty" and you need to "allow time before the curtain" for "warm" but "slow" service, regulars treasure it as a "true New Yorker."

44
19 | 22 | 18 | $52

Royalton Hotel, 44 W. 44th St. (bet. 5th & 6th Aves.), 212-944-8844;
www.ianschragerhotels.com
■ Its "now-classic Starck-designed" interior is as "smashing" as ever ("check out the bathrooms"), and the French food's been "surprisingly good" since Claude Troisgros took over the kitchen last year; though service can be "snobby" and prices are steep, even "after all these years", you may still spot a stray "rock star or fashionista" mingling amid the "visitors and publishing" types.

44 & X Hell's Kitchen ◐
21 18 18 $42
622 10th Ave. (44th St.), 212-977-1170

■ "A cook who has style" spins "upscale" "twists" on the "perfect mac 'n' cheese" and other American comfort classics at this "hip" "little slice of heaven in Hell's Kitchen"; "eye-candy" staff and an "interesting crowd" distract from the "din" and "Edward Hopper"–like view of a "Hess gas station."

FOUR SEASONS ⑤
26 27 26 $80
99 E. 52nd St. (bet. Lexington & Park Aves.), 212-754-9494

■ "Nothing speaks class and power better" than this "spectacular" (and spectacularly "pricey") Midtown "landmark", "Philip Johnson's grand monument to NYC", where the "superlative" Continental cuisine is "simply done", service is "on the money" and the wine list's "wonderful"; in sum, it's an "experience" in "luxurious dining" that "everyone should enjoy at least once"; N.B. cognoscenti congregate at the Grill Room for lunch and the Pool Room for dinner.

1492 Food ◐
▽ 19 17 16 $37
60 Clinton St. (bet. Rivington & Stanton Sts.), 646-654-1114

■ "Finally a tapas bar that understands the pace and flavors" of an "authentic" Spanish taperia, say fans of this Lower East Side "sleeper" whose "great vibe" and sharable portions are perfect "for groups"; just "go when you have time on your hands", and keep in mind those little plates can "add up."

14 Wall Street ⑤
20 21 21 $48
14 Wall St., 31st fl. (bet. Broad St. & B'way), 212-233-2780

■ Fans say it's "cool to be" "power-lunching" "with the financial kings of the world" "in J.P. Morgan's" former "aerie"; this "wood-paneled" Wall Street French is a "solid" bet with its "refined" cuisine, "lovely ambiance and "subtle" service, but just "don't dine late – you'll be all by yourself."

Franchia
– – – M
12 Park Ave. (bet. 34th & 35th Sts.), 212-213-1001;
www.franchia.com

At this new Murray Hill Korean teahouse, the all-vegetarian menu is homemade (down to the soy mock meat) and matched with an extensive list of infusions – and "they also offer tea workshops"; all in all, it's a promising hangout for the gourmet yoga set.

Francisco's Centro Vasco
21 12 17 $40
159 W. 23rd St. (bet. 6th & 7th Aves.), 212-645-6224

☑ "Claw your way" into this "boisterous" Chelsea Spaniard for "sweet, juicy" lobsters the "size of small children" at possibly the "best price per pound in the city"; it's "utterly unpretentious" and "a great place to party" but takes "no rezzies, so get there early."

Frank ◐⌿
22 14 15 $28
88 Second Ave. (bet. 5th & 6th Sts.), 212-420-0202

☑ "Frankly, it's damn good" declare East Villagers of this Southern Italian "hole-in-the-wall", whose "straight-ahead" fare is "cheap" and "scrumptious"; "young" things gladly endure "marathon waits" to get into its "thrift-store-eclectic" digs, calling it "all part of the charm."

Frankie & Johnnie's Steakhouse ⑤
21 12 19 $50
269 W. 45th St. (bet. B'way & 8th Ave.), 212-997-9494 ◐
32 W. 37th St. (bet. 5th & 6th Aves.), 212-947-8940
www.frankieandjohnnies.com

☑ "Once a speakeasy", this "walk-up relic" is still "*the* place" in the Theater District for "classic", "no-nonsense" steak in a "frenetic" setting that's "long on nostalgia", but short on space; its Garment District offshoot has the same "slabs" without the "bumping elbows."

Frank's `21  16  19  $52`
85 10th Ave. (15th St.), 212-243-1349
■ A "real he-man's" "haven" tucked "out of the way" behind the Chelsea Market, this frankly "non-trendy" Italian-accented steakhouse delivers "your basic" "red meat" in "solid", "clubby" style; the room and "personable staff" are from the "old school", though the "expense-account" pricing is right up to date.

Fraunces Tavern ⌧ `17  21  19  $42`
54 Pearl St. (Broad St.), 212-968-1776; www.frauncestavern.com
⌧ The "historical" flavor leaves you "patriotically fulfilled" at this Downtown "landmark", site of George Washington's "famous farewell" to his officers and now an American "mainstay"; it's a "charmer", though many find the "food isn't up to" the "revolutionary cachet."

Fred's `18  16  18  $29`
476 Amsterdam Ave. (83rd St.), 212-579-3076
⌧ "Even cat people" "feel at home" at this "dog-themed" Upper West Side "neighborhood hangout", which dishes up "reliable" American fare to "the over-30 set" and their pups; some growl the eating's "just ok", but it's a "popular" place to "come, sit" and "stay within budget."

Fred's at Barneys NY `20  19  18  $43`
Barneys NY, 660 Madison Ave., 9th fl. (60th St.), 212-833-2200
■ To keep "your gossip current" join the "chichi" "Barney's shoppers" doing "power lunch" at this "sleek", "airy" Eastsider, where "this season's" "fashionistas" and "famous faces" "nibble" "tasty" Tuscan–New American; though "laughably expensive", it's "quite the scene" for the "*Sex and the City*" crowd in real time."

French Roast ◗ `15  14  12  $24`
2340 Broadway (85th St.), 212-799-1533
458 Sixth Ave. (11th St.), 212-533-2233
⌧ "Open 24 hours" and a "handy" "relief" from "the local diner", this "passably French" pair does bistro bites "cheaply" for everyone from early-birds to "night-owls"; "alfresco" tables ease the "overcrowding", but the "flighty service" is a turnoff unless you're "lingering."

Frère Jacques ⌧ `▽ 19  16  19  $42`
13 E. 37th St. (bet. 5th & Madison Aves.), 212-679-9355
■ Sure, this "sweet", "unassuming" Murray Hill bistro is on the "small" side, but it's "not too crowded" for fans to "unwind and enjoy" the "accomplished" French cooking and "accommodating service"; those singing along say it's "easily missed" but a "satisfying find."

Fresco by Scotto ⌧ `22  20  21  $53`
34 E. 52nd St. (bet. Madison & Park Aves.), 212-935-3434;
www.frescobyscotto.com
■ Walk in and "become part of the family" at this "hospitable-to-the-max" Midtowner, a "media-politico" "power scene" with a "delightful" (if "pricey") Tuscan menu; "Page Six wanna-bes" keep the "noise" and "energy" level high, and most agree the Scotto clan "aims to please"; N.B. eat-and-run types hit the take-out arm next door.

fresh. `22  19  19  $58`
105 Reade St. (bet. Church St. & W. B'way), 212-406-1900;
www.freshrestaurant.com
■ Owner/seafood purveyor "Eric Tevrow knows his fish", so this "exciting" TriBeCan stays "true to its name" with "imaginative"

preparations of catch so recent "you can still taste the ocean"; anchored by a "splashy", "sea-blue room", it's "all the rage" with "trendy" types willing to "splurge" for the latest "fresh take."

Friendhouse ● 19 | 18 | 19 | $22

99 Third Ave. (bet. 12th & 13th Sts.), 212-388-1838
132 St. Marks Pl. (Ave. A), 212-598-1188

■ This "cool", "clublike" East Village Asian's Japanese and Chinese dishes "fare so well" together that it's "hard to choose" between them; staff as amiable "as the name suggests" and "unbelievable prices" also make fans; N.B. the new, unrated St. Marks location exclusively serves Japanese food.

Friend of a Farmer 17 | 17 | 15 | $27

77 Irving Pl. (bet. 18th & 19th Sts.), 212-477-2188

☑ "Country cute" with a "Vermont" vibe, this Gramercy brunch "standby" has enough "fresh" Americana and "farmhouse" frills to "charm" the gingham off "Laura Ingalls"; still, city slickers cite "pseudo-B&B decor" and "so-so food" as "underwhelming."

Frutti di Mare ●⊄ 18 | 12 | 16 | $25

84 E. Fourth St. (bet. Bowery & 2nd Ave.), 212-979-2034

☑ There's "no messing around" at this East Village "mainstay" for "solid" Italian seafood, featuring a "popular" early-bird deal that's "one of the best buys" going; never mind "haphazard service" and "chaotic" conditions, 'cause for a "date on the cheap" it "can't be beat."

Fujiyama Mama ● 20 | 18 | 17 | $39

467 Columbus Ave. (bet. 82nd & 83rd Sts.), 212-769-1144

☑ "Sushi and a DJ" keep the "very '80s" "party" alive at this West Side Japanese, a "crazy place" to "get a group" together and "embarrass someone for their birthday"; behind the "cheesy" "flash" and "blaring" "dance music", it's still "fun all the way."

Funky Broome 18 | 11 | 14 | $24

176 Mott St. (Broome St.), 212-941-8628

☑ A NoLita "original", this Cantonese offers a "promising menu" of "tasty", "unusual" fare to suit the "daring" and the "budget-conscious" alike; but the "fluorescent" interior is "funky" to a fault, and those after "more traditional" tastes are swept "farther south."

Gabriela's 17 | 12 | 16 | $27

315 Amsterdam Ave. (75th St.), 212-875-8532
685 Amsterdam Ave. (93rd St.), 212-961-0574
www.gabrielas.com

■ "Mexican, not Texican" "rocks the house" at these "lively", "kid-friendly" Westsiders with food "super-sized" so you "won't go away hungry"; "Speedy Gonzalez service" and "gaudy" dive decor define the "cheap and easy" spirit that keeps them "packed."

Gabriel's ⊠ 22 | 19 | 22 | $55

11 W. 60th St. (bet. B'way & Columbus Ave.), 212-956-4600

■ "Hands-on" host Gabriel Aiello and his "unflappable staff" "make you feel special" at this perennial "Lincoln Center-area" Italian "favorite"; despite demanding dinner prices, "top Tuscan" cuisine and "warm", "low-key" surroundings keep "upscale" fans ("many in show biz") coming back for more; P.S. the $20 lunch prix fixe menu is a steal.

Gaby ● ▽ 21 | 24 | 20 | $51

Sofitel, 44 W. 45th St. (bet. 5th & 6th Aves.), 212-354-3460

■ Those in-the-know hail this "unsung" Midtowner as a "wonderful surprise" thanks to its improved French fare, "chic but comfortable" "deco" digs and attached "outdoor cafe"; if the "price is high", the "elegant" feel makes it "seem worthwhile."

Gage & Tollner ☒   22 | 23 | 22 | $47

372 Fulton St. (Jay St.), Brooklyn, 718-875-5181; www.gageandtollner.com

■ Traditionalists "revel in" the "trip to yesteryear" at this circa-1879 Downtown Brooklyn "landmark" that delivers "succulent" surf 'n' turf and "formal" service by "gaslight"; once in the "beautiful wood-paneled" room it's easy to "forget" the "urban mall outside" and relish "old-world style" with "no shortcuts."

Gallagher's Steak House ❶   20 | 16 | 18 | $54

228 W. 52nd St. (bet. B'way & 8th Ave.), 212-245-5336; www.gallaghersnysteakhouse.com

☑ It's "nostalgiaville" at this Theater District chophouse, where "aging steaks in the window" are the prelude to "gut-buster" portions and "crusty" service in a "throwback setting"; it "holds its own" as an "old boys' club", but antis advise "don't expect old-fashioned prices."

Gam Mee Ok ❶   21 | 15 | 16 | $22

43 W. 32nd St. (bet. B'way & 5th Ave.), 212-695-4113

☑ Leading a "small menu" of "hearty" favorites, the "ambrosial" "house specialty *sullongtang*" (beef soup) is the name of the game at this "busy" Garment District Korean; since the "tab is cheap" and it's "open 24/7", most are ok with functional service and decor.

Garden Cafe ☒   ▽ 28 | 22 | 26 | $43

620 Vanderbilt Ave. (Prospect Pl.), Brooklyn, 718-857-8863

■ "A real labor of love", this "postage stamp–size" Prospect Heights "treasure" "actually caters to adults" with "stellar" "in-season" New American fare served in "intimate", "no-rush" style, and the "refined" result is "something special"; Manhattanites only "wish this was closer to home."

Gargiulo's   22 | 19 | 21 | $40

2911 W. 15th St. (bet. Mermaid & Surf Aves.), Brooklyn, 718-266-4891; www.gargiulos.com

■ At this "Coney Island mainstay" they've been providing "quality" "homestyle" Neapolitan "year after year" in an "expansive" "dining hall" that "echoes of old Brooklyn"; for the "genuine" goods at "fair prices", it's one "you can rely on."

Gascogne   22 | 20 | 21 | $46

158 Eighth Ave. (bet. 17th & 18th Sts.), 212-675-6564; www.gascognenyc.com

■ "Tucked away" in Chelsea, this "first-rate" bistro is the "real" Gallic deal with Southern French "country" cooking served in "dark", "cozy", "romantic" digs; "Francophiles" find it a "respite" especially when dining in the "delightful" garden.

Gennaro ⊘   24 | 13 | 15 | $34

665 Amsterdam Ave. (bet. 92nd & 93rd Sts.), 212-665-5348

■ "Lines to Milan and back form midweek in a snowstorm" at this *magnifico* Upper Westside Italian; the reasons, like the decor, are basic: you "can't beat the food-for-value ratio" and "everyone knows it" – just like they know it "needs to expand."

Ghenet   ▽ 22 | 14 | 17 | $27

284 Mulberry St. (bet. Houston & Prince Sts.), 212-343-1888; www.ghenet.com

☑ "Go with friends who like to share" and don't mind utensil-free eating – it's the formula for success at this low-budget NoLita Ethiopian; it's both a "change of pace" and "basic education" in a "laid-back" milieu with "sweet service" at "molasses" speed.

Giambelli ◐
21 | 17 | 21 | $55

46 E. 50th St. (bet. Madison & Park Aves.), 212-688-2760

◪ This '50s-era vet still "holds its own" as a "comfy" Midtown venue for "solid" Italian and "impeccable service"; naysayers knock it as "pricey" and "kinda dated", but the "quality remains high" and regulars consider it a "steady" "old friend."

Giando on the Water
▽ 17 | 21 | 17 | $42

400 Kent Ave. (Broadway), Brooklyn, 718-387-7000;
www.giandoonthewater.com

◪ The "spectacular" panoramic view of Downtown Manhattan from this Williamsburg Northern Italian helps "overcome" charges that the food and service are "just decent"; "good value" is also a draw for those who snare a "table by the window" and consider it the "poor man's River Cafe."

Gigino at Wagner Park
19 | 23 | 19 | $38

20 Battery Pl. (West St.), 212-528-2228

■ "On a clear day" the "gorgeous sunsets" and "view of Ms. Liberty" at this moderately priced Financial District Italian rank with "NYC's best" sights, so "who cares" if the food and service are "variable"; the "fab" visuals and "informal" vibes unite on a "harborside" patio that's "made for summer."

Gigino Trattoria
21 | 18 | 19 | $40

323 Greenwich St. (bet. Duane & Reade Sts.), 212-431-1112

■ If you think "rustic" "character" is hard to come by in TriBeCa, this "cheerful", modestly tabbed Tuscan trattoria proves the contrary with its "top-flight" "country" Italian fare, "comfortable" quarters and "caring service"; it's also a local star for being the "set of the movie *Dinner Rush*."

Gino ⇗
20 | 13 | 19 | $42

780 Lexington Ave. (bet. 60th & 61st Sts.), 212-758-4466

■ There's "a certain charm" "straight out of 1945" at this East Side Italian, where customers come weekly to savor "satisfying" red-gravy fare in a room with lotsa "charisma" but "no decor" (except "those zebras on the wall"); it's "hectic", but many "swear by" it – at least "for old times' sake."

Giorgione
▽ 22 | 20 | 18 | $47

307 Spring St. (bet. Greenwich & Hudson Sts.), 212-352-2269

■ An "attractive" "new face" in western SoHo, this "welcoming" (if pricey) Italian "surprises" with "excellent pizzas" and a "fresh" raw bar, on offer in a "simple" yet "elegant" space; it's "a little out of the way", but still getting the "buzz" it "deserves."

Giorgio's of Gramercy
23 | 19 | 21 | $41

27 E. 21st St. (bet. B'way & Park Ave. S.), 212-477-0007

■ Maybe a moniker like a "bad hairdresser" explains why this Flatiron New American is so darn "underappreciated", since the food and service are "way above par"; it's also "cozy" and "affordably romantic", so cash-strapped romeos are more than "glad the whole town doesn't know."

Giovanni
▽ 23 | 20 | 21 | $47

47 W. 55th St. (bet. 5th & 6th Aves.), 212-262-2828;
www.giovanni-ristorante.com

■ They "maintain high standards" at this Midtown "sleeper", matching "fine" Northern Italian fare with "gracious" service for those willing to "pay for quality"; despite the "prime location", it's "rarely crowded", making it a good choice for "business or romance."

Giovanni Venticinque

▽ 22 | 17 | 21 | $53

25 E. 83rd St. (bet. 5th & Madison Aves.), 212-988-7300

❚ "Only a block from the Met", this "warm", "old-world" Northern Italian "stands out" as a "sedate" "hideaway" for "fabulous food" "served with style"; *amici* deem it "worth the investment", though some consider the "sleepy decor and clientele" a snooze.

Girasole ◐

22 | 17 | 21 | $53

151 E. 82nd St. (bet. Lexington & 3rd Aves.), 212-772-6690

■ "Not much changes", and the "regulars like it that way" at this Upper East Side Italian, where the "superior eats" and "personable" staff are "popular" with the graying "Chanel crowd"; the "high prices" buy "few surprises", but for an "upscale" yet "homey feel" it's a "winner."

Global 33 ◐

19 | 19 | 15 | $33

99 Second Ave. (bet. 5th & 6th Sts.), 212-477-8427;
www.global33nyc.com

■ "Bring a group" because there's "tapas for everyone" at this "lounge-y" East Village Eclectic, an "'in' spot" for "urban hipsters" to play it "cool" over affordable "small plates" and "dangerously good" drinks; the food's "surprisingly" "original", but it's the "party" that makes the globe go round.

Gnocco Caffe ⊟

22 | 17 | 18 | $31

337 E. 10th St. (bet. Aves. A & B), 212-677-1913; www.gnocco.com

■ Still a "well-kept secret", this East Villager makes a "great date place" with its "lovely garden" and "delightful" "real Italian cooking", including the namesake fried dough antipasto that mavens "swear by"; "decent prices" compensate for the "cash-only" rule, but the service style is "imported" ("they take their time").

Gobo ◑

25 | 24 | 22 | $30

401 Sixth Ave. (bet. Waverly Pl. & W. 8th St.), 212-255-3242

■ "Finally", there's a "high-end" "place for vegans" thanks to this Village newcomer from the sons of the Zen Palate clan, where "unbelievable" vegetarian dishes with Asian leanings make for "adventurous", "guilt-free" eating in a "smart", "serene" setting; it may be slightly "pricey", but it's a "dream come true" where even "meat lovers" may find "enlightenment."

Golden Unicorn

20 | 12 | 13 | $23

18 E. Broadway, 3rd fl. (Catherine St.), 212-941-0911

❚ Experience "dim sum mania" at this "hectic" Chinatowner for "chowing down" on a "wide variety" of offerings in a "tacky" yet "colorful" upstairs hall; it's the "English-friendliest" of the "Hong Kong–style" houses, but insiders "go early" as the "mobs" make for nearly "unbearable" waits.

Gonzo ◐

22 | 18 | 19 | $40

140 W. 13th St. (bet. 6th & 7th Aves.), 212-645-4606

■ Chef Vincent Scotto goes for the "gusto" at this "hot" Village Italian, home to "distinctive" fare led by "super-thin" "grilled pizza" with "gourmet toppings"; for "affordable" "virtuosity" with "no attitude" it's "a real contender", where "major crowds" keep the "expansive" space "bustling" and "oh-so-loud."

good

20 | 16 | 17 | $33

89 Greenwich Ave. (bet. Bank & W. 12th Sts.), 212-691-8080;
www.goodrestaurantnyc.com

■ "As they promise", "good" vibes rule at this "satisfying" Village New American, serving "creative" "comfort food" with a "smile" in "inviting" digs; those who "pile in" for an "honest" bite or "killer brunch" say "the name's an understatement."

Good Enough to Eat
21 | 15 | 16 | $24

483 Amsterdam Ave. (bet. 83rd & 84th Sts.), 212-496-0163

■ The "Vermonty" "homespun" style at this Upper West Side American "hits the spot" when it's time to "fuel" up on "stick-to-the-ribs" "country-kitchen" fare; "blockbuster" lines on weekend mornings are "wearisome", but it's "totally worth" the wait and "the cholesterol."

Goody's
21 | 8 | 16 | $17

1 E. Broadway (bet. Catherine & Oliver Sts.), 212-577-2922

☑ Followers "can't get enough" of the "yummy" buns at this Chinatown soup-dumpling shop, a "wonderful", "fast" fix when you're going "cheap"; the "decor leaves much to be desired", but, in contrast to "rival" Joe's Shanghai, there's "no wait" here.

Googie's ●
15 | 11 | 13 | $21

1491 Second Ave. (78th St.), 212-717-1122

☑ "Take the kids" to this "stroller-friendly" East Side "standby" for "good old diner fare" "and lots of it"; despite "no-frills" digs and "spaced-out" service, it "beats eating at home" even if the weekend "brunch scene" is a "zoo."

GOTHAM BAR & GRILL
27 | 25 | 26 | $65

12 E. 12th St. (bet. 5th Ave. & University Pl.), 212-620-4020

■ An "all-time champ" that "delivers" "every time", this Village New American sets the "benchmark" with Alfred Portale's "inspired" "art on a plate", a "towering" mix of "sky-high presentations" and "subtle flavors"; the "stellar service" and "grand", "soaring" space ensure it's "tops" "in every detail"; P.S. the $25 "lunch prix fixe is a steal."

Grace ●
16 | 18 | 17 | $34

114 Franklin St. (bet. Church St. & W. B'way), 212-343-4200

☑ Maybe most "come for the martinis", but this TriBeCa New American is also graced with "inventive", "tapas-size dishes"; once you "push past" the "heavy-duty bar" crowd it's "decent" for a "light" bite or "really late" "late-night snack" – naturally the "drinks are perfect."

Grace's Trattoria
17 | 16 | 16 | $37

201 E. 71st St. (bet. 2nd & 3rd Aves.), 212-452-2323

☑ "Catering to the neighbors" with "fresh" "Italian home cooking", this "upbeat" annex to "quality" grocer Grace's Marketplace is a "relaxing" refuge from the prim Upper East Side; though "nice to have" around, ratings show it could be better.

Gradisca ●⊄
▽ 19 | 16 | 17 | $33

126 W. 13th St. (bet. 6th & 7th Aves.), 212-691-4886

☑ It's way "beyond dark" inside this candlelit Greenwich Village "hideaway", providing romantics with a "rustic" but "sexy" option for "hearty", "well-priced" Italian; "happening" regulars advise "be loud – it's part of the scene."

GRAMERCY TAVERN
27 | 26 | 27 | $71

42 E. 20th St. (bet. B'way & Park Ave. S.), 212-477-0777

■ Living "up to" its "well-deserved" reputation, Danny Meyer's "sublime" Flatironer "has it all", from chef Tom Colicchio's "superbly crafted" New American cuisine to "sinful" desserts to "seamless" service that makes everyone "feel like a VIP"; whether in the "classic Yankee" back rooms or the "more casual" and "economical" "front tavern", "essential NY" dining "doesn't get any better" – ergo, its No. 2 standing for overall popularity.

Grand Sichuan
22 8 14 $23

125 Canal St. (Bowery), 212-625-9212 ⊟
227 Lexington Ave. (bet. 33rd & 34th Sts.), 212-679-9770
745 Ninth Ave. (bet. 50th & 51st Sts.), 212-582-2288
229 Ninth Ave. (24th St.), 212-620-5200
1049 Second Ave. (bet. 55th & 56th Sts.), 212-355-5855

☑ "They don't kid around with the spices" at this "low-cost" "real Chinese" chain where "ownership differs" but the "encyclopedic menu" is always "filled with uncommon choices"; the "oh-boy" "hot" food can be exciting, but otherwise expect "no frills."

Grange Hall
20 19 17 $35

50 Commerce St. (Barrow St.), 212-924-5246

■ "When you miss mom's home cooking", this "easygoing" "true American" on a "picturesque" West Village block offers "wholesome" "heartland food"; it's a "sturdy", "old-style" setting for a "nifty brunch", and "cool retro drinks" keep the "young" bar gang "lively."

Grano Trattoria ●
18 15 19 $32

21 Greenwich Ave. (W. 10th St.), 212-645-2121

■ This "cozy", comfy Villager has "everything you'd want" in an "unpretentious" "neighborhood Italian", namely a "warm", "amusing" staff and a "well-rounded", moderately priced menu "direct from the wood-burning stove"; fans "go regularly" for "casual" "carbo-loading."

Gray's Papaya ●●⊟
20 4 13 $5

2090 Broadway (72nd St.), 212-799-0243
539 Eighth Ave. (37th St.), 212-904-1588
402 Sixth Ave. (8th St.), 212-260-3532

☑ "Rites of passage" for any "real NYer", these 24/7 "quickie" "stand-up" "pit stops" serve "juicy, crunchy" franks chased with "frosty" "fruit drinks" that attract "everyone from hookers to Wall Street execs"; the settings are "spartan", but "recession-buster" prices leave "change for a pack of Tums."

Great Jones Cafe ●●⊟
19 11 14 $23

54 Great Jones St. (bet. Bowery & Lafayette St.), 212-674-9304;
www.greatjones.com

■ You'd better "forget about your arteries" when you "grease" up on the "plentiful" "spicy" "bayou" food at this NoHo Cajun "closet"; it's a "cute dive" with a "roadhouse" jukebox and about the "funkiest brunch" going – if you can "score a table."

Great NY Noodle Town ●⊟
22 5 11 $16

28½ Bowery (Bayard St.), 212-349-0923

☑ Noodlephiles slurp up "sublimity in a bowl" at this Chinatown "staple" for "sensational" "cheap eats"; "jammed" "communal tables" and "unscenic" environs mean it's "not a place to linger."

Greek Captain ●⊟
▽ 23 8 14 $30

32-10 36th Ave. (bet. 32nd & 33rd Sts.), Queens, 718-786-6015

☑ Aye, it's an "unassuming" "dive", but this Long Island City Greek seafooder is "right on target" thanks to its "huge", "startlingly fresh" servings of marine cuisine; the "lunchroom atmosphere" won't keep "serious fish eaters" from getting "hooked."

Green Field Churrascaria
▽ 19 14 16 $31

108-01 Northern Blvd. (108th St.), Queens, 718-672-5202;
www.greenfieldchurrascaria.com

☑ Carnivore "control thyself", because the meat "just keeps coming" at this Corona Brazilian BBQ, a "protein" "pig-out" with a "well-stocked" salad bar" for roughage relief; the football stadium–size setting and "plate-banging" fans make it best for "big parties."

Grey Dog's Coffee ⇥　　　21 | 17 | 18 | $14

33 Carmine St. (bet. Bedford & Bleecker Sts.), 212-462-0041

■ A "morning must", the Village's own "San Fran coffeehouse" offers "creative sandwiches", "great joe" and "very little seating" to "young" pups sporting "J. Crew" "casual"; though "claustrophobic" at "peak hours", it's more of a "people place" "now that dogs aren't allowed."

Grifone ⒮　　　24 | 18 | 25 | $54

244 E. 46th St. (bet. 2nd & 3rd Aves.), 212-490-7275

◪ This "classic" UN-area Italian is "the real McCoy" when it comes to "first-rate" food and "impeccable" service in an "intimate" room suffused with "quiet conversation"; its champions claim the "under-30 crowd wouldn't appreciate" its "old-fashioned" feel and "hefty prices."

Grilled Cheese NYC ◑∅⇥　　　20 | 10 | 17 | $11

168 Ludlow St. (bet. Houston & Stanton Sts.), 212-982-6600

■ On a mission to "raise the humble grilled cheese" to a "new level", this "tiny" Lower East Side sandwich board boasts "oodles" of "inventive" options mom "never dreamed of"; it's a "hot", "gooey", "hip" dose of "pure nostalgia."

Grill Room ⒮　　　▽ 20 | 21 | 20 | $47

World Financial Ctr., 225 Liberty St. (West Side Hwy.), 212-945-9400

◪ "Beautiful" "waterfront" views set the scene for this World Financial Center surf 'n' turf house, now "back and better than ever" as an "upmarket" hangout for the "business set"; if the "unadventurous menu" "doesn't match the scenery, it suits most "after a hard workday"; N.B. closed weekends.

GRIMALDI'S ⇥　　　27 | 11 | 16 | $19

19 Old Fulton St. (bet. Front & Water Sts.), Brooklyn, 718-858-4300; www.grimaldis.com

■ Regular "pilgrimages" to this Dumbo "legend" are a "must for pizza lovers" who agree "the key" to the "masterpiece" coal-oven pies is a "light", "crispy crust" in "harmony" with the "freshest" possible toppings; "long waits" and outer-boro "attitude just make it that much more authentic."

GROCERY, THE ⒮　　　28 | 18 | 25 | $46

288 Smith St. (bet. Sackett & Union Sts.), Brooklyn, 718-596-3335

■ Cooking with "heart", this superlative Carroll Gardens New American "makes magic" with "consistently" "sumptuous" "seasonal fare" and "endearing" service in a "spare" "one-room" setting augmented in summer by a "great garden"; the "cost alone" beckons since such "incredible care" "would break the bank in Manhattan."

Guastavino's　　　18 | 25 | 17 | $52

409 E. 59th St. (bet. 1st & York Aves.), 212-980-2455; www.guastavinos.com

◪ To make "a big impression", Terence Conran's "must-see" East Side New American is built into the Queensboro Bridge, yielding an "awe-inspiring" "vaulted" space for "happening" dining and nightlife; but though a "feast for the eyes", some grumble the food and service "aren't as stunning" as the visuals, i.e. that "cool upper level" that's reserved for "private parties" and late-night lounging.

Gus' Place　　　19 | 17 | 20 | $36

149 Waverly Pl. (bet. 6th & 7th Aves.), 212-645-8511

■ Take it "easy" is the rule at this "wonderfully low-key" Villager, where the "varied" Greek-Med fare is "always satisfactory" and the "cheery" servers "don't push"; it's both "comfortable" and "affordable", so "you can linger" and "enjoy Gus' company" "without going broke."

Hacienda de Argentina ◑
▽ 22 | 22 | 23 | $43

339 E. 75th St. (bet. 1st & 2nd Aves.), 212-472-5300

■ "Definitely one to watch", this East Side Argentinean steakhouse's "perfectly handled" pampas preparations put "a nice twist" on red meat; boosters are bolo'd over by this newcomer's "rich", "dark" decor and "conscientious staff."

Haikara Grill
▽ 19 | 16 | 16 | $41

1016 Second Ave. (bet. 53rd & 54th Sts.), 212-355-7000

☑ This Eastsider's "Japanese done Jewish" gets noticed by the observant, who claim "kosher sushi never tasted so good"; skeptics cite "high prices" and service woes, but given the specialty "what choice do you have?"

Hakata Grill
22 | 16 | 19 | $31

230 W. 48th St. (bet. B'way & 8th Ave.), 212-245-1020

■ "Surprisingly peaceful" for the Theater District, this area "staple" presents a "first-rate" Japanese–Pacific Rim lineup in a "cozy", "contemporary" setting; "very reasonable" tabs help strapped ticket-holders, and desk-sitters "can count on" "efficient delivery."

Halcyon
21 | 23 | 21 | $55

Rihga Royal Hotel, 151 W. 54th St. (bet. 6th & 7th Aves.), 212-468-8888

☑ Set in an "upmarket" Midtown hotel, this "lovely", "formal" New American offers "loads of ambiance" to go with its "fine" food and "unrushed" service; the $39 prix fixe "bargain" is "the right first act" for a "theater night", though foes yawn the "stolid" style works best if you "take the grandparents."

Hale & Hearty Soups ⌀
20 | 8 | 12 | $10

Chelsea Mkt., 75 Ninth Ave. (bet. 15th & 16th Sts.), 212-255-2400
22 E. 47th St. (bet. 5th & Madison Aves.), 212-557-1900
Grand Central, lower level (42nd St. & Vanderbilt Ave.), 212-983-2845
849 Lexington Ave. (bet. 64th & 65th Sts.), 212-517-7600
630 Lexington Ave. (54th St.), 212-371-1330
462 Seventh Ave. (35th St.), 212-971-0605
685 Third Ave. (43rd St.), 212-681-6460 ☒
55 W. 56th St. (bet. 5th & 6th Aves.), 212-245-9200 ☒
49 W. 42nd St. (bet. 5th & 6th Aves.), 212-575-9090 ☒
32 Court St. (Remsen St.), Brooklyn, 718-596-5600

☑ Like "the Starbucks of soups and salads", this counter-service chain ladles a "zesty" "variety" for "efficient" "grab 'n' go"; but beware the "mad gauntlet" at lunchtime and "steep" prices for "a lot of broth."

Hallo Berlin
19 | 7 | 13 | $18

626 10th Ave. (bet. 44th & 45th Sts.), 212-977-1944
402 W. 51st St. (9th Ave.), 212-541-6248

☑ It's "Oktoberfest all the time" at this "kitschy" Hell's Kitchen pair, a "real trencherman's" delight for "German soul food" washed down with lotsa lager; sure, the "beer garden" motif is "silly", but for a "heapin'" feast on the "cheap" you could do wurst.

Hampton Chutney Co.
20 | 9 | 14 | $14

68 Prince St. (bet. B'way & Lafayette St.), 212-226-9996;
www.hamptonchutney.com

■ For a "hip alternative", this SoHo-via-Amagansett Indian specializes in "awesome", "oversized" dosa wraps with a "totally addictive" "new-wave" twist; the food "deserves better" than the "uncomfortable" quarters, so many tote it ohm.

HANGAWI
25 | 26 | 25 | $41

12 E. 32nd St. (bet. 5th & Madison Aves.), 212-213-0077;
www.hangawirestaurant.com

■ "So Zen" it's "like another world", this Murray Hill Korean vegetarian is all "tranquility" as patrons "sit low" and "shoeless" to "bliss out" on "enticing" cuisine and "sweet-natured" service; the "small portions" may be "costly", but it's a "transporting experience" for a "vegan date."

Harbour Lights ◑
19 | 23 | 18 | $42

South Street Seaport, Pier 17, 3rd fl. (bet. Fulton & South Sts.), 212-227-2800;
www.harbourlightsrestaurant.com

◪ The "balcony" perch commands a "spectacular" harbor panorama at this recently renovated American mariner in the South Street Seaport; it's "pricey" and "touristy" and the food's just "good", but the view "overlooking the Brooklyn Bridge" compensates.

Hard Rock Cafe ◑
12 | 20 | 13 | $28

221 W. 57th St. (bet. B'way & 7th Ave.), 212-489-6565; www.hardrock.com

◪ It's hard to deny this "high-decibel", low-price Midtown burger joint "has the formula down", delivering "music memorabilia" and "decent" eats for an "upbeat" outing "with the kids"; maybe the "tourist-trap" milieu is "getting old", but most join the chorus: "long live Rock!"

Harrison, The
23 | 21 | 22 | $53

355 Greenwich St. (Harrison St.), 212-274-9310; www.theharrison.com

■ "Everything clicks" at this "handsome" TriBeCa Med-American, a "comfortably chic" "class act" where "marvelous" food and "civilized" service make for "smooth", "grown-up" dining; the "smart" set keeps the "buzz" up, and the atmosphere "cool"; the only problem is how to score a reservation.

Harry Cipriani
21 | 20 | 20 | $73

Sherry Netherland, 781 Fifth Ave. (bet. 59th & 60th Sts.), 212-753-5566;
www.cipriani.com

◪ It's all about the "scene" at this East Side Venetian, where the "Bellini-swilling" "rich and famous" fork over "megabucks" to toy with sublime pasta and "rub elbows" at tiny, "tight" tables; an "intimate delight" for high "society", it also strikes some as a "haughty" place to pay the "prices of tomorrow today."

Harry's at Hanover Square ☒
17 | 15 | 19 | $46

1 Hanover Sq. (bet. Pearl & Stone Sts.), 212-425-3412; www.harrystogo.com

■ There's "nothing froufrou" about this "Wall Street stalwart", an "old-boys'" "bastion" for "solid" surf 'n' turf served with "no surprises" in "traditional", "clubby" digs; it's also a "classic" "watering hole", and the "suits" taking stock rate it "about as good as it gets down here"; N.B. closed weekends.

Harry's Burritos ◑
16 | 9 | 12 | $18

241 Columbus Ave. (71st St.), 212-580-9494
76 W. Third St. (Thompson St.), 212-260-5588

◪ "Big, fat" burritos with "no fuss" make these "laid-back" "dives" "popular" for "dirt-cheap" Tex-Mex and "stiff" margaritas ("bring your college ID"); critics harry the "bland pseudo-Mexican" fare and "flaky" service, but shrug "you get what you pay for."

HARU
22 | 17 | 17 | $37

433 Amsterdam Ave. (bet. 80th & 81st Sts.), 212-579-5655 ◑
280 Park Ave. (48th St.), 212-490-9680
1329 Third Ave. (76th St.), 212-452-2230 ◑

(continued)

(continued)
HARU

1327 Third Ave. (76th St.), 212-452-1028 ◐
205 W. 43rd St. (bet. B'way & 8th Ave.), 212-398-9810
www.harusushi.com

■ "Jumbo" sushi "slabs" raise this Japanese "empire" "a cut above" in the eyes of "youngish" fans who cheer the "sensational" food, "raw or cooked", that "won't bankrupt you"; though "loud, rushed" and prone to "painful" waits, it's "no wonder" given the "fail-safe" "quality."

Harvest   17 | 13 | 15 | $23

218 Court St. (Warren St.), Brooklyn, 718-624-9267

◪ A "greasy spoon without the grease", this Cobble Hill "Southern-style" American piles on "homey" "comfort food" with a few "funky" variations; the "price is right" and the "strollerfest brunches" "jam-packed", but "slow service" and "just-ok" eats harvest complaints.

Hasaki ◐   24 | 15 | 20 | $36

210 E. Ninth St. (bet. 2nd & 3rd Aves.), 212-473-3327

■ The "old-fashioned" "art of sushi comes alive" at this East Village Japanese standby, where the "delicate", "delectable" fish is so "fairly priced" that aficionados ask "how do they do it?"; combining a "sterling" rep with "cramped quarters" and "no reservations" means "come early" or "get ready to wait."

Hatsuhana ⌧   24 | 15 | 19 | $49

17 E. 48th St. (bet. 5th & Madison Aves.), 212-355-3345
237 Park Ave. (46th St.), 212-661-3400
www.hatsuhana.com

◪ Among "the first" of the city's "authentic" Japanese, these Midtown "sushi-bar" "standbys" "still hold up" with "melt-in-your-mouth fish" that's "as fresh as the sea" and worth bearing "expensive" tabs and "sparse" setups; though always "dependable", some feel the production is getting to be "perfunctory"; N.B. the Park Avenue branch is closed on weekends.

Havana Central   17 | 13 | 14 | $22

22 E. 17th St. (bet. B'way & 5th Ave.), 212-414-2298

◪ "Lots of energy" comes in a "little" package at this "casual" Union Square Cuban "joint" that goes "cafeteria-style" by day and full-service by night; it's "still finding its way" but is "so cheap" and "winning" that amigos are ready to "lift the embargo."

Havana Chelsea ⇄   ▽ 18 | 6 | 12 | $17

190 Eighth Ave. (bet. 19th & 20th Sts.), 212-243-9421

◪ Chelsea's "especial" "neighborhood" "hole-in-the-wall" is beloved for its "outstanding" "pressed Cuban sandwich" and impressive "low prices"; diehards "tolerate" the "bare-bones" decor for "gigantic portions" of "the real thing", but the less tolerant take it out.

Havana Village ◐   ▽ 18 | 11 | 16 | $23

94 Christopher St. (bet. Bedford & Bleecker Sts.), 212-242-3800

■ As a still-"secret" newcomer to the West Village, this "cool" Cuban is "underappreciated" but gaining ground with "good", "inexpensive" food; if it gets "too crowded", there's always the tranquil patio.

Haveli ◐   21 | 18 | 18 | $28

100 Second Ave. (bet. 5th & 6th Sts.), 212-982-0533

■ "Right off" the Sixth Street strip but far "above the norm", this East Village Indian is a "soothing" "haven" with "creative" food, "attentive" service and "roomy" environs; "it costs more", but it's "worth every penny" to shun the competition for something "tastefully done."

Heartbeat
19 | 21 | 19 | $50

W New York, 149 E. 49th St. (bet. Lexington & 3rd Aves.), 212-407-2900;
www.myriadrestaurantgroup.com

☑ Like a "spa without the workout", this "innovative" Midtown American "artfully concocts "cool, healthy eats" (sans butter, cream and saturated fats) served amid "sleek", "feng shui" surroundings; critics insist it's "too ascetic" and "pricey."

Heartland Brewery
14 | 14 | 14 | $27

1285 Sixth Ave. (51st St.), 212-582-8244
South Street Seaport, 93 South St. (Fulton St.), 646-572-2337
127 W. 43rd St. (bet. B'way & 6th Ave.), 646-366-0235
35 Union Sq. W. (bet. 16th & 17th Sts.), 212-645-3400 ◗
www.heartlandbrewery.com

☑ The "jazzed-up bar grub" and specialty suds at these "convenient", "Anywhere USA" microbreweries win over "rowdy", "post-frat" types and "worker bees" out to get a buzz on; meanwhile foes of "greasy" eats warn "heartburn" is "more like it."

Heidelberg
17 | 14 | 16 | $32

1648 Second Ave. (bet. 85th & 86th Sts.), 212-628-2332;
www.heidelbergrestaurant.com

■ A "time capsule" of "old Germantown", this "durable" Yorkville Deutschlander plies "classic" "*echt*-cholesterol" fare seemingly served by "extras from *The Sound of Music*"; unphased by "dusty", "faux-Bavarian" decor and limited "people skills", well-wishers hoist a stein to "one of the last" "old-world" "strongholds."

Hell's Kitchen
23 | 17 | 18 | $38

679 Ninth Ave. (bet. 46th & 47th Sts.), 212-977-1588

■ "Forget about tacos", because this "hot" Theater District "Nuevo fiesta" "redefines" Mexican; "blown-away" boosters attest the "new chef hasn't broken stride", though with "trendy" "crowds" packing the "small" space, it's "hellacious to get in."

Hemsin
▽ 21 | 11 | 16 | $23

39-17 Queens Blvd. (39th Pl.), Queens, 718-482-7998

■ "A real find near MoMA Queens", this "friendly" Sunnyside Turk draws art lovers with "excellent" food at "good prices", including housemade desserts and breads; the decor and service "could use some sprucing up", but the "easy" eating seems to "satisfy most."

Henry's ◗
16 | 18 | 17 | $30

2745 Broadway (105th St.), 212-866-0600

☑ "Younger" Westsiders dig this "everyday" American's "versatile menu" and "sidewalk cafe"; however, foes cite "unimaginative" food and "spotty" service, while admitting it's a "dependable" "default."

Henry's End
25 | 14 | 23 | $41

44 Henry St. (Cranberry St.), Brooklyn, 718-834-1776; www.henrysend.com

■ There's "no better game in town" than this Brooklyn Heights New American's "expertly prepared" and moderately priced lineup of elk, wildfowl and the like, served from an open kitchen in "duck blind"–size quarters; though the setting could be "more comfortable", the "charm" and "exotic" tastes win out in the end.

Henry's Evergreen
20 | 12 | 18 | $31

1288 First Ave. (bet. 69th & 70th Sts.), 212-744-3266;
www.henrysevergreen.com

☑ Why "schlep to Chinatown" when this East Side "original" boasts "authentic Cantonese" featuring "incredible dim sum", not to mention a "smart", "extensive wine list"; "ultimate host" Henry Leung is on hand to ensure a "civilized" experience despite the coffee shop–style digs.

Herban Kitchen ⊠
290 Hudson St. (Spring St.), 212-627-2257

∇ 18 14 16 $29

■ "Taste is not sacrificed" at this "totally organic" SoHo American, where the "imaginative" "health food" includes carnivorous choices for stray "meat-eating friends"; it takes the "low-key" road with "rundown" digs and "slow", "New Age-y" service, "the better to savor" the "guilt-free" grub.

Hill Diner
231 Court St. (bet. Baltic & Warren Sts.), Brooklyn, 718-522-2220

19 14 16 $18

■ It's "nothing exotic", but this "bright", "comfortable" Cobble Hill Eclectic gets "pretty tasty" results doing "diner food" with "a bit of culinary flair" for a "reasonable price"; "spacey service" aside, a "dependable" "standby" with a "bonus" "back garden" is "just what the neighborhood needs."

Hispaniola ●
839 W. 181st St. (Cabrini Blvd.), 212-740-5222

∇ 21 23 18 $35

■ "Very hip for Washington Heights", this island of "class" "surprises" with a "delicious" Nuevo Latino–Asian mix and an "upscale" space with a "splendid view of the GW Bridge"; "chaotic service" is "barely noticeable" since the food is a "culinary godsend" for the area.

Historic Old Bermuda Inn
2512 Arthur Kill Rd. (St. Lukes Ave.), Staten Island, 718-948-7600

∇ 16 23 15 $41

◪ Staten Islanders tout this "gorgeous" "historic mansion" as a Continental charmer where the "country feel" still lingers; but antis argue the effect is wrecked by "mediocre" food and a "tacky catering hall" doing "large parties and events."

Hog Pit BBQ
22 Ninth Ave. (13th St.), 212-604-0092; www.hogpit.com

17 9 14 $23

◪ Learn to "love the grease" is the motto at this "down-home" Meatpacking District pit stop; "roadhouse" regulars consider the "grungy" digs "an asset", and even "non-motorcycle types" can chug "PBR", feed the "honky-tonk jukebox" and "let loose."

Holy Basil ●
149 Second Ave. (bet. 9th & 10th Sts.), 212-460-5557

22 17 17 $29

■ East Villagers are wholly impressed with this "trustworthy" "gourmet Thai", where the food's "tops" for "spice and flavor", though "skimpy on portions"; the "discreet" service and "intimate", "low-lit" room are great for a date that "won't cost a mint", but "bring a flashlight."

Home
20 Cornelia St. (bet. Bleecker & W. 4th Sts.), 212-243-9579

20 15 18 $36

■ Everything's "homemade" by definition at this Greenwich Village American, supplying affordable, "creative" comfort food in a "teeny" dining room and "cute" "back garden"; ignoring the "tight seating and plain decor", those who revel in the "warm" reception could move right in and "never leave."

HONMURA AN
170 Mercer St. (bet. Houston & Prince Sts.), 212-334-5253

26 25 24 $51

■ Go to "noodle heaven" at this "otherworldly" SoHo Japanese, a "temple" to "silken" soba and other "ambrosial" "delicacies" set in a "sea of tranquility" with "calm", "courteous" service; converts call it "transcendent" for "all the senses", though "expensive" tabs bring back the material world.

Hope & Anchor
▽ 20 | 18 | 20 | $24

347 Van Brunt St. (Wolcott St.), Brooklyn, 718-237-0276

■ A diner with "added zip", this "find" marooned in Red Hook exhibits a "flair" for fresh takes on "American classics" and "economical" prices deemed "worth a detour"; it's more "modern" than salty (excepting the racy bathroom wall), so locals "hope for the best."

Houston's
20 | 18 | 18 | $33

Citigroup Ctr., 153 E. 53rd St. (enter at 54th St. & 3rd Ave.), 212-888-3828
NY Life Bldg., 378 Park Ave. S. (27th St.), 212-689-1090
www.houstons.com

■ "Yes, it's a chain", but this "cosmopolitan" pair draws "younger suits" who brave "crazy waits" for a table for "surprisingly good" "all-American" fare like the "must-have" spinach dip; extra incentives include "always-on" service and a "middle-management meet market" at the bar.

HSF ⇗
17 | 10 | 11 | $23

46 Bowery (bet. Bayard & Canal Sts.), 212-374-1319

◪ For "classic" dim sum you could do worse than this Chinatown "warhorse", offering "selections galore" from a "never-ending stream of carts"; it's an "affordable" way to "eat till you drop", though it "helps if you speak Chinese" and don't mind "jostling and noise."

Hudson Cafeteria ◑
18 | 23 | 17 | $43

Hudson Hotel, 356 W. 58th St. (bet. 8th & 9th Aves.), 212-554-6000;
www.ianschragerhotels.com

◪ The "super-cool" hold court at this neo-"gothic" West Side American, serving "dressed-up" "comfort food" at shared "long tables" in an indoor-outdoor space like an "ultra-stylish" "castle" "dining hall"; it's a great place for sating the "visual appetite", especially at night.

Hue ◑
– | – | – | E

91 Charles St. (Bleecker St.), 212-691-4575

A swank, sleek bi-level setup (complete with waterfall, stone fireplace and roomy front bar/lounge) plus crowd-pleasing Vietnamese nibbles and sushi add up to a happening scene straight out of the gate at this West Village newcomer; neighbors on this once-sleepy block will have to get used to the bouncers and town cars out front.

Hunan Park
17 | 9 | 15 | $21

235 Columbus Ave. (bet. 70th & 71st Sts.), 212-724-4411 ◑
721 Columbus Ave. (95th St.), 212-222-6511

◪ An "easy choice" for Upper Westsiders, these Chinese "staples" are good for "inexpensive" chow that's a "step above" typical takeout; if "zero atmosphere" detracts, the "world's fastest" delivery saves the day ("they must cook it on the way").

Icon
21 | 20 | 20 | $44

W Court Hotel, 130 E. 39th St. (Lexington Ave.), 212-592-8888;
www.myriadrestaurantgroup.com

■ Despite smoothly "subdued lighting", this "stylish" Murray Hill New American "really shines" with an "enjoyable" menu, "chic" room and "accommodating" "outdoor courtyard"; admirers applaud Drew Nieporent for a job "well done."

I Coppi
22 | 21 | 20 | $43

432 E. Ninth St. (bet. Ave. A & 1st Ave.), 212-254-2263

■ It's an "offbeat" locale for a "Tuscan getaway", but this "inviting" East Villager stays "faithful" to Northern Italy with "first-class" food, "solicitous" service and a "rustic" setting complete with "lovely garden"; though it's "a bit pricey", romantics requiring a "date place" are "not disappointed."

Ida Mae
– | – | – | E

111 W. 38th St. (bet. B'way & 6th Ave.), 212-704-0038; www.idamae.com
Stirring up a little excitement in the Garment District, this new Southern arrival comes with a classic French twist (think poached lobster with grilled grits and crawfish-butter foam); though the dining-room decor isn't exactly stylish, the adjoining bar/lounge is.

Ideya
∇ 18 | 16 | 15 | $36

349 W. Broadway (bet. Broome & Grand Sts.), 212-625-1441; www.ideya.net
■ "Refreshing" "island" currents tow a "mix of trendy" types to this "vibrant" SoHo Caribbean, home to "inventive" "spicy" food that leaves those who had no idea "happily surprised"; rather than waiting for the laid-back servers, partyers prefer "mingling" and getting "sauced" on the "best mojitos in town."

Il Bagatto ⌐
24 | 17 | 15 | $30

192 E. Second St. (bet. Aves. A & B), 212-228-0977
◪ Offering "primo" "true Italian" at an "unbeatable" cost, this "funky" little East Villager is "always mobbed" now that the *gatto's* out of the bag; "Mussolini"-style service and "insane waits" "even with reservations" are "part of the process", but the droves of customers show the "sensational food" is "worth" it.

Il Buco ◗
23 | 23 | 20 | $52

47 Bond St. (bet. Bowery & Lafayette St.), 212-533-1932; www.ilbuco.com
■ "If you want to impress", this "memorable" Med "tucked away" in NoHo matches "inspired" food and "interesting wines" in a transporting "old-world" setting; the "charming" service and "sophisticated" feel are "romantic as it gets", at least until the bill arrives.

Il Cantinori
22 | 21 | 21 | $56

32 E. 10th St. (bet. B'way & University Pl.), 212-673-6044; www.il-cantinori.com
■ "Bold-face names" descend on this "hyped" Villager for its "splendido" "high-end" Northern Italian cooking in "elegant", "floral" surroundings; high prices and "pompous" propensities reflect its "celeb-magnet" status, but most maintain it's "worth the splurge" – "if you can get in."

Il Corallo Trattoria ◗
21 | 14 | 18 | $24

176 Prince St. (bet. Sullivan & Thompson Sts.), 212-941-7119
◪ Pastaphiles can "savor" "lots of options" and "ample portions" at this SoHo "find", a "real bargain" for "honest" Italian; the "tight", bright space may be "light on the amenities" but does a "bustling" business nonetheless, so "be prepared" to wait.

Il Cortile ◗
23 | 21 | 19 | $44

125 Mulberry St. (bet. Canal & Hester Sts.), 212-226-6060
■ This "old favorite" "sets the bar" "a notch above" its Little Italy neighbors given its "rich" Italian fare made "with love" and presented in "attractive", "upmarket" environs featuring a "sunny" "back atrium"; some partialists say you "pay up" for the privilege, but with such a "sure performer" even they "enjoy every calorie."

Il Covo dell'Est
18 | 17 | 17 | $36

210 Ave. A (13th St.), 212-253-0777
■ "A most welcome" "oasis" in Alphabet City, this "friendly" Tuscan serves as a "comfortable" corner for "fair-priced", "full-flavor" fare;

it's an "unsung" "little secret", though not surprisingly the "crowds are getting thicker."

Il Fornaio
21 | 12 | 17 | $27

132A Mulberry St. (bet. Grand & Hester Sts.), 212-226-8306

☑ When "basic" "red sauce" is in order, this Little Italy "standby" slings "well-prepared" "homestyle" Italian at "bargain-basement prices"; critics complain there's "no atmosphere" and service is "not overly friendly", but pragmatic partisans proudly point to the *piccolo* price.

Il Gatto & La Volpe
19 | 15 | 19 | $38

1154 First Ave. (bet. 63rd & 64th Sts.), 212-688-8444; www.ilgattolavolpe.com

■ "Tiny but steady", this "low-key" Upper East Side Italian is an "easy choice" for a "better-than-average" bite in "homey, intimate" digs; the "quiet" style signals "nothing special", but "unexpectedly" "good quality" keeps "neighborhood" regulars coming back.

Il Gattopardo ●☒
23 | 18 | 23 | $54

33 W. 54th St. (bet. 5th & 6th Aves.), 212-246-0412

☑ It may be a "less-known" Midtown option, but this "civilized" Southern Italian is right on the meatball with "marvelous" cuisine and "caring", "professional" service; the "minimalist room" strikes some as "stark", but it's "brightened" by the staff's "aim-to-please" attitude and the "garden out back."

IL GIGLIO ☒
26 | 20 | 24 | $60

81 Warren St. (bet. Greenwich St. & W. B'way), 212-571-5555;
www.ilgiglionyc.com

■ "Go hungry" to this "classic" TriBeCa Northern Italian where "abundant" servings of "exceptional" food "tempt you the minute you're seated" and the "impeccable" staff "can't do enough" to please; the "inviting" ambiance rounds out a "superior" experience, but "bring two credit cards" as "the good life" "doesn't come cheap."

Il Menestrello ☒
21 | 17 | 22 | $56

14 E. 52nd St. (5th Ave.), 212-421-7588

☑ "Traditional" as ever, this Midtown Italian "does everything well" on a "familiar menu", making it an "old favorite" among "corporate" sorts for "biz luncheons"; though "a little long in the tooth", it's an all around "solid" performer with greatest appeal to the "expense-account" set.

Il Monello
22 | 19 | 23 | $56

1460 Second Ave. (bet. 76th & 77th Sts.), 212-535-9310

■ One to watch after "reopening with new ownership" last year, this Upper Eastsider is showing "aspirations" "beyond a neighborhood trattoria", but "keeping regulars happy" with "first-rate" Northern Italian and "seamless" service; the "special" care justifies "pricey" tabs, and even non-locals say it's "worth going out of the way" for.

IL MULINO ☒
27 | 18 | 24 | $74

86 W. Third St. (bet. Sullivan & Thompson Sts.), 212-673-3783

■ "Fast for two days" and "break open the piggy bank", because "there's nothing else like" this "compact" Village Italian "king", a "bacchanal" with "phenomenal service" supplying "endless" "ambrosial" food till you "beg them to stop" and "roll yourself out"; not surprisingly for "pure heaven", getting in "requires an act of God" so "use your connections" or "opt for lunch."

Il Nido ☒
24 | 18 | 23 | $61

251 E. 53rd St. (bet. 2nd & 3rd Aves.), 212-753-8450

■ "Old-fashioned" with "no gimmicks", this East Side "mainstay" is a "trip back" to "the good old days" with "top-notch" Northern Italian and "serious" "personalized" black-tie service for those disposed to drop "lotsa lire"; the room and patrons may seem "dated" to some, but most consider the "formal" feel to be right "on the mark."

Ilo

25 | 22 | 23 | $70

Bryant Park Hotel, 40 W. 40th St. (bet. 5th & 6th Aves.), 212-642-2255; www.bryantparkhotel.com
■ A "brilliant" "departure" from star chef Rick Laakkonen, this "smooth", "original" Bryant Park New American is "willing to take chances" to produce "sublime", "complex" fare; "classy all the way" from the "sleek", "modernistic" space to the "informed" staff and "ultrasophisticated" scene, it's pardoned for its "off-the-lobby" locale and "over-the-top" tabs.

Il Palazzo

25 | 19 | 22 | $40

151 Mulberry St. (bet. Grand & Hester Sts.), 212-343-7000
■ This rare "non-touristy" venue is voted "tops in Little Italy" thanks to its "perfectly prepared" dishes that "traditional" types consider a lesson in "how to cook" Italian; it's also popular for its stress-free style and "intimate" waterfall-enhanced garden that "sets the right mood."

Il Postino ●

23 | 19 | 21 | $62

337 E. 49th St. (bet. 1st & 2nd Aves.), 212-688-0033
◪ At this Turtle Bay Italian the "waiter recites" "a zillion" "fresh and delicious" specials, so "who needs a menu?"; loyalists laud the "first-class" food and "old-world warmth", but to avoid "a shock" you had better "check prices" first or "go when someone else is paying."

Il Riccio ●

▽ 22 | 15 | 20 | $45

152 E. 79th St. (bet. Lexington & 3rd Aves.), 212-639-9111
■ "The secret's out" on this "little" East Side trattoria offering "warm welcomes" and a "varied" repertoire of "wonderful Southern Italian" dishes that keeps "many regulars" (even Mayor Mike) faithful; though "pricey", it draws "a good crowd" who say there's "no attitude here."

Il Tinello ☒

23 | 19 | 22 | $59

16 W. 56th St. (bet. 5th & 6th Aves.), 212-245-4388
■ Catering to mature types inclined to "dine not just eat", this "first-class" Midtown Northern Italian boasts "*buonissimo*" cuisine delivered by a "top-notch" "tuxedoed staff"; though it may be a bit "stuffy" and "not for the financially faint-of-heart", they do "make you feel special."

Il Vagabondo ●

17 | 15 | 17 | $37

351 E. 62nd St. (bet. 1st & 2nd Aves.), 212-832-9221
◪ So "retro" it's a "novelty", this "popular" East Side Italian is known for "hearty" "red-sauce" staples with an "indoor bocce court" to "work off all those carbs"; if the "crusty" service and "stark" setting "could use some work", the "spirit" "holds up" and prices are held down.

Il Valentino

19 | 20 | 20 | $51

Sutton Hotel, 330 E. 56th St. (bet. 1st & 2nd Aves.), 212-355-0001; www.thesutton.com
■ "Sophisticated" Sutton Place denizens find this "upscale" Northern Italian, an "attractive" option for "fulfilling" meals and "charming" "continental" service; they suggest it "should be better known", especially now that the "mellow" "live music is back."

Inagiku

23 | 20 | 22 | $59

Waldorf-Astoria, 111 E. 49th St. (bet. Lexington & Park Aves.), 212-355-0440; www.inagiku.com
■ Importing "Tokyo to NY", the Waldorf's "elegant" Japanese features "immaculate", "fresh" fin fare (notably "excellent sushi"), plus a

"soothing" setting and service as "attentive" as a geisha; it's sure to "impress clients", especially if they see the bill.

Indochine ◐
20 | 20 | 16 | $47

430 Lafayette St. (bet. Astor Pl. & 4th St.), 212-505-5111
■ "Still going strong", this "sexy", "tropical" Astor Place "mainstay" serves "fab" French-Vietnamese to an "energetic crowd" of "oh-so-chic" "young things" who "can't get enough"; servers who "think they're on a runway" dampen the "exotic" "escape", but the "scene factor" is very much intact.

industry (food) ◐
18 | 23 | 16 | $46

509 E. Sixth St. (bet. Aves. A & B), 212-777-5920;
www.industryfood.com
☑ It's a "total scene" at this "hopping" East Villager where "*Wallpaper* people" meet for "delish" New American fare and designer drinks in "chic", "log cabin"-like digs; critics of the "club vibe" and "long waits" say that the staff is "out to lunch."

'ino ◐⊘
23 | 15 | 18 | $23

21 Bedford St. (bet. Downing St. & 6th Ave.), 212-989-5769
■ The acknowledged "sandwich shop" "champion", this West Village "shoebox" specializes in "awesome" panini and "great wines by the glass" at "kindly prices"; often "jammed", the concept is so good that fans wish there was "one on every corner."

'inoteca ◐
– | – | – | M

98 Rivington St. (Ludlow St.), 212-614-0473
The wine bar 'ino's new, improved, three-times-larger Lower East Side offspring serves the original's signature panini paired with a perfectly parsed, 200+ bottle wine list; people-wise, look for pretty young things pretending they're on *Sex and the City*.

Inside
21 | 18 | 20 | $41

9 Jones St. (bet. Bleecker & W. 4th Sts.), 212-229-9999
■ Chef Anne Rosenzweig has "hit her stride" at this "welcoming" Village New American, rendering a "remarkable" "rotating" menu with her trademark "panache"; the food shows more "inspiration" than the "simple" atmosphere, but insiders hail it as an "affordable find."

Intermezzo
18 | 16 | 17 | $30

202 Eighth Ave. (bet. 20th & 21st Sts.), 212-929-3433; www.intermezzony.com
☑ "Fresh", "inexpensive" Italian "makes regulars out of the Chelsea crew" even though the recent "redo" gets mixed reviews ("hot" vs. "postmodern bordello") and has done nothing to help the "loud" noise levels; on the plus side, the "flirtatious" waiters are "entertaining."

Iron Sushi
∇ 21 | 12 | 20 | $26

440 Third Ave. (bet. 30th & 31st Sts.), 212-447-5822
☑ Sushiphiles are "pleasantly surprised" by this "quiet, local" Murray Hill Japanese that turns out rolls "large" and "interesting" enough to satisfy "hearty appetites"; unfortunately, as its ratings show, this is "not the nicest-looking place on the block."

Isabella's ◐
20 | 19 | 18 | $37

359 Columbus Ave. (77th St.), 212-724-2100;
www.brguestrestaurants.com
■ "Steve Hanson keeps 'em coming back" to this "buzzing", "hectic" Westsider boasting crowd-pleasing "something-for-everyone" Med–New American cuisine and "fab" brunches; it gains a breezy "California feeling" in warmer months "when the doors open" and the "sidewalk" tables go out, providing prime Columbus Avenue "people-watching."

Island Burgers ⊄
22 | 8 | 12 | $14

766 Ninth Ave. (bet. 51st & 52nd Sts.), 212-307-7934

▣ When the "delicious shakes" and "none-better" burgers arrive, this "no-space", "no-frills" Hells Kitchen standby "suddenly becomes more comfortable"; however, "plan on waiting" and "stop at McD's first" if you want fries – there aren't any here.

Iso ●Ø☒
23 | 15 | 18 | $37

175 Second Ave. (11th St.), 212-777-0361

■ "Reasonable prices" for "super-fresh" sushi rolls like "works of art" make this "gracious" husband and wife–run East Village Japanese "deservedly popular"; "beautiful flower arrangements" add a touch of "elegance", even though some think the decor "needs to be revisited."

Isola ●
18 | 14 | 17 | $30

485 Columbus Ave. (bet. 83rd & 84th Sts.), 212-362-7400

▣ "Simple Italian" fare and pizzas from a "fragrant" "brick oven" make this Westsider a "standby" for a "casual" supper or "family brunch"; in summer you can enjoy it on the "elevated" patio.

Ithaka ●
∇ 21 | 17 | 19 | $42

308 E. 86th St. (bet. 1st & 2nd Aves.), 212-628-9100

■ "Transplanted" to the East Side after fire ravaged its original Village digs, this often "overlooked" taverna fills a niche with its "country-style Greek" food, including "some of the best fish" going; surveyors split when it comes to the weekend music (some say "noisy", others "a barrel of fun").

I Tre Merli ●
18 | 19 | 16 | $42

463 W. Broadway (bet. Houston & Prince Sts.), 212-254-8699; www.itremerli.it

▣ People are still "dying to get into" this "chic" Italian wine bar that's "functional" for a bite at outdoor tables with a "view of the SoHo" parade; though "lots of model types" provide eye-candy, "snooty" staffers can "sour" the experience.

I Trulli ☒
23 | 21 | 22 | $51

122 E. 27th St. (bet. Lexington Ave. & Park Ave. S.), 212-481-7372; www.itrulli.com

■ "Savor the aromas" of Apulia at this "elegant" Gramercy Southern Italian, where the impressively "deep" wine list matches the "trulli terrific" tastes, and patrons vie for "tables near the fireplace" in winter and "lovely garden" seating in summer; while a "fat wallet" surely helps, the "casual" Enoteca wine bar next door is a less-pricey option.

Itzocan Café ⊄
∇ 22 | 13 | 22 | $20

438 E. Ninth St. (bet. Ave. A & 1st Ave.), 212-677-5856

▣ Look for "wonderfully fresh" Mexican eats and an "attentive" staff at this "affordable" BYO East Village yearling; "intimate" (read: "closetlike") proportions mean that "as the word gets out, it's going to be hard to get in."

Ivo & Lulu ☒⊄
–|–|–|I

558 Broome St. (bet. 6th Ave. & Varick St.), 212-226-4399

The "hospitable" "husband-and-wife" owners of A in Morningside Heights have headed Downtown with this "cozy", inexpensive SoHo French-Caribbean BYO, where the slim selection of "flavorful", all-"organic" dishes come out of a closet-size kitchen.

Ivy's Cafe ●
18 | 9 | 18 | $23

154 W. 72nd St. (bet. B'way & Columbus Ave.), 212-787-3333

▣ "They serve it all" at this "very plain" Upper Westsider where you can "get your sushi fixes fast", not to mention "good Chinese" dishes;

if some say the spicing can be "timid" and the quality "uneven", at least "the price is right."

Jackson Diner ⊟
24 | 10 | 15 | $21

37-47 74th St. (bet. Roosevelt & 37th Aves.), Queens, 718-672-1232
■ "Swipe the metro card" and "bring an appetite" to this Jackson Heights Indian standout where even "Gandhi wouldn't have fasted"; the "delicious", "super-spiced" food (including a weekend brunch that "keeps you full until Tuesday") easily outweighs the "New Delhi cafeteria decor", "indifferent" service and "deafening" din.

Jackson Hole
16 | 9 | 13 | $18

517 Columbus Ave. (85th St.), 212-362-5177 ◑
232 E. 64th St. (bet. 2nd & 3rd Aves.), 212-371-7187 ◑
1270 Madison Ave. (91st St.), 212-427-2820
1611 Second Ave. (bet. 83rd & 84th Sts.), 212-737-8788 ◑
521 Third Ave. (35th St.), 212-679-3264 ◑
69-35 Astoria Blvd. (70th St.), Queens, 718-204-7070 ◑
35-01 Bell Blvd. (35th Ave.), Queens, 718-281-0330 ◑
☑ You'll need "three hands and lots of napkins" to tackle the "juicy" but "crumbly" burgers at these "greasy spoons"; they work best for "afternoons with the kids" or as "hangover" antidotes when "calories", "dingy" digs and "poor" service are the least of your worries.

Jacques Brasserie
19 | 17 | 17 | $41

204-206 E. 85th St. (bet. 2nd & 3rd Aves.), 212-327-2272
☑ "Love of the mussels" and other brasserie classics aided by "great" Belgian brews lead locals to this "charming" Yorkville French spot; if service strikes some as "friendly" and others as "uneven", all seem to agree that it's no bargain.

Jaiya Thai ◑
21 | 10 | 15 | $26

396 Third Ave. (28th St.), 212-889-1330; www.jaiya.com
☑ The Elmhurst original has closed, but this "authentic" inexpensive Gramercy Thai is still as fiery as ever; heat-seekers "ignore the service and decor", "wipe the sweat" from their brows and dig in.

Jane ◑
21 | 19 | 19 | $38

100 W. Houston St. (bet. La Guardia Pl. & Thompson St.), 212-254-7000;
www.janerestaurant.com
■ You'll "eat well", especially at brunch, at this "sleek", "spacious" New American on the Village-SoHo border; usually "hopping", its "charming" service, "great babe-watching" and "funky" cocktails outweigh the "noisy" acoustics.

Japonica
22 | 13 | 18 | $39

100 University Pl. (12th St.), 212-243-7752
☑ "Practically a Village landmark", this "reliable" Japanese sates seekers of "supreme sushi" with "obscenely large" portions; "tired" looks and "somewhat high prices" don't seem to stem the "long waits."

Jarnac
24 | 21 | 24 | $48

328 W. 12th St. (Greenwich St.), 212-924-3413; www.jarnacny.com
■ West Villagers have become "very attached" to this "cute-as-a-button" French bistro whose "*magnifique*" classics are "prepared with TLC"; "pampering" service and a chef who comes out to ensure "you're happy" bolster the overall "excellent" impression.

Jasmine
20 | 15 | 16 | $26

1619 Second Ave. (84th St.), 212-517-8854
☑ Addicts of this Upper East Side Thai's "fragrant", "tasty" dishes satisfy cravings "once a week", and even more often "in summer

when you can sit outside" and savor the flavors; others call it "run-of-the-mill", but "reliable", for "fast, cheap" meals.

Jean Claude ⊅　　　　　　23 | 15 | 20 | $39
137 Sullivan St. (bet. Houston & Prince Sts.), 212-475-9232
■ There are "no fake accents" at this SoHo slice "of real France" serving "wonderful" "bistro classics" à la "superb steak frites"; though "tight quarters" can be a problem, the "friendliest waiters" and "hard-to-beat value" keep it regularly "packed."

JEAN GEORGES ☒　　　　28 | 26 | 26 | $90
Trump Int'l Hotel, 1 Central Park W. (bet. 60th & 61st Sts.), 212-299-3900;
www.jean-georges.com
■ It's always "a thrill" to visit Jean-Georges Vongerichten's "icon of NY dining" on Columbus Circle, where "masterful" New French creations and "spectacular desserts", together with the "pampering" pro service and Adam Tihany's "cleanly minimalist" interior, make "you want your meal never to end"; you may have to save up for dinner here, but the "lovely", more casual lunch has earned a reputation as "one of NYC's best" culinary values.

Jean-Luc　　　　　　　21 | 20 | 18 | $50
507 Columbus Ave. (bet. 84th & 85th Sts.), 212-712-1700;
www.jeanlucrestaurant.com
☑ A "strong culinary addition" to the Upper West Side, this "hip" neo-Deco French bistro appeals both to "aging boomers" and "tan, attractive" youngish things who "mob" its bar on weekends; the less-contented contend it's "too noisy" and "costs more than it delivers."

Jefferson ☒　　　　　　23 | 22 | 19 | $54
121 W. 10th St. (bet. Greenwich & 6th Aves.), 212-255-3333
■ Cafe Asean owner Simpson Wong has gone upscale with this "refined" nearby Village New American boasting "inspired" "Asian-influenced" cuisine, a "light and airy" "minimalist" interior and "neighborly" service; a few find it "overpriced", but they're easily outvoted by those who consider it "the year's best newcomer."

Jekyll & Hyde Club　　　10 | 23 | 14 | $30
1409 Sixth Ave. (bet. 57th & 58th Sts.), 212-541-9517;
www.jekyllandhydeclub.com
☑ When you "owe your kids big time", have some "ghoulishly" "silly fun" and hit this "haunted house"–themed "little bit of Orlando" in Midtown; most agree "the scariest part" is the basic American food.

Jeollado ●⊅　　　　　　18 | 12 | 14 | $24
116 E. Fourth St. (bet. 1st & 2nd Aves.), 212-260-7696
☑ "Fun and cheap", this "wacky" East Village Japanese is "great for groups" given its "garage"-like space and "everything-under-the-sun" menu (including Korean dishes); a few detect a "quantity-over-quality" concept at work, but revelers who "rent the karaoke room" don't seem to notice.

Jerry's　　　　　　　　17 | 13 | 15 | $29
101 Prince St. (bet. Greene & Mercer Sts.), 212-966-9464; www.jerrysnyc.com
☑ A "tried-and-true" SoHo "hangout", this veteran "upscale diner" dishes out "dependable" chow; though "erratic" service and "aircraft-hangar" acoustics can annoy, it's hard to beat for "good-value" meals.

JEWEL BAKO ☒　　　　　27 | 25 | 25 | $68
239 E. Fifth St. (bet. 2nd & 3rd Aves.), 212-979-1012
■ "Extraordinary" sushi of nearly "unparalleled" quality (think "Harry Winston, not Tiffany") is the main attraction at this East Village

Japanese, but "lovely" owners Jack and Grace Lamb also "deserve praise" for their "hospitality" and "most beautiful use of a space" barely bigger than a "jewel box"; though you'll "pay top-dollar", for the ultimate "experience" insiders advise go for it – "order the tasting menu."

Jewel of India
20 | 20 | 19 | $36

15 W. 44th St. (bet. 5th & 6th Aves.), 212-869-5544

☑ "Myriad well-done dishes" glitter on the "ample lunch buffet" at this "old-reliable" Midtown Indian whose "bargain" prix fixes, "comfortable" setup and "solicitous" service seal its popularity; still, detractors call it "more rhinestone" than jewel.

Jezebel ☒
18 | 24 | 18 | $47

630 Ninth Ave. (45th St.), 212-582-1045; www.jezebelny.com

☑ You "feel like the belle of the ball" while savoring the succulent Southern fare at this Theater District standby; though the "escape"-to-"Charleston" decor is "better than the food" and the "slow-paced service" a little too authentic, overall it "still enchants."

J.G. Melon ●⊜
20 | 12 | 15 | $22

1291 Third Ave. (74th St.), 212-744-0585

☑ "In the battle for best burger joint", this Eastsider pub is a perennial contender despite "gruff" service and "cramped" digs; though lustier appetites lament "not-big" patty proportions, those in-the-know simply "order two."

Jimmy's Bronx Cafe ●
▽ 18 | 17 | 15 | $31

281 W. Fordham Rd. (Major Deegan Expwy.), Bronx, 718-329-2000

☑ "Fun"-seekers on a budget hit this Bronx "restaurant/bar/club" "for spirited late-evening" "dancing to salsa music" and Yankee-Met-Knick–watching rather than for its reliably good Latin eats; if it doesn't quite succeed in "trying to be all things" to all people, most agree it's well "worth a stop" when heading up the Deegan.

Jimmy's Downtown ●
19 | 21 | 17 | $51

400 E. 57th St. (bet. 1st Ave. & Sutton), 212-486-6400

☑ "Dress to impress" for visits to Jimmy Rodriguez's "sexy" splash of "Miami" on Sutton Place, whose bar is so "packed" with "beautiful people", the "hot" Nuevo Latino cuisine comes off "bland" in comparison; while "pushy" waiters and "noisy" acoustics dissuade some, most feel like they've landed a role in *Sex and the City.*"

Jimmy Sung's
18 | 19 | 20 | $36

219 E. 44th St. (bet. 2nd & 3rd Aves.), 212-682-5678

☑ Though "relatively unknown" outside of its UN area, this "upscale Chinese" is saluted for its "solid" fare and for staffers "so polite" they "treat you like you're paying a fortune" (though you're not); the less-diplomatic dismiss it as "so-so", but even they use it for "ordering in."

Jimmy's Uptown ●
18 | 24 | 18 | $42

2207 Seventh Ave. (bet. 130th & 131st Sts.), 212-491-4000

☑ "Hidden" beyond a "nondescript" facade is Jimmy Rodriguez's "sleek", "exciting" Harlem "hot, hot, hot" spot, whose "good", if pricey, Latin–soul food and smooth service have a hard time living up to the "wow" "bar scene."

Joanna's
18 | 17 | 20 | $47

30 E. 92nd St. (bet. 5th & Madison Aves.), 212-360-1103

■ Carnegie Hill dwellers seeking "a relaxing meal with a minimum of fuss" look to this "Italian hideaway that does it right", either in its "cozy" dining room or "romantic" back garden; "courteous" service is a plus, and the $24.75 pre-theater prix fixe is a "deal."

Joe Allen ◑
17 | 15 | 17 | $38

326 W. 46th St. (bet. 8th & 9th Aves.), 212-581-6464;
www.joeallenrestaurant.com

▨ "Oozing New Yawk", this "bustling" Theater District "landmark" gives "ordinary people" the chance to eat "nothing-tricky" American classics in the company of "Broadway folk", including "bored" "aspiring-actor" staffers; if some suspect it's "past its prime", most find it "surprisingly good."

Joe's Pizza
24 | 4 | 14 | $7

233 Bleecker St. (Carmine St.), 212-366-1182 ◑
7 Carmine St. (bet. Bleecker St. & 6th Ave.), 212-255-3946
137 Seventh Ave. (bet. Carroll St. & Garfield Pl.), Brooklyn, 718-398-9198 ⊅

▨ "Late-night" revelers, "cops" and everyone in between "stands on line" at these low-cost pizza "mainstays" for "satisfying", "thin-crust" slices that "don't get soggy"; they're decidedly "no-frills", leading some to wish there were "tables outside."

Joe's Shanghai
21 | 9 | 13 | $22

113 Mott St. (bet. Canal & Hester Sts.), 212-966-6613 ⊅
9 Pell St. (bet. Bowery & Mott St.), 212-233-8888 ◑⊅
24 W. 56th St. (bet. 5th & 6th Aves.), 212-333-3868
82-74 Broadway (bet. 45th & Whitney Aves.), Queens, 718-639-6888 ⊅
136-21 37th Ave. (bet. Main & Union Sts.), Queens, 718-539-3838 ⊅
www.joesshanghai.com

▨ "Fat, juicy" soup dumplings rank high on everyone's list at these "cramped", "bustling" Shanghai palaces, but it's worth "exploring the menu" for other "excellent" options as well; just don't expect much decor or "time to savor" the flavors given its rushed service; N.B. the Mott Street location is new and unrated.

Johnny Rockets ◑
15 | 15 | 15 | $14

42 E. Eighth St. (bet. B'way & University Pl.), 212-253-8175;
www.johnnyrockets.com

▨ "Chain" link though it is, this "retro-kitsch" Village diner is adored for its "fantastic" milkshakes and "greasy"-but-"good" burgers that appeal to more than just "kiddies"; still, it's a bit too "hokey" for some, especially "when the staff does disco."

John's of 12th Street ⊅
19 | 13 | 16 | $29

302 E. 12th St. (2nd Ave.), 212-475-9531

▨ "Bring back the romance" over "candlelight" and "heaping" portions of "red-sauce" pasta at this cash-only East Village Italian that's truly "old school" (since 1908); it's "not elegant", but it's got "its own charm" and is "cheap" enough to appeal to young lovers.

John's Pizzeria ◑
21 | 12 | 15 | $20

278 Bleecker St. (bet. 6th Ave. & 7th Ave. S.), 212-243-1680 ⊅
408 E. 64th St. (bet. 1st & York Aves.), 212-935-2895
260 W. 44th St. (bet. B'way & 8th Ave.), 212-391-7560

■ Pizzaholics don't complain about the "no-slice policy" because they're only too glad to down "entire" "oozey, cheesy, thin-crust" brick-oven pies at either the "Bleecker Street original" or its Uptown offshoots; "waits" are inevitable and service "harried", but for most, any "discomfort is irrelevant."

JoJo
24 | 23 | 22 | $65

160 E. 64th St. (bet. Lexington & 3rd Aves.), 212-223-5656;
www.jean-georges.com

■ It was the first "Jean-Georges masterpiece", and this East Side French remains a "favorite" for "simply sensational" haute bistro fare "professionally" served in a "beautiful", "romantic" townhouse setting; "expensive" tabs seem par for the course, but then there's always the "steal" of a $20 prix fixe lunch.

Jordan's Lobster Dock
▽ | 20 | 9 | 12 | $23

2771 Knapp St. (Belt Pkwy.), Brooklyn, 718-934-6300

☑ "Come in old clothes and prepare to get stained" because the "lobsters are good but the eating's messy" at this Sheepshead Bay seafooder; outdoor picnic tables offer "bay atmosphere" and the adjoining market sells fresh catch to take home.

Josephina ●
19 | 17 | 17 | $41

1900 Broadway (bet. 63rd & 64th Sts.), 212-799-1000; www.josephinanyc.com

■ A "solid" bet before a Lincoln Center event thanks to its "delish" fish and veggie-friendly choices, this "upscale" Westside Eclectic-American also offers "affable", "fast" service; it's most "enjoyable" at lunch or "after 8 PM" when you can actually "have a conversation."

Joseph's Ristorante ⊠
▽ | 21 | 14 | 21 | $52

3 Hanover Sq. (Pearl St.), 212-747-1300

☑ "You may "miss" this basement-level Italian "if you don't know it's there", but it's worth seeking out for "excellent" classic dishes and "warm" service in a "boys'-club" milieu; suitably for its Financial District address, it's "quiet enough to talk business", as well as expense-account worthy; N.B. closed weekends.

Josie's
21 | 16 | 17 | $30

300 Amsterdam Ave. (74th St.), 212-769-1212
565 Third Ave. (37th St.), 212-490-1558
www.josiesnyc.com

■ "Flavorful", "healthy" Eclectic cuisine with plenty of "vegetarian options" is why this "cramped" Upper West Side venue and its "more comfy", "modern" Murray Hill sibling are "always packed" "with the girls" animatedly dissecting the latest *Sex and the City* episode.

Joya ●⊝
23 | 19 | 18 | $21

215 Court St. (Warren St.), Brooklyn, 718-222-3484

■ "Go off-peak to avoid the lines" at this "upbeat", "ridiculously cheap" Cobble Hill Thai that bustles with "twentysomethings" enjoying "excellent" food, a "trendy bar scene" and "hip" artwork; a "spacious garden" offsets the "crowded" conditions and "bad acoustics."

Jubilee
23 | 15 | 18 | $43

347 E. 54th St. (bet. 1st & 2nd Aves.), 212-888-3569

■ "One never tires" of the "perfect" mussels and fries at this "solid French bistro" in the East 50s, a "long", "narrow", "neighborhood" venue with "convivial, insider-ish atmosphere" and "cozy seating that envelops you" (it's "perfect for a first date").

JUdson Grill ⊠
22 | 22 | 21 | $56

152 W. 52nd St. (bet. 6th & 7th Aves.), 212-582-5252; www.judsongrill.com

■ Chef Bill Telepan's "creative", "market-driven", "artistically presented" Contemporary American menu "soars" as much as the "high ceilings" at this "spacious", "sophisticated" Midtown "expense-account" brasserie that's also convenient "to the shows"; P.S. the bar works for dining alone, or to "pick up a suit" during the ".crowded after-work scene."

Jules ●
19 | 16 | 13 | $35

65 St. Marks Pl. (bet. 1st & 2nd Aves.), 212-477-5560

☑ "Live jazz is a nice touch" at this "fairly priced" East Village French bistro where you'll "feel like you're in Montmartre" as you down "steak frites that's tops" and try to "get the attention of the waiters"; "brunch specials" and the $20 pre-theater menu are a steal."

Julian's
19 | 17 | 18 | $36

802 Ninth Ave. (bet. 53rd & 54th Sts.), 212-262-4800

☑ "Not special, but convenient" as a "pre-theater standby" or for the "popular weekend brunch" is the scoop on this "basic", affordable West 50s Italian, which was "recently renovated" but still has sidewalk seating and a "cool" enclosed garden.

Junior's
18 | 9 | 14 | $20

Grand Central, lower level (42nd St. & Vanderbilt Ave.), 212-983-5257
386 Flatbush Ave. Ext. (DeKalb Ave.), Brooklyn, 718-852-5257 ◑
www.juniorscheesecake.com

☑ "Massive portions" of "average", "fattening" diner food" like "two-fisted burgers" are mere footnotes to the "awesome", "creamy" cheesecakes that have made this "bustling", "spacious", three-meal-a-day Downtown Brooklyn deli/diner venue (and its offshoot in Grand Central) a dessert "landmark."

Justin's ◑
▽ 11 | 17 | 14 | $36

31 W. 21st St. (bet. 5th & 6th Aves.), 212-352-0599;
www.justinsrestaurant.com

☑ "No less than three dishes, including 'The Mogul Platter', are named for his holiness", Sean 'P. Diddy' Combs, the owner of this "dark, candlelit" Flatiron District soul food entry, which gets rapped for "blah food, ok service" and a "mandatory 18-percent tip [for four or more on Fridays and Saturdays] that's insulting" – unless he's producing your next album.

J.W.'s Steakhouse ⌧
▽ 23 | 19 | 22 | $55

Marriott Marquis Hotel, 1535 Broadway, 8th fl. (bet. 45th & 46th Sts.),
212-704-8900; www.nymarriottmarquis.com

■ "Everything about it says 'hotel' but the steaks, which are great" at this "unknown" chophouse with "nice views of Times Square" and "friendly, efficient service"; it's an "excellent pre-theater choice", even if the bill will beef up the cost of your evening out.

Kai ⌧
▽ 25 | 24 | 23 | $69

Ito En, 822 Madison Ave. (bet. 68th & 69th Sts.), 212-988-7277;
www.itoen.com

■ "Enter kaiseki heaven" at this Japanese "jewel" on the Upper East Side where "daring" yet "subtle combinations" are elegantly presented by "doting servers"; the "perfect spot for Zen ladies who lunch" is attached to the Ito En tea emporium, so "don't forget to try" their "ethereal" brews, which help calm the inevitable "sticker shock."

Kam Chueh ◑
▽ 22 | 8 | 17 | $25

40 Bowery (bet. Bayard & Canal Sts.), 212-791-6868

■ At this low-budget Chinatown seafooder, the fish couldn't be fresher since it comes live from "the tanks" "moments" before you eat it; "if you don't mind Glad bag tablecloths" or the "fast" but "semi-fluent" servers, the "delicious" dishes "will rock your world", even "late at night."

Kang Suh ◑
22 | 12 | 15 | $30

1250 Broadway (32nd St.), 212-564-6845

■ "Anyone fancy 3 AM kimchi" or BBQ? – "hot coals" glow 'round the clock for "damn good" grilled meats at this "authentic", easily affordable, "no-frills" "hibachi" haunt in Little Korea; go with a "group" and "over-order" – you'll "manage to eat it all"; just "don't wear a sweater as you'll never get the smell out."

Kapadokya

▽ 19 | 19 | 21 | $29

142 Montague St., 2nd fl. (bet. Clinton & Henry Sts.), Brooklyn, 718-875-2211

☑ "Montague Street could use more great additions like this" Brooklyn Heights Turk, where diners "devour" both the "satisfying" savories and the sight of "scantily clad women" belly dancing on weekends; if the dishes "don't wow you", a puff of the hookah on the "veranda" should "make your night."

Karyatis ◐

▽ 20 | 17 | 18 | $35

35-03 Broadway (bet. 35th & 36th Sts.), Queens, 718-204-0666

☑ Though this "comfortable taverna" may be "a bit staid" for the area, fans feel its "fabulous" Greek fare "is worthy of the Astoria scene"; now that it's got "new owners", however, a few former regulars "see no reason to return", claiming the dining room may be "upscale" but the kitchen is "going downhill."

Katsuhama

▽ 21 | 11 | 14 | $24

11 E. 47th St. (bet. 5th & Madison Aves.), 212-758-5909; www.katsuhama.com

■ "Life won't be the same after you've had the katsu" at this simple, low-budget Midtowner because "they do everything" to keep the "Japanese schnitzel" "juicy inside, crispy outside" and "awfully yummy", bolstered by "endless supplies" of "rice, fine miso soup and shredded cabbage"; by any standard, it's a "killer" "bargain."

Katz's Delicatessen

23 | 8 | 11 | $18

205 E. Houston St. (Ludlow St.), 212-254-2246; www.homedelivery.com/katz.html

■ "Pastrami or corned beef?" – "New Yawk" "philosophers have debated the question since the beginning of time" at this huge Jewish deli "avatar of the old days" before "cholesterol" and "cardiac" ("oy") entered the vocabulary; with cured meat piled so "high" that it'll "make you cry", "who cares?" about "cranky countermen" and the "bleak setting" – "it's a nosh-talgia thing."

Keens Steakhouse

23 | 22 | 20 | $56

72 W. 36th St. (bet. 5th & 6th Aves.), 212-947-3636; www.keenssteakhouse.com

■ "You'll never have mutton anywhere else", so "step into the snug warmth" of this circa-1885 Garment District steakhouse-cum-pub where a "single-malt is apéritif" to a "chop deserving of its fame"; "from the antique clay pipe collection covering the low-hung ancient wood ceilings" to the fireplace in the "speakeasy" atmosphere of the "handsome" bar and the museumlike private-party rooms upstairs, it's "like a visit to olde New York" – except now Lily Langtry would be more than welcome.

Kelley & Ping

17 | 14 | 12 | $22

127 Greene St. (Prince St.), 212-228-1212

☑ "Imagine yourself in some back-alley Bangkok" joint, and you get an idea of this "dark and funky" "SoHo Pan-Asian noodle shop and faux grocery"; "cafeteria-style" lunch is "made to order for a fresh, hot", "oh-so-satisfying" "bargain", but the "no frills" service is decidedly "uninspired."

Kiev ◐

15 | – | 11 | $15

117 Second Ave. (7th St.), 212-420-9600

☑ "Dingy" no more, this 24/7 East Village Ukrainian's interior has undergone a total overhaul, but the "pierogi and kielbasa like your Polish grandma's" "haven't changed"; still, diehards who "miss the old" "dive" decor insist the "atmosphere has suffered."

Kiiroi-Hana
∇ 20 | 11 | 16 | $32

23 W. 56th St. (bet. 5th & 6th Aves.), 212-582-7499

☑ "Delicious, sizable pieces" of "excellent fresh fish" and bowls of hot soup are the draws at this Japanese that "consistently pleases, even if it never wows"; sure, the room is bland, but it's still a "dependable" stop for a "quick Midtown lunch" that "won't break the bank."

Killmeyer's Old Bavaria Inn
∇ 20 | 20 | 20 | $31

4254 Arthur Kill Rd. (Sharrotts Rd.), Staten Island, 718-984-1202; www.killmeyers.com

■ Staten Island Teuton touters attest "there's nothing like eating" "hearty portions" of affordable "authentic Bavarian food" served by "the beautiful fräuleins" "in traditional dress" at this "rustic German"; P.S. "don't miss the biergarten in summer."

King Cole Bar ●
18 | 28 | 23 | $44

St. Regis Hotel, 2 E. 55th St. (bet. 5th & Madison Aves.), 212-339-6721

■ The "height of swank", this "distinguished" "New York legend" "inside a glorious hotel" is "where the elite" "soak up history" – and "expensive", "strong", "civilized cocktails" – beneath a "famed" "Maxfield Parrish painting" of the merry old soul himself; its "stunning decor" and "unique atmosphere", if not its "limited [American] menu", "make it a classic" "no one should miss."

Kings' Carriage House
20 | 26 | 22 | $52

251 E. 82nd St. (bet. 2nd & 3rd Aves.), 212-734-5490

■ Set in an "absolutely charming carriage house" "tucked away" "on a side street", this "Upper East Side treasure" offers the equivalent of a "country getaway", not to mention "delightful service" and pleasing Continental dining via prix fixe lunch and dinner menus; P.S. its "lovely afternoon tea" will make you "feel like a queen", and its bill will make you feel like you need to be one.

Kin Khao
21 | 17 | 16 | $34

171 Spring St. (bet. Thompson St. & W. B'way), 212-966-3939; www.kinkhao.com

■ It's "still quite the scene" say Siam-savvy surveyors smitten with this "sexy" "standout", a "dark, romantic" "haven in Hipsville" (aka SoHo) for "pretty people" in search of "to-die-for martinis" and "inventive", "sensational Thai food" "at bargain rates"; no wonder regulars report it "can rapidly become an addiction."

Kitchen 22/Kitchen 82 ⌧
22 | 19 | 19 | $36

36 E. 22nd St. (bet. B'way & Park Ave. S.), 212-228-4399
461 Columbus Ave. (82nd St.), 212-875-1619
www.charliepalmer.com

☑ "Swank on a shoestring" is the "amazing concept delivered" by "top chef Charlie Palmer" at these "hip", dinner-only New Americans (a Flatiron yearling and an Upper West Side newcomer) that have "rapidly become favorites" for their "deeelish", "bargain $25 three-course prix fixe menus" and "reasonable", "idiot-proof wine lists"; still, a few are "underwhelmed" by the sometimes "rushed" turnover and "no-reservations policy."

Kitchen Club
∇ 19 | 18 | 22 | $43

30 Prince St. (Mott St.), 212-274-0025; www.thekitchenclub.com

■ Those who've "stumbled in" "look forward to returning" to this midpriced NoLita favorite where "quirky and friendly chef"-owner-host-"character" Marja Samsom "magically blends flavors" in her "unusual" yet "excellent Japanese-styled" "Eclectic" menu; still, some say "the best thing is [her French] bulldog", Chibi, whose name graces the adjacent sake bar.

Kitchenette
20 13 14 $20

1272 Amsterdam Ave. (bet. 122nd & 123rd Sts.), 212-531-7600
80 W. Broadway (Warren St.), 212-267-6740

■ A "teensy" "TriBeCa original" and its "more spacious" year-old Morningside Heights spin-off, this "down-home", down-priced Southern duo delivers "big portions" of "delicious", "no-frills comfort food"; they may be "low on ambiance", with "inconsistent service", but they're "always bustling"; N.B. both now serve dinner.

Kitsch ◐
– – – E

134 E. 61st St. (bet. Lexington & Park Aves.), 212-319-0900

Already a draw for privileged Euros, this new Med boîte off the Madison Avenue gold coast serves a medley of small plates at tabs that quickly add up; for distraction, there's mismatched decor (hence the name) and music that gets louder as the night progresses.

Knickerbocker Bar & Grill ◑
20 18 19 $41

33 University Pl. (bet. 8th & 9th Sts.), 212-228-8490;
www.knickerbockerbarandgrill.com

■ "Try the T-bone for two" at this "classic", "reliable" Village "steak joint" where the cuts, chops and burgers get "solid" marks; sure, the "nightly jazz" sometimes "gets too loud", but the "old-time ambiance" and "accommodating staff" are "so welcoming" that it still remains a "comfortable standby."

Kodama
19 12 17 $28

1465 Third Ave. (bet. 82nd & 83rd Sts.), 212-535-9661
301 W. 45th St. (bet. 8th & 9th Aves.), 212-582-8065 ◐

■ For "sashimi after the show" or a "quick", pre-play meal, this "pleasant" Japanese "convenient to the theaters" (it also has a Yorkville sibling) gets applause for "high-quality sushi" and "reasonable prices"; some say they're "nothing mind-blowing", but "they will get you out" before the curtain rises.

Korea Palace
19 13 18 $33

127 E. 54th St. (bet. Lexington & Park Aves.), 212-832-2350;
www.koreapalace.com

☑ For those "too lazy to go down to K-town", this brightly lit Midtown Korean offers a "very convenient" alternative with a "pretty varied selection" of "solid fare" along with a "sushi bar"; its decor is far from palace-y, but the "Asian-style service (they can't do enough)" brings a bit of royalty to the premises.

Krispy Kreme
23 7 12 $5

Penn Station, 2 Penn Plaza (33rd St. on Amtrak rotunda level), 212-947-7175
1497 Third Ave. (bet. 84th & 85th Sts.), 212-879-9111
141 W. 72nd St. (bet. B'way & Columbus Ave.), 212-724-1100
265 W. 23rd St. (bet. 7th & 8th Aves.), 212-620-0111
www.krispykreme.com

☑ Sugar fiends swear that this chain's "addictive" "little pillows" are "as good as a doughnut gets"; sure, you can "feel the cavities forming", "the staff is as sour as the product is sweet" and the setting is "too fast food–like", but with the taste of a "melt-in-your-mouth" original glazed "hot from the oven", who cares?

Kum Gang San ◐
21 16 16 $31

49 W. 32nd St. (bet. B'way & 5th Ave.), 212-967-0909
138-28 Northern Blvd. (Union St.), Queens, 718-461-0909

☑ The "barbecue is exceptional" and they've got the "best kalbi" claim cronies of these 24-hour Koreans that offer "well-executed and often blistering" fare; some find the Manhattan branch "a bit gaudy" and say the "decor is better in Queens", but the "lively atmosphere" and "bargain lunch specials" are "great for groups."

Kurio ⌧ ▽ 25 | 19 | 23 | $43
338 E. 92nd St. (bet. 1st & 2nd Aves.), 212-828-1267
■ This "surprisingly sophisticated" Upper East Side New American still "needs to be discovered" even after a few years on the scene; the "slightly edgy" vibe extends to the service and decor, drawing in an "entertaining mix of trendy and local" folks who "come back week after week" for the midpriced, seasonally changing menu.

Kuruma Zushi ⌧ 27 | 15 | 22 | $112
7 E. 47th St., 2nd fl. (bet. 5th & Madison Aves.), 212-317-2802
■ "You may never be able to eat sushi anywhere else" after trying this second-floor Midtown Japanese where the "flavorful" stars of the show are "flown in each day" and there's "extra attentive service"; lunch may be "crowded" and "the prices criminal", but for food this "fabulous", recidivists often "return to the scene."

Kyma ◑ 20 | 14 | 18 | $38
300 W. 46th St. (8th Ave.), 212-957-8830
☑ A "delightful find" for the Broadway bound, this modestly priced Theater District Greek serves up "tasty" fare including a "wonderful selection of fresh whole fish" in an "airy", "unassuming" space; the "gracious" service makes up for that "rushed pre-show feeling."

La Baraka 19 | 17 | 22 | $39
255-09 Northern Blvd. (Little Neck Pkwy.), Queens, 718-428-1461
■ "Everyone is family" at this "friendly French" in Little Neck, touted for its "authentic" fare, "served with love", and "cozy" surrounds; the $29.95 "prix fixe deal" gets special mention, and for "dessert", "a kiss" from owner Lucette has "become legend."

La Belle Vie 17 | 16 | 16 | $34
184 Eighth Ave. (bet. 19th & 20th Sts.), 212-929-4320
☑ "Solid and tasty" French bistro fare is found at this "easygoing", "well-priced" "taste of Paris" in Chelsea; if the overall sum can be "ho-hum", the "people-watching" potential and brunch at a "streetside table" can live up to the name.

La Bergamote ⇄ 25 | 13 | 15 | $10
169 Ninth Ave. (20th St.), 212-627-9010
☑ You're in "Chelsea, France" at this counter-service bakery/cafe with a "drooling cult" following for its "gorgeous", reasonably priced pastries and authentic feel that can, unfortunately, extend to staff "attitude"; limited seating suggests takeout.

La Boîte en Bois ⇄ 21 | 16 | 20 | $47
75 W. 68th St. (bet. Columbus Ave. & CPW), 212-874-2705
■ Fans of "tasty", "classic" French fare willingly "squeeze into" this "aptly named" "shoebox" ("reservations a must"), whose "bargain $17 prix fixe" is a "perennial" "pre–Lincoln Center" "treat"; though some say it's "not so cute to accept only cash", it's "worth every penny."

La Bouillabaisse 21 | 11 | 17 | $34
145 Atlantic Ave. (bet. Clinton & Henry Sts.), Brooklyn, 718-522-8275
☑ Sure, it's "small, cramped and noisy", however, given the quality of its "superb" "namesake" soup, devoted neighbors of this Brooklyn Heights French bistro couldn't care less; opinions diverge regarding the recent "ownership change" ("hasn't been kind" vs. "keeping up the tradition").

L'Absinthe
22 | 22 | 20 | $60

227 E. 67th St. (bet. 2nd & 3rd Aves.), 212-794-4950
■ To be transported "from Second Avenue straight to" "fin-de-siècle France", visit this "posh" brasserie whose etched-glass, tile-floor quarters are "authentic" as the "amazing" "you're-in-Paris" cuisine; its "very East Side crowd" doesn't flinch at the "expensive" tabs, but "snooty" service can Gaul.

L'Acajou ●⊠
20 | 12 | 17 | $40

53 W. 19th St. (bet. 5th & 6th Aves.), 212-645-1706
◪ Its "funky", unpretentious interior "belies" the "delicious" Alsatian dishes that are the specialty of this "casual", "friendly" Flatiron French bistro; it's generally "packed with regulars" who appreciate that the owners and staff "couldn't be nicer."

La Cantina
▽ 22 | 14 | 21 | $42

38 Eighth Ave. (Jane St.), 212-727-8787
■ Further evidence that "big things come in small packages", this tiny, "cramped" West Village Italian is beloved for its "delicious" classic dishes served with "warm, friendly" aplomb; wallet-watchers appreciate that it's "fairly" affordable "for high-class cuisine."

La Cantina Toscana
▽ 23 | 17 | 21 | $47

1109 First Ave. (bet. 60th & 61st Sts.), 212-754-5454
■ "Exceptional game" is the strong suit of this "neighborhood" Tuscan not widely known outside of the East 60s; "well prepared" fare, "excellent wines" and "friendly service" should earn it notice.

LA CARAVELLE ⊠
26 | 25 | 26 | $82

33 W. 55th St. (bet. 5th & 6th Aves.), 212-586-4252;
www.lacaravelle.com
■ André and Rita Jammet's 40-year-old Midtown French "grande dame" keeps "breezing along" "near the top of the haute dining" scene, thanks to chef Troy Dupuy's "sumptuous" cuisine, a "beautiful" setting enhanced by "heavenly murals" and "floral displays", and "pampering", "formal" service; though the à la carte menu can be very "expensive", the $38 lunch prix fixe is a fine introduction.

La Cocina/Ta Cocina
15 | 12 | 15 | $24

2608 Broadway (bet. 98th & 99th Sts.), 212-865-7333
714 Ninth Ave. (bet. 48th & 49th Sts.), 212-586-0821
430 Third Ave. (30th St.), 212-532-1887
217 W. 85th St. (bet. Amsterdam Ave. & B'way), 212-874-0770
◪ Given that it's "cheap, reliable and fast", "it's not rocket science" figuring out why this Mexican quartet is a popular "standby"; the tastes are "solid", and if it "looks like a dive", "happy" vibes compensate.

LA CÔTE BASQUE
26 | 25 | 25 | $75

60 W. 55th St. (bet. 5th & 6th Aves.), 212-688-6525
■ "Still *magnifique* after all these years", this "top-notch" Midtown French eatery is a "restful" place where diners lose themselves in "lovely murals" of the Basque seacoast as well as "masterful" chef Jean-Jacques Rachou's "delicious" cuisine; naturally, you pay for the privilege, but the $38 prix fixe lunch is "one of NY's best deals"; N.B. anyone who cares about fine dining should go before February 2004, when it's scheduled to close and convert to a brasserie.

Lady Mendl's
21 | 27 | 25 | $40

Inn at Irving Pl., 56 Irving Pl. (bet. 17th & 18th Sts.), 212-533-4466;
www.innatirving.com
■ You'll "forget what century you live in" (until the check comes) at this "sophisticated", "ultra-ladylike" Gramercy Park "townhouse"

tea salon whose "plush" appointments and "solicitous" service make for the "perfect girls' outing"; just be sure mom's paying, because these crumpets "aren't cheap."

La Flor Bakery & Cafe ⊄
▽ 26 | 16 | 18 | $24

53-02 Roosevelt Ave. (53rd St.), Queens, 718-426-8023

■ At this "sunny" "neighborhood" "oasis" on an unlikely Woodside corner, Viko Ortega (a "master chef and gentleman") whips up "innovative" Mexican-Eclectic fare, plus "delectable" pastries; best of all, it's "super-cheap" and "now has a liquor license."

La Focaccia ◐
▽ 22 | 19 | 19 | $33

51 Bank St. (W. 4th St.), 212-675-3754

■ On a "beautiful West Village corner" dwells this "lovely" Italian where the "wood-burning" oven and "friendly" service make for "warm" experiences; just don't "stuff yourself with the eponymous" flatbread or you won't appreciate the "delicious" dishes.

La Giara
20 | 15 | 19 | $34

501 Third Ave. (bet. 33rd & 34th Sts.), 212-726-9855; www.lagiara.com

◪ A "good pre-movie place" where your "wallet won't take a hit", Murray Hillers rely on this "solid" Italian for "simple, fresh food" and "warm service"; perhaps it's "nothing to write home about", but in mild weather the "people-watching" from its sidewalk seats may be.

La Gioconda ⊠
▽ 21 | 15 | 20 | $37

226 E. 53rd St. (bet. 2nd & 3rd Aves.), 212-371-3536

■ "Get there early to snag one of the 10 or so tables" at this "tiny" East Midtown Italian supplier of "housemade pastas" "with flair", because its "bargain" prix fixe lunches fill seats fast; come evening, it's the "quintessential romantic hideout" for cheap dates.

La Goulue ◐
21 | 20 | 18 | $56

746 Madison Ave. (bet. 64th & 65th Sts.), 212-988-8169

◪ As long as you "look gorgeous" and "speak French", you'll feel like a "VIP" at this attractive, wood-paneled East Side magnet for the "cool, rich" and "Euro"; the Gallic bistro standards are "pleasant" enough and, as for the bill, "if you're shopping at Hermès and Prada, it won't seem expensive at all."

LA GRENOUILLE ⊠
26 | 27 | 26 | $88

3 E. 52nd St. (bet. 5th & Madison Aves.), 212-752-1495; www.la-grenouille.com

■ A "Masson family jewel" since 1962, this "exquisite", "most romantic" East Side French remains a gourmet "mecca" where the "classic" fare is "flawless", the "flowers are amazingly beautiful" and "commoners are treated like royalty"; no wonder recession-proof NYers like Henry Kissinger, Diane Sawyer and Beverly Sills favor it (prix fixe lunch is $45, dinner $85); N.B. in case you haven't seen it, the private room upstairs may be NYC's best pricey party site.

La Grolla
21 | 13 | 19 | $40

413 Amsterdam Ave. (bet. 79th & 80th Sts.), 212-496-0890

◪ "Tasty, hearty" specialties from the Val D'Aosta region (including "delicious, gooey" *fonduta*) draw Upper Westsiders to this "cozy" Northern Italian when in the mood for "more than just pasta"; there's also a "small, unpretentious" cafe next door for "lighter, cheaper" fare.

La Houppa
▽ 19 | 19 | 19 | $44

26 E. 64th St. (bet. 5th & Madison Aves.), 212-317-1999

■ "Thinnest"-crust pizzas from a wood-burning oven and housemade pastas are the draw at this "charming" East Side "townhouse" Italian; it's most "fun" "in summertime" out in the garden.

Lake Club
▽ 18 | 24 | 19 | $44

*1150 Clove Rd. (Victory Blvd.), Staten Island, 718-442-3600;
www.lake-club.com*

▣ Be sure to "get a table next to the lake" if you visit this "beautiful", "pricey" Staten Island American set on an island in Clove Lakes Park; its "turn-of-the-century boathouse" setting enchants, but service can be "slow" and the "view's more dazzling than the food."

La Lanterna di Vittorio ◑
▽ 19 | 21 | 15 | $22

129 MacDougal St. (bet. W. 3rd & W. 4th Sts.), 212-529-5945

■ Known mostly for its "delicious coffee and Italian desserts", this "old Village haunt" lures tourists, locals and "NYU" types who vie for "fireside seats in winter" and "linger over cappuccino" and those "amazing pastries."

La Locanda dei Vini
21 | 16 | 20 | $42

737 Ninth Ave. (bet. 49th & 50th Sts.), 212-258-2900

■ "Hell's Kitchen's best-kept secret" may be this Italian whose "delicious" regional dishes and "caring staff" make it a pre-theater "godsend"; insiders suggest "go after eight" and "dine at leisure like they do in the old country."

La Lunchonette
21 | 15 | 18 | $39

130 10th Ave. (18th St.), 212-675-0342

■ Long before West Chelsea was a "gallery-hopping" destination, this "quirky" yet "endearing" "St. Germain-des-Hudson" French was turning out "comforting" bistro classics; still the domain of "locals in-the-know", it's among the area's "last" pre-"gentrification" holdouts.

La Mangeoire
20 | 19 | 20 | $45

1008 Second Ave. (bet. 53rd & 54th Sts.), 212-759-7086

■ "Like being in Provence for the evening", this "charming, little" East Side bistro pleases its Francophile crowd of "neighborhood regulars" with "pretty" Mediterranean decor and "tasty" traditional fare; N.B. closed at press time due to fire.

La Méditerranée
▽ 18 | 17 | 19 | $40

947 Second Ave. (bet. 50th & 51st Sts.), 212-755-4155

■ Eastsiders of a certain age "relax after a stressful day" at this "comfortable" French bistro with a "reassuring" menu, tinkling piano and "friendly, efficient" service; it hosts a "low-power but fun lunch", and the $22 post–9:30 PM prix fixe tempts locals.

La Mela ◑
19 | 10 | 16 | $34

167 Mulberry St. (bet. Broome & Grand Sts.), 212-431-9493

▣ Think of this affordable Little Italy "family-style gorge-fest" as one big "Italian bar mitzvah" where there's no menu, but no matter – "the food just keeps coming"; "fun with a group" and perfect for bringing "outta-towners", it's "always entertaining."

La Metairie
21 | 21 | 20 | $52

189 W. 10th St. (W. 4th St.), 212-989-0343; www.lametairie.com

■ As a "romantic escape to the French countryside", this West Village "date place" specializes in "gorgeous" Provençal fare; it may feel like "one of the smallest places on earth", but service from "people who care" ensures it's "worth the squeeze" – and the price.

La Mirabelle
21 | 16 | 22 | $45

102 W. 86th St. (bet. Amsterdam & Columbus Aves.), 212-496-0458

▣ There's "nothing nouvelle" about this West Side French "warhorse", and "that's just fine" with fans of "personal" service and "homey" fare; never mind if the decor (and the clientele) is on the "dated" side.

Lamu

∇ 20 | 16 | 20 | $45

(fka Adulis)

39 E. 19th St. (bet. B'way & Park Ave. S.), 212-358-7775; www.lamunyc.com

◪ Though named for an island off the coast of Kenya, this Gramercy newcomer proffers a midpriced Mediterranean menu; early reports of "simple but elegant" fare, pleasantly "intimate" digs and "attentive" service suggest it's off to a good start.

Lan ◐

∇ 20 | 17 | 16 | $39

56 Third Ave. (bet. 10th & 11th Sts.), 212-254-1959

■ No longer unsung, the "growing popularity" of this "chic" East Village Japanese's "nimble, artistic" specialties (notably "melt-in-your-mouth sushi") has begat "long lines"; "slightly bloated prices" and a "Downtown-trendified 'tude" are a further toll of success.

L & B Spumoni Gardens ⌿

22 | 9 | 15 | $19

2725 86th St. (bet. W. 10th & W. 11th Sts.), Brooklyn, 718-449-6921; www.spumonigardens.com

■ "It's hip to be square" at this Bensonhurst pizzeria/ice cream parlor whose "signature" Sicilian slices and spumoni will "make you sing 'That's Amore!'"; "long lines" and "not-much-to-look-at" digs deter few, especially since the outdoor seating's prime for "people-watching."

L'Annam ◐

17 | 12 | 16 | $21

121 University Pl. (13th St.), 212-420-1414
393 Third Ave. (28th St.), 212-686-5168

◪ "Always packed", this "Americanized" Vietnamese duo keeps the masses happy with "eat-yourself-silly" portions of "good, cheap" food; despite "distracted" service, minimal decor and overly tame offerings, it's the "best bang for your buck outside Hanoi."

Lansky Lounge ◐

∇ 19 | 21 | 17 | $39

104 Norfolk St. (bet. Delancey & Rivington Sts.), 212-677-9489

◪ "Getting there is half the fun" at this Lower East Side former "speakeasy"–turned–surf 'n' turfer reached via a semi-secret back-alley entrance; romeos note its "modern", "nightclub"-like quarters and "surprisingly good" food make it a "sexy date place."

La Paella

20 | 17 | 16 | $32

214 E. Ninth St. (bet. 2nd & 3rd Aves.), 212-598-4321; www.lapaella214.com

◪ The "small plates" mirror the "cozy, little" setup at this East Village Spaniard whose pricing "won't break even NYU students' budgets"; although "cramped", "noisy" and "so dark you can't see your food", it's "fun with a group" and an ice-cold "pitcher of sangria."

La Palapa ◐

21 | 19 | 18 | $33

359 Sixth Ave. (bet. Washington Pl. & W. 4th St.), 212-243-6870
77 St. Marks Pl. (bet. 1st & 2nd Aves.), 212-777-2537
www.lapalapa.com

■ "Sophisticated Mexico City cuisine" lands on "tacky St. Marks Place" at this "nuanced" taqueria turning out "rich, balanced" cooking; a "charming" interior and "lovely" garden add to the "grown-up" air; N.B. the West Village location is new and unrated.

La Petite Auberge

20 | 16 | 20 | $42

116 Lexington Ave. (bet. 27th & 28th Sts.), 212-689-5003

■ "Older" types say this laced-curtain Gramercy French bistro is good enough for "every day", what with its solid "1940s-style" food and "sincere" service; while the decor may be on the "dowdy" side, overall it's still "civilized" enough to "deserve its 27-year run."

La Pizza Fresca

22 | 16 | 18 | $34

31 E. 20th St. (bet. B'way & Park Ave. S.), 212-598-0141

☑ "Obviously, there are real Italians in the kitchen" at this "perennial" Flatiron "favorite" known for its "authentic Neapolitan pizza"; critics cite the sometimes "sluggish service" and "overpriced" vinos, but most call it a "melt-in-your-mouth" experience.

La Rambla

– | – | – | E

(fka Ernie's)

2150 Broadway (bet. 75th & 76th Sts.), 212-496-1588;
www.arkrestaurants.com

Now occupying the former Ernie's space is this colorful, boisterous Pan–Latin American that works well before a show at the nearby Beacon Theater and offers a vast sharing-friendly menu that sambas its way across the region with seviches, sopas, tapas and extensive seafood and vegetarian offerings.

La Ripaille ☻

21 | 19 | 20 | $44

605 Hudson St. (bet. Bethune & W. 12th Sts.), 212-255-4406

■ Even though it's "been around forever", this "old-fashioned" Village French bistro still "deserves all the praise it gets" for its "small but great menu" and "friendly", "hands-on owner"; in short, "you don't last this long in NYC with being good."

La Rivista ☻🗷

▽ 20 | 14 | 20 | $46

313 W. 46th St. (bet. 8th & 9th Aves.), 212-245-1707;
www.larivistanyc.com

■ This Restaurant Row Italian is "dependable" both for its "better-than-average" fare and "never-be-late-for-the-show" service; in addition, there are "free parking" vouchers as well as a nightly "piano player" for those not into a hasty tasting.

La Taza de Oro 🗷🖘

19 | 5 | 14 | $15

96 Eighth Ave. (bet. 14th & 15th Sts.), 212-243-9946

☑ Both "construction workers and Chelsea gym" bunnies squeeze into this "narrow" Puerto Rican coffee shop for its "simple, honest" cheap chow and "great cafe con leche" ("Starbucks, eat your heart out"); though there's "no decor to speak of", it "fills the stomach and satisfies the soul."

La Tour

18 | 16 | 16 | $37

1319 Third Ave. (bet. 75th & 76th Sts.), 212-472-7578

☑ "Decent French" fare can be had at this "low-key" East Side bistro that's often "noisy and crowded" owing to its "can't-be-beat", "all-you-can-eat mussels and fries" for $15; critics wish that "the welcome was as warm as the food."

Lattanzi ☻🗷

23 | 19 | 22 | $51

361 W. 46th St. (bet. 8th & 9th Aves.), 212-315-0980;
www.lattanziristorante.com

■ Now in its 20th year, this "winning" Restaurant Row Italian is renowned for its "Roman-style specialties" ("don't miss" those fried artichokes), "gracious service" and "above-average prices"; insiders show up "after the theater crowd departs for a more relaxed meal."

Lavagna

23 | 17 | 20 | $38

545 E. Fifth St. (bet. Aves. A & B), 212-979-1005; www.lavagnanyc.com

■ "Not a sleeper anymore", this "sweet and sexy" East Village Med offers "delectable" chow in a "secret hideaway" setting at prices that "won't break the bank"; "excellent wine" and "helpful" service enhance the "sit-down-and-enjoy-yourself" mood.

La Vineria

▽ 22 | 16 | 21 | $39

19 W. 55th St. (bet. 5th & 6th Aves.), 212-247-3400

■ Something of a "best-kept secret", this "simpatico" Midtown Southern Italian puts out an "imaginative", "delicious" menu in a setting that "feels like Positano"; granted, it's so "small you sit at more than one table" simultaneously.

Layla ☒

19 | 22 | 19 | $48

211 W. Broadway (Franklin St.), 212-431-0700;
www.myriadrestaurantgroup.com

☒ Analyze this: Robert De Niro and Drew Nieporent "continue to charm" TriBeCa with this "festive" Mideastern known for its "nifty Moroccan" decor and belly dancer; but when the "glitter" settles, some can't decide whether the "pricey" food is "exotic" or just "ho-hum."

LE BERNARDIN ☒

28 | 26 | 27 | $90

155 W. 51st St. (bet. 6th & 7th Aves.), 212-554-1515; www.le-bernardin.com

■ "Neptune's choice" for a "fabulous fish" "splurge", Maguy LeCoze's "*merveilleux*" Midtown French "temple" "takes your breath away" thanks to "genius" chef Eric Ripert's "sublime", "inventive" food (ranked No. 1 in our *Survey*), "impeccable" service and "ethereal" surroundings; granted, even the "gods of the sea" would blink at the price of "perfection" (prix fixe lunch $47, dinner $84), but mere mortals cheerfully "beg, borrow or steal" for this "ultimate dining experience"; what most don't know is that there's a handsome party room upstairs.

Le Bilboquet

20 | 14 | 14 | $45

25 E. 63rd St. (bet. Madison & Park Aves.), 212-751-3036

☒ Observe the East Side's Euro wildlife and sample "well-prepared" victuals at this très "hip", trop "cramped" French bistro; depending on your point of view, the "great people-watching" and severe elbow-rubbing will make for either "frenetic fun" or "noisy, rude" repasts.

Le Boeuf à la Mode

21 | 18 | 21 | $49

539 E. 81st St. (bet. East End & York Aves.), 212-249-1473

■ A "true hidden gem", this "charming", "old-school" East Side bistro serves "delicious", "classic dishes" (and a prix fixe that "can't be beat") in "cozy" environs; even if the regulars are a bit long in the tooth, younger diners don't mind.

Le Charlot ●

▽ 19 | 15 | 15 | $47

19 E. 69th St. (bet. Madison & Park Aves.), 212-794-1628

☒ It's "cheaper than a flight" to Paree to dine on the "solid" bistro fare at this East Side French; drawing lots of "good-looking" Euros, it can be "deafening", with a healthy dose of "attitude" on the side.

LE CIRQUE 2000

25 | 26 | 24 | $83

NY Palace Hotel, 455 Madison Ave. (bet. 50th & 51st Sts.), 212-303-7788;
www.lecirque.com

■ Ringmaster Sirio Maccioni's "posh" French Midtown "carnival of delights" is a "grand show" featuring a crowd of "glamorous" VIPs and wide-eyed "out-of-towners" feasting on "exceptional" dishes in "opulent" rooms, the whole spectacle choreographed by a "superb" staff; though tickets to this "top-notch" circus don't come cheap and the decor walks the tightrope between "glitter" and "glitz", the "entire package" is beyond "memorable" – it's a "masterpiece."

L'Ecole ☒

24 | 19 | 22 | $41

French Culinary Institute, 462 Broadway (Grand St.), 212-219-3300;
www.frenchculinary.com

■ The "classic French" "homework" tastes "delicious" when it's "prepared from the heart" by the "masterful students" at SoHo's

French Culinary Institute; add an "eager", "courteous" staff and "real bargain" prices (five courses for $29.95) and it's no wonder that these kids get good grades.

Le Colonial
`20` `23` `19` `$49`

149 E. 57th St. (bet. Lexington & 3rd Aves.), 212-752-0808

■ You can easily imagine "you're in pre-war Saigon" instead of the East Side at this "exotic" bi-level French-Vietnamese with such a "lush", "languorous" ambiance that it "feels like Catherine Deneuve might walk in at any moment"; the "tasty" offerings earn kudos, though bon tons prefer the sexy upstairs lounge and its "pretty" Euro crowd.

Le Gamin ☉
`18` `15` `13` `$21`

27 Bedford St. (Downing St.), 212-243-2846
536 E. Fifth St. (bet. Aves. A & B), 212-254-8409
183 Ninth Ave. (21st St.), 212-243-8864
132 W. Houston St. (bet. MacDougal & Sullivan Sts.), 212-673-4592
www.legamin.com

☑ "Paris on a budget" aptly describes these "inexpensive", "relaxed" French bistros with "crêpes from heaven" and "exceptional" café au lait; still, foes froth about "lackadaisical" service.

Le Gigot
`25` `20` `23` `$48`

18 Cornelia St. (bet. Bleecker & W. 4th Sts.), 212-627-3737

■ For a "cozy spot on a cold winter's night", try this "absolutely charming" Village bistro offering "scrumptious" Gallic fare matched with "super-friendly" service; granted, it's very "small" and "pricey for the area", but it's tough to beat for "authentic" French dining.

Le Jardin Bistro
`20` `18` `17` `$38`

25 Cleveland Pl. (bet. Kenmare & Spring Sts.), 212-343-9599;
www.lejardinbistro.com

■ A "memorable garden" complete with "trellises with grapes" provides the transporting experience at this "homey" NoLita French bistro; but whether inside or out, it's an "alluring" "escape" featuring "simple" cooking with "no pretension" at "reasonable" prices.

Le Madeleine
`20` `18` `19` `$44`

403 W. 43rd St. (bet. 9th & 10th Aves.), 212-246-2993; www.lemadeleine.com

■ Despite "frantic" pre-theater crowds and a "tight" space, this 25-year-old Hell's Kitchen French bistro will get you to the show on time, although the "satisfying food" and "congenial service" are best savored "after the curtain goes up."

Le Madri
`21` `21` `21` `$53`

168 W. 18th St. (7th Ave.), 212-727-8022

■ "After all these years", Pino Luongo's "charming" Chelsea Tuscan "never fails to please" with "haute" yet "hearty" fare so "authentic" it's as if "they imported Italian mamas to cook it"; numerous fans say the "special-occasion" pricing is "worth it."

Le Marais ☉
`20` `14` `17` `$44`

150 W. 46th St. (bet. 6th & 7th Aves.), 212-869-0900

☑ "Serious noise" meets "serious steak" at this "consistently solid" Restaurant Row French chophouse that "you wouldn't know is kosher, except for the prices"; despite "crowded" conditions and "nonchalant service", adherents insist this one "grows on you."

Lemongrass Grill
`16` `12` `15` `$22`

37 Barrow St. (7th Ave. S.), 212-242-0606
2534 Broadway (bet. 94th & 95th Sts.), 212-666-0888

(continued)

(continued)
Lemongrass Grill
138 E. 34th St. (bet. Lexington & 3rd Aves.), 212-213-3317
80 University Pl. (11th St.), 212-604-9870
61A Seventh Ave. (bet. Berkeley & Lincoln Pls.), Brooklyn, 718-399-7100
◪ At this "ubiquitous" "fast-food Thai" chain, you won't want to linger given the crowds, noise and frenetic service; while foes feel the "assembly-line" chow "lacks spice and spark", others say it "does the trick" for "inexpensive, tasty" grazing.

Lenox
19 | 20 | 19 | $52
1278 Third Ave. (bet. 73rd & 74th Sts.), 212-772-0404;
www.lenoxroom.com
■ Owner/maitre d' Tony Fortuna "continues to take great care of his customers" at this "civilized" New American, the "epitome of Waspdom" and the "lush life", Upper East Side–style; despite the "hip" trappings and late-night "Downtown" vibe, it mostly draws an "older" demographic who can easily swallow the "expensive" tabs.

Lentini
21 | 18 | 21 | $52
1562 Second Ave. (81st St.), 212-628-3131
■ Chef Giuseppe Lentini (ex Elio's) turns out "consistent", "upscale" Italiana "with price tags to match" at this "classy" East Side trattoria blessed with "cordial" service; puzzled fans wonder why a spot that "deserves to be packed" is so darn "quiet."

Lento's
20 | 11 | 16 | $23
7003 Third Ave. (Ovington Ave.), Brooklyn, 718-745-9197 ⌦
289-291 New Dorp Ln. (Richmond Rd.), Staten Island, 718-980-7709
■ "Phenomenal", "paper-thin" pizzas – but "*only* the pizzas" – are "worth the trek from Manhattan" to these outer-borough, no-frills, "family-friendly institutions"; connoisseurs are convinced "like everything else, it's better in Brooklyn than in Staten Island."

L'Entrecote ⊠
∇ 18 | 15 | 19 | $45
1057 First Ave. (bet. 57th & 58th Sts.), 212-755-0080
◪ You'll feel like you're eating in Paris at this "cozy" Sutton Place French bistro where fans "never tire of the simple menu"; still, some say "time has passed it by" and wonder "what will they do" now that Mayor "Mike made them put out the cigs"?

Leopard, The ⊠
∇ 19 | 19 | 21 | $59
253 E. 50th St. (bet. 2nd & 3rd Aves.), 212-759-3735
◪ A "wonderful" $55 prix fixe including "all the wine you can handle" is the raison d'être of this Midtown French-Continental top cat that attracts a "sedate, older crowd"; it "hasn't changed its spots" in years and may "need a new decorator", but most report "pleasurable dining."

Le Pain Quotidien
21 | 16 | 14 | $20
ABC Carpet & Home, 38 E. 19th St. (bet. B'way & Park Ave. S.), 212-673-7900
1336 First Ave. (bet. 71st & 72nd Sts.), 212-717-4800
100 Grand St. (bet. Greene & Mercer Sts.), 212-625-9009
833 Lexington Ave. (bet. 63rd & 64th Sts.), 212-755-5810
1131 Madison Ave. (bet. 84th & 85th Sts.), 212-327-4900
50 W. 72nd St. (bet. Columbus Ave. & CPW), 212-712-9600
www.painquotidien.com
■ "Quality breads" served in "homey", "farmhouse-style" setups "centered around communal tables" define this all-over-town Belgian patisserie/cafe chain; its simple, tasty food and modest prices appeal to both the "ladies who lunch" and the "quick-bite" workaday crowd.

Le Père Pinard ●

20 | 19 | 15 | $34

175 Ludlow St. (bet. Houston & Stanton Sts.), 212-777-4917;
www.perepinard.com

■ You can "taste the food" now that they "don't allow smoking anymore" at this "hopping" Lower East Side French bistro, but otherwise it's as "authentic" as ever, with a little "gem" of a garden as a bonus; its "air-kissing" customers say what it lacks in service, it "makes up in vibe."

Le Perigord

24 | 21 | 24 | $69

405 E. 52nd St. (bet. FDR Dr. & 1st Ave.), 212-755-6244; www.leperigord.com

■ "Omnipresent" owner Georges Briguet and his "proud" staff "oversee every loving detail" at this longtime Sutton Place French "oasis" boasting "superb old-school cooking"; though trendsters find it "somewhat dated", traditionalists insist "old-timers can still surprise."

Le Pescadou ●

∇ 19 | 15 | 19 | $47

18 King St. (6th Ave.), 212-924-3434

☑ "Dependable" cooking in happening SoHo makes this "casual" French seafood just the ticket for a "winning date"; but nitpickers natter if you're going to pay so much, it needs to give "more attention to detail", adding that "service is great – if you're great looking."

Le Refuge

22 | 20 | 21 | $53

166 E. 82nd St. (bet. Lexington & 3rd Aves.), 212-861-4505;
www.lerefugeinn.com

■ "Living up to its name", this French venue set in an East Side townhouse has the "air of a country inn" and offers a "true respite" from the "stress of the city", given its "solid cooking" and "impeccable" service sans "snobbery"; the only drawback is it's a "bit pricey for a neighborhood place."

Le Refuge Inn

∇ 24 | 23 | 21 | $49

Le Refuge Inn, 620 City Island Ave. (Sutherland St.), Bronx, 718-885-2478;
www.lerefugeinn.com

■ "True civilization in the Bronx" is no oxymoron at this "quaint" City Island inn, a spin-off of Le Refuge with the same "outstanding" Gallic fare served in the "parlor of a Victorian mansion"; romeos bent on a "romantic" recharging "book a room and stay overnight."

Le Rivage

19 | 15 | 20 | $38

340 W. 46th St. (bet. 8th & 9th Aves.), 212-765-7374; www.lerivagenyc.com

☑ Ok, it's a bit "short on decor", but pricewise you can't do much better than this Restaurant Row bistro's "super-value" $25.75 four-course prix fixe; they "get you to the show on time" without "making you feel that they were rushing you."

Les Halles ●

20 | 16 | 16 | $41

15 John St. (bet. B'way & Nassau St.), 212-285-8585
411 Park Ave. S. (bet. 28th & 29th Sts.), 212-679-4111

■ "Pretend you're in Paris" on Park Avenue South at *Kitchen Confidential* chef Anthony Bourdain's French bistro/butcher shop where "juicy steaks", "boisterous" crowds and "lackadaisical" actor/waiters contribute to the fantasy; those seeking a less frenetic scene opt for lunch or head for the "quieter" Financial District location.

Le Singe Vert ●

18 | 18 | 16 | $36

160 Seventh Ave. (bet. 18th & 19th Sts.), 212-366-4100

■ For a "quick trip to the Left Bank" ("attitude included"), try this "authentic" Chelsea French bistro that's "hip" but "never trendy"; though most praise its "something-for-everyone" menu and "flirty" air, some wonder if it will "lose its cool" now that "smoking is banned."

Le Souk ◐   17 21 15 $32

47 Ave. B (bet. 3rd & 4th Sts.), 212-777-5454; www.lesoukny.com
■ "You'll hardly notice the food" at this "seductive" East Village North African, what with the "hot belly dancers" and "young", "party"-hearty crowd; some say it "lost its charm" after a recent expansion, but you'll have to see for yourself.

Les Routiers   20 15 18 $44

568 Amsterdam Ave. (bet. 87th & 88th Sts.), 212-874-2742; www.les-routiers.com
■ "Overlooked" and "underrated", this "*très bon*" Upper West Side French bistro dishes out "Ouest-lite" chow at "normal" prices; despite a "threadbare" dining room and occasional bouts of "Gallic service", its "small" setup works even for "incognito" types.

Le Tableau   24 15 20 $37

511 E. Fifth St. (bet. Aves. A & B), 212-260-1333; www.letableaunyc.com
■ "*Quelle surprise*" – the East Village is the "unlikely" home to this "charming" French bistro offering "food prepared with thought and care" at "honest prices"; the trade-off is "tables thisclosetogether", so "hopefully your neighbor will have an interesting conversation."

Levana   ▽ 18 14 17 $51

141 W. 69th St. (bet. B'way & Columbus Ave.), 212-877-8457; www.levana.com
☑ The glatt kosher cooking's so tasty an "outsider wouldn't know it unless told" at this West Side New American that features "exotic choices like venison and bison" besides super steak; critics contend "it's time for a face-lift", but add "you come here to eat, not look."

Lever House   – – – VE

390 Park Ave. (enter on 53rd St., bet. Madison & Park Aves.), 212-888-2700
Located in the eponymous 1952 landmark edifice, this honeycomb-patterned Midtown neophyte attracts business big shots and celebs who buzz about its well-executed New American menu, lively bar and power-broker prices; a chic alternative to the dining options in another landmark, the nearby Seagram Building, it's more akin to the breezy Brasserie than the formal Four Seasons.

L'Express ◐   16 14 13 $28

249 Park Ave. S. (20th St.), 212-254-5858
☑ "Pretty standard" chow is redeemed by "fair prices" and a 24/7 open-door policy at this often "packed" Flatiron French bistro that's a "refuge for late-night" types; just don't expect to "talk and be heard" and brace yourself for "take-it-or-leave-it" service.

Le Zie 2000 ◐   22 14 19 $36

172 Seventh Ave. (bet. 19th & 20th Sts.), 212-206-8686; www.lezie.com
■ The Venetian food's "across-the-board delicious" at this "upbeat" Chelsea "neighborhood" spot whose "homemade pasta" will "make you regret going on Atkins"; though seating is "cheek-by-jowl", the "fair prices" are "magnifico."

Le Zinc ◐   19 16 18 $39

139 Duane St. (bet. Church St. & W. B'way), 212-513-0001; www.lezincnyc.com
☑ "Laid-back", fairly priced French bistro fare is the draw at this "casual" TriBeCan, a "lively" entrant from the Chanterelle folks with a "great zinc bar" and "decor in progress" (posters "pasted on the walls"); since it's often too "loud" to talk, insiders suggest it's "better at lunch" – or breakfast.

Le Zoccole
— | — | — | M

(fka Pisces)

95 Ave. A (6th St.), 212-260-6660

A "great new entrant in the East Village", this baby sister of Chelsea's popular Le Zie dishes out "creative" Northern Italian fare, with *chicchetti* (Venetian-style small plates) on the side; the double-decker setup is kind of "loud", suggesting it's already a hit.

Le Zoo
19 | 16 | 17 | $40

314 W. 11th St. (Greenwich St.), 212-620-0393

■ "Genuinely French", "mildly innovative" cookery sets the "civilized" tone at this "small" West Village bistro with a "personable" staff and "reasonable" prices; though "too crowded" and "cramped" on weekends, it's more "doable weekdays."

Liberta ●
▽ 19 | 15 | 17 | $30

1574 Second Ave. (bet. 81st & 82nd Sts.), 212-772-0752

☑ "Inexpensive" tabs for "good enough" grub keep this Upper East Side Italian a "solid" option for a "relaxing" repast; the unconvinced find "nothing distinguishable" about it, although a new pizzeria annex adds some "variety" to the menu.

Lil' Frankie's Pizza ●≠
24 | 16 | 18 | $21

19 First Ave. (bet. 1st & 2nd Sts.), 212-420-4900

■ "Baby brother" to nearby Frank, this jammin', "very East Village" joint is the "perfect neighborhood pizzeria" offering "mouthwatering", "super-thin-crust" pies and an overall "good vibe"; in short, this one's "poised and ready to become a neighborhood classic."

Lili's Noodle Shop & Grill
17 | 15 | 16 | $21

Embassy Suites, 102 North End Ave. (Vesey St.), 212-786-1300
1500 Third Ave. (bet. 84th & 85th Sts.), 212-639-1313

■ "Lightning-fast" service means you "don't dawdle" at these Chinese noodle shops boasting "vast menus" of "affordable" eats that are "always fresh, hot and good"; "discounted movie tickets" come with your meal at the Downtown outpost.

Lima's Taste ●
▽ 20 | 7 | 15 | $28

432 E. 13th St. (bet. Ave. A & 1st Ave.), 212-228-7900

■ "Authentic Peruvian food" rife with "bold flavors" is the draw at this petite East Village newcomer that's "already crowded" with adventurers seeking "unusual", low-budget dining; despite "slow" service and some serious decor challenges (the "red walls have to go"), most call it "truly special."

Limoncello
21 | 19 | 23 | $54

Michelangelo Hotel, 777 Seventh Ave. (50th St.), 212-582-7932

■ "Adults" dig this "quiet" Theater District Italian for its "unhurried atmosphere", "caring service" and "delicious", "upscale pasta" with "no surprises"; even if the decor's a bit "fusty", the "business and pre-show crowd" says it's "worth the extra dollars."

L'IMPERO ⌧
26 | 25 | 24 | $67

45 Tudor City Pl. (bet. 42nd & 43rd Sts.), 212-599-5045; www.limpero.com

■ "Sexy and sophisticated, yet totally relaxed", this "sublime" "high-end Italian" yearling "hidden away in Tudor City" "lives up to all the hype"; chef Scott Conant's "confident" cooking lets the "ingredients shine through", and combined with an "oceanic" wine list, "friendly" service and "dreamy" decor out of an "Antonioni movie", it's no wonder "it's so hard to get a reservation"; P.S. the $49 prix fixe dinner is a "bargain considering the quality."

Link
▽ 19 20 17 $37

120 E. 15th St. (Irving Pl.), 212-995-1010

■ "Interesting twists on New American standards" combined with a "great cocktail list" make for a "hopping lounge scene" at this new Gramercy Parker; its "attractive", window-lined space also offers plenty of people-watching opportunities.

Little Italy Pizza
22 6 13 $8

1 E. 43rd St. (bet. 5th & Madison Aves.), 212-687-3660 ⊠
11 Park Pl. (bet. B'way & Church St.), 212-227-7077 ⊠
180 Varick St. (bet. Charlton & King Sts.), 212-366-5566 ⊠
72 W. 45th St. (bet. 5th & 6th Aves.), 212-730-7575

■ You get a "good slice for the price" at these hyper-"popular", all-over-town pizzerias; sure, they're "hectic" at lunchtime, the staff "hasn't smiled in months" and there's little seating, but the "delectable" pies are "worth standing up for."

Lobster Box
17 14 15 $40

34 City Island Ave. (Belden St.), Bronx, 718-885-1952;
www.lobsterbox.com

☑ It's a "different world" at this circa-1946, "old-faithful" fish house anchored at the tip of City Island; "no surprises" here means "pleasing views" and "huge portions" of "reliable" seafood at prices that will keep 'em coming for another 50 years.

Locanda Vini & Olii
▽ 25 24 22 $39

129 Gates Ave. (Cambridge Pl.), Brooklyn, 718-622-9202;
www.locandavinieolii.com

■ "Hip meets quaint" at this "atmospheric" Clinton Hill Northern Italian housed in a "gorgeously restored old pharmacy" and dispensing midpriced, "mega-tasty" items in "micro-small" doses; an "incredibly helpful" staff "out of a Rossellini movie" makes it just the spot to "celebrate a slow, romantic birthday."

Lola
19 19 18 $45

30 W. 22nd St. (bet. 5th & 6th Aves.), 212-675-6700

☑ Fervent fans "praise the lord" over the "awesome" Sunday gospel brunch at this Flatiron French-Creole where "friendly" servers and a "lively atmosphere" usher believers to "N'Awlins"; still, some skeptics shrug it's "too noisy" and mighty "pricey."

Lombardi's ⊅
25 11 15 $21

32 Spring St. (bet. Mott & Mulberry Sts.), 212-941-7994

■ Pretenders "can't begin to replicate" the "smoky crisp" crust of the "superlative-defying" coal-fired pizzas at this Little Italy joint; though "seating is tight", service slack and the beer "warm", "there's always a line out the door."

Londel's Supper Club
▽ 18 16 14 $30

2620 Frederick Douglass Blvd. (bet. 139th & 140th Sts.), 212-234-6114

■ If you can't get "south of the Mason-Dixon Line", settle for this "wonderful" Uptown Southerner whose standards are dished out with "live jazz" on the side; the atmosphere is "about as old Harlem as you can get", and if that includes sluggish service, so-ul be it.

London Lennie's
20 14 17 $36

63-88 Woodhaven Blvd. (bet. Fleet Ct. & Penelope Ave.), Queens,
718-894-8084; www.londonlennies.com

■ The fish "never flounders" at this "long-running" Rego Park seafooder known for its "heavenly fried" fare, "affordable" tabs and "no-reservations" policy; ok, there's "always a wait" on weekends and service can be "slow", but its "senior crowd" has the "free time."

Long Tan ◐   20 | 21 | 18 | $27
196 Fifth Ave. (bet. Berkeley Pl. & Union St.), Brooklyn, 718-622-8444;
www.long-tan.com
■ "Cool", "skinny" types are drawn to this "hip" Park Slope Thai for
its "deliciously spiced", "decently priced" food, "deadly drinks" and
"slick", "Manhattan-ish" vibe; when it gets "crowded" and "too loud
by half", insiders escape to the "not-to-be-missed garden."

L'Orange Bleue ◐   17 | 18 | 17 | $38
430 Broome St. (Crosby St.), 212-226-4999; www.lorangebleue.com
■ "It's one big party" at this "down-to-earth" SoHo Med where the
mood "couldn't be friendlier or more lively" and the food's incidental
and "not too expensive"; b-day celebrants can expect a "memorable"
show – "flaming cakes", "belly dancers" and lots of enthusiasm.

L'Orto Ristorante Elegante ⓈⒺ   ▽ 24 | 26 | 26 | $61
5 Gold St. (bet. Maiden Ln. & Platt St.), 212-742-8524;
www.lortorestaurant.com
■ "As good as its name", this "top-notch Italian" may be "hard to find
for strangers to the Financial District", but is "worth seeking out" for
its "great seafood", "romantic" room and "impeccable" service; sure,
it's "expensive", but the "widely spaced" tables and "hidden" address
pay off when it comes to "discreet" dining.

Los Dos Molinos ⓈⒺ   17 | 16 | 15 | $31
119 E. 18th St. (bet. Irving Pl. & Park Ave. S.), 212-505-1574;
www.losdosmolinos.com
◪ "'Hot' means hot" at this Gramercy Southwesterner, a "fun, kitschy"
corner that cures "stuffy noses" with "highly spiced" food that'll also
"make you sweat"; regulars "put out the fire" and blot out the "inept"
service with margaritas so big "you can swim in them."

Lotus ◐ⓈⒺ   ▽ 14 | 22 | 13 | $57
409 W. 14th St. (bet. 9th Ave. & Washington St.), 212-243-4420;
www.lotusnewyork.com
◪ Renowned for its "sexy" crowds, "snobbish attitude" and "hectic
bar", this Meatpacking District hot spot raises the vital question "is it
a club or a restaurant?"; now with a post-*Survey* menu switch to 'urban
Asian street fare' at lower prices, we may learn the answer.

Loulou   ▽ 24 | 19 | 22 | $35
222 DeKalb Ave. (bet. Adelphi St. & Clermont Ave.), Brooklyn, 718-246-0633
■ "Exactly what one wants in a neighborhood restaurant", this
"charming" Fort Greene French bistro specializes in "top-quality
rustic cuisine" à la Brittany, served in a "cozy" (read: "tiny") setting;
bonuses include "friendly" staffers and a "back garden that seems a
world away from NYC."

Lozoo   ▽ 22 | 23 | 21 | $39
140 W. Houston St. (bet. MacDougal & Sullivan Sts.), 646-602-8888;
www.lozoo.net
■ "Not your usual Chinese", this "adventurous" new Villager offers
"modern Shanghai cuisine" in equally "cutting-edge", "minimalist"
digs; though the "upscale" cooking comes in "small portions",
surveyors see "great potential" and would "definitely go back."

Luca   21 | 16 | 19 | $37
1712 First Ave. (bet. 88th & 89th Sts.), 212-987-9260
■ Chef-owner Luca Marcato "roams the room greeting all" when he
isn't whipping up "outstanding" Northern Italiana at this "friendly",
"informal" Eastsider; the "decor isn't much" and the staff "can get
overwhelmed", but overall it's "deelish" – and a terrific "value."

Lucien ◑
∇ 18 | 15 | 16 | $36

14 First Ave. (bet. 1st & 2nd Sts.), 212-260-6481

■ They "do the bistro thing well" at this East Village French "hangout" that lures luridly tattooed locals with straight-up "traditional" cooking, "casual service" and "Parisian-hole-in-the-wall" looks; always busy, it "has the din of a neighborhood favorite", and is a "buy" to boot.

Lucky Cheng's
9 | 15 | 15 | $36

24 First Ave. (bet. 1st & 2nd Sts.), 212-473-0516;
www.planetluckychengs.com

☑ God knows "you don't go for the food" at this East Village Asian-Eclectic – rather you go to "gawk" at the "hilarious" "cross-dressing" staff who "tell dirty jokes", perform "impromptu floor shows" and offer "lap dances for dessert"; obviously, it "can be exhausting", and weary well-wishers suggest they "freshen up the menu – and their makeup."

Lucky Strike ◑
16 | 15 | 15 | $32

59 Grand St. (bet. W. B'way & Wooster St.), 212-941-0479;
www.luckystrikeny.com

☑ "After all these years" "Keith McNally's starter kit of a SoHo bistro" still draws "attractive" crowds with its "surprisingly good" grub, "late-night" hours and "hip-but-not-*too*-hip" vibe; still, cigarette users ask "what's the point?" now that the "no-smoking law" is in effect.

Luke's Bar & Grill ◑⊄
17 | 12 | 16 | $25

1394 Third Ave. (bet. 79th & 80th Sts.), 212-249-7070

■ "Basic bar food" provides "multigenerational appeal" at this East Side American, a "neighborhood" favorite for "casual" eats on the "maid's night off"; cynics see "nothing cool-handed" about the "no-credit-card" policy, but admire the "friendly" atmosphere.

Lumi ◑
∇ 19 | 17 | 18 | $48

963 Lexington Ave. (70th St.), 212-570-2335;
www.lumirestaurant.com

☑ An "attractive", bi-level townhouse setting and "interesting" cuisine place this "sedate", if pricey, East Side Italian a "cut above the pack", though a "lack of energy" cuts it back; oh well, at least it's "lovely to sit outside and watch the world go by."

Luna Piena
18 | 15 | 17 | $34

243 E. 53rd St. (bet. 2nd & 3rd Aves.), 212-308-8882

■ There are "no pretenses", just a "gracious staff" and a "homey" vibe at this Midtown Italian "mainstay" offering "large portions" of "solid", "good-for-the-price" cooking; even better, its "back garden is one of the prettiest around" and "perfect on a summer night."

Lunchbox Food Company ◑
∇ 20 | 17 | 18 | $31

357 West St. (bet. Clarkson & Leroy Sts.), 646-230-9466;
www.lunchboxnyc.com

☑ "They care about quality" at this "remote" West Village New American with a "diner" setting that belies its superior, three-meals-a-day menu; though they need to "get their service act together", this "offbeat" spot is "far from ordinary", starting with its homemade doughnuts and bagels.

Lundy Bros.
15 | 16 | 15 | $40

1901 Emmons Ave. (Ocean Ave.), Brooklyn, 718-743-0022

☑ "Suckers for nostalgia" take a "trip down Memory Lane" at this reinvented 1930s Sheepshead Bay seafood palace where the grub's "just okay" though "portions are large"; many call it a "shadow of its former self", but since the Times Square offshoot has shuttered, this "pale copy" is the only remnant of a former "Brooklyn legend."

LUPA ●
26 | 18 | 21 | $45

170 Thompson St. (bet. Bleecker & Houston Sts.), 212-982-5089;
www.luparestaurant.com

■ For the "earthiest Italian food this side of the Atlantic", try this "dynamite" Village "Roman trattoria" via the Batali-Bastianich-Denton team, where "Jets jerseys rub elbows with Armani cashmere" and everyone "gets fat" and happy on the "exceptional cooking"; the atmosphere's "relaxed", service "knowledgeable" and tabs "very fair", but without a coveted reservation, the wait can be mind-boggling.

Lusardi's ●
25 | 19 | 23 | $53

1494 Second Ave. (bet. 77th & 78th Sts.), 212-249-2020

■ "You feel welcome" at this "old-school" East Side Northern Italian staffed by "attentive" waiters who keep their "devoted older clientele" loyal; look for an "excellent", "carefully prepared" menu, a "world-class wine list", "clubby" digs and – no surprise – "expensive" pricing.

Lutèce ⊠
24 | 23 | 23 | $75

249 E. 50th St. (bet. 2nd & 3rd Aves.), 212-752-2225;
www.lutece.com

■ The "legend is back" crow fans after the "recent improvements" at this "serene" East Side French landmark where chef David Féau's "sumptuous" meals are accompanied by a "dizzying wine selection"; "discreet", "solicitous" service and "understatedly elegant" decor make this an "exquisite refuge from all those places posing as chic", and though you'll pay for the privilege, the $29 prix fixe lunch remains one of the "best deals in town."

Luxia ●
20 | 18 | 19 | $39

315 W. 48th St. (bet. 8th & 9th Aves.), 212-957-0800

■ "Better than expected", this "cute little" Theater District Italian serves "reasonably sized" portions of "surprisingly delicious food" at the "right price"; a "pretty garden" adds "romance" in good weather.

Luzia's
18 | 12 | 15 | $30

429 Amsterdam Ave. (bet. 80th & 81st Sts.), 212-595-2000

☑ Offering affordable, "unpretentious Portuguese comfort food", this West Side "sleeper" occupies a "small" space that "could really use some sprucing up" (ditto the service); but those seeking a "brunch alternative" say it's worth a try when the lines at EJ's are overwhelming.

Macelleria ●
22 | 19 | 18 | $45

48 Gansevoort St. (bet. Greenwich & Washington Sts.), 212-741-2555

■ Possibly NYC's "most unconventional steakhouse", this "relaxed", non-macho Northern Italian is housed in a "rustic", butcher shop–like space; given its Meatpacking District locale, the "beautiful", midpriced cuts of beef "don't have far to travel" to reach your plate, although the occasionally "rude" service has a ways to go.

Madiba ●
▽ 18 | 22 | 19 | $31

195 DeKalb Ave. (bet. Adelphi St. & Carlton Ave.), Brooklyn, 718-855-9190;
www.madibaweb.com

■ As one of the city's "few South Africans", this Fort Greene scene is an "excellent", easily affordable "ambassador", laying out an "unusual, diverse menu" in attractive, "rough-hewn" digs; a "hip" following and "live music" on weekends contribute to its "rocking party" rep.

Madison Bistro
19 | 17 | 20 | $43

238 Madison Ave. (bet. 37th & 38th Sts.), 212-447-1919;
www.madisonbistro.com

■ "Dependable Gallic fare" draws business lunchers and Murray Hill locals to this "nice quiet bistro", a "relaxed", midpriced neighborhood spot with "old-fashioned" food, "unobtrusive service" and "*très français*" decor; bargain hunters tout the prix fixes.

Madison's
▽ 21 | 18 | 19 | $35

5686 Riverdale Ave. (258th St.), Bronx, 718-543-3850

■ "Into the vast Riverdale culinary wasteland" comes this "much-needed Italian", a "cosmopolitan" place with a "well-presented" menu, "efficient staff" and a bonus "chatty" bar; since it's "only half the cost of your high-end Manhattan eatery", locals "thank God they're here."

Magnifico
▽ 25 | 17 | 25 | $44
(fka Sandro's)

200 Ninth Ave. (22nd St.), 212-633-8033

■ They "make you feel like family", except when you get the bill, at this new Chelsea Northern Italian (fka Sandro's) where the food's "adventurous", the atmosphere "cozy" and the service "professional" but "personal"; indeed, supporters swear this "best-kept secret" is "getting better all the time."

Magnolia
▽ 18 | 18 | 18 | $31

486 Sixth Ave. (12th St.), Brooklyn, 718-369-4814

◪ Boosters insist this "solid" Park Sloper is blossoming thanks to its "flavorful" New American menu, not to mention the "pretty" setup; sleuths say service can be "clueless" and the room too "noisy", though there's nothing wrong with that "live weekend jazz."

Maine Lobster
16 | 9 | 16 | $38

1631 Second Ave. (bet. 84th & 85th Sts.), 212-327-4800

◪ "Unpretentious seafood" surfaces on the Upper East Side at this "tiny" New England–style joint serving "flavorful fish" for not a lot of clams; critics carp about just "ok" food, "not-much-to-look-at" decor and "not-that-great service", all of which "could stand improvement."

Maison ●
– | – | – | M

1700 Broadway (bet. 53rd & 54th Sts.), 212-757-2233

To "feel like you're in Paris without ever leaving Manhattan", try this "worthy" new French brasserie that's best known for its big-for-Midtown outdoor seating area and 24/7 open-door policy; early visitors report settling in at an alfresco "table and debriefing over a glass of champagne and a yummy salad."

Malaga
18 | 8 | 17 | $35

406 E. 73rd St. (bet. 1st & York Aves.), 212-737-7659

◪ "Garlic permeates the air" at this East Side Spaniard that's been dishing out "hearty" grub and "sangria the way it should be" since '73; maybe it's "getting a little long in the tooth", but "once you get past the tacky decor" and focus on the "reasonable" tabs, it's easy to "sit back and enjoy the paella."

Malatesta Trattoria ●⊉
▽ 19 | 17 | 19 | $31

649 Washington St. (Christopher St.), 212-741-1207

■ "Cute waiters learning English" bring you "solid Italian food" at this "great little joint" parked in a "far-off" part of the West Village; "cheap", "charming" and churning "with twentysomethings", it really comes to life when the "wraparound French doors are opened."

Maloney & Porcelli ●
22 | 19 | 22 | $58

37 E. 50th St. (bet. Madison & Park Aves.), 212-750-2233;
www.maloneyandporcelli.com

■ "Fred Flintstone–size steaks" and a "show-stopping" "signature pork shank" draw everyone from "attorneys" to "Atkins dieters" to this Midtown chop shop whose decor and service "don't make women feel out of place"; it sports a "kicking bar scene" and grand upstairs party space, but for best results, "bring your boss' platinum card."

Mamá Mexico ◗

20 | 17 | 19 | $31

214 E. 49th St. (bet. 2nd & 3rd Aves.), 212-935-1316
2672 Broadway (bet. 101st & 102nd Sts.), 212-864-2323
www.mamamexico.com

■ "Go early or go deaf" at this "hyperactive", hyper-value Mexican duo where "every night's a fiesta", complete with "knock-you-for-a-loop" margaritas, "super-loud mariachi bands" and "too many college students" doing "tequila shots"; for more retiring folk, the Midtown yearling is "nowhere near as crowded."

Mama's Food Shop ⊠⇄

22 | 11 | 14 | $14

200 E. Third St. (bet. Aves. A & B), 212-777-4425
222 Sullivan St. (bet. Bleecker & W. 3rd Sts.), 212-505-8123
www.mamasfoodshop.com

☑ For food "tastier than your mama ever made", check out these Village Americans dishing out "monster portions" of "June Cleaver" comfort food on the "cheap"; ok, "service ain't grand", but the "lack of decor is endearing" – and the new West Side outpost is a "delightful surprise."

Mamlouk

▽ 22 | 19 | 20 | $39

211 E. Fourth St. (bet. Aves. A & B), 212-529-3477

■ To "live like a sultan", try this "exotic" East Village Mideasterner offering a set "six-course prix fixe" menu for a "recession-proof" $30 price tag; it's a "sensual dinner experience" with "more food than you can possibly finish", but sadly the "hookahs are gone" now, put out by the new nonsmoking law.

Mandarin Court

19 | 7 | 12 | $21

61 Mott St. (bet. Bayard & Canal Sts.), 212-608-3838

☑ It's "dim sum all the time" at this "heart of Chinatown" spot where nonstop carts offer a "wide variety of tasty little bits" at "bargain-basement prices"; although service is "indifferent", the decor "bottom-drawer" and the bathrooms "indescribable", the food's so "solid" that "nobody cares."

Manducatis

21 | 11 | 17 | $40

13-27 Jackson Ave. (47th Rd.), Queens, 718-729-4602

☑ The "queen of red sauce", aka Ida Cerbone, whips up "terrific" "old-school" dishes at this Long Island City Italian "sleeper" that's especially handy "if you're going to MoMA Queens"; an "awesome wine list" compensates for the "lack of decor" and "extremely slow service."

Manetta's ⊠

▽ 22 | 14 | 18 | $31

10-76 Jackson Ave. (49th Ave.), Queens, 718-786-6171

■ "Homemade pastas" and "too-good-to-be-true pizzas" are the hooks at this "consistent" Italian "tucked away in Long Island City"; though "uninspired" lookswise, "prices are reasonable" and "service is steady, even when it's busy."

Mangia ⊠

20 | 12 | 12 | $19

16 E. 48th St. (bet. 5th & Madison Aves.), 212-754-0637
Trump Bldg., 40 Wall St. (bet. Broad & William Sts.), 212-425-4040
50 W. 57th St. (bet. 5th & 6th Aves.), 212-582-5554
www.mangianet.com

■ "Redefining the solo corporate lunch", these Mediterranean "gourmet food bars" cater to "stylish executives on the go" with a "something-for-everyone" "smorgasbord" that's "worth the little-bit-higher prices"; despite "disorganized" service and a need for "more seating", many gladly "mangia here every day."

Mangiarini
22 | 14 | 19 | $34

1593 Second Ave. (bet. 82nd & 83rd Sts.), 212-734-5500;
www.mangiarini.com

■ "Good things come in small packages" at this "low-key", low-priced Upper East Side Italian where the "subtle" but "interesting" dishes mesh nicely with the "minimalist", "Calvin Klein–style" decor; the biggest drawback is its "tiny" size – they "need to move so more people can enjoy them."

Manhattan Chili Co.
16 | 13 | 15 | $23

1500 Broadway (43rd St.), 212-730-8666
Ed Sullivan Theater, 1697 Broadway (bet. 53rd & 54th Sts.),
212-246-6555
www.manhattanchilico.com

☑ "Chili every which way" – "from mild to *mamacita!*" – is the draw at these cheap Theater District Southwesterners that appeal to "tourists" and "vegetarians"; snobs say they "feel like a chain", what with their "laminated menus" and "frat house" at "happy hour" vibe.

Manhattan Grille
20 | 18 | 19 | $52

1161 First Ave. (bet. 63rd & 64th Sts.), 212-888-6556;
www.themanhattangrille.com

☑ "Get your cholesterol meter up and running" at this "clubby", comfortable East Side "neighborhood steakhouse", a "longtimer" that's popular with "mature" types ("saw Dick Clark there"); though some say it's too "pricey" and "stodgy", fans of "non-trendy", "non-fusion" dining argue it's "better than the big names."

Manhattan Ocean Club
25 | 22 | 22 | $63

57 W. 58th St. (bet. 5th & 6th Aves.), 212-371-7777;
www.manhattanoceanclub.com

■ "Honest seafood" "simply and superbly prepared" practically swims into the "classy", ocean liner–like environs of this "amazing" Midtowner; now in its 20th year and "still at the top of its game" with service that's equally "polished, without being pretentious", it remains NYC's "catch of the day" even if they know how to hook your wallet.

Maple Garden Duck House
23 | 14 | 21 | $37

236 E. 53rd St. (bet. 2nd & 3rd Aves.), 212-759-8260

■ "Out-of-this-world" "Peking duck on demand" (and "*only* the duck") keeps this Midtown Mandarin bustling, though the "really nice hosts" and "attentive" service help too; if its looks are "less than impressive", at least it's "nicer than Chinatown."

MARCH
26 | 25 | 26 | $89

405 E. 58th St. (bet. 1st Ave. & Sutton Pl.), 212-754-6272;
www.marchrestaurant.com

■ "Romance abounds" at this "dreamy" Sutton Place townhouse where the setting is "plush", service "telepathic" and chef Wayne Nish's New American tasting menus are "heavenly"; however, be "prepared to be stunned by the experience – especially the bill"; P.S. the new lunch service produces less "sticker shock."

Marchi's ⌀
▽ 20 | 17 | 20 | $50

251 E. 31st St. (bet. 2nd & 3rd Aves.), 212-679-2494;
www.marchirestaurant.com

☑ Perfect for big groups that don't like to make decisions, this Kips Bay Northern Italian proffers "no menu", having served the "same" five-course meal (antipasti, lasagna, fish, fowl, dessert) "every day" since 1930; though the feeling of "leisurely hospitality" is "wonderful", it's easy to "tire of the limited choices" here.

Marco Polo Ristorante
▽ 19 | 17 | 21 | $43

345 Court St. (Union St.), Brooklyn, 718-852-5015;
www.marcopoloristorante.com

☒ "Old-world service and charm" draw an "older crowd" to this "old-style" Carroll Gardens middle-income Italian that offers "valet parking" but thankfully "no checkered tablecloths"; foes find "no thrills or frills" here, only a *Godfather*-esque mood.

Mardi Gras ◑
18 | 17 | 17 | $30

70-20 Austin St. (bet. 70th Ave. & 70th Rd.), Queens, 718-261-8555

☒ The "Big Easy" alights in Forest Hills at this "very loud" Cajun-Creole where the "good food", "excellent Hurricanes" and "weekly jazz" make many imagine they're "back on Bourbon Street"; the unconvinced waver: it's a "lotta fun" but "not exactly the real thing."

Maria Pia
19 | 17 | 18 | $33

319 W. 51st St. (bet. 8th & 9th Aves.), 212-765-6463;
www.mariapianyc.com

■ This "simple", little Theater District Italian "covers all of the bases well", with "good standard fare", "warm" service and "intimate" environs "illuminated with romantic candlelight" – all at "prices that aren't overpowering"; icing the cake is a $19.95 prix fixe dinner.

Marichu
22 | 19 | 19 | $46

342 E. 46th St. (bet. 1st & 2nd Aves.), 212-370-1866;
www.marichu.com

■ "Unspoiled and undiscovered", this "authentic" Basque "somewhat isolated" near the UN lures an "international clientele" with its "carefully prepared" Spanish menu, "European" ambiance and "lovely backyard garden"; although it's on the "pricey" side, the payoff is "sophisticated", "civilized" dining.

Marina Cafe
▽ 18 | 19 | 18 | $39

154 Mansion Ave. (Hillside Terr.), Staten Island, 718-967-3077;
www.marinacafegrand.com

☒ "Everyone seems to know everyone else" at this "long-established" Staten Island seafooder where the "small-town" feel is abetted by a big-time, "water's-edge" panorama of Great Kills Harbor; though you "can't eat the view", the "food's pretty good", ditto the "cheery" service.

Marinella
▽ 20 | 16 | 22 | $37

49 Carmine St. (Bedford St.), 212-807-7472

■ "Charming and old-fashioned", this "friendly" Italian is "like the Village used to be", offering "authentic, savory" grub in a "comfortable atmosphere"; even though the "specials on the chalkboard always seem the same", it takes you back to a time "before pasta cost as much as caviar."

Marion's Continental ◑
▽ 15 | 18 | 16 | $31

354 Bowery (bet. 4th & Great Jones Sts.), 212-475-7621

☒ "Who goes for the food?" – the "kitschy" decor is "worth the price of admission" at this "campy" Bowery American where the "throwback" menu plays second fiddle to the "fancy martini" list; fans say the "fun-lovin' vibe" makes it perfect after an "Off-Off Broadway show."

Mario's
21 | 15 | 20 | $38

2342 Arthur Ave. (bet. 184th & 186th Sts.), Bronx, 718-584-1188

■ For "quintessential Arthur Avenue" dining, try this "neighborhood landmark" serving "huge" platters of "delicious" Southern Italiana, "1950s"-style (not to mention "fabulous pizza"); so even if the digs "could use refreshing", enthusiasts are thrilled that this "timeless" tradition "never changes."

Market Café ⊠
▽ 20 | 14 | 16 | $25

496 Ninth Ave. (bet. 37th & 38th Sts.), 212-967-3892

■ "Near the Javits Center", this "casual", "dinerlike" American offers "reliable" grub priced for folks "on tight budgets"; granted, they "need to hire more help" and looks are strictly "hole-in-the-wall", but for "a meal this good and cheap", consider squinting.

MarkJoseph Steakhouse ⊠
24 | 18 | 22 | $60

261 Water St. (Peck Slip), 212-277-0020;
www.markjosephsteakhouse.com

☑ "Thick-walleted" "white guys in ties" with "huge appetites" are all over this Downtown steakhouse, the latest "Wall Street hangout" for "amazing" chops, "outstanding" wine and refreshingly "pleasant" service; whether it's "better than Luger's" is a matter of debate: antis sneer "wanna-be" "knockoff", but pros proselytize it's "just as good", "without the trip to Brooklyn" – "*and* they take credit cards."

Mark's
24 | 25 | 25 | $66

Mark Hotel, 25 E. 77th St. (bet. 5th & Madison Aves.), 212-879-1864;
www.mandarinoriental.com

■ An "uncommon warmth and intimacy" pervades this "under-the-radar" East Side hotel dining room for "elegant, mature" types who call the French-American menu "sumptuous", the service haute and the "civilized setting" a haven of "serenity"; it's the "perfect place to overdose on butter, cream and eggs", so try Sunday brunch or the "wonderful tea" "after the Met."

Markt ◐
18 | 18 | 16 | $41

401 W. 14th St. (9th Ave.), 212-727-3314

■ "Singles mingle" at this "noisy" Meatpacking District Belgian brasserie, a "mussel beach" with a "wall-to-wall" beer selection and marvelous moules frites; the outdoor tables are so "like being in Europe" that it's easy to forgive the "indifferent" service.

Maroons
22 | 13 | 18 | $32

244 W. 16th St. (bet. 7th & 8th Aves.), 212-206-8640

■ When your "soul needs soothing", "squeeze" into this "tight" Chelsea Caribbean-Southerner where the "mixed marriage" menu is "heavy", "delicious" and "affordable"; a "bopping buppie scene" makes for long "waits" in the "loud" bar, but a "personable staff" and "killer cocktails" ease the pain.

Marseille
21 | 20 | 19 | $48

630 Ninth Ave. (44th St.), 212-333-2323; www.marseillenyc.com

☑ "Dining for grown-ups" is alive and well in "up-and-coming" Hell's Kitchen at this French-Med "foodie oasis" where chef Alex Ureña's "cutting-edge" cooking "shines" against the "dark, sexy" backdrop; maybe the "noise level is high and portions small", but regulars say it works "best after curtain time."

Mars 2112
9 | 21 | 13 | $28

1633 Broadway (51st St.), 212-582-2112; www.mars2112.com

☑ "Don't expect out-of-this-world" meals at this Martian-themed Theater District American – the "food isn't exactly stellar" and although "fun for five-year-olds", you'll need "blinders" to get the kids past the "gift shop"; thankfully, the "bumpy" "simulated spaceship ride" happens *before* the meal.

Marumi
▽ 22 | 12 | 17 | $32

546 La Guardia Pl. (bet. Bleecker & W. 3rd Sts.), 212-979-7055

■ At this NoHo "neighborhood" Japanese, "there's always a line" since the space is "tiny" and the "excellent" sushi "so reasonably priced that you almost feel guilty"; the "efficient", if overworked, staff keeps the "throngs" of "locals and NYU students" satisfied.

Maruzzella ◗   ▽ 21 | 16 | 21 | $34

1483 First Ave. (bet. 77th & 78th Sts.), 212-988-8877
■ Even irregulars "feel like a regulars" at this "comfy, cozy" Upper East Side Italian where the "caring" service is matched by a "nice simple menu" ("love what they do with veal"); many like it so well that they "don't want to tell the rest of NY."

Mary Ann's   16 | 12 | 14 | $24

2452 Broadway (bet. 90th & 91st Sts.), 212-877-0132
116 Eighth Ave. (16th St.), 212-633-0877 ⊟
1803 Second Ave. (93rd St.), 212-426-8350
1503 Second Ave. (bet. 78th & 79th Sts.), 212-249-6165
80 Second Ave. (5th St.), 212-475-5939 ⊟
107 W. Broadway (bet. Chambers & Reade Sts.), 212-766-0911
◪ "It's Cinco de Mayo every day" at these "loud" "Yank-Mex" outlets where "huge portions" of "decent" chow are washed down with "pitchers of margaritas"; given the "great happy-hour deals", no one cares that these "cheap", "cheerful dives" are just "so-so" foodwise.

Mary's Fish Camp ⊠   23 | 12 | 18 | $36

64 Charles St. (W. 4th St.), 646-486-2185; www.marysfishcamp.com
■ It's easy to pretend you're at a "beach-town shack" instead of the West Village at this "postage stamp–size" seafooder where the "kick-ass lobster rolls" make up for the "no-thrills" setting, "hard bench" seating and "excruciatingly long lines"; "once you start eating, you'll forget the wait" since the fish is so darn fresh "you'd think there's a lake out back."

Massimo al Ponte Vecchio   ▽ 24 | 14 | 24 | $39

206 Thompson St. (bet. Bleecker & W. 3rd Sts.), 212-228-7701
◪ Celebrating over "25 years of great food", this "reliable Village Italian" "neighborhood favorite" still "dishes out some of the most imaginative game offerings in town"; "caring service" compensates for decor heavy on the "Italian-American celeb portraits."

Mavi Turkish Cuisine ◗   ▽ 21 | 12 | 21 | $24

42-03 Queens Blvd. (42nd St.), Queens, 718-786-0206
◪ Those "in the mood for kebabs" "before or after MoMA Queens" stick by this low-budget Sunnyside Turk for its "delicious", "beautifully presented" chow; picky eaters say it's "not as good as Nazar" (its previous incarnation), although just as "friendly" as ever.

Max ◗⊟   23 | 15 | 16 | $25

1274 Amsterdam Ave. (123rd St.), 212-531-2221
51 Ave. B (bet. 3rd & 4th Sts.), 212-539-0111
394 Court St. (bet. Carroll St. & 1st Pl.), Brooklyn, 718-596-9797
www.maxrestaurantny.com
■ "Success hasn't spoiled" these "cheap" Southern Italian "dynamos" whose impossibly "crunched" setups are trumped by "fresh" "red gravy" grub that's simply "delish"; just be ready to "wait for everything", since "no reservations are taken."

Maya   24 | 21 | 20 | $48

1191 First Ave. (bet. 64th & 65th Sts.), 212-585-1818
■ "High-style" "gourmet" cuisine that's "light years ahead of the usual taco fare", "sexy señorita" servers and "mind-altering" margaritas lure "grown-up singles" to this "classy" Eastsider that's "na-cho typical" Mexican; though the "din" can be "deafening", most find it easy to "eat, drink and be merry" here, albeit at "premium prices."

Mayrose
15 | 11 | 13 | $20

920 Broadway (21st St.), 212-533-3663

◨ A former "Silicon Alley hot spot", this "retro" Flatiron diner has morphed into a "comfortable", low-budget non-scene (except for the "crowded brunch"); "huge windows" make for a "sun-filled" setting that's only overshadowed by "nonexistent service."

Maz Mezcal
21 | 18 | 19 | $34

316 E. 86th St. (bet. 1st & 2nd Aves.), 212-472-1599;
www.mazmezcal.com

■ Regulars feel like they're "part of *la familia*" at this "*mucho delicioso*" Yorkville cantina that's exactly "what a Mexican restaurant should be"; "darn good" dishes, "affordable" prices and a "festive", "hi-octane-margarita" air keep it "packed" most of the time.

McHales ◗⇗
18 | 9 | 13 | $19

750 Eighth Ave. (46th St.), 212-997-8885

■ Burgers "so big you need a crane to lift them" go down neatly with a tap brew at this "hard-boiled" Theater District bar and grill where the "frat-basement" decor "hasn't changed since the '50s"; too "down-at-the-heel" for tourists, it's an affordable mainstay for "stagehands" and slummers.

Mediterraneo ◗
19 | 14 | 15 | $33

1260 Second Ave. (66th St.), 212-734-7407

◨ "More scene than restaurant", this recently expanded "Euro-chic" East Side Italian offers a "mostly pasta" menu to pretty "young things" on "cell phones"; the "outdoor tables are the big draw" here as an ideal spot to "show off your new Manolos."

Mee Noodle Shop
17 | 4 | 12 | $15

219 First Ave. (13th St.), 212-995-0333
795 Ninth Ave. (53rd St.), 212-765-2929
922 Second Ave. (49th St.), 212-888-0027
547 Second Ave. (bet. 30th & 31st Sts.), 212-779-1596

■ It's "amazing what you can get for a few bucks" at this mini-priced "mini-chain" of "fast and furious", "decent" noodle shops; since service is "curt" and the decor "spartan", many adherents stick to "delivery."

Meet
18 | 21 | 16 | $46

71-73 Gansevoort St. (Washington St.), 212-242-0990; www.the-meet.com

◨ "So dark it must be trendy", this midpriced Meatpacking District Mediterranean was "cool for a nano-second" but still serves "scene cuisine" in a "sophisticated", "feng shui"–ish space; as is often the case, the "bar atmosphere's better than the food" and the food's better than the "lame" service.

MeKong
▽ 20 | 13 | 16 | $28

44 Prince St. (bet. Mott & Mulberry Sts.), 212-343-8169

■ "Popular, but not *too* popular", this "easygoing", "no-frills" NoLita Vietnamese serves "delicious classics" in usually "quiet" environs; ok, service is "haphazard" and the "decor could be better", but at least the price is right and you can "get a table right away."

Melrose
▽ 18 | 21 | 19 | $44

Stanhope Park Hyatt, 995 Fifth Ave. (81st St.), 212-650-4737;
www.stanhopepark.hyatt.com

◨ Right across from the Metropolitan Museum, this "welcoming" Upper Eastsider exhibits "very good" taste with its American standards, "classic" cream-colored dining room and ever popular sidewalk seating; as a bonus, crooner Steve Ross makes frequent appearances for supper-club dining.

Meltemi
19 | 16 | 19 | $41

905 First Ave. (51st St.), 212-355-4040

☑ "Fish is what it's all about" at this "airy" Sutton Place Greek where fin fans melt for the "freshness" of the catch, served with "no pretense" to regulars and "UN celebs" alike; but given the "basic" seafaring, some find the "hefty price tags" a little fishy.

Menchanko-tei ●
18 | 8 | 15 | $20

131 E. 45th St. (bet. Lexington & 3rd Aves.), 212-986-6805
43-45 W. 55th St. (bet. 5th & 6th Aves.), 212-247-1585
www.menchankotei.com

■ Blink and "you're in Tokyo" at these "real-deal" ramen-o-ramas, "quick" stops for "fabulous", "filling" noodle soups that "stick to the ribs" and "warm" the heart at a "good price"; they may have "utilitarian service" and "zero atmosphere", but hey, "all those Japanese businessmen can't be wrong."

Mercer Kitchen ●
22 | 22 | 18 | $54

Mercer Hotel, 99 Prince St. (Mercer St.), 212-966-5454;
www.jean-georges.com

☑ For a "SoHo experience" akin to *The Matrix* gone "underground", join all the "models and quasi-celebs" at Jean-Georges Vongerichten's "adventurous" French–New American; "plebeians" may protest the "doing-you-a-favor" service and "steep" prices, but with all the "action", it's a "mood-altering" experience.

Merchants, N.Y. ●
14 | 17 | 15 | $33

1125 First Ave. (62nd St.), 212-832-1551
112 Seventh Ave. (bet. 16th & 17th Sts.), 212-366-7267
www.merchantsny.com

☑ With food as much of a "gamble" as the "pickup scene", these affordable if "formulaic" New Americans satisfy a "younger bar contingent" right out of a "TV sitcom"; the "casual", "shopworn" digs are "enjoyable" enough for "B&T watching" or a "late date."

Mermaid Inn ●
▽ 25 | 21 | 23 | $40

96 Second Ave. (bet. 5th & 6th Sts.), 212-674-5870;
www.themermaidnyc.com

■ Already "making quite a splash" in the East Village, this "quaint" new seafooder from the Red Cat/Harrison crew sends out a siren call with "simple but brilliant" dishes and "kitschy" decor reminiscent of a "New England fish shack"; all hands hail this "instant winner" as a "much-needed" reminder that "you're actually on an island."

MESA GRILL
24 | 21 | 21 | $51

102 Fifth Ave. (bet. 15th & 16th Sts.), 212-807-7400; www.mesagrill.com

■ The "hype is true": Bobby Flay's "still got it" at this "energetic" Flatiron "favorite", the big-name chef's "premier" showcase for "snappy" SW fusion fare with enough "kick" to "jump-start your tongue"; the "stark", high-ceilinged room continues to "buzz" as Bobby proves he's "not just a pretty TV face" – his "sassy" act is definitely worth "paying for."

Meskerem ●
20 | 10 | 15 | $22

124 MacDougal St. (bet. Bleecker & W. 3rd Sts.), 212-777-8111
468 W. 47th St. (bet. 9th & 10th Aves.), 212-664-0520
www.meskeremrestaurant.com

■ "Convert a food xenophobe" to "finger-lickin' good" Ethiopian fare at this cutlery-free duo where the "yummy stews" are "scooped up" on flatbread ("extra napkins" come at no extra charge); despite an "utter lack of decor", most give a hand to this "cheap", "filling" experience.

Métisse
22 | 17 | 20 | $41

239 W. 105th St. (bet. Amsterdam Ave. & B'way), 212-666-8825
■ "Understated and underappreciated", this "petite" Upper West Side "hideaway" is a "delicious" French option for "casual" Columbia types who applaud its "cordial" air; it's the local answer to the "Downtown scene", "without the prices" and the hassle of "getting a table."

Métrazur ☒
19 | 23 | 18 | $46

Grand Central, East Balcony (42nd St. & Park Ave.), 212-687-4600; www.metrazur.com
☑ It's "hard to beat the show" at this "unique" New American on the "gloriously restored" balcony overlooking Grand Central Terminal's "mad" commuter "parade"; though diners split on the costly cooking – "solid" vs. "ordinary" – most concur it's served in the "prettiest room in the world."

Metro Fish ☒
21 | 15 | 20 | $40

8 E. 36th St. (bet. 5th & Madison Aves.), 212-683-6444; www.metrofishrestaurant.com
☑ "Not for the faint of appetite", this Murray Hill piscatorium proffers a "wide variety" of "first-rate fish" "served your way" in whopping "suburban portions"; the $25 prix fixe dinner remains a reel "steal", though the "dated", "LI-comes-to-NY" ambiance may seem designed for "your parents."

Metronome ☒
19 | 20 | 18 | $40

915 Broadway (21st St.), 212-505-7400; www.metronomenyc.com
■ The beat goes on at this "really cool" Flatiron Med–New American, a midpriced venue that's more about the "elegant" deco digs and "live jazz" than the "diverse menu"; still, the eating's "surprisingly decent" and the "loungey" rhythm just fine for "getting to know someone."

Metropolitan Cafe ●
16 | 16 | 15 | $34

959 First Ave. (bet. 52nd & 53rd Sts.), 212-759-5600; www.arkrestaurants.com
■ Expect "no surprises" at this Sutton Place "neighborhood anchor", just a "crowd-pleasing menu" of "functional", affordable Americana served in "typical" digs or in the great "garden room retreat"; though "hardly cosmopolitan", it works for brunch or with "little ones" in tow.

Metsovo ●
19 | 20 | 18 | $41

65 W. 70th St. (bet. Columbus Ave. & CPW), 212-873-2300
■ A "more atmospheric" Grecian formula, this Lincoln Center–area "hideaway" aims for "high class" with "subdued", "brick-walled" surroundings and a "cozy fire in the hearth"; the "tasty" "country Greek" specialties lean toward seafood with a "twist" and, as befits a "sleeper", the pace is "not rushed."

Mexicana Mama ⊄
25 | 10 | 16 | $30

525 Hudson St. (bet. Charles & W. 10th Sts.), 212-924-4119
■ "Quality and love" are mama's main ingredients at this inexpensive, "closet-size" West Village home to Nuevo Mexican fare; utilizing "unusual", "nontraditional" fixings, it "draws crowds" beyond its "cramped" capacity, causing compadres who can't "stand the waits" and parrying "other diners' elbows" to make one request: "expand!"

Mexican Radio ●
18 | 14 | 16 | $27

19 Cleveland Pl. (bet. Kenmare & Spring Sts.), 212-343-0140
■ "Young" Tijuana-bes turn to this "rowdy" NoLita cantina for "knock-your-socks-off" margaritas and "affordable" Mexican chow that "doesn't shortchange on the good fillings"; sure, it's on the "funky" side of the dial, but for most, this "fun scene" is coming in "just fine."

Mezzaluna ☽   `20` `13` `17` `$39`
1295 Third Ave. (bet. 74th & 75th Sts.), 212-535-9600
⬛ For the East Side upper crust's idea of a "neighborhood pizzeria", try this "thriving" Italian, a steady source of "quality pastas" and "thin pizzas"; critics say "everyone seems to know" this "standby", hence the "cramped" setup with tables "shoehorned" in.

Mezzogiorno ☽   `20` `17` `18` `$43`
195 Spring St. (Sullivan St.), 212-334-2112
⬛ A "familiar" refuge in SoHo, this "consistently solid" Italian offers brick-oven pizza and pasta that's "more authentic" than what's usually available in this trendy terrain; its Ray-Banned regulars tout the "outside cafe tables" for "sunny-day" primo "people-watching."

Michael Jordan's The Steak House NYC   `20` `20` `18` `$57`
Grand Central, North Balcony (42nd St. & Vanderbilt Ave.), 212-655-2300; www.theglaziergroup.com
⬛ Still in the game, this steakhouse parked a "jump shot above" Grand Central Concourse courts "business" players and "impressionable out-of-towners" with "championship" chunks of meat; but "benchwarmer" service and "over-the-top" tabs suggest that an "MVP" needs "more than just the MJ name."

Michael's ▨   `21` `21` `22` `$58`
24 W. 55th St. (bet. 5th & 6th Aves.), 212-767-0555; www.michaelsnewyork.com
⬛ To "hobnob with publishing demi-celebs", visit this airy, art-decorated Cal cuisine Midtowner where media execs cut their deals at "biz breakfasts" or lunches (making it easier to "get in at dinnertime"); though some say "you go for the people-watching, not the food" at this expense-accounter, most surveyors say you get the best of both.

Mickey Mantle's ☽   `12` `17` `14` `$34`
42 Central Park S. (bet. 5th & 6th Aves.), 212-688-7777
⬛ "Sports nuts" who "can't get to the game" keep this "memorabilia"-bedecked CPS dugout "lively" as they "pay respects" to the Mick on admittedly "touristy" turf; maybe the "overpriced bar food" "often strikes out", but fans know it's better than what they get at the ballpark and the viewing is easier on the plentiful TVs.

Mi Cocina   `22` `18` `19` `$41`
57 Jane St. (Hudson St.), 212-627-8273
⬛ Mexican grub moves a "notch above" the "usual rice and beans" at this "popular" West Villager, offering an "ambitious" menu of "high-end" "traditional" cooking plus a "serious tequila list" to keep things "interesting"; it's also a few pesos "classier than others."

MILOS, ESTIATORIO ☽   `26` `23` `21` `$67`
125 W. 55th St. (bet. 6th & 7th Aves.), 212-245-7400; www.milos.ca
⬛ "Heaven" is "pristine fish" "simply grilled" at this "exceptional" Midtown Greek where the "hospitality" and "cavernous", white "wide-open space" make for a thalassic classic; if the appetizers and prix fixes are sound "bargains", anyone choosing an entree from the "dazzling" iced array should "watch out for by-the-pound" pricing – or expect a "mighty expensive surprise."

Minado   `–` `–` `–` `l`
6 E. 32nd St. (bet. 5th & Madison Aves.), 212-725-1333; www.minado.com
All-you-can-eat, serve-yourself sushi, salads and hot dishes is the concept at this 600-seat, bi-level Murray Hill Japanese where for $13.95

at lunch and $23.95 at dinner (and $2 more for each on weekends) patrons can partake in a mind-boggling array of options.

Minetta Tavern ●
18 | 15 | 19 | $37

113 MacDougal St. (bet. Bleecker & W. 3rd Sts.), 212-475-3850

◪ Fans tout this "cozy", '30s-era Village Italian as a "convenient", "tried-and-true throwback" to "old-world" cooking, "warm" service and modest prices; though an "overhaul" may be overdue, its regulars "wouldn't want it any other way."

Mingala Burmese
19 | 11 | 17 | $21

1393-B Second Ave. (bet. 72nd & 73rd Sts.), 212-744-8008
21-23 E. Seventh St. (bet. 2nd & 3rd Aves.), 212-529-3656

■ "Adventurous eaters" are in for a "real treat" at these cheap and "cheery" Burmese Eastsiders, whose "intriguing" flavors offer an "addictive alternative" to the usual "Asian options"; since both the decor and service need work, many vote for "takeout."

Minnow
21 | 17 | 19 | $38

442 Ninth St. (bet. 6th & 7th Aves.), Brooklyn, 718-832-5500

■ They "do Poseidon proud" with "imaginative new takes" on "top-line" fish at this "small" Park Slope seafooder where the "TLC is evident" on every plate; despite sardine seating, locals who see it "improving all the time" spout "how lucky we are!"

Miracle Grill
20 | 17 | 17 | $33

415 Bleecker St. (bet. Bank & W. 11th Sts.), 212-924-1900
112 First Ave. (bet. 6th & 7th Sts.), 212-254-2353 ●
www.miracleny.com

■ Villagers have faith in these "unpretentious" Southwestern "mainstays" for "fine", "plentiful" food and "potent cocktails" at "reasonable prices"; both are "spicy brunch" meccas, and the East Side branch's garden is a "star attraction", but it's a "miracle if you can get a table" there.

Mirchi
20 | 18 | 18 | $32

29 Seventh Ave. S. (bet. Bedford & Morton Sts.), 212-414-0931;
www.mirchiny.com

■ "Hot stuff" awaits at this "different" West Village Indian where "imaginative" street food "not seen" elsewhere is generously spiced for a "mouthwatering", "mouth-tingling" effect; the "modern" look and open kitchen "add a touch of chic", and fired-up fans believe it "blows others away."

Mishima
22 | 13 | 18 | $31

164 Lexington Ave. (bet. 30th & 31st Sts.), 212-532-9596

■ Your "friendly" "neighborhood sushi joint", this Murray Hill Japanese is a "reliable", reasonably priced resource for "large pieces" of "quality fish"; it's a "little secret" that "too many have discovered", so seating is usually "tight", despite the somewhat "roomier" addition upstairs.

Miss Mamie's/Miss Maude's
▽ 22 | 14 | 18 | $21

547 Lenox Ave. (bet. 137th & 138th Sts.), 212-690-3100
366 W. 110th St. (bet. Columbus & Manhattan Aves.), 212-865-6744
www.spoonbreadinc.com

■ "When you're very hungry", these simply charming Harlem sisters (by way of North Carolina) are "just right" for "heavenly", "home-cooked soul food" in "substantial" helpings seldom seen outside of "grandma's kitchen" ("ask for extra napkins"); regulars who "can't get too much" of the "warm" service and "rib-stickin'" eats advise "leave room for dessert."

Miss Saigon
18 | 11 | 16 | $25

1425 Third Ave. (bet. 80th & 81st Sts.), 212-988-8828

☑ The show goes on at this Yorkville "fixture" for "fast", "flavorful" Vietnamese that's a "dependable" choice for a "decent", "fairly priced" performance; the low-budget scenery's "nothing special", so those who "take it out" don't miss much.

Miss Williamsburg Diner ⊭
▽ 20 | 13 | 15 | $33

206 Kent Ave. (bet. Metropolitan Ave. & N. 3rd St.), Brooklyn, 718-963-0802; www.mswilliamsburg.com

☑ Easy to miss given an address on the Williamsburg "fringes", this "beat-up diner" is a "surprise" source of "fresh, imaginative Italian" grub; often "cramped" with "arty" types emitting "too much attitude", it's still an "interesting" experience with "outdoor seating" as a bonus.

Mitali ◐
18 | 12 | 16 | $27

296 Bleecker St. (7th Ave. S.), 212-989-1367
334 E. Sixth St. (bet. 1st & 2nd Aves.), 212-533-2508

☑ Among the "better" bets for "honest Indian" food and "value", these separately managed Village vets are "favorites" when well-spiced "basics" will do; critics contend they're "coasting" when it comes to decor and service, but they go back anyway.

Mix in New York
– | – | – | E

68 W. 58th St. (bet. 5th & 6th Aves.), 212-583-0300

The combination of brilliant chef Alain Ducasse and showman restaurateur Jeffrey Chodorow has produced this exciting Midtown mix of modern French-American cooking (think bison pot-au-feu) and sleek design featuring rose-hued suspended glass panels; foodies who can't swing the gold-plated prices at Ducasse's eponymous eatery will appreciate the more affordable (though still expensive) tabs here.

Mizu Sushi
24 | 17 | 21 | $31

29 E. 20th St. (bet. B'way & Park Ave. S.), 212-505-6688

■ This "spirited" Flatiron Japanese "rocks" with "huge", "delectable rolls" priced for its "twentysomething" clientele; it "outshines the local competition" with "prompt" service and a "hip", "cozy" space, so everyone's "finally finding out about it – unfortunately."

MJ Grill
▽ 22 | 20 | 21 | $41

110 John St. (Cliff St.), 212-346-9848

■ "Same quality, lower price" is the lowdown on this "casual" new MarkJoseph steakhouse "spin-off"; its "slick pub" setup and "well-executed" American menu are a "welcome addition" to the underserved Financial District.

Mocca ⊭
17 | 9 | 16 | $24

1588 Second Ave. (bet. 82nd & 83rd Sts.), 212-734-6470

☑ "Captured in time", this "one-of-a-kind" Yorkville Hungarian doles out "huge" helpings of Budapest's best "old-country" cooking that's "really filling" and "unbelievably cheap"; sure, the room's "shabby" and the "mama" waitresses make you "clean your plate", but that's all "part of the charm."

Moda
▽ 18 | 18 | 16 | $53

Flatotel, 135 W. 52nd St. (bet. 6th & 7th Aves.), 212-887-9880

☑ "One of the hipper" Midtowners, this hotel dining room offers "fine" Med-Italian fare amid "classy", "minimalist decor" that's tailor-made for "pricey" indulgence; phrasemakers who dub it "SoHo North" "can't believe it hasn't caught on", though critics of the "hit-or-miss" menu and service shrug "style isn't enough."

Molyvos

23 | 20 | 20 | $49

871 Seventh Ave. (bet. 55th & 56th Sts.), 212-582-7500; www.molyvos.com
■ Hellenic food with "gusto" that's "handy to Carnegie Hall" attracts "appreciative" crowds to this "lively winner" known for its "terrific", taverna-style dishes, "amiable" Aegean service and "noisy hustle-bustle"; most love the "warm, rustic" atmosphere, but not the "big-fat-Greek-expense-account" prices.

Mombar ⌧

▽ 23 | 20 | 23 | $36

25-22 Steinway St. (bet. 25th & 28th Aves.), Queens, 718-726-2356
■ Mideastern eats get a "big-time upgrading" at this "funky" Astoria Egyptian, a "wonderful", "hand-tiled" "hole-in-the-wall" run by a "super-friendly" chef-owner whose "excellent" specialties run "from the familiar up to the adventurous" on the food pyramid; it's "hard to find", but those who shun the "schlep" are "missing out."

Monkey Bar

19 | 22 | 19 | $53

Elysée Hotel, 60 E. 54th St. (bet. Madison & Park Aves.), 212-838-2600; www.theglaziergroup.com
■ A tribute to a "more glamorous time", this Midtown ode to "old NY" wows with a "well-executed" steakhouse menu "served with flair" in "elegant" art deco digs just off of the swinging bar; though an "expensive date", it's "still a place to be" and seekers of "chic" are bananas about the "retro" atmo.

Monsoon ◗

19 | 14 | 17 | $26

435 Amsterdam Ave. (81st St.), 212-580-8686
■ The "big menu" of "fresh" choices has droves of Upper Westsiders taking shelter at this "solid neighborhood Vietnamese" known for its "exotic" flavors, "fast service" and "reasonable prices"; fans gladly weather the "crowded", "unremarkable" quarters for "everyday" quality they can "count on."

Monster Sushi

17 | 11 | 15 | $28

535 Hudson St. (Charles St.), 646-336-1833
22 W. 46th St. (bet. 5th & 6th Aves.), 212-398-7707 ⌧
158 W. 23rd St. (bet. 6th & 7th Aves.), 212-620-9131
www.monstersushi.com
☑ "They're not kidding" about the "absurdly large" slices of sushi at this "no-nonsense" Japanese trio where a "monster of a deal" helps compensate for "lacking" decor and service; they "fill the bill" for a "bargain binge", but don't expect subtlety, just "super-sized McSushi."

Montparnasse

19 | 19 | 17 | $44

Pickwick Arms, 230 E. 51st St. (bet. 2nd & 3rd Aves.), 212-758-6633; www.montparnasseny.com
■ Paris "without the attitude" is "right under your nose" at this "upbeat" East Side bistro, a "real Frenchie" with "surprisingly good" "traditional" food and a staff "just off an Air France flight"; it's *un peu* "pricey" but "hard to top" for "authenticity", and followers feel it "should be more crowded."

MONTRACHET ⌧

26 | 20 | 24 | $69

239 W. Broadway (bet. Walker & White Sts.), 212-219-2777; www.myriadrestaurantgroup.com
■ "Still up there" with the "heavy hitters", Drew Nieporent's TriBeCa French "stalwart" works "magic" matching "phenomenal food", "exceptional wines" and "top-notch" service; compared to the normal high prices, Friday's $20 prix fixe lunch remains an "incredible deal", and despite snipes that the "outdated" decor is "beyond shabby chic", those who "go there to eat" are in for a "special treat."

Moran's Chelsea
18 | 19 | 20 | $42

146 10th Ave. (19th St.), 212-627-3030; www.moransny.com

☑ "You don't have to be Irish" to appreciate this midpriced Chelsea "period piece", an outpost of "hospitality" sparkling with "Tiffany lamps, Waterford crystal" and "blazing" fireplaces; the "basic" steak-and-seafood menu is "decent" enough, but it's the auld "ambiance that can't be beat."

Morrells
∇ 25 | 26 | 25 | $55

900 Broadway (bet. 19th & 20th Sts.), 212-253-0900
1 Rockefeller Plaza (on 49th St., bet. 5th & 6th Aves.), 212-262-7700
www.morrellsrestaurant.com

☑ In addition to their casual cafe near the Rock Center skating rink, the famed wine merchants have uncorked this eponymous new Flatiron outpost, an ambitious New American where wine infuses many sauces (and even the desserts); the by-the-glass roster numbers over 150, all stored above the spacious bar and accessed by an overhead catwalk.

Morton's, The Steakhouse ●
23 | 20 | 22 | $61

551 Fifth Ave. (45th St.), 212-972-3315; www.mortons.com

☑ A Chi-town chain "formula that works", this "he-man's steakhouse" draws a "big-boy" crowd that leaves "happily stuffed" with their wallets "empty"; the "business-y", wood-paneled room and "pro service" hold "no surprises", but many wish the "pre-meal", "shrink-wrapped meat parade" would "stay in the Midwest."

Mosto Osteria ●
∇ 19 | 19 | 20 | $30

87 Second Ave. (5th St.), 212-228-9912; www.mostoosteria.com

■ East Villagers make the most of this "friendly standby" for "simple", inexpensive, but "well-prepared Northern Italian" meals; consensus calls the eating "better than you'd expect for the price", and the "enthusiastic" staff is "accommodating", if "eccentric."

Moustache ●⊄
21 | 12 | 15 | $21

265 E. 10th St. (bet. Ave. A & 1st Ave.), 212-228-2022
90 Bedford St. (bet. Barrow & Grove Sts.), 212-229-2220

■ "Plenty of character" keeps these "cozy" Village Mideasterns plenty "packed" with folks lined up for their "signature pita-based pitzas"; even with "looong" waits and hardly a whisker of "elbow room", they're "worth it" for a "satisfying nosh" that "won't break the bank."

Moutarde ●
21 | 21 | 17 | $39

239 Fifth Ave. (Carroll St.), Brooklyn, 718-623-3600

■ Already a "popular" Park Slope "scene", this "pretty" new bistro does "bustling" business whipping up "creative" "country French" cooking "worthy of a more expensive" venue; recalling every Gallic "cliché in the book" – including a "loud", "packed" room and "spotty service" – it still cuts the mustard.

Mr. Chow ●
22 | 20 | 19 | $66

324 E. 57th St. (bet. 1st & 2nd Aves.), 212-751-9030

☑ Get "back to '80s excess" at this East Side "gourmet Chinese" "hyper-scene", a "chic", "art deco stage" for "major stargazing" at an A-list cast that includes "supermodels" and the "who's who of hip-hop"; don't bother ordering since "the waiter will know" what to bring on, but do expect a "way expensive" bill.

Mr. K's
23 | 24 | 25 | $52

570 Lexington Ave. (51st St.), 212-583-1668

■ No one does "glam Chinese" with the "flair" of this "exemplary" Eastsider, ever "on the mark" with "sublime" food to match its "posh", "pretty-in-pink" setting and "very personal" service; granted, the "over-the-top" "pomp" comes at "royal prices", but "if you want pampering, this is the place."

Mughlai ●
19 | 12 | 16 | $30

320 Columbus Ave. (75th St.), 212-724-6363

■ Upper Westsiders who "don't want to travel" for "reliable", cheap Indian fare find it at this "longtime" local "staple"; if the sari atmosphere "lacks authenticity", at least the "broader-than-usual" menu is a "cut above" the competition.

My Most Favorite Dessert Co.
17 | 14 | 14 | $33

120 W. 45th St. (bet. B'way & 6th Ave.), 212-997-5130;
www.mymostfavorite.com

■ Forget the calories and "eat like a kid" at this Theater District kosher emporium where the name suggests the "main focus" and regulars "order accordingly"; the rest of the menu's "passable", but beware of "borderline" service and upside tabs.

Ñ ●⊘
19 | 19 | 17 | $28

33 Crosby St. (bet. Broome & Grand Sts.), 212-219-8856

■ "Squeeze in" for "funky" grazing at this bite-sized bargain SoHo tapas bar, a "top" draw for "sharing portions" of "tasty" Spanish apps chased with "delish sangria"; just think thin, as the "dark", "cool" Latin atmosphere ñ-tices "overspilling" crowds.

Nam
22 | 20 | 19 | $37

110 Reade St. (W. B'way), 212-267-1777

■ "Delighting all the senses" as well as the wallet, this "higher-end Vietnamese" is a "hit" with "trendy" TriBeCans enamored of its "innovative" food, "stylish" environs and "gracious" service; it's "desperately needed" in an area starved for "attitude-free" dining.

Nana ●⊘
▽ 22 | 20 | 18 | $27

155 Fifth Ave. (bet. Lincoln & St. John's Pls.), Brooklyn,
718-230-3749

■ Park Slopers say this new Pan-Asian is an "affordable" "original" thanks to an "inspired" menu ("fabulous sushi") and a "cool industrial" setting that comes with a bonus patio; "growing pains" include "haphazard service", but overall most call it a "winner."

Nanni ⌧
23 | 13 | 23 | $52

146 E. 46th St. (bet. Lexington & 3rd Aves.), 212-697-4161

■ For "old-style" Northern Italian cooking near Grand Central, this old "faithful" "expense-accounter" sets the "gold standard"; even though the "homey" decor may be "showing its age", the staff remains as cordial as ever.

Napa & Sonoma Steak House
▽ 20 | 19 | 16 | $48

15-01 149th St. (15th Ave.), Queens, 718-746-3446;
www.napaandsonoma.net

■ Whitestone's no wine country, but wayfarers still like the looks of this natty chop shop and the taste of its "extensive" lineup of surf 'n' turf; still, some say it will take more "hospitality" to match the "steakhouses of repute."

Naples 45 ⌧
19 | 17 | 18 | $31

MetLife Bldg., 200 Park Ave. (45th St.), 212-972-7001;
www.restaurantassociates.com

■ "Crispy brick-oven pizza" and an affordable range of Italian eats are the draws at this "cavernous" "dining hall" near Grand Central; given the fact that it's as "noisy and hectic" as it is "quick and convenient", the "outdoor" seating can be a real relief.

Nar ⌷

152 Metropolitan Ave. (Berry St.), Brooklyn, 718-599-3027

– | – | – | I

At this new Williamsburg Turkish meze joint, expect cash-only small plates; its low-key space consists of a nosh-and-run bar and a dining room fitted with curved booths for festive, low-budget group gatherings.

Neary's ◑

16 | 12 | 19 | $38

358 E. 57th St. (1st Ave.), 212-751-1434

■ Puckish Jim Neary, the "prince of schmooze", presides with "warmth and cheer" at this "clubby" Irish pub serving "simple", moderately priced American "comfort food"; it's a haunt for "mature" Sutton Place locals who say Jimmy has "more stories than the NY Public Library."

Nebraska Steak House

∇ 20 | 13 | 21 | $48

15 Stone St. (bet. Broad St. & B'way), 212-952-0620 ⌷
566 E. 187th St. (Hoffman St.), Bronx, 718-584-6167

■ Using "old-fashioned" cow sense, this Wall Street yearling and its Bronx offshoot "quietly get the job done" with "huge steaks", a "men's-club feel" and service that "aims to please"; but critics cry "pricey", and even "girl bartenders" can't rescue the rooms' appearance.

Negril ◑

19 | 17 | 17 | $32

70 W. Third St. (bet. La Guardia Pl. & Thompson St.), 212-477-2804
362 W. 23rd St. (bet. 8th & 9th Aves.), 212-807-6411
www.negrilvillage.com

■ "Cool vibes and hot food" sum up these "sassy" Jamaicans, islands of "fine times" fueled by "wicked umbrella drinks" and "killer jerk everything"; the Chelsea cay is "cramped, mon" while the Villager has "lots of room", but "laid-back" service keeps both leisurely.

Nellie's ◑

∇ 18 | 18 | 20 | $37

146 W. Houston St. (MacDougal St.), 212-375-1727

■ "Whoa, Nellie, that's some fine eating" say locals hoarse from "spreading the word" about this Village New American "neighborhood" noshery with "enjoyable" chow and "attentive" service; it's a "comfy" spot to just "lay low" that "more people need to know about."

Nello ◑

19 | 17 | 16 | $65

696 Madison Ave. (bet. 62nd & 63rd Sts.), 212-980-9099

◪ "Definitely a scene", this "lively" East Side Italian scoping spot serves "solid food" to "pretty people" who ignore the "crazy prices" and "Euro attitude" for the chance to sit at "prime sidewalk seats" and watch the svelte "shoppers stroll by" on Madison.

Nëo Sushi ◑

23 | 17 | 18 | $55

2298 Broadway (83rd St.), 212-769-1003; www.neosushi.com

◪ The "next best thing to Nobu" for Upper Westsiders, this "cute" Japanese "reaches new heights" with "exquisite, unusual" sushi that seems "priced by the carat"; still, devotees with "deep pockets" insist it's "worth the cost."

New Green Bo ◑⌷

23 | 6 | 14 | $17

66 Bayard St. (bet. Elizabeth & Mott Sts.), 212-625-2359

◪ Featuring prices and "soup dumplings beyond compare", the "so-tasty" "Shanghai-style" chow at this "hole-in-the-wall" is what C-town is all about; it's "crowded as ever" with the faithful whose idea of "heaven" is to "cram" in, "smile and eat."

New Leaf Cafe

∇ 19 | 24 | 18 | $31

Fort Tryon Park, 1 Margaret Corbin Dr. (190th St.), 212-568-5323; www.nyrp.org

■ It's "hard to find" a more pleasing (or less costly) setting than at this "rustic escape" in Fort Tryon Park, serving "good" New American grub "for a good cause" (Bette Midler's NY Restoration Project, which uses the proceeds for area upkeep); only a "stroll" from the Cloisters, it's blossoming "in all the right directions."

New Lok Kee ●⪥

▽ 21 | 11 | 13 | $21

36-50 Main St. (37th Ave.), Queens, 718-762-6048

◪ This Flushing "reincarnation" of an ex-Chinatowner proves "as tasty as ever", despite its new lok-ation; sure, things can get "crowded" and "noisy", but hey, "you go for the food."

New Pasteur ⪥

20 | 6 | 15 | $16

85 Baxter St. (bet. Bayard & Canal Sts.), 212-608-3656

◼ When on "jury duty", this Chinatown Vietnamese is a "reliable" place to adjourn to for "generous portions" of "awesome, spicy" fare; it "doesn't look like much", but the verdict is it's "authentic" – and "so cheap it's crazy."

Nha Trang

21 | 7 | 14 | $17

87 Baxter St. (bet. Bayard & Canal Sts.), 212-233-5948 ⪥
148 Centre St. (bet. Walker & White Sts.), 212-941-9292

◼ "Don't wait for a jury summons" to try these "popular" Chinatown Vietnamese twins where you can "stuff your face" with "fabulous" food at "amazingly low prices"; no one cares about the "nonexistent" decor and too-fast service since they're among "the best bargains" going.

Nice

20 | 12 | 14 | $25

35 E. Broadway (bet. Catherine & Market Sts.), 212-406-9510

◪ "It really is nice" when the carts roll out "delectable dim sum" at this Chinatown Cantonese chowdown; however, with weekenders competing with "banquet" throngs, this "massive hall" can make even natives "feel like tourists."

Nice Matin ●

▽ 23 | 21 | 19 | $43

201 W. 79th St. (Amsterdam Ave.), 212-873-6423

◼ "So far so good" is the word on this "sophisticated" new French-Med "brasserie", now "charming" Upper Westsiders with a reprise of Paris; perhaps the staff is "still getting its act together", but for most it's a "pleasing" dose of "class" "without attitude."

Nick & Stef's Steakhouse ☒

24 | 20 | 22 | $53

9 Penn Plaza (on 33rd St., bet. 7th & 8th Aves.), 212-563-4444;
www.restaurantassociates.com

◪ To score some "good, hearty" "dry-aged beef" near Madison Square Garden, try this LA-based steakhouse named for owner Joachim Splichal's sons; despite a "somewhat sterile" setting and "scalpers' prices", "pumped" "pre-game" crowds insist it's a "safe bet."

Nick and Toni's Cafe

19 | 15 | 17 | $45

100 W. 67th St. (bet. B'way & Columbus Ave.), 212-496-4000

◪ This Lincoln Center "spin-off" of the "Hamptons classic" plies a "fine", "uncomplicated" Med menu featuring "wood-oven specialties", but it's "priced a bit high" and served a bit low to be more than a "handy way stop."

Nick's

24 | 13 | 16 | $20

1814 Second Ave. (bet. 93rd & 94th Sts.), 212-987-5700
108-26 Ascan Ave. (bet. Austin & Burns Sts.), Queens,
718-263-1126 ⪥

◪ Despite having the standard pizzeria problems when it comes to decor and service, this Forest Hills "brick-oven" original and its new Upper East Side spin-off proffer toppings and "thin crusts" that are "as good as it gets."

Nicola Paone ⊠
▽ 18 | 16 | 22 | $49

207 E. 34th St. (bet. 2nd & 3rd Aves.), 212-889-3239

Murray Hill feels "far from the madding crowd" at this '50s-"vintage" (but 21st century–priced) Tuscan "oasis" where "very traditional" food comes with choice Italian wines; though its "quiet", "old-world" ways seem "tired" to some, chances are "your parents will like it."

Nicola's ◑
23 | 17 | 21 | $55

146 E. 84th St. (Lexington Ave.), 212-249-9850

Regulars rely on this Upper East Side Italian for "solid", "old-style" food and service, knowing that the reception is always "better" for "members of the club"; some suggest a "makeover" to justify the prices, but in the eyes of its "older" admirers who "don't feel like experimenting" it will "never fade."

Niko's Mediterranean Grill ◑
18 | 9 | 15 | $28

2161 Broadway (76th St.), 212-873-7000

A "menu longer than *The Odyssey*" offers "tons" of options at this "lively" West Side Greek-Med where the "diner" ethos extends to "huge portions" and "everyday value"; despite "close" quarters "cluttered" with mementos, the "neighborhood loves it" and the mega-burgers are among NYC's best.

92
15 | 15 | 15 | $42

45 E. 92nd St. (Madison Ave.), 212-828-5300

"Join the locals" at this Carnegie Hill "standby" where "well-heeled" "prepsters" with their "Ralph Lauren kids on parade" convene for "upscale" all-American diner fare; foes find the "easy eating" eroded by "spacey service" and tedious tyke-tolerant turmoil.

Nino's ◑
23 | 19 | 24 | $56

1354 First Ave. (bet. 72nd & 73rd Sts.), 212-988-0002

"They know how to treat people" at this East Side Northern Italian where the "well-dressed" habitués "feel at home" relishing "fabulous" food, "suave" service and a "warm" setting complete with "live piano"; if prices are "first class" too, at least "you get what you pay for."

Nino's Positano
20 | 17 | 19 | $46

890 Second Ave. (bet. 47th & 48th Sts.), 212-355-5540

"Less formal than the Uptown" flagship, this "middle-of-the-road", midpriced Midtowner does Italian "like it's homemade" in "quiet", "accommodating" style, with a $20 prix fixe lunch that's a "real find"; though some say "standard", more say "safe."

Nippon ⊠
▽ 22 | 13 | 19 | $46

155 E. 52nd St. (bet. Lexington & 3rd Aves.), 212-758-0226; www.restaurantnippon.com

There's nothing "neo-fake" about this '63 vintage Midtown Japanese or its "traditional" "fresh, fresh" sushi and soba fare; if it's "looking a little frayed", "business" lunchers still insist it's "worth rediscovering."

Nisos ◑
17 | 17 | 15 | $40

176 Eighth Ave. (19th St.), 646-336-8121

"Simplest is best" on the "decent" Med menu highlighting "fresh fish" at this Chelsea "standby"; though service seems somewhat "uneven" lately, the "breezy" environs with "open-air", "see-and-be-seen" tables make serious staffing superfluous.

NL
▽ 19 | 17 | 19 | $40

169 Sullivan St. (bet. Bleecker & Houston Sts.), 212-387-8801; www.nl-ny.com

Plugging an "unusual niche" with "wonderfully different" food via Holland and Indonesia, this Village Dutch "treat" makes for a "likable change of pace"; though the space may be "cramped", that's outweighed by a staff that is clearly "trying to please."

NOBU
28 | 23 | 24 | $76

105 Hudson St. (Franklin St.), 212-219-0500;
www.myriadrestaurantgroup.com

■ "Taste buds you never knew you had" find their "bliss" at Nobu Matsuhisa's "celeb-jammed" TriBeCa "mecca" where the "ingenious Japanese-Peruvian" cuisine is "high art" and saying "'omakase' is a must" to sample the chef's choice of "mind-blowing" flavors; the "dynamic" David Rockwell–designed space and "sharp" servers are equally rousing, so "hock the grandchildren" and "call way in advance", since the reservation ritual "puts the 'no'" in the name; to avoid the hassle, go for lunch.

NOBU, NEXT DOOR ●⊠
27 | 22 | 23 | $63

105 Hudson St. (bet. Franklin & N. Moore Sts.), 212-334-4445;
www.myriadrestaurantgroup.com

■ Those tired of "praying for" entree to Nobu find a "substitute sent from heaven" in this next-door TriBeCa "crowd-pleaser", which serves "basically the same divine", "pricey" Japanese-Peruvian fare; since "no reservations except for large parties" are taken, "almost everyone can get in" who's willing to wait.

Nocello
22 | 17 | 21 | $43

257 W. 55th St. (bet. B'way & 8th Ave.), 212-713-0224

☑ A "small gem" with a "civilized setting", this "no-surprises" Northern Italian is a "reasonable" option for "solid", "homey" cooking near Carnegie Hall; though "packed" at peak times, it's reliably "genuine."

Noche ⊠
19 | 24 | 18 | $46

1604 Broadway (bet. 48th & 49th Sts.), 212-541-7070

☑ David Emil's "flashy fiesta" in the Theater District salsas to a "different" drummer, serving "pretty decent" New Americana with "funky" Latin accents; the "striking", "multilevel" space, "mean mojitos" and live performances supply enough "sizzle" to make the food almost a "second thought."

NoHo Star ●
18 | 14 | 16 | $28

330 Lafayette St. (Bleecker St.), 212-925-0070; www.nohostar.com

☑ Still twinkling "bright", this "animated", affordable NoHo "standby" offers a "varied" New American–Asian "blend" that's "perennially good" for a "casual" munch or "damn fine brunch"; it's usually a "pleasure", so bear with "loud" acoustics and "distracted" service.

Noodle Pudding ⊅
23 | 17 | 21 | $33

38 Henry St. (bet. Cranberry & Middagh Sts.), Brooklyn,
718-625-3737

■ A "silly name" and "no sign" notwithstanding, this "friendly" Brooklyn Heights Italian is "always busy" with "locals and families" out for a "fabulous" "home-cooked meal away from home"; there's "limited elbow room", but "consistent quality" that "won't break the bank" keeps 'em "smiling."

Norma's
25 | 19 | 21 | $33

Le Parker Meridien, 118 W. 57th St. (6th Ave.), 212-708-7460;
www.leparkermeridien.com

■ "Definitely better than what mom used to make", breakfast reaches "unheard-of heights" at this Midtown American where there are "no wrong choices" on the "heavenly", "calorific" menu; with "friendly" service and "all the little extras", it's "well worth" the difference in price from that of your local coffee shop.

North Square
23 | 20 | 20 | $39

Washington Sq. Hotel, 103 Waverly Pl. (MacDougal St.), 212-254-1200; www.northsquareny.com

■ "Civilized" is the word on this "snug" "hideaway for adults" just off Washington Square, where "creative, upscale" New American food, a "fine wine list" and "aim-to-please" service come at a "really fair" price; it's a "find" with a "great jazz brunch" as a bonus.

Notaro
18 | 14 | 19 | $31

635 Second Ave. (bet. 34th & 35th Sts.), 212-686-3400; www.notaro.com

■ An "underused" Murray Hill "local", this "comfortable", "family-run" Tuscan is "notable" for its "consistently tasty renditions of the standards"; given the "real Italian" hospitality and prix fixe "bargains", it's no wonder cognoscenti "will return."

Novecento ◑
▽ 22 | 18 | 19 | $40

343 W. Broadway (bet. Duane & Worth Sts.), 212-925-4706; www.novecentogroup.com

■ SoHo "trendy" meets "Argentine authentic" at this "carnivore's delight", a "plain" but "cozy" spot to dig into a "fantastic steak" or brunch gaucho-style while chic "shoppers stroll by outside"; the "gorgeous" "international party people" say "see you there."

Novitá
24 | 19 | 22 | $49

102 E. 22nd St. (bet. Lexington Ave. & Park Ave. S.), 212-677-2222

■ The search for "perfect pasta" ends at this Gramercy Park Piedmontese "neighborhood secret" where a "delicious" menu is "served graciously" in a "civilized" subterranean space; for "hassle-free" dining that's "worth the price", most maintain there's "nothing not to like."

Nyonya ◑⇄
23 | 13 | 14 | $20

194 Grand St. (bet. Mott & Mulberry Sts.), 212-334-3669
5323 Eighth Ave. (54th St.), Brooklyn, 718-633-0808

☑ "When your wallet's hurting", these "authentic", "no-nonsense" Chinatown–Sunset Park Malaysians provide relief with "flavorful" food and "rock-bottom pricing"; "packed" quarters, "rushed" service and "lacking" decor are unfortunately part of the "bargain."

Oak Room ⌘
19 | 24 | 21 | $61

Plaza Hotel, 768 Fifth Ave. (59th St.), 212-546-5330; www.fairmont.com

☑ An "establishment tradition" and "quintessential old NY" experience, the Plaza's "dark", oak-lined enclave oozes "staid elegance" from the "formal" service to the "fine steaks and seafood"; sure, it caters to "tourists", pricing is "over the top" and many share that "classic look", but "the show" always goes on, especially in the adjoining Oak Bar.

OCEANA ⌘
27 | 25 | 25 | $72

55 E. 54th St. (bet. Madison & Park Aves.), 212-759-5941; www.oceanarestaurant.com

■ Seafood lovers, "your ship has come in" at this Midtowner where the "across-the-board quality never dips" as "flawless fish" and "white-glove service" make for "top-deck" dining in "elegant, yachtlike" quarters; it remains "at the crest" and "hard to best" for those "willing to pay", and is "even better" on a "corporate-account splurge"; N.B. prix fixe only in the dining room, à la carte in the upstairs bar.

Ocean Grill
23 | 20 | 20 | $47

384 Columbus Ave. (bet. 78th & 79th Sts.), 212-579-2300; www.brguestrestaurants.com

☑ "The bait is great fish" at this West Side seafood house that "packs 'em in" with a "vast array" of "extra-fresh" marine "delights", including a super raw bar; it's a "cheerful" "dating place" but "loud" at "peak hours", so "sit outside" – or learn "sign language."

Ocean Palace ●
21 | 11 | 17 | $24

1414-1418 Ave. U (bet. E. 14th & 15th Sts.), Brooklyn, 718-376-3838

☑ "Why go to Chinatown" to "test your palate" when "it's all here" at this Brooklyn Chinese where the daytime "dim sum is yum-yum" and dinner features a "wide variety" of "authentic Hong Kong" dishes; "don't expect much" by way of decor or service, but no one's complaining when the eating's this "cheap."

Ocean's ●
– | – | – | E

(fka Marylou's)

21 W. Ninth St. (bet. 5th & 6th Aves.), 212-475-1551

Located in the Central Village space that long housed Marylou's, this Rat Pack–style restaurant/lounge offers an upscale New American menu and updates on mid-century cocktails; you can almost see Sinatra holding court in the wood-and-leather library.

Odeon ●
18 | 17 | 18 | $41

145 W. Broadway (bet. Duane & Thomas Sts.), 212-233-0507

■ "hats off to consistency" at this TriBeCan "old faithful" for "solid" French-American "bistro grub" and "all-around good times"; the "retro room's "perennially hip vibe" attracts an "eclectic mix of everybody", who confirm that the fabled late-night scene here "still rocks."

O.G. ●
▽ 22 | 13 | 19 | $31

507 E. Sixth St. (bet. Aves. A & B), 212-477-4649

■ Oh gee, there's "something for everyone" on this East Villager's "creative" menu, a "cool fusion" of "appealing Asian flavors" presented in "dishes suitable for sharing"; it may be a "small", "simple" setup, but it's got "downscale prices" to match.

Ola ☒
▽ 23 | 19 | 18 | $51

304 E. 48th St. (2nd Ave.), 212-759-0590; www.olarestaurant.com

■ "Carb counters' dreams come true" at Douglas Rodriguez's "sassy" UN-area upstart, where "bold" Nuevo Latino cooking with an "Atkins-friendly" twist yields "terrific tapaslike" creations and "mouthwatering seviches"; the decor hasn't changed much from when it was called the Alamo, but it's a "new hot spot" so bring "ola-ta money."

Old Devil Moon
17 | 17 | 15 | $19

511 E. 12th St. (bet. Aves. A & B), 212-475-4357; www.olddevilmoon.com

☑ The East Village's idea of a "hick roadside diner", this Southerner slings "down-home cooking from the heart" amid "astoundingly bad" "back-country kitsch" decor; though "fun" for a "greasy truck-stop" brunch, its "white-trash camp" ethic works best if you're "25 or under."

Old Homestead
22 | 15 | 19 | $56

56 Ninth Ave. (bet. 14th & 15th Sts.), 212-242-9040; www.oldhomesteadsteakhouse.com

☑ "Like going home" for "steak lovers", this circa-1868 Meatpacking District "throwback" upholds its rep with "enormous" cuts of "serious beef" "done right" in a "stodgy men's club setting"; traditionalists think there's "no wonder" that it endures, but modernists yawn it's "way past its prime" and problematically priced.

Old San Juan
▽ 20 | 10 | 17 | $23

765 Ninth Ave. (bet. 51st & 52nd Sts.), 212-262-6761

☑ "Take advantage of the variety" at this "casual" Hell's Kitchen spot where a "super mix of Argentinean and Puerto Rican" chow satisfies "large" appetites "on the cheap"; though service is "irregular" and the "decor isn't much", for that "home-cooked feeling", it "rivals grandma."

Olica ☒

23 22 21 $64

145 E. 50th St. (bet. Lexington & 3rd Aves.), 212-583-0001; www.olicanyc.com

■ A "worthy successor" to Destinée, chef Jean-Yves Schillinger's Midtown French cafe ranks with the "best" for "superb" food enhanced by a "beautiful", "dramatic" room and "pro" service; those in on this "find" admit the "quiet", "formal feel" is best enjoyed with lots of "money" in your pocket.

Oliva ●

▽ 18 12 15 $32

161 E. Houston St. (Allen St.), 212-228-4143; www.olivanyc.com

☑ Boasting a "real Basque kitchen", this "quaint" Lower East Side Spaniard supplies "intriguing" tapas and "delicious" sangria chasers; the "crowded" setup is "chaotic" but "convivial" as boosters bask in a "lo-fi", "hip" milieu "without the attitude."

Olives

22 21 21 $52

W Union Sq., 201 Park Ave. S. (E. 17th St.), 212-353-8345; www.toddenglish.com

■ Yes, they do "interesting things with olives" at this "seductive" Union Square outpost of Todd English's Boston empire, where the Med menu "shines" with "rich", "original combinations that work"; "informed service" and a "sleek" open-kitchen layout add to the "chicness of it all", and the "ever-packed scene" is showing "staying power."

Olive Vine Cafe ⇪

20 12 17 $15

362 15th St. (7th Ave.), Brooklyn, 718-499-0555
81 Seventh Ave. (bet. Berkeley Pl. & Union St.), Brooklyn, 718-622-2626
131 Sixth Ave. (bet. Park & Sterling Pls.), Brooklyn, 718-636-4333

■ Both food and prices "hit the spot" at these "bargain" Park Slope Mideasterners; "dependable" stops for "fast", "simple" eats, like the "fresh pita pizzas", these "serviceable local joints" may be "nothing extraordinary", but sure are "nice in a pinch."

Ollie's ●

16 9 13 $20

2957 Broadway (116th St.), 212-932-3300
2315 Broadway (84th St.), 212-362-3111
1991 Broadway (bet. 67th & 68th Sts.), 212-595-8181
200-B W. 44th St. (bet. B'way & 8th Ave.), 212-921-5988

☑ "Giant bowls of soup" that "cost less than Campbell's" account for the "wild popularity" of this West Side Chinese "noodle chain"; the "supersonic" service and "functional" decor may "lack charm", but delivery arrives "quicker than you can say 'moo shu.'"

O Mai

21 17 17 $35

158 Ninth Ave. (bet. 19th & 20th Sts.), 212-633-0550

■ "No run-of-the-mill Vietnamese", this Chelsea newcomer from the owners of Nam "dares to be special" with "inventive" food and "stylish" if "minimalist" digs; though "crowded" conditions and "spotty" service "diminish the Zen", so far the "happy" throngs sigh "O Mai goodness."

Omen ●

▽ 24 18 21 $48

113 Thompson St. (bet. Prince & Spring Sts.), 212-925-8923

■ "If you're from Kyoto", you'll find "delectable down-home cooking" at this SoHo Japanese standby that serves "artful" cuisine that's a "refreshing change from the sushi houses"; as a "kinesthetic" extra, the "serene" atmosphere "soothes the nerves" just as the food "enlightens the palate."

Omonia Cafe ❷
19 | 14 | 15 | $18

7612-14 Third Ave. (bet. 76th & 77th Sts.), Brooklyn, 718-491-1435
32-20 Broadway (33rd St.), Queens, 718-274-6650
☑ "Forget the calories": "traditional Greek pastries" are the "name of the game" at these Bay Ridge/Astoria coffeehouses, sites of many a "sweet", "self-induced bellyache"; nearly 24/7 availability leads to "late-night reverse dieting", while "erratic" service suits the "cafe lifestyle" of "lingering for hours."

Once Upon a Tart
21 | 13 | 14 | $15

135 Sullivan St. (bet. Houston & Prince Sts.), 212-387-8869;
www.onceuponatart.com
☑ When a "snack" attack strikes, "sweet tooths in SoHo" call this "cute counter-service cafe" "irresistible" for "scrumptious baked goodies" and "fresh" sandwiches; it's also "convenient", though the "tiny" space is "not that wonderful" once the "weekend strollers" roll in.

One C.P.S. ❷
21 | 23 | 21 | $54

Plaza Hotel, 1 Central Park S. (5th Ave. & 59th St.), 212-583-1111;
www.onecps.com
■ One with "class", the Plaza's "stunning" New American brasserie is a "true NY experience", offering "excellent" food and an "amazing space" defined by a "great view of Central Park" and Adam Tihany's "elegant", high-ceilinged design; the "efficient staff" adds to a "polished but comfortable" feel so "sexy" that the outing may "end in a room upstairs."

ONE IF BY LAND, TIBS
24 | 27 | 24 | $71

17 Barrow St. (bet. 7th Ave. S. & W. 4th St.), 212-228-0822;
www.oneifbyland.com
■ Savor the "ultimate romantic night out" at this "dreamy" Village New American set in Aaron Burr's former carriage house, famed for "atmospheric" "candlelit interludes" with "superb food" and "marvelous" service on the side; though you'll be "dropping big bucks", given everything "from the roses to the piano player", it "does wonders" as a casanova's "deal closer."

101 ❷
20 | 17 | 18 | $33

10018 Fourth Ave. (bet. 100th & 101st Sts.), Brooklyn, 718-833-1313
☑ Lots of "local flavor" qualifies this "friendly", easily affordable Bay Ridge Italian–New American as a "definite" for "robust homemade dishes" served straight from "stove to table"; conversationalists "stick to off-peak" hours before the "young crowd" hits the bar and it "gets very noisy."

107 West
16 | 12 | 15 | $25

2787 Broadway (bet. 107th & 108th Sts.), 212-864-1555
811 W. 187th St. (bet. Ft. Washington & Pinehurst Aves.), 212-923-3311
www.107west.com
☑ Though "far from exotic", this "neighborhoody" duo delivers "decent value" and a "dependable" Cajun–Tex-Mex menu that's "welcome" on the "food-barren" stretches of the Upper West Side and Inwood; those who dis the "stark diner" decor say you'd "better carry out."

Onieal's Grand St.
▽ 18 | 20 | 17 | $40

174 Grand St. (bet. Centre & Mulberry Sts.), 212-941-9119; www.onieals.com
■ An "unexpected retreat" on the "outskirts of Little Italy", this New American purveys "surprisingly good" grub in an "old-world" setting embellished by "beautiful mahogany"; though "little known", the "hybrid" of eatery and "energetic bar scene" makes it a "favorite" with local hipsters.

Ony

▽ 19 | 14 | 17 | $22

357 Sixth Ave. (bet. Washington Pl. & W. 4th St.), 212-414-9885 ●
158 W. 72nd St. (bet. B'way & Columbus Ave.), 212-362-3504
www.ony-usa.com
■ "Choose your broth" at this Village noodle dispenser, serving "slurpalicious" "Japanese comfort food" by the bowl in "friendly", stripped-down environs; the "passable sushi" also makes the cut, but it's ony fair to say the "satisfying" soups and "unbelievable value" are the main attractions; P.S. the West Side sibling is new and unrated.

Orbit East Harlem ●

– | – | – | M

2257 First Ave. (116th St.), 212-348-7818; www.orbiteastharlem.com
"Cool and tasty" dining at modest prices wins applause at this Eclectic Harlemite where a globally accented menu harmonizes with live performances and a "funky" yet "understated" space; locals laud it as a "great addition" to a "neighborhood that's definitely changing", while its "sleeper" status means "you can still get in."

Oriental Garden ●

23 | 13 | 15 | $28

14 Elizabeth St. (bet. Bayard & Canal Sts.), 212-619-0085
■ "You can't get fresher fish" than the selection "swimming in tanks" at this "Chinatown seafood favorite" admired for its "impressive variety" and "truly fine" Hong Kong–style preparations including "popular" dim sum; never mind the bright white digs, "jam-packed" tables and brusque service: overall, it's a "cut above" – way above!

Orsay ●

18 | 21 | 17 | $54

1057 Lexington Ave. (75th St.), 212-517-6400
☑ "After a day of shopping", the "elite meet" at this "buzzing" East Side brasserie to "hobnob" over "well-prepared" French cooking in "stylish" environs; you'll pay "top dollar" for "much attitude", but the "chic people scene" is a "movable feast for the eyes."

Orso ●

22 | 17 | 20 | $49

322 W. 46th St. (bet. 8th & 9th Aves.), 212-489-7212; www.orsorestaurant.com
■ "Yup, that's whazhizname" gape "celeb-spotting" gawkers at this Restaurant Row "theater hangout" where mortals "mingle with the stars" over "outstanding" Northern Italian fare in a "warm", "non-fussy" setting; since "popularity" makes reservations "maddening", "call a month ahead" or so – and "keep trying."

Osaka

24 | 18 | 19 | $28

272 Court St. (bet. DeGraw & Kane Sts.), Brooklyn, 718-643-0044
■ Access to the "freshest fish" "without having to cross the bridge" leaves sushiphiles "totally spoiled" at this Cobble Hill Japanese that rolls out "some inventive twists" on its "wide" menu; "fresh air" fans adjourn to the "great garden" to avoid the "rushed" atmosphere inside.

Oscar's

19 | 17 | 18 | $40

Waldorf-Astoria, 570 Lexington Ave. (50th St.), 212-872-4920;
www.waldorfastoria.com
☑ This "comfortable" "all-day dining option" in the tony Waldorf-Astoria is a "hospitable place to meet" for "basic" American brasserie fare that's "good" though a bit "expensive for what it is"; despite a marked improvement in its Food rating, skeptics see a "glorified coffee shop" whose performance doesn't merit any awards yet.

Osteria al Doge ●

20 | 16 | 18 | $44

142 W. 44th St. (bet. B'way & 6th Ave.), 212-944-3643;
www.osteria-doge.com
☑ The "rustic charm" keeps showgoers "coming back" to this midpriced Times Square Northern Italian for a "hearty taste of

Venice"; despite "tight" quarters and a "loud" scene, it "stands out above" many of its "pre- and post-theater" peers.

Osteria del Circo

| 22 | 23 | 21 | $57 |

120 W. 55th St. (bet. 6th & 7th Aves.), 212-265-3636;
www.osteriadelcirco.com

■ Sirio's sons and spouse have their "upbeat" act together at Le Cirque's "whimsical" Midtown spin-off, a culinary carnival serving "imaginative Tuscan" fare in a "delightful" "circuslike setting"; most agree that the Maccioni family tastefully delivers "diverting" dining.

Osteria del Gallo Nero ●

| ▽ 21 | 19 | 20 | $40 |

192 Bleecker St. (bet. MacDougal St. & 6th Ave.), 212-475-2355;
www.galloneronyc.com

■ There's no fiddling around at this "tiny" Village trattoria that "takes you right to Tuscany" with its "great homemade" meals and "wonderful, warm" service; maybe the "cute country decor" attracts "tourists", but most "feel like family" – "it's that kind of place."

Osteria del Sole ●

| 22 | 18 | 20 | $39 |

267 W. Fourth St. (Perry St.), 212-620-6840

■ A "real treat" solely for its "fabulous" Sardinian-style food, this "quaint" West Village Italian adds "fair prices" and "enthusiastic" service to the "bargain"; the "secret's out", however, so try to "beat the crowds" since it can get "loud" and "cramped."

Osteria Laguna ●

| 20 | 17 | 18 | $40 |

209 E. 42nd St. (bet. 2nd & 3rd Aves.), 212-557-0001; www.osteria-laguna.com

■ "Popular with the business crowd" as a "working-lunch staple" near the UN, this "inviting" Italian is "reliable" for "well-executed" Tuscan fare and "pro" service; "bustling" by day, it's "much less crazy" for a "leisurely dinner."

Otabe

| 23 | 21 | 21 | $52 |

68 E. 56th St. (bet. Madison & Park Aves.), 212-223-7575

■ A "traditional" Japanese that's "close to the real thing", this "serene" Midtowner features "first-rate sushi" up front plus "teppan grill specialties" in a handsome back room that "makes Benihana look like McDonald's"; yeasayers call the prices "worth it", but be prepared for "quiet" – it's more "empty" than it deserves to be.

Ota-ya

| ▽ 20 | 17 | 21 | $33 |

1572 Second Ave. (bet. 81st & 82nd Sts.), 212-988-1188

■ "Better than the usual midrange Japanese", this Upper Eastsider serves as a good "neighborhood sushi" source offering a "varied" menu and "more-than-attentive" service but thankfully modest prices; as a "relative unknown", it's also "not as crowded" as the bigger names.

Otto ●

| 20 | 19 | 18 | $34 |

(fka Clementine)

1 Fifth Ave. (8th St.), 212-995-9559; www.ottopizzeria.com

■ "Star power" lures the "masses" to Batali and Bastianich's new Village "train station" simulation where the front bar boasts an "endless" Italian wine list and the rear is a "gourmet" pizzeria; despite "deafening" acoustics and "ridiculous" waits, it's the kind of place that "everybody otto go to" – at least once.

OUEST

| 25 | 22 | 22 | $57 |

2315 Broadway (bet. 83rd & 84th Sts.), 212-580-8700; www.ouestny.com

■ "Everyone raves" about chef Tom Valenti's "divine" New American menu at this solid "gold standard" that's generally considered to be the "cream of the Upper West Side crop"; done up in "men's club leather" with "cozy circular booths", it's a "destination" for both "celebs" and locals who revel in its "restaurant-as-theater" air; in short, "Ouestward go."

Our Place
22 | 17 | 21 | $31

141 E. 55th St. (bet. Lexington & 3rd Aves.), 212-753-3900
1444 Third Ave. (82nd St.), 212-288-4888
■ "A cut above" the "run-of-the-mill C-town" joints, this "civilized" East Side duo offers "tasty" Chinese cooking along with a "gracious" staff; regulars are thrilled that the Uptown branch has been "recently renovated", even if "higher-than-normal tabs" are the trade-off.

Outback Steakhouse
15 | 12 | 15 | $31

919 Third Ave. (enter on 56th St., bet. 2nd & 3rd Aves.), 212-935-6400
60 W. 23rd St. (6th Ave.), 212-989-3122
1475 86th St. (15th Ave.), Brooklyn, 718-837-7200
Bay Terrace, 23-48 Bell Blvd. (26th Ave.), Queens, 718-819-0908
Queens Pl., 88-01 Queens Blvd. (56th Ave.), Queens, 718-760-7200
www.outbacksteakhouse.com
☑ To "feel like a tourist again", try these "formulaic" chain steakhouses that are often "jammed" despite "cloying Aussie lingo" on the menu, "overly spiced" chops on the plate and "been-in-one, been-in-them-all" atmospheres; diehards say the "bloomin' onion appetizer is obligatory."

Oyster Bar ⊠
20 | 16 | 14 | $43

Grand Central, lower level (42nd St. & Vanderbilt Ave.), 212-490-6650;
www.oysterbarny.com
☑ This Grand Central "grande dame" is famed for serving reasonably priced "fresh seafood without pomp and circumstance"; sure, it's "as loud as a nightclub" and service can be "as cold as the fish", but just "stick to the counter" and "focus on the raw oysters" and pan roasts and "you'll be very happy" at this "quintessential NY experience"; P.S. check out the white wines.

Oyster Bar at the Plaza ●
18 | 17 | 17 | $49

Plaza Hotel, 768 Fifth Ave. (enter on 58th St., bet. 5th & 6th Aves.),
212-546-5340; www.fairmont.com
☑ A "surprisingly good" "tourist landmark", this Plaza Hotel seafooder offers "delicious oysters on the half shell" and other deep-sea dishes in a faux seaside pub setting; though some say it's "too expensive for what it is", it's hard to put a price on "classic NY style."

Oznot's Dish ●
21 | 19 | 18 | $31

79 Berry St. (N. Ninth St.), Brooklyn, 718-599-6596
■ For a "novel twist" on Med/Mideastern cooking, check out this Williamsburg cafe where the "creative" dishes arrive in "abundant", "affordable" portions; an "innovative wine list", "funky garden" and a "steal" of a brunch compensate for the somewhat "spotty" service.

Pad Thai
19 | 14 | 17 | $24

114 Eighth Ave. (bet. 15th & 16th Sts.), 212-691-6226
■ Strictly a "neighborhood favorite", this Chelsea Thai supplies "reliable" "Americanized food" at a "moderate price", making the "less than exciting" setting easier to swallow; though it "tends to be crowded", service here is usually "cordial" and "fast."

Paladar ⇗
20 | 16 | 16 | $30

161 Ludlow St. (bet. Houston & Stanton Sts.), 212-473-3535; www.paladar.ws
■ After several mojitos, "twentysomething" "bargain-hunters" scream "*dios mio*" about chef Aaron Sanchez's "fresh", cheap Nuevo Latino eats at this "festive" Lower Eastsider; just be prepared for staffers who are "biding their time till their next modeling job comes through."

PALM

24 | 16 | 20 | $59

837 Second Ave. (bet. 44th & 45th Sts.), 212-687-2953 ⊠
840 Second Ave. (bet. 44th & 45th Sts.), 212-697-5198
250 W. 50th St. (bet. B'way & 8th Ave.), 212-333-7256 ☾
www.thepalm.com

☑ "Go hungry and rich" to this "old-fashioned" East Side chop shop (and its two siblings), a "classic joint" where theatrically "grumpy" waiters dish out "man-size portions of beef" in a "sawdust" and "celebrity caricature"–laden space that's as "loud as the floor of the NYSE"; though some say it's "not like the old days", diehards insist this is "still the granddaddy of NY steakhouses."

Palm Court

21 | 27 | 22 | $57

Plaza Hotel, 768 Fifth Ave. (Central Park S. & 59th St.), 212-546-5350; www.fairmont.com

■ "Eloise would still be content" having a "lavish" ("wear your pearls") Sunday brunch under the palms in this "palatial" Plaza space that's almost "like being in the movies"; though the British high tea is veddy "high priced", the experience remains "charming, even for natives."

Pamir

20 | 16 | 20 | $32

1437 Second Ave. (bet. 74th & 75th Sts.), 212-734-3791

■ It's "like being in Kabul – the good side of town" – at this East Side Afghan where the "fab kebabs" make for "awesome" dining; hanging "carpets muffle the sound so you can actually have a conversation" in the "cavelike", "relaxed" room.

Pampa ⊅

22 | 16 | 17 | $32

768 Amsterdam Ave. (bet. 97th & 98th Sts.), 212-865-2929; www.pamparestaurant.com

☑ "Juicy, flavorful steaks" are "grilled to perfection" at this Upper West Side Argentinean, a "meat eater's delight" priced for those on "burger budgets"; while the crowds and "arrogant waiters" are turnoffs, it's a natural when you're yearning for "real gaucho food."

Pampano

▽ 25 | 25 | 23 | $52

209 E. 49th St. (bet. 2nd & 3rd Aves.), 212-751-4545

■ Co-owner Placido Domingo gets a standing ovation for this "pretty", if "pricey", Midtown newcomer purveying self-described 'modern Mexican seafood'; it's the tenor's third try in this spot, and now as before, the "amazing" skylit upstairs dining room is the place to be; with ratings like these, it's worth a visit on his public's part.

Pam Real Thai Food ⊅

▽ 23 | 7 | 19 | $18

404 W. 49th St. (bet. 9th & 10th Aves.), 212-333-7500

■ "BYOB and an appetite" to this Theater District Thai dishing out "simple, authentic" chow; maybe the "waiting room" decor "looks cheap", but the food "tastes and costs like Bangkok."

Panino'teca 275 ⊅

22 | 19 | 20 | $18

275 Smith St. (bet. DeGraw & Sackett Sts.), Brooklyn, 718-237-2728

■ "Light", "lovely" and "relaxing", this Italian sandwich supplier draws Carroll Gardens locals craving "affordable", "delicious panini" and "solid wines"; expect a "distinctly hip yet baby-friendly" ambiance, the "naked lady" artwork on the bar notwithstanding.

Pão!

▽ 19 | 14 | 20 | $37

322 Spring St. (Greenwich St.), 212-334-5464; www.paony.com

☑ There's "nothing fancy or pretentious" going on at this "Portuguese comfort food" purveyor on the western "outskirts of SoHo", just "authentic" eats and an "attentive" staff; to avoid the "shabby looks", dine alfresco and make friends with the "bikers at the bar next door."

Paola's
22 | 18 | 20 | $48

245 E. 84th St. (bet. 2nd & 3rd Aves.), 212-794-1890

■ Fans of Paola (that's everyone who knows her) and her "unusual homemade pastas" consider this "mildly elegant" East Side Italian standby a "romantic" favorite thanks to "lighting that makes everyone look good"; despite scattered gripes, the consistent "excellence of the food" keeps the trade brisk.

Papaya King ⇄
20 | 3 | 10 | $6

179 E. 86th St. (3rd Ave.), 212-369-0648 ●
121 W. 125th St. (bet. Lenox & 7th Aves.), 212-665-5732
www.papayaking.com

■ "Real meals for less than $5" draw "all walks of life" to these strictly stand-up wiener wonderlands well known for their "hot diggity dogs" and "fab fruit drinks"; sure, they may be "short on ambiance" (unless layers of grease count), and service is of the whaddya-want variety, but in a world of "tax hikes" and budget cuts, their prices "can't be beat."

Paper Moon Milano ▣
20 | 18 | 18 | $43

39 E. 58th St. (bet. Madison & Park Aves.), 212-758-8600

◪ "Airy", "stylish" digs and "reliable" Northern Italian cooking make for a "bustling working lunch scene" at this Midtowner that's a "much quieter option" come suppertime; although a few shrug "*comme ci, comme ça*", the clear consensus is "safe bet."

Paradou
· 21 | 17 | 17 | $34

8 Little W. 12th St. (bet. Greenwich & Washington Sts.), 212-463-8345
426A Seventh Ave. (bet. 14th & 15th Sts.), Brooklyn, 718-499-5557
www.paradounyc.com

■ "Strong word of mouth" keeps this Meatpacking District French cafe hopping with fans touting its "awesome grilled sandwiches", "full-bodied wines" and "especially nice back garden" – the "surly staff whose love you have to earn" is another story; N.B. the Park Slope outpost is new and unrated.

Paris Commune
19 | 18 | 18 | $32

411 Bleecker St. (bet. Bank & W. 11th Sts.), 212-929-0509

■ Known for its "reliable brunch" and "long weekend waits", this "cozy" West Village Franco-American attracts a "decidedly non-proletarian" crowd ("handsome gay men", "models galore"); though a tad "tired" and "oddly forgotten at dinnertime", it's "so much better since the smoking law" went into effect.

Parish & Co. ●
∇ 19 | 18 | 21 | $41

202 Ninth Ave. (22nd St.), 212-414-4988; www.parishandco.com

■ "Picky eaters with eclectic tastes" prefer this Chelsea New American neophyte for its "unconventional menu" that offers a "choice of portion size"; the "thumping bass beat" may attract brickbats, but its "comfy" environs and "well-informed service" draw applause.

Park, The ●
15 | 24 | 14 | $45

118 10th Ave. (bet. 17th & 18th Sts.), 212-352-3313; www.theparknyc.com

◪ "Trendy to a fault", this West Chelsea Med has eye-popping decor that includes spectacular gardens and even "hot tubs", plus a crowd of "wanna-bes and used-to-bes" who "think they're on *Sex and the City*"; P.S. the Food and Service ratings speak for themselves.

Park Avalon ●
20 | 21 | 19 | $41

225 Park Ave. S. (bet. 18th & 19th Sts.), 212-533-2500;
www.brguestrestaurants.com

■ "Romance is in the air" at this "vibrant" Flatiron New American where an abundance of "candles sets the perfect mood" and the "food never fails"; regulars report it's "not as expensive as it looks" and is "still cool after all these years", an "accomplishment in itself"; P.S. "don't miss the Sunday jazz brunch."

Park Avenue Cafe

25 | 22 | 23 | $63

100 E. 63rd St. (bet. Lexington & Park Aves.), 212-644-1900; www.parkavenuecafe.com

■ "Still pushing the boundaries of the 'New' in New American", this "first-class" Midtowner showcases chef Neil Murphy's "sumptuous" food, starting with a "habit-forming bread basket"; the "Americana decor" and "staff that's able to explain every morsel" add to the "warm", "comfortable" vibe that's only jarred by "Park Avenue prices."

Park Bistro

20 | 17 | 19 | $49

414 Park Ave. S. (bet. 28th & 29th Sts.), 212-689-1360

☑ Fans find this "old-fashioned" Gramercy bistro "as good as ever", touting its "French soul food" and "ever-present owner" who "keeps standards high"; though a few fret it's "frayed around the banquettes", the "cacophonous" acoustics suggest it's as popular as ever.

Park Place

▽ 20 | 17 | 20 | $33

5816 Mosholu Ave. (Broadway), Bronx, 718-548-0977

■ "In a neighborhood without many decent restaurants", this Riverdale Continental near Van Cortlandt Park "never disappoints", offering "Manhattan quality" at good Bronx prices; if a few feel it's "losing focus", the "packed" main room doesn't show it.

Park Side ◑

24 | 20 | 21 | $42

107-01 Corona Ave. (51st Ave.), Queens, 718-271-9321; www.parksiderestaurant.com

■ "They come from miles around" to this "excellent, unashamed" "old-school" Corona Italian making reservations hard to get on weekends; the "waiters wear tuxes", the crowd's right out of a "Scorsese flick" and after dinner you can "watch bocce ball across the street."

Parma ◑

21 | 15 | 22 | $50

1404 Third Ave. (bet. 79th & 80th Sts.), 212-535-3520

☑ Think "country club" to get an idea of the atmosphere at this "old-fashioned" East Side Northern Italian where "the regulars all know each other" and the staff in turn "treats them all like kings"; it might be time to "update the decor", but fortunately, there's no need to tinker with the "*delicioso*", "home-cooked" food.

Parsonage

▽ 21 | 21 | 20 | $45

74 Arthur Kill Rd. (Clarke Ave.), Staten Island, 718-351-7879

☑ You'll "forget you're in Staten Island" at this Richmondtown Continental where the "colonial" setting is brought up to date by the more "modern fare"; while some warn "don't set your expectations too high", most agree that "history is worth repeating" here.

Pascalou

20 | 13 | 17 | $38

1308 Madison Ave. (bet. 92nd & 93rd Sts.), 212-534-7522

☑ "Imaginative" "French home cooking" and a "terrific early-bird" draw bargain-hunters to this "feels-like-Paris" bistro "near Museum Mile"; it "helps to be slim" to fit into the ultra-"tiny" setup, but it's "hard to stay that way" given the "great meals" served.

Pasha

21 | 19 | 18 | $37

70 W. 71st St. (bet. Columbus Ave. & CPW), 212-579-8751; www.pashanewyork.com

■ There's "romance for the budget conscious" at this "exotic" West Side Turk where one can dine on "flavorful" food in a "sumptuous" setting right out of "Istanbul" "without emptying your wallet"; it's an agreeable "change from the usual", especially for those who are Lincoln Center bound.

Pasticcio
∇ 18 | 16 | 18 | $32

447 Third Ave. (bet. 30th & 31st Sts.), 212-679-2551; www.pasticcionyc.com

☑ The quality's "consistent" even if the "menu's a little predictable" at this Murray Hill Italian that's been offering "great value" for nearly 25 years; some squawk the kitchen's "uneven", but most surveyors report having a "pleasant enough" time.

Pastis ●
20 | 21 | 16 | $41

9 Ninth Ave. (Little W. 12th St.), 212-929-4844; www.pastisny.com

■ "When you want to be trendy", try Keith McNally's Meatpacking District French bistro that gets its "buzz" from a mix of "pretty young things", "Page Six" names, "hipsters" and "hangers-on", not to mention "beautiful" staffers who tend to "forget you exist"; still, the food's "solid" and the faux "bohemian" setting's "fabulous", so settle back and "get ready to make friends – they pack in as many tables as possible."

Patio Dining
∇ 21 | 15 | 17 | $40

31 Second Ave. (bet. 1st & 2nd Sts.), 212-460-9171

■ Formerly Mugsy's Chow Chow, this "funky" East Village Med offers a daily-changing, midpriced menu featuring "fresher than fresh" ingredients, best enjoyed in warm weather in its "namesake setting"; a chef change has some asking "what happens now?"

Patois
21 | 17 | 18 | $37

255 Smith St. (bet. DeGraw & Douglass Sts.), Brooklyn, 718-855-1535

■ Experience the "City of Lights", Carroll Gardens–style at this French bistro "standard" that "started the Smith Street craze" and "still anchors" the scene; devotees delight in its "delicious" food and "lively ambiance" as well as the "toasty fireplace" and cute "little patio."

Patria
24 | 22 | 21 | $57

250 Park Ave. S. (20th St.), 212-777-6211

■ "Still the king of Nuevo Latino" cooking, Phil Suarez's "happening" Flatiron "multilevel spot" draws a "snazzy crowd" with food that's "beautiful to look at and wonderful to eat"; sure, it's "loud" and a "little pricey", but the payoff's "experimental", "never boring" chow that will sure "wake up those taste buds."

Patroon ⊠
21 | 20 | 22 | $62

160 E. 46th St. (bet. Lexington & 3rd Aves.), 212-883-7373

■ "More than a steakhouse" now, Ken Aretsky's "elegant" duplex Midtowner has rejiggered its menu to add more New American dishes and has also opened a rooftop terrace for the legal smoking of stogies; its "power broker", "boys' club" followers admit "deep pockets" are a necessity, but insist it's "worth it" for the "sophistication" alone.

Patsy's
20 | 15 | 19 | $43

236 W. 56th St. (bet. B'way & 8th Ave.), 212-247-3491; www.patsys.com

☑ "Sinatra tributes" abound at this "venerable" Southern Italian standby near Carnegie Hall that was an erstwhile "favorite" of the Chairman of the Board; today, surveyors are split, with most considering it a shrine to "fine red-sauce" cooking, though a few foes find it "inconsistent" and "past its prime."

Patsy's Pizzeria
21 | 12 | 15 | $22

206 E. 60th St. (bet. 2nd & 3rd Aves.), 212-688-9707
2287-91 First Ave. (bet. 117th & 118th Sts.), 212-534-9783 ⇗

(continued)

(continued)
Patsy's Pizzeria
1312 Second Ave. (69th St.), 212-639-1000 ⊐
509 Third Ave. (bet. 34th & 35th Sts.), 212-689-7500 ⊐
61 W. 74th St. (bet. Columbus Ave. & CPW), 212-579-3000 ⊐
318 W. 23rd St. (bet. 8th & 9th Aves.), 646-486-7400 ⊐
67 University Pl. (bet. 10th & 11th Sts.), 212-533-3500 ⊐
■ For a "full-bodied" pizza with a crust "so thin you can almost see through it", check out these "classic", all-over-town pie palaces, especially the separately owned East Harlem branch that's "the best" of the bunch and maybe the best in town; the trade-offs are predictable: "gruff service" and "step-below-a-diner decor."

Paul & Jimmy's
| 19 | 17 | 21 | $39 |

123 E. 18th St. (bet. Irving Pl. & Park Ave. S.), 212-475-9540
■ At this "traditional" Gramercy "old-timer", you "feel like family" over meals reminiscent of "going to your Italian grandma's" for dinner; "neighborhood" types tout the "reasonable prices" and "accommodating" service, even though it's a bit "unexciting."

Payard Bistro 🗗
| 24 | 21 | 18 | $50 |

1032 Lexington Ave. (bet. 73rd & 74th Sts.), 212-717-5252; www.payard.com
■ François Payard's "art-on-a-plate" pastries are "almost too beautiful to eat" at his eponymous East Side split-level patisserie/bistro where the impatient "start with dessert and work backwards" to his partner Phillipe Bertineau's "savory" entrees; sure, service can be "churlish" and you may need "two credit cards", but for those who can remember, this is better than Schrafft's or Sherry's were on their best days.

Peanut Butter & Co.
| 20 | 12 | 14 | $12 |

240 Sullivan St. (bet. Bleecker & W. 3rd Sts.), 212-677-3995; www.ilovepeanutbutter.com
■ To "channel your childhood", try this "novelty" Villager that serves "retro sandwiches", specializing in variations on a peanut-butter theme; though this "wacky", "only-in-NY" experiment is surely "more inventive than what mom used to make", "slow" service drags it down.

PEARL OYSTER BAR 🗗
| 27 | 14 | 20 | $37 |

18 Cornelia St. (bet. Bleecker & W. 4th Sts.), 212-691-8211; www.pearloysterbar.com
■ "You can almost hear the ocean roar" at this "spartan", low-budget Village "clam shack" where chef Rebecca Charles provides "perfection on the half shell" along with maybe the "best lobster roll south of Cape Cod"; fortunately, the call for "more seats" has been answered – they've just "doubled their seating capacity" – but you can still expect to "stand in line" for the chance to "die and go to chowder heaven."

Pearl Room
| ∇ 21 | 21 | 20 | $43 |

8201 Third Ave. (82nd St.), Brooklyn, 718-833-6666
■ "Bay Ridge's version of sophistication" is yours at this "pretty" neighborhood seafood room that supplies "special evenings" with the "freshest fish", "delightfully prepared"; "friendly" service and a "beautiful garden" net schools of customers.

Pearson's Texas BBQ ⊐
| 22 | 6 | 14 | $19 |

Legends Sports Bar & Grill, 71-04 35th Ave. (bet. 71st & 72nd Sts.), Queens, 718-779-7715
170 E. 81st St. (bet. Lexington & 3rd Aves.), 212-288-2700
■ "Worth the trek" to the "middle of nowhere" – the "back of an old-man bar" in Jackson Heights – this "close-to-perfect" Texas BBQ specialist dishes out "tender, juicy" ribs and "excellent sides"; while the food and prices "meet Southern-boy standards", the trade-offs

are "no decor" or service; P.S. an Upper East Side outpost is in the works at press time.

Peasant
22 | 20 | 18 | $47

194 Elizabeth St. (bet. Prince & Spring Sts.), 212-965-9511

■ "Plates are simple but big on flavor" at this "stylish" NoLita Italian where the room's "medieval" air complements the "pleasant" peasant food "cooked over a wood fire"; though the Italian-language menu may be "indecipherable", that's definitely not the case when it comes to the "hefty" tabs.

Peep
21 | 21 | 17 | $31

(fka Quilty's)

177 Prince St. (bet. Sullivan & Thompson Sts.), 212-254-7337

■ For a dose of "Downtown energy", check out SoHo's "trendy" new "restaurant du jour", a "nightclub"-like Thai whose "pink neon" looks nearly overwhelm the "affordable", "tasty" chow; it's already famous for its "peekaboo bathrooms" equipped with "two-way mirrors" – "you can see the dining room", but "they can't see you" – you hope!

Peking Duck House
22 | 16 | 16 | $32

28 Mott St. (bet. Chatham Sq. & Pell St.), 212-227-1810

■ The "awesome" marquee duck "carved tableside" is the "thing to order" at this cheap Chinatown spot whose "name defines the place"; though the rest of the menu and the "shiny new" decor draw mixed notices, overall it's "much more pleasant" than the competition.

Pelagos
▽ 19 | 15 | 17 | $40

103 W. 77th St. (bet. Amsterdam & Columbus Aves.), 212-579-1112

☒ "For a Milos-type experience without breaking the bank", try this simple new West Side Greek where "fresh fish" is on display, "sold by weight" and then "cooked to perfection"; although much "needs to improve", most "hope they make it."

Pellegrino's ◑
24 | 19 | 22 | $37

138 Mulberry St. (bet. Grand & Hester Sts.), 212-226-3177

■ "Better than most" on Mulberry Street, this "*delicioso*" Italian is "genuinely good", even if the "specials include special pricing"; still, its "friendly crowd", "terrific staff" and "authentic" menu make it a "standout" that any visitor to Little Italy should try.

Penang ◑
18 | 16 | 15 | $28

240 Columbus Ave. (71st St.), 212-769-3988
1596 Second Ave. (83rd St.), 212-585-3838
109 Spring St. (bet. Greene & Mercer Sts.), 212-274-8883
38-04 Prince St. (bet. 38th & 39th Aves.), Queens, 718-321-2078 ⊟

☒ Amid "bamboo and palm frond" "pseudo tiki" decor, a "noisy college crowd" revels in "satisfying" Malaysiana at this widespread chainlet; though the grub may be "far from authentic", it stays "busy" for a reason: it's "cheap, fast and decent."

Pepe ... To Go
21 | 11 | 15 | $19

Grand Central, lower level (42nd St. & Vanderbilt Ave.), 212-867-6054
559 Hudson St. (bet. Perry & W. 11th Sts.), 212-255-2221 ⊟
149 Sullivan St. (bet. Houston & Prince Sts.), 212-677-4555 ⊟
253 10th Ave. (bet. 24th & 25th Sts.), 212-242-6055
200 Smith St. (Baltic St.), Brooklyn, 718-222-8279

■ "Every neighborhood should have one" of these "down-home" Italian "fast-food shacks" serving "heaps" of "above-average eats" "for a song"; given the "grumpy service" and "nothing-to-write-home-about" decor, regulars report "delivery's the way to go."

Pepolino ⬤
24 | 16 | 22 | $43
281 W. Broadway (bet. Canal & Lispenard Sts.), 212-966-9983

■ "Much easier than flying to Florence", this "tiny" Tuscan treasure off Canal Street is a "real surprise find" for "earthy, top-flight" food and "accommodating" service in "cramped" but "charming" digs; no wonder it's "getting noticed, finally."

Perbacco ⬤⇱
▽ 25 | 19 | 21 | $26
234 E. Fourth St. (bet. Aves. A & B), 212-253-2038

☑ "Tasty Italian-style tapas" is yours at this "cozy", inexpensive new East Villager where the "lovingly prepared" tidbits are complemented by a "great by-the-glass wine list"; "waiters who seem to have been in the country for mere months" add to the "old-world charm."

Periyali ⌧
25 | 20 | 23 | $51
35 W. 20th St. (bet. 5th & 6th Aves.), 212-463-7890; www.periyali.com

■ Way "above the usual peasant Greek", this "haute" Flatiron institution's "gold-standard" cooking leaves some asking "could Athens be more delicious?"; ok, it's "not cheap", and "unlike years ago, it now has lots of competition", but its "grown-up" followers say it's "eternally consistent."

Persepolis
18 | 12 | 17 | $32
1423 Second Ave. (bet. 74th & 75th Sts.), 212-535-1100

☑ The "delicious sour cherry rice" (an "Atkins nightmare") is "as bittersweet as ever" at this East Side Persian where the "out-of-the-ordinary" fare comes in "copious" portions; despite a "claustrophobic" setup, it's "affordable" and service comes "with a smile."

Pershing Square
15 | 17 | 15 | $37
90 E. 42nd St. (Park Ave.), 212-286-9600; www.pershingsquare.com

☑ A "great location [opposite Grand Central] but average everything else" sums up this attractive American brasserie where the "not exciting" chow and "fouled-up" service need work; still, fans insist it has "potential", pointing to one of the "best undiscovered breakfasts" in town and a super after-work bar scene.

Pescatore
19 | 15 | 17 | $34
955-957 Second Ave. (bet. 50th & 51st Sts.), 212-752-7151;
www.pescatorerestaurant.com

■ "Always busy and for a good reason" – namely, its "well-executed", seafood-specific Italian menu – this "neighborhood" Midtown "mainstay" also delivers a "solid bang for your buck"; the only drawback is the price of popularity: "noise."

Petaluma ⬤
17 | 15 | 18 | $41
1356 First Ave. (73rd St.), 212-772-8800

■ Though "not the trendy place it once was", this "classy" East Side Italian remains a "neighborhood standard" thanks to its always "enjoyable" food and "comfortable" environs; usually "quiet and relaxing", it gets "really busy when Sotheby's has an auction."

PETER LUGER STEAK HOUSE ⇱
28 | 14 | 20 | $61
178 Broadway (Driggs Ave.), Brooklyn, 718-387-7400;
www.peterluger.com

■ "Nothing compares" to this "grand high poobah" of steakdom, a Williamsburg "temple of testosterone" (and "shrine to Dr. Atkins") that's voted the top chop shop in this *Survey* for the 20th year running; look for a "glorious porterhouse" that you can "cut with a butter knife", "cantankerous" waiters right "out of central casting", German "beer-hall" decor and a "cash-only" policy; in sum, it's "right on the money" when it comes to the "best steak in the known world."

Pete's Downtown

∇ | 18 | 16 | 19 | $39

2 Water St. (Old Fulton St.), Brooklyn, 718-858-3510

◪ A "great bargain (compared to River Cafe across the street)", this red-sauce Italian shares the same "beautiful" waterfront vistas, but offers a more "basic" menu for more "reasonable prices"; although critics consider it "anachronistic", with a little work it could be smokin'.

Pete's Tavern ●

14 | 15 | 15 | $28

129 E. 18th St. (Irving Pl.), 212-473-7676; www.petestavern.com

◪ There's "lots of history" to see at this circa-1864 Gramercy tavern once frequented by O. Henry, though the "food's nothing to write a short story about" anymore; fans stick to "burgers and beers only" since "nostalgia's the best thing on the menu."

Petite Abeille

20 | 13 | 16 | $24

466 Hudson St. (Barrow St.), 212-741-6479
134 W. Broadway (Duane St.), 212-791-1360
107 W. 18th St. (bet. 6th & 7th Aves.), 212-604-9350
400 W. 14th St. (9th Ave.), 212-727-1505 ⊟

■ "Brussels feels a little closer" at these West Side "Belgian comfort food" outlets where "Tintin and Asterix books" are scattered around the "homey", "matchbox-size" setups; expect a "busy", buzzy scene with "simple" fare, "bargain prices" and "cheeky but friendly service."

Petrosino ●⊟

∇ | 21 | 20 | 18 | $42

190 Norfolk St. (Houston St.), 212-673-3773

■ Attractive, "understated" looks and "inventive" Southern Italian cooking make this "sexy" Lower East Side yearling popular with a "hip but not trendy" crowd; although the "service may need a little more work", the "superb wine list" is fine as is.

Petrossian ●

24 | 24 | 24 | $70

182 W. 58th St. (7th Ave.), 212-245-2214; www.petrossian.com

■ For those "who just won the lottery" and have the "big bucks" to "indulge in the caviar-and-champagne lifestyle" in "plush deco" digs, this "decadent" French-Continental near Carnegie Hall is your opportunity; however, thanks to the $20 lunch and $39 dinner prix fixe menus, there's room for bargain-hunters too.

Philip Marie

20 | 17 | 20 | $40

569 Hudson St. (W. 11th St.), 212-242-6200; www.philipmarie.com

■ "Delicious-sounding and even better-tasting entrees" prove that "someone's paying attention in the kitchen" at this "cute" West Village New American; insiders have a "romantic dinner for two" in the downstairs "private wine room" and feel "like movie stars."

Pho Bang

19 | 6 | 13 | $14

6 Chatham Sq. (Mott St.), 212-587-0870
157 Mott St. (bet. Broome & Grand Sts.), 212-966-3797 ⊟
3 Pike St. (bet. Division St. & E. B'way), 212-233-3947 ⊟
82-90 Broadway (Elmhurst Ave.), Queens, 718-205-1500 ⊟
41-07 Kissena Blvd. (Main St.), Queens, 718-939-5520 ⊟

◪ You "can't beat the value" at these Vietnamese noodle shops where "nickels and dimes" buy "high-quality meals" that are "filling but not too heavy"; many judge them "convenient for jury duty" despite the "early Depression" decor and "'yeah, whatever' service."

Phoenix Garden ⊟

23 | 8 | 12 | $27

242 E. 40th St. (bet. 2nd & 3rd Aves.), 212-983-6666

■ "BYOB and be merry" at this Tudor City Cantonese, a "terrific value" provided you overlook the "couldn't-care-less" service and bare brick-walled setting; meanwhile, the "high-quality Cantonese" cooking is good enough for those who remember to say "Chinatown's loss is Midtown's gain."

Pho Viet Huong

19 | 11 | 13 | $20

73 Mulberry St. (bet. Bayard & Canal Sts.), 212-233-8988

❏ "Cult followers" of this Chinatown Vietnamese are bowled over by its "generous" servings of "wonderful" noodle soups and "cheap" tabs; despite having "not much looks" or service, it's popular with "judges and jurors" from the "nearby Foley Square courthouses."

Piadina ●⏱

▽ 20 | 17 | 18 | $30

57 W. 10th St. (bet. 5th & 6th Aves.), 212-460-8017

■ "Romantic candlelight" sets the mood at this "quaint little" West Village Northern Italian with a "hip" quotient that works well for a "first date"; unfortunately, this "hidden treasure" is "no longer a secret" – word's out on how "cozy" and "affordable" it is.

Piccola Venezia

25 | 16 | 22 | $52

42-01 28th Ave. (42nd St.), Queens, 718-721-8470; www.piccola-venezia.com

■ "Everyone's a VIP" at this Astoria Italian where it's "first class all the way" from the "Manhattan-level food" and the "A+ service" to the "pricey-for-the-neighborhood" tabs; though the decor may be "dated", the "large tables and large personalities" occupying them are timeless.

Piccolo Angolo

25 | 13 | 20 | $34

621 Hudson St. (Jane St.), 212-229-9177

■ It's "worth a trip" just to hear owner Renato Migliorini list the specials at this West Village Italian, an "always entertaining" spot serving "rich food" at low prices; just "be prepared to wait for long lines" and brace yourself for a setup so "tight" you can't avoid getting to know the people next to you.

PICHOLINE

27 | 24 | 26 | $74

35 W. 64th St. (bet. B'way & CPW), 212-724-8585

■ For "masterpiece dining" near Lincoln Center, it's tough to top Terry Brennan's "extravagant" French-Med where the food's "inventive without being precious", service "attentive without being smothering" and *fromager* Max McCalman's cheese course is "heaven on a plate"; of course, you should "be prepared to spend big", but after you add in an "opera at the Met, life doesn't get much better."

Pie

21 | 11 | 14 | $11

124 Fourth Ave. (bet. 12th & 13th Sts.), 212-475-4977

■ Some "unique concepts" highlight this new Village pizzeria: the "surfboard"-shaped pies, "innovative" toppings (like bacon and egg), "cutting to order with scissors", "pricing by the pound" and eating at communal tables; the only things that aren't exceptional are the decor and service deficits that typify pizzerias.

Pierre au Tunnel

20 | 17 | 21 | $45

250 W. 47th St. (bet. B'way & 8th Ave.), 212-575-1220; www.pierreautunnel.com

■ "After all these years", this "reliable" Gallic "chestnut" remains a "Theater District standard" for "straightforward bistro" eats; perhaps the decor is getting "tired", but its caring, "old-line French waitresses" and "good value" will never go out of style.

Pietrasanta

20 | 13 | 18 | $32

683 Ninth Ave. (47th St.), 212-265-9471; www.pietrasanta47th.com

■ An "easy walk to the theaters", this Hell's Kitchen Northern Italian dishes out "generous portions" of "zippy" pastas; although "heavy patronage" has left it looking "a little shabby", the "rock-bottom" prices will never wear out their welcome.

Pietro's ⊠   23 | 13 | 21 | $58
232 E. 43rd St. (bet. 2nd & 3rd Aves.), 212-682-9760; www.pietros.com
■ "No longer the secret of the UN set", this "old-fashioned" Grand Central–area Italian steakhouse is "heaven for hearty appetites", turning out "generous" servings and possibly the "best Caesar" in town; sure, the "retro decor" could "stand a spruce-up", but the "precision" service is fine as is.

Pigalle ◑   18 | 18 | 16 | $33
Days Hotel, 790 Eighth Ave. (48th St.), 212-489-2233; www.pigallenyc.com
■ Prepare yourself for a "persuasive Parisian bistro feel" at this "casual" Theater District French best known for its "pleasant, open air" setup, "relative pittance" pricing and 24/7 open-door policy; the grub's "surprisingly good for a Days Hotel restaurant."

Pig Heaven ◑   18 | 14 | 18 | $31
1540 Second Ave. (bet. 80th & 81st Sts.), 212-744-4333
■ Now in its 20th year, this East Side Chinese "keeps reinventing itself" serving "above-average" pork (and non-pork) items "with style"; given its "gracious hostess", "precise service" and decent pricing, most are willing to ignore the "terrible name."

Ping's Seafood ◑   22 | 13 | 15 | $26
22 Mott St. (bet. Bayard & Pell Sts.), 212-602-9988
83-02 Queens Blvd. (Goldsmith St.), Queens, 718-396-1238
◪ The "trademark", live-from-the-tank Hong Kong–style seafood is "divine" at this Chinese duo that also carts out "unsurpassed dim sum"; loyal subjects say the "Queens location is king", though both suffer from "sterile" decor and "stuff-'em-and-shove-'em service."

Pink Tea Cup ◑⊄   20 | 10 | 15 | $20
42 Grove St. (bet. Bedford & Bleecker Sts.), 212-807-6755;
www.thepinkteacup.com
◪ "Everything's fried" at this "funky" little West Villager dishing out "soul food extraordinaire" to "displaced Southerners"; even though it's the size of a "phone booth", the "hangover-cure" cuisine comes at such an "amazing price" that the "weekend lines" are understandable.

Pinocchio   ▽ 23 | 15 | 26 | $41
1748 First Ave. (bet. 90th & 91st Sts.), 212-828-5810
◪ Given the "lovingly prepared" Italian food, "friendly" service and an "owner who makes you feel like a long-lost relative", it's no wonder Eastsiders say this is a real "find"; now if only they'd address that "narrow", "squeezed" space.

Pintaile's Pizza   17 | 6 | 12 | $14
26 E. 91st St. (bet. 5th & Madison Aves.), 212-722-1967
1237 Second Ave. (bet. 64th & 65th Sts.), 212-752-6222
1577 York Ave. (bet. 83rd & 84th Sts.), 212-396-3479
1443 York Ave. (bet. 76th & 77th Sts.), 212-717-4990
◪ "Upper East Side anorexics" are thrilled by these "niche pizzerias", a "change from the usual" owing to their "wafer-thin" crusts and "crazy toppings"; but traditionalists hiss the "girly" pies and suggest having a back-up plan "if you're looking for something filling."

Pioneer   – | – | – | E
1303 Third Ave. (bet. 74th & 75th Sts.), 212-717-6600
If you're game, the daily-changing menu at this new East Side Midwestern meat-and-freshwater-fish specialist has patrons dining

on the likes of antelope, wild boar, pike and trout; to get you in the mood, it's decorated with stuffed animal heads.

Pipa
20 | 23 | 18 | $40

ABC Carpet & Home, 38 E. 19th St. (bet. B'way & Park Ave S.), 212-677-2233

■ "Eat and shop under one roof" (ABC Carpet & Home) at this "destination" Spaniard that looks like "13th-century Segovia" by way of the "*Phantom of the Opera*"; its "young" followers tout its "*delicioso*" tapas and sangria, but note that "tabs run up quite quickly" and wonder what will happen "now that chef Douglas Rodriguez is gone."

Pisticci ⊅
∇ 22 | 21 | 20 | $26

125 La Salle St. (B'way), 212-932-3500

■ It's "worth the trip Uptown" to this new, Columbia-area Southern Italian offering a "carefully chosen menu" at an "unbelievable price"; despite "tight" space and a staff still "working out the kinks", it's a "great addition to a neglected neighborhood."

Pizza 33 ●
22 | 10 | 13 | $9

489 Third Ave. (33rd St.), 212-545-9191

☑ "It ain't much to look at, but the pizza's outstanding" at this Murray Hill brick-oven pie purveyor proffering a "great topping selection" and "unusually crispy, tasty crusts"; it's quite the scene after an "evening on the town" given its "late-night" weekend hours.

Pizzeria Uno Chicago ●
13 | 12 | 13 | $20

432 Columbus Ave. (81st St.), 212-595-4700
220 E. 86th St. (bet. 2nd & 3rd Aves.), 212-472-5656
391 Sixth Ave. (bet. 8th St. & Waverly Pl.), 212-242-5230
South Street Seaport, 89 South St. (Pier 17), 212-791-7999
55 Third Ave. (bet. 10th & 11th Sts.), 212-995-9668
9201 Fourth Ave. (92nd St.), Brooklyn, 718-748-8667
39-02 Bell Blvd. (39th Ave.), Queens, 718-279-4900
107-16 70th Rd. (bet. Austin St. & Queens Blvd.), Queens, 718-793-6700
37-11 35th Ave. (38th St.), Queens, 718-706-8800
www.unos.com

☑ As "chain restaurant food goes", these "low-brow" pizzerias dish out "decent" deep dish pies to "teens" with "coupons"; cynics see "poker lounge" ambiances, "irritable" servers and "sticky tables", and sigh "no wonder it's called the Second City."

P.J. Clarke's ●
16 | 17 | 16 | $31

915 Third Ave. (55th St.), 212-317-1616; www.pjclarkes.com

■ "Finally, the revamp's complete" at this "old faithful", circa-1884 Midtown saloon, but you may not notice since it has the "same great ambiance" and "terrific burgers" abetted by "subtle changes" like "no smoke"; upstairs, there's a brand-new dining room called the Sidecar, which requires reservations when not taken over by private parties.

Place, The
22 | 24 | 22 | $46

310 W. Fourth St. (bet. Bank & W. 12th Sts.), 212-924-2711

■ Take "refuge from the hubbub of the city" at this "sooo romantic" Village Med–New American, a "secret underground spot" enhanced by "twinkling lights" and a fireplace – "if your date doesn't fall in love with you here, forget it."

Plain Canvas
– | – | – | M

406 E. Ninth St. (bet. Ave. A & 1st Ave.), 212-777-2120; www.plaincanvas.com
There's nothing plain about the looks of this small East Village Eclectic, whose shiny op art–style space resembles a high-tech kitchen; the menu truly trots the globe, offering fish balls from Iceland, potato pancakes from Lithuania, curried beef from Bangladesh and a

hamburger from you-know-where; smiling servers skillfully navigate the bi-level digs.

Planet Thailand ●⊟
22 | 20 | 14 | $24

133 N. Seventh St. (bet. Bedford Ave. & Berry St.), Brooklyn, 718-599-5758

■ It "doesn't get any trendier" than this "cavernous" Williamsburg Japanese/Thai "warehouse" offering a "phonebook-size menu" of "delicious", "cheap" eats; more "like a disco than a restaurant", it's so "wildly popular" that it actually "draws reverse commuters."

Pó
25 | 16 | 21 | $45

31 Cornelia St. (bet. Bleecker & W. 4th Sts.), 212-645-2189

■ "No matter who owns" this "charming" Village Italian (formerly the domain of Mario Batali), it "remains delicious", with "earthy, ethereal" meals highlighted by a bargain six-course, $40 tasting menu; granted, it's "no bigger than a good-size closet", but the "big flavors" fully compensate.

Poke
▽ 27 | 11 | 20 | $27

305 E. 85th St. (bet. 1st & 2nd Aves.), 212-249-0569

■ Ok, "atmosphere is severely lacking" at this "tiny" East Side Japanese "hole-in-the-wall", but "what it lacks in size it makes up for" with "positively addictive fresh sushi" and a popular "BYO" policy.

Pomodoro Rosso
22 | 15 | 20 | $34

229 Columbus Ave. (bet. 70th & 71st Sts.), 212-721-3009

■ The line at this Lincoln Center Italian is easily explained: you're instantly transported "to Italy for the price of a meal"; and even though they "don't take reservations", the "dependable" food, "reasonable" prices and "feel-at-home" vibe are "worth the wait."

Pongal
23 | 14 | 12 | $25

110 Lexington Ave. (bet. 27th & 28th Sts.), 212-696-9458

☑ The "most delectable dosas on the planet" are the "must-try" items at this low-budget Curry Hill Vegetarian Indian that not only boasts "inventive flavors" but is "kosher to boot"; given the "unbelievably slow service", you'd best put off going unless you have "lots of time to spare."

Pongsri Thai
20 | 11 | 16 | $25

311 Second Ave. (18th St.), 212-477-2727
244 W. 48th St. (bet. B'way & 8th Ave.), 212-582-3392 ●

☑ These "bargain" Thais draw "melting-pot crowds" with "plentiful" servings of "tasty" chow, in spite of service and decor that leave "much to be desired"; in sum, they're not exactly a "culinary adventure."

Ponticello
▽ 23 | 16 | 20 | $42

46-11 Broadway (bet. 46th & 47th Sts.), Queens, 718-278-4514;
www.ponticelloristorante.com

■ The "food tastes like mama made it" at this "old-fashioned" Astoria Italian where the "efficient" staff also "makes you feel like family"; fortunately, they've just completed renovations, so you no longer have to ignore the decor.

Popover Cafe
17 | 14 | 16 | $23

551 Amsterdam Ave. (bet. 86th & 87th Sts.), 212-595-8555;
www.popovercafe.com

☑ "Popovers as light as clouds" are the draw at this "snuggle"-worthy Upper Westsider, a brunch "institution" so you should "expect long weekend waits"; surveyors split on the "teddy bear decor" ("cute as a button" vs. "sickeningly sweet") but most agree that beside the namesake dish, this "one-trick pony" is "not exceptional."

Porters ◐
▽ 19 | 18 | 19 | $42

216 Seventh Ave. (bet. 22nd & 23rd Sts.), 212-229-2878; www.portersnyc.com
☑ "Why isn't this place busier?" ask fans of this "pleasant" Chelsea Med–New American offering "comforting" food, "well-intentioned" service and "unusual ocean-liner looks"; some point to a "menu without focus" and "not the coolest of crowds" as the answer.

Portofino Grille
19 | 23 | 18 | $42

1162 First Ave. (bet. 63rd & 64th Sts.), 212-832-4141;
www.portofinogrille.com
◼ So authentic that "it feels like you need a passport to eat here", this "charming" East Side Italian is known for its faux "village square" decor with "twinkling stars" on the ceiling – they're "beautiful" to some, "wonderfully tacky" to others.

Positano ◐
▽ 21 | 15 | 19 | $31

122 Mulberry St. (bet. Canal & Hester Sts.), 212-334-9808
◼ For "authentic food in Little Italy", this "cozy staple" supplies "tasty", old-school vittles in a setting that's "fun for tourists", though perhaps not quite ready for *Architectural Digest*; service for the most part is "warm and caring", even if a "smile is not always included."

Post House
24 | 20 | 22 | $64

Lowell Hotel, 28 E. 63rd St. (bet. Madison & Park Aves.), 212-935-2888;
www.theposthouse.com
◼ "More pleasant" than the "testosterone-drenched" competition, this Americana-filled, "woman-friendly" East Side steakhouse rolls out "T-rex-size" hunks of beef and a "serious wine list" in an "elegant but not snobbish" atmosphere (think "Smith & Wollensky without the noise"); like the hotel that houses it, it caters to "old money" types who accept nothing less than across-the-board quality.

Press 195 ⇄
▽ 20 | 13 | 17 | $17

195 Fifth Ave. (bet. Sackett & Union Sts.), Brooklyn, 718-857-1950;
www.press195.com
☑ Wasting away in "paniniville", Park Slope layabouts like this "casual" spot for its "piping hot, crunchy" sandwiches and "huge salads", though some say the pressed items are a tad too "Americanish"; a "cute garden" and "interesting" vinos compensate.

Primavera ◐
24 | 21 | 24 | $63

1578 First Ave. (82nd St.), 212-861-8608; www.primaveranyc.com
◼ "Still primo after all these years", this "classic, classy" Upper East Side Italian led by the ever hospitable Nicola Civetta remains a "solid favorite" thanks to "impeccable" food, "committed waiters" and a "cosmopolitan" ambiance; sure, it's "expensive", but its "mature" following (including the likes of Walter Cronkite, Arthur Schlesinger, etc.) would have it no other way.

Prime Grill
24 | 21 | 19 | $55

60 E. 49th St. (bet. Madison & Park Aves.), 212-692-9292;
www.theprimegrill.com
◼ "So nice you can't tell it's kosher" is the word on this "upscale" Midtown steakhouse (and sushi bar) that "utilizes excellent ingredients and creative cooking" to draw nondenominational "sophisticates"; of course, you pay for it, but "dollar for dollar, it may be the best" of its genre in town and leaves most just "glatt" to have visited.

Primola ◐
23 | 16 | 20 | $54

1226 Second Ave. (bet. 64th & 65th Sts.), 212-758-1775
◼ "Larger than life" owner Giuliano Zuliani "puts on a great show" at this "clubby", expensive East Side Italian where it's "helpful to be a

regular" – otherwise, you'll probably "end up waiting" for everything; payoffs include "excellent" food and "mature" "celeb watching" along the lines of "Woody, Soon-Yi" and "Barbara Walters."

Provence ⬤
22 | 22 | 20 | $52

38 MacDougal St. (Prince St.), 212-475-7500;
www.provence-soho.com
■ "Bringing new meaning to the word 'romantic'", this "sweet" SoHo bistro that "feels like Arles" serves "wonderful" Provençal cuisine in a flower-bedecked front room or out back in its "stunning" year-round garden; devotees say this near "perfect", albeit pricey, experience demonstrates "why you can't stay mad at the French."

Provence en Boite
▽ 22 | 20 | 20 | $36

8303 Third Ave. (bet. 83rd & 84th Sts.), Brooklyn, 718-759-1515;
www.provenceenboite.com
■ "'Bay Ridge' and 'French bistro'" are no longer an "oxymoron" thanks to this modestly priced, "quaint little" Gallic "gem" that also specializes in "beautiful pastries baked on the premises"; fans say there's "no need to go to Paris" when you can "just get on the R train."

Prune
23 | 13 | 19 | $44

54 E. First St. (bet. 1st & 2nd Aves.), 212-677-6221
■ A "foodie's dream", this East Village New American from chef Gabrielle Hamilton sports a "gutsy" "adventure" of a menu served by a quirky "staff eager to share their passion for the food"; the downside is a space so "pocket-sized" that it's comfortable only for "contortionists" or "hipsters without hips."

Pump Energy Food
19 | 5 | 15 | $13

113 E. 31st St. (bet. Lexington Ave. & Park Ave. S.), 212-213-5733 ⬗
31 E. 21st St. (bet. B'way & Park Ave. S.), 212-253-7676
40 W. 55th St. (bet. 5th & 6th Aves.), 212-246-6844 ⬗
112 W. 38th St. (bet. B'way & 6th Ave.), 212-764-2100
www.thepumpenergyfood.com
◩ "Heart-healthy fare" that's "always fresh, never processed" draws "vegan rock stars" and other "neurotic eaters" to these Midtowners that get really busy during "pre–bathing suit season"; critics consider it "short on flavor", with "all the atmosphere of a prison cafeteria."

Punch ⬤
19 | 17 | 18 | $35

913 Broadway (bet. 20th & 21st Sts.), 212-673-6333
◩ Amusing "circus-inspired decor" sets the "whimsical" mood at this "sexy" Flatiron Eclectic where the "clever menu descriptions" are "fun to read" but may need "translation" from your server; although the kitchen is "all over the culinary map", counter-punchers say "nothing really knocks you out" here.

Puttanesca
17 | 14 | 15 | $33

859 Ninth Ave. (56th St.), 212-581-4177; www.puttanesca.com
◩ For "casual dining" convenient to both Lincoln Center and the Theater District, try this Hell's Kitchen Italian that serves "above-average" food at below-average prices; though sometimes "harried" and "noisy", it stays "crowded" for good reason.

Q, a Thai Bistro
20 | 18 | 19 | $33

108-25 Ascan Ave. (bet. Austin & Burns Sts.), Queens,
718-261-6599
■ Radiating "Manhattan-like flair" but not prices, this Forest Hills Thai offers "well-presented food" in an "upscale wanna-be" ambiance; it's "always packed" since the setup's "compact" with "tables on top of each other."

Q 56

▽ 18 | 17 | 19 | $46

Swissôtel-The Drake, 65 E. 56th St. (bet. Madison & Park Aves.), 212-756-3925; www.q56restaurant.com

◨ "Spacious, airy" environs set the "comfortable" mood at this Drake Hotel seafooder that "deserves to be better known"; though some find the "limited menu" too "ho-hum" for the price, its "convenient" Midtown address makes it "good for a business lunch."

Quartino

▽ 20 | 19 | 18 | $31

21-23 Peck Slip (Water St.), 212-349-4433

■ Far "away from everything", this South Street Seaport Ligurian conjures up the "Italian Riviera" with its "relaxed", "rustic" air and affordable, heart-"healthy" cooking (i.e. nothing's fried); a few "wish the portions were larger."

Quatorze Bis

20 | 19 | 19 | $52

323 E. 79th St. (bet. 1st & 2nd Aves.), 212-535-1414

■ "Deservedly popular", this "consistent" East Side French bistro is "better than a visit to Alsace" (and "handier"); the "oh-so-*bonne*" cooking, "mellow" ambiance and pleasing service compensate for "unreal" pricing.

Quattro Gatti

20 | 17 | 20 | $41

205 E. 81st St. (bet. 2nd & 3rd Aves.), 212-570-1073

■ "Leisurely meals" with "treat-you-like-family" service make this "old-line" Upper East Side Italian "feel like home" to many, even if it "could use some renovations"; "there's a reason it's been there forever": supporters say the "food's fantastic."

Queen

24 | 13 | 19 | $37

84 Court St. (bet. Livingston & Schermerhorn Sts.), Brooklyn, 718-596-5955

■ Try not to "kiss the chef" at this Brooklyn Heights Italian where the kitchen is "inventive" yet "unpretentious"; too bad about the "ordinary" "Ramada Inn decor", but "nobody cares when the food and service are this good."

Quercy ⇗

▽ 22 | 16 | 20 | $40

242 Court St. (Baltic St.), Brooklyn, 718-243-2151

■ From the owners of Chelsea's La Lunchonette comes this new Cobble Hill French bistro with a menu that's just as "original and inventive" as its sibling's and decor that's just as "spare"; though the location has a history of "quick turnovers", fans say "this one will last."

Quintessence

17 | 13 | 17 | $25

566 Amsterdam Ave. (bet. 87th & 88th Sts.), 212-501-9700
353 E. 78th St. (bet. 1st & 2nd Aves.), 212-734-0888
263 E. 10th St. (bet. Ave. A & 1st Ave.), 646-654-1823
www.raw-q.com

◨ "Scare your meat-eating friends" at these "live food" outlets where the fare is "all vegetarian" and "all uncooked" – or "cold, wet and raw", depending on your point of view; diehards dub it a "whole new level of healthy", while "once-is-enough" types cite "ditsy service" and "not-so-cheap" tabs.

Rachel's American Bistro

18 | 12 | 17 | $34

608 Ninth Ave. (bet. 43rd & 44th Sts.), 212-957-9050;
www.rachels9thavenue.com

■ "Surprisingly satisfying" meals come at "moderate prices" at this "unassuming" (verging on "shopworn") Theater District New American; just be prepared to "love thy neighbor" – the seating seems calibrated for "sardines."

Radio Perfecto ⏺
16 | 16 | 16 | $2
190 Ave. B (bet. 11th & 12th Sts.), 212-477-3366
■ "Vintage" Bakelite radios set the background for this Alphabet City "comfort food outpost" famed for a rotisserie chicken dinner that "everybody loves"; a "fun garden" and "oh-so-affordable" pricing leave most listeners all "warm and fuzzy."

Rafaella ⏺
21 | – | 20 | $36
384 Bleecker St. (Perry St.), 212-229-9885
■ This Village Northern Italian "treasure" has relocated across the street but still offers plenty of inherent "romantic" possibilities; "reliable", "well-priced" food and "knee-to-knee" seating further embellish its "date place" rep.

Raga
▽ 23 | 16 | 20 | $35
433 E. Sixth St. (bet. Ave. A & 1st Ave.), 212-388-0957
■ For "Uptown sophistication at Downtown prices", try this East Village Indian whose "unusual fusion" cooking ("without the curry overload") sure "beats the other end of Sixth Street"; although many consider it the "poor man's Tabla", some wonder "why it's so empty."

Rain
21 | 20 | 18 | $39
1059 Third Ave. (bet. 62nd & 63rd Sts.), 212-223-3669
100 W. 82nd St. (bet. Amsterdam & Columbus Aves.), 212-501-0776
◪ Still drawing "black-clad" hepcats (and "baseball-capped frat boys"), these Uptown Pan-Asians "haven't lost their touch"; the "different but not too unusual" cuisine is "safe enough for first-timers", while the "happening bar" and "attractive" pricing produce a "noisy", "partylike" scene.

RAINBOW ROOM
20 | 27 | 22 | $82
GE Bldg., 30 Rockefeller Plaza, 65th fl. (bet. 49th & 50th Sts.), 212-632-5100; www.cipriani.com
■ "Art deco lovers' hearts beat faster" at this circa-1934, "top-of-the-world" Italian featuring dancing and magical views 65 stories above Rock Center; though it's "only open on select Fridays and Saturdays" (and for a "wonderful" Sunday brunch), there's an alternative: the serviceable if unsensational Rainbow Grill, just down the hall, open nightly; either way, "bring money, bags of it."

Rao's ☒⋈
21 | 15 | 21 | $57
455 E. 114th St. (Pleasant Ave.), 212-722-6709; www.raos.com
■ "Getting in is next to impossible" at this legendary East Harlem Southern Italian – "unless you know a regular" – but once inside, the select few say the Damon Runyon–esque "environment is everything", from the "homestyle" cooking and the "celebs galore" to Nick the Vest at the bar and owner Franky 'No' Pellegrino's "floor show"; wanna-eats moan it's "easier to dine in the Oval Office" and have to settle for the next best thing: "buying Rao's sauce at Gristede's."

Raoul's ⏺
23 | 20 | 20 | $51
180 Prince St. (bet. Sullivan & Thompson Sts.), 212-966-3518
■ Ok, it "won't be the same without the smoking", but this longtime SoHo French bistro "cornerstone" still has a "sexy throb", luring both the famous and infamous with one of the "best vibes Downtown"; "heavenly steak au poivre" and an "attractive" glass-topped garden don't hurt either.

Rare Bar & Grill
▽ 26 | 16 | 19 | $24
Shelburne Murray Hill Hotel, 303 Lexington Ave. (37th St.), 212-481-1999
■ "Deserted Murray Hill" gets a "dash of style" via this upscale burger palace's pleasantly priced, "perfectly prepared" patties that come

...ings and are served by an "earnest" staff; though ...ther "blah", word is this newcomer's a "winner."

Rasputin
V 22 | 23 | 19 | $63

2670 Coney Island Ave. (Ave. X), Brooklyn, 718-332-8111

■ It helps to take a "liberal approach to vodka" at this "decadent" Brighton Beach Russian cabaret known for its "flashy, trashy" floor show and "dancing" till the wee hours; though its "traditional" fare is surprisingly good, it plays second balalaika to the general "craziness", and if you stay late enough, you can order a second meal – "breakfast."

Raymond's Cafe
V 20 | 16 | 20 | $31

88 Seventh Ave. (bet. 15th & 16th Sts.), 212-929-1778

◪ A "genuine bargain" given its Chelsea locale, this "quiet" American offers a "consistently good" menu with a "clean, light touch"; still, some find the decor "institutional" and the overall package "boring", despite the "friendly professional staff."

Red
17 | 15 | 17 | $32

356 W. 44th St. (bet. 8th & 9th Aves.), 212-445-0131; www.red44th.com

◪ As "affordable theater options go", this Hell's Kitchen New American keeps you "*out* of the red" with its "large portions" of "reliable" bites at "reasonable" tabs; but the somewhat "confused" service and crimson color scheme (like dining "in a blood vessel") draw brickbats.

Red Cat
23 | 19 | 21 | $47

227 10th Ave. (bet. 23rd & 24th Sts.), 212-242-1122;
www.theredcat.com

■ "Just the right balance of serious cooking and boho ambiance" keeps hepcats meowing about this "breezy" West Chelsea Med–New American, a "buzzing", red-"hot scene" that seems to grow more "popular" every year; "country-inn" looks and "purrfect service" make it a favorite "destination après–gallery hopping."

Redeye Grill ☻
21 | 19 | 19 | $49

890 Seventh Ave. (56th St.), 212-541-9000; www.redeyegrill.com

■ "Young, lively" and "popular" as can be, Shelley Fireman's "showy", spacious Midtown New American is a "fine catch" for "excellent" fresh food served to everyone from "tourists" to "business" folk to "singles on the make"; it's famed as the "home of the dancing shrimp" and for its sensational Cobb salad.

Red Garlic ☻
19 | 12 | 16 | $27

916 Eighth Ave. (bet. 54th & 55th Sts.), 212-489-5237; www.redgarlic.com

◪ There's a "superior price-to-quality ratio" at this Hell's Kitchen Thai seafood joint where a pronounced French accent enlivens the "respectable" repasts; still, "inept service", "typical" decor and "small portions" lead some calculators to figure there's "nothing extraordinary" going on here.

Red Snapper
V 18 | 15 | 17 | $28

494 Amsterdam Ave. (84th St.), 212-579-7907

■ "Spicy Thai food at a downright reasonable price" is the recipe for success at this Upper West Side seafooder boasting "prompt" service and "modern" decor bathed in "cool blue lighting"; still, some wonder "why this place isn't more popular."

Regency
V 19 | 20 | 21 | $56

Regency Hotel, 540 Park Ave. (61st St.), 212-339-4050; www.loewshotels.com

■ Offering two lobby restaurants (540 Park and The Library), this Tisch-owned Midtown hotel American is famed for its quintessential "power breakfast scene" that's a magnet for business and political types; after sundown, 540 Park morphs into Feinstein's at the Regency, one of the city's top cabarets.

Regional Thai
19 | 14 | 16 | $26

1479 First Ave. (77th St.), 212-744-6374
208 Seventh Ave. (22nd St.), 212-807-9872 ●
◩ As "cheap and cheerful as they come", this Thai duo is "nothing flashy" but does the job with "authentic" cooking that's a "step above average"; "shabby" looks and "space-cadet" servers are turnoffs.

Relish ●
▽ 20 | 21 | 17 | $27

225 Wythe Ave. (bet. Metropolitan Ave. & N. 3rd St.), Brooklyn, 718-963-4546
■ "Retro cool" is alive and well at this "film noir" Williamsburg American, a stainless-steel diner where "cooler-than-thou" cats come for "couture" comfort food; depending on the season, "hungover hipsters" head for the "velvety" rear lounge or "spectacular" patio.

Remi
23 | 22 | 20 | $52

145 W. 53rd St. (bet. 6th & 7th Aves.), 212-581-4242
■ Only "getting better with age", this stylish Midtown Venetian supplies heavy-duty "event dining" thanks to its "first-rate" fare and "splendid" Adam Tihany decor (highlighted by a "giant mural" of Venice); it's "great for business dinners" and its carry-out satellite, Remi To Go, "can't be beat" for a "quick, excellent lunch"; P.S. check out the "knockout" private-party rooms.

René Pujol ⊠
24 | 21 | 23 | $55

321 W. 51st St. (bet. 8th & 9th Aves.), 212-246-3023
■ For "civilized dining", this "stress-free" Theater District French "mainstay" "still has what it takes": "authentic regional cuisine", "pleasant surroundings" and "waiters who do it right"; sure, it can be "expensive", but its "senior" following says it's "too good to save for special occasions."

Republic
18 | 14 | 15 | $20

37 Union Sq. W. (bet. 16th & 17th Sts.), 212-627-7172; www.thinknoodles.com
■ Picture an "airplane hangar" with "hard bench" seating and "communal tables" to get an idea of this Union Square Pan-Asian where "oodles of noodles" come at "Cup O' Noodles prices"; though the decibel level is not unlike a "NASCAR racetrack", it's worth shouting about if you're "on a budget."

Re Sette
▽ 25 | 23 | 24 | $48

7 W. 45th St. (bet. 5th & 6th Aves.), 212-221-7530
■ As its across-the-board high ratings show, this regal new Midtown Italian lives up to its name (which translates as 'Seven Kings') and offers "lick-the-plate" cuisine from Italy's Barese region, fired up in a wood-burning brick oven; a "warm" private room upstairs with a communal table for up to 32 may convince you to bring your court.

Rhône ●⊠
17 | 20 | 15 | $42

63 Gansevoort St. (bet. Greenwich & Washington Sts.), 212-367-8440; www.rhonenyc.com
◩ Better known as a wine bar, this "trendy" Meatpacking District Franco-American also offers "chic portions" of "decent" chow; though the minimalist decor splits voters – "cool" vs. "cold" – there's agreement on the "high" prices and "iffy" service.

Riazor ●
▽ 17 | 9 | 17 | $26

245 W. 16th St. (bet. 7th & 8th Aves.), 212-727-2132
◩ Chances are you could be the "only non-Spanish speaker" at this *muy* "authentic" Chelsea Spaniard that dishes out "well-seasoned"–

as in garlic laden – chow; granted, this "little backwater" is an "absolute dive", but penny pinchers say you "can't beat the value."

Ribollita
| 19 | 16 | 18 | $37 |

260 Park Ave. S. (bet. 20th & 21st Sts.), 212-982-0975

■ For "unfussy" dining in a high-maintenance neighborhood, this Flatiron Northern Italian offers "wholesome", "medium priced" fare that "should get more press"; since the setup's on the "funky" side, regulars "close their eyes" and channel "Tuscany."

Rice ⊅
| 18 | 14 | 14 | $18 |

227 Mott St. (bet. Prince & Spring Sts.), 212-226-5775 ◑
81 Washington St. (bet. Front & York Sts.), Brooklyn, 718-222-9880
www.riceny.com

☑ "Quick, small meals" come at "bargain-basement" prices at these "thimble-size" NoLita/Dumbo Pan-Asians that are also "geared toward takeout"; critics claim the food's "bland", even if the "menu holds a lot of promise."

Rice Avenue
| – | – | – | M |

72-19 Roosevelt Ave. (bet. 72nd & 73rd Sts.), Queens, 718-803-9001

A spin-off of Manhattan's Spice mini-chain, this new Jackson Heights Thai apes its siblings' minimalist aesthetic with "attractive" yet spare digs that makes it "feel like Manhattan"; in keeping with the local competition, the food's heat level is high and prices are "low" here.

Rice 'n' Beans
| 20 | 7 | 16 | $21 |

744 Ninth Ave. (bet. 50th & 51st Sts.), 212-265-4444;
www.ricenbeansrestaurant.com

☑ There's "good value" to be had at this Midtown Brazilian "hole-in-the-wall" where the "well-prepared peasant food" comes in "plentiful" portions; but if you're "claustrophobic", be ready for "tight" quarters.

Rincón de España
| ▽ 20 | 11 | 17 | $36 |

226 Thompson St. (bet. Bleecker & W. 3rd Sts.), 212-260-4950

■ "Irresistible paella" and "alluring sangria" supply the "robust" notes at this "landmark" Village Spaniard that's been on the scene since 1966 with the same "original owner"; fans overlook its "rundown" looks in exchange for "guitar serenades" and "prices that won't break the bank."

Rio Mar ◑
| 17 | 12 | 17 | $31 |

7 Ninth Ave. (Little W. 12th St.), 212-242-1623

■ "Seedy" and "garlicky" sums up the scene at this "workingman's" Meatpacking District Spaniard, a pleasingly priced, "pre-Pastis" pioneer known for "authentic tapas", "dangerous sangria" and "lots of local color"; sure, it's a "dump", but "hard-core" holdouts "hope it stays around for a long time."

Risotteria
| 21 | 10 | 15 | $21 |

270 Bleecker St. (Morton St.), 212-924-6664; www.risotteria.com

■ "Luxurious comfort food" gets a boost at this low-budget Village "concept" Italian specializing in "dozens of risottos"; most call it a "cute idea", but given the fact that the "rather cramped" space is "nothing to look at", many "opt for home delivery."

Rive Gauche
| 17 | 16 | 14 | $30 |

560 Third Ave. (37th St.), 212-949-5400

☑ "Inside is loud, but outside is comfy" at this "casual" Murray Hill French bistro where the "straightforward", inexpensive food "tastes even better in such a slim-pickings neighborhood"; though foes find "no ooh-la-la" here, realists relish this "poor man's Montparnasse."

River
17 | 17 | 17 | $27 |

345 Amsterdam Ave. (bet. 76th & 77th Sts.), 212-579-1888

☑ A "great tiki interior" augments the low-cost cooking at this Viet-Thai that has the "fastest takeout" on the Upper West Side; critics claim it's "not a force of nature", dubbing it a "less creative version of Rain."

RIVER CAFE
25 | 28 | 24 | $80 |

1 Water St. (bet. Furman & Old Fulton Sts.), Brooklyn, 718-522-5200;
www.rivercafe.com

■ Perhaps the "most romantic spot in (or out of) town", restaurateur Buzzy O'Keeffe's "breathtaking showplace" on the Brooklyn waterfront is best known for its panorama of lower Manhattan, though the spectacular American "food matches the view" and is backed up by a "wine list longer than your SUV"; granted, prices are steep ($70 prix fixe only), but the "cost is justified" for a dining experience "without equal"; for a low-key, lower-priced experience, go for lunch.

rm ☒
24 | 21 | 23 | $72 |

33 E. 60th St. (bet. Madison & Park Aves.), 212-319-3800

■ An "instant success", star chef Rick Moonen's "sublime" East Side seafood yearling is moving "full steam ahead" with a "just-caught" menu reminiscent of his work at "Oceana, only better"; a "stylish" room and "seamless service" help justify the "expensive" tabs; N.B. $58 prix fixe only in the dining room, à la carte available at the bar.

Roberto's
27 | 15 | 19 | $40 |

632 E. 186th St. (Belmont Ave.), Bronx, 718-733-9503

■ There's "no need to look at the menu" at this "unassuming" Bronx Italian – "just put yourself in chef Roberto Paciullo's hands" for an "old-fashioned" "taste of the old country"; it's no surprise, this "tiny" spot is "always jammed", and since "they don't take reservations", regulars "arrive when the doors open" to avoid "long waits."

Roc ◉
22 | 21 | 22 | $50 |

190-A Duane St. (Greenwich St.), 212-625-3333

■ Everything's "top-notch – including the price" – at this "upscale" TriBeCa Italian, a "happening" locus for Downtown types seeking "simple yet creative" food in "hip" yet "appealing" environs; "friendly, knowledgeable service" adds a "welcoming" touch.

Rocco
∇ 20 | 14 | 20 | $30 |

181 Thompson St. (bet. Bleecker & Houston Sts.), 212-677-0590;
www.roccorestaurant.com

■ "Live out that Billy Joel song" at this "unpretentious", "red-sauce" Italian, a "vintage" "blast from the past" that's been on the Village scene since 1922; it "hasn't changed in years, which is good for the food but bad for the decor."

Rocco's 22nd Street
– | – | – | E |

12 E. 22nd St. (bet. B'way & Park Ave. S.), 212-353-0500;
www.roccosrestaurant.com

Thank God the show's over and the hidden microphones are gone now from Rocco DiSpirito's new Flatiron entry, the subject of a TV reality show entitled *The Restaurant*; look for family-affair Italian-American cooking (Rocco's mom, aunt and uncle are all on the payroll) served in slick digs by a staff still trying to get over its 15 minutes of notoriety.

Rock Center Café
18 | 22 | 18 | $42 |

Rockefeller Ctr., 20 W. 50th St. (bet. 5th & 6th Aves.), 212-332-7620;
www.restaurantassociates.com

☑ "Watch the ice skaters" glide by in winter (or "dine outdoors in summer") at this Rockefeller Center American "in the heart of it all" where the "standard" "food takes a backseat to the atmosphere"; it's perfect for a drink after work, if you don't mind "paying for the location."

Rocking Horse
| 22 | 18 | 18 | $34 |

182 Eighth Ave. (bet. 19th & 20th Sts.), 212-463-9511

■ You "can't go wrong with a burrito and a mojito" at this "unwaveringly popular", "upscale" Mexican in "swinging Chelsea"; best known for its "unique south-of-the-border" cuisine and "boisterous bar scene", it also has "festive" mod decor and plenty of "pumped-up hunks."

Rolf's
| 17 | 20 | 14 | $37 |

281 Third Ave. (22nd St.), 212-477-4750

■ "Schnitzel lovers dream about" this "kitschy" Gramercy German where the "heavy", "rib-sticking" preparations arrive in portions so "oversized" that "you'll be eating leftovers for a week"; though service can be "lackadaisical", the place is a "blast at Christmas" when the "over-the-top" decorations transport you to the "North Pole."

Roppongi ❷
| 21 | 16 | 19 | $33 |

434 Amsterdam Ave. (81st St.), 212-362-8182

■ "Move over Haru!" – this across-the-street Japanese has some Westsiders claiming it's "just as good", but "less crowded" and "slightly cheaper" (though some say it's "less glamorous" as well); still, given its "fresh sushi without the frenzy", it "should be more popular."

ROSA MEXICANO
| 22 | 20 | 20 | $46 |

61 Columbus Ave. (62nd St.), 212-977-7700
1063 First Ave. (58th St.), 212-753-7407 ❷
www.rosamexicano.com

■ "Gourmet Mexican isn't an oxymoron" at these "hot spots" famed for guacamole "made fresh at your table" and "stupendous" pomegranate margaritas that knock you under the table; both locations are appealing, except perhaps when it comes time to pay.

Rose Water
| 24 | 19 | 23 | $38 |

787 Union St. (6th Ave.), Brooklyn, 718-783-3800

■ The "seasonal" menu made from "fresh greenmarket" ingredients is "right on the money" at this Park Slope New American; a "surefire crowd-pleaser" that's "inventive without being precious", this place may be on the "small" side, but so are its "Brooklyn prices."

Rossini's ❷
| 22 | 18 | 23 | $51 |

108 E. 38th St. (bet. Lexington & Park Aves.), 212-683-0135

■ "Still ticking", this Murray Hill Northern Italian standby draws a sedate crowd with its tasty, "old-fashioned" menu and tuxedoed, "old-world" service; fans feel like they're "in another world" here – a world where there's peace and "quiet", and weekend "opera singers."

Rothmann's
| 21 | 20 | 21 | $57 |

3 E. 54th St. (bet. 5th & Madison Aves.), 212-319-5500;
www.rothmannssteakhouse.com

☑ One of the newer entrants in "NY's meat wars", this "polished" Midtown chop shop may not enjoy the same "hustle-bustle" as its competitors but does manage to turn out "succulent steaks" for power-lunching "suits" with "big bucks"; still, snipers say this "cookie-cutter" joint is "indistinguishable from dozens of others."

Roth's Westside Steak
| 20 | 17 | 19 | $44 |

680 Columbus Ave. (93rd St.), 212-280-4103;
www.rothswestsidesteakhouse.net

☑ A "live jazz combo plays in the background" as you tuck into "steaks done as they should be" at this Upper West Side steakhouse with a "friendly vibe" and "attentive, not intrusive" service; foes see "nothing special" going on except for tabs "too pricey for the neighborhood."

Roumeli Taverna ❷
▽ 22 | 10 | 18 | $29

33-04 Broadway (33rd St.), Queens, 718-278-1001

☑ You'll "often see the owner cooking" in the open kitchen at this "authentic", underdecorated Hellenic in Astoria, where "good food" at a "good price" retains a loyal following; needless to say, "they're extra nice if you speak Greek."

Route 66 Cafe ❷
17 | 13 | 17 | $21

858 Ninth Ave. (bet. 55th & 56th Sts.), 212-977-7600

■ "Quality diner food" "served fast and on the cheap" sums up the scene at this "low-key" Hell's Kitchen Eclectic "rest stop" with appropriate "road-travel decor"; picky eaters don't "find much to write home about", save the "giant", "unfinishable portions."

Royal Siam
19 | 13 | 19 | $24

240 Eighth Ave. (bet. 22nd & 23rd Sts.), 212-741-1732

■ "Darn good Thai" dishes keep "taste buds tingling" at this "relaxed", "no-frills" Chelsea spot where the staff is "always courteous"; though "nothing to look at", the "decent" prices are worth examining.

Roy's New York
24 | 21 | 22 | $49

Marriott Financial Ctr., 130 Washington St. (bet. Albany & Carlisle Sts.), 212-266-6262; www.roysrestaurant.com

■ "Aloha comes to Manhattan Island" at this Financial District link of star chef Roy Yamaguchi's empire, where the "flavorful" Hawaiian fusion fare issuing from an "open kitchen" is "different from anything else in the city"; it's "off the beaten path" and thus "underappreciated", but roy-alists are willing to travel for a "taste of paradise."

RUBY FOO'S ❷
19 | 22 | 17 | $40

1626 Broadway (49th St.), 212-489-5600
2182 Broadway (77th St.), 212-724-6700
www.brguestrestaurants.com

☑ "Bring on the party" cheer the youthful "crowds" at these "vibrant" "extravaganzas" known for "entry-level" Pan-Asian grub served amid "glitzy", "old Hollywood" decor right out of *Auntie Mame*; though some say it's "more an entertainment destination than a restaurant", many even call this "over-the-top" experience "totally cool."

Rue 57 ❷
19 | 18 | 17 | $43

60 W. 57th St. (6th Ave.), 212-307-5656

☑ Somehow sushi and French bistro fare "work together" at this something-for-everyone Midtown brasserie; though it can produce a "deafening cacophony" and "service isn't up to par with the food", the "upbeat" mood and "convenient location" keep it "busy all the time."

Rughetta
▽ 22 | 18 | 23 | $40

347 E. 85th St. (bet. 1st & 2nd Aves.), 212-517-3118; www.rughetta.com

■ Upper Eastsiders seeking "romance" turn to this Southern Italian where the quarters may be "tight" but the mood's still "inviting"; the food's "fine", the prices "fair" and service comes "with a genuine smile" – no wonder many consider it their neighborhood "standout."

Russian Samovar ❷
20 | 17 | 18 | $43

256 W. 52nd St. (bet. B'way & 8th Sts.), 212-757-0168; www.russiansamovar.com

■ There's "no need to go to Brighton Beach (or Moscow)" to indulge in "czarist-era" cuisine and an "astounding variety" of flavored vodkas when you can steppe into this Theater District Russian; bonuses include an "excellent pianist" leading festive "sing-alongs" and "celebrity sightings" along the lines of "Oksana Baiul."

Ruth's Chris Steak House
23 | 19 | 21 | $58

885 Second Ave. (bet. 47th & 48th Sts.), 212-759-9496
148 W. 51st St. (bet. 6th & 7th Aves.), 212-245-9600
www.ruthschris.com

☑ What's "bad for the waistline is good for the taste buds" at these crosstown chop shop chain links famed for their "high-priced" "steaks dripping in butter"; though some find "too much showbiz" and too many "tourists" here, fans insist "if you love sizzle", you "can't go wrong."

Sabor ●
19 | 16 | 17 | $35

462 Amsterdam Ave. (bet. 82nd & 83rd Sts.), 212-579-2929
1725-1727 Second Ave. (89th St.), 212-828-0003

☑ "Tasty" mini-plates fill out the menu of this Upper West Side South American tapas dispenser, a "bustling" scene despite "expensive", "tiny portions" that "leave you either light in the stomach or the wallet"; N.B. the East Side outpost is new and unrated.

S'Agapo ●
21 | 13 | 17 | $32

34-21 34th Ave. (35th St.), Queens, 718-626-0303

☑ "Low-key and homey", this Astoria Greek is known for "super-fresh fish" at swimmingly "reasonable prices"; regulars "take advantage of the outdoor seating" to avoid the "fluorescent-lit interior", though the "raggedy service" is harder to escape.

Sage ●
23 | 23 | 21 | $43

331 Park Ave. S. (bet. 24th & 25th Sts.), 212-253-8400; www.sagenyc.com

☑ Formerly the aloof TanDa, this Gramercy New American is now a more "mellow" spot "with no attitude" in evidence; "someone cares in the kitchen" too, turning out "on-target", "value"-priced comfort food; P.S. the "civilized bar upstairs" makes a good venue for a nightcap.

Sahara ●
21 | 15 | 15 | $23

2337 Coney Island Ave. (bet. Aves. T & U), Brooklyn, 718-376-8594

■ This big Gravesend Middle Eastern "treat" "keeps expanding and getting noisier"; given the "inconsistent service" and overall "tumult", it's a "place to eat, not to dine", leading many to opt for "takeout."

Saigon Grill ●
23 | 9 | 15 | $19

620 Amsterdam Ave. (90th St.), 212-875-9072
1700 Second Ave. (88th St.), 212-996-4600
www.saigongrill.com

☑ Brace yourself for "clatter", since these "hectic" crosstown Vietnamese "godsends" are "incredibly busy, for good reason": "fabulous food" at "astonishingly affordable" tabs; trade-offs include "bus-stop decor" and often "sloppy service."

Sala ●
21 | 22 | 19 | $35

344 Bowery (Great Jones St.), 212-979-6606

■ "Sangria to die for" and "amazing tapas" keep this "rustic", moderately priced Bowery Spaniard "jumping on weekend nights"; its young demographic uses it for both "birthdays" and "romance", alternating between the narrow street-level dining room and the "dark, sexy" downstairs lounge.

Salaam Bombay
21 | 18 | 19 | $36

317 Greenwich St. (bet. Duane & Reade Sts.), 212-226-9400;
www.salaambombay.com

■ A "delicious reason to support Downtown", this TriBeCa Indian is "many notches above the typical Sixth Street" spot offering "unusual", "fragrant" choices abetted by "royal-treatment" service; although it's a tad "expensive" overall, the "phenomenal" $12.95 all-you-can-eat lunch buffet comes "highly recommended."

Salam Cafe
20 | 17 | 16 | $31

104 W. 13th St. (bet. 6th & 7th Aves.), 212-741-0277

■ Parked on a "beautiful Village block" is this "blessedly low-key" and modestly priced Mideastern that supplies "consistently reliable" chow in a "comfortable casbah" setting; "slooow service" drags it down, but the "imaginative" kitchen gives things a boost.

Sal Anthony's
16 | 15 | 18 | $36

168 First Ave. (bet. 10th & 11th Sts.), 212-674-7014
55 Irving Pl. (bet. 17th & 18th Sts.), 212-982-9030
133 Mulberry St. (bet. Grand & Hester Sts.), 212-925-3120
www.salanthonys.com

☑ These Italian "survivors" are "convenient in a pinch", despite "never-changing menus" and decor that's getting "a little long in the tooth"; on the plus side, they're priced right and are known quantities; N.B. the new First Avenue branch (fka Lanza) has been on the East Village scene since 1904.

Sala Thai ●
22 | 13 | 18 | $27

1718 Second Ave. (bet. 89th & 90th Sts.), 212-410-5557

☑ "Still going strong" after over 20 years, this Yorkville Thai remains a "faithful joint" purveying "beautiful food" to a "respectable-looking crowd"; "cramped" quarters result in a demand to "expand."

Salon Mexico ●
22 | 19 | 22 | $43

136 E. 26th St. (bet. Lexington & 3rd Aves.), 212-685-9400;
www.salonmexiconyc.com

■ Bringing a "haute" jolt to Mexican cooking, this "upscale" Gramercy "sophisticate" features an "imaginative" menu enlivened by Sino-French accents and "potent" margaritas; an adjoining lounge with "live jazz" adds to the "amazing experience" – just bring *"mucho dinero."*

Salsa y Salsa
– | – | – | I

206 Seventh Ave. (bet. 21st & 22nd Sts.), 212-929-2678

Try this casual new Mexican for a cheap 'n' cheerful source for south-of-the-border stuff; its margarita-slinging bar is already drawing enough passersby to become a local staple.

Salt
21 | 17 | 17 | $40

58 MacDougal St. (bet. Houston & Prince Sts.), 212-674-4968
29A Clinton St. (bet. Houston & Stanton Sts.), 212-979-8471 ● ☒

■ "Comfort food with an edge" is yours at this new, "salt shaker–size" SoHo American known for its "trendy" crowd, "communal tables" and unique ordering concept (sort of like "Craft on the cheap"); the even newer Lower East Side spin-off offers a more limited menu in moodier digs.

Salute!
17 | 16 | 15 | $38

270 Madison Ave. (39th St.), 212-213-3440

☑ Rescuing locals from Murray Hill's "restaurant limbo" is this "bustling" Tuscan "bright spot" where the "pasta dishes make up for the bad pickup lines at the bar"; regulars say it's "better at lunch", as the dinner "entrees can use some work", ditto the "sleepwalking waiters."

Sambuca
19 | 16 | 19 | $34

20 W. 72nd St. (bet. Columbus Ave. & CPW), 212-787-5656

☑ "It doesn't have the hype of Carmine's", but this "family-style" West Side Southern Italian "doesn't have the long waits" either, rather "super-size portions" of "garlicky" grub at "reasonable prices"; though a few disparage the "food-by-the-pound" concept, for most it's an unbeatable "bargain."

Sammy's ◐
17 | 8 | 14 | $19

301-303 Sixth Ave. (Carmine St.), 212-337-9888
453 Sixth Ave. (11th St.), 212-924-6688
◪ "Everything happens fast" at these "lickety-split" Village Chinese noodle shops where they "want you in and out as fast as possible" (those wishing to "relax and talk", "get it to go"); otherwise, expect "huge portions", "low prices" and "no atmosphere."

Sammy's Roumanian
19 | 9 | 16 | $45

157 Chrystie St. (Delancey St.), 212-673-0330
■ It's a schmaltz world at this at-least-once-in-a-lifetime Lower East Side "experience", a "year-round bar mitzvah" celebrating "Jewish home cooking", where there's "nothing green on the plate" and "everything comes with a side of chicken fat"; wags say "if you leave without heartburn, you ordered the wrong thing!"; P.S. check in advance to get your cardiologist's clearance.

Sandobe ◐⊄
21 | 7 | 13 | $23

330 E. 11th St. (bet. 1st & 2nd Aves.), 212-780-0328
◪ Some "like it raw" at this "popular" East Village Japanese that serves "only sushi" and takes only cash; despite "long waits", "cramped" quarters and a "total dive" feel, "you don't have to be rich to get your fill" – though many still opt to "eat and run."

San Domenico
22 | 22 | 22 | $68

240 Central Park S. (bet. B'way & 7th Ave.), 212-265-5959;
www.sandomenicony.com
■ It's amore for the "older clientele" that patronizes Tony May's "civilized" Central Park South Italian, a magnet for "sophisticated palates" thanks to "spacious surroundings", "formal service" and chef Odette Fada's "sublime", modern cooking; however, some say this "ultimate experience" is undermined by Tony's frequent absences and a dining room that's beginning to show its age.

San Pietro ◐⊠
23 | 21 | 22 | $64

18 E. 54th St. (bet. 5th & Madison Aves.), 212-753-9015;
www.sanpietro.net
■ Shop-till-you-drop types relish "relaxing" lunches (and occasional "Giuliani sightings") at this Midtown Southern Italian where the "top-notch" food arrives in "elegantly modest" surroundings; the "gracious service" may be "better if you're a regular", but even irregulars can "blow a lot" of dough here.

Santa Fe
18 | 18 | 18 | $37

72 W. 69th St. (bet. Columbus Ave. & CPW), 212-724-0822
◪ There may be "no surprises" at this Southwestern "workhorse", but Lincoln Center–neighborhood amigos are *loco* for its "cozy fireplace" and similarly cozy cuisine with "just enough spice to warm your heart"; "beyond-this-planet" margaritas keep it hopping with a youngish demographic.

Sapori d'Ischia
▽ 24 | 16 | 22 | $42

55-15 37th Ave. (56th St.), Queens, 718-446-1500
■ "Hidden" in "semi-industrial" Woodside, this "specialty shop by day" transforms itself into a "wonderful" Southern Italian after dark offering "delicious pastas" (not to mention "live opera" twice a week); even better, the overall cost is a "fraction" of what you'd expect to pay in Manhattan.

Sapphire Indian
20 | 19 | 19 | $40

1845 Broadway (bet. 60th & 61st Sts.), 212-245-4444; www.sapphireny.com

■ "Not your run-of-the-mill Indian", this Columbus Circle eatery is nevertheless something of a "best-kept secret" – "at least until the Time Warner Building opens", that is; though it's a tad "expensive", you can't beat the $11.95 lunch buffet.

Sapporo East ◑
20 | 10 | 16 | $23

245 E. 10th St. (1st Ave.), 212-260-1330

■ "If you can find a seat, you're doing well" at this East Village Japanese "staple" for "NYU and Cooper Union students" – it doesn't take reservations, "so get there early"; "rushed service" and dumpy decor are trumped by the "dependable", "dirt-cheap" sushi.

Sarabeth's
21 | 17 | 17 | $31

423 Amsterdam Ave. (bet. 80th & 81st Sts.), 212-496-6280
Chelsea Mkt., 75 Ninth Ave. (bet. 15th & 16th Sts.), 212-989-2424
Wales Hotel, 1295 Madison Ave. (bet. 92nd & 93rd Sts.), 212-410-7335
Whitney Museum, 945 Madison Ave. (75th St.), 212-570-3670
www.sarabeth.com

■ "Brunch is the thing" at these "insanely popular" Americans with "English teacup ambiances" that are one part "J. Crew", one part "Martha Stewart"; since the "waits to get in are impossible" ("can't they open more locations?"), "arm yourself with patience and comfortable shoes" or opt for dinner when they're "less crowded."

Sardi's
15 | 20 | 18 | $46

234 W. 44th St. (bet. B'way & 8th Ave.), 212-221-8440; www.sardis.com

◪ Maybe the "show-biz caricatures on the walls" are "better than the food" at this ancient Theater District Continental, but it's still a White Way "mainstay" for starry-eyed Broadway babies who order drinks and "make believe they're in *All About Eve*"; otherwise, this "bygone" "cliché" works when you have unsophisticated "tourists" in tow.

Sarge's Deli ◑
19 | 7 | 14 | $21

548 Third Ave. (bet. 36th & 37th Sts.), 212-679-0442; www.sargesdeli.com

■ "Towering sandwiches", "vats of cole slaw" and "tons of Jewish comfort food" can be had at this 24/7 Murray Hill deli "relic"; given the "über-crotchety" staff and "early-Formica" decor, regulars opt for "takeout – and suffer the heartburn at home."

Saul
26 | 20 | 23 | $46

140 Smith St. (bet. Bergen & Dean Sts.), Brooklyn, 718-935-9844

■ "Despite all the nearby competition", this "ambitious" New American "pioneer" remains in the forefront of "Brooklyn's renaissance" thanks to the "sublime" cooking of namesake chef Saul Bolton; the "down-to-earth" staff "couldn't be nicer", and even if prices are a "little expensive" for the area, they're still "lower than Manhattan."

Savann
∇ 20 | 15 | 18 | $37

414 Amsterdam Ave. (bet. 79th & 80th Sts.), 212-580-0202;
www.savannrestaurant.com

■ Folks "tired of culinary roulette" are gambling on this Upper West Side French for "above-average" food "without the long lines of its neighbors"; alright, the "low-key" quarters are on the "tight" side, but the payoff is "exceptional value", notably that $17.95 early-bird.

Savannah Steak ◑⌧
∇ 21 | 21 | 19 | $51

7 E. 48th St. (bet. 5th & Madison Aves.), 212-935-2500;
www.savannahsteak.com

■ "Making a splash" with "young, attractive" types, this new Midtown steakhouse offers "excellent" chops in "stark" but airy environs; the weakest link – service – "needs to come up to speed", but all in all this is an "impressive start."

Savoia
∇ 21 16 19 $30

277 Smith St. (bet. DeGraw & Sackett Sts.), Brooklyn, 718-797-2727
■ "They may not speak your language" but the "food speaks volumes" at this Carroll Gardens Italian, particularly the "lovely" thin-crust brick-oven pizzas and "wonderful Sicilian dishes" (the "handsome" waiters included); right now the "tiny" setup is a "little uncomfortable", since they're in the process of expanding.

Savoy
22 20 21 $54

70 Prince St. (Crosby St.), 212-219-8570
■ "Tranquil, understated" and "refreshingly untrendy", this longtime SoHo Mediterranean with "remarkable staying power" showcases chef Peter Hoffman's "inventive", "market-driven menu"; but "recent renovations" moving the bar to street level have some saying the setup's "not as good" as before.

Sazerac House
18 16 17 $30

533 Hudson St. (Charles St.), 212-989-0313;
www.sazerachouse.com
■ This "trustworthy" jambalaya joint housed in a "historic" 1826 Village building shows plenty of "staying power" (39 years in the business) thanks to its "stick-to-your-ribs" Cajun-American chow at "moderate prices"; though the "decor needs some uplift", it's always "good in a pinch."

Scaletta
22 19 24 $48

50 W. 77th St. (bet. Columbus Ave. & CPW), 212-769-9191;
www.scalettaristorante.com
■ There's "nothing nouvelle" going on at this "civilized" West Side Northern Italian catering to a "sedate senior" set with "good if not adventurous food" and "comforting" service; though "a tad pricey", it offers a "roomy" setup and that allows "quiet" conversation.

SCALINATELLA ●
25 19 23 $65

201 E. 61st St. (3rd Ave.), 212-207-8280
■ "Don't let the basement location faze you" – this "charming" East Side Italian "powerhouse" has a "scrumptious" seafood-heavy menu and "waiters who spoil you from the moment you walk in"; though "pricey", the experience is always "memorable", with regulars insisting it's one of the best in NYC.

SCALINI FEDELI ⌧
26 25 25 $79

165 Duane St. (bet. Greenwich & Hudson Sts.), 212-528-0400;
www.scalinifedeli.com
■ You can be transported "straight to the Italian countryside" at this TriBeCa Tuscan, a "NJ transplant" where many feel "like royalty" as they tuck into Michael Cetrulo's "divine" cooking; "superb service" and a "romantic" vaulted space (the "former Bouley") add to the overall "wonderful experience", and though it's priced "for expense accounts", "you get more than enough for your money" here.

Schiller's ●
– – – M

131 Rivington St. (Norfolk St.), 212-260-4555; www.schillersny.com
The latest from restaurateur Keith McNally, this hip new Lower Eastsider sports the same faux bistro looks he developed at Balthazar and Pastis, albeit on a smaller scale; foodwise, the Eclectic menu offers everything from Cuban sandwiches to Wiener schnitzel, and it's all exceptionally low-priced (as is the abbreviated but well-parsed wine list); P.S. a trip to the bathroom is de rigueur here.

Sciuscià ●
▽ 19 | 16 | 20 | $45

Giraffe Hotel, 365 Park Ave. S. (26th St.), 212-213-4008;
www.sciuscianyc.com

☑ "Hope springs eternal" at this revamped "underground" Gramercy Mediterranean (fka Chinoiserie) where a "high-reaching chef" and a "movie star–look-alike" staff turn out "reasonably good food"; detractors find the "minimalist" mood as "chilly" and "cold" as its "cool, young" following.

Scopa
20 | 16 | 17 | $39

79 Madison Ave. (28th St.), 212-686-8787

☑ "Consistent" Northern Italian cooking "rewards virtually anyone's food fancy" at this Gramercy Parker that's a "popular" locus both at lunch and "after work"; but bashers see a "mishmash of concepts" at work and think it's "overpriced" for pasta.

SEA
22 | 21 | 16 | $24

75 Second Ave. (bet. 4th & 5th Sts.), 212-228-5505
114 N. Sixth St. (Berry St.), Brooklyn, 718-384-8850 ●

■ Thai is "cool again" at this new "ultrahip" Williamsburger whose "club vibe" includes a "reflecting pool", a giant "Buddha", gimmicky "unisex bathrooms" and, not incidentally, a restaurant serving "amazing food"; decorwise, its smaller East Village sibling pales in comparison, although both share really "reasonable pricing."

Sea Grill ⊠
24 | 23 | 22 | $58

Rockefeller Ctr., 19 W. 49th St. (bet. 5th & 6th Aves.), 212-332-7610;
www.restaurantassociates.com

■ "Even though the pond outside is frozen", some of "NY's best seafood" still surfaces at this Rock Center grill known for its "rinkside" address, modern setting and chef Ed Brown's "passion" for "pristine, perfectly prepared", "premium-priced" poisson; ok, it's a bit "touristy", but it's "nice to be a tourist in your own town once in a while."

Second Avenue Deli ●
23 | 9 | 14 | $24

156 Second Ave. (10th St.), 212-677-0606; www.2ndavedeli.com

■ It takes "chutzpah" to nab a table (or even "make it to the take-out counter") at this East Village "granddaddy" of kosher delis where "gluttony is no crime" given "plotz"-worthy food with enough "schmaltz to grease a jumbo jet"; fans say its great "late hours", "fab prices" and "big-haired", big-hearted staff combine to make it the "last of a dying breed" – if you wanna learn deli, start here.

Seo
▽ 23 | 16 | 18 | $41

249 E. 49th St. (bet. 2nd & 3rd Aves.), 212-355-7722

■ "Top sushi" and "divine noodles" beckon at this UN-area Japanese offering a "small but creative" menu served amid "simple, serene decor"; a "predominately Japanese clientele" validates its authenticity, right down to those "Tokyo prices."

Seppi's ●
18 | 17 | 16 | $44

Le Parker Meridien, 123 W. 56th St. (bet. 6th & 7th Aves.), 212-708-7444;
www.leparkermeridien.com

☑ "Worth remembering" in Midtown, this Parker Meridien French bistro offers "unexpectedly well-executed dishes" till 2 AM, a closing time that's a "rarity" in this area; too bad the "slow service" and immodest prices drag down the otherwise "solid" performance.

Serafina ●
18 | 17 | 15 | $38

38 E. 58th St. (bet. Madison & Park Aves.), 212-832-8888
29 E. 61st St. (bet. Madison & Park Aves.), 212-702-9898

(continued)

(continued)
Serafina
393 Lafayette St. (4th St.), 212-995-9595
1022 Madison Ave. (79th St.), 212-734-2676
www.serafinarestaurant.com
☑ There's plenty of "good energy" at this "vogueish" Italian quartet where "oh-so-cool" Euros nibble on "chichi pasta and pizza" at "above-average" prices and cope with a staff that's "one bulb short of a chandelier"; P.S. expect a "prep school crowd" on Madison, and "lots of models" on Lafayette.

Serendipity 3 ◑

19 20 14 $26

225 E. 60th St. (bet. 2nd & 3rd Aves.), 212-838-3531;
www.serendipity3.com
■ "Skip dinner and go right to dessert" at this East Side ice cream parlor/toy store, a "child's delight/parent's nightmare" renowned for its "signature frozen hot chocolate"; "impossible waits" and service "as cold as the sundaes" are turnoffs, but nothing else comes close for an afternoon of parent-child bonding.

Sesumi

▽ 22 14 17 $30

1649 Second Ave. (bet. 85th & 86th Sts.), 212-879-1024
■ Don't expect anything "flashy" or "trendy" at this Upper East Side Japanese, a "secret sushi" "standby" that startles since there's "never a wait"; insiders ignore the "tired environs" and focus instead on the "attentive service" and "reasonable prices."

Sette Mezzo ◑≠

23 14 19 $51

969 Lexington Ave. (bet. 70th & 71st Sts.), 212-472-0400
☑ The "standard against which others are measured", this "elitist" East Side Italian serves "reliable, tasty" fare in a "private-club" atmosphere; downsides include "brusque service if you're not a regular" and a "cash-only policy" that's a "pain" given the price.

Seven ◑

18 17 18 $38

350 Seventh Ave. (bet. 29th & 30th Sts.), 212-967-1919
☑ A "nice departure" in the "no-man's-land of Penn Station", this New American offers more than "serviceable" chow that's just the ticket "before the action at the Garden"; it may be a bit "expensive for what it offers", but the "upbeat" ambiance and "pleasant staff" compensate.

71 Clinton Fresh Food

25 16 20 $54

71 Clinton St. (bet. Rivington & Stanton Sts.), 212-614-6960;
www.71clintonfreshfood.com
■ Since chef "Wylie Dufresne is gone", this Lower East Side New American that "started the Clinton Street rage" has "lost a bit of its buzz – but not its sting" – so you can expect the same "brilliant" food at the same "pricey-for-the-neighborhood" tabs; despite the "shoebox" size, this "must-try-or-die" spot remains as "hip" as can be.

71 Irving Place

18 18 16 $17

71 Irving Pl. (bet. 18th & 19th Sts.), 212-995-5252; www.irvingfarm.com
■ "Everything Starbucks isn't", this "European-style" Gramercy coffeehouse is "cozy" and "quirky" with a "community atmosphere"; regulars who enjoy spotting "celebs at their AM worst" call it their "fantasy of a perfect cafe", even if "tables are hard to come by."

Sevilla ◑

23 15 20 $36

62 Charles St. (W. 4th St.), 212-929-3189;
www.sevillarestaurantandbar.com
■ "What it lacks in subtlety, it makes up for in quantity" at this "inexpensive", circa-1941 Village Spaniard, a "paella heaven" and

"garlic lovers' paradise"; sure, it's "crowded", the decor's "outdated" and service can be over-"exuberant", but like everything else in life, it gets "better after two pitchers of sangria."

Shaan
22 | 21 | 20 | $38

Rockefeller Ctr., 57 W. 48th St. (bet. 5th & 6th Aves.), 212-977-8400
■ "Exquisite food" and "service fit for a raja" are yours at this "serene" Rock Center Indian "change of pace", a "delightfully spacious" place where "high ceilings" add to the "beautiful decor"; even better, the "delicious" $25 dinner prix fixe "doesn't cost too many rupees."

Shabu-Tatsu ●
20 | 13 | 17 | $34

216 E. 10th St. (bet. 1st & 2nd Aves.), 212-477-2972
■ "Decently priced" "Japanese comfort food" that you "cook yourself" is the draw at this simple East Village "hot pot" specialist that's both "fun for the family" and a "great ice-breaker" for first dates; sadly, the "Uptown branch has closed."

Shaffer City Oyster Bar & Grill ☒
23 | 16 | 21 | $46

5 W. 21st St. (bet. 5th & 6th Aves.), 212-255-9827
■ A "pearl among oyster houses", this Flatiron seafooder is one of the "best-kept secrets in town", offering a "super-fresh" spread of "beautiful" bivalves; "high-profile" chef-owner Jay Shaffer overcomes the "bare-bones" decor with his "extremely welcoming" personality.

Shallots NY
▽ 20 | 20 | 19 | $59

Sony Atrium, 550 Madison Ave. (bet. 55th & 56th Sts.), 212-833-7800; www.shallotsny.com
☑ Quite possibly the "most stylish kosher restaurant in Manhattan", this "fancy-Delancey" Midtown Mediterranean features David Rockwell decor that plays well against the "interesting" menu; still, critics kvetch about the "chutzpah" of charging so much for such "small portions."

Shanghai Cuisine ⌐
21 | 13 | 15 | $21

89 Bayard St. (Mulberry St.), 212-732-8988
☑ "Delicious" Shanghai dishes fill out the menu of this "dependable" C-towner, aka the "emperor of juicy meat dumplings"; low prices and service that's "prompt" (and definitely "not fawning") offset the annoying "no-reservations", "cash-only" policies.

Shark Bar
20 | 16 | 18 | $32

307 Amsterdam Ave. (bet. 74th & 75th Sts.), 212-874-8500; www.sharkbar.com
■ "Serious" soul food feeders find there's "no need to go way Uptown" thanks to this "upscale", midpriced Westsider parlaying great "down-home" grub with some impressive buppie "celeb-gazing" on the side; it's always "packed on weekends", so regulars prefer weeknights when it's "calmer."

Sharz Cafe & Wine Bar
21 | 13 | 18 | $39

435 E. 86th St. (bet. 1st & York Aves.), 212-876-7282
■ Following a move "further east" to somewhat "bigger" digs, this Yorkville Mediterranean is "still a bit tight", though the food remains "top-notch" and "reasonably priced"; a "glorious by-the-glass wine list" helps keep the mood "friendly."

Shelly's New York ●
19 | 18 | 19 | $49

104 W. 57th St. (bet. 6th & 7th Aves.), 212-245-2422; www.shellysnewyork.com
■ It's "hard to imagine" that this multilevel Midtown surf 'n' turfer was "once a Horn & Hardart cafeteria" given its "glitzy" decor, "phenomenal seafood" and a raw bar that's an "attraction in itself";

"live jazz upstairs" also hits high notes, though a few feel that owner Shelly Fireman should take another look at his prices.

Sherwood Cafe ●⊅ ▽ 18 | 25 | 16 | $24
195 Smith St. (bet. Baltic & Warren Sts.), Brooklyn, 718-596-1609
■ Perhaps the "coolest looking" spot on Smith Street, this "right-on" Boerum Hiller is one part French bistro and one part "antique store" with "nostalgic items for sale all over the place"; its "simple" menu is "always tasty", ditto that "lovely" garden out back.

Shinjuku – | – | – | M
177 Atlantic Ave. (bet. Clinton & Court Sts.), Brooklyn, 718-935-1300
This new Atlantic Avenue Japanese's large, moderately priced menu and airy, industrial-chic interior (complete with a custom-made sushi bar) prompts plenty of interest from Brooklyn Heights locals; however, it's still too soon to tell.

Shore – | – | – | M
41 Murray St. (bet. Church St. & W. B'way), 212-962-3750
The one shore thing near City Hall these days is this new New England–style seafooder; despite the plain interior, it's already a magnet for bureaucrats in the mood for clams and oysters, chased with lobster rolls and pot pies.

Shula's Steak House ▽ 20 | 18 | 21 | $57
Westin NY Times Sq., 270 W. 42nd St. (8th Ave.), 212-201-2776; www.donshula.com
☑ Recently touched down in Times Square, this new "football-themed" steakhouse from renowned NFL coach Don Shula is a "promising" purveyor of "perfect porterhouses", though critics complain this chain link doesn't score "any advantage over the competition"; as for that "cumbersome" menu printed on pigskin, pundits plead "punt it."

Shun Lee Cafe ● 20 | 15 | 17 | $37
43 W. 65th St. (bet. Columbus Ave. & CPW), 212-769-3888
■ There's "dim sum extraordinaire" available at this "snappy, black-and-white checked" West Side Chinese that's more than a "satisfactory substitute" for its "formal" next-door sibling, given its "lower prices"; sure, it's often "noisy", but overall it's an "efficient, agreeable" prelude to nearby Lincoln Center events.

Shun Lee Palace ● 24 | 21 | 22 | $51
155 E. 55th St. (bet. Lexington & 3rd Aves.), 212-371-8844
■ "Everyone's first choice" for "Chinese fine dining", Michael Tong's "elegant" Midtowner has fans licking their chopsticks over the fact that you "need no menu" here – just "leave it up to the staff to order for you"; the "spiffy" setting makes this a place to "dress up" for, and though you'll "pay dearly" for the privilege, it more than "lives up to the hype."

Shun Lee West ● 23 | 21 | 21 | $48
43 W. 65th St. (bet. Columbus Ave. & CPW), 212-595-8895
■ For "Chinese food with glamour", it's hard to beat this "solid-gold" Westsider where the "extraordinary" cuisine and "tuxedoed", "treat-you-like-royalty" service are just as "spectacular" as the "stylish" black-and-white decor; granted, this "Shangri-la" may be "more expensive" than other Chinese, but it clearly deserves to be.

Siam Inn ● ▽ 22 | 15 | 18 | $28
854 Eighth Ave. (bet. 51st & 52nd Sts.), 212-757-4006; www.siaminn.com
■ The "curry puff is the stuff" dreams are made of at this "convenient" if "uncrowded" Theater District Thai; though the decor may not "lure

you off the street", the "authentic" fare and "sweet staff" make for an "experience worth coming back for."

Silver Spurs
16 11 14 $17

771 Broadway (9th St.), 212-473-5517
490 La Guardia Pl. (Houston St.), 212-228-2333
■ "Burgers the size of your head" corral wanna-be cowpokes into these Western-themed Downtown diners known for their "jumbo portions" and "inexpensive" tabs; too bad the "rude" servers and "cutesy" menus are so doggone "irritating."

Sipan ●
20 18 16 $38

702 Amsterdam Ave. (94th St.), 212-665-9929
☑ "Unusual" Peruvian dishes are washed down with "killer Pisco sours" at this Upper Westsider where the "made-with-love" grub comes at irresistibly "moderate" prices; drawbacks include "*mañana* service" and weekend "noise", but overall, the mood's "pleasant."

Sirabella's
23 15 22 $40

72 East End Ave. (bet. 82nd & 83rd Sts.), 212-988-6557
■ Something of an Upper East Side "sleeper", this "teeny-weeny" Tuscan has "superlative food" and a "sweetheart" of an owner, the hands-on Mario Sirabella; "delivery may be the best option if you don't show your face weekly" here.

Sistina ●
▽ 24 19 22 $65

1555 Second Ave. (bet. 80th & 81st Sts.), 212-861-7660
■ "High-quality" cuisine comes at appropriately "high prices" at this "classy" Upper East Side Northern Italian where both the service and wines are "welcoming"; as a bonus, "talking to your dinner companions is easy" as everything's usually calm and "quiet."

66 ●
22 25 22 $58

241 Church St. (Leonard St.), 212-925-0202; www.jean-georges.com
■ *The* "place of the moment", this new TriBeCa Chinese via supertoque Jean-Georges Vongerichten simply "crackles with flavor" according to those "hip" enough to snag a coveted reservation (hint: the long "communal table" in front is held for walk-ins); the 'in' crowd says Richard Meier's "minimalist Zen" design, equally stylish staffers and a "celeb"-heavy following make it worth every "expensive" penny.

Slice of Harlem
▽ 22 13 19 $19

308 Lenox Ave. (bet. 125th & 126th Sts.), 212-426-7400
■ Any way you slice it, this Harlem "brick-oven" pizza purveyor produces "excellent" pies for the dough, and the adventurous "expand their horizons" to sample the rest of its *bella cucina*; while decor is not its strong suit, name a pizza place where it is!

Smith & Wollensky
22 16 20 $60

797 Third Ave. (49th St.), 212-753-1530;
www.smithandwollensky.com
■ It's "bloody rare" to find a well-run steakhouse these days, but this two-story Midtown "staple" is the real deal with "massive" steaks ("straight from the moo to you"), "terrific" wines, a "clubby" feel and "old-fashioned NY waiters" who make it all run smoothly; bargain-hunters may nickname it "Smith & Expensy" but owner Alan Stillman has anticipated that with his cheaper Wollensky's Grill right next door.

Snack
23 11 18 $21

105 Thompson St. (bet. Prince & Spring Sts.), 212-925-1040
■ Greek right down to its "spartan" decor, this "offbeat" SoHo Hellenic may be "one of the city's smallest eateries" but compensates with

"big fresh flavors" and "superb value", even though getting a seat can be a "game of chance."

Snackbar
— | — | — | M

111 W. 17th St. (bet. 6th & 7th Aves.), 212-627-3700
Contemporary French cooking gets the small-plate treatment at this new Chelsea-ite that's drawing a young crowd with its casual pricing and straight-out-of-*Architectural-Digest* looks; mix 'n' match is the idea here, with meat or fish served with a choice of ten sauces, while cocktails come in shot, martini, highball or pitcher sizes.

Snack Taverna
— | — | — | M

63 Bedford St. (7th Ave. S.), 212-929-3499
Lovers of SoHo's Snack gain elbow room at this more upscale West Village offshoot; glass-fronted and big enough to house a small bar, it has an ambitious kitchen that ramps up rustic Greek dishes backed by an interesting all-Hellenic wine list.

Soba Nippon
∇ 21 | 16 | 19 | $31

19 W. 52nd St. (bet. 5th & 6th Aves.), 212-489-2525;
www.sobanippon.com
■ "Wonderfully fresh soba" and udon noodles are made on-site at this "solid" Japanese slurpeteria where there's "not much decor", yet prices are "reasonable for Midtown"; although "bustling at midday", it's a "calm oasis" come suppertime.

Sobaya
23 | 19 | 20 | $26

229 E. Ninth St. (bet. 2nd & 3rd Aves.), 212-533-6966;
www.ticakean.com/restaurant.html
■ A "great little pocket of Zen", this "bargain" East Village Japanese is known for "first-rate, hand-rolled noodles" and "great sake selection" served in a "serene", "jewel-box" setting; indeed, its "expat"-heavy crowd finds it "so like Tokyo" that many say it "cures homesickness."

Soho Steak ⌀
∇ 19 | 14 | 18 | $38

90 Thompson St. (bet. Prince & Spring Sts.), 212-226-0602
◪ For a "decent steak at a decent price", check out this "cash-only" SoHo chop shop where the fit's "tight" but the crowd's "not afraid to sit on each other's laps"; the herd agrees what it "lacks in panache", it makes up for with "vibe."

Solera ⊠
22 | 19 | 20 | $51

216 E. 53rd St. (bet. 2nd & 3rd Aves.), 212-644-1166; www.solerany.com
■ There's a "refined atmosphere" at this "sunny" if "pricey" Midtown Spaniard where the "incredible tapas", "fabulous paella" and "stiff sangria" all "shine"; add "warm service", and sighs of "*mi enchanta*" accompany a perfect Iberian "epicurean escapade."

Son Cubano ●⊠
20 | 22 | 17 | $39

405 W. 14th St. (bet. 9th Ave. & Washington St.), 212-366-1640
■ Explore "Havana's golden age" at this "sexy" Meatpacking District Cuban tapas dispenser with an ambiance "straight out of a Hemingway novel" and a "conversation-prohibitive" noise level; a "mammoth dark-wood bar" and "live bands" fuel the "party atmosphere."

Sosa Borella
19 | 16 | 18 | $35

832 Eighth Ave. (50th St.), 212-262-7774
460 Greenwich St. (bet. Desbrosses & Watts Sts.), 212-431-5093
■ "Down-to-earth" dining in "relaxed" environs is yours at this Italian-Argentinean duo known for their "great little pizzas" and other "interesting", "fairly priced" items; the "out-of-the-way" TriBeCa branch is a notably "calm oasis" when you need to get away from it all.

Soul Cafe
▽ 16 | 16 | 13 | $36

444 W. 42nd St. (bet. 9th & 10th Aves.), 212-244-7685;
www.soulcaferestaurant.com

☑ Expect a "noisy, crowded" bar scene augmented by "loud" live bands at this soul food joint "convenient to 42nd Street Theater Row"; despite its stab at "sophisticated", "down-home" cooking, many find things just "average" here – except for the partying.

Soup Kitchen International, Al's 🗷⇗
24 | 2 | 8 | $13

259 W. 55th St. (bet. B'way & 8th Ave.), 212-757-7730;
www.therealsoupman.com

☑ "NY's best-behaved clientele" still line up at this Midtown soupeteria "made famous on *Seinfeld*" for its "piping hot" bowls of "liquid heaven" and the strict "rules" of its owner, "laugh-a-minute" Al Yeganeh; be aware that it's "only open for lunch" from November to May, and Al is doing so well now that you may have to ask him to yell at you.

South Shore Country Club 🗷
▽ 19 | 22 | 21 | $50

200 Huguenot Ave. (Arthur Kill Rd.), Staten Island, 718-356-7017;
www.south-shore.com

☑ "One of Staten Island's best", this "above-average" Continental is a "wedding" and "anniversary" magnet boasting a "beautiful" layout and "aim-to-please" service; its "lovely setting" in the midst of a "lush green" fairway suits most to a tee, though some birdies tweet the food's "not always up to par" here.

SouthWest NY
13 | 18 | 13 | $31

2 World Financial Ctr. (Liberty St.), 212-945-0528;
www.southwestny.com

☑ "You can't beat" the "spectacular harbor view" from this indoor/outdoor Southwesterner overlooking the WFC marina, though critics contend both the food and service are "shaky"; more reliable is the "after-work bar scene" featuring "Jersey girls" in pursuit of the "endangered investment banker species."

SPARKS STEAK HOUSE 🗷
25 | 19 | 21 | $64

210 E. 46th St. (bet. 2nd & 3rd Aves.), 212-687-4855;
www.sparksnyc.com

■ "You know you're in NY" after a trip to this Midtown steakhouse where "testosterone meets cholesterol" in "dark", "clubby" digs populated by "power brokers" and "big shots" sporting "oversized jewelry"; given the "melt-in-your-mouth" steaks, "incredible wine list" and "crisp, professional service", there's "nothing more you could ask for – except maybe a price reduction."

Sparky's American Food ●⇗
▽ 18 | 11 | 14 | $9

135A N. Fifth St. (Bedford Ave.), Brooklyn, 718-302-5151

■ Forget Westminster: some of the "best dogs" around are found at this Williamsburg "cookout-style" joint where the "digs are spare" but the free-range, organic wieners are "delish"; bonus "homemade condiments" and "killer fries" have fans sitting up and begging for more.

Spice
20 | 16 | 16 | $22

199 Eighth Ave. (bet. 20th & 21st Sts.), 212-989-1116
1411 Second Ave. (bet. 73rd & 74th Sts.), 212-988-5348
60 University Pl. (10th St.), 212-982-3758

■ For "Thai on the fly", it's tough to top this "repeat visit"–worthy trio where the spice is "right", ditto the "bargain-basement prices"; not surprisingly, they're often "buzzing" with "starving college students" who don't mind "noise" and "slow service."

Spring Street Natural ◐
18 | 16 | 16 | $26

62 Spring St. (Lafayette St.), 212-966-0290

■ If you want to turn over a "wholesome" "new leaf", try this longtime NoLita health fooder that offers "earth-conscious" options for vegetarians, as well as fish and poultry for the less virtuous; a "calming fern bar" setting and "spaced-out staff" come with the territory.

SQC
19 | 14 | 17 | $38

270 Columbus Ave. (bet. 72nd & 73rd Sts.), 212-579-0100; www.sqcnyc.com

☑ "Magician" chef Scott Q. Campbell brings an "imaginative twist to New American food" at this "reasonably priced" Upper Westsider best known for its "to-die-for hot chocolate"; on the downside, "impersonal service" and "congestion" may make it hard to enjoy.

Sripraphai ⊅
∇ 26 | 6 | 18 | $18

64-13 39th Ave. (bet. 64th & 65th Sts.), Queens, 718-899-9599

☑ "When they say spicy, they mean it" at this Woodside Thai whose "fire extinguisher"–worthy fare really "tastes like Bangkok"; alright, the "no-frills", "Formica-and-fluorescent environment" needs work, but the "bargain" prices and "accommodating staff" are fine as is.

Stage Deli
18 | 10 | 14 | $24

1481 Second Ave. (77th St.), 212-439-9989
834 Seventh Ave. (bet. 53rd & 54th Sts.), 212-245-7850 ◐
www.stagedeli.com

☑ "Big is an understatement" at this deli twosome known for "monster sandwiches" that leave some groaning that "too much is not necessarily a good thing"; maybe the original "doesn't compare" to its arch-rival, Carnegie Deli, but the East Side satellite is a "welcome addition" for those who "don't feel like schlepping to Midtown."

Stamatis ◐
23 | 12 | 17 | $28

31-14 Broadway (bet. 31st & 32nd Sts.), Queens, 718-204-8964
29-12 23rd Ave. (bet. 29th & 31st Sts.), Queens, 718-932-8956

■ The "food really shines" at these "authentic" Astoria Greeks boasting "good home cooking" and "reasonable prices" that keep it "plenty crowded"; oracles advise "go early", ignore the "plain" decor and "listen to the servers, they know what's good."

St. Andrews ◐
17 | 14 | 18 | $36

120 W. 44th St. (bet. B'way & 6th Ave.), 212-840-8413

■ "Down-to-earth" surf 'n' turf comes at affordable prices at this Theater District pub best known for its "huge single-malt selection" poured by "lads in kilts"; once you "fight your way past the bar", it's a "surprisingly pleasant", transporting experience.

Starbucks
13 | 11 | 12 | $9

13-25 Astor Pl. (Lafayette St.), 212-982-3563 ◐
241 Canal St. (Centre St.), 212-219-2725
152-154 Columbus Ave. (67th St.), 212-721-0470 ◐
1117 Lexington Ave. (78th St.), 212-517-8476
682 Ninth Ave. (47th St.), 212-397-2288
141-143 Second Ave. (9th St.), 212-780-0024
585 Second Ave. (32nd St.), 212-684-1299
1642 Third Ave. (92nd St.), 212-360-0425
140 Varick St. (Spring St.), 646-230-9816
77 W. 125th St. (Lenox Ave.), 917-492-2454
Additional locations throughout the NY area
www.starbucks.com

☑ "Love 'em" or "loathe 'em", these ubiquitous java huts "spread the gospel" of "rocket fuel in a cup" as they "sprout like weeds" on "every corner"; though foes complain the "Stepford coffee" is "burnt" and "overpriced", at least it's "legal and wakes you up."

Starfoods ⦿   ▽ 19 19 20 $27
64 E. First St. (1st Ave.), 212-260-3189
■ After two brief-lived incarnations (as Smith and 64), this "hip" new East Villager has been reinvented as a self-described 'French-American roadhouse' dishing out the likes of hush puppies and chicken-fried steak; a "super-nice staff" and a "Max's Kansas City–redux" vibe add up to "indie flair."

Steak Frites ⦿   17 16 16 $39
9 E. 16th St. (bet. 5th Ave. & Union Sq. W.), 212-463-7101
◪ The "Left Bank" alights near Union Square at this "essential bistro" offering "all the usual [French] suspects" for moderate prices; though some say there's "better beef-for-the-buck elsewhere", it's still a better-than-decent alternative.

Steamers Landing   ▽ 18 20 18 $37
1 Esplanade Plaza (bet. Albany & Liberty Sts., Hudson River), 212-432-1451;
www.steamerslanding.com
■ It's "hard to imagine you're in NY" at this Financial District seafooder boasting two outdoor terraces with "outstanding water views" of "fabulous sunsets"; a "terrific menu priced just right" leaves fans wondering "what more can you ask."

Stella del Mare 🖂   ▽ 22 19 23 $51
346 Lexington Ave. (bet. 39th & 40th Sts.), 212-687-4425;
www.stelladelmareny.com
■ "Still a star", this longtime Murray Hill Italian seafooder is a "romantic", "third date"–worthy spot with an "excellent" menu and an "entertaining" staff; even if "prices are high for the neighborhood", its "convenience to Grand Central" makes it popular with commuters.

St. Maggie's Cafe 🖂   18 18 18 $38
120 Wall St. (bet. Front & South Sts.), 212-943-9050
◪ "Popular with the Wall Street crowd" (and those who've "missed the ferry"), this "comfortable but not stodgy" Financial District American set in "interesting Victorian" digs proffers "solid'' fare at "reasonable" tabs; what's more, the bar's "in a class by itself."

St. Michel   ▽ 22 19 21 $44
7518 Third Ave. (bet. Bay Ridge Pkwy. & 76th St.), Brooklyn, 718-748-4411;
www.stmichelrestaurant.com
■ You'll quickly "forget you're in Bay Ridge" at this little taste of "Paris", where a "creative" kitchen turns out "delicious" French fare; "friendly service" and a "romantic", "intimate atmosphere" also make for "consistently good", if not saintly, times.

Strip House   25 23 21 $61
13 E. 12th St. (bet. 5th Ave. & University Pl.), 212-328-0000;
www.theglaziergroup.com
■ "If the Playboy Mansion had a steakhouse", it would be this "modern" take on the genre, a "sexy, seductive" Villager with "playful" decor that's one part "bordello", one part "Moulin Rouge"; "cooked-to-perfection" chops and "creative spins on traditional sides" add to its allure, and "women-friendly" service ices the cake.

Suan   ▽ 18 13 16 $24
872 Lexington Ave. (bet. 65th & 66th Sts.), 212-288-1821
◪ "Huge portions" of "fresh" Thai food at "reasonable prices" make this "neighborhood" Eastsider "hard to beat", and its "fast" service

seals the deal; though aesthetes warn "don't expect much decor", there is a "pretty outdoor area."

SUBA
19 | 27 | 19 | $47

109 Ludlow St. (bet. Delancey & Rivington Sts.), 212-982-5714; www.subanyc.com

◩ It's "all about the atmosphere" at this Lower East Side Spaniard where the "good but not great" "avant-garde" grub plays second fiddle to NY's "sexiest" dining room – a "subterranean" grotto surrounded by a "calming", illuminated moat; it "can't be beat for a first date", and for "added adventure", try their monthly "dinner in the dark", which is just what it sounds like.

Sueños ●
– | – | – | E

(fka Alley's End)

311 W. 17th St. (bet. 8th & 9th Aves.), 212-243-1333

Chef Sue Torres (Rocking Horse, Hell's Kitchen) returns to Chelsea with this inventive new Mexican, hidden in the hard-to-find space that formerly housed Alley's End; it features the same glassed-in garden and psychedelic bathroom as before, but now there's a four-course chile tasting menu, an extensive tequila list and a staffer on hand rolling fresh tortillas.

Sugar Hill Bistro
∇ 20 | 22 | 17 | $39

458 W. 145th St. (bet. Amsterdam & Convent Aves.), 212-491-5505; www.sugarhillbistro.com

◼ A "historic, four-story brownstone" is the "stunning" setting for this Harlem American-Eclectic bringing some "class and elegance" to the scene; the "well-meaning" service "may not be very polished", but no one minds much given the "good", midpriced grub, live weekend jazz and "great" Sunday gospel brunch.

Sugiyama ⑤
26 | 20 | 26 | $95

251 W. 55th St. (bet. B'way & 8th Ave.), 212-956-0670

◼ To feel like a "judge on the *Iron Chef*", try this Midtown Japanese where master toque Nao Sugiyama oversees the "most innovative kaiseki kitchen in NYC"; sure, it's plenty "expensive", and savoring the 12-course option can "take all night", but foodies who imagine they've "died and gone to Tokyo" think this "culinary high-water mark" "couldn't be improved."

Sultan ●
21 | 15 | 20 | $33

1435 Second Ave. (bet. 74th & 75th Sts.), 212-861-0200; www.sultan-nyc.com

◼ For a "nice change from all the Italian places on Second Avenue", check out this "exotic" Turk turning out "tasty", "moderately priced" food, with "sweet servers" as a bonus; maybe the "tacky" decor is a deficit, but the "outside seating is a big plus."

Summit ⑤
– | – | – | E

308 E. 49th St. (bet. 1st & 2nd Aves.), 212-759-1964; www.summitnyc.com

The spirit of Sinatra is alive and swinging at this New American neophyte near the UN that celebrates the Chairman of the Board in all his Rat Pack grandeur, complete with zebra-skin rugs, a mural of Palm Springs and a luck-be-a-lady-tonight piano lounge; the food's just as snappy, and the staff's coolly engaging.

Superfine
∇ 17 | 18 | 15 | $30

126 Front St. (Pearl St.), Brooklyn, 718-243-9005; www.eatatsuperfine.com

◩ "Is it NY or Seattle in the '90s?" ask hipsters about this "bohemian" Dumbo bar/eatery, a "roomy", "no-attitude" joint that gets "crowded" as the night wears on; its "straightforward" but "limited" Med menu is "tasty" enough, but "go early or risk the popular items being gone."

Supper ●⌀
156 E. Second St. (bet. Aves. A & B), 212-477-7600

22 | 18 | 18 | $32

■ "Just as good as its sister restaurant, Frank", this East Village Tuscan is "like eating at your hipster Italian grandma's", albeit with "communal tables", a "no-reservations", "cash-only" policy and "excruciatingly long waits"; the consensus is the "heavenly" grub is "worth it", especially given tabs that are most "welcome in this economy."

Sur ●
232 Smith St. (bet. Butler & Douglass Sts.), Brooklyn, 718-875-1716

21 | 19 | 18 | $34

■ Brooklyn "beef bingers" tout this Cobble Hill Argentinean for its "dependable" meats and "must-try" grill; though "service continues to be an issue" and seating is "tight", it's more than "affordable" and "not too trendy", despite the Smith Street address.

Surya
302 Bleecker St. (bet. Grove St. & 7th Ave. S.), 212-807-7770

▽ 21 | 17 | 18 | $36

■ An "antidote to Sixth Street", this "inventive" Village Indian offers "nouveau" cooking featuring "subtle spicing"; other pluses include a "soothing" interior, "terrific garden" and a "bargain brunch."

Sushi Ann ⌧
(fka Sushisay)
38 E. 51st St. (bet. Madison & Park Aves.), 212-755-1780

▽ 21 | 16 | 19 | $67

■ "Tokyo-quality" sushi lures purists to this "low-key" Midtown Japanese (fka Sushisay) whose "name change makes no difference": the "impeccably fresh, perfectly handled" goods, "sterile" surroundings and "ridiculous" tabs mirror its predecessor.

Sushiden
19 E. 49th St. (bet. 5th & Madison Aves.), 212-758-2700
123 W. 49th St. (bet. 6th & 7th Aves.), 212-398-2800 ⌧
www.sushiden.com

23 | 17 | 20 | $51

■ "Worth the splurge" for "exotic appetizers" and "perfectly prepared fish", these somewhat "expensive" crosstown Japanese draw business types seeking a "fast" lunch; come dinnertime, the mood's more relaxed and "quiet", allowing you to appreciate the "pleasant" staff and "traditional" atmosphere all the more.

Sushi Hana ●
466 Amsterdam Ave. (bet. 82nd & 83rd Sts.), 212-874-0369
1501 Second Ave. (78th St.), 212-327-0582
www.sushihana.com

22 | 17 | 18 | $34

■ "Always crowded, and with good reason", these "low-key", modestly priced Japanese twins are "standard bearers" for "superfresh" "designer sushi" and a "variety of cooked foods"; fans say the "swanky" West Side branch is the "hipper" of the two, although the East Side's 'round-the-corner sake bar evens the score.

SUSHI OF GARI
402 E. 78th St. (bet. 1st & York Aves.), 212-517-5340

26 | 11 | 18 | $53

■ "Sushi doesn't come any fresher" than at this Upper East Side Japanese where regulars "don't order from the menu" but rather let chef "Gari choose"; sure, it may cost a lot, but this "ultimate experience" is "worth it" so long as you don't mind "zero" decor and "patrons packed in like sardines"; P.S. reservations are "mandatory."

Sushi Rose ⌧
248 E. 52nd St., 2nd fl. (bet. 2nd & 3rd Aves.), 212-813-1800

21 | 13 | 17 | $37

☑ Now that the "secret is out" about Saturday's "half-price sushi" deal, there are "lines out the door" at this always-"affordable", somewhat "unknown" Japanese hidden on the second floor of a Midtown block; "cramped" quarters and not much decor are the trade-offs.

SushiSamba ●
22 | 22 | 16 | $45

245 Park Ave. S. (bet. 19th & 20th Sts.), 212-475-9377
87 Seventh Ave. S. (bet. Bleecker & W. 4th Sts.), 212-691-7885
www.sushisamba.com

☑ "Young jet-setters" and "wanna-be celebs" rev up at these "energetic" Brazilian/Japanese "total scenes" where "sexy sushi" and "juicy seviches" are washed down with "designer" Latin cocktails; despite "hit-or-miss" service, "long waits" and "pricey" tabs, most say they appreciate the experience – especially on the West Side outlet's "joy" of a rooftop deck.

Sushi Seki ●
26 | 15 | 21 | $54

1143 First Ave. (bet. 62nd & 63rd Sts.), 212-371-0238

■ "Breaking new ground", this "heavenly" new East Side Japanese is overseen by a "disciple of Sushi of Gari" with "nouvelle" ideas that guarantee an "amazing omakase"; be prepared to "pay an arm and a shark's fin", but bonuses include "knowledgeable servers" and late-"late hours" (till 3 AM nightly).

Sushi Sen-nin
27 | 14 | 23 | $46

49 E. 34th St. (bet. Madison & Park Aves.), 212-889-2208;
www.sushisennin.com

■ Somehow, this Murray Hill Japanese "sleeper" is "still somewhat unknown", despite some of the "highest quality" sushi around as well as "accommodating", "above-and-beyond" service; just "get ready to open your wallet" for the privilege, though diehards say "they could charge even more if they redid the decor."

Sushiya
▽ 21 | 12 | 18 | $30

28 W. 56th St. (bet. 5th & 6th Aves.), 212-247-5760

☑ "Better-than-average" sushi at "price-is-right" tabs sums up this "consistent" Midtown Japanese; its "typical decor" may be "nothing fancy" and the staff "friendly if not totally competent", but the overall performance here is "solid" and "reliable."

SUSHI YASUDA ☒
27 | 23 | 24 | $70

204 E. 43rd St. (bet. 2nd & 3rd Aves.), 212-972-1001;
www.sushiyasuda.com

■ "Hard-to-find specialties" of "pristine" fish make for "sushi as art" at this "ethereal" Japanese near the UN, where "omakase is the best way to explore chef Maomichi Yasuda's ability"; the "Calvin Klein decor" and "sublime" service also contribute to the overall "out-of-body experience", brought to an abrupt climax by the "astronomical bill."

Sushi Zen ☒
25 | 19 | 22 | $50

108 W. 44th St. (bet. B'way & 6th Ave.), 212-302-0707; www.sushizen-ny.com

■ They're on a roll at this Theater District "Japanese treasure" that's all the more "pleasant" since relocating to "bigger" digs last year; fans say if the "first-class" sushi "got any fresher", they'd be "standing in water" to eat it, though the "Uptown prices" have a few over a barrel.

Svenningsen's
▽ 20 | 13 | 20 | $35

292 Fifth Ave. (bet. 30th & 31st Sts.), 212-465-1888;
www.svenningsensnyc.com

■ The "underserved" Garment District gets a boost with the arrival of this new, "decently priced" seafooder from the former chef of nearby Marble Collegiate Church; supporters shrug off the "suburban mall" appearance and focus instead on its "to-die-for lobster rolls" and "genuine live pianist."

Sweet Melissa ⌐

23 18 19 $16

276 Court St. (bet. Butler & Douglass Sts.), Brooklyn, 718-855-3410

■ To "indulge in buttery naughtiness" or just "a spot of tea", try this "tiny", "laid-back" Cobble Hill patisserie that dishes out light cafe fare and "delicate desserts"; life is particularly *dolce* in the "lovely" back garden where you can BYO and "pretend you're in Europe."

Sweet-n-Tart Cafe ◑⌐

20 12 13 $16

76 Mott St. (Canal St.), 212-334-8088
136-11 38th Ave. (Main St.), Queens, 718-661-3380
www.sweetntart.com

■ *Tong shui* "healing soups" and other "hip Chinese foods" highlight the "something-for-everyone" menus of these "cheeky Hong Kong–style" joints whose "name doesn't do justice to their range of tastes"; though service can be "tart", they're "cheap" and "open late."

Sweet-n-Tart Restaurant ◑

21 14 15 $21

20 Mott St. (Chatham Sq.), 212-964-0380; www.sweetntart.com

■ "It's worth being on jury duty" for the chance to lunch at this "cheap" Chinatown "destination" where most opt for the "tantalizing" dim sum, although there are a lot of other choices on the menu; the tri-level setup provides "much more room" than its Cafe siblings, even if the decor is almost as "tacky."

Swifty's ◑

17 18 17 $55

1007 Lexington Ave. (bet. 72nd & 73rd Sts.), 212-535-6000; www.swiftysny.com

◪ "Social butterflies", "old moguls" and the "Dominick Dunne set" ("Hi Nan! Hi Binky!") patronize this "clubby" Mario Buatta–designed, East Side "heir to Mortimer's"; the American WASP fare is only "fair" and plays second fiddle to the "bold-faced name people-watching."

Sylvia's

17 11 17 $29

328 Lenox Ave. (bet. 126th & 127th Sts.), 212-996-0660;
www.sylviassoulfood.com

◪ "Down-home" soul food "served with Southern hospitality" keeps the trade brisk at this longtime Harlem "gorgefest" famed for its weekend jazz and gospel brunches; though a few find it "too busy and touristy" and in "need of renovation", the "huge lines to get in" are the bottom line.

Symposium

19 14 19 $22

544 W. 113th St. (bet. Amsterdam Ave. & B'way), 212-865-1011

◪ "Not much has changed in over 30 years" at this "folksy" Greek taverna that's been a long-standing "Columbia University hangout"; sure, it may be in "need of a rehab", but its "easy-on-the-pocketbook" pricing and "secret back garden" keep lots of students from starving.

TABLA

25 25 24 $61

11 Madison Ave. (25th St.), 212-889-0667

■ "Your palate will have a field day" at Danny Meyer's Madison Square "fusion superstar" where chef Floyd Cardoz puts a "postmodern spin" on New American cooking via some "dazzling" Indian accents; the "royal-welcome" service and "awe-inspiring" space will make you "feel like a raja", but once you reach nirvana plan to "pull out the platinum card" – though the $25 prix fixe lunch (or the downstairs Bread Bar) is a "cheaper way to experience it."

Table d'Hôte

21 16 21 $45

44 E. 92nd St. (bet. Madison & Park Aves.), 212-348-8125

■ Bring your "skinny friends" to this Carnegie Hill Franco-American "charmer" that's "smaller than an elevator" but still works for a "sophisticated" bite; even those who find that "'intimate' turns to 'cramped' by the second course" admit that the $22 pre-theater "bargain" is "worth the squeeze."

Tai Hong Lau
▽ 18 | 10 | 12 | $22

70 Mott St. (bet. Bayard & Canal Sts.), 212-219-1431

⬛ Though the "limited dim sum selection" comes from a list (not a cart) at this C-town Cantonese seafooder, the tiny bites are "excellent", ditto the "intriguing wild cards" on the menu; though the "tattered decor" and service could use help, overall it's still a "solid" choice.

Taka
25 | 15 | 20 | $40

61 Grove St. (bet. Bleecker St. & 7th Ave. S.), 212-242-3699

⬛ "Lovingly prepared sushi" with "attention to detail" arrives on "homemade plates" at this midpriced but "top-class" Village Japanese that's the domain of Takako Yoneyama, its "chef and pottery maker" (the "only thing she doesn't do is eat the food for you"); although it's "somewhat of a secret", there can be "lines" since it's so "small."

Takahachi
▽ 23 | 13 | 18 | $28

145 Duane St. (bet. Church St. & W. B'way), 212-571-1830
85 Ave. A (bet. 5th & 6th Sts.), 212-505-6524 ●

⬛ This East Village Japanese "neighborhood stalwart" goes "beyond sushi and tempura" with its "creative daily specials"; "crowded" conditions make for a "clangy atmosphere", but the "reasonable prices" fully compensate; N.B. the TriBeCa outpost is new and unrated.

Talia's Steakhouse
– | – | – | E

668 Amsterdam Ave. (bet. 92nd & 93rd Sts.), 212-580-3770;
www.taliassteakhouse.com

Wear your yarmulke to fit in with the modern orthodox crowd at this bustling, *haimishe* neighborhood glatt kosher steakhouse on the Upper West Side; though the small, pricey menu is less steak-focused than its name would suggest, there's a small bar to meet a J-Date.

Tamarind ●
24 | 23 | 21 | $47

41-43 E. 22nd St. (bet. B'way & Park Ave. S.), 212-674-7400;
www.tamarinde22.com

⬛ "Head and shoulders above" most of its peers, this "high-end", "high-style" Flatiron Indian "soothes the soul" with "distinctive fusion" dishes that "transcend the genre"; the "modern", "minimalist" digs and "knowledgeable" staff help make it "well worth the extra rupees."

Tangerine ●Ⓢ
▽ 18 | 20 | 16 | $40

228 W. 10th St. (bet. Bleecker & Hudson Sts.), 212-463-9670

⬛ As "sleek and trendy" as its patrons, this "sceney" bi-level West Villager also offers "tasty" Thai cooking; critics explain the "inflated prices" by saying you're "paying for the decor."

Tang Pavilion
23 | 17 | 22 | $35

65 W. 55th St. (bet. 5th & 6th Aves.), 212-956-6888

⬛ "Consistent high quality" is the hallmark of this "no-nonsense" Midtown Chinese serving "reliable" Shanghai-style fare that's "great for the price" and just right for "pleasant business" lunching; "blazing quick service" means you'll get "in and out fast."

Tanti Baci Caffé
▽ 18 | 13 | 18 | $28

513 E. Sixth St. (bet. Aves. A & B), 212-979-8184
163 W. 10th St. (bet. 7th Ave. S. & Waverly Pl.), 212-647-9651

⬛ For "simple, well-prepared" Italian food with "lots of garlic", this crosstown Village duo is a "cheap and reliable" option with a "casual" mood; those who find it "mediocre" advise "stick to the pastas"; N.B. the East Village location is closed at press time.

TAO ●

| 22 | 26 | 17 | $53 |

42 E. 58th St. (bet. Madison & Park Aves.), 212-888-2288; www.taonyc.com

■ There's no place better to "show off your sexy clothes" than this Midtown "hot spot" set in a "cavernous" room complete with a "two-story-high Buddha"; sure, "service could be better" and the "prolonged waits" are a drag, but supporters swear the "excellent" Pan-Asian eats are even tastier when you're "sitting next to Paris Hilton."

Taormina ●

| ∇ 21 | 19 | 19 | $40 |

147 Mulberry St. (bet. Grand & Hester Sts.), 212-219-1007

■ It's "fun to sit outside and people-watch" at this longtime Mulberry Street Italian, an "old reliable" for "consistently fine" food and service that "makes you feel like family"; old-timers say it used to be John "Gotti's favorite place, so you know it had to be good" – and if it wasn't, nobody would dare argue.

Tapas Lounge ●

| 17 | 20 | 15 | $39 |

1078 First Ave. (59th St.), 212-421-8282

■ The "atmosphere's suitably moody" at this Spanish tapas joint opposite the Queensboro Bridge serving "savory" small plates and "merciless sangria"; despite brickbats for "snooty service" and "hefty prices", there's applause for its "*Casablanca*"-esque vibe.

Tartine ∉

| 22 | 12 | 15 | $25 |

253 W. 11th St. (W. 4th St.), 212-229-2611

■ They "don't take rezzies" (or plastic) at this "likable", "inexpensive" Village French bistro, so be prepared for "long lines", particularly for its "wonderful" weekend brunch; in return, there's "dependably tasty" food, a "love-that-BYO" policy and a "non-hurried" ambiance.

Taste

| ∇ 21 | 16 | 18 | $48 |

Eli's Manhattan, 1413 Third Ave. (80th St.), 212-717-9798;
www.elizabar.com

■ Formerly Eli's Restaurant, this "inventive" New American bistro/ wine bar "for adults" features "delicious", market-fresh items paired with a "great by-the-glass" wine list; though some "wish the prices were slightly less", most agree the place "certainly lives up to its name."

TASTING ROOM ⧄

| 25 | 18 | 26 | $53 |

72 E. First St. (bet. 1st & 2nd Aves.), 212-358-7831

■ Ok, the "wine list may be bigger than the restaurant", but no one minds much at this "brilliant" East Village New American where the "chef loves to experiment and never seems to miss"; blend in "deft service" and "interesting" vinos drawn from "American micro-vineyards", and the "expensive" pricing and absurdly "small setup" loses its sting.

Tatany

| 22 | 11 | 16 | $31 |

250 E. 52nd St. (bet. 2nd & 3rd Aves.), 212-593-0203 ●
380 Third Ave. (bet. 27th & 28th Sts.), 212-686-1871
www.tatany.com

■ "Rock-solid sushi" "served with flair" at "exceptional-value" prices explains the popularity of these East Side Japanese twins; they may be "nothing fancy" and their freshness "includes the staff", but these "neighborhood godsends" are certainly "better than most."

Taverna Kyclades ●

| 24 | 11 | 18 | $27 |

33-07 Ditmars Blvd. (bet. 33rd & 35th Sts.), Queens, 718-545-8666

■ "Heavenly Greek seafood" "simply prepared" is the hallmark of this Hellenic "hot spot" that's among the "best in Astoria", and since they don't take reservations, you should expect a wait; since there's "no decor", insiders head for the "outside terrace."

Taverna Vraka ▽ 18 16 17 $35

*23-15 31st St. (bet. 23rd & 24th Aves.), Queens, 718-721-3007;
www.vraka.com*

■ "Not the place to go if you want to talk", this "lively" Astoria Greek taverna is known for its "solid", midpriced meals accompanied by rousing "music on the weekends"; if the "good spirits" become too frenzied, "sit in the back" where it's a bit more "relaxing."

TAVERN ON THE GREEN 15 25 17 $59

*Central Park W. (bet. 66th & 67th Sts.), 212-873-3200;
www.tavernonthegreen.com*

■ "Everyone's inner child" finds this Central Park "fantasyland" an "enchanting" experience, from the "gorgeous Crystal Room" to the "convivial" garden; even if a few find the American food "expensive for the quality" and the decor too reminiscent of "Elvis' bedroom", its "evergreen appeal" extends beyond "tourists" to "hardened NYers" who insist it can't be beat for a party or for a bargain prix fixe lunch.

Tea & Sympathy 20 16 16 $24

*108 Greenwich Ave. (bet. 12th & 13th Sts.), 212-807-8329;
www.teaandsympathynewyork.com*

■ "Peckish" Brits "look homeward" at this Village tea shop that also purveys "simple English favorites" like shepherd's pie and bangers 'n' mash; it's comparable to a "trip to London without the rain", despite "sassy" service and a "seriously claustrophobic" space.

Tea Box ▽ 20 19 17 $29

Takashimaya, 693 Fifth Ave. (bet. 54th & 55th Sts.), 212-350-0180

■ "Midafternoon sugar crises" are averted at this "serene" Midtown department store tearoom offering a chance to "pause and collect yourself when shopping"; regulars report everything on the Japanese-American menu is "small and delicate – except the prices."

teany ● ▽ 18 17 16 $15

*90 Rivington St. (bet. Ludlow & Orchard Sts.), 212-475-9190;
www.teany.com*

☑ "It's hip, it's affordable, it's vegan" – and this Lower East Side tea cafe is also co-owned by pop star Moby, hence the "save-the-planet" vibe and "trendy" followers decked out in "vintage" threads; despite "flighty service" and "sterile" decor, this is one of the rare places "without pretension or staidness."

Tello's 18 16 19 $34

263 W. 19th St. (bet. 7th & 8th Aves.), 212-691-8696

☑ "Straight out of *The Godfather*", this "old-fashioned" Chelsea Italian is just the ticket for a "flavorful", "uncomplicated" dinner "before going to the Joyce"; the "staff's so sweet" that it's "good to be a regular" here, even if some surveyors find "nothing to write home about."

Telly's Taverna ●✦ ▽ 23 12 17 $33

28-13 23rd Ave. (bet. 28th & 29th Sts.), Queens, 718-728-9056

■ Since it's been "newly expanded", "you don't have to wait as long to be seated" at this "marvelous" Greek seafooder, one of "Astoria's finest" thanks to its "wonderful" grilled fish; even better, service is "friendly", the "outdoor garden's fantastic" and you won't drop a lot of drachmas.

Tennessee Mountain 16 11 14 $29

143 Spring St. (Wooster St.), 212-431-3993; www.tnmountain.com

☑ "Roll up your sleeves" and dig right in at this "cheap" SoHo BBQ specialist that "keeps Lipitor in business" with endless platters of "basic", "bib"-worthy ribs; its "youngish" following digs the $14.95

all-you-can-eat deals on Mondays and Tuesdays, and tolerates the "lousy" service and "tired" decor.

Ten Sushi ●
— | — | — | M

116 Ave. C (bet. 7th & 8th Sts.), 212-505-9471
The name means 'heaven' in Japanese, and this "super-cool" Alphabet City newcomer goes beyond "beautifully presented sushi" with items like seared tuna tempura roll and crispy oyster with tomato confit; locals ask "who would have thought Avenue C could look like this?"

Teodora
21 | 15 | 19 | $45

141 E. 57th St. (bet. Lexington & 3rd Aves.), 212-826-7101
■ "Bountiful portions" of first-rate Italian food explain the "cramped" feeling at this midpriced Midtowner that's a bit more spacious upstairs; the kitchen specializes in "true tastes" from the Emilia-Romagna region, injecting an element of "surprise" into a somewhat "lacking area."

Teresa's
18 | 10 | 13 | $18

103 First Ave. (bet. 6th & 7th Sts.), 212-228-0604
80 Montague St. (Hicks St.), Brooklyn, 718-797-3996
■ There are "no diets allowed" at these "belly-stuffing" Polish coffee shops, purveyors of "stick-to-your-ribs" Eastern European comfort food; ok, there's also "no flare", and service ranges from "perfunctory" to "unfriendly", but for "cheap home cooking", they're hard to top.

Terrace in the Sky
22 | 25 | 22 | $63

400 W. 119th St. (bet. Amsterdam Ave. & Morningside Dr.), 212-666-9490
■ "Breathtaking" 360-degree city views make for "destination" dining at this Morningside Heights French-Med rooftop that's a no-brainer for "Columbia graduation" celebrations; though "you'll pay plenty" for the privilege, in return you get "well-prepared" food and "romantic harp music" that enhance the "celestial" vistas.

Terra 47
— | — | — | M

47 E. 12th St. (bet. B'way & University Pl.), 212-358-0103; www.terra47.com
This "health-conscious" Village organic supplies "earth-friendly" salads and sandwiches as well as "full-blown dinners"; the "serene" setup is as "revitalizing" as the repasts, ditto the fair pricing.

Terrance Brennan's
Seafood & Chop House
21 | 19 | 19 | $66

(fka An American Place)

Benjamin Hotel, 565 Lexington Ave. (bet. 50th & 51st Sts.), 212-715-2400;
www.thebenjamin.com
■ Take a "trip down memory lane" at this "old-school" Midtown surf 'n' turfer via Terry Brennan that unabashedly celebrates "retro" dining with dishes like steak Diane and baked Alaska; "tableside" preparations, a "plush" setting and "decadent", à-la-carte-only side dishes make it a must-visit, preferably on "someone else's expense account."

Tevere
∇ 21 | 19 | 20 | $51

155 E. 84th St. (bet. Lexington & 3rd Aves.), 212-744-0210
■ "You won't believe it's kosher" at this Upper East Side Italian, what with its "basic, well-done" preparations; though the "tight quarters" and "expensive" pricing are distractions, regulars report it's "always reliable" and thus "always crowded."

T.G.I. Friday's
10 | 10 | 11 | $24

1680 Broadway (bet. 52nd & 53rd Sts.), 212-767-8326 ●
1552 Broadway (46th St.), 212-944-7352 ●
196 Broadway (bet. Fulton & John Sts.), 212-240-1280

(continued)

(continued)
T.G.I. Friday's
47 Broadway (Exchange Pl.), 212-483-8322
47 E. 42nd St. (bet. Madison & Vanderbilt Aves.), 212-681-8458
484 Eighth Ave. (34th St.), 212-630-0307
604 Fifth Ave. (bet. 48th & 49th Sts.), 212-767-8335
677 Lexington Ave. (56th St.), 212-339-8858
761 Seventh Ave. (50th St.), 212-767-8350
www.tgifridays.com

"If you've got imagination", these "generic" chain Americans might not be your cup of T given their "shopping-mall" meals, "depressing decor", "slow service" and "expensive" pricing; but on the positive side, "seats are usually available."

Thai House Cafe ⊠⇄
▽ 21 | 8 | 19 | $19

151 Hudson St. (Hubert St.), 212-334-1085

Regulars "go with the owner's suggestions" at this "reliable" TriBeCa Thai that "doesn't take credit cards" but dishes out "always delicious" food for "extremely reasonable" prices; aesthetes dis the decor as "garish" and "stick to takeout or delivery."

Thailand
22 | 10 | 14 | $21

106 Bayard St. (Baxter St.), 212-349-3132

"One reason to look forward to jury duty", this C-town Thai draws everyone from "district attorneys to defendants" with its "authentically spiced" chow that's "just as cheap as it is scrumptious"; "too-fast service" and minimal decor are downsides.

Thalassa
▽ 23 | 24 | 22 | $59

179 Franklin St. (bet. Greenwich & Hudson Sts.), 212-941-7661;
www.thalassanyc.com

A "dramatic addition to the TriBeCa scene", this new, Milos-style Greek seafooder lays out a dizzying spread of pristine fish that's "so fresh you can taste the sea"; the "beautiful, airy" digs reflect the "high-end" mood, complete with "platinum card"–worthy, "by-the-pound" pricing; P.S. there's an equally posh party space downstairs.

Thalia ●
21 | 22 | 19 | $47

828 Eighth Ave. (50th St.), 212-399-4444;
www.restaurantthalia.com

The "classiest thing to happen to Eighth Avenue" in some time, this "sophisticated" Theater District New American features an "imaginative" menu full of "interesting choices"; as for the decor, there are "soaring ceilings" and "huge windows" offering a view of the "world going by."

36 Bar and BBQ ●
– | – | – | M

5 W. 36th St. (5th Ave.), 212-563-3737

"Authentic", do-it-yourself Korean barbecue is nothing unusual in the Garment District, but this new arrival ups the ante with one of the "sleekest, most modern" setups in the genre; you should dress as if attending a "SoHo" event, but pick clothes that you won't mind "smelling like barbecued beef" afterward.

Thom
20 | 22 | 18 | $54

60 Thompson Hotel, 60 Thompson St. (bet. Broome & Spring Sts.),
212-219-2000; www.60thompson.com

"Atmosphere is everything" at this "too cool for school" SoHo hotel establishment where the "chic environment" and "gorgeous" crowd nearly trump the Asian-inflected New American cuisine; "uneven" service, "black card"–worthy pricing and "so much attitude" keep the "wanna-bes" at bay.

Thomas Beisl ●
▽ 21 | 20 | 20 | $38

25 Lafayette Ave. (Ashland Pl.), Brooklyn, 718-222-5800
■ A "welcome addition to the Fort Greene dining scene", this "charming" new Austrian bistro via chef Thomas Ferlesch (ex Café des Artistes) produces "perfect renditions" of Viennese classics at "better prices" than Manhattan; culture vultures are thrilled it's arrived in the "culinary wasteland near BAM."

Three Bow Thais ⊄
▽ 18 | 14 | 19 | $17

278 Smith St. (bet. DeGraw & Sackett Sts.), Brooklyn, 718-834-0511
◪ Despite the "terrible name", this Smith Street Thai comes through with "basic", "cheap eats"; detractors find it "boring" spending "not many bucks" for "not much bang", but at least delivery's "prompt."

Three of Cups ●
18 | 14 | 16 | $24

83 First Ave. (5th St.), 212-388-0059; www.threeofcupsnyc.com
■ "From pizza to pasta, no plate is left unturned" at this East Village Italian "staple" where the brick-oven pies come at "appealing prices" and are served "late" into the night; though the space is a bit "rundown", the "laid-back" mood and "fun downstairs lounge" make it a youth magnet.

360
– | – | – | M

360 Van Brunt St. (bet. Dikeman & Wolcott Sts.), Brooklyn, 718-246-0360
It's open Thursday–Sunday only, so reservations are suggested at this new Red Hook French bistro that's already known for its bargain $20 prix fixe, though there are a few à la carte items available too; an interesting list of inexpensive wines helps fill the bill.

325 Spring Street ◐
▽ 22 | 19 | 20 | $53

(fka Théo)
325 Spring St. (bet. Greenwich & Washington Sts.), 212-414-1344
■ A self-described 'truffle bistro', this "promising" new West SoHo spot successfully employs the delicacy along with a short list of tasty Provençal items; not surprisingly, given its choice ingredients and slick art moderne looks, it's on the pricey side, but solid ratings across the board indicate it's delivering the goods; P.S. there's also a "trendy" upstairs lounge.

Tierras Colombianas ⊄
▽ 20 | 11 | 18 | $21

33-01 Broadway (33rd St.), Queens, 718-956-3012
82-18 Roosevelt Ave. (82nd St.), Queens, 718-426-8868
■ "Plates the size of Bogotá" come piled with "hearty" grub at these "busy" Queens Columbians where the food's "light on the wallet but heavy on the belly"; "hungry hombres" applaud the "friendly" staff and tolerate the plain-Juanita decor.

Time Cafe
15 | 13 | 14 | $28

2330 Broadway (85th St.), 212-579-5100 ●
380 Lafayette St. (Great Jones St.), 212-533-7000
www.timecafenyc.com
◪ Clock-watchers say it's about "time for some updating" at these "uninspiring" Uptown/Downtown Americans that strike many as "glorified diners" given the only "decent" eats and "space-cadet" service; oh well, at least the attached Moroccan bars make for "convenient after-dinner drinks."

Tio Pepe ●
▽ 21 | 18 | 20 | $31

168 W. Fourth St. (bet. 6th & 7th Aves.), 212-242-9338; www.tiopepenyc.com
■ Whether for a "romantic evening" or "relaxing with friends", this Spanish-Mexican Villager offers "very good" standards at "prices

that won't send you to the poorhouse"; perhaps it's "not the most lively spot" around, but its "skylit garden" is a "great place to get started."

Titou
21 | 18 | 19 | $33

259 W. Fourth St. (bet. Charles & Perry Sts.), 212-691-9359

■ "Too bad the sidewalk isn't bigger" outside this "tiny" West Village French bistro given all the folks hoping to "grab a table" curbside; a sibling of Tartine, it's just as "reasonably priced", with the same "dinner-party" feel, but you have a "better shot of getting seated."

TOCQUEVILLE
26 | 22 | 24 | $62

15 E. 15th St. (bet. 5th Ave. & Union Sq. W.), 212-647-1515

■ "Civilized" dining thrives at this "intimate" Union Square French-American "bijou" that's right "up there with the best in the city"; "masterful" service, a "lovely" (if "sparely decorated") room and "exquisite" meals make the prices easier to swallow, and even if it's "overshadowed by nearby heavy-hitters", connoisseurs consider it close to "perfection."

Toledo ⊠
∇ 23 | 21 | 23 | $50

6 E. 36th St. (bet. 5th & Madison Aves.), 212-696-5036;
www.toledorestaurant.com

■ "Like being in Madrid – only closer" – this Murray Hill Spaniard offers "authentic" dining in a "sumptuous" setting replete with a "view of the Empire State Building from the back room"; though the "huge portions" come with "matching prices", its mature following doesn't mind.

Tommaso's
∇ 22 | 18 | 21 | $40

1464 86th St. (bet. 14th & 15th Aves.), Brooklyn, 718-236-9883

☑ "Arias" come free with the "great" osso buco at this "traditional" Bensonhurst Italian where owner-tenor Thomas Verdillo "serenades" diners "when moved to do so", and the "amazing wine list" also wins bravos; all-you-can-eat dinners make it really "fun during Carnevale."

TOMOE SUSHI ⊠
27 | 7 | 16 | $35

172 Thompson St. (bet. Bleecker & Houston Sts.), 212-777-9346

☑ Ok, "ambiance doesn't exist" at this "small" Village Japanese and there are always "painfully long lines", but the payoff is sushi "fit for royalty at prices affordable to serfs"; so until they "get a bigger space", it's "best to go early" and "bring a good book to read" since the sushi here would be "superlative even in Kyoto."

Tomo Sushi & Sake Bar ❶
17 | 16 | 17 | $24

2850 Broadway (bet. 110th & 111th Sts.), 212-665-2916

☑ "Hugely popular with the Columbia crowd", this Morningside Heights Japanese slices "basic" sushi for "low prices", but those who find "no thrills" cite "erratic" quality and "iffy service."

Tom's ⊠⊖
∇ 21 | 19 | 24 | $14

782 Washington Ave. (Sterling Pl.), Brooklyn, 718-636-9738

■ Chock-full of "character and charm", this Prospect Heights "throwback" shop (circa 1936) dishes out "classic" Americana, including fab egg creams, in "soda fountain" surroundings; "zoom-zoom" service and "retro" pricing make this a "trip down memory lane, when life was simpler"; N.B. breakfast and lunch only, closed Sundays.

Tony's Di Napoli
18 | 14 | 17 | $31

1606 Second Ave. (83rd St.), 212-861-8686
147 W. 43rd St. (bet. B'way & 6th Ave.), 212-221-0100
www.tonysdinapoli.com

■ "Go starving" to these "kid-friendly" "crowd-pleasers" known for their "hefty, family-style portions" of red-sauce Italian food ("even the bathroom soap has garlic in it"); critics call them "Carmine's wanna-bes", but have no complaints about those "budget" tabs; P.S. the new Times Square outpost is already a "total zoo."

Topaz Thai
21 | 11 | 15 | $26

127 W. 56th St. (bet. 6th & 7th Aves.), 212-957-8020

⚹ "Perfect pre–Carnegie Hall", this "tiny" Midtown Thai is "justifiably packed" at lunchtime given its "terrific" cooking, "breakneck-speed" service and budget prices; but unless you get the coveted "window seat", the setting may be a "bit too intimate."

Top of the Tower
∇ 14 | 25 | 18 | $44

Beekman Tower, 3 Mitchell Pl. (1st Ave. & 49th St.), 212-980-4796;
www.mesuite.com

■ The "breathtaking", 360-degree "rooftop" view is the raison d'être of this sexy art deco Midtown American-Continental, not the "so-so" food or "steep pricing", ergo many settle for a "drink at the bar" and an earful of live piano music; since it's often closed for private parties, phone first.

Toraya ⊠
∇ 18 | 20 | 18 | $30

17 E. 71st St. (bet. 5th & Madison Aves.), 212-861-1700;
www.toraya-america.com

■ To "get away from the cacophony of the city", try this "meditative", lunch-only East Side Japanese teahouse, a reminder that the "word 'restaurant' is derived from the word 'restorative'"; expect "micro portions" of "interesting snacks", as well as "tea and sympathy."

Torre di Pisa ⊠
18 | 21 | 19 | $49

19 W. 44th St. (bet. 5th & 6th Aves.), 212-398-4400

⚹ The "whimsical" "leaning"-Tower-of-Pisa design (from David Rockwell) nearly overwhelms the basic, "hearty" chow at this "airy" Midtown Northern Italian; penny-pinchers say the "expensive" pricing is similarly "off-kilter", but Broadway babies like the feeling of "eating on a stage set."

Tossed
17 | 8 | 13 | $16

295 Park Ave. S. (bet. 22nd & 23rd Sts.), 212-674-6700
30 Rockefeller Plaza Concourse (bet. 49th & 50th Sts.),
212-218-2525 ⊠
www.tossed.com

⚹ Making salads "less boring" is this "choose-your-own"-ingredients duo offering "all the fixings" imaginable; while the Rock Center outlet only does takeout, the Flatiron location is "all-purpose", cafeteria-style at lunch and full-service come dinnertime.

Totonno Pizzeria Napolitano
23 | 11 | 15 | $20

1544 Second Ave. (bet. 80th & 81st Sts.), 212-327-2800
1524 Neptune Ave. (bet. W. 15th & 16th Sts.), Brooklyn,
718-372-8606 ⊅
www.totonnos.com

■ Diehards declare the "quest for perfect pizza ends" at this circa-1924 Coney Island pie purveyor also famed for "lovingly gruff" service that "adds to its allure"; though its full-menu Yorkville sibling may be "minor league" in comparison, it's just as "busy" as the original.

Tournesol ◗
23 | 16 | 21 | $36

50-12 Vernon Blvd. (bet. 50th & 51st Aves.), Queens, 718-472-4355;
www.tournesolny.com

■ "Cramped or cozy depending on your point of view", this "très petite" Long Island City bistro offers "fabulous French fare without French attitude", and thus is a "perfect stop after MoMA Queens"; better yet, the tabs run "less than Manhattan."

TOWN
25 **25** **23** **$71**

Chambers Hotel, 15 W. 56th St. (bet. 5th & 6th Aves.), 212-582-4445;
www.townnyc.com

■ "Oozing sophistication" and drawing "beautiful" folk, this "fashionable" New American from chef Geoffrey Zakarian wows crowds with a "well-thought-out" menu "executed with skill and efficiency", "impeccable service" and a "lofty, sweeping" dining room; alright, the prices are "Uptown", but the feeling is Downtown.

Trata Estiatorio
21 **15** **17** **$52**

1331 Second Ave. (bet. 70th & 71st Sts.), 212-535-3800;
www.trata.com

■ At this "low-key" East Side Greek seafooder, if you "close your eyes, you can taste Mykonos", thanks to the "fantastic selection of fresh fish", "simply yet tastefully prepared"; sure, the "by-the-pound pricing can be deceiving", but the "quality-to-price ratio" is clear as can be.

Trattoria Alba ⌾
20 **18** **19** **$38**

233 E. 34th St. (bet. 2nd & 3rd Aves.), 212-689-3200

■ Everything a "neighborhood restaurant should be", this Murray Hill Northern Italian lures an "older crowd" with "solid" cooking and "professional service"; though it doesn't get many raves, locals laud its "inexpensive" pricing and consistent performance.

Trattoria Dell'Arte ●
21 **19** **19** **$50**

900 Seventh Ave. (bet. 56th & 57th Sts.), 212-245-9800;
www.trattoriadellarte.com

■ For "invigorating dining", try this ever-"busy", ever-"friendly" Midtown Italian that's famed for its "glorious" antipasti bar and "distinctive" body-part wall art; it "hasn't skipped a beat in years", and given a location opposite Carnegie Hall, it attracts everyone from music-lovers to tourists.

Trattoria Dopo Teatro ●
16 **16** **16** **$38**

125 W. 44th St. (bet. B'way & 6th Ave.), 212-869-2849;
www.dopoteatro.com

☑ When "you're in a rush to see a show", "they turn tables fast" at this "handy" if "not exceptional" Theater District Italian most liked for its "reasonably priced" prix fixe, workmanlike service and "restaurant movie set" decor (i.e. the "romantic" indoor garden).

TRATTORIA L'INCONTRO
26 **18** **23** **$41**

21-76 31st St. (Ditmars Blvd.), Queens, 718-721-3532;
www.trattorialincontro.com

■ An Italian "gem amid Astoria's Greeks", this "unbeatable" venue is famed for its "mile-long list" of specials, all part of the "innovative" work from chef Rocco Sacramone; it's "worth the money", so don't even think about "Saturday night without reservations."

Trattoria Pesce & Pasta
19 **13** **17** **$30**

262 Bleecker St. (bet. 6th Ave. & 7th Ave. S.), 212-645-2993 ●
625 Columbus Ave. (bet. 90th & 91st Sts.), 212-579-7970
1079 First Ave. (59th St.), 212-888-7884 ●
1562 Third Ave. (bet. 87th & 88th Sts.), 212-987-4696
www.pescepasta.com

■ This Italian foursome "must be doing something right" given the crowds "queuing up early" for "robust" antipasti, "tasty seafood" and "inexpensive wines" ferried between "cramped" tables by "helpful" staffers; inescapably "noisy", they're also endearingly "comfy" and "bargains" to boot.

Trattoria Romana
24 | 15 | 22 | $39

1476 Hylan Blvd. (Benton Ave.), Staten Island, 718-980-3113;
www.trattoriaromana.com

■ Among the "best Staten Island has to offer", this "family-oriented" Italian used to be "small and noisy" but since expanding has become "big and noisy"; "tasty, hearty" food, "reasonable" prices and "at-your-beck-and-call" service keep it "head and shoulders above the rest."

Trattoria Rustica
21 | 17 | 21 | $39

343 E. 85th St. (bet. 1st & 2nd Aves.), 212-744-1227; www.paolasrestaurant.com

■ "Hidden away in the netherworld" of Yorkville, this "quaint" Italian may be "nothing flashy" but comes across with a "varied menu", "cordial" service and "old-house" decor; "potentially romantic" and moderately priced, it's got "date spot" written all over it.

Trattoria Trecolori
∇ 20 | 16 | 21 | $34

133 W. 45th St. (bet. 6th & 7th Aves.), 212-997-4540; www.trattoriatrecolori.com

☑ "Convenient" before a show, this Theater District Italian earns solid marks for its "great bang for the buck", a staff that "treats you like royalty" and "reliable" dishes (particularly the "homemade tiramisu"); the only drawback: a "noise level that makes conversation difficult."

Tre Pomodori
18 | 11 | 18 | $24

210 E. 34th St. (bet. 2nd & 3rd Aves.), 212-545-7266
1742 Second Ave. (bet. 90th & 91st Sts.), 212-831-8167

☑ "When you need to stretch that dollar", try these "dependable" if "not innovative" East Side Italians where the "decor isn't exactly Le Cirque, but neither are the prices"; the "closet"-like quarters make for "great eavesdropping", but most wish they'd just "bust down a wall" and expand.

Triangolo ●≠
20 | 15 | 21 | $38

345 E. 83rd St. (bet. 1st & 2nd Aves.), 212-472-4488

■ A "quiet" Yorkville side street is home to this "quality" Italian that's a "notch above" in food and service and a notch below in price; despite its solid, "homestyle" preparations, surveyors sigh "if they took credit cards, we'd eat here more often."

Tribeca Grill
22 | 20 | 21 | $53

375 Greenwich St. (Franklin St.), 212-941-3900;
www.myriadrestaurantgroup.com

☑ "Stylish people" steep in the "understated cool" of Drew Nieporent and Robert De Niro's TriBeCa anchor eatery, an "old standby" that's "not trendy anymore" and perhaps in need of a "face-lift and a food-lift"; still, diehards deem it "reliable", whether for cocktails "pre-Nobu" or a "creative" New American meal paired with a "terrific" wine.

Trio
∇ 24 | 19 | 24 | $42

167 E. 33rd St. (bet. Lexington & 3rd Aves.), 212-685-1001

■ "Delicious Croatian specialties are what to order" at this "relatively undiscovered" Murray Hill Mediterranean "standout"; supporters say the "pleasant" service, "live piano" music and "strong homemade grappa" burnish this "jewel in a dining wasteland."

Triomphe
22 | 22 | 22 | $59

Iroquois Hotel, 49 W. 44th St. (bet. 5th & 6th Aves.), 212-453-4233;
www.iroquoisny.com

■ An "oasis of calm in the busy Theater District", this "extremely relaxing" New French is so "small and intimate" you can actually "have a conversation"; despite a rather "limited" menu, it's just the ticket to "impress someone special" – at least when nearby db Bistro Moderne is full.

Trois Marches ⌧
∇ 19 | 14 | 17 | $47

306 E. 81st St. (bet. 1st & 2nd Aves.), 212-639-1900
◪ French "basics" enlivened by some "Asian influences" make up the "limited" but "well-prepared" menu at this "hidden", "seldom crowded" Yorkville venue; sure, service can be "strained at times", but the winning prix fixe "deserves a try."

Tropica ⌧
23 | 20 | 22 | $47

MetLife Bldg., 200 Park Ave. (enter on 45th St., bet Lexington & Park Aves.), 212-867-6767; www.restaurantassociates.com
■ "Escape the reality" of nearby Grand Central at this "hard-to-find" seafooder whose "Hemingway-in-Key-West" feel extends from the food and decor to its "rum"-based drinks; despite lots of "hustle and bustle", it's a "safe bet" for "business" lunching – and even better for an "unrushed", commuter-free dinner; N.B. closed weekends.

T Salon
17 | 19 | 15 | $25

11 E. 20th St. (bet. B'way & 5th Ave.), 212-358-0506; www.tsalon.com
◪ "Cheers" for the "finger sandwich" set, this "civilized" yet "funky" Flatiron emporium purveys a "proper" high tea selected from an "incredible" array of brews with "tasty" American nibbles on the side; "indifferent" service, "pricey" tabs and a controversial owner are the tempests in this pot.

Tsampa ◑
∇ 19 | 21 | 17 | $24

212 E. Ninth St. (bet. 2nd & 3rd Aves.), 212-614-3226
◪ "Enlighten" your spirit and wallet at this "serene", low-wattage East Village Tibetan that puts forth a "plethora of veggies" among its "healthy", "calming" choices; still, those hoping to "get in touch with their inner Buddha" find things "politically correct" but "flavorless."

Tse Yang
23 | 23 | 23 | $55

34 E. 51st St. (bet. Madison & Park Aves.), 212-688-5447
■ "There's Chinese food and then there's *Chinese food*" say devotees of this "exquisite, upscale" Midtowner long renowned for its "awesome Peking duck"; other "splendid" fare, a "beautiful, aquarium-filled" setting and "royal-treatment" service help justify the empty-the-"money-market-fund" pricing.

Tsuki ◑
∇ 24 | 13 | 20 | $34

1410 First Ave. (bet. 74th & 75th Sts.), 212-517-6860
■ The "Upper East Side sushi wars" have another player in this "sweet" "ma and pa" Japanese where the "unassuming storefront" belies the "always fresh", "attractively presented" fish within; though many "wish the decor was better", the "eager-to-please" service is fine as is.

Tuk Tuk ⇗
∇ 20 | 15 | 19 | $21

204 Smith St. (bet. Baltic & Butler Sts.), Brooklyn, 718-222-5598
◪ "Authentic" dishes with plenty of "spice" have Cobble Hillers making a "weekly pilgrimage" to this "sure bet" Thai; granted, not everyone digs the "live weekend jazz" (the "venue's not large enough"), but there's harmony about the modest prices.

Tupelo Grill ⌧
18 | 17 | 17 | $45

1 Penn Plaza (33rd St., bet. 7th & 8th Aves.), 212-760-2700; www.tupelogrill.com
■ Helping fill the "good restaurant void" around Penn Station, this American grill works for a "pre-game meal", a "quick business lunch" and especially for "blind dates", given its "proximity to transportation for quick getaways"; N.B. closed on weekends.

Turkish Kitchen
22 | 19 | 18 | $36

386 Third Ave. (bet. 27th & 28th Sts.), 212-679-6633

■ "Beam yourself to Istanbul" and savor "delicious" meze and "succulent" meats at this "crimson-walled" Gramercy Turk whose upstairs room is "quieter" than the more convivial ground floor; while service gets mixed marks ("warm" vs. "rushed"), most guests "walk away satisfied and stuffed."

Turkuaz
18 | 21 | 18 | $33

2637 Broadway (100th St.), 212-665-9541; www.turkuazrestaurant.com

■ Sense that "pasha feeling" coming on at this "exotic" Turk where "savory" cooking and "tented", *"Ali Baba and the Forty Thieves"* decor help you "leave the Upper West Side behind"; though a few find "nothing exciting" about it, it sure is "different" and the weekend belly dancing is "fun."

Tuscan
20 | 23 | 20 | $56

622 Third Ave. (40th St.), 212-404-1700

☑ "Get the meatballs" is the new rallying cry at this Midtown Italian where the manly meat menu has been "triumphantly reimagined" by consulting chef Rocco DiSpirito; while the "upbeat" bar scene remains the same, some detect shrinkage in portions, inflation in prices and occasional service outages.

Tuscan Square ☒
18 | 18 | 16 | $45

16 W. 51st St. (bet. 5th & 6th Aves.), 212-977-7777

☑ Imagine you're dining in a "Tuscan restaurant movie set" (instead of Rock Center) at this "busy" Northern Italian that's "convenient" for a "biz lunch" or to amuse "out-of-towners"; quibblers cite "slow service" and "high-rent" pricing, wishing for "more restaurant and less theme park."

Tuscany Grill
23 | 18 | 19 | $41

8620 Third Ave. (bet. 86th & 87th Sts.), Brooklyn, 718-921-5633

■ For "simple, homey" Northern Italian fare "just like from mama's cucina", try this "congenial" Bay Ridge "family favorite" where "both the food and the clientele are a feast for the eyes"; though it can get "crowded", it's thankfully free of "Manhattan attitude."

12th St. Bar & Grill
22 | 20 | 20 | $34

1123 Eighth Ave. (bet. 11th & 12th Sts.), Brooklyn, 718-965-9526

■ "There's no reason to go into the city" since this "imminently civilized" Park Slope New American provides a "wonderful" menu at prices that are "less than Manhattan" – probably even "cheaper than cooking" at home; it's just the spot to "bring your parents to show them that Brooklyn's not so bad" after all.

'21' CLUB ☒
21 | 22 | 23 | $65

21 W. 52nd St. (bet. 5th & 6th Aves.), 212-582-7200;
www.21club.com

■ "Nothing's changed except the prices" at this circa-1929 erstwhile speakeasy, a place where NYC's power elite gladly don jackets and ties to dine on chef Erik Blauberg's "refreshed" American "comfort-food" menu accompanied by "world-class" wine from a "spectacular" cellar; "polished", "do-it-right" service and a plethora of "stylish private-party rooms" (check out the Wine Cellar and the new 'Upstairs at 21' space) complete the picture at this "venerable institution."

26 Seats
▽ 23 | 18 | 21 | $35

168 Ave. B (bet. 10th & 11th Sts.), 212-677-4787; www.26seats.com

■ Ok, it's really in the East Village, but this "adorable French hideaway" could be on the "Left Bank" thanks to its "outstanding" yet modestly priced bistro fare; a "hospitable" staff and "close quarters" lend the illusion that you're "dining among friends" – 25 of them to be exact.

Two Boots

| 19 | 10 | 13 | $14 |

42 Ave. A (3rd St.), 212-254-1919 ●
37 Ave. A (bet. 2nd & 3rd Sts.), 212-505-2276
74 Bleecker St. (B'way), 212-777-1033 ●
Grand Central, lower level (42nd St. & Lexington Ave.), 212-557-7992
30 Rockefeller Plaza, downstairs (bet. 49th & 50th Sts.), 212-332-8800 Ⓢ
201 W. 11th St. (7th Ave. S.), 212-633-9096 ●
514 Second St. (bet. 7th & 8th Aves.), Brooklyn, 718-499-3253
www.twoboots.com

■ "Bootiful", cornmeal-dusted, "crispy-bottomed" pizzas studded with "tangy" bayou-inspired toppings distinguish these pie palaces from the rest of the pack and result in "long lines" of "kids" and their keepers; separately managed, the "jolly" Park Slope outlet features a full Cajun menu and a patio.

212 ●

| 17 | 17 | 16 | $41 |

133 E. 65th St. (Lexington Ave.), 212-249-6565; www.212restaurant.com

☑ "Like its patrons", this "long, skinny" East Side French-Italian is "loud but fun", offering "casual" fare to "preppies with kids" for brunch and attracting "Euros" after dark; sure, the setup's "tight", the menu "uninspired" and service "haughty", but the "extensive vodka" selection "makes you get over these things pretty fast."

2 West

| ▽ 21 | 22 | 23 | $58 |

Ritz-Carlton Battery Park, 2 West St. (Battery Pl.), 917-790-2525;
www.ritzcarlton.com

■ This "pleasant surprise" off Battery Park offers "imaginative" New Americana in "swanky" environs; while a few are "disappointed" at the "steep" price tags and "lack of harbor views", at least the "spoil-you-rotten" service is "what you'd expect from the Ritz-Carlton people."

Typhoon Ⓢ

| 16 | 17 | 16 | $37 |

22 E. 54th St. (bet. 5th & Madison Aves.), 212-754-9006

☑ Best known for its "noisy ground-floor bar scene", this "earnest" Midtowner also supplies Thai-fusion fare upstairs at prices that "won't swamp your wallet"; pragmatists point to its "meat-market" vibe and smirk the "food isn't what you're here for."

Ubol's Kitchen

| ▽ 24 | 11 | 21 | $23 |

24-42 Steinway St. (bet. Astoria Blvd. & 25th Ave.), Queens, 718-545-2874

■ "More like your aunt's kitchen than a restaurant", this "cheap" Thai "hot sauce" "standout" draws intra-borough crowds who swear it's "worth the schlep to the edge of Astoria"; just be prepared for "difficult parking" and "simple" (putting it kindly) decor.

Uguale ●

| ▽ 20 | 18 | 18 | $41 |

396 West St. (W. 10th St.), 212-229-0606

■ "As far west as you can get without falling in the river", this Village "waterfront" Franco-Italian has certified "date" appeal thanks to a "cozy fireplace", "cute" little bar and "sunset" views; even better, the food is "quality" and "reservations not too difficult" to come by.

Ulrika's

| 23 | 18 | 21 | $44 |

115 E. 60th St. (bet. Lexington & Park Aves.), 212-355-7069; www.ulrikas.com

■ Imagine you're "in the Swedish countryside (instead of near Bloomie's)" at this "unpretentious" Midtown Scandinavian where "leggy, blonde" waitresses serve "homey" classics ("meatballs just like *mormor's*") in "modern yet cozy" digs; it's "not well known", which is all the more reason why "regulars love it."

Ulysses ◐
95 Pearl St. (off Hanover Sq.), 212-482-0400

– | – | – | M

On pleasant nights, this sprawling Downtown Irish tavern opens its rear doors to Stone Street, where hundreds of young financial types gather to meet and greet; as a sibling to nearby Bayard's, it's not surprising that they also produce some mighty fine pub grub.

Umberto's Clam House ◐
178 Mulberry St. (Broome St.), 212-343-2053; www.umbertosclamhouse.com

18 | 12 | 15 | $32

☑ "Go for the clams" to this Little Italy "old favorite" where there's "nothing nuevo" going on, just "simple" Italian cooking; critics say it's "famous for all the wrong reasons", citing the abundance of "touristy *Sopranos*" fans who won't "sit with their backs to the window."

Uncle George's ◐≠
33-19 Broadway (34th St.), Queens, 718-626-0593; www.unclegeorges.us

18 | 7 | 13 | $20

☑ "Abundant" portions of "authentic Greek" grub for "pocket change" is the formula for success at this 24/7 Astoria taverna that's definitely "not pretty" but "busy at all hours"; luckily, it's "open all night", since you may have to "wait that long for your check."

Uncle Jack's Steakhouse
39-40 Bell Blvd. (40th Ave.), Queens, 718-229-1100

25 | 18 | 21 | $62

■ This "avuncular" Bayside chop shop lures "meat lovers" ("Mayor Mike" among them) with "supple steaks" that rank among the "city's best"; the waiters are "characters who treat you like gold", but it still "can't hurt to have an extra million laying around" when the check comes; N.B. a new outpost near Penn Station is in the works.

Uncle Nick's
747 Ninth Ave. (bet. 50th & 51st Sts.), 212-245-7992

21 | 12 | 16 | $30

■ "*Opa!*" is the word at this "raucous" Hell's Kitchen "dynamo" where "huge portions" of "rustic" Greek dishes at "bargain-basement prices" make for "rousing" repasts; critics of the "threadbare" digs and "uneven" service escape to the adjoining Ouzaria for "quieter dining."

UNION PACIFIC ⌧
111 E. 22nd St. (bet. Lexington Ave. & Park Ave. S.), 212-995-8500; www.unionpacificrestaurant.com

26 | 26 | 25 | $71

■ As "dazzling" as ever, this Gramercy New American "winner" from "Big Apple wonder boy" Rocco DiSpirito is akin to a "culinary spa", matching "exciting" food with a "calming", "ultra-sleek" setting; proponents pile praise on everything from the "mesmerizing waterfall" to the "solicitous" service, and though you must "bring lots of plastic", "you get what you pay for" here; P.S. economists say the $20 prix fixe lunch is a "gift to the city."

UNION SQUARE CAFE
21 E. 16th St. (bet. 5th Ave. & Union Sq. W.), 212-243-4020

27 | 23 | 26 | $60

■ The "good mood is contagious" at Danny Meyer's "paradigm of a NY restaurant", again voted Most Popular in this *Survey* thanks to "extraordinary", "unfussy" New American cooking from chef Michael Romano, a "casually elegant" ambiance with a choice of seating areas and a staff whose "manners you wish you could teach your kids"; it may be "tough" to secure a prime-time table, but short of "marrying into Meyer's family", "seats at the bar always ensure a great meal" without "planning too far in advance."

United Noodles
349 E. 12th St. (bet. 1st & 2nd Aves.), 212-614-0155

▽ 20 | 18 | 19 | $29

☑ For a "unique" Pan-pasta experience, "use your noodle" and head for this "narrow", moderately priced East Village nook where the soba shows up in an "ultramodern" setting right out of "*2001: A Space Odyssey*"; its "sparse", "where's-the-ramen?"–size portions lead some to see "more style than substance" here.

Unity
▽ | 18 | 20 | 18 | $42 |

Embassy Suites, 102 North End Ave. (Vesey St.), 646-769-4200

☑ A "well-kept secret", this "overlooked" New American is a "solid choice" in Battery Park; critics complain the "up-and-down menu" is crying for "unification", though the "comfortable" setup is fine as is.

Üsküdar
| 20 | 10 | 18 | $31 |

1405 Second Ave. (bet. 73rd & 74th Sts.), 212-988-2641

■ The food "tastes like a million bucks", the staff's "caring" and the "tiny" prices mirror the "hobbit-size" dimensions of this "no-frills" East Side Turk; it's a "great date place" – there's nowhere else to gaze except across the table.

Utsav
| 21 | 20 | 18 | $36 |

1185 Sixth Ave. (enter on 46th or 47th St., bet. 6th & 7th Aves.), 212-575-2525

■ "Escape the Midtown throngs" at this "calming", second-floor Indian that's so well "hidden", "you'll get the Lewis and Clark award" if you can find it; discoverers report dishes that appeal to "vegetarians and meat eaters" alike, as well as a $13.95 "bargain lunch buffet."

Va Bene
▽ | 21 | 19 | 19 | $45 |

1589 Second Ave. (bet. 82nd & 83rd Sts.), 212-517-4448

☑ "Dairy kosher" cooking gets a Roman spin at this "upscale" Eastsider offering a "taste of real Italian"; though a bit "pricey" and "unwelcoming" if you don't have a reservation", the observant insist it's "interesting."

Vago ⊠
| – | – | – | M |

29 W. 56th St. (bet. 5th & 6th Aves.), 212-765-5155

"Distinctive" Italian fare is yours at this Midtown "find" where fans tout its "great" $19.95 lunch prix fixe; even better, there's "enough room between the tables" to conduct your business "in private."

Vanderbilt Station
▽ | 18 | 22 | 18 | $46 |

4 Park Ave. (33rd St.), 212-889-3369

■ A "newcomer with history", this Murray Hill "landmark" was once part of the Vanderbilt Hotel and still sports its "low-slung" Guastavino "tile ceiling" and "grotto"-like bar, decor that's nicely mirrored in its "old-style" American menu; those on board say it has all the "elements" for a "classy" night out.

V&T ●
| 19 | 8 | 12 | $18 |

1024 Amsterdam Ave. (bet. 110th & 111th Sts.), 212-666-8051

☑ Almost an extension of the "Columbia campus", this "authentically retro" Morningside Heights Italian has been feeding "broke" students "primo" pizzas since 1945; along with the "surly waiters" and "plastic decor", it "hasn't changed" in decades.

Vatan
| 22 | 23 | 22 | $31 |

409 Third Ave. (29th St.), 212-689-5666

■ Wear "loose pants" and "go hungry" to this "endless" all-you-can-eat Gramercy Park Vegetarian with a transporting Indian "village" setting; the $21.95 "fixed menu" means "no decisions needed", just let the "solicitous" servers bring "more" (and more) of "what you like."

Va Tutto!
▽ | 20 | 18 | 18 | $36 |

23 Cleveland Pl. (bet. Kenmare & Spring Sts.), 212-941-0286

☑ "Eating in the garden is lovely" at this "tranquil" NoLita Italian where the "good" homemade pastas and desserts taste even better alfresco; but high-maintenance types find things only "average at best", citing uneven entrees and "slow" service.

Vegetarian Paradise

19 | 9 | 14 | $18

33-35 Mott St. (Canal St.), 212-406-6988
144 W. Fourth St. (bet. MacDougal St. & 6th Ave.), 212-260-7130
◪ Serving up "good-deal", "mock-meat" menus "tasty" enough to make "even the most" carnivorous "lick their lips", these separately owned Chinatown and Greenwich Village Chinese Vegetarians cater to alterna-eaters willing to be "flexible about atmosphere and service"; the less convinced counter "far from paradise."

Veniero's ◐

23 | 13 | 13 | $14

342 E. 11th St. (bet. 1st & 2nd Aves.), 212-674-7070; www.venierospastry.com
◪ "Not for dieters or impatient types", this East Village "dessert institution" may offer "cattle-call lines", "where's my waiter?" service and "smushed" seating, but it's "worth the trip" for "addictive", "sugar-high" inducing Italian sweets served in "old-time", circa-1895 digs.

Vera Cruz ◐

▽ 19 | 14 | 16 | $24

195 Bedford Ave. (bet. N. 6th & 7th Sts.), Brooklyn, 718-599-7914
■ Though not well-known outside its Williamsburg locale, this simple Mexican is a pleasant "place to kick back" with "good food, good margaritas, no complaints"; in summer, this "trip to Puerto Vallarta" feel is enhanced if you can "snag a table on the back patio."

Verbena

23 | 20 | 21 | $57

54 Irving Pl. (bet. 17th & 18th Sts.), 212-260-5454
■ "Still lovely after all these years", chef-owners (and spouses) Diane Forley and Michael Otsuka's Gramercy Park Med-Asian has its "heart in the right place", impressing with a "polished, confident" (and "pricey") experience and "delicate, innovative food"; the spacious back garden is a "delight" as well.

VERITAS

27 | 23 | 26 | $78

43 E. 20th St. (bet. B'way & Park Ave. S.), 212-353-3700; www.veritas-nyc.com
■ An "oenophile's delight" offering "more selections than you can drink in a lifetime", this "sleek, subdued but hip" Flatiron "splurge" is also "paradise for lovers of [chef Scott Bryan's] sophisticated" New American fare; our sated surveyors "raise glasses" to the "dreamy" ($68) prix fixe dinners – "perfection on a plate."

Vermicelli

20 | 17 | 18 | $29

1492 Second Ave. (bet. 77th & 78th Sts.), 212-288-8868
■ A "Zen feeling comes over" one at this "cozy" Vietnamese "best-kept secret" in Yorkville; blessed with a "friendly", "courteous" staff and a wide selection of "unique" offerings, it "delights different tastes", especially its "phenomenal $6.95 bargain box lunch."

Veronica ⌧

▽ 21 | 4 | 13 | $17

240 W. 38th St. (bet. 7th & 8th Aves.), 212-764-4770
◪ You can "satisfy your cravings" for American breakfasts and Italian lunches at this "no-frills", "no-nonsense" cafeteria, a good fit if "you happen to be in the Garment District" on weekdays; the wide selection of "homemade" dishes come in "plentiful" portions at picayune prices.

Veselka ◐

19 | 11 | 13 | $17

144 Second Ave. (9th St.), 212-228-9682
■ "Eat like a king for the price of a servant" at this "bustling" 24/7 East Village Ukrainian "blintz-eria" that "feels like a socialist coffeehouse"; "the young and art-inclined" and just plain hungry report that "it's dynamite" for breakfast or "late-night noshing."

Via Brasil

▽ 19 | 14 | 19 | $36

34 W. 46th St. (bet. 5th & 6th Aves.), 212-997-1158

■ For a "different treat", samba over to this Rio-esque Midtowner offering "wonderfully fresh" "Brazilian soul food", "potent caipirinhas" and service that's "warm, but not in your face"; Wednesday–Saturday there's "great live music", so "relax and enjoy the experience."

Via Emilia ⌺⇗

21 | 12 | 17 | $30

240 Park Ave. S. (bet. 19th & 20th Sts.), 212-505-3072

■ A cash-only "treasure" for price-conscious Italian food lovers, this "charming hole-in-the-wall" on "trendy" Park Avenue South delights diners with "simple", "satisfying" dishes straight out of Emilia-Romagna and an "unmatched selection of chilled Lambrusco" wines; "go early to beat the crowds" because they don't take reservations.

Viand

17 | 8 | 16 | $18

2130 Broadway (75th St.), 212-877-2888 ◗
300 E. 86th St. (2nd Ave.), 212-879-9425 ◗
1011 Madison Ave. (78th St.), 212-249-8250
673 Madison Ave. (bet. 61st & 62nd Sts.), 212-751-6622 ⇗

■ It's worth "shooing away other patrons" for that "awesome turkey sandwich" at these "jammed little coffee shops"; they've "saved many a Saturday morn'" and are perfect for an affordable "quickie lunch", with a "bantering staff" that has the "skill of anticipation"; N.B. the East 80s and new Upper West Side location are open 24/7.

Via Oreto

21 | 15 | 19 | $42

1121-23 First Ave. (bet. 61st & 62nd Sts.), 212-308-0828

■ You're sure to "become a cult follower" if you "bring the *familia*" to this "friendly" Eastsider for "plentiful" portions of "hearty", "homemade Italian favorites", especially the "super pastas" and "Sundays-only meatballs"; with mama and son "running the ship", it's as "warm" and "inviting" as your "talented Sicilian grandmother's kitchen."

Via Quadronno

22 | 15 | 16 | $32

25 E. 73rd St. (bet. 5th & Madison Aves.), 212-650-9880;
www.viaquadronno.com

◪ A "panini palazzo" that's "like being in Milano" chorus customers who consider this cafe tucked off Madison a "little Italian oasis" for a post-shopping lunch or a cuppa "espresso that can't be beat"; *si*, the "tables are the size of a large dinner napkin", and the sandwiches may be "expensive", but it comes in handy.

ViceVersa ⌺

23 | 22 | 22 | $50

325 W. 51st St. (bet. 8th & 9th Aves.), 212-399-9291

■ "They have the whole package" at this "delicious surprise" in Hell's Kitchen, from "innovative" Italian cuisine "magnificently presented" to an "upbeat atmosphere" with a "lovely garden" to an "approachable staff – the icing on the cake"; it's a "pure delight" for "pre-theater meals without too much fanfare" and "worthwhile anytime."

Vico ◗⇗

20 | 13 | 18 | $52

1302 Madison Ave. (bet. 92nd & 93rd Sts.), 212-876-2222

◪ Paying with plastic is prohibited at this "expensive", "clubby" Italian, which courts "the Carnegie Hill crowd" with "reliably delicious" classics ("great veal") served by staffers who are "so nice" if you're "a regular"; non-regulars reply, "all cash, no flash – don't dash."

Victor's Cafe ◗

21 | 19 | 19 | $43

236 W. 52nd St. (bet. B'way & 8th Ave.), 212-586-7714; www.victorscafe.com

■ Even Castro would approve of the "must-order mojitos" and "super sangria" that wash down the "solid, tasty" treats ("pork, black beans and rice – need I say more?") at this "festive" Hell's Kitchen Cuban; though a *poco* pricey, it's "popular pre-theater" *gracias* to "fast-but-not-rushed service."

View, The
17 | 24 | 19 | $50

Marriott Marquis Hotel, 1535 Broadway (bet. 45th & 46th Sts.), 212-704-8900; www.nymarriottmarquis.com

☑ With its "cool city views", the 47th-floor "revolving dining room" of "this Times Square mainstay" remains a "great place to go for a spin"; even if the surf 'n' turf "menu doesn't quite deliver", supporters shrug "who cares about the food when you're this high up?"

Villa Berulia
▽ 22 | 18 | 24 | $45

107 E. 34th St. (bet. Lexington & Park Aves.), 212-689-1970

■ The owners ooze "old-world charm" and "terrific" staffers "treat everyone like family" at this "warm, comfortable", midpriced Murray Hill Northern Italian; ok, "so it's not super-trendy", but when "you get a craving for those traditional dishes, this is the place."

Village ◑
20 | 20 | 20 | $40

62 W. Ninth St. (bet. 5th & 6th Aves.), 212-505-3355; www.villagerestaurant.com

■ West Villagers whisper "shhh, don't tell" about their "neighborhood joy" that "deftly prepares" New American and "innovative French bistro" delights; "friendly service" further brightens the "spacious", "skylit dining room."

Village 247
– | – | – | I

247 Smith St. (bet. DeGraw & Douglass Sts.), Brooklyn, 718-855-2848

This new Cobble Hill American offers a cute, Main Street USA look, backed up by a downstairs bar and outdoor garden; the menu is equally patriotic (burgers and such), and priced to move.

Villa Mosconi ☒
20 | 15 | 22 | $40

69 MacDougal St. (bet. Bleecker & Houston Sts.), 212-673-0390; www.villamosconi.com

■ "Regulars and newcomers alike are treated well" at this "real Italian" Villager that "hasn't changed in 20 years" – "and rightly so"; its "delicious homemade pasta" is "worth the calories" and its "old-fashioned" setting is custom-made for "celebrating all the life events."

Vince and Eddie's
18 | 16 | 18 | $45

70 W. 68th St. (bet. Columbus Ave. & CPW), 212-721-0068

☑ "Close to Lincoln Center", this "cute" little place features "flavorful American fare", a "thoughtful" staff and a "back garden" complete with a "wonderful fireplace"; however, the "cozy" digs get "cramped" "pre- or post-show", and "pricey" tabs pinch too.

Vincent's ◑
20 | 12 | 17 | $32

119 Mott St. (Hester St.), 212-226-8133

☑ "My father went, I go and my children now go" to this 100-year-old "typical Little Italy" address; "despite the cafeteria decor", "those in-the-know" agree it's "still the best for a bargain late-night fix of red sauce" and a "spicy" Southern Italian shrimp-calamari combo.

Vine ☒
20 | 18 | 18 | $51

25 Broad St. (Exchange Pl.), 212-344-8463; www.vinefood.com

☑ "Across from the Stock Exchange", this "slick New American" is "full of power brokers" "bullish" on its "well-presented", "dependable" dishes; but while the old bank "vault downstairs is great for private parties", bears sell short the "limited" options on the "overpriced", seafood-surfeited menu.

Vinnie's Pizza ●⇗
22 | – | 14 | $11

285 Amsterdam Ave. (bet. 73rd & 74th Sts.), 212-874-4382
■ Back on the scene following "renovations", this Upper West Side pizza palace is once again turning out "thick, cheesy" pies that "go a long way" because they're so darn "filling"; regulars report its "redesigned interior threatens to end its reputation as a takeout-only" joint; stay tuned.

Virgil's Real BBQ
21 | 14 | 17 | $30

152 W. 44th St. (bet. B'way & 6th Ave.), 212-921-9494; www.virgilsbbq.com
☑ "Bring your appetite" and "stretch pants" to this Times Square joint serving "surprisingly authentic" BBQ that "goes straight to your arteries"; however, be prepared for "tourists", "long" waits and digs that are "more Disney than down-home."

Vittorio Cucina
▽ 20 | 15 | 19 | $38

308-310 Bleecker St. (bet. Grove St. & 7th Ave. S.), 212-463-0730; www.vittoriocri.com
■ For *amici* of this Village Italian, the "only problem is choosing" from the "huge" regular menu that's augmented by specials "from a new region each month"; service is "on the mark" and the back garden serves as an "oasis on a sunny day."

Vivolo ●
18 | 18 | 19 | $44

140 E. 74th St. (bet. Lexington & Park Aves.), 212-737-3533; www.vivolonyc.com
■ An "uncomplicated menu" of "solid", "traditional" Italian dishes served by an "amiable" staff in "lovely, quiet" duplex digs draws a "steady", "genteel" (read: "older") crowd to this "longtime" Upper Eastsider; for "early-birds", the pre-theater prix fixe "can't be beat."

Volare ⌦
▽ 22 | 14 | 26 | $38

147 W. Fourth St. (6th Ave.), 212-777-2849
■ "You're welcomed like family" at this "friendly", "low-key" Village stalwart that's "like a second home to many"; expect "enormous portions" of "delicious" Northern Italian fare served in a "cozy", "below-street-level" space with "charming", if "outdated" decor.

Vong
24 | 24 | 22 | $60

200 E. 54th St. (3rd Ave.), 212-486-9592; www.jean-georges.com
■ Jean-Georges Vongerichten's Midtown "dowager of fusion can still show newcomers a thing or two" with its "marvelous, inventive" French-Thai cuisine served by a "professional" staff in an "ultrachic" room that "drips with Zen glamour"; while some find the portions "silly" for the prices, "you can't go vong" with the "bargain" lunch and pre-theater prix fixes.

Voyage ⌦
▽ 20 | 19 | 16 | $43

117 Perry St. (Greenwich St.), 212-255-9191
☑ Sojourners to this "bright" West Village newcomer predict smooth sailing for chef Scott Barton's (ex Heartbeat) "confident, polished" New American cuisine with Southern and Latin American accents; though the "swank" space with a peripatetic theme is "inviting", occasionally "confused" service and "waits at the door" are potential bumps in the road.

Vuli
▽ 21 | 17 | 20 | $39

Radisson Lexington Hotel, 134 E. 48th St. (Lexington Ave.), 212-583-0847; www.radisson.com
■ A "sleeper" if ever there was one, this Midtown Northern Italian is "never crowded", despite "consistently good pastas" served by "waiters straight off the plane from Rome"; fans, who dub it their personal "favorite", are just as happy having it to themselves.

Walker's ◐
16 | 13 | 16 | $27
16 N. Moore St. (Varick St.), 212-941-0142
■ A "beloved local haunt", this TriBeCa "classic" tavern (set in a historic 19th-century space) attracts a "diverse" crowd from "yuppies to firefighters" with "reliable" "pub favorites" and "surprisingly good" specials, "friendly" service and a "down-to-earth atmosphere."

Wallsé
25 | 21 | 22 | $60
344 W. 11th St. (Washington St.), 212-352-2300; www.wallserestaurant.com
■ Chef-owner Kurt Gutenbrunner's "new takes" on Austrian cuisine make this "sophisticated" West Villager a "winner"; while the signature Wiener schnitzel displays an "uncomplicated perfection", the wine list "encourages exploration" and the staff's "informed", "gracious" performance is just icing on the Sachertorte.

Washington Park
21 | 20 | 21 | $61
24 Fifth Ave. (9th St.), 212-529-4400; www.washingtonparknyc.com
☑ Jonathan Waxman, the talented chef who made Jams a hot spot in the '80s, is back with "delicious", "classic" American cuisine that's drawing a smart crowd to this popular Villager; although most surveyors are enthusiastic fans, a few detractors dis "bumpy service" and "way-high prices" (though the "prix fixe lunch is an excellent buy").

Water Club
21 | 24 | 21 | $58
East River at 30th St. (enter on E. 23rd St.), 212-683-3333;
www.thewaterclub.com
■ "A treat for lovers of city lights", this "forever favorite" on an East River barge boasts "intoxicating" views from its nautically themed interior; the "diverse" American menu's equally shipshape, with "outstanding seafood" and a "superb" brunch buffet; add a "wonderful" staff and plentiful party space and it's hard not to be buoyed up by a visit.

WATER'S EDGE ⊠
23 | 26 | 23 | $61
44th Dr. & East River (Vernon Blvd.), Queens, 718-482-0033
■ "Some enchanted evening" can be had at this high-budget Long Island City cynosure affording "spectacular" panoramas of the Manhattan skyline and New American seafood-focused fare that "exceeds expectations"; if this weren't enough, the "free ferry ride" from East 34th Street ratchets up the "romance" quotient.

WD-50 ⊠
∇ 24 | 20 | 22 | $61
50 Clinton St. (bet. Rivington & Stanton Sts.), 212-477-2900
☑ Most diners say "risk-taking" chef Wylie Dufresne "pulls it off" at this new Lower East Side American-Eclectic, citing "brilliant", "incredibly sophisticated flavor combinations"; however, some bash the menu as "just plain weird" with "too much flash and no attention to taste"; your call.

West Bank Cafe ◐
19 | 16 | 18 | $37
Manhattan Plaza, 407 W. 42nd St. (bet. 9th & 10th Aves.), 212-695-6909
■ A "great Theater District haunt", this "convenient", "comfortable", "consistent" New American offers a "good range of tasty", "moderately priced" fare in a "pleasant", if undistinguished, setting; service is "friendly", and you can bank on the fact that "you'll make it to the show."

Westville
– | – | – | I
210 W. 10th St. (bet. Bleecker & W. 4th Sts.), 212-741-7971;
www.westville-nyc.com
A new little white-washed Village spot dishing out dirt-cheap New American savories, home-baked sweets and daily-changing veggie sides fresh from the farmer; from muffins in the morning till po' boys late-night, it's a casual respite from the area's tag-inflated tourist traps.

Whim

▽ | 18 | 13 | 15 | $37

243 DeGraw St. (Clinton St.), Brooklyn, 718-797-2017; www.gotlemon.com
For a "bit of the Village in Carroll Gardens", fans favor this "bustling" newcomer offering "innovative" seafood, a "good raw bar" and an $8 brunch served to the backdrop of Grateful Dead tunes; however, a few whimper the dishes are "uneven" and the "small" space "cramped."

White Horse Tavern ◑⇎

13 | 15 | 13 | $19

567 Hudson St. (11th St.), 212-989-3956
Its "Dylan Thomas drank here" history makes this circa-1880 West Village vet worth a visit, along with its "dark", "comfortable" interior, "great outdoor seating" and "cheap beer"; neighsayers knock the Traditional American eats as "average", but there's no denying that it remains one of the "city's best saloons."

'wichcraft ⊠

– | – | – | I

49 E. 19th St. (bet. B'way & Park Ave. S.), 212-780-0577
Tom Colicchio (Craft, Craftbar) extends his Flatiron empire with this new low-budget eatery serving high-quality, all-day breakfast vittles as well as hot and cold sandwiches; toss in pastry chef Karen DeMasco's creations and early word has it you've got a winning dining spot.

Wild Ginger ◑

20 | 21 | 19 | $23

51 Grove St. (bet. Bleecker St. & 7th Ave. S.), 212-367-7200;
www.wildginger-ny.com
A "wonderful variety" of "solid" Thai classics in "welcoming", "soothing" environs make this inexpensive West Village waterfall-and-bamboo haven an "amazing value"; if you really want to impress her, "don't let your date see the prices."

Wild Tuna

18 | 15 | 18 | $42

1081 Third Ave. (bet. 63rd & 64th Sts.), 212-838-7570; www.thewildtuna.com
The "latest incarnation" of a "constantly changing" spot, this East Side fish house from Shelly Fireman "screams beachside clam shack" but teems with "solid", midpriced seafood selections; though a few find "nothing special" going on, finicky fans find it's "worth a return" visit.

Willow

19 | 17 | 18 | $48

1022 Lexington Ave. (73rd St.), 212-717-0703
"Take your mother-in-law" to this "comfortable" East Side duplex offering "tasty" French-American food in a "charming" townhouse space; its "older-generation" crowd may "dine here for the lighting" alone, but it's also "quiet" enough to be "conducive to conversation."

Wo Hop ◑⇎

20 | 5 | 13 | $16

17 Mott St. (Canal St.), 212-267-2536
"No frills" is putting it mildly at this "venerable" C-town Chinese where "service comes with a grunt"; still, the "cheap", "basic" grub "hits the spot" and its 24/7 open-door policy lures late-nighters who've "never been here sober."

Wolf's ◑

17 | 14 | 15 | $23

41 W. 57th St. (bet. 5th & 6th Aves.), 212-888-4100; www.wolfsdeli.com
"Major chopped liver" and other "great" Jewish classics fill out the menu of this Midtown corned beef and pastrami purveyor that boasts a "pleasant" upscale feel; the prices may be "premium" but, hey, you could "open your own deli" with those "gargantuan" leftovers.

Wollensky's Grill ◑

22 | 16 | 19 | $46

201 E. 49th St. (3rd Ave.), 212-753-0444; www.smithandwollensky.com
For the "same great steaks" and "awesome burgers" at "lower prices" than its "big brother next door", try this more "modest" adjunct

of Smith & Wollensky; "open later" than the mothership, it's a favorite "media hang" for "publishers and their posses."

Wondee Siam
22 | 8 | 14 | $20

792 Ninth Ave. (bet. 52nd & 53rd Sts.), 212-459-9057
813 Ninth Ave. (bet. 53rd & 54th Sts.), 917-286-1726
☑ "Authentic to a T", this Hell's Kitchen duo provides a "veritable culinary trip to Thailand", right down to the "rock-bottom prices"; while the northernmost outpost might be the "prettier of the two", aesthetes say that given their deficiencies of decor and service, the chow is "best eaten elsewhere."

Won Jo ◑
▽ 21 | 11 | 15 | $26

23 W. 32nd St. (bet. B'way & 5th Ave.), 212-695-5815
☑ It's fun to keep those "taste buds stimulated" at this budget-conscious Garment District Korean renowned for its "interactive", grill-it-yourself BBQ ("fortunately the new smoking laws don't apply to smoke from hibachis"); though decor and service are "not the best", it's open 24/7 if you want to "make a night of it."

Woo Lae Oak
22 | 23 | 20 | $46

148 Mercer St. (bet. Houston & Prince Sts.), 212-925-8200;
www.woolaeoaksoho.com
■ "Sceney" types say this SoHo "haute Korean" offers the "hippest BBQ" around with "optional do-it-yourself preparation"; while it may be "pricey", the "starkly modern" setup and "informative staff" make it "great for groups" – but maybe not for dates: the "grill aroma stays with you."

World Yacht
▽ 17 | 21 | 17 | $72

Pier 81, W. 41st St. & Hudson River (12th Ave.), 212-630-8100;
www.worldyacht.com
☑ "Better-than-expected food" drawn from "famous chefs' recipes" and "phenomenal views" that remind you "how beautiful Manhattan is" are the attractions of this dining-and-dancing boat cruise that "everyone should do at least once" – still, spoilers suggest the "boilerplate" grub and "steep prices" are for "tourists" only.

Wu Liang Ye
20 | 12 | 15 | $27

215 E. 86th St. (bet. 2nd & 3rd Aves.), 212-534-8899
338 Lexington Ave. (bet. 39th & 40th Sts.), 212-370-9648
36 W. 48th St. (bet. 5th & 6th Aves.), 212-398-2308
☑ "When they say hot, they mean it" at these "authentic" Szechuan triplets where the "eye-opening" menu veers from the "traditional" to the "super-spicy"; despite "no atmosphere" and not much service, they're still "more interesting than the competition" – especially when there are "pocketbook concerns."

X.O.
19 | 11 | 12 | $15

148 Hester St. (bet. Bowery & Elizabeth St.), 212-965-8645
96 Walker St. (bet. Centre & Lafayette Sts.), 212-343-8339
☑ "Nontraditional but still tasty", this C-town Chinese duo offers a "wide selection" of Hong Kong–style dishes made for adventurous types with "obscure cravings"; sure, the staff's "proficiency in English wavers", but they're "always crowded" since they're also "cheap."

Xunta
21 | 13 | 13 | $26

174 First Ave. (bet. 10th & 11th Sts.), 212-614-0620; www.xuntatapas.com
■ "Cheap, yummy tapas" arrives in a "super-crowded" space at this "festive", "very East Village" Spaniard popular with younger folk; even though service is "slooow" and the seating is "uncomfortable", no one seems to notice after "downing large quantities of sangria."

Yakiniku JuJu
▽ 25 | 17 | 22 | $26

157 E. 28th St. (bet. Lexington & 3rd Aves.), 212-684-7830

■ "Cook-it-yourselfers" like this "tiny" Japanese-Korean barbecue specialist near Curry Hill for its "tasty" fixin's, "upbeat service" and "incredible value" (i.e. "all-you-can-eat BBQ for only $20"); sincere stalwarts swear "shabu-shabu is the reason to come."

YAMA
25 | 11 | 16 | $36

38-40 Carmine St. (bet. Bedford & Bleecker Sts.), 212-989-9330
122 E. 17th St. (Irving Pl.), 212-475-0969 ⧉
92 W. Houston St. (bet. La Guardia Pl. & Thompson St.), 212-674-0935
www.yamarestaurant.com

◪ "Colossal pieces" of "right-out-of-the-water" sushi at "yamazing" prices make for "packed" conditions at this "too popular" Japanese trio; granted, the service and "decor ain't much" and they "don't take reservations" (except at Carmine Street), but "fins down" they "deliver the goods"; hint: the "lines are shorter at lunch."

Ye Waverly Inn
16 | 22 | 18 | $39

16 Bank St. (Waverly Pl.), 212-929-4377; www.yewaverlyinn.com

◪ Conjuring up "turn of the 18th century NY", this "historic" Village "standby" charms diners with its "wonderful fireplaces", "nice garden" and "warm, cozy" ambiance; picky eaters say the American-Continental menu is "not too exciting", but what it "lacks in food, it makes up for in personality."

York Grill
22 | 20 | 22 | $42

1690 York Ave. (bet. 88th & 89th Sts.), 212-772-0261

■ Terrific "word of mouth" via "grown-up, sophisticated" types keeps this "classy, old-fashioned" Yorkville American "always busy"; fans of its "adventurous comfort food" say "thank God it's in the middle of nowhere – or else we'd never get in!"

Yujin
▽ 24 | 24 | 20 | $50

24 E. 12th St. (bet. 5th Ave. & University Pl.), 212-924-4283

■ Radiating urbane "chic", this "trendy" new Village spot is "coolly minimalist" but "reaching for the heights" with "imaginative, delicious" "jazz riffs on Japanese" fare; a few sniff this "Nobu wanna-be" "needs time to work out the kinks", but for most it's "worth the trip – and the high prices."

Yuka
20 | 12 | 18 | $26

1557 Second Ave. (bet. 80th & 81st Sts.), 212-772-9675

◪ "Big rolls at low prices" is the formula for success at this East Side Japanese famed for its $18 "all-you-can-eat sushi deal" that's a strong candidate for "best value in town"; trade-offs include "long waits" and a "cluttered, hole-in-the-wall" setting, but most leave "stuffed" and happy.

Yuki Sushi ●
22 | 15 | 20 | $27

656 Amsterdam Ave. (92nd St.), 212-787-8200

■ A "ray of light in a limited culinary neighborhood", this "much-needed" West Side Japanese brightens up the area with its "creative rolls", "civilized" air and "always-glad-to-see-you" service; "one of the best price-to-quality ratios" around is a further bonus.

Yura & Co.
19 | 11 | 13 | $23

1292 Madison Ave. (92nd St.), 212-860-8060
1645 Third Ave. (92nd St.), 212-860-8060
1659 Third Ave. (93rd St.), 212-860-8060

◪ "Simple but fine home cooking" brings "mommies", "Dalton School teens" and "92nd St. Y"–goers to these "heavenly smelling" bakery/

cafes in Carnegie Hill; true, the menu is "limited", service "amateurish" and seats are few, but they do the trick when you're "on the run."

Zabar's Cafe ⊅
— — — M

2245 Broadway (80th St.), 212-787-2000; www.zabars.com
Though the decor amounts to little more than white Formica and linoleum, the availability of fresh Zabar's products keeps this little West Side joint jumping; the main problem is getting a seat – especially on weekends when everyone reads their *Sunday Times* here.

Zarela
21 16 17 $40

953 Second Ave. (bet. 50th & 51st Sts.), 212-644-6740; www.zarela.com
■ "It's always a party" at this colorful, "totally upbeat" East Side Mexican where the "tasty, uncomplicated" cooking competes with "kick-ass margaritas" for your attention – along with "seductive" owner Zarela Martinez, who "stops by the tables to chat" with the diners.

Zaytoons
23 13 17 $16

283 Smith St. (Sackett St.), Brooklyn, 718-875-1880
472 Myrtle Ave. (bet. Hall St. & Washington Ave.), Brooklyn, 718-623-5555
■ "Scrumptious" Middle Eastern chow "on the cheap" brings Brooklynites to this "interesting" Smith Street BYO (and its Fort Greene sibling, a "Pratt students" magnet); since they "don't take reservations" and service can be "very slow", high-maintenance types "have it delivered."

Za Za ◗
∇ 20 15 19 $34

1207 First Ave. (bet. 65th & 66th Sts.), 212-772-9997; www.zazanyc.com
■ "Your favorite Italian dishes" turn up at this Eastsider that "holds its own" against the competition with "delicious", "reasonably priced" fare and "earnest service"; the only drawback is it's so "cramped" that the "waiter sits in your lap to take your order."

Zebú Grill
∇ 20 16 20 $34

305 E. 92nd St. (bet. 1st & 2nd Aves.), 212-426-7500
■ "Bold flavors" jazz up the menu at this East Side Brazilian whose "fusionlike touches" alternate with "Americanized" food; spacewise, it's either "extremely cozy" or "small and noisy", but the "treat-you-like-family service" and modest prices make it "charming" enough.

Zenith Vegetarian Cuisine
∇ 19 15 17 $26

311 W. 48th St. (bet. 8th & 9th Aves.), 212-262-8080
☑ Now in a "new space", this Theater District Vegetarian purveys "interesting combinations" of "picturesquely named" food that's "surprisingly tasty", even if foes say the "quality varies drastically"; there's no debate, however, that it's "cheap" and "different."

Zen Palate
19 17 16 $26

2170 Broadway (bet. 76th & 77th Sts.), 212-501-7768
663 Ninth Ave. (46th St.), 212-582-1669
34 Union Sq. E. (16th St.), 212-614-9291
www.zenpalate.com
☑ "Faux never tasted so good" as at these "cheap" "beans-and-sprouts" Vegetarians that also deserve architecture awards for their "Zentastic" decor; but those with an "urge for real food" find the cuisine "dull and flavorless", the service "whimsical" and the overall vibe "slightly holier than thou."

Zerza ◗
— — — M

304 E. Sixth St. (bet. 1st & 2nd Aves.), 212-529-8250; www.zerzabar.com
Breaking the Indian eatery monopoly on this Christmas tree–lit East Village block is this new Med-Moroccan duplex, an homage

to Casablanca complete with tagines and belly dancers; look for a smooth bar/lounge at street level and a cozy upstairs dining room offering a variety of small plates at small prices.

Zitoune
▽ 21 19 20 $41

46 Gansevoort St. (Greenwich St.), 212-675-5224

■ For a "lovely change of pace", check out this Meatpacking District Moroccan that offers a "tantalizing menu" of "refined" dishes served by a "helpful staff"; respondents report it's already setting a "standard" for its genre.

Zócalo
19 16 16 $36

174 E. 82nd St. (bet. Lexington & 3rd Aves.), 212-717-7772
Grand Central, lower level (42nd St. & Vanderbilt Ave.), 212-687-5666
www.zocalo.us

■ The "way-too-lively bar area" at this East Side Mexican makes it a place "to eat, not talk", though amigos still shout about its "rockin' guac" and "fabu margaritas"; more sedate types like the quieter Midtown offshoot as "one of the tastier options in Grand Central."

Zoë
22 20 20 $47

90 Prince St. (bet. B'way & Mercer St.), 212-966-6722

■ A once "trendy comer that's evolved into a classy institution", this SoHo New American succeeds thanks to its "creative" open kitchen, "well-oiled" service and "stylish cafe setting"; though sometimes "noisy", it works best "après shopping" or for brunch.

Zum Schneider ⊅
17 15 14 $22

107 Ave. C (7th St.), 212-598-1098; www.zumschneider.com

☑ "Bar food with a German twist" is yours at this inexpensive East Village "beer garden" where the grub is "nowhere near as interesting" as the "hard-to-find draft brews"; its young, "backpacking" followers dig the "kitschy" looks, though the "slow service" is a drag.

Zum Stammtisch
22 17 19 $34

69-46 Myrtle Ave. (bet. 69th Pl. & 70th St.), Queens, 718-386-3014;
www.zumstammtisch.com

■ "Like eating in Bavaria", this "traditional" Glendale German boasts perpetual "Oktoberfest" decor right down to "waitresses in dirndls" toting "giant portions" of "hearty", "*ach-du-lieber*" food; if you don't feel like "going off your diet", weight-watchers suggest the "goulash soup, a meal in itself."

Zuni ◑
19 12 16 $33

598 Ninth Ave. (43rd St.), 212-765-7626

☑ "Stick to the basics" and you won't go wrong at this "modest" Hell's Kitchen New American, a "decent neighborhood joint" that's "inexpensive and adequate" pre-theater; still, some deplore the "funky" ambiance and "dependably slow service."

Zutto
22 18 19 $38

62 Greenwich Ave. (bet. 7th Ave. S. & W. 11th St.), 212-367-7204
77 Hudson St. (Harrison St.), 212-233-3287

■ "If you aren't famous enough to get into Nobu", make an entrance at this "almost-as-good" Japanese duo where the "sushi isn't California-ized" and the cooked food is prepared with "haikulike simplicity"; even better, the "serene" decor makes for "inviting" repasts.

Indexes

CUISINES
LOCATIONS
SPECIAL FEATURES

Indexes list the best of many within each category.

CUISINES

(Restaurant Names, Food ratings and neighborhoods)

Afghan

Afghan Kebab Hse/18/multi. loc.
Pamir/20/E 70s

American (New)

Abigael's/19/Garment
Above/19/W 40s
Aesop's Tables/23/Staten Is.
Alias/22/Low E Side
Ambassador Grill/18/E 40s
Amuse/22/Chelsea
Angus McIndoe/18/W 40s
Annisa/26/G Vil.
Aureole/27/E 60s
AZ/23/Flatiron
Beacon/23/W 50s
Black Duck/20/Gramercy
Blue Hill/25/G Vil.
Blue Ribbon/25/multi. loc.
Blue Ribbon Bak./24/G Vil.
Blue Water Grill/23/Union Sq.
Boat House/16/E 70s
Bridge Cafe/21/Seaport
Bull Run/17/Fin. District
Butter/18/G Vil.
Cafe Atlas/22/W 50s
Café Botanica/20/W 50s
Cafe S.F.A./17/E 40s
Café St. Barts/17/E 50s
Candela/18/Union Sq.
Canteen/18/SoHo
Capitale/21/Little Italy
Carriage House/17/Chelsea
Caviar Russe/24/E 50s
Chadwick's/21/Bay Ridge
Charlotte/18/W 40s
Chickenbone Cafe/–/Williamsburg
Chop't Salad/21/Union Sq.
Cibo/20/E 40s
Citarella/23/W 40s
Cocotte/21/Park Slope
Compass/22/W 70s
Cornelia St. Cafe/17/G Vil.
Craft/26/Flatiron
Craftbar/21/Flatiron
Cub Room/20/SoHo
Deborah/21/G Vil.
Dish/18/Low E Side
Dishes/22/E 40s
District/21/W 40s
Downtown Atlantic/–/Boerum Hill
Druids/19/W 50s
Duane Park Cafe/24/TriBeCa
DuMont/21/Williamsburg
Eatery/18/W 50s
Eleven Madison/25/Gramercy
elmo/14/Chelsea

Essex/20/Low E Side
Etats-Unis/25/E 80s
55 Wall/21/Fin. District
Fifty Seven 57/23/E 50s
First/20/E Vil.
Five Front/21/Dumbo
Five Points/22/NoHo
Fives/26/W 50s
44 & X/21/W 40s
Fraunces Tavern/17/Fin. District
Fred's at Barneys/20/E 60s
Garden Cafe/28/Prospect Heights
Giorgio's Gramercy/23/Flatiron
good/20/W. Vil.
Gotham B&G/27/G Vil.
Grace/16/TriBeCa
Gramercy Tavern/27/Flatiron
Grocery, The/28/Carroll Gdns.
Guastavino's/18/E 50s
Halcyon/21/W 50s
Harbour Lights/19/Seaport
Harrison/23/TriBeCa
Heartbeat/19/E 40s
Henry's/16/W 100s
Henry's End/25/Bklyn Hts.
Herban Kitchen/18/SoHo
Hope & Anchor/20/Red Hook
Icon/21/Murray Hill
Ilo/25/W 40s
industry (food)/18/E Vil.
Inside/21/G Vil.
Isabella's/20/W 70s
Jane/21/G Vil.
Jefferson/23/G Vil.
Jerry's/17/SoHo
Josephina/19/W 60s
JUdson Grill/22/W 50s
Kitchen 22/82/22/multi. loc.
Kurio/25/E 90s & Up
Lenox/19/E 70s
Levana/18/W 60s
Lever House/–/E 50s
Link/19/Gramercy
Lunchbox Food/20/W. Vil.
Magnolia/18/Park Slope
March/26/E 50s
Mark's/24/E 70s
Mercer Kitchen/22/SoHo
Merchants, N.Y./14/multi. loc.
Métrazur/19/E 40s
Metronome/19/Flatiron
Mix in NY/–/W 50s
Monkey Bar/19/E 50s
Morrells/25/multi. loc.
My Most Favorite/17/W 40s
Nellie's/18/G Vil.
New Leaf/19/Wash. Hts. & Up

92/15/E 90s & Up
Noche/19/W 40s
NoHo Star/18/NoHo
Norma's/25/W 50s
North Sq./23/G Vil.
Oceana/27/E 50s
Ocean's/–/G Vil.
One C.P.S./21/W 50s
One if by Land/24/G Vil.
101/20/Bay Ridge
Onieal's Grand St./18/Little Italy
Oscar's/19/E 50s
Ouest/25/W 80s
Parish & Co./19/Chelsea
Park Avalon/20/Flatiron
Park Avenue Cafe/25/E 60s
Patroon/21/E 40s
Philip Marie/20/W. Vil.
Pioneer/–/E 70s
Place/22/W. Vil.
Porters/19/Chelsea
Prune/23/E Vil.
Rachel's American/18/W 40s
Radio Perfecto/16/E Vil.
Red/17/W 40s
Red Cat/23/Chelsea
Redeye Grill/21/W 50s
Regency/19/E 60s
Relish/20/Williamsburg
Rhône/17/Meatpacking
River Cafe/25/Dumbo
Rose Water/24/Park Slope
Sage/23/Gramercy
Salt/21/multi. loc.
Saul/26/Boerum Hill
Seven/18/Chelsea
71 Clinton/25/Low E Side
Snackbar/–/Chelsea
SQC/19/W 70s
Summit/–/E 40s
Tabla/25/Gramercy
Table d'Hôte/21/E 90s & Up
Taste/21/E 80s
Tasting Room/25/E Vil.
Tavern on Green/15/W 60s
Tea Box/20/E 50s
Thalia/21/W 50s
Thom/20/SoHo
Time Cafe/15/multi. loc.
Tocqueville/26/Union Sq.
Town/25/W 50s
Tribeca Grill/22/TriBeCa
12th St. Bar & Grill/22/Park Slope
'21' Club/21/W 50s
2 West/21/Fin. District
Union Pacific/26/Gramercy
Union Sq. Cafe/27/Union Sq.
Unity/18/Fin. District
Vanderbilt Station/18/Murray Hill
Veritas/27/Flatiron
View/17/W 40s

Village/20/G Vil.
Vine/20/Fin. District
Voyage/20/W. Vil.
Washington Park/21/G Vil.
Water's Edge/23/LIC
WD-50/24/Low E Side
West Bank Cafe/19/W 40s
Westville/–/W. Vil.
'wichcraft/–/Flatiron
Willow/19/E 70s
World Yacht/17/W 40s
York Grill/22/E 80s
Zoë/22/SoHo
Zuni/19/W 40s

American (Traditional)

Algonquin Hotel/16/W 40s
Alias/22/Low E Side
America/14/Flatiron
American Grill/21/Staten Is.
American Park/18/Fin. District
Annie's/16/E 70s
Bar 89/16/SoHo
Barking Dog/17/multi. loc.
Bayard's/25/Fin. District
Billy's/16/E 50s
Boat Basin Cafe/11/W 70s
Brennan & Carr/–/Sheepshead Bay
Brooklyn Diner USA/16/W 50s
Bryant Park Grill/Cafe/16/W 40s
Bubby's/19/TriBeCa
Cafe Nosidam/16/E 60s
Cafeteria/17/Chelsea
Chelsea Grill/17/Chelsea
Chick-Inn/–/W. Vil.
City Grill/16/W 70s
City Hall/21/TriBeCa
Coffee Shop/16/Union Sq.
Comfort Diner/14/multi. loc.
Corner Bistro/24/W. Vil.
Cupping Room/17/SoHo
Diner/22/Williamsburg
E.A.T./19/E 80s
Edward's/17/TriBeCa
EJ's Luncheonette/17/multi. loc.
Elephant & Castle/17/G Vil.
Empire Diner/14/Chelsea
ESPN Zone/12/W 40s
Etoile/18/E 80s
Fairway Cafe/20/W 70s
Fanelli's Cafe/15/SoHo
Fred's/18/W 80s
Friend of a Farmer/17/Gramercy
Good Enough to Eat/21/W 80s
Grange Hall/20/W. Vil.
Grilled Cheese/20/Low E Side
Hard Rock Cafe/12/W 50s
Heartland Brew./14/multi. loc.
Home/0/G Vil.
Houston's/20/multi. loc.
Hudson Cafeteria/18/W 50s

Jackson Hole/16/multi. loc.
Jekyll & Hyde/10/W 50s
J.G. Melon/20/E 70s
Joe Allen/17/W 40s
Johnny Rockets/15/G Vil.
Junior's/18/Downtown
King Cole Bar/18/E 50s
Kitchenette/20/multi. loc.
Lake Club/18/Staten Is.
Lucky Strike/16/SoHo
Luke's Bar & Grill/17/E 70s
Maloney & Porcelli/22/E 50s
Mama's Food /22/multi. loc.
Manhattan Grille/20/E 60s
Marion's/15/NoHo
Market Café/20/Garment
Mars 2112/9/W 50s
Mayrose/15/Flatiron
McHales/18/W 40s
Melrose/18/E 90s & Up
Metropolitan Cafe/16/E 50s
Michael Jordan's/20/E 40s
Mickey Mantle's/12/W 50s
MJ Grill/22/Fin. District
Neary's/16/E 50s
Odeon/18/TriBeCa
Once Upon a Tart/21/SoHo
Paris Commune/19/W. Vil.
Pershing Square/15/E 40s
Pete's Tavern/14/Gramercy
Pizzeria Uno/13/multi. loc.
P.J. Clarke's/16/E 50s
Popover Cafe/17/W 80s
Press 195/20/Park Slope
Raymond's Cafe/20/Chelsea
Rocco's 22nd St./–/Flatiron
Rock Center Café/18/W 50s
Sarabeth's/21/multi. loc.
Sazerac House/18/W. Vil.
Serendipity 3/19/E 60s
Silver Spurs/16/multi. loc.
Sparky's American/18/Williamsburg
St. Maggie's/18/Fin. District
Sugar Hill Bistro/20/Harlem
Swifty's/17/E 70s
T.G.I. Friday's/10/multi. loc.
Top of the Tower/14/E 40s
T Salon/17/Flatiron
Tupelo Grill/18/Garment
'21' Club/21/W 50s
Village 247/–/Cobble Hill
Vince and Eddie's/18/W 60s
Walker's/16/TriBeCa
Water Club/21/Murray Hill
Westville/–/W. Vil.
White Horse Tavern/13/W. Vil.
Wollensky's Grill/22/E 40s
Ye Waverly Inn/16/W. Vil.
Yura & Co./19/E 90s & Up

Argentinean

Azul Bistro/20/Low E Side
Chimichurri Grill/21/W 40s
Hacienda Argentina/22/E 70s
Novecento/22/SoHo
Old San Juan/20/W 50s
Pampa/22/W 90s
Sosa Borella/19/multi. loc.
Sur/21/Cobble Hill

Asian

Asia de Cuba/23/Murray Hill
AZ/23/Flatiron
bluechili/23/W 50s
Bright Food Shop/19/Chelsea
China Grill/22/W 50s
Chow Bar/20/W. Vil.
Citrus Bar & Grill/19/W 70s
Daily Chow/18/E Vil.
Faan/18/Cobble Hill
Gobo/25/G Vil.
Hispaniola/21/Wash. Hts. & Up
Lotus/14/Meatpacking
Lucky Cheng's/9/E Vil.
Nana/22/Park Slope
NoHo Star/18/NoHo
O.G./22/E Vil.
Rain/21/multi. loc.
Rice/18/multi. loc.
Roy's NY/24/Fin. District
Ruby Foo's/19/multi. loc.
Tao/22/E 50s
Verbena/23/Gramercy

Australian

Eight Mile Creek/21/Little Italy

Austrian

Café Sabarsky/20/E 80s
Cafe Steinhof/17/Park Slope
Danube/27/TriBeCa
Thomas Beisl/21/Ft. Greene
Wallsé/25/W. Vil.

Bakeries

Amy's Bread/23/multi. loc.
City Bakery/22/Flatiron
Columbus Bakery/19/multi. loc.
Le Pain Quotidien/21/multi. loc.
Yura & Co./19/E 90s & Up

Barbecue

Blue Smoke/19/Gramercy
Brother Jimmy's BBQ/16/multi. loc.
Cho Dang Gol/23/Garment
Dallas BBQ/14/multi. loc.
Do Hwa/21/G Vil.
Hog Pit BBQ/17/Meatpacking
Kang Suh/22/Garment
Kum Gang San/21/multi. loc.
Pearson's Texas BBQ/22/multi. loc.
Tennessee Mtn./16/SoHo

Cuisine Index

36 Bar & BBQ/–/Garment
Virgil's Real BBQ/21/W 40s
Woo Lae Oak/22/SoHo

Belgian

Brasserie 360/18/E 60s
Café de Bruxelles/20/W. Vil.
Le Pain Quotidien/21/multi. loc.
Markt/18/Meatpacking
Petite Abeille/20/multi. loc.

Brazilian

Casa/22/W. Vil.
Churrascaria Plata./22/W 40s
Circus/19/E 60s
Green Field Churr./19/Corona
Rice 'n' Beans/20/W 50s
Via Brasil/19/W 40s
Zebú Grill/20/E 90s & Up

Burmese

Mingala Burmese/19/multi. loc.

Cajun

Acme B&G/15/NoHo
Bayou/19/Harlem
Cooking with Jazz/25/Whitestone
Delta Grill/20/W 40s
Great Jones Cafe/19/NoHo
Mardi Gras/18/Forest Hills
107 West/16/multi. loc.
Sazerac House/18/W. Vil.
Two Boots/19/Park Slope

Californian

Cal. Pizza Kitchen/16/E 60s
Michael's/21/W 50s

Caribbean

A/22/W 100s
Bambou/21/E Vil.
Brawta Caribbean/19/Boerum Hill
Ideya/18/SoHo
Ivo & Lulu/–/SoHo
Justin's/11/Flatiron
Maroons/22/Chelsea
Negril/19/multi. loc.
Tropica/23/E 40s

Chinese

(* dim sum specialist)
Au Mandarin/22/Fin. District
Big Wong/22/Ctown
Bill Hong's/20/E 50s
Canton/24/Ctown
Chef Ho's/20/E 80s
Chiam*/21/E 40s
Chin Chin/23/E 40s
Dim Sum Go Go*/20/Ctown
East Lake*/21/Flushing
Empire Szechuan/15/multi. loc.
Evergreen Sh.*/17/multi. loc.
Excellent Dumpling/18/Ctown

Flor de Mayo/21/multi. loc.
Friendhouse/19/E Vil.
Funky Broome/18/NoLita
Golden Unicorn*/20/Ctown
Goody's/21/Ctown
Grand Sichuan/22/multi. loc.
Great NY Noodle/22/Ctown
Henry's Evergreen*/20/E 60s
HSF*/17/Ctown
Hunan Park/17/multi. loc.
Ivy's Cafe/18/W 70s
Jimmy Sung's/18/E 40s
Joe's Shanghai/21/multi. loc.
Kam Chueh/22/Ctown
Lili's Noodle Shop/17/multi. loc.
Lozoo/22/G Vil.
Mandarin Court*/19/Ctown
Maple Garden/23/E 50s
Mee Noodle Shop/17/multi. loc.
Mr. Chow/22/E 50s
Mr. K's/23/E 50s
New Green Bo/23/Ctown
New Lok Kee/21/Flushing
Nice*/20/Ctown
Ocean Palace*/21/Ocean Parkway
Ollie's/16/multi. loc.
Oriental Garden*/23/Ctown
Our Place*/22/multi. loc.
Peking Duck/22/Ctown
Phoenix Garden/23/E 40s
Pig Heaven/18/E 80s
Ping's Seafood*/22/multi. loc.
Sammy's/17/G Vil.
Shanghai Cuisine/21/Ctown
Shun Lee Cafe*/20/W 60s
Shun Lee Palace/24/E 50s
Shun Lee West/23/W 60s
66*/22/TriBeCa
Sweet-n-Tart Cafe*/20/multi. loc.
Sweet-n-Tart Rest.*/21/Ctown
Tai Hong Lau*/18/Ctown
Tang Pavilion/23/W 50s
Tse Yang/23/E 50s
Veg. Paradise*/19/multi. loc.
Wo Hop/20/Ctown
Wu Liang Ye/20/multi. loc.
X.O.*/19/Ctown

Coffeehouses

Cafe Lalo/20/W 80s
Caffe Reggio/16/G Vil.
DT.UT/17/E 80s
Edgar's Cafe/18/W 80s
Ferrara/22/multi. loc.
French Roast/15/multi. loc.
Grey Dog's Coffee/21/G Vil.
Le Pain Quotidien/21/multi. loc.
Omonia Cafe/19/multi. loc.
Once Upon a Tart/21/SoHo
71 Irving Place/18/Gramercy
Starbucks/13/multi. loc.

Coffee Shops/Diners

Brooklyn Diner USA/16/W 50s
Burger Heaven/16/multi. loc.
Chat n' Chew/17/Union Sq.
Comfort Diner/14/multi. loc.
Edison Cafe/15/W 50s
EJ's Luncheonette/17/multi. loc.
Empire Diner/14/Chelsea
Florent/19/Meatpacking
Googie's/15/E 70s
Hill Diner/19/Cobble Hill
Junior's/18/E 40s
Mayrose/15/Flatiron
Tom's/21/Prospect Heights
Veselka/19/E Vil.
Viand/17/multi. loc.

Colombian

Tierras Colomb./20/multi. loc.

Continental

Café Pierre/22/E 60s
Four Seasons/26/E 50s
Historic Bermuda Inn/16/Staten Is.
Kings' Carriage/20/E 80s
Leopard/19/E 50s
Melrose/18/W 90s & Up
Palm Court/21/W 50s
Park Place/20/Bronx
Parsonage/21/Staten Is.
Petrossian/24/W 50s
Sardi's/15/W 40s
South Shore Country/19/Staten Is.
Top of the Tower/14/E 40s
Ye Waverly Inn/16/W. Vil.

Creole

Bayou/19/Harlem
Delta Grill/20/W 40s
Great Jones Cafe/19/NoHo
Lola/19/Flatiron
Mardi Gras/18/Forest Hills
Two Boots/19/Park Slope

Cuban

Agozar/18/NoHo
Asia de Cuba/23/Murray Hill
Cafe Con Leche/17/multi. loc.
Café Habana/22/NoLita
Cuba Libre/18/Chelsea
Don Pedro's/21/E 90s & Up
Havana Central/17/Union Sq.
Havana Chelsea/18/Chelsea
Havana Vil./18/W. Vil.
Son Cubano/20/Meatpacking
Victor's Cafe/21/W 50s

Delis

Artie's Deli/17/W 80s
Barney Greengrass/23/W 80s
Ben's Kosher Deli/18/multi. loc.
Carnegie Deli/21/W 50s
Eisenberg Sandwich/19/Flatiron
Ess-a-Bagel/23/multi. loc.
Junior's/18/E 40s
Katz's Deli/23/Low E Side
Sarge's Deli/19/Murray Hill
Second Ave. Deli/23/E Vil.
Stage Deli/18/multi. loc.
Wolf's/17/W 50s

Dessert

Amy's Bread/23/multi. loc.
Cafe Lalo/20/W 80s
Café Sabarsky/20/E 80s
Caffe Rafaella/17/W. Vil.
Caffe Reggio/16/G Vil.
ChikaLicious/–/E Vil.
City Bakery/22/Flatiron
Edgar's Cafe/18/W 80s
Ferrara/22/multi. loc.
Junior's/18/Downtown
Krispy Kreme/23/multi. loc.
La Bergamote/25/Chelsea
Lady Mendl's/21/Gramercy
Le Pain Quotidien/21/multi. loc.
My Most Favorite/17/W 40s
Omonia Cafe/19/multi. loc.
Once Upon a Tart/21/SoHo
Park Avenue Cafe/25/E 60s
Payard Bistro/24/E 70s
Provence en Boite/22/Bay Ridge
Serendipity 3/19/E 60s
Sweet Melissa/23/Cobble Hill
Toraya/18/E 70s
Veniero's/23/E Vil.

Dominican

Cafe Con Leche/17/multi. loc.
Don Pedro's/21/E 90s & Up
El Malecon/21/multi. loc.

Dutch

NL/19/G Vil.

Eclectic

aka Cafe/20/Low E Side
Aki/24/G Vil.
Alice's Tea Cup/18/W 70s
B. Smith's/18/W 40s
Café Boulud/27/E 70s
Cal. Pizza Kitchen/16/E 60s
Carol's Cafe/25/Staten Is.
Caviarteria/24/E 50s
Chickenbone Cafe/–/Williamsburg
Chubo/–/Low E Side
Danube/27/TriBeCa
Delegates Dining Rm./20/E 40s
Dishes/22/E 40s
East of Eighth/15/Chelsea
Global 33/19/E Vil.
Josephina/19/W 60s
Josie's/21/multi. loc.
Kitchen Club/19/Little Italy

Cuisine Index

La Flor Bakery Cafe/26/Woodside
Lucky Cheng's/9/E Vil.
Orbit East Harlem/–/Harlem
Plain Canvas/–/E Vil.
Punch/19/Flatiron
Route 66 Cafe/17/W 50s
Schiller's/–/Low E Side
Sugar Hill Bistro/20/Harlem
WD-50/24/Low E Side
World Yacht/17/W 40s

Egyptian

Casa La Femme/15/SoHo
Mombar/23/Astoria

English

(See also Fish and Chips)
Cafe Topsy/17/W. Vil.
Tea & Sympathy/20/W. Vil.

Ethiopian

Ethiopian/19/E 80s
Ghenet/22/NoLita
Meskerem/20/multi. loc.

Filipino

Cendrillon/23/SoHo

Fish and Chips

A Salt & Battery/19/multi. loc.
Chip/CurryShop/19/Park Slope
Chipper/19/Sunnyside
F & B/20/Chelsea

French

A.O.C./–/W. Vil.
Arabelle/25/E 60s
Bambou/21/E Vil.
Bayard's/25/Fin. District
Bouterin/21/E 50s
Box Tree/20/E 40s
Café Boulud/27/E 70s
Café des Artistes/22/W 60s
Café Pierre/22/E 60s
Chez Oskar/19/Ft. Greene
Cocotte/21/Park Slope
Fives/26/W 50s
Fleur de Sel/25/Flatiron
44/19/W 40s
Gaby/21/W 40s
Gascogne/22/Chelsea
Indochine/20/G Vil.
Ivo & Lulu/–/SoHo
La Baraka/19/Little Neck
La Bergamote/25/Chelsea
La Boîte en Bois/21/W 60s
La Caravelle/26/W 50s
La Côte Basque/26/W 50s
La Grenouille/26/E 50s
La Mirabelle/21/W 80s
Le Bernardin/28/W 50s
L'Ecole/24/SoHo
Le Colonial/20/E 50s

Leopard/19/E 50s
Le Refuge/22/E 80s
Le Refuge Inn/24/Bronx
Le Rivage/19/W 40s
Lola/19/Flatiron
Lutèce/24/E 50s
Mark's/24/E 70s
Mercer Kitchen/22/SoHo
Mix in NY/–/W 50s
Montrachet/26/TriBeCa
Once Upon a Tart/21/SoHo
Paradou/21/multi. loc.
Rasputin/22/Brighton Beach
Red Garlic/19/W 50s
René Pujol/24/W 50s
Rhône/17/Meatpacking
Sherwood Cafe/18/Boerum Hill
Starfoods/19/E Vil.
Table d'Hôte/21/E 90s & Up
Terrace in the Sky/22/W 100s
325 Spring St./22/SoHo
26 Seats/23/E Vil.
Uguale/20/W. Vil.
Vong/24/E 50s
Willow/19/E 70s

French (Bistro)

A/22/W 100s
Alouette/19/W 90s
À Table/21/Ft. Greene
Avenue/19/W 80s
Balthazar/23/SoHo
Banania Cafe/22/Cobble Hill
Bandol Bistro/19/E 70s
BarTabac/17/Boerum Hill
Bienvenue/20/Murray Hill
Bistro du Nord/19/E 90s & Up
Bistro Les Amis/21/SoHo
Bistro Le Steak/18/E 70s
Bistro St. Mark's/24/Park Slope
Bistro Ten 18/19/W 100s
Bouchon/22/G Vil.
Brasserie Julien/18/E 80s
Cafe du Pont/18/E 50s
Cafe Joul/19/E 50s
Cafe Lebowitz/17/NoLita
Cafe Loup/18/G Vil.
Cafe Luluc/21/Cobble Hill
Cafe Luxembourg/21/W 70s
Cafe Un Deux Trois/15/W 40s
CamaJe/19/G Vil.
Capsouto Frères/23/TriBeCa
Casimir/21/E Vil.
Chelsea Bistro/22/Chelsea
Chez Brigitte/17/W. Vil.
Chez Jacqueline/20/G Vil.
Chez Josephine/20/W 40s
Chez Michallet/23/W. Vil.
Chez Napoléon/18/W 50s
Cosette/21/Murray Hill
Country Café/19/SoHo

Cuisine Index

Danal/21/E Vil.
D'Artagnan/20/E 40s
db Bistro Moderne/24/W 40s
Epicerie/18/Low E Side
Félix/16/SoHo
Ferrier Bistro/18/E 60s
Flea Market Cafe/19/E Vil.
Florent/19/Meatpacking
French Roast/15/multi. loc.
Frère Jacques/19/Murray Hill
Jarnac/24/W. Vil.
Jean Claude/23/SoHo
Jean-Luc/21/W 80s
JoJo/24/E 60s
Jubilee/23/E 50s
Jules/19/E Vil.
La Belle Vie/17/Chelsea
La Bouillabaisse/21/Bklyn Hts.
L'Acajou/20/Flatiron
La Goulue/21/E 60s
La Lunchonette/21/Chelsea
La Mangeoire/20/E 50s
La Mediterranée/18/E 50s
La Petite Auberge/20/Gramercy
La Ripaille/21/W. Vil.
La Tour/18/E 70s
Le Bilboquet/20/E 60s
Le Boeuf à la Mode/21/E 80s
Le Charlot/19/E 60s
Le Gamin/18/multi. loc.
Le Gigot/25/G Vil.
Le Jardin Bistro/20/NoLita
Le Madeleine/20/W 40s
Le Marais/20/W 40s
L'Entrecote/18/E 50s
Le Père Pinard/20/Low E Side
Le Pescadou/19/SoHo
Les Halles/20/multi. loc.
Le Singe Vert/18/Chelsea
Les Routiers/20/W 80s
Le Tableau/24/E Vil.
L'Express/16/Flatiron
Le Zinc/19/TriBeCa
Le Zoo/19/W. Vil.
Loulou/24/Ft. Greene
Lucien/18/E Vil.
Lucky Strike/16/SoHo
Madison Bistro/19/Murray Hill
Marseille/21/W 40s
Montparnasse/19/E 50s
Moutarde/21/Park Slope
Odeon/18/TriBeCa
Orsay/18/E 70s
Paris Commune/19/W. Vil.
Park Bistro/20/Gramercy
Pascalou/20/E 90s & Up
Pastis/20/Meatpacking
Patois/21/Carroll Gdns.
Payard Bistro/24/E 70s
Pierre au Tunnel/20/W 40s
Pigalle/18/W 40s

Provence/22/SoHo
Provence en Boite/22/Bay Ridge
Quatorze Bis/20/E 70s
Quercy/22/Cobble Hill
Raoul's/23/SoHo
Rive Gauche/17/Murray Hill
Seppi's/18/W 50s
Soho Steak/19/SoHo
Steak Frites/17/Union Sq.
St. Michel/22/Bay Ridge
Tartine/22/W. Vil.
Titou/21/W. Vil.
Tournesol/23/LIC
Village/20/G Vil.

French (Brasserie)

Artisanal/23/Murray Hill
Balthazar/23/SoHo
Brasserie/20/E 50s
Brasserie 8½/21/W 50s
Brasserie Julien/18/E 80s
Brasserie 360/18/E 60s
Django/20/E 40s
Jacques Brasserie/19/E 80s
L'Absinthe/22/E 60s
Maison/–/W 50s
Marseille/21/W 40s
Nice Matin/23/W 70s
One C.P.S./21/W 50s
Orsay/18/E 70s
Oscar's/19/E 50s
Pershing Square/15/E 40s
Pigalle/18/W 40s
Rue 57/19/W 50s

French (New)

Aix/23/W 80s
Alain Ducasse/27/W 50s
Atelier/26/W 50s
Bleu Evolution/17/Wash. Hts. & Up
Bouley/28/TriBeCa
Chanterelle/27/TriBeCa
Daniel/28/E 60s
Dumonet/22/E 70s
Elephant/22/E Vil.
14 Wall Street/20/Fin. District
Jacques Brasserie/19/E 80s
Jean Georges/28/W 60s
Le Cirque 2000/25/E 50s
Le Madeleine/20/W 40s
Le Perigord/24/E 50s
Métisse/22/W 100s
Olica/23/E 50s
Pascalou/20/E 90s & Up
Petrossian/24/W 50s
Picholine/27/W 60s
Savann/20/W 70s
Shaffer City/23/Flatiron
360/–/Red Hook
Tocqueville/26/Union Sq.
Triomphe/22/W 40s
Trois Marches/19/E 80s

212/17/E 60s
Village/20/G Vil.

German

Hallo Berlin/19/multi. loc.
Heidelberg/17/E 80s
Killmeyer's/20/Staten Is.
Rolf's/17/Gramercy
Zum Schneider/17/E Vil.
Zum Stammtisch/22/Glendale

Greek

Avra Estiatorio/23/E 40s
Café Bar/21/Astoria
Christos Hasapo/23/Astoria
Eliá/25/Bay Ridge
Elias Corner/23/Astoria
Esperides/22/Astoria
Ethos/–/Murray Hill
Greek Captain/23/LIC
Gus' Place/19/G Vil.
Ithaka/21/E 80s
Karyatis/20/Astoria
Kyma/20/W 40s
Meltemi/19/E 50s
Metsovo/19/W 70s
Milos, Estiatorio/26/W 50s
Molyvos/23/W 50s
Niko's Med. Grill/18/W 70s
Omonia Cafe/19/multi. loc.
Pelagos/19/W 70s
Periyali/25/Flatiron
Roumeli Taverna/22/Astoria
S'Agapo/21/Astoria
Snack/23/SoHo
Snack Taverna/–/W. Vil.
Stamatis/23/Astoria
Symposium/19/W 100s
Taverna Kyclades/24/Astoria
Taverna Vraka/18/Astoria
Telly's Taverna/23/Astoria
Thalassa/23/TriBeCa
Trata Estiatorio/21/E 70s
Uncle George's/18/Astoria
Uncle Nick's/21/W 50s

Hamburgers

Better Burger/16/multi. loc.
Big Nick's Burger/18/W 70s
Blue 9 Burger/17/E Vil.
Burger Heaven/16/multi. loc.
burger joint/23/W 50s
Chelsea Grill/17/Chelsea
Cité Grill/20/W 50s
Corner Bistro/24/W. Vil.
Cozy Soup/Burger/19/G Vil.
db Bistro Moderne/24/W 40s
DuMont/21/Williamsburg
Fanelli's Cafe/15/SoHo
Hard Rock Cafe/12/W 50s
Houston's/20/Gramercy
Island Burgers/22/W 50s

Jackson Hole/16/multi. loc.
J.G. Melon/20/E 70s
Johnny Rockets/15/G Vil.
Luke's Bar & Grill/17/E 70s
McHales/18/W 40s
P.J. Clarke's/16/E 50s
Rare Bar & Grill/26/Murray Hill
Silver Spurs/16/multi. loc.
'21' Club/21/W 50s
White Horse Tavern/13/W. Vil.
Wollensky's Grill/22/E 40s

Hawaiian

Roy's NY/24/Fin. District

Health Food

Chop't Salad/21/Union Sq.
Dojo/15/multi. loc.
Heartbeat/19/E 40s
Herban Kitchen/18/SoHo
Josie's/21/multi. loc.
Pump Energy Food/19/multi. loc.
Quintessence/17/multi. loc.
Spring St. Natural/18/NoLita
Terra 47/–/G Vil.
Tossed/17/multi. loc.

Hot Dogs

F & B/20/Chelsea
Gray's Papaya/20/multi. loc.
Papaya King/20/multi. loc.
Sparky's American/18/Williamsburg

Hungarian

Mocca/17/E 80s

Ice Cream Parlor

Emack & Bolio's/24/multi. loc.
L & B Spumoni/22/Bensonhurst

Indian

Adä/21/E 50s
Amma/23/E 50s
Baluchi's/18/multi. loc.
Banjara/22/E Vil.
Bay Leaf/21/W 50s
Bombay Palace/18/W 50s
Bread Bar at Tabla/24/Gramercy
Brick Lane Curry/21/E Vil.
Bukhara Grill/22/multi. loc.
Cafe Spice/18/multi. loc.
Chip/CurryShop/19/Park Slope
Chola/24/E 50s
Curry Leaf/20/Gramercy
Dakshin Indian/20/multi. loc.
Dawat/23/E 50s
Delhi Palace/23/Jackson Hts.
Diwan/21/E 40s
Hampton Chutney/20/SoHo
Haveli/21/E Vil.
Jackson Diner/24/Jackson Hts.
Jewel of India/20/W 40s
Mirchi/20/G Vil.

Mitali/*18/multi. loc.*
Mughlai/*19/W 70s*
Pongal/*23/Gramercy*
Raga/*23/E Vil.*
Salaam Bombay/*21/TriBeCa*
Sapphire Indian/*20/W 60s*
Shaan/*22/W 40s*
Surya/*21/W. Vil.*
Tabla/*25/Gramercy*
Tamarind/*24/Flatiron*
Utsav/*21/W 40s*
Vatan/*22/Gramercy*

Indonesian
Bali Nusa Indah/*19/W 40s*

Irish
Cafe Topsy/*17/W. Vil.*
Chipper/*19/Sunnyside*
Neary's/*16/E 50s*
Ulysses/*–/Fin. District*

Israeli
Azuri Cafe/*24/W 50s*

Italian
(N=Northern; S=Southern)
Acappella (N)/*24/TriBeCa*
Acqua (N)/*18/W 90s*
Acqua Pazza/*24/W 50s*
Al Di La (N)/*25/Park Slope*
Aleo (N)/*24/Flatiron*
Alfredo of Rome/*18/W 40s*
Amarone/*18/W 40s*
Amici Amore I (N)/*20/Astoria*
Anche Vivolo/*18/E 50s*
Angelina's/*22/Staten Is.*
Angelo's (S)/*22/Little Italy*
ápizz/*20/Low E Side*
Areo/*24/Bay Ridge*
Arezzo/*23/Flatiron*
Arqua (N)/*21/TriBeCa*
Arté (N)/*18/G Vil.*
Arturo's Pizzeria/*20/G Vil.*
Assaggio/*18/W 80s*
Azalea (N)/*–/W 50s*
Babbo/*27/G Vil.*
Baci/*23/Bay Ridge*
Baldoria/*20/W 40s*
Baldo Vino (N)/*18/E Vil.*
Bamonte's (N)/*23/Williamsburg*
Baraonda (N)/*18/E 70s*
Barbalùc (N)/*17/E 60s*
Barbetta (N)/*20/W 40s*
Barolo (N)/*19/SoHo*
Bar Pitti (N)/*21/G Vil.*
Basso Est/*24/Low E Side*
Basta Pasta/*21/Flatiron*
Becco/*21/W 40s*
Bella Blu (N)/*19/E 70s*
Bella Donna/*18/multi. loc.*
Bella Luna (N)/*17/W 80s*

Bella Via/*18/LIC*
Bellavista Cafe/*19/Bronx*
Bellini/*22/E 50s*
Bello (N)/*20/W 50s*
Belluno (N)/*20/Murray Hill*
Beppe (N)/*22/Flatiron*
Bice (N)/*20/E 50s*
Biricchino (N)/*20/Chelsea*
Borgo Antico/*18/G Vil.*
Bottino (N)/*19/Chelsea*
Bravo Gianni/*21/E 60s*
Bread/*22/TriBeCa*
Bricco (S)/*19/W 50s*
Brick Cafe (N)/*19/Astoria*
Brio/*18/E 60s*
Bruculino (S)/*20/W 70s*
Brunelli/*19/E 70s*
Bruno/*20/E 50s*
Bussola Ristorante/*21/G Vil.*
Cafe Nosidam/*16/E 60s*
Cafe Picasso/*18/W. Vil.*
Cafe Trevi (N)/*21/E 80s*
Caffe Buon Gusto/*18/multi. loc.*
Caffe Cielo (N)/*18/W 50s*
Caffe Grazie/*18/E 80s*
Caffe Linda/*19/E 40s*
Caffé/Green (N)/*21/Bayside*
Caffe Rafaella (N)/*17/W. Vil.*
Caffe Reggio/*16/G Vil.*
Campagnola (S)/*24/E 70s*
Canaletto (N)/*20/E 60s*
Cara Mia/*19/W 40s*
Carino (S)/*19/E 80s*
Carmine's (S)/*20/multi. loc.*
Casa Di Meglio (N)/*18/W 40s*
Casa Mia/*20/Gramercy*
Caserta Vecch. (S)/*20/Carroll Gdns.*
Celeste (S)/*22/W 80s*
Cellini (N)/*20/E 50s*
Centolire (N)/*20/E 80s*
'Cesca (S)/*–/W 70s*
Chelsea Ristorante (N)/*20/Chelsea*
Chianti/*22/Bay Ridge*
Cibo/*20/E 40s*
Cicciolino/*22/E Vil.*
Cinque Terre (N)/*19/Murray Hill*
Cipriani Dolci/*20/E 40s*
Coco Pazzo (N)/*20/multi. loc.*
Col Legno (N)/*20/E Vil.*
Cono & Sons/*21/Williamsburg*
Convivium Osteria/*25/Park Slope*
Coppola's/*20/multi. loc.*
Cotto/*–/E Vil.*
Crispo/*22/W. Vil.*
Cucina (N)/*20/Park Slope*
Cucina di Pesce/*18/E Vil.*
Culinaria/*23/W 40s*
Da Andrea (N)/*22/W. Vil.*
Da Antonio/*20/E 50s*
Da Ciro/*21/Murray Hill*
Da Filippo (N)/*21/E 60s*

Cuisine Index

Da Nico/*22/Little Italy*
Daniella/*21/Chelsea*
Da Silvano (N)/*21/G Vil.*
Da Tommaso (N)/*19/W 50s*
Da Umberto (N)/*24/Chelsea*
Deck, The (S)/*--/Chelsea*
DeGrezia (N)/*22/E 50s*
Di Fara/*28/Midwood*
Divino (N)/*18/E 80s*
Dominic/*--/TriBeCa*
Dominick's (S)/*23/Bronx*
Don Giovanni (N)/*18/multi. loc.*
Don Peppe (N)/*25/Ozone Park*
Downtown (N)/*20/SoHo*
Due (N)/*21/E 70s*
East Post/*19/E Vil.*
Ecco/*21/TriBeCa*
Ecco-la/*16/E 90s & Up*
Elaine's/*12/E 80s*
Elio's/*24/E 80s*
Ennio & Michael/*22/NoHo*
Enzo's/*25/Bronx*
Erminia/*25/E 80s*
Esca (S)/*23/W 40s*
Etrusca (N)/*--/W 50s*
F & J Pine (S)/*21/Bronx*
Felidia/*25/E 50s*
Ferdinando's (S)/*21/Carroll Gdns.*
Ferrara/*22/multi. loc.*
Fiamma Osteria/*25/SoHo*
F.illi Ponte/*20/TriBeCa*
Fino (N)/*19/multi. loc.*
Fiorello's Cafe/*19/W 60s*
Fiorentino's/*20/Gravesend*
Firenze (N)/*19/E 80s*
Fontana di Trevi (N)/*20/W 50s*
Frank (S)/*22/E Vil.*
Fred's at Barneys (N)/*20/E 60s*
Fresco by Scotto (N)/*22/E 50s*
Frutti di Mare/*18/E Vil.*
Gabriel's (N)/*22/W 60s*
Gargiulo's (S)/*22/Coney Island*
Gennaro (N)/*24/W 90s*
Giambelli (N)/*21/E 50s*
Giando/Water (N)/*17/Williamsburg*
Gigino Trattoria/*21/TriBeCa*
Gigino/Wagner Pk./*19/Fin. District*
Gino (S)/*20/E 60s*
Giorgione/*22/SoHo*
Giovanni (N)/*23/W 50s*
Giovanni 25 (N)/*22/E 80s*
Girasole/*22/E 80s*
Gnocco Caffe (N)/*22/E Vil.*
Gonzo/*22/G Vil.*
Grace's Trattoria/*17/E 70s*
Gradisca/*19/G Vil.*
Grano Trattoria/*18/G Vil.*
Grifone (N)/*24/E 40s*
Harry Cipriani (N)/*21/E 50s*
I Coppi (N)/*22/E Vil.*
Il Bagatto/*24/E Vil.*

Il Buco/*23/NoHo*
Il Cantinori (N)/*22/G Vil.*
Il Corallo/*21/SoHo*
Il Cortile/*23/Little Italy*
Il Covo dell'Est (N)/*18/E Vil.*
Il Fornaio/*21/Little Italy*
Il Gatto & La Volpe/*19/E 60s*
Il Gattopardo (S)/*23/W 50s*
Il Giglio (N)/*26/TriBeCa*
Il Menestrello/*21/E 50s*
Il Monello (N)/*22/E 70s*
Il Mulino (N)/*27/G Vil.*
Il Nido (N)/*24/E 50s*
Il Palazzo/*25/Little Italy*
Il Postino/*23/E 40s*
Il Riccio (S)/*22/E 70s*
Il Tinello (N)/*23/W 50s*
Il Vagabondo (N)/*17/E 60s*
Il Valentino (N)/*19/E 50s*
'ino/*23/W. Vil.*
'inoteca/*--/Low E Side*
Intermezzo/*18/Chelsea*
Isola/*18/W 80s*
I Tre Merli (N)/*18/SoHo*
I Trulli (S)/*23/Gramercy*
Joanna's (N)/*18/E 90s & Up*
John's 12th Street/*19/E Vil.*
John's Pizzeria/*21/W 40s*
Joseph's/*21/Fin. District*
Julian's/*19/W 50s*
La Cantina (S)/*22/W. Vil.*
La Cantina Toscana (N)/*23/E 60s*
La Focaccia (N)/*22/W. Vil.*
La Giara/*20/Murray Hill*
La Gioconda/*21/E 50s*
La Grolla (N)/*21/W 70s*
La Houppa/*19/E 60s*
La Lanterna/*19/G Vil.*
La Locanda Vini/*21/W 40s*
La Mela/*19/Little Italy*
L & B Spumoni/*22/Bensonhurst*
La Pizza Fresca (N)/*22/Flatiron*
La Rivista/*20/W 40s*
Lattanzi/*23/W 40s*
Lavagna/*23/E Vil.*
La Vineria (S)/*22/W 50s*
Le Madri (N)/*21/Chelsea*
Lentini/*21/E 80s*
Lento's/*20/multi. loc.*
Le Zie 2000 (N)/*22/Chelsea*
Le Zoccole (N)/*--/E Vil.*
Liberta/*19/E 80s*
Lil' Frankie's Pizza/*24/E Vil.*
Limoncello/*21/W 50s*
L'Impero/*26/E 40s*
Locanda Vini (N)/*25/Clinton Hill*
L'Orto/*24/Fin. District*
Luca (N)/*21/E 80s*
Lumi/*19/E 70s*
Luna Piena/*18/E 50s*
Lupa/*26/G Vil.*

Cuisine Index

Lusardi's (N)/*25/E 70s*
Luxia/*20/W 40s*
Macelleria (N)/*22/Meatpacking*
Madison's/*21/Bronx*
Magnifico (N)/*25/Chelsea*
Malatesta (N)/*19/W. Vil.*
Manducatis/*21/LIC*
Manetta's/*22/LIC*
Mangia/*20/E 40s*
Mangiarini/*22/E 80s*
Marchi's (N)/*20/Murray Hill*
Marco Polo/*19/Carroll Gdns.*
Maria Pia/*19/W 50s*
Marinella/*20/G Vil.*
Mario's (S)/*21/Bronx*
Maruzzella/*21/E 70s*
Massimo/*24/G Vil.*
Max (S)/*23/multi. loc.*
Mediterraneo (N)/*19/E 60s*
Mezzaluna/*20/E 70s*
Mezzogiorno/*20/SoHo*
Minetta Tavern (N)/*18/G Vil.*
Miss Williamsburg/*20/Williamsburg*
Moda (S)/*18/W 50s*
Mosto Osteria (N)/*19/E Vil.*
Nanni (N)/*23/E 40s*
Naples 45 (S)/*19/E 40s*
Nello (N)/*19/E 60s*
Nick's/*24/multi. loc.*
Nicola Paone (N)/*18/Murray Hill*
Nicola's/*23/E 80s*
Nino's (N)/*23/E 70s*
Nino's Positano/*20/E 40s*
Nocello/*22/W 50s*
Noodle Pudding/*23/Bklyn Hts.*
Notaro (N)/*18/Murray Hill*
Novitá/*24/Gramercy*
101/*20/Bay Ridge*
Orso (N)/*22/W 40s*
Osteria al Doge (N)/*20/W 40s*
Osteria del Circo (N)/*22/W 50s*
Osteria del Sole (S)/*22/W. Vil.*
Oster. Gallo Nero (N)/*21/G Vil.*
Osteria Laguna (N)/*20/E 40s*
Otto/*20/G Vil.*
Palm (N)/*24/E 40s*
Panino'teca 275/*22/Carroll Gdns.*
Paola's/*22/E 80s*
Paper Moon Milano (N)/*20/E 50s*
Park Side/*24/Corona*
Parma (N)/*21/E 70s*
Pasticcio/*18/Murray Hill*
Patsy's (S)/*20/W 50s*
Paul & Jimmy's/*19/Gramercy*
Peasant/*22/NoLita*
Pellegrino's/*24/Little Italy*
Pepe ... To Go/*21/multi. loc.*
Pepolino (N)/*24/TriBeCa*
Perbacco/*25/E Vil.*
Pescatore/*19/E 50s*
Petaluma/*17/E 70s*

Pete's Downtown/*18/Dumbo*
Petrosino (S)/*21/Low E Side*
Piadina (N)/*20/G Vil.*
Piccola Venezia/*25/Astoria*
Piccolo Angolo (N)/*25/W. Vil.*
Pietrasanta (N)/*20/W 40s*
Pietro's (N)/*23/E 40s*
Pinocchio/*23/E 90s & Up*
Pisticci (S)/*22/W 100s*
Pó/*25/G Vil.*
Pomodoro Rosso/*22/W 70s*
Ponticello (N)/*23/Astoria*
Portofino Grille/*19/E 60s*
Positano (S)/*21/Little Italy*
Primavera (N)/*24/E 80s*
Primola/*23/E 60s*
Puttanesca/*17/W 50s*
Quartino (N)/*20/Seaport*
Quattro Gatti/*20/E 80s*
Queen/*24/Bklyn Hts.*
Rafaella (N)/*21/W. Vil.*
Rainbow Room (N)/*20/W 40s*
Rao's (S)/*21/Harlem*
Remi (N)/*23/W 50s*
Re Sette/*25/W 40s*
Ribollita (N)/*19/Flatiron*
Risotteria (N)/*21/G Vil.*
Roberto's/*27/Bronx*
Roc/*22/TriBeCa*
Rocco (S)/*20/G Vil.*
Rocco's 22nd St./*–/Flatiron*
Rossini's (N)/*22/Murray Hill*
Rughetta (S)/*22/E 80s*
Sal Anthony's/*16/multi. loc.*
Salute! (N)/*17/Murray Hill*
Sambuca (S)/*19/W 70s*
San Domenico (S)/*22/W 50s*
San Pietro (S)/*23/E 50s*
Sapori d'Ischia (S)/*24/Woodside*
Savoia (S)/*21/Carroll Gdns.*
Scaletta (N)/*22/W 70s*
Scalinatella/*25/E 60s*
Scalini Fedeli (N)/*26/TriBeCa*
Scopa (N)/*20/Gramercy*
Serafina/*18/multi. loc.*
Sette Mezzo/*23/E 70s*
Sirabella's (N)/*23/E 80s*
Sistina (N)/*24/E 80s*
Sosa Borella/*19/multi. loc.*
Stella del Mare (N)/*22/Murray Hill*
Supper (N)/*22/E Vil.*
Tanti Baci Caffé/*18/multi. loc.*
Taormina/*21/Little Italy*
Tello's/*18/Chelsea*
Teodora (N)/*21/E 50s*
Tevere/*21/E 80s*
Three of Cups/*18/E Vil.*
Tommaso's/*22/Bensonhurst*
Tony's Di Napoli (S)/*18/multi. loc.*
Torre di Pisa (N)/*18/W 40s*
Totonno Pizzeria/*23/E 80s*

Cuisine Index

Trattoria Alba (N)/*20/Murray Hill*
Trattoria Dell'Arte/*21/W 50s*
Trattoria Dopo Teatro/*16/W 40s*
Trattoria L'incontro/*26/Astoria*
Trattoria Pesce/*19/multi. loc.*
Trattoria Romana/*24/Staten Is.*
Trattoria Rustica/*21/E 80s*
Trattoria Trecolori/*20/W 40s*
Tre Pomodori/*18/multi. loc.*
Triangolo/*20/E 80s*
Tuscan (N)/*20/E 40s*
Tuscan Square (N)/*18/W 50s*
Tuscany Grill (N)/*23/Bay Ridge*
212/*17/E 60s*
Uguale/*20/W. Vil.*
Umberto's Clam/*18/Little Italy*
Va Bene/*21/E 80s*
Vago/*–/W 50s*
V&T (S)/*19/W 100s*
Va Tutto! (N)/*20/NoLita*
Veniero's/*23/E Vil.*
Veronica/*21/Garment*
Via Emilia (N)/*21/Flatiron*
Via Oreto (S)/*21/E 60s*
Via Quadronno/*22/E 70s*
ViceVersa (N)/*23/W 50s*
Vico/*20/E 90s & Up*
Villa Berulia (N)/*22/Murray Hill*
Villa Mosconi (N)/*20/G Vil.*
Vincent's (S)/*20/Little Italy*
Vittorio Cucina/*20/W. Vil.*
Vivolo/*18/E 70s*
Volare (N)/*22/G Vil.*
Vuli (N)/*21/E 40s*
Za Za (N)/*20/E 60s*

Japanese

Aki/*24/G Vil.*
Aki Sushi/*19/multi. loc.*
Avenue A Sushi/*18/E Vil.*
Benihana/*16/multi. loc.*
Blue Ribbon Sushi/*25/multi. loc.*
Bond Street/*25/NoHo*
Choshi/*18/Gramercy*
Dojo/*15/multi. loc.*
East/*16/multi. loc.*
Evergreen Sh./*17/multi. loc.*
Friendhouse/*19/E Vil.*
Fujiyama Mama/*20/W 80s*
Haikara Grill/*19/E 50s*
Hakata Grill/*22/W 40s*
Haru/*22/multi. loc.*
Hasaki/*24/E Vil.*
Hatsuhana/*24/E 40s*
Honmura An/*26/SoHo*
Inagiku/*23/E 40s*
Iron Sushi/*21/Murray Hill*
Iso/*23/E Vil.*
Ivy's Cafe/*18/W 70s*
Japonica/*22/G Vil.*
Jeollado/*18/E Vil.*

Jewel Bako/*27/E Vil.*
Kai/*25/E 60s*
Katsuhama/*21/E 40s*
Kiiroi-Hana/*20/W 50s*
Kitchen Club/*19/Little Italy*
Kodama/*19/multi. loc.*
Korea Palace/*19/E 50s*
Kum Gang San/*21/multi. loc.*
Kuruma Zushi/*27/E 40s*
Lan/*20/E Vil.*
Marumi/*22/NoHo*
Menchanko-tei/*18/multi. loc.*
Minado/*–/Murray Hill*
Mishima/*22/Murray Hill*
Mizu Sushi/*24/Flatiron*
Monster Sushi/*17/multi. loc.*
Nëo Sushi/*23/W 80s*
Nippon/*22/E 50s*
Nobu/*28/TriBeCa*
Nobu Next Door/*27/TriBeCa*
Omen/*24/SoHo*
Ony/*19/multi. loc.*
Osaka/*24/Cobble Hill*
Otabe/*23/E 50s*
Ota-ya/*20/E 80s*
Planet Thailand/*22/Williamsburg*
Poke/*27/E 80s*
Roppongi/*21/W 80s*
Sandobe/*21/E Vil.*
Sapporo East/*20/E Vil.*
Seo/*23/E 40s*
Sesumi/*22/E 80s*
Shabu-Tatsu/*20/E Vil.*
Shinjuku/*–/Bklyn Hts.*
Soba Nippon/*21/W 50s*
Sobaya/*23/E Vil.*
Sugiyama/*26/W 50s*
Sushi Ann/*21/E 50s*
Sushiden/*23/multi. loc.*
Sushi Hana/*22/multi. loc.*
Sushi of Gari/*26/E 70s*
Sushi Rose/*21/E 50s*
SushiSamba/*22/multi. loc.*
Sushi Seki/*26/E 60s*
Sushi Sen-nin/*27/Murray Hill*
Sushiya/*21/W 50s*
Sushi Yasuda/*27/E 40s*
Sushi Zen/*25/W 40s*
Taka/*25/W. Vil.*
Takahachi/*23/multi. loc.*
Tatany/*22/multi. loc.*
Tea Box/*20/E 50s*
Ten Sushi/*–/E Vil.*
Tomoe Sushi/*27/G Vil.*
Tomo Sushi/*17/W 100s*
Toraya/*18/E 70s*
Tsuki/*24/E 70s*
Won Jo/*21/Garment*
Yakiniku JuJu/*25/Gramercy*
Yama/*25/multi. loc.*
Yujin/*24/G Vil.*

Yuka/20/E 80s
Yuki Sushi/22/W 90s
Zutto/22/multi. loc.

Korean

Cho Dang Gol/23/Garment
Dae Dong/20/Garment
Do Hwa/21/G Vil.
Dok Suni's/21/E Vil.
Franchia/–/Murray Hill
Gam Mee Ok/21/Garment
Hangawi/25/Murray Hill
Jeollado/18/E Vil.
Kang Suh/22/Garment
Korea Palace/19/E 50s
Kum Gang San/21/multi. loc.
36 Bar & BBQ/–/Garment
Won Jo/21/Garment
Woo Lae Oak/22/SoHo
Yakiniku JuJu/25/Gramercy

Kosher

Abigael's/19/Garment
Azuri Cafe/24/W 50s
Ben's Kosher Deli/18/multi. loc.
Box Tree/20/E 40s
Curry Leaf/20/Gramercy
Darna/20/W 80s
Haikara Grill/19/E 50s
Le Marais/20/W 40s
Levana/18/W 60s
My Most Favorite/17/W 40s
Pongal/23/Gramercy
Prime Grill/24/E 40s
Second Ave. Deli/23/E Vil.
Shallots NY/20/E 50s
Talia's Steakhouse/–/W 90s
Tevere/21/E 80s
Va Bene/21/E 80s
Veg. Paradise/19/Ctown

Lebanese

Al Bustan/21/E 50s

Malaysian

Nyonya/23/multi. loc.
Penang/18/multi. loc.

Mediterranean

Aesop's Tables/23/Staten Is.
Aigo/–/E 80s
Aleo/24/Flatiron
Alma Blue/–/SoHo
Amaranth/18/E 60s
A.O.C. Bedford/–/G Vil.
Beyoglu/21/E 80s
Branzini/20/E 40s
Café Bar/21/Astoria
Café Botanica/20/W 50s
Cafe Centro/21/E 40s
Cafe Ronda/21/W 70s
Cripplebush Road/–/Williamsburg
Cupping Room/17/SoHo

Django/20/E 40s
Epices du Traiteur/20/W 70s
Five Points/22/NoHo
Gus' Place/19/G Vil.
Harrison/23/TriBeCa
Il Buco/23/NoHo
Isabella's/20/W 70s
Jarnac/24/W. Vil.
Kitsch/–/E 60s
Lamu/20/Flatiron
Lavagna/23/E Vil.
Layla/19/TriBeCa
L'Orange Bleue/17/SoHo
Mangia/20/multi. loc.
Marseille/21/W 40s
Meet/18/Meatpacking
Mermaid Inn/25/E Vil.
Metronome/19/Flatiron
Moda/18/W 50s
Nice Matin/23/W 70s
Nick and Toni's/19/W 60s
Niko's Med. Grill/18/W 70s
Nisos/17/Chelsea
Olives/22/Union Sq.
Oznot's Dish/21/Williamsburg
Park/15/Chelsea
Patio Dining/21/E Vil.
Picholine/27/W 60s
Place/22/W. Vil.
Porters/19/Chelsea
Provence/22/SoHo
Red Cat/23/Chelsea
Savann/20/W 70s
Savoy/22/SoHo
Sciuscià/19/Gramercy
Shallots NY/20/E 50s
Sharz Cafe/21/E 80s
Solera/22/E 50s
Superfine/17/Dumbo
Terrace in the Sky/22/W 100s
Trio/24/Murray Hill
Uncle Nick's/21/W 50s
Verbena/23/Gramercy
Zerza/–/E Vil.

Mexican

Alma/23/Carroll Gdns.
Benny's Burritos/17/multi. loc.
Bonita/22/Williamsburg
Bright Food Shop/19/Chelsea
Burritoville/17/multi. loc.
Café Frida/21/W 70s
Café Habana/22/NoLita
Chango/16/Flatiron
Cosmic Cantina/19/E Vil.
Dos Caminos/20/multi. loc.
El Parador Cafe/20/Murray Hill
El Teddy's/14/TriBeCa
Gabriela's/17/multi. loc.
Hell's Kitchen/23/W 40s
Itzocan Café/22/E Vil.

Cuisine Index

La Cocina/Ta Cocina/15/multi. loc.
La Flor Bakery Cafe/26/Woodside
La Palapa/21/multi. loc.
Mamá Mexico/20/multi. loc.
Maya/24/E 60s
Maz Mezcal/21/E 80s
Mexicana Mama/25/W. Vil.
Mexican Radio/18/NoLita
Mi Cocina/22/W. Vil.
Pampano/25/E 40s
Rocking Horse/22/Chelsea
Rosa Mexicano/22/multi. loc.
Salon Mexico/22/Gramercy
Salsa y Salsa/–/Chelsea
Sueños/–/Chelsea
Tio Pepe/21/G Vil.
Vera Cruz/19/Williamsburg
Zarela/21/E 50s
Zócalo/19/multi. loc.

Middle Eastern

Layla/19/TriBeCa
Mamlouk/22/E Vil.
Moustache/21/multi. loc.
Olive Vine Cafe/20/Park Slope
Oznot's Dish/21/Williamsburg
Sahara/21/Gravesend
Salam Cafe/20/G Vil.
Zaytoons/23/multi. loc.

Moroccan

Bleu Evolution/17/Wash. Hts. & Up
Cafe Mogador/22/E Vil.
Chez Es Saada/18/E Vil.
Country Café/19/SoHo
Darna/20/W 80s
Zerza/–/E Vil.
Zitoune/21/Meatpacking

New England

Church & Dey/–/Fin. District
Maine Lobster/16/E 80s
Mary's Fish Camp/23/W. Vil.
Pearl Oyster/27/G Vil.
Shore/–/TriBeCa

Noodle Shops

Big Wong/22/Ctown
Bo-Ky/19/Ctown
Great NY Noodle/22/Ctown
Honmura An/26/SoHo
Kelley & Ping/17/SoHo
Lili's Noodle Shop/17/multi. loc.
Mee Noodle Shop/17/multi. loc.
Menchanko-tei/18/multi. loc.
Ollie's/16/multi. loc.
Ony/19/multi. loc.
Pho Bang/19/multi. loc.
Pho Viet Huong/19/Ctown
Republic/18/Union Sq.
Sammy's/17/G Vil.
Soba Nippon/21/W 50s

Sobaya/23/E Vil.
Sweet-n-Tart Cafe/20/multi. loc.
Sweet-n-Tart Rest./21/Ctown
United Noodles/20/E Vil.

North African

Le Souk/17/E Vil.

Nuevo Latino

Beso/19/Park Slope
Cabana/20/multi. loc.
Calle Ocho/22/W 80s
Citrus Bar & Grill/19/W 70s
Cuba Libre/18/Chelsea
DR-K/23/Wash. Hts. & Up
Esperanto/20/E Vil.
Hispaniola/21/Wash. Hts. & Up
Jimmy's Bronx/18/Bronx
Jimmy's Downtown/19/E 50s
Jimmy's Uptown/18/Harlem
La Rambla/–/W 70s
OLA/23/E 40s
Paladar/20/Low E Side
Patria/24/Flatiron
Sabor/19/multi. loc.

Pacific Rim

Hakata Grill/22/W 40s

Persian

Persepolis/18/E 70s

Peruvian

Coco Roco/21/Park Slope
Flor de Mayo/21/multi. loc.
Lima's Taste/20/E Vil.
Sipan/20/W 90s

Pizza

Angelo's Pizzeria/20/multi. loc.
ápizz/20/Low E Side
Arturo's Pizzeria/20/G Vil.
Bella Blu/19/E 70s
Bellavista Cafe/19/Bronx
Cafe Picasso/18/W. Vil.
Cal. Pizza Kitchen/16/E 60s
Caserta Vecchia/20/Carroll Gdns.
Cotto/–/E Vil.
Cripplebush Road/–/Williamsburg
Dee's Pizza/22/Forest Hills
Denino's/23/Staten Is.
Di Fara/28/Midwood
Don Giovanni/18/multi. loc.
Gonzo/22/G Vil.
Grimaldi's/27/Dumbo
Joe's Pizza/24/multi. loc.
John's Pizzeria/21/multi. loc.
L & B Spumoni/22/Bensonhurst
La Pizza Fresca/22/Flatiron
Lento's/20/multi. loc.
Liberta/19/E 80s
Lil' Frankie's Pizza/24/E Vil.
Little Italy Pizza/22/multi. loc.

Lombardi's/*25/NoLita*
Mediterraneo/*19/E 60s*
Naples 45/*19/E 40s*
Nick's/*24/multi. loc.*
Otto/*20/G Vil.*
Patsy's Pizzeria/*21/multi. loc.*
Pie/*21/E Vil.*
Pintaile's Pizza/*17/multi. loc.*
Pizza 33/*22/Murray Hill*
Pizzeria Uno/*13/multi. loc.*
Savoia/*21/Carroll Gdns.*
Slice of Harlem/*22/Harlem*
Three of Cups/*18/E Vil.*
Totonno Pizzeria/*23/multi. loc.*
Two Boots/*19/multi. loc.*
V&T/*19/W 100s*
Vinnie's Pizza/*22/W 70s*

Polish

Teresa's/*18/multi. loc.*

Portuguese

Alfama/*20/W. Vil.*
Alphabet Kitchen/*20/E Vil.*
Convivium Osteria/*25/Park Slope*
Luzia's/*18/W 80s*
Pão!/*19/SoHo*

Puerto Rican

La Taza de Oro/*19/Chelsea*
Old San Juan/*20/W 50s*

Romanian

Sammy's Roumanian/*19/Low E Side*

Russian

Caviarteria/*24/E 50s*
FireBird/*20/W 40s*
Rasputin/*22/Brighton Beach*
Russian Samovar/*20/W 50s*

Sandwiches

Amy's Bread/*23/multi. loc.*
Artie's Deli/*17/W 80s*
Barney Greengrass/*23/W 80s*
BB Sandwich/*21/G Vil.*
Ben's Kosher Deli/*18/multi. loc.*
Bread/*22/NoLita*
Brennan & Carr/*–/Sheepshead Bay*
Carnegie Deli/*21/W 50s*
Cosi/*17/multi. loc.*
E.A.T./*19/E 80s*
Edgar's Cafe/*18/W 80s*
Eisenberg Sandwich/*19/Flatiron*
Ess-a-Bagel/*23/multi. loc.*
Ferrara/*22/multi. loc.*
Grilled Cheese/*20/Low E Side*
Hale & Hearty Soups/*20/Bklyn Hts.*
Katz's Deli/*23/Low E Side*
Lady Mendl's/*21/Gramercy*
Panino'teca 275/*22/Carroll Gdns.*
Peanut Butter/Co./*20/G Vil.*
Press 195/*20/Park Slope*

Sarge's Deli/*19/Murray Hill*
Second Ave. Deli/*23/E Vil.*
71 Irving Place/*18/Gramercy*
Stage Deli/*18/multi. loc.*
Sweet Melissa/*23/Cobble Hill*
Via Quadronno/*22/E 70s*
'wichcraft/*–/Flatiron*
Wolf's/*17/W 50s*
Zabar's Cafe/*–/W 80s*

Scandinavian

AQ Cafe/*20/Murray Hill*
Aquavit/*26/W 50s*
Ulrika's/*23/E 60s*

Seafood

Acqua Pazza/*24/W 50s*
American Park/*18/Fin. District*
Aquagrill/*26/SoHo*
Atlantic Grill/*22/E 70s*
Avra Estiatorio/*23/E 40s*
Blue Fin/*22/W 40s*
Blue Water Grill/*23/Union Sq.*
Citarella/*23/W 40s*
City Crab/Lobster/*17/multi. loc.*
City Hall/*21/TriBeCa*
Crudo/*–/Low E Side*
Docks Oyster Bar/*19/multi. loc.*
Dolphins/*18/E Vil.*
Elias Corner/*23/Astoria*
Esca/*23/W 40s*
Fish/*19/G Vil.*
Foley's Fish House/*21/W 40s*
Francisco's Centro/*21/Chelsea*
fresh./*22/TriBeCa*
Frutti di Mare/*18/E Vil.*
Gage & Tollner/*22/Downtown*
Greek Captain/*23/LIC*
Grill Room/*20/Fin. District*
Harry's/*17/Fin. District*
Jordan's/*20/Sheepshead Bay*
Jubilee/*23/E 50s*
Kam Chueh/*22/Ctown*
La Bouillabaisse/*21/Bklyn Hts.*
Lake Club/*18/Staten Is.*
Lansky Lounge/*19/Low E Side*
Le Bernardin/*28/W 50s*
Le Pescadou/*22/SoHo*
Lobster Box/*17/Bronx*
London Lennie's/*20/Rego Park*
Lundy Bros./*15/Sheepshead Bay*
Maine Lobster/*16/E 80s*
Mandarin Court/*19/Ctown*
Manhattan OceanClub/*25/W 50s*
Marina Cafe/*18/Staten Is.*
Mary's Fish Camp/*23/W. Vil.*
Meltemi/*19/E 50s*
Mermaid Inn/*25/E Vil.*
Metro Fish/*21/Murray Hill*
Metsovo/*19/W 70s*
Milos, Estiatorio/*26/W 50s*

Minnow/21/Park Slope
Moran's Chelsea/18/Chelsea
Oak Room/19/W 50s
Oceana/27/E 50s
Ocean Grill/23/W 70s
Oriental Garden/23/Ctown
Oyster Bar/20/E 40s
Oyster Bar at Plaza/18/W 50s
Pampano/25/E 40s
Pão!/19/SoHo
Pearl Oyster/27/G Vil.
Pearl Room/21/Bay Ridge
Pelagos/19/W 70s
Pescatore/19/E 50s
Ping's Seafood/22/multi. loc.
Q 56/18/E 50s
Red Garlic/19/W 50s
Red Snapper/18/W 80s
rm/24/E 60s
Roy's NY/24/Fin. District
Sea Grill/24/W 40s
Shaffer City/23/Flatiron
Shelly's New York/19/W 50s
Shore/–/TriBeCa
St. Andrews/17/W 40s
Steamers/18/Fin. District
Stella del Mare/22/Murray Hill
Svenningsen's/20/Garment
Taverna Kyclades/24/Astoria
Telly's Taverna/23/Astoria
Terrance Brennan's/21/E 50s
Thalassa/23/TriBeCa
Trata Estiatorio/21/E 70s
Tropica/23/E 40s
Umberto's Clam/18/Little Italy
View/17/W 40s
Water's Edge/23/LIC
Whim/18/Carroll Gdns.
Wild Tuna/18/E 60s

Soul Food

Amy Ruth's/20/Harlem
Brother Jimmy's BBQ/16/multi. loc.
Charles' Southern/24/multi. loc.
Duke's/16/Gramercy
Great Jones Cafe/19/NoHo
Jimmy's Uptown/18/Harlem
Justin's/11/Flatiron
Kitchenette/20/multi. loc.
Miss Mamie's/22/Harlem
Old Devil Moon/17/E Vil.
Pink Tea Cup/20/W. Vil.
Shark Bar/20/W 70s
Soul Cafe/16/W 40s
Sylvia's/17/Harlem

Soup

Hale & Hearty Soups/20/multi. loc.
71 Irving Place/18/Gramercy
Soup Kitchen Int'l/24/W 50s

South African

Madiba/18/Ft. Greene

South American

Boca Chica/20/E Vil.
Cafe Ronda/21/W 70s
Calle Ocho/22/W 80s
Paladar/20/Low E Side
Patria/24/Flatiron
Sabor/19/multi. loc.
SushiSamba/22/multi. loc.

Southeast Asian

Cafe Asean/21/G Vil.

Southern

Amy Ruth's/20/Harlem
Brother Jimmy's BBQ/16/multi. loc.
Charles' Southern/24/multi. loc.
Chat n' Chew/17/Union Sq.
Church & Dey/–/Fin. District
Duke's/16/Gramercy
Great Jones Cafe/19/NoHo
Harvest/17/Cobble Hill
Ida Mae/–/Garment
Jezebel/18/W 40s
Justin's/11/Flatiron
Kitchenette/20/multi. loc.
Londel's Supper Club/18/Harlem
Maroons/22/Chelsea
Miss Mamie's/22/Harlem
Old Devil Moon/17/E Vil.
Pink Tea Cup/20/W. Vil.
Soul Cafe/16/W 40s
Starfoods/19/E Vil.
Sylvia's/17/Harlem

Southwestern

Agave/18/W. Vil.
Canyon Road/20/E 70s
Cilantro/17/multi. loc.
Cowgirl/16/W. Vil.
Los Dos Molinos/17/Gramercy
Manhattan Chili Co./16/multi. loc.
Mesa Grill/24/Union Sq.
Miracle Grill/20/multi. loc.
Santa Fe/18/W 60s
SouthWest NY/13/Fin. District

Spanish

(* tapas specialist)
Allioli*/24/Williamsburg
Alphabet Kitchen/20/E Vil.
Azafran*/24/TriBeCa
Bolo*/22/Flatiron
Cafe Español/19/G Vil.
Convivium Osteria/25/Park Slope
Don Pedro's*/21/E 90s & Up
El Charro Español/19/G Vil.
El Cid*/22/Chelsea
El Faro/22/W. Vil.
El Pote/21/Murray Hill

El Quijote/19/Chelsea
Euzkadi/21/E Vil.
Flor de Sol/20/TriBeCa
1492 Food*/19/Low E Side
Francisco's Centro/21/Chelsea
La Paella/20/E Vil.
Malaga/18/E 70s
Marichu*/22/E 40s
Ñ*/19/SoHo
Oliva/18/Low E Side
Pipa*/20/Flatiron
Riazor*/17/Chelsea
Rincón/España/20/G Vil.
Rio Mar*/17/Meatpacking
Sala/21/NoHo
Sevilla/23/W. Vil.
Solera*/22/E 50s
Suba/19/Low E Side
Tapas Lounge*/17/E 50s
Tio Pepe/21/G Vil.
Toledo/23/Murray Hill
Xunta*/21/E Vil.

Spanish (Basque)

Euzkadi/21/E Vil.
Marichu/22/E 40s
Oliva/18/Low E Side

Steakhouses

Angelo & Maxie's/21/multi. loc.
Ben Benson's/22/W 50s
Benihana/16/multi. loc.
Billy's/16/E 50s
Bobby Van's Steak/23/E 40s
Bull & Bear/20/E 40s
Carne/18/W 100s
Chadwick's/21/Bay Ridge
Christos Hasapo/23/Astoria
Churrascaria Plata./22/W 40s
Cité/21/W 50s
Cité Grill/20/W 50s
Del Frisco's/24/W 40s
Delmonico's/20/Fin. District
Dylan Prime/22/TriBeCa
Embers/21/Bay Ridge
Fairway Cafe/20/W 70s
Frankie & Johnnie's/21/multi. loc.
Frank's/21/Meatpacking
Gage & Tollner/22/Downtown
Gallagher's Steak/20/W 50s
Green Field Churr./19/Corona
Grill Room/20/Fin. District
Hacienda Argentina/22/E 70s
Harry's/17/Fin. District
J.W.'s Steakhouse/23/W 40s
Keens Steakhouse/23/Garment
Knickerbocker B&G/20/G Vil.
Lansky Lounge/19/Low E Side
Le Marais/20/W 40s
Les Halles/20/multi. loc.
Macelleria/22/Meatpacking
Maloney & Porcelli/22/E 50s

Manhattan Grille/20/E 60s
MarkJoseph Steak/24/Fin. District
Michael Jordan's/20/E 40s
Monkey Bar/19/E 50s
Moran's Chelsea/18/Chelsea
Morton's Steak/23/E 40s
Napa/Son. Steak/20/Whitestone
Nebraska Steak/20/multi. loc.
Nick & Stef's Steak/24/Garment
Oak Room/19/W 50s
Old Homestead/22/Meatpacking
Otabe/23/E 50s
Outback Steak/15/multi. loc.
Palm/24/multi. loc.
Patroon/21/E 40s
Peter Luger/28/Williamsburg
Pietro's/23/E 40s
Post House/24/E 60s
Prime Grill/24/E 40s
Rothmann's/21/E 50s
Roth's Steak/20/W 90s
Ruth's Chris/23/multi. loc.
Savannah Steak/21/E 40s
Shelly's New York/19/W 50s
Shula's Steak/20/W 40s
Smith & Wollensky/22/E 40s
Soho Steak/19/SoHo
Sparks Steak/25/E 40s
St. Andrews/17/W 40s
Steak Frites/17/Union Sq.
Strip House/25/G Vil.
Talia's Steakhouse/–/W 90s
Terrance Brennan's/21/E 50s
Tupelo Grill/18/Garment
Tuscan/20/E 40s
Uncle Jack's Steak/25/Bayside
View/17/W 40s
Wollensky's Grill/22/E 40s

Tearooms

Franchia/–/Murray Hill
Tea & Sympathy/20/W. Vil.
Tea Box/20/E 50s
teany/18/Low E Side
Toraya/18/E 70s
T Salon/17/Flatiron

Tex-Mex

Burritoville/17/multi. loc.
Harry's Burritos/16/multi. loc.
Mary Ann's/16/multi. loc.
107 West/16/multi. loc.

Thai

Bann Thai/22/Forest Hills
Basil/19/Chelsea
Chanpen Thai/19/W 50s
Elephant/22/E Vil.
Holy Basil/22/E Vil.
Jaiya Thai/21/Gramercy
Jasmine/20/E 80s
Joya/23/Cobble Hill

Kin Khao/21/SoHo
Lemongrass Grill/16/multi. loc.
Long Tan/20/Park Slope
Pad Thai/19/Chelsea
Pam Real Thai/23/W 40s
Peep/21/SoHo
Planet Thailand/22/Williamsburg
Pongsri Thai/20/multi. loc.
Q, a Thai Bistro/20/Forest Hills
Red Garlic/19/W 50s
Red Snapper/18/W 80s
Regional Thai/19/multi. loc.
Rice Avenue/–/Jackson Hts.
River/17/W 70s
Royal Siam/19/Chelsea
Sala Thai/22/E 80s
SEA/22/multi. loc.
Siam Inn/22/W 50s
Spice/20/multi. loc.
Sripraphai/26/Woodside
Suan/18/E 60s
Tangerine/18/W. Vil.
Thai House Cafe/21/TriBeCa
Thailand/22/Ctown
Three Bow Thais/18/Carroll Gdns.
Topaz Thai/21/W 50s
Tuk Tuk/20/Cobble Hill
Typhoon/16/E 50s
Ubol's Kitchen/24/Astoria
Vong/24/E 50s
Wild Ginger/20/W. Vil.
Wondee Siam/22/W 50s

Tibetan
Tsampa/19/E Vil.

Tunisian
Epices du Traiteur/20/W 70s

Turkish
Bereket/20/Low E Side
Beyoglu/21/E 80s
Dervish Turkish/20/W 40s
Efendi/20/E 50s
Hemsin/21/Sunnyside
Kapadokya/19/Bklyn Hts.
Mavi Turkish/21/Sunnyside
Nar/–/Williamsburg
Pasha/21/W 70s
Sultan/21/E 70s
Turkish Kitchen/22/Gramercy
Turkuaz/18/W 100s
Üsküdar/20/E 70s

Ukrainian
Kiev/15/E Vil.

Vegan
Angelica Kitchen/20/E Vil.
Candle Cafe/Candle 79/21/E 70s
Hangawi/25/Murray Hill
Quintessence/17/multi. loc.
teany/18/Low E Side

Vegetarian
Angelica Kitchen/20/E Vil.
Candle Cafe/Candle 79/21/E 70s
Chop't Salad/21/Union Sq.
Counter/23/E Vil.
Franchia/–/Murray Hill
Gobo/25/G Vil.
Hangawi/25/Murray Hill
Pongal/23/Gramercy
Quintessence/17/multi. loc.
Spring St. Natural/18/NoLita
Terra 47/–/G Vil.
Tossed/17/multi. loc.
Tsampa/19/E Vil.
Vatan/22/Gramercy
Veg. Paradise/19/multi. loc.
Zenith Vegetarian/19/W 40s
Zen Palate/19/multi. loc.

Venezuelan
Flor's Kitchen/21/E Vil.

Vietnamese
Bao 111/22/E Vil.
Bo-Ky/19/Ctown
Cyclo/20/E Vil.
Hue/–/W. Vil.
Indochine/20/G Vil.
L'Annam/17/multi. loc.
Le Colonial/20/E 50s
MeKong/20/NoLita
Miss Saigon/18/E 80s
Monsoon/19/W 80s
Nam/22/TriBeCa
New Pasteur/20/Ctown
Nha Trang/21/Ctown
O Mai/21/Chelsea
Pho Bang/19/multi. loc.
Pho Viet Huong/19/Ctown
River/17/W 70s
Saigon Grill/23/multi. loc.
Vermicelli/20/E 70s

Manhattan

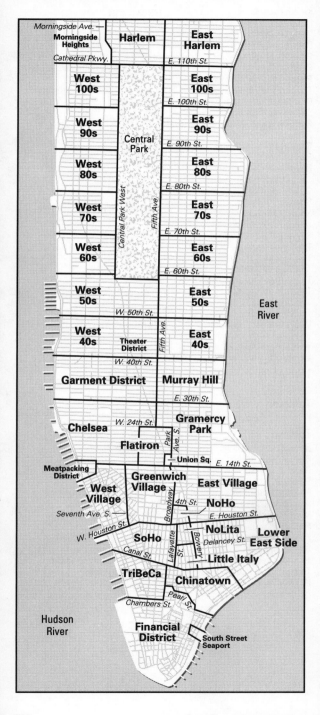

Morningside Ave. —
Morningside Heights
Cathedral Pkwy.

Harlem

East Harlem

E. 110th St.

West 100s

East 100s

E. 100th St.

West 90s

Central Park

East 90s

E. 90th St.

West 80s

East 80s

E. 80th St.

Central Park West

Fifth Ave.

West 70s

East 70s

E. 70th St.

West 60s

East 60s

E. 60th St.

West 50s

East 50s

East River

W. 50th St.

West 40s

Theater District

Fifth Ave.

East 40s

W. 40th St.

Garment District

Murray Hill

E. 30th St.

Chelsea

W. 24th St.

Gramercy Park

Flatiron

Park Ave. S.

Union Sq.

E. 14th St.

Meatpacking District

Greenwich Village

East Village

West Village

Broadway

4th St.

NoHo

Seventh Ave. S. —

E. Houston St.

W. Houston St.

SoHo

Lafayette St.

NoLita

Bowery

Delancey St.

Lower East Side

Little Italy

Canal St.

TriBeCa

Chinatown

Pearl St.

Chambers St.

Hudson River

Financial District

South Street Seaport

LOCATIONS

(Restaurant name followed by its street location.
A=Avenue, s=Street, e.g. 1A/116s=First Ave. at 116th St.;
3A/82-3s=Third Ave. between 82nd & 83rd Sts.)

MANHATTAN

Chelsea
(30th to 24th Sts., west of 5th
Ave., and 24th to 14th Sts.,
west of 6th Ave.)
Amuse *18s/6-7A*
Amy's Bread *9A/15-6s*
Basil *23s/7-8A*
Better Burger *8A/19s*
Biricchino *29s/8A*
Bottino *10A/24-5s*
Bright Food Shop *8A/21s*
Burritoville *23s/7-8A*
Cafeteria *7A/17s*
Carriage House *18s/6-7A*
Chelsea Bistro *23s/8-9A*
Chelsea Grill *8A/16-7s*
Chelsea Ristorante *8A/15-6s*
Cosi *6A/23s*
Cuba Libre *8A/18-9s*
Dallas BBQ *8A/23s*
Daniella *8A/26s*
Da Umberto *17s/6-7A*
Deck, The *18s/Hudson River*
Don Giovanni *10A/22-3s*
East of Eighth *23s/7-8A*
El Cid *15s/8-9A*
elmo *7A/19-20s*
El Quijote *23s/7-8A*
Empire Diner *10A/22s*
F & B *23s/7-8A*
Francisco's Centro *23s/6-7A*
Gascogne *8A/17-8s*
Grand Sichuan *9A/24s*
Hale & Hearty Soups *9A/15-6s*
Havana Chelsea *8A/19-20s*
Intermezzo *8A/20-1s*
Krispy Kreme *23s/7-8A*
La Belle Vie *8A/19-20s*
La Bergamote *9A/20s*
La Lunchonette *10A/18s*
La Taza de Oro *8A/14-5s*
Le Gamin *9A/21s*
Le Madri *18s/6-7A*
Le Singe Vert *7A/18-9s*
Le Zie 2000 *7A/19-20s*
Magnifico *9A/22s*
Maroons *16s/7-8A*
Mary Ann's *8A/16s*
Merchants, N.Y. *7A/16-7s*
Monster Sushi *23s/6-7A*

Moran's Chelsea *10A/19s*
Negril *23s/8-9A*
Nisos *8A/19s*
O Mai *9A/19-20s*
Pad Thai *8A/15-6s*
Parish & Co. *9A/22s*
Park *10A/17-8s*
Patsy's Pizzeria *23s/8-9A*
Pepe ... To Go *10A/24-5s*
Petite Abeille *18s/6-7A*
Porters *7A/22-3s*
Raymond's Cafe *7A/15-6s*
Red Cat *10A/23-4s*
Regional Thai *7A/22s*
Riazor *16s/7-8A*
Rocking Horse *8A/19-20s*
Royal Siam *8A/22-3s*
Salsa y Salsa *7A/21-2s*
Sarabeth's *9A/15-6s*
Seven *7A/29-30s*
Snackbar *17s/6-7A*
Spice *8A/20-1s*
Sueños *17s/8-9A*
Tello's *19s/7-8A*

Chinatown
(South of Hester St. & north of
Pearl St., bet. Bowery &
B'way)
Big Wong *Mott/Bayard-Canal*
Bo-Ky *Bayard/Mott-Mulberry*
Canton *Division/Bowery-Market*
Dim Sum Go Go *Bway/Chatham*
Evergreen Sh. *Mott/Bayard-Canal*
Excellent Dumpling *Lafayette/Canal*
Golden Unicorn *E. Bway/Catherine*
Goody's *E. Bway/Catherine-Oliver*
Grand Sichuan *Canal/Bowery*
Great NY Noodle *Bowery/Bayard*
HSF *Bowery/Bayard-Canal*
Joe's Shanghai *multi. loc.*
Kam Chueh *Bowery/Bayard-Canal*
Mandarin Court *Mott/Bayard-Canal*
New Green Bo *Bayard/Elizabeth*
New Pasteur *Baxter/Bayard-Canal*
Nha Trang *multi. loc.*
Nice *Bway/Catherine-Market*
Oriental Garden *Elizabeth/Bayard*
Peking Duck *Mott/Chatham Sq.-Pell*
Pho Bang *multi. loc.*
Pho Viet Huong *Mulberry/Bayard*

Ping's Seafood *Mott/Bayard-Pell*
Shanghai Cuisine *Bayard/Mulberry*
Starbucks *Canal/Centre*
Sweet-n-Tart Cafe *Mott/Canal*
Sweet-n-Tart Rest. *Mott/Chatham*
Tai Hong Lau *Mott/Bayard-Canal*
Thailand *Bayard/Baxter*
Veg. Paradise *Mott/Canal*
Wo Hop *Mott/Canal*
X.O. *multi. loc.*

East Village

(14th to Houston Sts., east of B'way)

Alphabet Kitchen *Ave. A/10-1s*
Angelica Kitchen *12s/1-2A*
A Salt & Battery *2A/4-5s*
Avenue A Sushi *Ave. A/6-7s*
Baldo Vino *7s/Ave. A-1A*
Baluchi's *2A/6s*
Bambou *14s/2-3A*
Banjara *1A/6s*
Bao 111 *Ave. C/7s*
Benny's Burritos *Ave. A/6s*
Blue 9 Burger *3A/12s*
Boca Chica *1A/1s*
Brick Lane Curry *6s/1-2A*
Burritoville *2A/8-9s*
Cafe Mogador *St. Marks/Ave A.-1A*
Casimir *Ave. B/6-7s*
Chez Es Saada *1A/1-2s*
ChikaLicious *10s/1-2A*
Cicciolino *4s/1-2A*
Col Legno *9s/2-3A*
Cosmic Cantina *3A/13s*
Cotto *Ave. C/8-9s*
Counter *1A/6-7s*
Cucina di Pesce *4s/Bowery-2A*
Cyclo *1A/12-3s*
Daily Chow *2s/Bowery*
Dallas BBQ *2A/St. Marks*
Danal *10s/3-4A*
Dojo *St. Marks/2-3A*
Dok Suni's *1A/St. Marks-7s*
Dolphins *Cooper Sq./5-6s*
East Post *2A/5-6s*
Elephant *1s/1-2A*
Esperanto *Ave. C/9s*
Euzkadi *4s/1A*
First *1A/5-6s*
Flea Market Cafe *Ave. A/9s*
Flor's Kitchen *1A/9-10s*
Frank *2A/5-6s*
Friendhouse *multi. loc.*
Frutti di Mare *4s/Bowery-2A*
Global 33 *2A/5-6s*
Gnocco Caffe *10s/Aves.A-B*
Hasaki *9s/2-3A*
Haveli *2A/5-6s*
Holy Basil *2A/9-10s*
I Coppi *9s/Ave.A-1A*

Il Bagatto *2s/Aves. A-B*
Il Covo dell'Est *Ave. A/13s*
industry (food) *6s/Aves. A-B*
Iso *2A/11s*
Itzocan Café *9s/Ave.A-1A*
Jeollado *4s/1-2A*
Jewel Bako *5s/2-3A*
John's 12th Street *12s/2A*
Jules *St. Marks/1-2A*
Kiev *2A/7s*
Lan *3A/10-1s*
La Paella *9s/2-3A*
La Palapa *St. Marks/1-2A*
Lavagna *5s/Aves. A-B*
Le Gamin *5s/Aves. A-B*
Le Souk *Ave. B/3-4s*
Le Tableau *5s/Aves. A-B*
Le Zoccole *Ave. A/6s*
Lil' Frankie's Pizza *1A/1-2s*
Lima's Taste *13s/Ave. A-1A*
Lucien *1A/1-2s*
Lucky Cheng's *1A/1-2s*
Mama's Food *3s/Aves. A-B*
Mamlouk *4s/Aves. A-B*
Mary Ann's *2A/5s*
Max *Ave. B/3-4s*
Mee Noodle Shop *1A/13s*
Mermaid Inn *2A/5-6s*
Mingala Burmese *7s/2-3A*
Miracle Grill *1A/6-7s*
Mitali *6s/1-2A*
Mosto Osteria *2A/5s*
Moustache *10s/Ave. A-1A*
O.G. *6s/Aves. A-B*
Old Devil Moon *12s/Ave. A-B*
Patio Dining *2A/1-2s*
Perbacco *4s/Ave. A-B*
Pie *4A/12-3s*
Pizzeria Uno *3A/10-1s*
Plain Canvas *9s/Ave. A-1A*
Prune *1s/1-2A*
Quintessence *10s/Ave. A-1A*
Radio Perfecto *Ave. B/11-2s*
Raga *6s/Ave.A-1A*
Sal Anthony's *1A/10-1s*
Sandobe *11s/1-2A*
Sapporo East *10s/1A*
SEA *2A/4-5s*
Second Ave. Deli *2A/10s*
Shabu-Tatsu *10s/1-2A*
Sobaya *9s/2-3A*
Starbucks *multi. loc.*
Starfoods *1s/1A*
Supper *2s/Aves. A-B*
Takahachi *Ave. A/5-6s*
Tanti Baci Caffé *6s/Aves. A-B*
Tasting Room *1s/1-2A*
Ten Sushi *Ave. C/7-8s*
Teresa's *1A/6-7s*
Three of Cups *1A/5s*
Tsampa *9s/2-3A*

26 Seats *Ave. B/10-1s*
Two Boots *multi. loc.*
United Noodles *12s/1-2A*
Veniero's *11s/1-2A*
Veselka *2A/9s*
Xunta *1A/10-1s*
Zerza *6s/1-2A*
Zum Schneider *Ave. C/7s*

East 40s

Ambassador Grill *44s/1-2A*
Avra Estiatorio *48s/Lex-3A*
Bobby Van's Steak *Park/46s*
Box Tree *49s/2-3A*
Branzini *Mad/41s*
Bukhara Grill *49s/2-3A*
Bull & Bear *Lex/49s*
Burger Heaven *multi. loc.*
Cafe Centro *Park/45s-Vanderbilt*
Cafe S.F.A. *5A/49-50s*
Cafe Spice *42s/Lex*
Caffe Linda *49s/Lex-3A*
Chiam *48s/Lex-3A*
Chin Chin *49s/2-3A*
Cibo *2A/41-2s*
Cipriani Dolci *42s/Vanderbilt*
Comfort Diner *45s/2-3A*
D'Artagnan *46s/Lex-3A*
Delegates Dining Rm. *1A/45s*
Dishes *multi. loc.*
Diwan *48s/Lex-3A*
Django *Lex/46s*
Docks Oyster Bar *3A/40s*
East *44s/2-3A*
Ferrara *Mad/45-6s*
Grifone *46s/2-3A*
Hale & Hearty Soups *multi. loc.*
Haru *Park/48s*
Hatsuhana *multi. loc.*
Heartbeat *49s/Lex-3A*
Il Postino *49s/1-2A*
Inagiku *49s/Lex-Park*
Jimmy Sung's *44s/2-3A*
Junior's *42s/Park*
Katsuhama *47s/5A-Mad*
Kuruma Zushi *47s/5A-Mad*
L'Impero *Tudor City/42-3s*
Little Italy Pizza *43s/5A-Mad*
Mamá Mexico *49s/2-3A*
Mangia *48s/5A-Mad*
Marichu *46s/1-2A*
Mee Noodle Shop *2A/49s*
Menchanko-tei *45s/Lex-3A*
Métrazur *42s/Park*
Michael Jordan's *Vanderbilt/43-4s*
Morton's Steak *5A/45s*
Nanni *46s/Lex-3A*
Naples 45 *Park/45s*
Nino's Positano *2A/47-8s*
OLA *48s/2A*
Osteria Laguna *42s/2-3A*

Oyster Bar *42s/Vanderbilt*
Palm *2A/44-5s*
Pampano *49s/2-3A*
Patroon *46s/Lex-3A*
Pepe ... To Go *Lex/42s*
Pershing Square *42s/Park*
Phoenix Garden *40s/2-3A*
Pietro's *43s/2-3A*
Prime Grill *49s/Mad-Park*
Ruth's Chris *2A/47-8s*
Savannah Steak *48s/5A-Mad*
Seo *49s/2-3A*
Smith & Wollensky *3A/49s*
Sparks Steak *46s/2-3A*
Summit *49s/1-2A*
Sushiden *49s/5A-Mad*
Sushi Yasuda *43s/2-3A*
T.G.I. Friday's *multi. loc.*
Top of the Tower *1A/49s*
Tropica *45s/Lex-Park*
Tuscan *3A/40s*
Two Boots *42s/Lex*
Vuli *48s/Lex*
Wollensky's Grill *49s/3A*
Zócalo *42s/Vanderbilt*

East 50s

Adä *58s/2-3A*
Al Bustan *3A/50-1s*
Amma *51s/2-3A*
Anche Vivolo *58s/2-3A*
Angelo's Pizzeria *2A/55s*
Baluchi's *53s/2-3A*
Bellini *52s/2-3A*
Bice *54s/5A-Mad*
Bill Hong's *56s/2-3A*
Billy's *1A/52-3s*
Bouterin *59s/1A-Sutton*
Brasserie *53s/Lex-Park*
Bruno *58s/2-3A*
Bukhara Grill *58s/2-3A*
Burger Heaven *multi. loc.*
Burritoville *3A/52s*
Cafe du Pont *1A/56-7s*
Cafe Joul *1A/58-9s*
Café St. Barts *50s/Park*
Caffe Buon Gusto *2A/53-4s*
Caviar Russe *Mad/54-5s*
Caviarteria *Park/59s*
Cellini *54s/Mad-Park*
Chola *58s/2-3A*
Columbus Bakery *1A/52-3s*
Cosi *56s/Mad-Park*
Da Antonio *55s/Lex-3A*
Dawat *58s/2-3A*
DeGrezia *50s/2-3A*
Efendi *2A/54-5s*
Ess-a-Bagel *3A/50-1s*
Felidia *58s/2-3A*
Fifty Seven 57 *57s/Mad-Park*
Four Seasons *52s/Lex-Park*

Fresco by Scotto *52s/Mad-Park*
Giambelli *50s/Mad-Park*
Grand Sichuan *2A/55-6s*
Guastavino's *59s/1A-York*
Haikara Grill *2A/53-4s*
Hale & Hearty Soups *Lex/54s*
Harry Cipriani *5A/59-60s*
Houston's *53s/54s-3A*
Il Menestrello *52s/Mad-Park*
Il Nido *53s/2-3A*
Il Valentino *56s/1-2A*
Jimmy's Downtown *57s/1A-Sutton*
Jubilee *54s/1-2A*
King Cole Bar *55s/5A-Mad*
Korea Palace *54s/Lex-Park*
La Gioconda *53s/2-3A*
La Grenouille *52s/5A-Mad*
La Mangeoire *2A/53-4s*
La Mediterranée *2A/50-1s*
Le Cirque 2000 *Mad/50-1s*
Le Colonial *57s/Lex-3A*
L'Entrecote *1A/57-8s*
Leopard *50s/2-3A*
Le Perigord *52s/FDR-1A*
Lever House *53s/Mad-Park*
Luna Piena *53s/2-3A*
Lutèce *50s/2-3A*
Maloney & Porcelli *50s/Mad-Park*
Maple Garden *53s/2-3A*
March *58s/1A-Sutton*
Meltemi *1A/51s*
Metropolitan Cafe *1A/52-3s*
Monkey Bar *54s/Mad-Park*
Montparnasse *51s/2-3A*
Mr. Chow *57s/1-2A*
Mr. K's *Lex/51s*
Neary's *57s/1A*
Nippon *52s/Lex-3A*
Oceana *54s/Mad-Park*
Olica *50s/Lex-3A*
Oscar's *Lex/50s*
Otabe *56s/Mad-Park*
Our Place *55s/Lex-3A*
Outback Steak *56s/2-3A*
Paper Moon Milano *58s/Mad-Park*
Pescatore *2A/50-1s*
P.J. Clarke's *3A/55s*
Q 56 *56s/Mad-Park*
Rosa Mexicano *1A/58s*
Rothmann's *54s/5A-Mad*
San Pietro *54s/5A-Mad*
Serafina *58s/Mad-Park*
Shallots NY *Mad/55-6s*
Shun Lee Palace *55s/Lex-3A*
Solera *53s/2-3A*
Sushi Ann *51s/Mad-Park*
Sushi Rose *52s/2-3A*
Tao *58s/Mad-Park*
Tapas Lounge *1A/59s*
Tatany *52s/2-3A*
Tea Box *5A/54-5s*

Teodora *57s/Lex-3A*
Terrance Brennan's *Lex/50-1s*
T.G.I. Friday's *Lex/56s*
Trattoria Pesce *1A/59s*
Tse Yang *51s/Mad-Park*
Typhoon *54s/5A-Mad*
Vong *54s/3A*
Zarela *2A/50-1s*

East 60s

Amaranth *62s/5A-Mad*
Arabelle *64s/Mad*
Aureole *61s/Mad-Park*
Baluchi's *1A/63s*
Barbalùc *65s/Lex*
Benihana *56s/Lex-Park*
Brasserie 360 *60s/3A*
Bravo Gianni *63s/2-3A*
Brio *Lex/61s*
Burger Heaven *Lex/62s*
Cabana *3A/60-1s*
Cafe Nosidam *Mad/66s*
Café Pierre *61s/5A*
Cal. Pizza Kitchen *60s/2-3A*
Canaletto *60s/2-3A*
Circus *Lex/62-3s*
Da Filippo *2A/69-70s*
Daniel *65s/Mad-Park*
East *66s/1-2A*
Ferrier Bistro *65s/Mad-Park*
Fred's at Barneys *Mad/60s*
Gino *Lex/60-1s*
Hale & Hearty Soups *Lex/64-5s*
Henry's Evergreen *1A/69-70s*
Il Gatto & La Volpe *1A/63-4s*
Il Vagabondo *62s/1-2A*
Jackson Hole *64s/2-3A*
John's Pizzeria *64s/1A-York*
JoJo *64s/Lex-3A*
Kai *Mad/68-9s*
Kitsch *61s/Lex-Park*
L'Absinthe *67s/2-3A*
La Cantina Toscana *1A/60-1s*
La Goulue *Mad/64-5s*
La Houppa *64s/5A-Mad*
Le Bilboquet *63s/Mad-Park*
Le Charlot *69s/Mad-Park*
Le Pain Quotidien *Lex/63-4s*
Manhattan Grille *1A/63-4s*
Maya *1A/64-5s*
Mediterraneo *2A/66s*
Merchants, N.Y. *1A/62s*
Nello *Mad/62-3s*
Park Avenue Cafe *63s/Lex-Park*
Patsy's Pizzeria *multi. loc.*
Pintaile's Pizza *2A/64-5s*
Portofino Grille *1A/63-4s*
Post House *63s/Mad-Park*
Primola *2A/64-5s*
Rain *3A/62-3s*
Regency *Park/61s*

rm *60s/Madison-Park*
Scalinatella *61s/3A*
Serafina *61s/Mad-Park*
Serendipity 3 *60s/2-3A*
Suan *Lex/65-6s*
Sushi Seki *1A/62-3s*
212 *65s/Lex*
Ulrika's *60s/Lex-Park*
Viand *Mad/61-2s*
Via Oreto *1A/61-2s*
Wild Tuna *3A/63-4s*
Za Za *1A/65-6s*

East 70s
Afghan Kebab Hse *2A/70-1s*
Aki Sushi *York/75-6s*
Amy's Bread *Lex/70-1s*
Annie's *3A/78-9s*
Atlantic Grill *3A/76-7s*
Baluchi's *1A/74s*
Bandol Bistro *78s/Lex-3A*
Baraonda *2A/75s*
Barking Dog *York/77s*
Bella Blu *Lex/70-1s*
Bella Donna *77s/1-2A*
Bistro Le Steak *3A/75s*
Boat House *72s/CPD N.*
Brother Jimmy's BBQ *2A/77-8s*
Brunelli *York/75s*
Burritoville *2A/77-8s*
Café Boulud *76s/5A-Mad*
Caffe Buon Gusto *77s/2-3A*
Campagnola *1A/73-4s*
Candle Cafe/Candle 79 *multi. loc.*
Canyon Road *1A/76-7s*
Cilantro *multi. loc.*
Coco Pazzo *74s/5A-Mad*
Dallas BBQ *3A/72-3s*
Due *3A/79-80s*
Dumonet *76/Mad*
EJ's Luncheonette *3A/73s*
Evergreen Sh. *3A/78-9s*
Googie's *2A/78s*
Grace's Trattoria *71s/2-3A*
Hacienda Argentina *75s/1-2A*
Haru *3A/76s*
Il Monello *2A/76-7s*
Il Riccio *79s/Lex-3A*
J.G. Melon *3A/74s*
La Tour *3A/75-6s*
Lenox *3A/73-4s*
Le Pain Quotidien *1A/71-2s*
Luke's Bar & Grill *3A/79-80s*
Lumi *Lex/70s*
Lusardi's *2A/77-8s*
Malaga *73s/1A-York*
Mark's *77s/5A-Mad*
Maruzzella *1A/77-8s*
Mary Ann's *2A/78-9s*
Mezzaluna *3A/74-5s*
Mingala Burmese *2A/72-3s*

Nino's *1A/72-3s*
Orsay *Lex/75s*
Pamir *2A/74-5s*
Parma *3A/79-80s*
Payard Bistro *Lex/73-4s*
Persepolis *2A/74-5s*
Petaluma *1A/73s*
Pintaile's Pizza *York/76-7s*
Pioneer *3A/74-5s*
Quatorze Bis *79s/1-2A*
Quintessence *78s/1-2A*
Regional Thai *1A/77s*
Sarabeth's *Mad/75s*
Serafina *Mad/79s*
Sette Mezzo *Lex/70-1s*
Spice *2A/73-4s*
Stage Deli *2A/77s*
Starbucks *Lex/78s*
Sultan *2A/74-5s*
Sushi Hana *2A/78s*
Sushi of Gari *78s/1A-York*
Swifty's *Lex/72-3s*
Toraya *71s/5A-Mad*
Trata Estiatorio *2A/70-1s*
Tsuki *1A/74-5s*
Üsküdar *2A/73-4s*
Vermicelli *2A/77-8s*
Viand *Mad/78s*
Via Quadronno *73s/5A-Mad*
Vivolo *74s/Lex-Park*
Willow *Lex/73s*

East 80s
Aigo *1A/83-4s*
Baluchi's *multi. loc.*
Bella Donna *1A/86-7s*
Beyoglu *3A/81s*
Brasserie Julien *3A/80-1s*
Café Sabarsky *5A/86s*
Cafe Trevi *1A/81-2s*
Caffe Grazie *84s/5A-Mad*
Carino *2A/88-9s*
Centolire *Mad/85-6s*
Chef Ho's *2A/89-90s*
Cilantro *2A/88-9s*
Dakshin Indian *1A/88-9s*
Divino *2A/80-1s*
DT.UT *2A/84-5s*
E.A.T. *Mad/80-1s*
Elaine's *2A/88-9s*
Elio's *2A/84-5s*
Erminia *83s/2-3A*
Etats-Unis *81s/2-3A*
Ethiopian *York/83-4s*
Etoile *56s/Lex-Park*
Firenze *2A/82-3s*
Giovanni 25 *83s/5A-Mad*
Girasole *82s/Lex-3A*
Heidelberg *2A/85-6s*
Ithaka *86s/1-2A*
Jackson Hole *2A/83-4s*

Jacques Brasserie *85s/2-3A*
Jasmine *2A/84s*
Kings' Carriage *82s/2-3A*
Kodama *3A/82-83s*
Krispy Kreme *3A/84-5s*
Le Boeuf à la Mode *81s/E. End-York*
Lentini *2A/81s*
Le Pain Quotidien *Mad/84-5s*
Le Refuge *82s/Lex-3A*
Liberta *2A/81-2s*
Lili's Noodle Shop *3A/84-5s*
Luca *1A/88-9s*
Maine Lobster *2A/84-5s*
Mangiarini *2A/82-3s*
Maz Mezcal *86s/1-2A*
Miss Saigon *3A/80-1s*
Mocca *2A/82-3s*
Nicola's *84s/Lex*
Ota-ya *2A/81-2s*
Our Place *3A/82s*
Paola's *84s/2-3A*
Papaya King *86s/3A*
Pearson's Texas BBQ *81s/Lex-3A*
Penang *2A/83s*
Pig Heaven *2A/80-1s*
Pintaile's Pizza *York/83-4s*
Pizzeria Uno *86s/2-3A*
Poke *85s/1-2A*
Primavera *1A/82s*
Quattro Gatti *81s/2-3A*
Rughetta *85s/1-2A*
Sabor *2A/89s*
Saigon Grill *2A/88s*
Sala Thai *2A/89-90s*
Sesumi *2A/85-6s*
Sharz Cafe *86s/1A-York*
Sirabella's *East End A/82-3s*
Sistina *2A/80-1s*
Taste *3A/80s*
Tevere *84s/Lex-3A*
Tony's Di Napoli *2A/83s*
Totonno Pizzeria *2A/80-1s*
Trattoria Pesce *3A/87-8s*
Trattoria Rustica *85s/1-2A*
Triangolo *83s/1-2A*
Trois Marches *81s/1-2A*
Va Bene *2A/82-3s*
Viand *86s/2A*
Wu Liang Ye *86s/2-3A*
York Grill *York/88-9s*
Yuka *2A/80-1s*
Zócalo *82s/Lex-3A*

East 90s & Up

Barking Dog *3A/94s*
Bistro du Nord *Mad/93s*
Brother Jimmy's BBQ *3A/93s*
Don Pedro's *2A/96s*
Ecco-la *3A/93s*
Jackson Hole *Mad/91s*
Joanna's *92s/5A-Mad*

Kurio *92s/1-2A*
Mary Ann's *2A/93s*
Melrose *5A/81s*
Nick's *2A/93-4s*
92 *92s/Mad*
Pascalou *Mad/92-3s*
Pinocchio *1A/90-1s*
Pintaile's Pizza *91s/5A-Mad*
Sarabeth's *Mad/92-3s*
Starbucks *3A/92s*
Table d'Hôte *92s/Mad-Park*
Tre Pomodori *2A/90-1s*
Vico *Mad/92-3s*
Yura & Co. *multi. loc.*
Zebú Grill *92s/1-2A*

Financial District

(South of Chambers St.)
American Park *Battery Park/State*
Au Mandarin *Vesey/Bway*
Bayard's *Hanover/Pearl*
Bull Run *William/Pine*
Church & Dey *Church/Dey*
Cosi *Vesey/W. Side Hwy.*
Delmonico's *Beaver/William*
55 Wall *Wall/Hanover-William*
Fino *Wall/Pearl*
14 Wall Street *Wall/Broad-Bway*
Fraunces Tavern *Pearl/Broad*
Gigino/Wagner Pk. *Battery/West*
Grill Room *Liberty/West Side Hwy.*
Harry's *Hanover/Pearl-Stone*
Joseph's *Hanover/Pearl*
Les Halles *John/Bway-Nassau*
Lili's Noodle Shop *North End/Vesey*
Little Italy Pizza *Park Pl./Bway*
L'Orto *Gold/Maiden-Platt*
Mangia *Wall/Broad-William*
MarkJoseph Steak *Water/Peck Slip*
MJ Grill *John/Cliff*
Nebraska Steak *Stone/Broad-Bway*
Roy's NY *Washington/Albany-Carlisle*
SouthWest NY *World Fin. Ctr./Liberty*
Steamers *Esplanade Plz./Albany*
St. Maggie's *Wall/Front-South*
T.G.I. Friday's *multi. loc.*
2 West *West/Battery Pl.*
Ulysses *Pearl/Hanover Sq.*
Unity *North End/Vesey*
Vine *Broad/Exchange Pl.*

Flatiron District

(Bounded by 24th & 14th Sts.,
bet. 6th Ave. & Park Ave. S.,
excluding Union Sq.)
Aleo *20s/5A*
America *18s/Bway-5A*
Angelo & Maxie's *Park S./19s*
Anju *20s/Bway-Park S.*
Arezzo *22s/5-6A*
AZ *17s/5-6A*

Basta Pasta *17s/5-6A*
Beppe *22s/Bway-Park S.*
Bolo *22s/Bway-Park S.*
Chango *Park S./19-20s*
City Bakery *18s/5-6A*
City Crab/Lobster *Park S./19s*
Comfort Diner *23s/5-6A*
Cosi *Park S./21s*
Craft *19s/Bway-Park S.*
Craftbar *19s/Bway-Park S.*
Eisenberg Sandwich *5A/22-3s*
Fleur de Sel *20s/Bway-5A*
Giorgio's Gramercy *21s/Bway*
Gramercy Tavern *20s/Bway-Park S.*
Justin's *21s/5-6A*
Kitchen 22/82 *22s/Bway-Park S.*
L'Acajou *19s/5-6A*
Lamu *19s/Bway-Park S.*
La Pizza Fresca *20s/Bway-Park S.*
Le Pain Quotidien *19s/Bway-Park S.*
L'Express *Park S./20s*
Lola *22s/5-6A*
Mayrose *Bway/21s*
Metronome *Bway/21s*
Mizu Sushi *20s/Bway-Park S.*
Morrells *Bway/19-20s*
Outback Steak *23s/6A*
Park Avalon *Park S./18-9s*
Patria *Park S./20s*
Periyali *20s/5-6A*
Pipa *19s/Bway-Park S.*
Pump Energy Food *21s/Bway-Park*
Punch *Bway/20-1s*
Ribollita *Park S./20-1s*
Rocco's 22nd St. *22s/Bway-Park S.*
Shaffer City *21s/5-6A*
SushiSamba *Park S./19-20s*
Tamarind *22s/Bway-Park S.*
Tossed *Park S./22-3s*
T Salon *20s/Bway-5A*
Veritas *20s/Bway-Park S.*
Via Emilia *Park S./19-20s*
'wichcraft *19s/Bway-Park S.*

Garment District

(40th to 30th Sts., west of 5th Ave.)

Abigael's *Bway/38-9s*
Ben's Kosher Deli *38s/7-8A*
Burritoville *39s/9A*
Cho Dang Gol *35s/5-6A*
Cosi *7A/36-7s*
Dae Dong *32s/Bway-5A*
Frankie & Johnnie's *37s/5-6A*
Gam Mee Ok *32s/Bway-5A*
Gray's Papaya *8A/37s*
Hale & Hearty Soups *7A/35s*
Ida Mae *38s/Bway-6A*
Kang Suh *Bway/32s*
Keens Steakhouse *36s/5-6A*

Krispy Kreme *Penn Plaza/33s*
Kum Gang San *32s/Bway-5A*
Market Café *9A/37-8s*
Nick & Stef's Steak *33s/7-8A*
Pump Energy Food *38s/Bway-6A*
Svenningsen's *5A/30-1s*
T.G.I. Friday's *8A/34s*
36 Bar & BBQ *36s/5A*
Tupelo Grill *33s/7-8A*
Veronica *38s/7-8A*
Won Jo *32s/Bway-5A*

Gramercy Park

(30th St. to 24th St., east of 5th Ave., and 24th St. to 14th St., east of Park Ave. S.)

Black Duck *28s/Lex-Park S.*
Blue Smoke *27s/Lex-Park*
Bread Bar at Tabla *Mad/25s*
Casa Mia *24s/2-3A*
Choshi *Irving/19s*
Coppola's *3A/27-8s*
Curry Leaf *Lex/27s*
Dos Caminos *Park S./26-7s*
Duke's *19s/Park S.*
East *multi. loc.*
Eleven Madison *Mad/24s*
Empire Szechuan *3A/27-8s*
Ess-a-Bagel *1A/21s*
Friend of a Farmer *Irving/18-9s*
Houston's *Park S./27s*
I Trulli *27s/Lex-Park S.*
Jaiya Thai *3A/28s*
Lady Mendl's *Irving Pl./17-8s*
L'Annam *3A/28s*
La Petite Auberge *Lex/27-8s*
Les Halles *Park S./28-9s*
Link *15s/Irving*
Los Dos Molinos *18s/Irving-Park S.*
Novità *22s/Lex-Park S.*
Park Bistro *Park S./28-9s*
Paul & Jimmy's *18s/Irving-Park S.*
Pete's Tavern *18s/Irving*
Pongal *Lex/27-8s*
Pongsri Thai *2A/18s*
Rolf's *3A/22s*
Sage *Park S./24-5s*
Sal Anthony's *Irving/17-8s*
Salon Mexico *26s/Lex-3A*
Sciuscià *Park S./26s*
Scopa *Mad/28s*
71 Irving Place *Irving/18-9s*
Tabla *Mad/25s*
Tatany *3A/27-8s*
Turkish Kitchen *3A/27-8s*
Union Pacific *22s/Lex-Park S.*
Vatan *3A/29s*
Verbena *Irving/17-8s*
Yakiniku JuJu *28s/Lex-3A*
Yama *17s/Irving*

Greenwich Village

(14th to Houston Sts., bet.
B'way & 7th Ave. S., excluding
NoHo)

Aki *4s/Barrow-Jones*
Annisa *Barrow/7A S.-W. 4s*
A.O.C. Bedford *Bedford/Downing*
Arté *9s/5A-University*
Arturo's Pizzeria *Houston/Thompson*
Babbo *Waverly/MacDougal-6A*
Baluchi's *6A/Washington*
Bar Pitti *6A/Bleecker-Houston*
BB Sandwich *3s/MacDougal-6A*
Blue Hill *Washingtion Pl./Wash. Sq.*
Blue Ribbon Bak. *Downing/Bedford*
Borgo Antico *13s/5A-University*
Bouchon *Greenwich A/Charles-Perry*
Bussola Ristorante *4A/9-10s*
Butter *Lafayette/Astor Pl.-4s*
Cafe Asean *10s/Greenwich-6A*
Cafe Español *multi. loc.*
Cafe Loup *13s/6-7A*
Cafe Spice *University/10-1s*
Caffe Reggio *MacDougal/Bleecker*
CamaJe *MacDougal/Bl.-Houston*
Chez Jacqueline *MacDougal/Blckr*
Cornelia St. Cafe *Cornelia/Bleecker*
Cosi *multi. loc.*
Cozy Soup/Burger *Bway/Astor*
Dallas BBQ *University/8s*
Da Silvano *6A/Bleecker-Houston*
Deborah *Carmine/Bedford-Bleecker*
Do Hwa *Carmine/Bedford-7A S.*
EJ's Luncheonette *6A/9-10s*
El Charro Español *Charles/7A S.*
Elephant & Castle *Greenwich A/6-7s*
Empire Szechuan *multi. loc.*
Evergreen Sh. *Bway/10s*
Fish *Bleecker/Jones*
French Roast *6A/11s*
Gobo *6A/8s-Waverly Pl.*
Gonzo *13s/6-7A*
Gotham B&G *12s/5A-University*
Gradisca *13s/6-7A*
Grano Trattoria *Greenwich A/W. 10s*
Gray's Papaya *6A/8s*
Grey Dog's Coffee *Carmine/Bedford*
Gus' Place *Waverly Pl./6-7A*
Harry's Burritos *3s/Thompson*
Home *Cornelia/Bleecker-W. 4s*
Il Cantinori *10s/Bway-University*
Il Mulino *3s/Sullivan-Thompson*
Indochine *Lafayette/Astor-4s*
Inside *Jones/Bleecker-W. 4s*
Jane *Houston/La Guardia-Thompson*
Japonica *University/12s*
Jefferson *10s/Greenwich-6A*
Joe's Pizza *multi. loc.*
Johnny Rockets *8s/Bway-University*
John's Pizzeria *Bleecker/6A-7A S.*

Knickerbocker B&G *University/8-9s*
La Lanterna *MacDougal/W. 3-4s*
L'Annam *University/13s*
La Palapa *6A/Washington Pl.-W. 4s*
Le Gamin *multi. loc.*
Le Gigot *Cornelia/Bleecker-W. 4s*
Lemongrass Grill *University/11s*
Lozoo *Houston/MacDougal-Sullivan*
Lupa *Thompson/Bleecker-Houston*
Mama's Food *Sullivan/Bleecker*
Marinella *Carmine/Bedford*
Massimo *Thompson/Bleecker-W. 3s*
Meskerem *MacDougal/Bleecker-3s*
Minetta Tavern *MacDougal/3s*
Mirchi *7A S./Bedford-Morton*
Negril *3s/La Guardia-Thompson*
Nellie's *Houston/MacDougal*
NL *Sullivan/Bleecker-Houston*
North Sq. *Waverly/MacDougal*
Ocean's *9s/5-6A*
One if by Land *Barrow/7A S.-4s*
Ony *6A/Washington Pl.-W. 4s*
Oster. Gallo Nero *Bl./MacDougal*
Otto *5A/8s*
Patsy's Pizzeria *University/10-1s*
Peanut Butter/Co. *Sullivan/Bleecker*
Pearl Oyster *Cornelia/Bleecker*
Piadina *10s/5-6A*
Pizzeria Uno *6A/8s-Waverly Pl.*
Pó *Cornelia/Bleecker-W. 4s*
Rincón/España *Thompson/3s*
Risotteria *Bleecker/Morton*
Rocco *Thompson/Bleecker-Houston*
Salam Cafe *13s/6-7A*
Sammy's *multi. loc.*
Silver Spurs *Bway/9s*
Spice *University/10s*
Strip House *12s/5A-University*
SushiSamba *7A S/Bleecker-W. 4s*
Tanti Baci Caffé *10s/7A S-Waverly*
Terra 47 *12s/Bway-University*
Tio Pepe *4s/6-7A*
Tomoe Sushi *Thompson/Bl.- Houston*
Trattoria Pesce *Bleecker/6A-7A S.*
Veg. Paradise *4s/MacDougal*
Village *9s/5-6A*
Villa Mosconi *MacDougal/Houston*
Volare *4s/6A*
Washington Park *5A/9s*
Yama *multi. loc.*
Yujin *12s/5A-University*
Zutto *Greenwich A/7A S.-W. 11s*

Harlem

(North of W. 110th St. & south of
W. 157th St.; east of
Morningside Ave./St. Nicholas
Ave. & west of 5th Ave.)

Amy Ruth's *116s/Lenox-7A*
Bayou *Lenox/125-26s*

Charles' Southern *8A/151s*
Jimmy's Uptown *7A/130-31s*
Londel's Supper Club *FDB/139-40s*
Miss Mamie's *multi. loc.*
Orbit East Harlem *1A/116s*
Papaya King *125s/Lenox-7A*
Patsy's Pizzeria *1A/117-8s*
Rao's *114s/Pleasant*
Slice of Harlem *Lenox/125-6s*
Starbucks *125s/Lenox*
Sugar Hill Bistro *145s/Amst.*
Sylvia's *Lenox/126-7s*

Little Italy
(South of Delancey St. & north
of Canal St., bet. Bowery &
Lafayette St.)

Angelo's *Mulberry/Grand-Hester*
Capitale *Bowery/Broome-Grand*
Da Nico *Mulberry/Broome-Grand*
Eight Mile Creek *Mulberry/Prince*
Ferrara *Grand/Mott-Mulberry*
Il Cortile *Mulberry/Canal-Hester*
Il Fornaio *Mulberry/Grand-Hester*
Il Palazzo *Mulberry/Grand-Hester*
Kitchen Club *Prince/Mott*
La Mela *Mulberry/Broome-Grand*
Nyonya *Grand/Mott-Mulberry*
Onieal's Grand St. *Grand/Centre*
Pellegrino's *Mulberry/Grand-Hester*
Pho Bang *Mott/Broome-Grand*
Positano *Mulberry/Canal-Hester*
Sal Anthony's *Mulberry/Grand*
Taormina *Mulberry/Grand-Hester*
Umberto's Clam *Mulberry/Broome*
Vincent's *Mott/Hester*

Lower East Side
(Houston to Canal Sts., east of
Bowery)

aka Cafe *Clinton/Rivington-Stanton*
Alias *Clinton/Rivington*
ápizz *Eldridge/Rivington-Stanton*
Azul Bistro *Stanton/Suffolk*
Basso Est *Orchard/Stanton*
Bereket *Houston/Orchard*
Chubo *Clinton/Houston-Stanton*
Crudo *Clinton/Rivington-Stanton*
Dish *Allen/Rivington-Stanton*
Epicerie *Orchard/Rivington-Stanton*
Essex *Essex/Rivington*
1492 Food *Clinton/Rivington-Stanton*
Grilled Cheese *Ludlow/Houston*
'inoteca *Rivington/Ludlow*
Katz's Deli *Houston/Ludlow*
Lansky Lounge *Norfolk/Delancey*
Le Père Pinard *Ludlow/Houston*
Oliva *Houston/Allen*
Paladar *Ludlow/Houston-Stanton*
Petrosino *Norfolk/Houston*

Salt *Clinton/Houston-Stanton*
Sammy's *Chrystie/Delancey*
Schiller's *Rivington/Norfolk*
71 Clinton *Clinton/Rivington-Stanton*
Suba *Ludlow/Delancey-Rivington*
teany *Rivington/Ludlow-Orchard*
WD-50 *Clinton/Rivington-Stanton*

Meatpacking District
(Gansevoort to W. 15th Sts.,
west of 9th Ave.)

Florent *Gansevoort/Greenwich-Wash.*
Frank's *10A/15s*
Hog Pit BBQ *9A/13s*
Lotus *14s/9A-Washington*
Macelleria *Gansevoort/Greenwich*
Markt *14s/9A*
Meet *Gansevoort/Washington*
Old Homestead *9A/14-5s*
Paradou *Little W. 12s/Greenwich*
Pastis *9A/Little W. 12s*
Petite Abeille *14s/9A*
Rhône *Gansevoort/Greenwich-Wash.*
Rio Mar *9A/Little W. 12s*
Son Cubano *14s/9A-Washington*
Zitoune *Gansevoort/Greenwich s*

Murray Hill
(40th to 30th Sts., east of 5th
Ave.)

AQ Cafe *Park/37-8s*
Artisanal *32s/Mad-Park*
Asia de Cuba *Mad/37-8s*
Barking Dog *34s/Lex-3A*
Belluno *Lex/39-40s*
Better Burger *3A/37s*
Bienvenue *36s/Mad*
Cinque Terre *38s/Mad-Park*
Cosette *33s/Lex-3A*
Da Ciro *Lex/33-4s*
El Parador Cafe *34s/1-2A*
El Pote *2A/38-9s*
Ethos *3A/33-4s*
Evergreen Sh. *38s/5A-Mad*
Fino *36s/5A-Mad*
Franchia *Park/34-5s*
Frère Jacques *37s/5A-Mad*
Grand Sichuan *Lex/33-4s*
Hangawi *32s/5A-Mad*
Icon *39s/Lex*
Iron Sushi *3A/30-1s*
Jackson Hole *3A/35s*
Josie's *3A/37s*
La Cocina/Ta Cocina *3A/30s*
La Giara *3A/33-4s*
Lemongrass Grill *34s/Lex-3A*
Madison Bistro *Mad/37-8s*
Marchi's *31s/2-3A*
Mee Noodle Shop *2A/30-31s*
Metro Fish *36s/5A-Mad*
Minado *32s/5A-Mad*

Mishima *Lex/30-1s*
Nicola Paone *34s/2-3A*
Notaro *2A/34-5s*
Pasticcio *3A/30-1s*
Patsy's Pizzeria *3A/34-5s*
Pizza 33 *3A/33s*
Pump Energy Food *31s/Lex-Park S.*
Rare Bar & Grill *Lex/37s*
Rive Gauche *3A/37s*
Rossini's *38s/Lex-Park*
Salute! *Mad/39s*
Sarge's Deli *3A/36-7s*
Starbucks *2A/32s*
Stella del Mare *Lex/39-40s*
Sushi Sen-nin *34s/Mad-Park*
Toledo *36s/5A-Mad*
Trattoria Alba *34s/2-3A*
Tre Pomodori *34s/2-3A*
Trio *33s/Lex-3A*
Vanderbilt Station *Park/33s*
Villa Berulia *34s/Lex-Park*
Water Club *30s/E. 23s*
Wu Liang Ye *Lex/39-40s*

NoHo
(Bet. 4th & Houston Sts., bet. Bowery and W. B'way)
Acme B&G *Gr. Jones/Bway*
Agozar *Bowery/Bleecker-Bond*
Bond Street *Bond/Bway-Lafayette*
Dojo *4s/Mercer*
East *University/10-1s*
Ennio & Michael *La Guardia/W. 3s*
Five Points *Gr. Jones/Lafayette*
Great Jones Cafe *Gr. Jones/Bowery*
Il Buco *Bond/Bowery-Lafayette*
Marion's *Bowery/4s-Gr. Jones*
Marumi *La Guardia/Bleecker-W. 3s*
NoHo Star *Lafayette/Bleecker*
Sala *Bowery/Greaty Jones*
Serafina *Lafayette/4s*
Silver Spurs *La Guardia/Houston*
Time Cafe *Lafayette/Great Jones*
Two Boots *Bleecker/Bway*

NoLita
(South of Houston St. & north of Delancey St., bet. Bowery & Lafayette St.)
Bread *Spring/Elizabeth-Mott*
Café Habana *Prince/Elizabeth*
Cafe Lebowitz *Spring/Elizabeth*
Funky Broome *Mott/Broome*
Ghenet *Mulberry/Houston-Prince*
Le Jardin Bistro *Clev./Kenmare*
Lombardi's *Spring/Mott-Mulberry*
MeKong *Prince/Mott-Mulberry*
Mexican Radio *Clev./Kenmare*
Peasant *Elizabeth/Prince-Spring*
Rice *Mott/Prince-Spring*

Spring St. Natural *Spring/Lafayette*
Va Tutto! *Cleveland/Kenmare-Spring*

SoHo
(South of Houston St. & north of Canal St., west of Lafayette St.)
Alma Blue *Prince/Sullivan-Thompson*
Aquagrill *Spring/6A*
Balthazar *Spring/Bway-Crosby*
Baluchi's *Spring/Sullivan-Thompson*
Bar 89 *Mercer/Broome-Spring*
Barolo *W. Bway/Broome-Spring*
Bistro Les Amis *Spring/Thompson*
Blue Ribbon *Sullivan/Prince-Spring*
Blue Ribbon Sushi *Sullivan/Prince*
Canteen *Mercer/Prince*
Casa La Femme *Wooster/Houston*
Cendrillon *Mercer/Broome-Grand*
Country Café *Thompson/Broome*
Cub Room *Sullivan/Prince*
Cupping Room *W. Bway/Broome*
Dos Caminos *W. Bway/Houston*
Downtown *W. Bway/Broome-Spring*
Fanelli's Cafe *Prince/Mercer*
Félix *W. Bway/Grand*
Fiamma Osteria *Spring/6A-Sullivan*
Giorgione *Spring/Greenwich-Hudson*
Hampton Chutney *Prince/Bway*
Herban Kitchen *Hudson/Spring*
Honmura An *Mercer/Houston-Prince*
Ideya *W. Bway/Broome-Grand*
Il Corallo *Prince/Sullivan*
I Tre Merli *W. Bway/Houston-Prince*
Ivo & Lulu *Broome/6A-Varick*
Jean Claude *Sullivan/Houston*
Jerry's *Prince/Greene-Mercer*
Kelley & Ping *Greene/Prince*
Kin Khao *Spring/Thompson-W. Bway*
L'Ecole *Bway/Grand*
Le Pain Quotidien *Grand/Greene*
Le Pescadou *King/6A*
Little Italy Pizza *Varick/Charlton*
L'Orange Bleue *Broome/Crosby*
Lucky Strike *Grand/W. Bway*
Mercer Kitchen *Prince/Mercer*
Mezzogiorno *Spring/Sullivan*
Ñ *Crosby/Broome-Grand*
Novecento *W. Bway/Duane-Worth*
Omen *Thompson/Prince-Spring*
Once Upon a Tart *Sullivan/Houston*
Pão! *Spring/Greenwich s*
Peep *Prince/Sullivan-Thompson*
Penang *Spring/Greene-Mercer*
Pepe *Sullivan/Houston-Prince*
Provence *MacDougal/Prince*
Raoul's *Prince/Sullivan-Thompson*
Salt *MacDougal/Houston-Prince*
Savoy *Prince/Crosby*
Snack *Thompson/Prince-Spring*
Soho Steak *Thompson/Prince-Spring*

Starbucks *Varick/Spring*
Tennessee Mtn. *Spring/Wooster*
Thom *Thompson/Broome-Spring*
325 Spring St. *Spring/Greenwich*
Woo Lae Oak *Mercer/Houston*
Zoë *Prince/Bway-Mercer*

South Street Seaport
Bridge Cafe *Water/Dover*
Cabana *South/Fulton-John*
Harbour Lights *Pier 17/Fulton-South*
Heartland Brew. *South/Fulton*
Pizzeria Uno *South/Pier 17*
Quartino *Peck/Water*

TriBeCa
(South of Canal St. & north of
Chambers St., west of B'way)
Acappella *Hudson/Chambers*
Arqua *Church/White*
Azafran *Warren/Greenwich-W. Bway*
Bouley *W. Bway/Duane*
Bread *Church/Walker*
Bubby's *Hudson/N. Moore*
Burritoville *multi. loc.*
Capsouto Frères *Washington/Watts*
Chanterelle *Harrison/Hudson*
City Hall *Duane/Church-W. Bway*
Danube *Hudson/Duane-Reade*
Dominic *Greenwich s/Harrison-Jay*
Duane Park Cafe *Duane/Hudson*
Dylan Prime *Laight/Greenwich*
Ecco *Chambers/Church-W. Bway*
Edward's *W. Bway/Duane-Thomas*
El Teddy's *W. Bway/Franklin-White*
F.illi Ponte *Desbrosses/W. Side Hwy.*
Flor de Sol *Greenwich/Franklin*
fresh. *Reade/Church-W. Bway*
Gigino Trattoria *Greenwich/Duane*
Grace *Franklin/Church-W. Bway*
Harrison *Greenwich s/Harrison*
Il Giglio *Warren/Greenwich-W. Bway*
Kitchenette *W. Bway/Warren*
Layla *W. Bway/Franklin*
Le Zinc *Duane/Church-W. Bway*
Mary Ann's *W. Bway/Chambers*
Montrachet *W. Bway/Walker-White*
Nam *Reade/W. Bway*
Nobu *Hudson/Franklin*
Nobu Next Door *Hudson/Franklin*
Odeon *W. Bway/Duane-Thomas*
Pepolino *W. Bway/Canal-Lispenard*
Petite Abeille *W. Bway/Duane*
Roc *Duane/Greenwich s*
Salaam Bombay *Green. s/Duane*
Scalini Fedeli *Duane/Greenwich s*
Shore *Murray/Church-W. Bway*
66 *Church/Leonard*
Sosa Borella *Greenwich s/Watts*
Takahachi *Duane-Church/W. Bway*
Thai House Cafe *Hudson/Hubert*

Thalassa *Franklin/Greenwich*
Tribeca Grill *Greenwich s/Franklin*
Walker's *N. Moore/Varick*
Zutto *Hudson/Harrison*

Union Square
(Bounded by 17th & 14th Sts.,
bet. Union Sq. E. & Union Sq.
W.)
Blue Water Grill *Union Sq. W./16s*
Candela *16s/Irving-Park S.*
Chat n' Chew *16s/5A-Union Sq. W*
Chop't Salad *17s/Bway-5A*
Coffee Shop *Union Sq. W./16s*
Havana Central *17s/Bway-5A*
Heartland Brew. *Union Sq. W./16s*
Mesa Grill *5A/15-6s*
Olives *Park S./17s*
Republic *Union Sq. W./16-7s*
Steak Frites *16s/5A-Union Sq. W.*
Tocqueville *15s/5A-Union*
Union Sq. Cafe *16s/5A-Union Sq. W.*
Zen Palate *Union Sq. E./16s*

Washington Hts. & Up
(North of W. 157th St.)
Bleu Evolution *187s/Ft. Washington*
Dallas BBQ *Bway/166s*
DR-K *Dyckman/Nagle*
El Malecon *Bway/175s*
Empire Szechuan *Bway/170-71s*
Hispaniola *181s/Cabrini Blvd.*
New Leaf *M. Corbin/190s*
107 West *187/Ft. Washington-Pinehurst*

West Village
(14th to Houston Sts., west of
7th Ave. S., excluding
Meatpacking District)
Agave *7A S./Charles-W. 10s*
Alfama *Hudson/Perry*
A.O.C. *Bleecker/Grove*
A Salt & Battery *Greenwich A/12-3s*
Benny's Burritos *Greenwich A/Jane*
Burritoville *Bleecker/7A S.*
Café de Bruxelles *Greenwich A/13s*
Cafe Picasso *Bleecker/Charles-10s*
Cafe Topsy *Hudson/Bank-11s*
Caffe Rafaella *7A S./Charles-W. 10s*
Casa *Bedford/Commerce*
Chez Brigitte *Greenwich A/Bank-7A*
Chez Michallet *Bedford/Grove*
Chick-Inn *Hudson/St. Luke's Pl.*
Chow Bar *4s/W. 10s*
Corner Bistro *W. 4s/Jane*
Cowgirl *Hudson/W. 10s*
Crispo *14s/7-8A*
Da Andrea *Hudson/Perry-W. 11s*
El Faro *Greenwich s/Horatio*

Emack & Bolio's *7A/13-4s*
good *Greenwich A/Bank-W. 12s*
Grange Hall *Commerce/Barrow*
Havana Vil. *Christopher/Bedford*
Hue *Charles/Bleecker*
'ino *Bedford/Downing-6A*
Jarnac *12s/Greenwich s*
La Cantina *8A/Jane*
La Focaccia *Bank/W. 4s*
La Metairie *10s/W. 4s*
La Ripaille *Hudson/Bethune-W. 12s*
Lemongrass Grill *Barrow/7A S.*
Le Zoo *11s/Greenwich s*
Lunchbox Food *West/Clarkson*
Malatesta *Washington/Christopher*
Mary's Fish Camp *Charles/W. 4s*
Mexicana Mama *Hudson/Charles*
Mi Cocina *Jane/Hudson*
Miracle Grill *Bleecker/Bank-W. 11s*
Mitali *Bleecker/7A S.*
Monster Sushi *Hudson/Charles*
Moustache *Bedford/Barrow-Grove*
Osteria del Sole *4s/Perry*
Paris Commune *Bleecker/Bank*
Pepe ... To Go *Hudson/Perry-11s*
Petite Abeille *Hudson/Barrow*
Philip Marie *Hudson/11s*
Piccolo Angolo *Hudson/Jane*
Pink Tea Cup *Grove/Bleecker*
Place *4s/Bank-W. 12s*
Rafaella *Bleecker/Perry*
Sazerac House *Hudson/Charles*
Sevilla *Charles/W. 4s*
Snack Taverna *Bedford/7A S.*
Surya *Bleecker/Grove-7A S.*
Taka *Grove/Bleecker-7A S*
Tangerine *10s/Bleecker-Hudson*
Tartine *11s/W. 4s*
Tea & Sympathy *Greenwich A/12-3s*
Titou *4s/Charles-Perry*
Two Boots *11s/7A S.*
Uguale *West/W. 10s*
Vittorio Cucina *Bleecker/Grove-7A*
Voyage *Perry/Greenwich s*
Wallsé *11s/Washington*
Westville *10s/Bleecker-W. 4s*
White Horse Tavern *Hudson/11s*
Wild Ginger *Grove/Bleecker-7A S.*
Ye Waverly Inn *Bank/Waverly*

West 40s

Above *42s/7-8A*
Afghan Kebab Hse *46s/6-7A*
Alfredo of Rome *49s/5-6A*
Algonquin Hotel *44s/5-6A*
Amarone *9A/47-8s*
Amy's Bread *9A/46-7s*
Angus McIndoe *44s/Bway-8A*
Baldoria *49s/Bway-8A*
Bali Nusa Indah *9A/45-6s*
Barbetta *46s/8-9A*

Becco *46s/8-9A*
Blue Fin *Bway/47s*
Bryant Park Grill/Cafe *40s/5-6A*
B. Smith's *46s/8-9A*
Burritoville *9A/44s*
Cafe Un Deux Trois *44s/Bway-6A*
Cara Mia *9A/45-6s*
Carmine's *44s/Bway-8A*
Casa Di Meglio *48s/Bway-8A*
Charlotte *44s/Bway-6A*
Chez Josephine *42s/9-10A*
Chimichurri Grill *9A/43-4s*
Churrascaria Plata. *49s/8-9A*
Citarella *6A/49s*
City Crab/Lobster *49s/6-7A*
Coco Pazzo *49s/Bway-8A*
Cosi *42s/5-6A*
Culinaria *40s/7-8A*
Dallas BBQ *43s/Bway-6A*
db Bistro Moderne *44s/5-6A*
Del Frisco's *6A/49s*
Delta Grill *9A/48s*
Dervish Turkish *47s/6-7A*
District *46s/6-7A*
Don Giovanni *44s/8-9A*
Esca *43s/9A*
ESPN Zone *Bway/42s*
FireBird *46s/8-9A*
Foley's Fish House *7A/47-8s*
44 *44s/5-6A*
44 & X *10A/44s*
Frankie & Johnnie's *45s/Bway-8A*
Gaby *45s/5-6A*
Hakata Grill *48s/Bway-8A*
Hale & Hearty Soups *42s/5-6A*
Hallo Berlin *10A/44-5s*
Haru *43s/Bway-8A*
Heartland Brew. *43s/Bway-6A*
Hell's Kitchen *9A/46-7s*
Ilo *40s/5-6A*
Jewel of India *44s/5-6A*
Jezebel *9A/45s*
Joe Allen *46s/8-9A*
John's Pizzeria *44s/Bway-8A*
J.W.'s Steakhouse *Bway/45-6s*
Kodama *45s/8-9A*
Kyma *46s/8A*
La Cocina/Ta Cocina *9A/48-9s*
La Locanda Vini *9A/49-50s*
La Rivista *46s/8-9A*
Lattanzi *46s/8-9A*
Le Madeleine *43s/9-10A*
Le Marais *46s/6-7A*
Le Rivage *46s/8-9A*
Little Italy Pizza *45s/5-6A*
Luxia *48s/8-9A*
Manhattan Chili Co. *Bway/43s*
Marseille *9A/44s*
McHales *8A/46s*
Meskerem *47s/9-10A*
Monster Sushi *46s/5-6A*

Morrells *49s/5-6A*
My Most Favorite *45s/Bway-6A*
Noche *Bway/48-9s*
Ollie's *44s/Bway-8A*
Orso *46s/8-9A*
Osteria al Doge *44s/Bway-6A*
Pam Real Thai *49s/9-10A*
Pierre au Tunnel *47s/Bway-8A*
Pietrasanta *9A/47s*
Pigalle *8A/48s*
Pongsri Thai *48s/Bway-8A*
Rachel's American *9A/43-4s*
Rainbow Room *Rock Plz./49-50s*
Red *44s/8-9A*
Re Sette *45s/5-6A*
Ruby Foo's *Bway/49s*
Sardi's *44s/Bway-8A*
Sea Grill *49s/5-6A*
Shaan *48s/5-6A*
Shula's Steak *42s/8A*
Soul Cafe *42s/9-10A*
St. Andrews *44s/Bway-6A*
Starbucks *9A/47s*
Sushiden *49s/6-7A*
Sushi Zen *44s/Bway-6A*
T.G.I. Friday's *Bway/46s*
Tony's Di Napoli *43s/Bway-6A*
Torre di Pisa *44s/5-6A*
Tossed *Rockefeller Plaza/49-50s*
Trattoria Dopo Teatro *44s/Bway-6A*
Trattoria Trecolori *45s/6-7A*
Triomphe *44s/5-6A*
Two Boots *Rockefeller Plaza/49-50s*
Utsav *46s/6-7A*
Via Brasil *46s/5-6A*
View *Bway/45-6s*
Virgil's Real BBQ *44s/Bway-6A*
West Bank Cafe *42s/9-10A*
World Yacht *41s/12A*
Wu Liang Ye *48s/5-6A*
Zenith Vegetarian *48s/8-9A*
Zen Palate *9A/46s*
Zuni *9A/43s*

West 50s

Acqua Pazza *52s/5-6A*
Afghan Kebab Hse *9A/51-2s*
Aki Sushi *52s/8-9A*
Alain Ducasse *58s/6-7A*
Angelo & Maxie's *6A/51-2s*
Angelo's Pizzeria *57s/6-7A*
Aquavit *54s/5-6A*
Atelier *CPS/6A*
Azalea *51s/Bway-8A*
Azuri Cafe *51s/9-10A*
Baluchi's *56s/Bway-8A*
Bay Leaf *56s/5-6A*
Beacon *56s/5-6A*
Bello *9A/56s*
Ben Benson's *52s/6-7A*

Benihana *56s/5-6A*
bluechili *51s/8A-Bway*
Bombay Palace *52s/5-6A*
Brasserie 8½ *57s/5-6A*
Bricco *56s/8-9A*
Brooklyn Diner USA *57s/Bway-7A*
burger joint *56s/6-7A*
Cafe Atlas *CPS/5-6A*
Café Botanica *CPS/6-7A*
Caffe Cielo *8A/52-3s*
Carnegie Deli *7A/55s*
Chanpen Thai *9A/51s*
Chez Napoléon *50s/8-9A*
China Grill *53s/5-6A*
Cité *51s/6-7A*
Cité Grill *51s/6-7A*
Cosi *Bway/51s*
Dakshin Indian *9A/50s*
Da Tommaso *8A/53-4s*
Druids *10A/50-1s*
East *55s/Bway-8A*
Eatery *9A/53s*
Edison Cafe *47s/Bway-8A*
Etrusca *53s/6-7A*
Fives *5A/55s*
Fontana di Trevi *57s/6-7A*
Gallagher's Steak *52/Bway-8A*
Giovanni *55s/5-6A*
Grand Sichuan *9A/50-1s*
Halcyon *54s/6-7A*
Hale & Hearty Soups *56s/5-6A*
Hallo Berlin *51s/9A*
Hard Rock Cafe *57s/Bway-7A*
Heartland Brew. *6A/51s*
Hudson Cafeteria *58s/8-9A*
Il Gattopardo *54s/5-6A*
Il Tinello *56s/5-6A*
Island Burgers *9A/51-2s*
Jekyll & Hyde *6A/57-8s*
Joe's Shanghai *56s/5-6A*
JUdson Grill *52s/6-7A*
Julian's *9A/53-4s*
Kiiroi-Hana *56s/5-6A*
La Caravelle *55s/5-6A*
La Côte Basque *55s/5-6A*
La Vineria *55s/5-6A*
Le Bernardin *51s/6-7A*
Limoncello *7A/50s*
Maison *Bway/53-4s*
Mangia *57s/5-6A*
Manhattan Chili Co. *Bway/53-4s*
Manhattan OceanClub *58s/5-6A*
Maria Pia *51s/8-9A*
Mars 2112 *Bway/51s*
Mee Noodle Shop *9A/53s*
Menchanko-tei *55s/5-6A*
Michael's *55s/5-6A*
Mickey Mantle's *CPS/5-6s*
Milos, Estiatorio *55s/6-7A*
Mix in NY *58s/5-6A*

Location Index

Moda *52s/6-7A*
Molyvos *7A/55-6s*
Nocello *55s/Bway-8A*
Norma's *57s/6A*
Oak Room *5A/59s*
Old San Juan *9A/51-2s*
One C.P.S. *5A-59s*
Osteria del Circo *55s/6-7A*
Oyster Bar at Plaza *58s/5-6A*
Palm *50s/Bway-8A*
Palm Court *5A/CPS-59s*
Patsy's *56s/Bway-8A*
Petrossian *58s/7A*
Pump Energy Food *55s/5-6A*
Puttanesca *9A/56s*
Redeye Grill *7A/56s*
Red Garlic *8A/54-5s*
Remi *53s/6-7A*
René Pujol *51s/8-9A*
Rice 'n' Beans *9A/50-1s*
Rock Center Café *50s/5-6A*
Route 66 Cafe *9A/55-6s*
Rue 57 *57s/6A*
Russian Samovar *52s/Bway-8A*
Ruth's Chris *51s/6-7A*
San Domenico *CPS/Bway-7A*
Seppi's *56s/6-7A*
Shelly's New York *57s/6-7A*
Siam Inn *8A/51-2s*
Soba Nippon *52s/5-6A*
Sosa Borella *8A/50s*
Soup Kitchen Int'l *55s/Bway-8A*
Stage Deli *7A/53-4s*
Sugiyama *55s/Bway-8A*
Sushiya *56s/5-6A*
Tang Pavilion *55s/5-6A*
T.G.I. Friday's *multi. loc.*
Thalia *8A/50s*
Topaz Thai *56s/6-7A*
Town *56s/5-6A*
Trattoria Dell'Arte *7A/56-7s*
Tuscan Square *51s/5-6A*
'21' Club *52s/5-6A*
Uncle Nick's *9A/50-1s*
Vago *56s/5-6A*
ViceVersa *51s/8-9A*
Victor's Cafe *52s/Bway-8A*
Wolf's *57s/5-6A*
Wondee Siam *multi. loc.*

West 60s

Café des Artistes *67s/Col.-CPW*
Empire Szechuan *Col./68-9s*
Fiorello's Cafe *Bway/63-4s*
Gabriel's *60s/Bway-Col.*
Jean Georges *CPW/60-1s*
Josephina *Bway/63-4s*
La Boîte en Bois *68s/Col.-CPW*
Levana *69s/Bway-Col.*
Nick and Toni's *67s/Bway-Col.*

Ollie's *Bway/67-8s*
Picholine *64s/Bway-CPW*
Rosa Mexicano *Col./62s*
Santa Fe *69s/Col.-CPW*
Sapphire Indian *Bway/60-1s*
Shun Lee Cafe *65s/Col.-CPW*
Shun Lee West *65s/Col.-CPW*
Starbucks *Col./67s*
Tavern on Green *CPW/66-7s*
Vince and Eddie's *68s/Col.-CPW*

West 70s

Alice's Tea Cup *73s/Amst.-Col.*
Baluchi's *Col./73-4s*
Big Nick's Burger *Bway/77s*
Boat Basin Cafe *79s/Hudson River*
Bruculino *Col./70s*
Burritoville *72s/Amst.-Col.*
Café Frida *Col./77-8s*
Cafe Luxembourg *70s/Amst.-W. End*
Cafe Ronda *Col./71-2s*
'Cesca *75s/Amst.*
Citrus Bar & Grill *Amst./75s*
City Grill *Col./72-3s*
Compass *70s/Amst.-West End*
Coppola's *W. 79s/Amst.-Bway*
Cosi *Bway/76s*
Dallas BBQ *72s/Col.-CPW*
Emack & Bolio's *Amst./78-9s*
Empire Szechuan *72s/Bway-W. End*
Epices du Traiteur *70s/Col.*
Fairway Cafe *Bway/74s*
Gabriela's *Amst./75s*
Gray's Papaya *Bway/72s*
Harry's Burritos *Col./71s*
Hunan Park *Col./70-1s*
Isabella's *Col./77s*
Ivy's Cafe *72s/Bway-Col.*
Josie's *Amst./74s*
Krispy Kreme *72s/Bway-Col.*
La Grolla *Amst./79-80s*
La Rambla *Bway/75-6s*
Le Pain Quotidien *72s/Col.-CPW*
Metsovo *70s/Col.-CPW*
Mughlai *Col./75s*
Nice Matin *79s/Amst.*
Niko's Med. Grill *Bway/76s*
Ocean Grill *Col./78-9s*
Ony *72s/Bway-Columbus*
Pasha *71s/Col.-CPW*
Patsy's Pizzeria *74s/Col.-CPW*
Pelagos *77s/Amst.-Col.*
Penang *Col./71s*
Pomodoro Rosso *Col./70-1s*
River *Amst./76-7s*
Ruby Foo's *Bway/77s*
Sambuca *72s/Col.-CPW*
Savann *Amst./79-80s*
Scaletta *77s/Col.-CPW*
Shark Bar *Amst./74-5s*

SQC *Col./72-3s*
Viand *Bway/75s*
Vinnie's Pizza *Amst./73-4s*
Zen Palate *Bway/76-7s*

West 80s

Aix *Bway/88s*
Artie's Deli *Bway/82-3s*
Assaggio *Col./82-3s*
Avenue *Col./85s*
Barney Greengrass *Amst./86-7s*
Bella Luna *Col./88-9s*
Brother Jimmy's BBQ *Amst./80-1s*
Cafe Con Leche *Amst./80-1s*
Cafe Lalo *83s/Amst.-Bway*
Calle Ocho *Col./81-2s*
Celeste *Amst./84-5s*
Columbus Bakery *Col./82-3s*
Darna *Col./89s*
Docks Oyster Bar *Bway/89-90s*
Edgar's Cafe *84s/Bway-West End*
EJ's Luncheonette *Amst./81-2s*
Flor de Mayo *Amst./83-4s*
Fred's *Amst./83s*
French Roast *Bway/85s*
Fujiyama Mama *Col./82-3s*
Good Enough to Eat *Amst./83-4s*
Haru *Amst./80-1s*
Isola *Col./83-4s*
Jackson Hole *Col./85s*
Jean-Luc *Col./84-5s*
Kitchen 22/82 *Col./82s*
La Cocina *85s/Amst.-Bway*
La Mirabelle *86s/Amst.-Col.*
Les Routiers *Amst./87-8s*
Luzia's *Amst./80-1s*
Monsoon *Amst./81s*
Nëo Sushi *Bway/83s*
Ollie's *Bway/84s*
Ouest *Bway/83-4s*
Pizzeria Uno *Col./81s*
Popover Cafe *Amst./86-7s*
Quintessence *Amst./87-8s*
Rain *82s/Amst.-Col.*
Red Snapper *Amst./84s*
Roppongi *Amst./81s*
Sabor *Amst./82-3s*
Sarabeth's *Amst./80-1s*

Sushi Hana *Amst./82-3s*
Time Cafe *Bway/85s*
Zabar's Cafe *Bway/80s*

West 90s

Acqua *Amst./94-5s*
Alouette *Bway/97-8s*
Cafe Con Leche *Amst./95-6s*
Carmine's *Bway/90-1s*
El Malecon *Amst./97-8s*
Empire Szechuan *Bway/97s*
Gabriela's *Amst./93s*
Gennaro *Amst./92-3s*
Hunan Park *Col./95s*
La Cocina/Ta Cocina *Bway/98-9s*
Lemongrass Grill *Bway/94-5s*
Mary Ann's *Bway/90-1s*
Pampa *Amst./97-8s*
Roth's Steak *Col./93s*
Saigon Grill *Amst./90s*
Sipan *Amst./94s*
Talia's Steakhouse *Amst./92-3s*
Trattoria Pesce *Col./90-1s*
Yuki Sushi *Amst./92s*

West 100s
(West of Morningside Ave.)

A *Col./106-7s*
Afghan Kebab Hse *Bway/102s*
Bistro Ten 18 *Amst./110s*
Carne *Bway/105s*
Empire Szechuan *Bway/100s*
Flor de Mayo *Bway/101s*
Henry's *Bway/105s*
Kitchenette *Amst./122-23s*
Mamá Mexico *Bway/101-2s*
Max *Amst./123s*
Métisse *105s/Amst.-Bway*
Ollie's *Bway/116s*
107 West *Bway/107-8s*
Pisticci *La Salle/Bway*
Symposium *113s/Amst.-Bway*
Terrace/Sky *119s/Amst.-Morningside*
Tomo Sushi *Bway/110-11s*
Turkuaz *Bway/100s*
V&T *Amst./110-11s*

BRONX

Bellavista Cafe *235s/Johnson*
Charles' Southern *165s/Woodycrest*
Dominick's *Arthur/Crescent-E. 187s*
El Malecon *Bway/231s*
Enzo's *Williamsbridge/Neill*
F & J Pine *Bronxdale/White Plains*
Jimmy's *Fordham/Major Deegan*

Le Refuge Inn *City Is./Southerland*
Lobster Box *City Island/Belden*
Madison's *Riverdale/258s*
Mario's *Arthur/184-86s*
Nebraska Steak *187/Hoffman*
Park Place *Mosholu/Bway*
Roberto's *186s/Belmont*

BROOKLYN

Bay Ridge

Areo *3A/84-5s*
Baci *3A/71s*
Chadwick's *3A/89s*
Chianti *3A/86s*
Eliá *3A/86-7s*
Embers *3A/95-6s*
Lento's *3A/Ovington*
Omonia Cafe *3A/76-7s*
101 *4A/100-1s*
Pearl Room *4A/82s*
Pizzeria Uno *4A/92s*
Provence en Boite *3A/83-4s*
St. Michel *3A/Bay Ridge-76s*
Tuscany Grill *3A/86-7s*

Bensonhurst

L & B Spumoni *86s/W.10-11s*
Tommaso's *86s/14-5A*

Boerum Hill

BarTabac *Smith/Dean*
Brawta Caribbean *Atlantic/Hoyt*
Downtown Atlantic *Atlantic/Bond*
Saul *Smith/Bergen-Dean*
Sherwood Cafe *Smith/Baltic*

Brighton Beach

Rasputin *Coney Island A/Ave. X*

Brooklyn Heights

Caffe Buon Gusto *Montague/Henry*
Hale & Hearty Soups *Court/Remsen*
Henry's End *Henry/Cranberry*
Kapadokya *Montague/Clinton-Henry*
La Bouillabaisse *Atlantic/Clinton*
Noodle Pudding *Henry/Cranberry*
Queen *Court/Livingston*
Shinjuku *Atlantic/Clinton-Court*
Teresa's *Montague/Hicks*

Carroll Gardens

Alma *Columbia/DeGraw*
Caserta Vecchia *Smith/Baltic-Butler*
Ferdinando's *Union/Columbia-Hicks*
Grocery, The *Smith/Sackett-Union*
Marco Polo *Court/Union*
Max *Court/Carroll-1st Pl.*
Panino'teca 275 *Smith/DeGraw*
Patois *Smith/DeGraw-Douglass*
Savoia *Smith/DeGraw-Sackett*
Three Bow Thais *Smith/DeGraw*
Whim *DeGraw/Clinton*
Zaytoons *Smith/Sackett*

Clinton Hill

Locanda Vini *Gates/Cambridge*

Cobble Hill

Banania Cafe *Smith/Douglass*
Cafe Luluc *Smith/Baltic*

Faan *Smith/Baltic*
Harvest *Court/Warren*
Hill Diner *Court/Baltic-Warren*
Joya *Court/Warren*
Osaka *Court/DeGraw-Kane*
Pepe ... To Go *Smith/Baltic*
Quercy *Court/Baltic*
Sur *Smith/Butler-Douglass*
Sweet Melissa *Court/Butler*
Tuk Tuk *Smith/Baltic-Butler*
Village 247 *Smith/DeGraw-Douglass*

Coney Island

Gargiulo's *15s/Mermaid-Surf*
Totonno Pizzeria *Neptune/W. 15-6s*

Downtown

Gage & Tollner *Fulton/Jay*
Junior's *Flatbush/DeKalb*

Dumbo

Five Front *Front/Old Fulton*
Grimaldi's *Old Fulton/Front-Water*
Pete's Downtown *Water/Old Fulton*
Rice *Washington/Front-York*
River Cafe *Water/Furman-Old Fulton*
Superfine *Front/Pearl*

Dyker Heights

Outback Steak *86s/15A*

Fort Greene

À Table *Lafayette/Adelphi-Clermont*
Chez Oskar *DeKalb/Adelphi*
Loulou *DeKalb/Adelphi-Clermont*
Madiba *DeKalb/Adelphi-Carlton*
Thomas Beisl *Lafayette/Ashland*
Zaytoons *Myrtle/Hall-Washington*

Gravesend

Fiorentino's *Ave. U/McDonald-West*
Sahara *Coney Island A/Aves. T-U*

Midwood

Di Fara *Ave. J/E. 14-15s*

Ocean Parkway

Ocean Palace *Ave. U/E. 14-5s*

Park Slope

Al Di La *5A/Carroll*
Beso *5A/Union*
Bistro St. Mark's *St. Mark's/Flatbush*
Blue Ribbon *5A/1s-Garfield*
Blue Ribbon Sushi *5A/1s-Garfield*
Cafe Steinhof *7A/14s*
Chip/CurryShop *5A/6-7s*
Coco Roco *5A/6-7s*
Cocotte *5A/4s*
Convivium Osteria *5A/Bergen*

Cucina *5A/Carroll-Garfield*
Joe's Pizza *7A/Carroll-Garfield*
Lemongrass Grill *7A/Berkeley*
Long Tan *5A/Berkeley-Union*
Magnolia *6A/12s*
Minnow *9s/6-7A*
Moutarde *5A/Carroll*
Nana *5A/Lincoln-St. John's*
Olive Vine Cafe *multi. loc.*
Paradou *7A/14-5s*
Press 195 *5A/Sackett-Union*
Rose Water *Union St./6A*
12th St. Bar & Grill *8A/11-2s*
Two Boots *2s/7-8A*

Prospect Heights

Garden Cafe *Vanderbilt/Prospect*
Tom's *Washington/Sterling*

Red Hook

Hope & Anchor *Van Brunt/Wolcott*
360 *Van Brunt/Dikeman-Wolcott*

Sheepshead Bay

Brennan & Carr *Nostrand/Ave. U*
Jordan's Lobster *Knapp/Belf Pkwy*
Lundy Bros. *Emmons/Ocean*

Sunset Park

Nyonya *8A/54s*

Williamsburg

Allioli *Grand/Havemeyer-Roebling*
Bamonte's *Withers/Lorimer-Union*
Bonita *Bedford/S. 2-3s*
Chickenbone Cafe *S. 4s/Driggs*
Cono & Sons *Graham/Ainslie*
Cripplebush Road *Wythe/N. 7s*
Diner *Bway/Berry*
DuMont *Union/Devoe-Metropolitan*
Giando/Water *Kent/Bway*
Miss Williamsburg *Kent/N. 3s*
Nar *Metropolitan/Berry*
Oznot's Dish *Berry/N. 9s*
Peter Luger *Bway/Driggs*
Planet Thailand *N. 7s/Bedford-Berry*
Relish *Wythe/Metropolitan-N. 3s*
SEA *N. 6s/Berry*
Sparky's American *N. 5s/Bedford*
Vera Cruz *Bedford/N. 6-7s*

QUEENS

Astoria

Amici Amore I *Newtown/30s*
Brick Cafe *33s/31A*
Café Bar *36s/34A*
Christos Hasapo *23A/41s*
Elias Corner *31s/24A*
Esperides *30A/37s*
Karyatis *Bway/35-6s*
Mombar *Steinway/25-8A*
Omonia Cafe *Bway/33s*
Piccola Venezia *28A/42s*
Pizzeria Uno *35A/38s*
Ponticello *Bway/46-7s*
Roumeli Taverna *Bway/33s*
S'Agapo *34A/35s*
Stamatis *multi. loc.*
Taverna Kyclades *Ditmars/33-4s*
Taverna Vraka *31s/23-4A*
Telly's Taverna *23A/28-9s*
Tierras Colomb. *Bway/33s*
Trattoria L'incontro *31s/Ditmars*
Ubol's Kitchen *Steinway/Astoria-25A*
Uncle George's *Bway/34s*

Bayside

Ben's Kosher Deli *26A/211s*
Caffé/Green *Cross Is./Clearview*
Jackson Hole *Bell Blvd./35A*
Outback Steak *Bell/26A*
Pizzeria Uno *Bell Blvd./39A*
Uncle Jack's Steak *Bell Blvd./40A*

Corona

Green Field Churr. *Northern/108s*
Park Side *Corona/51A*

Elmhurst

Joe's Shanghai *Bway/45A-Whitney*
Outback Steak *Queens Blvd./56A*
Pho Bang *Bway/Elmhurst*
Ping's Seafood *Queens/Goldsmith*

Flushing

East Lake *Main/Franklin*
Joe's Shanghai *37A/Main-Union*
Kum Gang San *Northern Blvd./Union*
New Lok Kee *Main/37A*
Penang *Prince/38-9A*
Pho Bang *Kissena/Main*
Sweet-n-Tart Cafe *38s/Main*

Forest Hills

Bann Thai *Austin/Yellowstone*
Cabana *70/Austin-Queens Blvd.*
Dee's Pizza *Metropolitan/71D*
Mardi Gras *Austin/70A-70Rd.*
Nick's *Ascan/Austin-Burns*
Pizzeria Uno *70 Rd./Austin-Queens*
Q, a Thai Bistro *Ascan/Austin-Burns*

Glendale

Zum Stammtisch *Myrtle/69 Pl.-70s*

Jackson Heights
Afghan Kebab Hse *37A/74-5s*
Delhi Palace *74s/Roosevelt-37A*
Jackson Diner *74s/Roosevelt-37A*
Jackson Hole *Astoria/ 70s*
Pearson's Texas BBQ *35A/71-2s*
Rice Avenue *Roosevelt/72-3s*
Tierras Colomb. *Roosevelt/82s*

Little Neck
La Baraka *Northern Blvd/Little Neck*

Long Island City
Bella Via *Vernon/48A*
Greek Captain *36A/32-3s*
Manducatis *Jackson/47Rd*
Manetta's *Jackson/49A*
Tournesol *Vernon/50-1A*
Water's Edge *44 Dr. & East River*

Ozone Park
Don Peppe *Lefferts Blvd./135A*

Rego Park
London Lennie's *Woodhaven Blvd./ Fleet Ct.-Penelope*

Sunnyside
Chipper *Queens Blvd/42s*
Hemsin *Queens Blvd./39 Pl.*
Mavi Turkish *Queens Blvd./42s*

Whitestone
Cooking with Jazz *154s/12A*
Napa/Son. Steak *149s/15A*

Woodside
La Flor Bakery Cafe *Roosevelt/53s*
Sapori d'Ischia *37A/56s*
Sripraphai *39A/64-5s*

STATEN ISLAND

Aesop's Tables *Bay/Maryland*
American Grill *Forest/Bard-Hart*
Angelina's *Jefferson/Annadale*
Carol's Cafe *Richmond/Four Corners*
Denino's *Pt. Richmond/Hooker*
Historic Bermuda *Arthur Kill/St. Lukes*
Killmeyer's *Arthur Kill/Sharrotts*

Lake Club *Clove/Victory*
Lento's *New Dorp/Richmond*
Marina Cafe *Mansion/Hillside*
Parsonage *Arthur Kill/Clarke*
South Shore Country *Huguenot*
Trattoria Romana *Hylan/Benton*

SPECIAL FEATURES

(For multi-location restaurants, the availability of index features may vary by location.)

Breakfast

(See also Hotel Dining)
A Salt & Battery
Balthazar
Barney Greengrass
Brasserie
Brooklyn Diner USA
Bubby's
Cafe Con Leche
Cafe Lebowitz
City Bakery
Columbus Bakery
Comfort Diner
Cupping Room
E.A.T.
EJ's Luncheonette
Empire Diner
Florent
Good Enough to Eat
Googie's
Havana Central
Hill Diner
Home
Hope & Anchor
Katz's Deli
Kiev
Kitchenette
La Bergamote
Le Pain Quotidien
L'Express
Lunchbox Food
Mayrose
Michael's
NoHo Star
Once Upon a Tart
Pastis
Payard Bistro
Pershing Square
Pigalle
Pink Tea Cup
Popover Cafe
Sarabeth's
Second Ave. Deli
SQC
Tartine
Tea & Sympathy
Teresa's
Tom's
Veronica
Veselka
Viand
Zabar's Cafe

Brunch

Aix
Ambassador Grill
America
Aquagrill
Aquavit
Artisanal
Atelier
Avenue
Balthazar
Bistro St. Mark's
Blue Water Grill
Brasserie 360
Bryant Park Grill/Cafe
Bubby's
Café Botanica
Café de Bruxelles
Café des Artistes
Cafe Luxembourg
Capsouto Frères
Chez Michallet
Chez Oskar
Cornelia St. Cafe
Danal
Eleven Madison
Gascogne
good
Grange Hall
Halcyon
Isabella's
JoJo
Le Gigot
Lola
L'Orange Bleue
Maloney & Porcelli
Manhattan Grille
Mark's
Metropolitan Cafe
Odeon
One C.P.S.
Palm Court
Park Avenue Cafe
Patois
Provence
Quatorze Bis
River Cafe
Rocking Horse
Sarabeth's
Saul
Shark Bar
Spring St. Natural
Sylvia's
Tavern on Green
Town
Tribeca Grill

Ulysses
View
Water Club
World Yacht
Zoë

Buffet Served

(Check availability)
Ambassador Grill
Aquavit
Bukhara Grill
Charlotte
Chola
Delegates Dining Rm.
Dumonet
Fives
Green Field Churr.
Killmeyer's
Mangia
Palm Court
Roy's NY
Shark Bar
Turkish Kitchen
View
Water Club
World Yacht

BYO

Amy Ruth's
Angelica Kitchen
Bella Donna
Brawta Caribbean
Chipper
Efendi
Fairway Cafe
Havana Chelsea
Hemsin
Itzocan Café
Ivo & Lulu
Kitchenette
La Bouillabaisse
La Taza de Oro
Mama's Food
Mandarin Court
Olive Vine Cafe
Pam Real Thai
Peking Duck
Pho Bang
Phoenix Garden
Pink Tea Cup
Poke
Quintessence
Sparky's American
Sripraphai
Tartine
Tea & Sympathy
T Salon
Yura & Co.
Zaytoons

Celebrity Chefs

Aix, *Didier Virot*
Alain Ducasse, *Alain Ducasse*
Aquavit, *Marcus Samuelsson*
Arezzo, *Margherita Aloi*
Atelier, *Gabriel Kreuther*
Aureole, *Charlie Palmer*
Babbo, *Mario Batali*
Bayard's, *Eberhard Müller*
Beacon, *Waldy Malouf*
Bouley, *David Bouley*
Chanterelle, *David Waltuck*
City Hall, *Henry Meer*
Coco Pazzo, *Mark Strausman*
Craft, *Tom Colicchio*
Daniel, *Daniel Boulud*
Felidia, *Lidia Bastianich*
44, *Claude Troisgros*
Four Seasons, *Christian Albin*
Gotham B&G, *Alfred Portale*
Gramercy Tavern, *Tom Colicchio*
Harrison, *Jimmy Bradley*
Ilo, *Rick Laakkonen*
Jean Georges, *J.G. Vongerichten*
JUdson Grill, *Bill Telepan*
La Côte Basque, *J.J. Rachou*
Le Bernardin, *Eric Ripert*
Les Halles, *Anthony Bourdain*
L'Impero, *Scott Conant*
Lutèce, *David Féau*
March, *Wayne Nish*
Mesa Grill, *Bobby Flay*
Nobu, *Nobu Matsuhisa*
Oceana, *Cornelius Gallagher*
OLA, *Douglas Rodriguez*
Olives, *Todd English*
Ouest, *Tom Valenti*
Park Avenue Cafe, *Neil Murphy*
Patroon, *John Villa*
Payard Bistro, *Payard, Bertineau*
Pearl Oyster, *Rebecca Charles*
Pearson's Texas BBQ, *R. Pearson*
Picholine, *Terrance Brennan*
Prune, *Gabrielle Hamilton*
rm, *Rick Moonen*
San Domenico, *Odette Fada*
Sea Grill, *Ed Brown*
Town, *Geoffrey Zakarian*
'21' Club, *Erik Blauberg*
Union Pacific, *Rocco DiSpirito*
Union Sq. Cafe, *Michael Romano*
Verbena, *D. Forley, M. Otsuka*
Veritas, *Scott Bryan*
Washington Park, *J. Waxman*
WD-50, *Wylie Dufresne*
Zarela, *Zarela Martinez*

Cheese Trays

Amici Amore I
A.O.C. Bedford
Artisanal

Babbo
Cafe Atlas
Café Boulud
Cafe Lebowitz
Café Pierre
CamaJe
Chanterelle
Charlotte
Chelsea Bistro
Chick-Inn
Culinaria
Daniel
Django
Etats-Unis
Garden Cafe
Jarnac
Melrose
Morrells
Olica
Olives
Oznot's Dish
Parish & Co.
Picholine
Sciuscià

Chef's Table
(Book in advance)
Alain Ducasse
Guastavino's
Le Cirque 2000
Olives
One C.P.S.
Park Avenue Cafe
Patroon
Remi
Smith & Wollensky

Child-Friendly
Alice's Tea Cup
America
Amy Ruth's
Barking Dog
Benihana
Brooklyn Diner USA
Brother Jimmy's BBQ
Bubby's
Cafe Un Deux Trois
Carmine's
'Cesca
Charles' Southern
Chat n' Chew
Chez Oskar
Churrascaria Plata.
Comfort Diner
Cowgirl
Dallas BBQ
EJ's Luncheonette
ESPN Zone
Friend of a Farmer

Gargiulo's
Good Enough to Eat
Googie's
Hard Rock Cafe
Heidelberg
Houston's
Jackson Hole
Jekyll & Hyde
Johnny Rockets
Junior's
La Mela
L & B Spumoni
London Lennie's
Madison's
Manhattan Chili Co.
Mars 2112
Mary Ann's
Mickey Mantle's
Mr. K's
Outback Steak
Peanut Butter/Co.
Pizzeria Uno
Rock Center Café
Sammy's Roumanian
Sarabeth's
Serendipity 3
Sylvia's
Tavern on Green
Tony's Di Napoli
Two Boots
Umberto's Clam
Virgil's Real BBQ
Yura & Co.
Zum Stammtisch

Cool Loos
AZ
Bar 89
Blue Hill
Brasserie
Butter
Compass
ESPN Zone
Guastavino's
Hope & Anchor
Kai
Meet
Mix in NY
Paradou
Pastis
Peep
P.J. Clarke's
Schiller's
SEA
Tao
Town
Tuscan
WD-50

Critic-Proof

(Get lots of business despite so-so food)

Acme B&G
America
Boat Basin Cafe
Cafe Un Deux Trois
Comfort Diner
Dallas BBQ
Dojo
East of Eighth
Edison Cafe
elmo
El Teddy's
Empire Diner
Empire Szechuan
ESPN Zone
French Roast
Googie's
Hard Rock Cafe
Heartland Brew.
Jekyll & Hyde
Lundy Bros.
Mars 2112
Mayrose
Merchants, N.Y.
92
Outback Steak
Park
Pershing Square
Pete's Tavern
Pizzeria Uno
Sardi's
Starbucks
Tavern on Green
T.G.I. Friday's
Time Cafe

Dancing

Jimmy's Bronx
Jimmy's Uptown
Long Tan
Lotus
Noche
Rainbow Room
Rasputin
Tavern on Green
World Yacht

Entertainment

(Call for days and times of performances)

Algonquin Hotel (cabaret)
Allioli (flamenco/tango)
Barbetta (piano)
Blue Fin (jazz)
Blue Smoke (jazz)
Blue Water Grill (jazz)
B. Smith's (jazz/R&B)
Café Pierre (piano player/singer)
Campagnola (piano bar)
Casa La Femme (belly dancing)
Chez Es Saada (DJ/belly dancing)
Chez Josephine (jazz/piano)
Cooking with Jazz (jazz/blues)
FireBird (harp/piano)
Fives (piano/vocals)
Flor de Sol (flamenco)
Jimmy's Bronx (Latin)
Jules (jazz)
King Cole Bar (piano)
Knickerbocker B&G (jazz)
La Mediterranée (piano)
Layla (belly dancing)
Le Madeleine (jazz guitar)
Lola (Latin/R&B)
Londel's Supper Club (jazz)
Lucky Cheng's (drag shows)
Madiba (DJ/South African bands)
Mardi Gras (jazz)
Marion's (burlesque)
Melrose (jazz/vocals)
Metronome (jazz)
Metropolitan Cafe (jazz)
Monkey Bar (piano)
Ñ (flamenco)
Noche (Latin band)
Porters (comedy/jazz)
Rainbow Room (orchestra)
Rasputin (cabaret/international)
River Cafe (piano)
Russian Samovar (guitar/vocals)
Salon Mexico (piano)
Soul Cafe (gospel/jazz)
Sugar Hill Bistro (jazz)
Sylvia's (blues/gospel/jazz)
Terrace in the Sky (harp)
Tommaso's (piano/singers)
Top of the Tower (piano)
Walker's (jazz)
Zarela (mariachi)

Fireplaces

Adä
Bayard's
Beppe
Bruno
Caffé/Green
Capitale
Centolire
Chelsea Bistro
Circus
Cornelia St. Cafe
Delta Grill
Gage & Tollner
Heartbeat
Heidelberg
I Trulli
Keens Steakhouse
La Lanterna
Lumi

March
Metsovo
Moran's Chelsea
One if by Land
Park
Patois
Piccola Venezia
Place
Portofino Grille
René Pujol
Savoy
Shaffer City
Uguale
Vince and Eddie's
Vivolo
Water Club
Water's Edge
Ye Waverly Inn

Game in Season
Aesop's Tables
Al Di La
Annisa
Aquavit
Aureole
Babbo
Barbetta
Bayard's
Beacon
Beppe
Café des Artistes
Capitale
Chez Oskar
Craft
Daniel
Danube
D'Artagnan
Da Umberto
Eight Mile Creek
Felidia
Fiamma Osteria
Four Seasons
Gabriel's
Gascogne
Gotham B&G
Gramercy Tavern
Grocery, The
Henry's End
Il Mulino
Il Postino
I Trulli
Jean Georges
JUdson Grill
L'Absinthe
La Grenouille
La Lunchonette
Le Perigord
Madiba
Massimo
Ouest
Peasant

Piccola Venezia
Picholine
Remi
River Cafe
San Domenico
San Pietro
Saul
Savoy
Tocqueville
Trattoria L'incontro
Union Pacific
Veritas
Washington Park

Gracious Hosts
Atelier, *Ronan Haneff*
Bellini, *Donatella Arpaia*
Canton, *Eileen Leong*
Chanterelle, *Karen Waltuck*
Chez Josephine, *J.C. Baker*
Chin Chin, *James Chin*
Eliá, *Christina & Pete Lekkas*
Four Seasons, *von Bidder, Niccolini*
Fresco by Scotto, *Marion Scotto*
Gus' Place, *Gus Theodoro*
Harry's, *Harry Poulakakos*
Jean Georges, *P. Vongerichten*
Jewel Bako, *Grace & Jack Lamb*
Kitchen Club, *Marja Samsom*
La Caravelle, *Rita/André Jammet*
La Grenouille, *Charles Masson*
La Mirabelle, *Annick Le Douaron*
Le Cirque 2000, *Sirio Maccioni*
Lenox, *Tony Fortuna*
Le Perigord, *Georges Briguet*
Neary's, *Jimmy Neary*
Nino's, *Nino Selimaj*
Paola's, *Paola Marracino*
Piccolo Angolo, *R. Migliorini*
Primavera, *Nicola Civetta*
Rao's, *Frank Pellegrino*
San Domenico, *Tony May*
San Pietro, *Gerardo Bruno*
Tocqueville, *Jo-Ann Makovitzky*
Tommaso's, *Thomas Verdillo*

Historic Places
(Year opened; * building)
1726 One if by Land*
1763 Fraunces Tavern*
1794 Bridge Cafe*
1826 Sazerac House*
1832 Historic Bermuda Inn*
1851 Bayard's*
1863 City Hall*
1864 Pete's Tavern
1868 Old Homestead
1870 Billy's
1875 Harry's*
1875 Vivolo*
1879 Gage & Tollner

1880 White Horse Tavern
1884 P.J. Clarke's
1885 Keens Steakhouse
1887 Peter Luger
1888 Katz's Deli
1889 Amuse*
1890 Walker's*
1892 Ferrara
1893 Capitale*
1894 Veniero's
1896 Rao's
1900 Bamonte's
1902 Algonquin Hotel
1902 Angelo's/Mulberry
1904 Ferdinando's
1904 Vincent's
1906 Barbetta
1907 Gargiulo's*
1907 Oak Room
1907 Oyster Bar at Plaza*
1907 Palm Court
1908 Barney Greengrass
1908 John's 12th Street
1909 Guastavino's*
1910 Vanderbilt Station*
1913 Oyster Bar
1917 Café des Artistes
1919 Caffé/Green*
1919 Mario's
1920 Ye Waverly Inn
1921 Sardi's
1922 Fanelli's Cafe
1922 Rocco
1924 Totonno Pizzeria
1925 El Charro Español
1926 Frankie & Johnnie's
1926 Lento's
1926 Palm
1927 Caffe Reggio
1927 El Faro
1927 Gallagher's Steak
1927 L'Impero*
1929 Eisenberg Sandwich
1929 Eleven Madison*
1929 John's Pizzeria
1929 '21' Club
1930 El Quijote
1930 Marchi's
1931 Café Pierre
1932 Patsy's Pizzeria
1932 Pietro's
1934 Papaya King
1934 Rainbow Room
1936 Tom's
1937 Carnegie Deli
1937 Denino's
1937 Minetta Tavern
1937 Stage Deli
1938 Brennan & Carr
1938 Wo Hop
1939 Heidelberg

1941 Sevilla
1943 Burger Heaven
1944 Patsy's
1945 Gino
1945 V&T
1946 Lobster Box
1947 Delegates Dining Rm.
1949 King Cole Bar
1949 L & B Spumoni
1950 Junior's
1950 Marion's
1950 Paul & Jimmy's
1950 Pierre au Tunnel
1952 Lever House*
1953 McHales
1954 Pink Tea Cup
1954 Second Ave. Deli
1954 Serendipity 3
1954 Veselka

Holiday Meals

Ambassador Grill
Aquavit
Arezzo
Artisanal
Beacon
Bellini
Café Botanica
Café des Artistes
Chelsea Bistro
Chez Michallet
Duane Park Cafe
Dumonet
Fifty Seven 57
FireBird
44
Four Seasons
Fresco by Scotto
Gotham B&G
Gramercy Tavern
Halcyon
Ilo
Mark's
Mercer Kitchen
Molyvos
Olives
One C.P.S.
One if by Land
Osteria al Doge
Ouest
Park Avenue Cafe
Patria
Petrossian
Pietrasanta
Provence
Raoul's
Redeye Grill
River Cafe
Rock Center Café
Rosa Mexicano
Ruby Foo's

San Domenico
Sea Grill
Seppi's
Tavern on Green
Terrace in the Sky
Trattoria Dell'Arte
View
Water Club
Water's Edge
Ye Waverly Inn

Hotel Dining
Algonquin Hotel
  Algonquin Hotel
Beekman Tower
  Top of the Tower
Benjamin Hotel
  Terrance Brennan's
Bryant Park Hotel
  Ilo
Carlyle Hotel
  Dumonet
Chambers Hotel
  Town
City Club Hotel
  db Bistro Moderne
Club Quarters Hotel
  Bull Run
Days Hotel
  Pigalle
Dumont Plaza Hotel
  Barking Dog
Edison Hotel
  Edison Cafe
Elysée Hotel
  Monkey Bar
Embassy Suites
  Lili's Noodle Shop
  Unity
Essex House
  Alain Ducasse
  Café Botanica
Flatotel
  Moda
Four Seasons Hotel
  Fifty Seven 57
Giraffe Hotel
  Sciuscià
Hilton NY
  Etrusca
Hudson Hotel
  Hudson Cafeteria
Inn at Irving Pl.
  Lady Mendl's
Iroquois Hotel
  Triomphe
Jolly Madison Towers
  Cinque Terre

Le Parker Meridien
  burger joint
  Norma's
  Seppi's
Le Refuge Inn
  Le Refuge Inn
Library Hotel
  Branzini
Lombardy Hotel
  Etoile
Lowell Hotel
  Post House
Mark Hotel
  Mark's
Marriott Financial Ctr.
  Roy's NY
Marriott Marquis Hotel
  J.W.'s Steakhouse
  View
Mercer Hotel
  Mercer Kitchen
Michelangelo Hotel
  Limoncello
Millenium Hilton
  Church & Dey
Millennium Broadway Hotel
  Charlotte
Millennium UN Plaza Hotel
  Ambassador Grill
Morgans Hotel
  Asia de Cuba
Muse Hotel
  District
NY Palace Hotel
  Le Cirque 2000
Park South Hotel
  Black Duck
Peninsula Hotel
  Fives
Pickwick Arms
  Montparnasse
Pierre Hotel
  Café Pierre
Plaza Athénée Hotel
  Arabelle
Plaza Hotel
  Oak Room
  One C.P.S.
  Palm Court
Radisson Lexington Hotel
  Vuli
Regency Hotel
  Regency
Regent Wall St.
  55 Wall
Renaissance NY Hotel
  Foley's Fish House
Rihga Royal Hotel
  Halcyon
Ritz-Carlton Battery Park
  2 West

Ritz-Carlton Central Park
  Atelier
Roosevelt Hotel
  Ferrara
Royalton Hotel
  44
Shelburne Murray Hill Hotel
  Rare Bar & Grill
Sherry Netherland
  Harry Cipriani
60 Thompson Hotel
  Thom
Sofitel
  Gaby
Stanhope Park Hyatt
  Melrose
St. Regis Hotel
  King Cole Bar
Surrey Hotel
  Café Boulud
Sutton Hotel
  Il Valentino
Swissôtel-The Drake
  Q 56
Time Hotel
  Coco Pazzo
Trump Int'l Hotel
  Jean Georges
Waldorf-Astoria
  Bull & Bear
  Inagiku
  Oscar's
Wales Hotel
  Sarabeth's
Washington Sq. Hotel
  North Sq.
W Court Hotel
  Icon
Westin NY Times Sq.
  Shula's Steak
W Hotel Times Sq.
  Blue Fin
W New York
  Heartbeat
W Union Sq.
  Olives

"In" Places

Aquagrill
Artisanal
Atelier
Babbo
Balthazar
Barbalùc
Beppe
Blue Ribbon
Blue Water Grill
Bond Street
Bouley
Cafe Lebowitz
Café Sabarsky

Craft
db Bistro Moderne
Deck, The
Dos Caminos
elmo
Fiamma Osteria
fresh.
Gabriel's
Gobo
Gonzo
Gramercy Tavern
Harrison
Jean-Luc
Jefferson
Jimmy's Downtown
Joya
Le Cirque 2000
L'Impero
Lupa
Mermaid Inn
Nam
Nobu
Ocean's
OLA
Olives
O Mai
Otto
Ouest
Paradou
Pastis
Pearl Oyster
Peep
Rao's
Red Cat
Sage
Schiller's
Strip House
Suba
SushiSamba
Sushi Yasuda
Tasting Room
325 Spring St.
WD-50

Jacket Required
(* Tie also required)
Alain Ducasse*
Aureole
Box Tree
Café Pierre
Daniel*
Delegates Dining Rm.
Dumonet
Four Seasons
Gramercy Tavern
Harry Cipriani
Il Mulino
Jean Georges
King Cole Bar
La Caravelle
La Côte Basque

La Grenouille*
Le Bernardin
Le Cirque 2000*
Le Perigord*
Le Refuge Inn
Picholine
Rainbow Room*
River Cafe
San Domenico
Tse Yang
'21' Club*
World Yacht

Jury Duty

(Near Manhattan
courthouses)

Arqua
Big Wong
Bo-Ky
Bouley
Bridge Cafe
City Hall
Da Nico
Dim Sum Go Go
Duane Park Cafe
Ecco
Goody's
Grand Sichuan
Great NY Noodle
HSF
Il Cortile
Il Fornaio
Il Palazzo
Joe's Shanghai
L'Ecole
New Green Bo
New Pasteur
Nha Trang
Nobu
Odeon
Onieal's Grand St.
Oriental Garden
Peking Duck
Pho Bang
Pho Viet Huong
Ping's Seafood
Roc
Shanghai Cuisine
Tai Hong Lau
Taormina
Thailand
Wo Hop

Late Dining

(In addition to most diners and
delis; weekday closing hour)

Avenue A Sushi (2 AM)
Balthazar (1 AM)
Bao 111 (2 AM)
Baraonda (1 AM)
Bereket (24 hrs.)

Blue Ribbon (2 AM, 4 AM)
Blue Ribbon Sushi (2 AM)
Brasserie (1 AM)
Brennan & Carr (1 AM)
Cafe Lalo (2 AM)
Cafe Lebowitz (1 AM)
Cafeteria (24 hrs.)
Caffe Reggio (2 AM)
Carriage House (1 AM)
Chez Josephine (1 AM)
Chick-Inn (2 AM)
Coffee Shop (5:30 AM)
Corner Bistro (3:30 AM)
Cosmic Cantina (5 AM)
Cripplebush Road (2 AM)
East Lake (2 AM)
Edgar's Cafe (1 AM)
Eight Mile Creek (1 AM)
Elaine's (2 AM)
elmo (1 AM)
Faan (1 AM)
Ferrier Bistro (1 AM)
Fiorello's Cafe (2 AM)
First (2 AM)
Florent (5 AM)
Frank (1 AM)
French Roast (24 hrs.)
Gam Mee Ok (24 hrs.)
Grace (4 AM)
Great NY Noodle (3:30 AM)
Hard Rock Cafe (2 AM)
Havana Vil. (1 AM)
Hue (2 AM)
'ino (2 AM)
'inoteca (3 AM)
I Tre Merli (1 AM)
J.G. Melon (2:30 AM)
Jimmy's Bronx (2 AM)
Jimmy's Uptown (1 AM)
Jules (1 AM)
Kam Chueh (3:30 AM)
Kang Suh (24 hrs.)
Kiev (24 hrs.)
Kitsch (1 AM)
Kum Gang San (24 hrs.)
La Lanterna (3 AM)
La Mela (2 AM)
Le Souk (2 AM)
L'Express (24 hrs.)
Liberta (1 AM)
Lucien (2 AM)
Lucky Strike (2 AM)
Maison (24 hrs.)
Marion's (2 AM)
Mermaid Inn (1 AM)
Ñ (2 AM)
Nana (1 AM)
Omen (1 AM)
Orbit East Harlem (1 AM)
Parish & Co. (1 AM)
Park (1 AM)

Pastis (1 AM)
Perbacco (1 AM)
Pigalle (24 hrs.)
Planet Thailand (1 AM)
Raoul's (2 AM)
Rio Mar (1:15 AM)
Sage (2 AM)
Sahara (5 AM)
Sandobe (1 AM)
Schiller's (2 AM)
Seppi's (2 AM)
Son Cubano (1 AM)
Stamatis (1 AM)
Starfoods (1 AM)
Sueños (2 AM)
SushiSamba (1 AM)
Sushi Seki (3 AM)
Tao (1 AM)
Three of Cups (1 AM)
212 (1 AM)
Ulysses (3 AM)
Umberto's Clam (4 AM)
Uncle George's (4 AM)
Veselka (24 hrs.)
Vincent's (2 AM)
West Bank Cafe (1 AM)
Wo Hop (24 hrs.)
Wollensky's Grill (2 AM)
Won Jo (24 hrs.)

Meet for a Drink

(Most top hotels, bars and the
following standouts)
Allioli
Amaranth
Amuse
Artisanal
Balthazar
Barbalùc
Boat Basin Cafe
Boat House
Bond Street
Brasserie 8½
Bread Bar at Tabla
Brick Cafe
Bryant Park Grill/Cafe
B. Smith's
Cafe Centro
Cafe Luxembourg
Chango
City Hall
Compass
Dos Caminos
Eight Mile Creek
elmo
El Teddy's
Four Seasons
Gotham B&G
Grace
Gramercy Tavern
Guastavino's

Houston's
Jimmy's Downtown
Joe Allen
JUdson Grill
Keens Steakhouse
Le Colonial
Lenox
L'Impero
Maloney & Porcelli
March
Mark's
Markt
Marseille
Meet
Metronome
Nisos
Noche
Odeon
Osteria del Circo
Pampano
Paper Moon Milano
Park
Park Avalon
Pastis
Petrossian
Punch
Quatorze Bis
Sage
Salute!
Scopa
Shelly's New York
SouthWest NY
Tao
Top of the Tower
Town
212
Vong
Wollensky's Grill
Zarela

Natural/Organic

A
Angelica Kitchen
Candle Cafe/Candle 79
Cho Dang Gol
Chop't Salad
Cosmic Cantina
Counter
Dojo
Friend of a Farmer
Gobo
Grocery, The
Heartbeat
Herban Kitchen
Ivo & Lulu
Josephina
Josie's
Luxia
Morrells
Parish & Co.
Popover Cafe

Special Feature Index

Quartino
Quintessence
Saul
Seo
Spring St. Natural
Terra 47
Toraya
Tossed
T Salon
Tsampa
Zebú Grill
Zenith Vegetarian
Zen Palate

Noteworthy Newcomers (174)

(Name, cuisine; * not open at press time, but looks promising)

Acqua Pazza, *Italian*
Agave, *Southwestern*
Agozar, *Cuban*
Aigo, *Mediterranean*
Aix, *French*
Aleo, *Italian/Mediterranean*
Alma Blue, *Mediterranean*
Amuse, *American*
A.O.C., *French*
A.O.C. Bedford, *Mediterranean*
Arawaks*, *Latin Carib.*
Asiate*, *French/Japanese*
Azalea, *Italian*
Baldo Vino, *Italian*
Bao 111, *Vietnamese*
Barbalùc, *Italian*
Bar Toto*, *Italian*
Basso Est, *Italian*
Bella Via, *Italian*
Biltmore Room*, *American*
Blue 9 Burger, *Burgers*
bluechili, *Asian*
Boi*, *Vietnamese*
Bottega del Vino*, *Italian*
Box Tree, *Kosher French*
Brasserie 360, *Belgian/French*
Brick Cafe, *Italian*
burger joint, *Burgers*
Cafe Atlas, *American/Continental*
Cafe Ronda, *Med./South Amer.*
Cafe Topsy, *British*
Capitale, *American*
Carriage House, *American*
Carvao*, *Med./American*
Caserta Vecchia, *Italian*
'Cesca, *Italian*
Chickenbone Cafe, *Eclectic*
Chick-Inn, *American*
ChikaLicious, *Dessert*
Chipper, *Fish & Chips*
Chubo, *Eclectic*
Church & Dey, *American*
Cicciolino, *Italian*

Cotto, *Mediterranean*
Counter, *Vegetarian*
Cripplebush Road, *Mediterranean*
Crudo, *Seafood*
Culinaria, *Italian*
David Burke & Donatella*, *Amer.*
Deck, The, *Italian*
Delouvrier*, *French*
Diner 24*, *American*
Dish, *American*
Dominic, *American/Italian*
Don Pedro's, *Latin Caribbean*
Downtown Atlantic, *American*
DR-K, *Nuevo Latino*
Dumonet, *French*
Efendi, *Turkish*
Ethiopian, *Ethiopian*
Ethos, *Greek*
Five Front, *American*
5 Ninth*, *American*
Geisha*, *Asian*
Giorgione, *Italian*
Gobo, *Vegetarian*
Grotta Azzurra*, *Italian*
Hacienda Argentina, *Argentine*
Havana Vil., *Cuban*
Hearth*, *American/Italian*
Hue, *Vietnamese*
Ida Mae, *American*
'inoteca, *Italian*
Ivo & Lulu, *French/Caribbean*
Jack's Oyster Bar*, *Seafood*
Jefferson, *American*
Kapadokya, *Turkish*
Kitchen 22/82, *American*
Kitsch, *French/Eclectic*
Lamu, *Mediterranean*
Landmarc*, *French*
La Rambla, *Pan-Latin*
Lever House, *American*
Le Zoccole, *Italian*
Link, *American*
Lozoo, *Chinese*
Lucy*, *Mexican*
Lunchbox Food, *American*
Magnifico, *Italian*
Maison, *French*
Matsuri*, *Japanese*
Mavi Turkish, *Turkish*
Megu*, *Japanese*
Mermaid Inn, *Seafood*
Minado, *Japanese*
Mix in NY, *American/French*
MJ Grill, *American*
Moutarde, *French*
Nana, *Asian*
New Lok Kee, *Chinese*
Nice Matin, *French/Med.*
Ocean's, *American*
OLA, *Nuevo Latino*

O Mai, *Vietnamese*
Ono*, *Japanese*
Open.*, *Seafood*
Orbit East Harlem, *Eclectic*
Otto, *Italian/pizzeria*
Pampano, *Mexican Seafood*
Parish & Co., *American*
Peep, *Thai*
Pelagos, *Greek*
Perbacco, *Italian*
Petrosino, *Italian*
Pie, *Pizzeria*
Pinch*, *Pizzeria*
Pioneer, *American*
Pisticci, *Italian*
Plain Canvas, *Eclectic*
Public*, *International*
Quercy, *French*
Rare Bar & Grill, *Hamburgers*
Red Cafe*, *American*
Re Sette, *Italian*
Rice Avenue, *Thai*
Riingo*, *American/Sushi*
Rocco's 22nd St., *Italian*
Sage, *American*
Salsa y Salsa, *Mexican*
Salt, *American*
Savannah Steak, *Steakhouse*
Schiller's, *Eclectic*
Sciuscià, *Mediterranean*
718*, *French*
Shinjuku, *Japanese*
Shore, *New England*
Shula's Steak, *Steakhouse*
66, *Chinese*
Snackbar, *American*
Snack Taverna, *Greek*
Sparky's American, *American*
Spice Market*, *Southeast Asian*
Starfoods, *French/Southern*
Sueños, *Mexican*
Sui*, *Eclectic*
Sumile*, *Japanese*
Summit, *American*
Sushi Ann, *Japanese*
Svenningsen's, *Seafood*
Talia's Steakhouse, *Kosher*
Taste, *American*
Ten Sushi, *Japanese*
Tent*, *Moroccan*
Terra 47, *Health Food*
Terrance Brennan's, *Sea/Steak*
Terre*, *French*
Thalassa, *Greek Seafood*
36 Bar & BBQ, *Korean*
Thomas Beisl, *Austrian*
360, *French*
325 Spring St., *French*
Twilight 101*, *Mediterranean*
Ulysses, *Irish*
Vento Trattoria*, *Italian*

Village 247, *American*
Voyage, *American*
WD-50, *American*
West 79*, *American*
Westville, *American*
Whim, *Seafood*
'wichcraft, *American sandwiches*
Yujin, *Japanese*
Zerza, *Moroccan/Mediterranean*
Zona Rosa*, *Mexican*

Noteworthy Closings (91)

Abajour
Adulis
Anglers & Writers
Artusi
Beekman Kitchen
Bistro Latino
Blue Elephant
Bondi Ristorante
Bot
Boughalem
Bulgin' Waffles
Butterfield 81
Cal's
Campagna
Castellano
Cent'Anni
Chicama
Christer's
Ciao Europa
Cinnabar
Ci Vediamo
Clay
Commissary
Commune
Della Femina
Dias
Dining Room, The
Dokpa
Domicile
Emily's
Emo's
Ernie's
Gebhardt's
Good Health Cafe
Grappa Café
Grove
Gus' Figs Bistro
Independent, The
Irving on Irving
Isla
Isobel
Juniper Cafe
La Bicyclette
La Brunette
Lawrence Scott
Lenny's Corner
Le Petit Hulot
Les Deux Gamins
Leshko's

Special Feature Index

Lespinasse
Little Basil
Lotfi's Moroccan Restaurant
Luce
Maison Saigon
Mammino
Max & Moritz
Medi
Mekka
Melissa Blue
Mme. Romaine de Lyon
Mooza
Nazar Turkish Cuisine
Nong
Nyla
Other Foods
Papillon
Pazo
Pico
Pisces
Plate 347
Plumeri
Q'ori
64
Smith Street Kitchen
Sushisay
Sweet Mama's
Tappo
3333 Restaurant
TanDa
Tazza
Théo
Tja!
Tonic, The
Tru Bliss
Two Two Two
Uncle Pho
Vida
Vietnam
Wong Kee
World, The
Wyanoka

Outdoor Dining
(G=garden; P=patio;
S=sidewalk; T=terrace)

Aesop's Tables (G)
Allioli (G)
Alma (T)
American Park (P, T)
Aquagrill (T)
Azalea (S)
Barbetta (G)
Barolo (G)
Bar Pitti (S)
Ben Benson's (S, T)
Bistro St. Mark's (G)
Blue Hill (G, P)
Blue Water Grill (T)

Boat Basin Cafe (P)
Boat House (T)
Bottino (G)
Bread Bar at Tabla (P)
Bryant Park Grill/Cafe (G, P, S)
Bubby's (S)
Cafe Centro (S)
Cafe Nosidam (S)
Café St. Barts (T)
Caffe Rafaella (S)
Caffe Reggio (S)
Chez Oskar (T)
Coffee Shop (S)
Convivium Osteria (G)
Da Silvano (S)
Dolphins (G)
Downtown (S, T)
Druids (G)
East of Eighth (G)
Empire Diner (S)
Esca (P)
Fiorello's Cafe (S)
Gaby (P)
Gascogne (G)
Giando/Water (P)
Gigino/Wagner Pk. (P)
Grocery, The (G)
Guastavino's (T)
Harbour Lights (T)
Harvest (G)
Home (G)
I Coppi (G)
Il Palazzo (G, S)
Isabella's (S)
I Trulli (G)
Jordan's Lobster (S)
Josephina (T)
Joya (G, P)
Julian's (G, S)
La Goulue (T)
Lattanzi (G)
Le Jardin Bistro (G)
Le Refuge (P)
Le Zoccole (S)
L'Impero (P)
Long Tan (P)
Loulou (G)
Luna Piena (G)
Lundy Bros. (S)
Madiba (S)
Maison (P)
March (T)
Marichu (P)
Markt (S, T)
Marseille (S)
Melrose (T)
Metropolitan Cafe (G)
Mezzogiorno (S)
Mickey Mantle's (S)
Miracle Grill (G)
Naples 45 (T)

New Leaf (P)
Nice Matin (S)
Nisos (S)
Ocean Grill (S)
Osteria del Circo (T)
Oznot's Dish (S)
Pampano (T)
Paradou (G)
Park (G)
Pastis (T)
Patio Dining (P)
Patois (G)
Patroon (T)
Pete's Tavern (S)
Place (T)
Porters (G, S)
Radio Perfecto (G)
River Cafe (G)
Rocco's 22nd St. (T)
Rose Water (P)
Sahara (G)
San Pietro (T)
Sherwood Cafe (G)
SouthWest NY (T)
Steak Frites (T)
Steamers (T)
Surya (G)
Sweet Melissa (G)
Tartine (S)
Tavern on Green (G)
Terrace in the Sky (T)
Thom (T)
Top of the Tower (T)
Ulysses (S)
Va Tutto! (G)
Vera Cruz (G)
Verbena (G)
ViceVersa (G)
Vittorio Cucina (G)
Water Club (P)
Water's Edge (P)
White Horse Tavern (S)
Wollensky's Grill (G, S)

People-Watching

Asia de Cuba
Atlantic Grill
Babbo
Balthazar
Bar Pitti
Bice
Blue Water Grill
Bond Street
Cafe Lebowitz
Cafe Luxembourg
Cafe Nosidam
Chez Es Saada
Da Silvano
Deck, The
Downtown
Elio's

Fresco by Scotto
Gabriel's
Hudson Cafeteria
Il Cantinori
Indochine
Isabella's
Joe Allen
La Grenouille
Le Cirque 2000
Markt
Melrose
Mercer Kitchen
Monkey Bar
Mr. Chow
Nam
Nobu
Pampano
Park
Pastis
San Domenico
Sardi's
Smith & Wollensky
Thom
Town
Vong

Power Scenes

Bayard's
Ben Benson's
Bobby Van's Steak
Bull & Bear
Chanterelle
City Hall
Craft
Daniel
Delegates Dining Rm.
Del Frisco's
Delmonico's
Elio's
44
Four Seasons
Fresco by Scotto
Gabriel's
Gotham B&G
Harry Cipriani
Harry's
Jean Georges
La Grenouille
Le Bernardin
Le Cirque 2000
Michael's
Milos, Estiatorio
Nicola's
Nobu
Peter Luger
Post House
Rao's
Regency
San Domenico
San Pietro
Smith & Wollensky

Sparks Steak
'21' Club

Pre-Theater/ Prix Fixe Menus

(See also Tasting Menus, and pages 21-22, plus the following good bets; call for prices and times)

Aix
Amuse
Barbetta
Bice
Cafe Atlas
Cafe Centro
Cafe du Pont
Casa Di Meglio
Cité
Cité Grill
Cucina di Pesce
Da Antonio
Da Nico
District
Divino
Do Hwa
55 Wall
Foley's Fish House
Fontana di Trevi
44
14 Wall Street
fresh.
I Coppi
Il Menestrello
Kai
Kings' Carriage
La Belle Vie
La Boîte en Bois
La Goulue
Le Madeleine
Le Refuge Inn
Le Rivage
L'Orange Bleue
Loulou
Meet
Minado
Montparnasse
Ocean Grill
Old Homestead
Olives
Palm Court
Pigalle
Provence en Boite
Rocking Horse
Ruby Foo's
Sardi's
Seppi's
Strip House
Taste
Thalia
360

Trattoria Dopo Teatro
Trois Marches
Veritas
View
Villa Berulia
Village

Private Rooms

(Restaurants charge less at off times; call for capacity)

Alain Ducasse
American Park
Amuse
AZ
Barbetta
Bayard's
Beacon
Beppe
Boat House
Bottino
Bouley
Capitale
Cellini
Centolire
Chez Josephine
Citarella
City Hall
Compass
Daniel
Danube
D'Artagnan
Del Frisco's
Eleven Madison
Fiamma Osteria
F.illi Ponte
FireBird
Four Seasons
Gabriela's
Gage & Tollner
Gramercy Tavern
Guastavino's
Harbour Lights
Il Buco
Il Cortile
I Trulli
Jean Georges
Jezebel
Keens Steakhouse
La Côte Basque
La Grenouille
La Petite Auberge
Le Bernardin
Le Cirque 2000
Le Perigord
Le Refuge
L'Impero
Lola
Lotus
Lutèce
Maloney & Porcelli
March

Mark's
Marseille
Metronome
Michael's
Mi Cocina
Milos, Estiatorio
Moda
Moran's Chelsea
Morton's Steak
Mr. K's
Nino's
Oceana
Ocean's
Old Homestead
One C.P.S.
One if by Land
Oyster Bar
Park
Park Avenue Cafe
Patroon
Periyali
Philip Marie
Piccola Venezia
Picholine
Primavera
Redeye Grill
Remi
René Pujol
Re Sette
River Cafe
rm
Rock Center Café
San Domenico
San Pietro
Sardi's
Scopa
Shelly's New York
Sparks Steak
Tao
Tavern on Green
Terrace in the Sky
Toledo
Town
Trattoria Dopo Teatro
Tribeca Grill
Triomphe
Tuscan
'21' Club
Union Pacific
Vine
Water Club
Water's Edge

Pubs/Microbreweries

(See *Zagat NYC Nightlife*)
Angus McIndoe
Corner Bistro
Druids
Fanelli's Cafe
Gramercy Tavern
Heartland Brew.

J.G. Melon
Joe Allen
Keens Steakhouse
King Cole Bar
Knickerbocker B&G
Luke's Bar & Grill
Markt
McHales
Moran's Chelsea
Neary's
Onieal's Grand St.
Pete's Tavern
P.J. Clarke's
St. Andrews
T.G.I. Friday's
Typhoon
Village 247
Walker's
White Horse Tavern
Wollensky's Grill

Quick Bites

Amy's Bread
AQ Cafe
A Salt & Battery
Azuri Cafe
BB Sandwich
Bereket
Better Burger
Big Nick's Burger
Blue 9 Burger
Brennan & Carr
Burger Heaven
Burritoville
Chip/CurryShop
Chipper
City Bakery
Columbus Bakery
Cosi
Cosmic Cantina
Cozy Soup/Burger
Dishes
Eisenberg Sandwich
F & B
Flor de Mayo
Gray's Papaya
Grilled Cheese
Hampton Chutney
Harry's Burritos
Havana Chelsea
'ino
Joe's Pizza
Mee Noodle Shop
Ollie's
Once Upon a Tart
Oyster Bar
Papaya King
Popover Cafe
Press 195
Pump Energy Food
Quintessence

Rice 'n' Beans
Risotteria
Silver Spurs
Westville
'wichcraft
Zabar's Cafe

Quiet Conversation

Alain Ducasse
Arabelle
Atelier
Bouterin
Box Tree
Café Botanica
Café Pierre
Chanterelle
Citarella
Danube
DeGrezia
Dumonet
Four Seasons
Hangawi
Honmura An
Jean Georges
Kai
La Caravelle
La Grenouille
Le Bernardin
Lutèce
March
Mark's
Montrachet
Mr. K's
Petrossian
Picholine
Primavera
Regency
rm
Sushi Yasuda
Tea Box
Terrace in the Sky
Tocqueville
Toraya
Tsampa

Raw Bars

American Park
Aquagrill
Atlantic Grill
Balthazar
Blue Fin
Blue Water Grill
City Crab/Lobster
City Hall
Crudo
Docks Oyster Bar
Fish
Guastavino's
Jordan's Lobster
London Lennie's
Markt
Mercer Kitchen

Mermaid Inn
Milos, Estiatorio
Ocean Grill
Oyster Bar
Oyster Bar at Plaza
P.J. Clarke's
Scopa
Shaffer City
Shelly's New York
Shore
SushiSamba
Ulysses
Whim

Romantic Places

Algonquin Hotel
Alma
Aureole
Bambou
Barbetta
Barolo
Boat House
Box Tree
Café des Artistes
Casa La Femme
Chanterelle
Chez Es Saada
Chez Josephine
Chez Michallet
Daniel
Danube
Erminia
FireBird
Gascogne
Giando/Water
Harbour Lights
Il Buco
Jezebel
King Cole Bar
Lady Mendl's
La Grenouille
La Lanterna
La Metairie
Le Cirque 2000
Le Refuge
Le Refuge Inn
L'Impero
March
Mark's
One if by Land
Periyali
Petrossian
Piccola Venezia
Place
Primavera
Rainbow Room
Raoul's
River Cafe
Sistina
Suba
Terrace in the Sky

Top of the Tower
Town
View
Water's Edge
World Yacht

Senior Appeal

Ambassador Grill
Aureole
Barbetta
Bouterin
Café Botanica
Café des Artistes
Cafe Trevi
Fontana di Trevi
Il Nido
Il Tinello
La Côte Basque
La Goulue
La Petite Auberge
Lattanzi
Le Perigord
Lusardi's
Lutèce
Mark's
Oak Room
Pierre au Tunnel
Pietro's
Sardi's
Tavern on Green
Teresa's

Singles Scenes

Angelo & Maxie's
Artisanal
Atlantic Grill
Balthazar
Blue Fin
Bonita
Brasserie 8½
Bryant Park Grill/Cafe
Canyon Road
Chez Es Saada
Citrus Bar & Grill
Coffee Shop
Dos Caminos
DT.UT
elmo
El Teddy's
Ferrier Bistro
First
Grace
Guastavino's
Hog Pit BBQ
Hudson Cafeteria
Isabella's
Jane
Jimmy's Downtown
Joya
JUdson Grill
Lansky Lounge

Le Zinc
Marion's
Merchants, N.Y.
Mesa Grill
Metronome
Monkey Bar
Park Avalon
Punch
Schiller's
Scopa
Shark Bar
Soul Cafe
Suba
Tao
325 Spring St.
Town
Tribeca Grill

Sleepers

(Good to excellent food, but
little known)
Adä
Arabelle
Azul Bistro
Baci
Café Bar
Casa
Di Fara
DuMont
Eliá
Essex
Euzkadi
Giovanni
Hispaniola
Joseph's
Kam Chueh
Kurio
La Cantina
La Cantina Toscana
La Vineria
Locanda Vini
L'Orto
Marinella
Market Café
Marumi
Massimo
Mombar
Oster. Gallo Nero
Patio Dining
Pinocchio
Poke
Sesumi
Sripraphai
Sugar Hill Bistro
Veronica
Vittorio Cucina
Volare
Vuli
Yakiniku JuJu

Special Feature Index

Sunday – Best Bets
(See also Hotel Dining)

America
Amy Ruth's
Annisa
Aquagrill
Artisanal
Avenue
Balthazar
Blue Smoke
Blue Water Grill
Boat House
Bouley
Café de Bruxelles
Café des Artistes
Capsouto Frères
Centolire
Chez Michallet
Chiam
Compass
Gonzo
Gramercy Tavern
Grange Hall
Gus' Place
Isabella's
La Lunchonette
La Mediterranée
Lupa
Madiba
Markt
Marseille
Mesa Grill
Molyvos
Ocean Grill
Odeon
Ouest
Park Avenue Cafe
Peter Luger
River Cafe
Salaam Bombay
Shun Lee Palace
66
Tavern on Green
Thomas Beisl
Trattoria Dell'Arte
Water Club
Zoë

Tasting Menus
($ minimum)

Alain Ducasse (185)
Annisa (68)
Aquavit (90)
Atelier (128)
Aureole (85)
Babbo (59)
Blue Hill (65)
Bouley (75)
Café Boulud (105)
Chanterelle (95)
Citarella (68)
Craft (85)
Daniel (120)
Danube (75)
Eleven Madison (60)
Esca (65)
Four Seasons (120)
Gramercy Tavern (85)
Grocery, The (65)
Il Buco (65)
Ilo (95)
Jean Georges (118)
La Caravelle (95)
La Grenouille (115)
Le Bernardin (98)
Le Cirque 2000 (105)
L'Impero (85)
Marseille (65)
Michael's (90)
Montrachet (76)
Nino's (70)
Oceana (110)
One if by Land (75)
Osteria del Circo (65)
Patria (59)
Payard Bistro (62)
Picholine (85)
River Cafe (90)
rm (100)
San Domenico (70)
Scalini Fedeli (85)
Solera (65)
Tabla (75)
Terrace in the Sky (90)
Tocqueville (75)
'21' Club (70)
Union Pacific (85)
Vong (68)
Washington Park (65)

Tea Service

Alice's Tea Cup
Café Botanica
Café Pierre
Cafe S.F.A.
Danal
55 Wall
Kai
Kings' Carriage
Lady Mendl's
Mark's
Melrose
Palm Court
Payard Bistro
Sarabeth's
Sweet Melissa
Tea Box
Toraya
T Salon

Theme Restaurants
Brooklyn Diner USA
ESPN Zone
Hard Rock Cafe
Jekyll & Hyde
Johnny Rockets
Lucky Cheng's
Mars 2112
Mickey Mantle's
Shula's Steak

Transporting Experiences
Aquavit
Bayard's
Boat House
Café des Artistes
Casa La Femme
Chez Es Saada
Chez Josephine
FireBird
Hangawi
Il Buco
Jewel Bako
Jezebel
Keens Steakhouse
La Grenouille
Le Colonial
Nobu
One if by Land
Rainbow Room
Rao's
Tabla
Tavern on Green
Vatan
Water's Edge

Visitors on Expense Account
Alain Ducasse
Aquavit
Bouley
Chanterelle
Del Frisco's
Felidia
Four Seasons
Harry Cipriani
Il Cantinori
Il Mulino
Il Nido
Jean Georges
Kai
Kuruma Zushi
La Caravelle
La Côte Basque
La Grenouille
Le Bernardin
March
Milos, Estiatorio
Nobu
Petrossian
Picholine

Primavera
San Domenico
San Pietro
Scalinatella
Scalini Fedeli
Tavern on Green
Terrance Brennan's
Veritas

Winning Wine Lists
Alain Ducasse
Aquavit
Artisanal
Atelier
Aureole
Babbo
Barbetta
Barolo
Bayard's
Ben Benson's
Bouley
Café Boulud
Cafe Centro
Capitale
Chanterelle
Chiam
Cité
City Hall
Craft
Daniel
Danube
DeGrezia
Del Frisco's
Dumonet
Eleven Madison
Felidia
Fiamma Osteria
F.illi Ponte
Four Seasons
Fresco by Scotto
Gabriel's
Giovanni
Gotham B&G
Gramercy Tavern
Harry's
Henry's End
Henry's Evergreen
Ilo
'inoteca
I Trulli
Jean Georges
JUdson Grill
La Cantina Toscana
La Caravelle
La Côte Basque
La Grenouille
Le Bernardin
Le Cirque 2000
L'Ecole
Le Perigord
Le Zie 2000

Special Feature Index

L'Impero
Lusardi's
Lutèce
Maloney & Porcelli
Manhattan OceanClub
March
MarkJoseph Steak
Michael's
Montrachet
Morrells
Ñ
Nick & Stef's Steak
Nicola Paone
Oceana
Olives
One C.P.S.
One if by Land
Onieal's Grand St.
Otto
Ouest
Oyster Bar
Oznot's Dish
Park Avenue Cafe
Patria
Piccola Venezia
Picholine
Ponticello
Post House
Primavera
Raoul's

Remi
René Pujol
Rhône
River Cafe
rm
Rothmann's
Ruth's Chris
San Domenico
San Pietro
Scalini Fedeli
Sistina
Smith & Wollensky
Sparks Steak
Strip House
Tasting Room
Tavern on Green
Terrace in the Sky
Tocqueville
Tommaso's
Town
Tribeca Grill
Tropica
Tse Yang
'21' Club
Union Pacific
Union Sq. Cafe
Verbena
Veritas
Washington Park
Water Club

Wine Vintage Chart

This chart is designed to help you select wine to go with your meal. It is based on the same 0 to 30 scale used throughout this *Survey.* The ratings (prepared by our friend **Howard Stravitz,** a law professor at the University of South Carolina) reflect both the quality of the vintage and the wine's readiness for present consumption. Thus, if a wine is not fully mature or is over the hill, its rating has been reduced. We do not include 1987, 1991–1993 vintages because they are not especially recommended for most areas. A dash indicates that a wine is either past its peak or too young to rate.

	'85	'86	'88	'89	'90	'94	'95	'96	'97	'98	'99	'00	'01	'02
WHITES														
French:														
Alsace	24	18	22	28	28	26	25	24	24	26	24	26	27	–
Burgundy	26	25	–	24	22	–	29	28	24	23	25	24	21	–
Loire Valley	–	–	–	–	24	–	20	23	22	–	24	25	23	–
Champagne	28	25	24	26	29	–	26	27	24	24	25	25	26	–
Sauternes	21	28	29	25	27	–	21	23	26	24	24	24	28	–
California (Napa, Sonoma, Mendocino):														
Chardonnay	–	–	–	–	–	–	25	21	25	24	24	22	26	–
Sauvignon Blanc/Semillon	–	–	–	–	–	–	–	–	–	25	25	23	27	–
REDS														
French:														
Bordeaux	24	25	24	26	29	22	26	25	23	25	24	27	24	–
Burgundy	23	–	21	24	27	–	26	28	25	22	28	22	20	24
Rhône	25	19	27	29	29	24	25	23	24	28	27	26	25	–
Beaujolais	–	–	–	–	–	–	–	–	22	21	24	25	18	20
California (Napa, Sonoma, Mendocino):														
Cab./Merlot	26	26	–	21	28	29	27	25	28	23	26	23	26	–
Pinot Noir	–	–	–	–	–	26	23	23	25	24	26	25	27	–
Zinfandel	–	–	–	–	–	25	22	23	21	22	24	–	25	–
Italian:														
Tuscany	26	–	24	–	26	22	25	20	29	24	28	26	25	–
Piedmont	26	–	26	28	29	–	23	27	27	25	25	26	23	–